George Vance Smith, John Scott Porter

The Holy Scriptures of the old covenant

George Vance Smith, John Scott Porter

The Holy Scriptures of the old covenant

ISBN/EAN: 9783337281618

Printed in Europe, USA, Canada, Australia, Japan

Cover: Foto ©Lupo / pixelio.de

More available books at **www.hansebooks.com**

THE

HOLY SCRIPTURES

OF THE

OLD COVENANT,

IN

A REVISED TRANSLATION

BY

THE LATE REV. CHARLES WELLBELOVED,
THE REV. GEORGE VANCE SMITH, B.A.,
THE REV. JOHN SCOTT PORTER.

VOLUME I.

CONTAINING THE FIVE BOOKS OF MOSES, WITH THE BOOKS OF
JOSHUA, JUDGES, AND RUTH,

BY THE LATE

REV. CHARLES WELLBELOVED.

LONDON:
LONGMAN, BROWN, GREEN, LONGMANS, AND ROBERTS,
PATERNOSTER ROW.
M.DCCC.LIX.

PREFACE.

The necessity for a revision of the Common Version of the Holy Scriptures is so generally recognised, that it would be superfluous here to repeat the arguments in its favour. At the same time, the obstacles to a revision by authority are so numerous, that there is little prospect of its being speedily accomplished. It cannot be thought presumptuous, therefore, if individuals take upon themselves an office, which seems to be declined by those public bodies to which it more properly belongs; and endeavour to offer to readers of the Scriptures a more faithful representation of their text and meaning, than they can obtain from the Common Version.

The Authors of this revision have not, however, undertaken either the establishment of a new text or the production of a new translation of the Scriptures. They have assumed the Common Version as a basis, and have departed from it only where, in their judgment, the text was clearly corrupt, the rendering inaccurate, or the phraseology obsolete or obscure. In the part now published, the Masoretic text of the original, as exhibited in the edition of Van der Hooght, has been followed, with such occasional variations as appeared to be at once important and adequately supported by the authority of manuscripts and versions. The truth is, that little aid towards the establishment of a new text is to be derived from the Hebrew manuscripts, none of which carry us back beyond the æra of the Masoretic revision, in the seventh century after Christ; and that most of their various readings are either unimportant in themselves, or inappreciable in a translation. And though biblical scholars are unanimous in the opinion, that our present text is in many passages incorrect, they are by no means agreed as to the manner in which it is to be corrected. The present publication is intended for the use of a class of readers, who have no means of weighing critical evidence; and its purpose being practical, the Editors have, in doubtful cases, admitted the prescriptive right of a version, which two centuries and a half have rendered sacred to the religious mind of England. Its style and idiom have been carefully preserved, where change seemed the duty of a faithful translator.

In regard to the use of Italics, this revision differs somewhat from the Common Version. It has not been thought necessary to employ them, as is done in our Bibles, wherever the translation contains a word which has no equivalent in the original; as, for instance, in the systematic omission in Hebrew of the substantive verb, and similar cases of merely grammatical idiom. Nor, again, are they used when words are inserted which are not now found in the present Hebrew text, but which the Editors believe, on the authority of manuscripts or versions, to have originally stood there. Thus, in Genesis iv. 8, the words "Let us go into the field," though wanting in the Hebrew, are printed in the common character, the author of the revision believing, on critical evidence, that they have been accidentally lost; on the other hand, in Joshua xi. 2, and other passages of the same book, the words "*of the Jordan*," which have no separate equivalent in the original, are added in Italics, because the word *Arabah* is here used in the Hebrew, not in the general sense of *plain*, but specifically of that great plain or valley through which the Jordan runs, from the Lake of

Gennesareth to the Dead Sea. No words of importance have ever been added, without such a notice to the readers.

After all that can be done to exhibit a faithful rendering of the Scriptures, obscurities will remain which only a commentary can remove. It has not been thought expedient, however, to add explanatory notes to this translation; but, should the undertaking be favourably received, a volume of brief notes might be added, in which the reasons of the changes introduced into the revision should be stated, and difficult passages be explained.

The late Rev. Charles Wellbeloved published some years ago a new translation of the Five Books of Moses, with Job and the Psalms, Proverbs, Ecclesiastes, and Solomon's Song, as a part of a Family Bible, which he did not complete. He had been engaged before his death in revising what he had published, with a view to its incorporation in the present work, but had proceeded no further than the end of Deuteronomy. He had, however, left in manuscript a revision of Joshua, Judges, and Ruth, from which the translation of these books has been prepared by the Rev. John Kenrick. The Books of Samuel, Ezra, Nehemiah, Esther, Isaiah, Jeremiah, and Lamentations, have been undertaken by the Rev. George Vance Smith; the Books of Kings, Chronicles, Ezekiel, and Daniel, by the Rev. John Scott Porter. The Psalms and the other Books included in Mr. Wellbeloved's Bible will be printed from a revised copy of that work, and the Minor Prophets from a manuscript which he had prepared for the press several years before his death. It is expected that the whole will be comprised in three volumes.

Such a work as the present has, of course, not been undertaken without concert and mutual understanding among the persons engaged in it, and it is hoped that a general uniformity will by this means be preserved. Each translator, however, must be regarded as responsible only for his own share.

Among independent translators, diversities of taste and opinion will necessarily exist, giving rise to varieties in their translations, but the sense of the original may be faithfully represented by different modes of expression.

The Authors of this revision have engaged in it with no view to any personal or party object, but solely in the hope of furnishing a correct and intelligible version of the Scriptures, and they commit their work to the judgment of the serious and candid reader, and to the blessing of Him whose Word is Truth.

THE BOOK OF GENESIS.

1 CHAP. I.—In the beginning God created the heavens
2 and the earth. And the earth was without form, and void; and darkness was upon the face of the deep; and the Spirit of God brooded on the face of the waters.
3 And God said, "Let there be light:" and there was light.
4 And God saw that the light was good: and God separated
5 the light from the darkness. And God called the light Day, and the darkness he called Night. And the evening came and the morning came, the first day.
6 And God said, "Let there be a firmament in the midst of the waters, and let it separate the waters from the waters."
7 And God made the firmament, and separated the waters below the firmament from the waters above the firmament:
8 and it was so. And God called the firmament Heaven. And the evening came and the morning came, the second day.
9 And God said, "Let the waters under the heavens be gathered together into one place, and let the dry land ap-
10 pear:" and it was so. And God called the dry land Earth; and the gathering together of the waters he called Seas:
11 and God saw that it was good. And God said, "Let the earth bring forth grass, *and* herbs yielding seed, *and* fruit-trees yielding fruit according to their kinds, the seed of which shall be in itself upon the earth:" and it was
12 so. For the earth brought forth grass, *and* herbs yielding seed according to their kinds, and trees yielding fruit, the seed of which was in itself according to their kinds:
13 and God saw that it was good. And the evening came and the morning came, the third day.
14 And God said, "Let there be lights in the firmament of

heaven to separate the day from the night; and let them be for signs and seasons, days and years; and let them be for lights in the firmament of heaven, to give light upon the earth:" and it was so. For God made two great lights; the greater light to rule the day, and the smaller light to rule the night: *he made* the stars also. And God set them in the firmament of heaven, to give light upon the earth, and to rule over the day and over the night, and to separate the light from the darkness: and God saw that it was good. And the evening came and the morning came, the fourth day.

And God said, "Let the waters swarm with living things, and let flying creatures fly above the earth under the firmament of heaven:" and it was so. For God created great sea animals, and all the moving things with which the waters swarmed, according to their kinds, and every winged fowl according to its kind: and God saw that it was good. And God blessed them, saying, "Be fruitful, and multiply, and fill the waters of the seas; and let the fowl multiply on the earth." And the evening came and the morning came, the fifth day.

And God said, "Let the earth bring forth living creatures according to their kinds, cattle, and creeping things, and wild beasts according to their kinds:" and it was so. For God made the wild beasts according to their kinds, and cattle according to their kinds, and every thing that creepeth on the ground according to its kind: and God saw that it was good. And God said, "Let us make man in our image, according to our likeness; and let them have dominion over the fishes of the sea, and over the fowls of heaven, and over the cattle, and over all the earth, and over every creeping thing that creepeth upon the earth." So God created man in his own image; in the image of God created he him. Male and female he created them. And God blessed them, and God said to them, "Be fruitful, and multiply, and fill the earth, and subdue it; and have dominion over the fishes of the sea, and over the fowls of heaven, and over the cattle, and over every living thing that creepeth upon the earth. And God said, "Lo, I give to you every herb bearing seed, which is upon the face of the whole earth, and every tree, in which is fruit yielding seed; it shall be food for yourselves, and for all the beasts of the earth and for all the fowls of heaven, and for every thing that creepeth upon the earth, in which is

31 life: every green herb *I give* for food:" and it was so. And God saw everything that he had made, and, behold, it was very good. And the evening came and the morning came, the sixth day.

1 CHAP. II.—Thus the heavens and the earth were finished,
2 and all their hosts. So on the seventh day God had finished his work which he had made; and he rested on the seventh
3 day from all his work which he had made. God therefore blessed the seventh day, and sanctified it; because that on it he rested from all his work which God had created and made.

4 This is the Account of the heavens and the earth, at their creation when Jehovah God made the heavens and the
5 earth. And every plant of the field had not yet been on the earth, and every herb of the field had not yet grown: for Jehovah God had not caused rain to fall upon the earth, nor
6 was there a man to till the ground; but there went up a mist from the earth, and watered the whole face of the
7 ground. And Jehovah God formed man of the dust of the ground, and breathed into his nostrils the breath of life; and man became a living soul.
8 And Jehovah God planted a garden in Eden eastward:
9 and there he put the man whom he had formed. And out of the ground Jehovah God caused to grow every tree that is pleasant to the sight and good for food; the tree of life also in the midst of the garden, and the tree of the knowledge of good and evil.
10 And a river flowed from Eden to water the garden; and
11 thence it was divided, and became four heads. The name of the first is Phison: it is that which surroundeth the
12 whole land of Havilah, where there is gold; and the gold of
13 that land is good: there is bdellium and the onyx-stone. And the name of the second river is Gihon: it is that which sur-
14 roundeth the whole land of Cush. And the name of the third river is Hiddekel: it is that which runneth towards the east of Assyria. And the fourth river is Euphrates.
15 And Jehovah God took the man, and put him into the
16 garden of Eden, to till it and to keep it. And Jehovah God charged the man, saying, "Of every tree of the garden
17 thou mayest freely eat; but of the tree of the knowledge of good and evil, thou shalt not eat: for in the day that thou eatest of it thou shalt surely die."

And Jehovah God said, "It is not good that the man 18
[ADAM] should be alone; I will make for him a helpmate."
Then out of the ground Jehovah God formed every beast of 19
the field and all the fowls of heaven; and brought them to
Adam to see what he would call them: and whatsoever Adam
called every living creature, that was its name. So Adam 20
gave names to all cattle, and to the fowls of heaven, and to
every beast of the field: but for Adam no helpmate was
found. Therefore Jehovah God caused a deep sleep to fall 21
upon Adam, and while he slept, he took one of his ribs, and
closed up the flesh instead thereof: and the rib, which 22
Jehovah God had taken from man, he made a woman, and
brought her to Adam. And Adam said, "This now is bone 23
of my bone, and flesh of my flesh: she shall be called
Woman, because she was taken out of man." Therefore 24
shall a man leave his father and his mother, and shall cleave
unto his wife; and they shall be one flesh. And they were 25
both naked, the man and his wife, and were not ashamed.

CHAP. III.—Now the serpent was more subtle than any 1
beast of the field which Jehovah God had made. And he
said to the woman, "Hath God indeed said, 'Ye shall not
eat of every tree of the garden?'" And the woman said to 2
the serpent, "Of the fruit of the trees of the garden we
may eat: but of the fruit of the tree which is in the midst 3
of the garden, God hath said, 'Ye shall not eat of it, neither
shall ye touch it, lest ye die.'" And the serpent said to 4
the woman, "Ye shall not surely die: but God doth know, 5
that in the day ye eat of it your eyes will be opened; and
ye will be as God, knowing good and evil." And when the 6
woman saw that the tree was good for food, and that it was
pleasant to the eyes, and a tree to be desired as making
wise, she took of the fruit of it and did eat, and gave also
to her husband with her, and he did eat. And the eyes of 7
them both were opened, and they knew that they were naked:
and they sewed fig-leaves together, and made themselves
girdles. And they heard the voice of Jehovah God walk- 8
ing in the garden in the cool of the day: and Adam and his
wife hid themselves from the presence of Jehovah God,
amongst the trees of the garden. And Jehovah God called 9
to Adam, and said to him, "Where art thou?" And he 10
said, "I heard thy voice in the garden, and I was afraid,
because I was naked; and I hid myself." And he said, 11

"Who told thee that thou wast naked? Hast thou eaten
12 of the tree, of which I commanded thee not to eat?" And
Adam said, "The woman, whom thou gavest to be with me,
13 she gave me of the tree, and I did eat." And Jehovah God
said to the woman, "Why hast thou done this?" And the
woman said, "The serpent beguiled me, and I did eat."
14 And Jehovah God said to the serpent, "Because thou hast
done this, thou art cursed above all cattle, and above every
beast of the field: upon thy belly shalt thou go, and dust
15 shalt thou eat all the days of thy life. And I will put
enmity between thee and the woman, and between thy seed
and her seed: it shall bruise thy head, and thou shalt bruise
16 its heel." *And* to the woman he said, "I will greatly multiply the sorrow of thy conception: in sorrow thou shalt
bring forth children; and thy desire *shall be* to thy husband,
17 and he shall rule over thee." And to Adam he said, "Because thou hast hearkened to the voice of thy wife, and hast
eaten of the tree of which I commanded thee, saying, 'Thou
shalt not eat of it;' cursed is the ground for thy sake: in
18 sorrow shalt thou eat of it all the days of thy life: thorns
also and thistles shall it bring forth to thee; and thou shalt
19 eat the herb of the field. In the sweat of thy face shalt thou
eat bread, till thou return to the ground: for out of it wast
thou taken: for dust thou art, and to dust thou shalt
20 return." And Adam called his wife's name Eve [LIFE];
21 because she was the mother of all living. And Jehovah God
made for Adam and his wife garments of skins, and clothed
22 them. And Jehovah God said, "Behold, the man is become as one of us, to know good and evil: and now, lest he
put forth his hand, and take also of the tree of life, and eat,
23 and live for ever." Therefore Jehovah God sent him forth
from the garden of Eden, to till the ground whence he had
24 been taken. So he drove out the man; and he placed on
the east of the garden of Eden cherubim, and a flaming
sword which turned every way, to guard the way of the tree
of life.

1 CHAP. IV.—And Adam knew Eve his wife; and she conceived, and bare Cain [ACQUISITION], for she said, "I have
2 acquired a man from Jehovah." And again she bare his
brother Abel [VANITY]. And Abel was a keeper of sheep,
but Cain was a tiller of the ground.
3 Now in process of time Cain brought of the fruit of the

ground an offering to Jehovah. And Abel also brought of 4
the first-born and of the fattest of his flock. And Jehovah
had respect to Abel and to his offering: but to Cain and to 5
his offering he had not respect. And Cain was very wroth,
and his countenance fell. And Jehovah said to Cain, "Why 6
art thou wroth? and why is thy countenance fallen? If 7
thou doest well, shalt not thou be accepted? and if thou
doest not well, sin lieth at the door. And unto thee *shall be*
his desire, and thou shalt rule over him."

And Cain said to Abel his brother, "Let us go into the 8
field;" and when they were in the field, Cain rose up against
Abel his brother and slew him. And Jehovah said to Cain, 9
"Where is Abel thy brother?" And he said, "I know
not. Am I my brother's keeper?" And *Jehovah* said, 10
"What hast thou done? the voice of thy brother's blood
crieth to me from the ground. And now art thou cursed 11
from the ground, which hath opened its mouth to receive
thy brother's blood from thy hand. If thou tillest the 12
ground it will no more yield to thee its strength: a fugitive
and a wanderer shalt thou be in the earth." And Cain said 13
to Jehovah, "My punishment is greater than I can bear.
Lo, thou art driving me out this day from the face of this 14
land; and from thy presence I shall be hidden; and I shall
be a fugitive and a wanderer in the earth: and it shall come
to pass that whosoever shall find me will slay me." And 15
Jehovah said to him, "Not so; whosoever slayeth Cain, vengeance
shall be taken on him sevenfold." And Jehovah gave
a token to Cain, that no one who might find him should kill
him.

And Cain went out from the presence of Jehovah, and 16
dwelt in the land of Nod, on the east of Eden. And Cain 17
knew his wife; and she conceived, and bare Enoch; and he
built a city, and called the name of the city, after the
name of his son Enoch. And to Enoch was born Irad: 18
and Irad begat Mehujael: and Mehujael begat Methusael:
and Methusael begat Lamech. And Lamech took unto him 19
two wives: the name of the one was Adah, and the name of
the other Zillah. And Adah bare Jabal: he was the father 20
of such as dwell in tents, and *tend* cattle. And his brother's 21
name was Jubal: he was the father of all such as play upon
the harp and the psaltery. And Zillah also bare Tubal-cain, 22
an instructer of every artificer in brass and iron: and the
sister of Tubal-cain was Naamah.

23 And Lamech said to his wives:
"Adah and Zillah, hear my voice;
Ye wives of Lamech, hearken to my speech:
For I have slain a man on his wounding me,
And a young man on his bruising me.
24 If Cain shall be avenged sevenfold,
Lamech *shall be avenged* seventy and sevenfold."
25 And Adam knew his wife again; and she bare a son, and called his name Seth [APPOINTMENT] : "For God," *said she*, "hath appointed me another seed instead of Abel, whom
26 Cain slew." And to Seth also was born a son; and he called his name Enos: then began men to call upon the name of Jehovah.

1 CHAP. V.—This is the Book of the descendants of Adam. In the day that God created man, in the likeness of God he
2 made him; male and female he created them; and he blessed them, and called their name Adam [MAN], in the day when they were created.
3 And Adam lived a hundred and thirty years and begat *a son* in his own likeness, after his own image, and called
4 his name Seth: and the days of Adam, after he begat Seth, were eight hundred years: and he begat sons and
5 daughters: so all the days that Adam lived were nine hundred and thirty years: and he died.
6 And Seth lived a hundred and five years, and begat
7 Enos: and Seth lived, after he begat Enos, eight hundred and seven years, and begat sons and daughters: so all
8 the days of Seth were nine hundred and twelve years: and he died.
9 And Enos lived ninety years, and begat Cainan: and
10 Enos lived, after he begat Cainan, eight hundred and
11 fifteen years, and begat sons and daughters: so all the days of Enos were nine hundred and five years: and he died.
13 And Cainan lived seventy years and begat Mahalaleel: and Cainan lived, after he begat Mahalaleel, eight hundred and
14 forty years, and begat sons and daughters: so all the days of Cainan were nine hundred and ten years: and he died.
15 And Mahalaleel lived sixty-five years and begat Jared:
16 and Mahalaleel lived, after he begat Jared, eight hundred
17 and thirty years, and begat sons and daughters: so all the days of Mahalaleel were eight hundred and ninety-five years: and he died.

And Jared lived a hundred and sixty-two years, and begat 18
Enoch: and Jared lived, after he begat Enoch, eight hun- 19
dred years, and begat sons and daughters: so all the days 20
of Jared were nine hundred and sixty-two years: and he
died.

And Enoch lived sixty-five years and begat Methuselah: 21
and Enoch walked with God, after he begat Methuselah, 22
three hundred years, and begat sons and daughters: so all 23
the days of Enoch were three hundred and sixty-five years:
and Enoch walked with God, and he was not: for God took 24
him.

And Methuselah lived a hundred and eighty-seven years, 25
and begat Lamech: and Methuselah lived, after he begat 26
Lamech, seven hundred and eighty-two years, and begat
sons and daughters: so all the days of Methuselah were 27
nine hundred and sixty-nine years: and he died.

And Lamech lived a hundred and eighty-two years, and 28
begat a son; and he called his name Noah [COMFORTER or 29
REST] saying, "This *child* shall comfort us concerning our
work and the toil of our hands, because of the ground which
Jehovah hath cursed." And Lamech lived, after he begat 30
Noah, five hundred and ninety-five years, and begat sons
and daughters: so all the days of Lamech were seven hun- 31
dred and seventy-seven years: and he died.

And Noah was five hundred years old; and Noah begat 32
Shem, Ham, and Japheth.

CHAP. VI.—And it came to pass that when men began 1
to multiply on the face of the earth, and daughters were
born to them, the sons of God saw the daughters of men 2
that they were beautiful, and they took to themselves for
wives whomsoever they chose. And Jehovah said, "My 3
Spirit shall not be always judging men on account of their
transgressions: they are flesh, and their days shall be a hundred and twenty years."

There were giants in the earth in those days; and also 4
after that, when the sons of God had gone in unto the
daughters of men, and they had borne children to them,
these became mighty men, who of old were men of renown.
When Jehovah saw that the wickedness of man was great 5
in the earth, and that every imagination of the thoughts of
his heart was only evil continually, Jehovah repented that he 6
had made man on the earth, and was grieved in his heart.

GENESIS VII.

7 And Jehovah said, "I will destroy man, whom I have created, from the face of the earth; both man and beast, and the creeping thing, and the fowls of heaven: for I repent that I
8 have made them." But Noah found favour in the eyes of Jehovah.
9 This is the Account of Noah. Noah was the most just and upright man of his age, *and* Noah walked with God:
10 and Noah begat three sons, Shem, Ham, and Japheth. But the earth was corrupt in the sight of God; and the earth
12 was filled with violence. And God looked upon the earth, and, lo, it was corrupt; for all flesh had corrupted their way
13 upon the earth. And God said to Noah, "The end of all flesh is come before me; because through them the earth is filled with violence: therefore, lo, I will destroy them
14 with the earth. Make for thyself an ark of gopher-wood; rooms shalt thou make in the ark, and thou shalt cover it within
15 and without with bitumen. After this *form* thou shalt make it: the length of the ark shall be three hundred cubits, the breadth of it fifty cubits, and the height of it thirty cubits.
16 A sloping roof shalt thou make to the ark, and *at the height of* a cubit shalt thou finish it above; and the door of the ark shalt thou place in the side of it: a lower, a second,
17 and a third *story* shalt thou make in it. For, lo, I, even I, am about to bring a flood of waters upon the earth, to destroy all flesh, in which is the breath of life, from under the heavens; everything that is in the earth shall die.
18 But with thee will I establish my covenant: and thou shalt go into the ark; thou, and thy sons, and thy wife, and thy
19 sons' wives with thee. And of every living thing of all flesh, two of every *kind* shalt thou take into the ark, to be
20 kept alive with thee; they shall be male and female. Of birds according to their kinds, and of beasts according to their kinds, and of every thing that creepeth on the ground according to their kinds, two of every *kind* shall come unto thee
21 to be kept alive. Take thou therefore every sort of food that is eaten, and store it up with thee; that it may be for food for
22 thee, and for them." Thus did Noah; according to all that God commanded him, so he did.

1 CHAP. VII.—And Jehovah said to Noah, "Go thou and all thy household into the ark: for thee have I seen
2 righteous before me in this generation. Of all clean beasts thou shalt take with thee seven pairs, the male and his

female; and of beasts that are not clean one pair, the male and his female. Of fowls of heaven also seven pairs, the 3 male and the female, to keep alive *their* seed upon the face of all the earth. For after seven days I will cause it to 4 rain upon the earth forty days and forty nights; and every living creature that I have made will I destroy from off the face of the earth." And Noah did according to all 5 that Jehovah commanded him.

And Noah was six hundred years old when the flood of 6 waters was upon the earth. And Noah with his sons, and 7 his wife, and his sons' wives went into the ark, because of the waters of the flood. Of clean beasts, and of beasts 8 not clean, and of birds, and of everything that creepeth upon the ground, there went in two and two unto Noah 9 into the ark, the male and the female, as God had commanded Noah.

And it came to pass after seven days, that the waters 10 of the flood were upon the earth. In the six hundredth 11 year of the life of Noah, in the second month, the seventeenth day of the month, on that same day were all the fountains of the great deep broken up, and the windows of heaven were opened. And the rain came upon the earth 12 forty days and forty nights. In that very day Noah, and 13 Shem, and Ham, and Japheth, the sons of Noah, and Noah's wife, and the three wives of his sons with them, entered into the ark; they, and every beast according to its kind, and 14 all cattle according to their kinds, and every thing that creepeth upon the ground according to its kind, and every fowl according to its kind, every bird of every sort. And they went in unto Noah into the ark, two and 15 two of all flesh, in which was the breath of life. And they 16 that went in, went in male and female of all flesh, as God had commanded him: and Jehovah shut him in.

And the flood was forty days upon the earth; and the 17 waters increased, and bare up the ark, and it was raised above the earth.

And the waters prevailed, and increased greatly upon 18 the earth, and the ark floated upon the surface of the waters. And the waters prevailed exceedingly upon the earth, so that 19 all the high mountains, which were under the whole heaven, were covered. Fifteen cubits upward did the waters prevail: 20 and the mountains were covered. And all flesh died that 21 moved upon the earth, both of fowl, and of cattle, and of

beasts, and of every creeping thing that creepeth upon the
22 earth, and every man : all in whose nostrils was the breath of
23 life, of all that was in the dry *land*, died. And every living creature was destroyed which was upon the face of the ground, both man, and cattle, and creeping things, and the fowls of heaven ; and they were destroyed from the earth : and Noah only remained *alive*, and they who were with him in
24 the ark. And the waters prevailed upon the earth a hundred and fifty days.

1 CHAP. VIII.—But God remembered Noah, and every beast, and all the cattle that were with him in the ark: and God made a wind to pass over the earth, to
2 assuage the waters. The fountains also of the deep and the windows of heaven were stopped, and the rain from
3 heaven was restrained; and the waters gradually returned from off the earth : and at the end of the hundred and fifty
4 days the waters were abated, so that the ark rested in the seventh month, on the seventh day of the month, upon the
5 mountains of Ararat. And the waters decreased continually until the tenth month : in the tenth *month*, on the first *day* of the month, were the tops of the mountains seen.
6 And it came to pass at the end of forty days, that Noah
7 opened the window of the ark which he had made: and he sent forth a raven, which went out, going and returning,
8 until the waters were dried up from off the earth. He also sent forth a dove from him, to see if the waters were abated
9 from off the face of the ground: but the dove found no rest for the sole of her foot, and she returned unto him into the ark; for the waters were on the face of the whole earth. Then he put forth his hand, and took her, and pulled
10 her in unto him into the ark. And he stayed seven days more, and again he sent forth the dove out of the ark:
11 and the dove came in unto him in the evening, and, lo, in her mouth was an olive-leaf plucked off. So Noah knew
12 that the waters were abated from off the earth. And he stayed seven days more and sent forth the dove, which returned not again unto him.
13 And in the six hundredth and first year, in the first *month*, the first *day* of the month, the waters were dried up from off the earth : and Noah removed the covering of the ark, and looked, and, lo, the face of the ground was dry.

And in the second month, on the twenty-seventh day of the month, the earth was dried. 14

And God spake to Noah, saying, "Go forth from the ark, thou and thy wife, and thy sons, and thy sons' wives with thee. Bring forth with thee every living thing that is with thee of every kind; fowl and cattle and every creeping thing that creepeth upon the ground; that they may breed abundantly on the earth, and be fruitful, and multiply upon the earth." And Noah went forth, and his wife, and his sons, and his sons' wives with him. Every beast, every creeping thing and every fowl, whatsoever moveth upon the earth according to their kinds, went forth out of the ark. 15 17 18 19

And Noah built an altar to Jehovah, and took of every sort of clean beasts, and of every sort of clean birds, and offered burnt offerings on the altar. And Jehovah smelled the acceptable smell: and Jehovah said in his heart, "I will not again curse the ground any more for man's sake; although the imagination of man's heart be evil from his youth: neither will I again smite any more every thing living as I have done. While the earth remaineth, seedtime and harvest, and cold and heat, and summer and winter, and day and night shall not cease." 20 21 22

CHAP. IX.—And God blessed Noah and his sons, and said to them, "Be fruitful and multiply, and replenish the earth. And let the fear of you and the dread of you be upon all the beasts of the earth, and upon all the fowls of heaven, upon every thing which creepeth on the ground, and upon all the fishes of the sea: into your hand are they delivered. Every moving thing that liveth shall be food for you; even as the green herb I give you them all; but flesh with the life thereof, *that is* the blood thereof, ye shall not eat. And surely of your blood of your lives will I require an account; at the hand of every beast will I require it, and at the hand of man; at the hand of every man's brother will I require an account of the life of man. Whosoever sheddeth man's blood, by man shall his blood be shed: for in the image of God he hath made man. And be ye fruitful and multiply; bring forth abundantly in the earth, and multiply therein." 1 2 3 4 5 6 7

And God spake to Noah and to his sons with him, saying, "Behold I now establish my covenant with you, 8 9

10 and with your seed after you, and with every living creature that is with you, of fowl, of cattle, and wild beasts with you; from all that came out of the ark to every beast
11 of the earth. I establish my covenant with you, that no more shall all flesh be cut off by the waters of a flood; nor shall there any more be a flood to destroy the earth."
12 And God said, "This is the sign of the covenant which I make between me and you, and every living creature that is
13 with you, for perpetual generations. I have set my bow in the cloud, and it shall be for a sign of a covenant between
14 me and the earth. And it shall come to pass, when I bring a cloud over the earth, the bow shall appear in the cloud;
15 and I will remember my covenant, which is between me and you, and every living creature of all flesh; and the waters shall no more become a flood to destroy all flesh.
16 For the bow shall be in the cloud, and I will look upon it, that I may remember the everlasting covenant between God and every living creature of all flesh that is upon the earth."
17 And God said to Noah, "This is the sign of the covenant which I have established between me and all flesh that is upon the earth."
18 And the sons of Noah, who went forth from the ark, were Shem, and Ham, and Japheth: now Ham is the father
19 of Canaan. These are the three sons of Noah: and from them was the whole earth overspread.
20 And Noah began to be a husbandman, and he planted a
21 vineyard; and he drank of the wine, and was drunken;
22 and he was uncovered within his tent. And Ham, the father of Canaan, saw the nakedness of his father, and told
23 his two brethren who were without. And Shem and Japheth took a garment, and laid it upon both their shoulders, and went backward and covered the nakedness of their father; and their faces were backward, and they saw not their father's nakedness.
24 And when Noah awoke from his wine, and knew what his younger son had done unto him, he said:
25   "Cursed be Canaan!
    A slave of slaves shall he be to his brethren."
26 He also said:
    " Blessed of Jehovah, my God, be Shem!
    And Canaan shall be his slave.
27   God shall enlarge Japheth,

And he shall dwell in the tents of Shem;
And Canaan shall be his slave."

And Noah lived after the flood three hundred and fifty 28 years. And all the days of Noah were nine hundred and 29 fifty years: and he died.

CHAP. X.—Now this is the Account of the descendants 1 of the sons of Noah, Shem, Ham, and Japheth: and to them sons were born after the deluge.

The sons of Japheth; Gomer, and Magog, and Madai, 2 and Javan, and Tubal, and Meschech, and Tiras. And the 3 sons of Gomer; Ashkenaz, and Riphath, and Togarmah. And the sons of Javan; Elisha, and Tarshish, Chetim, and 4 Dodanim. By these were the coasts of the nations divided 5 in their lands; each according to its language, according to their families, in their nations.

And the sons of Ham; Cush, and Mizraim, and Phut, 6 and Canaan. And the sons of Cush; Seba, and Havilah, 7 and Sabtah, and Raamah, and Sabtecha: and the sons of Raamah; Sheba and Dedan. Cush also begat Nimrod; he 8 began to be a mighty one in the earth: he was a mighty 9 hunter before Jehovah: wherefore it is said, "Even as Nim- 10 rod the mighty hunter before Jehovah." And the beginning of his kingdom was Babel, and Erech, and Accad, and Calneh, in the land of Shinar. From that land he went 11 into Assyria, and builded Nineveh, and the city Rehoboth, and Calah, and Resen, between Nineveh and Calah: the 12 same is a great city. And Mizraim begat Ludim, and Ana- 13 mim, and Lehabim, and Naphtuhim, and Pathrusim, and 14 Casluhim (from whom came Philistim), and Caphtorim. And 15 Canaan begat Zidon his first-born, and Heth, and the Jebu- 16 site, and the Amorite, and the Girgasite, and the Hivite, 17 and the Arkite, and the Sinite, and the Arvadite, and the 18 Zemarite, and the Hamathite. And afterwards the families of the Canaanites were spread abroad, and the boundaries 19 of the Canaanites were from Zidon to Gerar and Gaza; thence to Sodom, and Gomorrah, and Admah, and Zeboim, even unto Lasha. These are the sons of Ham, according to 20 their families, *and* their language, in their lands, *and* in their nations.

Unto Shem also, the father of all the children of Eber, the 21 elder brother of Japheth, even to him were *children* born.

22 The sons of Shem; Elam, and Asshur, and Arphaxad, and
23 Lud, and Aram.   And the children of Aram; Uz, and Hul,
24 and Gether, and Mash.   And Arphaxad begat Salah; and
25 Salah begat Eber.   And unto Eber were born two sons; the
name of one was Peleg [DIVISION]; for in his days was the
26 earth divided; and his brother's name was Joktan.   And
Joktan begat Almodad, and Sheleph, and Hazarmaveth, and
27 Jerah, and Adoram, and Uzal, and Diklah, and Obal, and
29 Abimael, and Sheba, and Ophir, and Havilah, and Jobab:
30 all these were the sons of Joktan.   And their dwelling was
31 from Mesha unto Sephar, a mountain of the east.   These
are the sons of Shem, according to their families, *and* their
language, in their lands, according to their nations.
32   These are the families of the sons of Noah, according to
their descents, in their nations: and by these were the
nations divided in the earth after the flood.

1   CHAP. XI.—And the whole earth was of one language,
2 and of one speech.   And it came to pass as they moved
from the east that they found a plain in the land of Shinar;
3 and they settled there; and they said to one another,
"Come, let us make bricks, and burn them thoroughly."
4 So they had brick for stone, and bitumen for mortar.   And
they said, "Come, let us build for ourselves a city, and a
tower the top of which *may reach* unto heaven; and let us
make for ourselves a *land*-mark, lest we be scattered abroad
5 over the face of the whole earth."   And Jehovah came down
to see the city and the tower which the sons of men were
6 building.   And Jehovah said, "Lo, they are one people, and
they have all one language; and this they begin to do: and
now they will be restrained from nothing which they pur-
7 pose to do.   Come, let us go down, and there confound
their language, that they may not understand one another's
8 speech."   So Jehovah scattered them thence over the face
of all the earth: and they ceased from building the city.
9 Therefore the name of it is called Babel [CONFUSION];
because Jehovah did there confound the language of all
the earth: and thence did Jehovah scatter them over the
face of all the earth.
10   This is the Account of the descendants of Shem.   Shem was
a hundred years old when he begat Arphaxad, two years after
11 the flood: and Shem lived, after he begat Arphaxad, five hundred years, and begat sons and daughters.

And Arphaxad lived thirty-five years, and begat Salah: 12
and Arphaxad lived, after he begat Salah, four hundred 13
and three years, and begat sons and daughters.

And Salah lived thirty years, and begat Eber: and Salah 14
lived, after he begat Eber, four hundred and three years, and
begat sons and daughters.

And Eber lived thirty-four years, and begat Peleg: and 16
Eber lived, after he begat Peleg, four hundred and thirty
years, and begat sons and daughters.

And Peleg lived thirty years, and begat Reu: and Peleg 18
lived, after he begat Reu, two hundred and nine years, and
begat sons and daughters.

And Reu lived thirty-two years, and begat Serug: and 20
Reu lived, after he begat Serug, two hundred and seven
years, and begat sons and daughters.

And Serug lived thirty years, and begat Nahor: and 22
Serug lived, after he begat Nahor, two hundred years, and
begat sons and daughters.

And Nahor lived twenty-nine years, and begat Terah: 24
and Nahor lived, after he begat Terah, a hundred and nine- 25
teen years, and begat sons and daughters.

And Terah lived seventy years, and begat Abram, Nahor, 26
and Haran.

And this is the Account of the descendants of Terah: Terah 27
begat Abram, Nahor, and Haran. Haran begat Lot: and Haran 28
died before his father Terah in the land of his nativity, in Ur
of Chaldæa. And Abram and Nahor took unto themselves 29
wives: the name of Abram's wife was Sarai, and the name
of Nahor's wife Milcah, the daughter of Haran, who was
the father of Milcah and the father of Iscah. But Sarai 30
was barren; she had no child. And Terah took his son 31
Abram and his grandson Lot the son of Haran, and Sarai
his daughter-in-law, his son Abram's wife; and brought
them out from Ur of Chaldæa, to go into the land of
Canaan. But when they came unto Haran, they settled 32
there. And the days of Terah were two hundred and five
years: and Terah died in Haran.

CHAP. XII.—Now Jehovah had said to Abram, "Depart 1
from thy country, and from thy kindred, and from thy
father's house, into a land that I will shew thee: and I 2
will make thee a great nation, and I will bless thee,
and make thy name great; and thou shalt be a bless-

GENESIS XII.

3 ing: and I will bless them who bless thee, and curse him who curseth thee; and in thee shall all families of the earth be
4 blessed." So Abram departed as Jehovah had commanded him; and Lot went with him. And Abram was seventy-five years old when he went from Haran.
5 And Abram took Sarai his wife, and Lot his brother's son, and all their substance which they had gathered, and the persons whom they had gotten in Haran: and they went forth to go into the land of Canaan. And when they
6 were come into the land of Canaan, Abram passed through the land to the place of Sichem, to the terebinth tree of Moreh.
7 Now the Canaanites were then in the land. And Jehovah appeared to Abram, and said "To thy seed will I give this land." And there he built an altar to Jehovah,
8 who had appeared to him. And he removed thence to the mountainous country on the east of Beth-el, and pitched his tent, *having* Beth-el on the west, and Hai on the east; and there he built an altar to Jehovah, and called upon the
9 name of Jehovah. And Abram journeyed, going on still toward the south.
10 And there was a famine in the land: and Abram went down into Egypt to sojourn there; for the famine was
11 grievous in the land *of Canaan*. And it came to pass when he drew near to enter into Egypt, that he said to Sarai his wife, "Lo now, I know that thou art a beautiful
12 woman to look upon: when, therefore, the Egyptians see thee, they will say, 'This is his wife;' and they will kill me,
13 but they will save thee alive. Say, I pray thee, thou art my sister, that it may be well with me on thy account, and that
14 my life may be preserved for thy sake." And it came to pass, that when Abram was come into Egypt, the Egyptians
15 saw that the woman was very beautiful. The princes of Pharaoh also saw her, and commended her before Pharaoh,
16 and the woman was taken into Pharaoh's house. And he treated Abram well for her sake: and he had flocks and herds, and he-asses, and men-servants and maid-servants,
17 and she-asses, and camels. But Jehovah plagued Pharaoh and his house with great plagues, because of Sarai, Abram's
18 wife. Pharaoh therefore called Abram, and said, "What is this that thou hast done to me? why didst thou not tell me
19 that she was thy wife? Why saidst thou, 'She is my sister?' so I might have taken her to be my wife: now, therefore,
20 behold thy wife take her, and go." And Pharaoh gave

c

orders to *certain* men concerning him: and they sent him away, and his wife, and all that he had.

CHAP. XIII.—And Abram went up out of Egypt, he, 1 and his wife, and all that he had, and Lot with him, into the south *part of Canaan*. Now Abram was very rich in 2 cattle, in silver, and in gold. And he went on in his jour- 3 neys from the south to Beth-el, to the place where his tent had been before, between Beth-el and Hai; to the place 4 where he had formerly built an altar; and there Abram called on the name of Jehovah. And Lot also, who went 5 with Abram, had flocks, and herds, and tents. And the 6 land was not able to bear them to dwell together: for their substance was great, so that they could not dwell together. And there was strife between the herdmen of Abram's cattle 7 and the herdmen of Lot's cattle. Now the Canaanites and the Perizzites dwelt then in the land. And Abram said to 8 Lot, "Let there be no strife, I pray thee, between me and thee, and between my herdmen and thy herdmen: for we are kinsmen. Is not the whole land before thee? Separate 9 thyself, I pray thee, from me. If *thou wilt go* to the left hand, then I will go to the right; or if *thou wilt go* to the right hand, then I will go to the left." Then Lot lifted up 10 his eyes, and beheld all the plain of Jordan, that it was well watered every where, before Jehovah had destroyed Sodom and Gomorrah, all the way to Zoar, as the garden of Jehovah, as the land of Egypt. Lot therefore chose 11 for himself all the plain of Jordan; and Lot journeyed eastward: thus they separated themselves the one from the other: Abram dwelt in the land of Canaan, and Lot dwelt amongst 12 the cities of the plain, and pitched his tent by Sodom. Now 13 the men of Sodom were exceedingly wicked and sinful in the sight of Jehovah.

And Jehovah said to Abram, after Lot was separated from 14 him, "Lift up now thine eyes, and look from the place where thou art, northward and southward and eastward and westward: for all the land which thou seest, to thee will I give 15 it, and to thy seed for ever. And I will make thy seed as 16 the dust of the earth: so that if any one can number the dust of the earth, thy seed also may be numbered. Arise, 17 walk through the land, in the length of it and in the breadth of it: for I will give it to thee." Then Abram 18 pitched his tent and went and dwelt at the terebinth trees of Mamre, which are by Hebron, and built there an altar to Jehovah.

1 CHAP. XIV.—And it came to pass in the days of Amraphel king of Shinar, and Arioch king of Ellasar, Chedorlao-
2 mer king of Elam, and Tidal king of Goim, *that they* made
war with Bera king of Sodom, and with Birsha king of Gomorrah, Shinab king of Admah, and Shemeber king of Ze-
3 boim, and the king of Bela, which is Zoar. All these
were joined together in the vale of Siddim, which is the
4 Salt Sea. Twelve years had they been subject to Chedorlao-
5 mer, but in the thirteenth year they revolted. And in the
fourteenth year came Chedorlaomer, and the kings who were
with him, and smote the Rephaites in Ashteroth-karnaim,
and the Zuzites in Ham, and the Emites in Shaveh-kiria-
6 thaim, and the Horites in their mount Seir, unto El-paran,
7 which is by the desert. And they turned and came to
En-mishpat, which is Kadesh, and smote all the country of
the Amalekites, and also the Amorites that dwelt in Hazezon-
8 tamar. And the king of Sodom, and the king of Gomorrah,
and the king of Admah, and the king of Zeboim, and the
king of Bela, which is Zoar, went out and joined battle
9 with them in the vale of Siddim; with Chedorlaomer the
king of Elam, and with Tidal king of Goim, and Amraphel
king of Shinar, and Arioch king of Ellasar; four kings with
10 five. Now the vale of Siddim was full of pits of bitumen:
and the kings of Sodom and of Gomorrah fled, and fell
11 there; and they who remained fled to the mountains. Then
they took all the goods of Sodom and Gomorrah, and all their
12 victuals, and departed. They took Lot also, Abram's
brother's son, who dwelt in Sodom, and his goods, and
departed.
13 But one who had escaped came and told Abram the
Hebrew; for he dwelt by the terebinth trees of Mamre the
Amorite, brother of Eshcol, and brother of Aner: and these
14 were in alliance with Abram. And when Abram heard that
his kinsman was taken captive, he mustered his trained *servants*, born in his own house, three hundred and eighteen,
15 and pursued *them* unto Dan. And he and his servants divided
themselves and fell upon them by night, and smote them, and
pursued them unto Hobah, which is on the left of Damascus.
16 And he brought back all the goods; his kinsman Lot also,

and his goods he brought back, with the women also, and the people.

And after his return from smiting Chedorlaomer, 17 and the kings that were with him, the king of Sodom went out to meet him, at the valley of Shaveh, which is the King's Dale. Melchizedek also, king of Salem, brought forth 18 bread and wine; and he was a priest of God Most High. And he blessed him, and said, "Blessed be Abram by God Most 19 High, possessor of the heavens and the earth: and blessed 20 be God Most High, who hath delivered thine enemies into thy hands." And *Abram* gave him a tenth part of all.

And the king of Sodom said to Abram, "Give me the per- 21 sons, and take the goods to thyself." And Abram said to 22 the king of Sodom, "I have lifted up my hand to Jehovah God Most High, possessor of the heavens and the earth, that 23 I will not take anything that is thine, from a thread even to a sandal string, lest thou shouldest say, 'I have made Abram rich:' save only that which the young men have eaten, and 24 the portion of the men who went with me, Aner, Eshcol, and Mamre; let them take their portion."

CHAP. XV.—After these things the word of Jehovah 1 came to Abram in a vision, saying, "Fear not, Abram: I am a shield to thee, thy exceeding great reward." And 2 Abram said, "Lord Jehovah, what wilt thou give me, seeing I am still childless, and the steward of my house is this Eliezer of Damascus?" Abram also said, "Lo, to me thou 3 hast given no seed: and, lo, one born in my house will be my heir." And, lo, the word of Jehovah *came* to him, say- 4 ing, "This shall not be thine heir; but one who shall spring from thyself shall be thine heir." And he brought him forth 5 abroad, and said, "Look now towards the heavens, and number the stars, if thou be able to number them." And he said to him, "So shall thy seed be." And he believed 6 Jehovah; and he accounted it to him for righteousness. And 7 he said to him, "I am Jehovah who brought thee out of Ur of the Chaldees, to give thee this land for an inheritance." And *Abram* said, "Lord Jehovah, by what shall I know that 8 I shall inherit it?" And he said to him, "Bring to me a 9 heifer three years old, and a she-goat three years old, and a ram three years old, and a turtle-dove, and a young pigeon." And he brought to him all these, and divided them in halves, 10

and laid each piece one against another; but the birds he
11 divided not. And the birds of prey came down upon the car-
12 cases, and Abram drove them away. And when the sun was
going down, a deep sleep fell upon Abram; and, lo, a horror
13 with great darkness fell upon him. And *Jehovah* said to
Abram, "Know surely, that thy seed shall be sojourners in
a land not their own, which will reduce them into slavery,
14 and will afflict them four hundred years: but that nation,
whom they shall serve, I will judge; and afterwards they
15 shall come out with great substance. Thou indeed shalt go
to thy fathers in peace; thou shalt be buried in a good old
16 age. But in the fourth generation they shall come hither
again; for the iniquity of the Amorites is not yet complete."
17 And it came to pass that when the sun had gone down, and
it was dark, lo, a smoking furnace and a burning lamp which
18 passed between those pieces. At that time Jehovah made a
covenant with Abram, saying, "To thy seed I give this
land, from the river of Egypt unto the great river, the river
19 Euphrates: the *land of the* Kenites, and the Kenizzites,
20 and the Kadmonites, and the Hittites, and the Perizzites,
21 and the Rephaites, and the Amorites, and the Canaanites,
and the Girgashites, and the Jebusites."

1 CHAP. XVI.—Now Sarai, Abram's wife, bare him no
children: and she had an Egyptian hand-maid, whose
2 name was Hagar. And Sarai said to Abram, "Lo now,
Jehovah hath restrained me from bearing: I pray thee, go
in unto my handmaid; I may, perhaps, obtain children by
3 her." And Abram hearkened to the voice of Sarai. And
Sarai, Abram's wife, took Hagar the Egyptian, her handmaid, after Abram had dwelt ten years in the land of Canaan,
4 and gave her to her husband Abram to be his wife. And
he went in unto Hagar, and she conceived: and, when she
saw that she had conceived, her mistress was despised in her
5 eyes. And Sarai said to Abram, "My wrong *lieth* upon
thee: I have given my hand-maid into thy bosom; and
when she saw that she had conceived, I was despised in her
6 eyes: may Jehovah judge between me and thee." But
Abram said to Sarai, "Behold, thy hand-maid is in thy
power: do to her as it pleaseth thee."

And Sarai treated her harshly, so that she fled from her
7 face. And an angel of Jehovah found her by a fountain of

water in the desert, by the fountain in the way to Shur.
And he said, "Hagar, Sarai's hand-maid, whence camest 8
thou? and whither wouldst thou go?" And she said, "I flee
from the face of my mistress Sarai." And the angel of Jeho- 9
vah said to her, "Return to thy mistress, and submit thyself
to her power." And the angel of Jehovah said to her, "I will 10
multiply thy seed exceedingly, so that it shall not be numbered
for multitude." The angel of Jehovah also said to her, 11
"Behold, thou hast conceived, and shalt bear a son, and
shalt call his name Ishmael [GOD WILL HEAR]; because God
hath heard *thee* in thine affliction. And he will be a wild 12
man; his hand against every man, and every man's hand
against him: yet he shall dwell in the presence of all his
brethren." And she called the name of Jehovah who spake 13
to her, 'Thou God seest me:' for she said, "Have I also here
looked after him who seeth me?" Wherefore the well was 14
called Beer-lahai-roi: lo, it is between Kadesh and Bered.

And Hagar bare Abram a son; and Abram called the 15
name of his son, whom Hagar bare, Ishmael. And Abram 16
was eighty-six years old when Hagar bare Ishmael to
Abram.

CHAP. XVII.—And when Abram was ninety-nine years 1
old, Jehovah appeared to Abram, and said to him, "I am
God Almighty. Walk before me, and be perfect; and I will 2
make a covenant between me and thee, and will multiply thee
exceedingly." And Abram fell on his face; and God talked 3
with him, saying, "Lo, I make a covenant with thee, and 4
thou shalt be the father of a multitude of nations. And thy 5
name shall not any more be called Abram [EXALTED
FATHER]; but thy name shall be called Abraham [FATHER
OF A MULTITUDE]: for the father of a multitude of nations have I appointed thee to be. And I will make thee 6
exceedingly fruitful, and I will make nations of thee,
and kings shall come from thee. And I will establish 7
my covenant between me and thee, and thy seed after
thee in their generations, for an everlasting covenant, to be
a God to thee, and to thy seed after thee. And I will give 8
to thee, and to thy seed after thee, the land in which thou art
a stranger, all the land of Canaan, for an everlasting possession; and I will be their God." And God said to Abraham, 9
"Thou shalt keep my covenant therefore, thou, and thy seed

10 after thee, in their generations. This is my covenant, between me and you, and thy seed after thee, which ye shall keep. Every male-child among you shall be circumcised:
11 and ye shall circumcise the flesh of your foreskin; and it shall be a mark of the covenant between me and you.
12 Every male-child among you eight days old, whether he be born in the house, or bought with money of any alien, who is not of thy seed, shall, through your generations,
13 be circumcised. He that is born in thy house, and he that is bought with thy money, must without fail be circumcised, that my covenant may be in your flesh, an everlasting cove-
14 nant. But the uncircumcised male-child, whose flesh of his foreskin is not circumcised, shall be cut off from his people; he hath broken my covenant."
15 And God said to Abraham, "As for Sarai thy wife, thou shalt not call her name Sarai [MY PRINCESS], but Sarah [A
16 FRUITFUL WOMAN] shall her name be. And I will bless her, and give thee a son also of her; yea I will bless her, and she shall be *a mother of* nations, and kings of peoples
17 shall come from her." Then Abraham fell upon his face, and laughed, and said in his heart, "Shall a child be born to him who is a hundred years old? and shall Sarah, who is
18 ninety years old, bear?" And Abraham said unto God,
19 "Oh that Ishmael might live before thee!" And God said "Sarah thy wife shall indeed bear thee a son; and thou shalt call his name Isaac [LAUGHTER]: and I will establish my covenant with him and with his seed after him, for an
20 everlasting covenant. For Ishmael also I have heard thee; lo, I have blessed him, and will make him fruitful, and will multiply him exceedingly: twelve princes shall he beget,
21 and I will make him a great nation. But my covenant will I establish with Isaac, whom Sarah shall bear to thee at
22 this very time the next year." And he left off talking with him, and God went up from Abraham.
23 Then Abraham took Ishmael his son, and all that had been born in his house, and all that had been bought with his money, every male of Abraham's household, and circumcised the flesh of their foreskin on that selfsame day, as God
24 had commanded him. And Abraham was ninety-nine years old when he was circumcised in the flesh of his foreskin.
25 And Ishmael his son was thirteen years old when he was
26 circumcised in the flesh of his foreskin. In the same day
27 was Abraham circumcised and Ishmael his son; and all the

men of his house, born in the house, and bought with money of an alien, were circumcised with him.

CHAP. XVIII.—And Jehovah appeared to him at the terebinth trees of Mamre, as he sat in the tent-door in the heat of the day. And he lifted up his eyes and looked, and lo, three men stood over against him: and when he saw them, he ran to meet them from the tent-door, and bowed himself toward the ground, and said, "My lord, if now I have found favour in thy sight, pass not away, I pray thee, from thy servant: let a little water, I pray you, be fetched, and wash your feet, and rest yourselves under the tree: and I will fetch a morsel of bread, that ye may refresh yourselves; after that ye shall pass on: for with this intent are ye come to your servant." And they said, "So do as thou hast said." And Abraham hastened into the tent to Sarah, and said, "Make ready quickly three measures of fine meal, knead it, and made hearth-cakes." And Abraham ran to the herd, and fetched a calf tender and good, and gave it to a young man, who hastened to dress it. And he took butter and milk, and the calf which he had dressed, and set it before them; and he stood by them under the tree, and they did eat. And they said to him, "Where is Sarah thy wife?" And he said, "Lo, in the tent." And he said, "I will certainly return unto thee according to the time of life; and, lo, Sarah thy wife shall have a son." And Sarah heard it in the tent-door, which was behind him. Now Abraham and Sarah were far advanced in years; *and* it had ceased to be with Sarah after the manner of women. Therefore Sarah laughed within herself, saying, "After I am grown old shall I have pleasure, my lord being old also?" And Jehovah said to Abraham, "Wherefore did Sarah laugh, saying, 'Shall I who am old surely bear a child?' Is anything too hard for Jehovah? At the time appointed will I return unto thee, according to the time of life, and Sarah shall have a son." Then Sarah denied, saying, "I laughed not;" for she was afraid. And he said, "Nay; but thou didst laugh."

And the men rose up thence, and turned towards Sodom; and Abraham went with them to conduct them on the way. And Jehovah said, "Shall I hide from Abraham that which I am about to do; seeing that Abraham shall surely become a great and mighty nation, and all the nations of the

19 earth shall be blessed in him? For I know that he will
command his children and his household after him, to keep
the way of Jehovah, by doing justice and judgment; that
Jehovah may bring upon Abraham that which he hath
20 spoken concerning him." And Jehovah said, "Because
the cry of Sodom and Gomorrah is great, and because their
21 sin is very grievous, I will go down now, and see whether
they have done altogether according to the cry against it,
which is come unto me; and if not, I will know."
22 Then the men turned their faces thence, and were going towards Sodom: but Abraham stood yet before Jehovah. And
23 Abraham drew near, and said, "Wilt thou also destroy the
24 righteous with the wicked? Peradventure there may be fifty
righteous *persons* within the city: wilt thou also destroy and
not spare the place for the fifty righteous that are therein?
25 Far be it from thee to do after this manner, to slay the
righteous with the wicked; and to make the righteous and the
wicked alike; that be far from thee. Shall not the Judge of all
26 the earth do right?" And Jehovah said, "If I find in
Sodom fifty righteous *persons* within the city, then I will
27 spare the whole place, for their sakes." And Abraham
answered and said, "Lo, now, I have taken upon me to speak
28 to my Lord, though I am but dust and ashes: peradventure
there may be wanting five of the fifty righteous: wilt thou
destroy the whole city for *the want of* five?" And he said, "If
29 I find there forty-five, I will not destroy it." And he spake
to him yet again, and said, "Peradventure there may be forty
found there." And he said, "I will not do it for the sake
30 of forty." And he said "Oh let not my Lord be angry,
and I will speak: peradventure there may be thirty found
there." And he said, "I will not do it, if I find thirty
31 there." And he said, "Lo, now, I have taken upon me to
speak to my Lord: peradventure there may be twenty
found there." And he said, "I will not destroy it for
32 the sake of twenty." And he said, "Oh let not my Lord
be angry, and I will speak yet but this once: peradventure
ten may be found there." And he said, "I will not destroy
33 it for the sake of ten." And Jehovah went away, when he
had left off talking with Abraham: and Abraham returned
to his own place.

1 CHAP. XIX.—And the two angels came to Sodom in
the evening; and Lot was sitting in the gate of Sodom:

and Lot saw them, and rose up to meet them; and having bowed himself with his face toward the ground, he said, 2 "Lo now, my lords, turn in, I pray you, into your servant's house, and tarry all night, and wash your feet, and ye shall rise up early and go on your way." And they said, "Nay; we will abide in the street all night." But when he pressed 3 them greatly, they turned in unto him, and entered into his house: and he made them a feast, and baked unleavened bread, and they did eat.

They had not yet lain down, when the men of the city, 4 the men of Sodom, both young and old, all the people together, surrounded the house; and they called to Lot, and 5 said to him, "Where are the men who came in to thee this night? bring them out to us, that we may know them." And Lot went out at the door to them, and shut the door 6 after him, and said, "I pray you, brethren, do not so 7 wickedly. Lo now, I have two daughters who have not 8 known man; let me, I pray you, bring them out to you, and do ye to them as is right in your eyes: only to these men do nothing; for therefore came they under the shadow of my roof." And they said, "Stand back." And they said *again*, 9 "Shall one who came in to sojourn, make himself a judge? now will we deal worse with thee than with them." So they pressed hard on the man, on Lot, and were approaching to break the door. But the men put forth their hand, and 10 pulled Lot into the house to them, and shut the door. And 11 they smote the men who were at the door of the house, both small and great, with blindness; so that they wearied themselves to find the door. And the men said to Lot, 12 "Who of thy kindred besides are here? Thy sons-in-law, thy sons and thy daughters, and whomsoever thou hast in the city, bring out of this place: for we are about to de- 13 stroy this place, because the cry against them is become great before the face of Jehovah; and Jehovah hath sent us to destroy it." And Lot went out and spake to his sons-in- 14 law, who had married his daughters, and said, "Arise, go ye out of this place; for Jehovah is about to destroy this city." But he seemed, in the eyes of his sons-in-law, as one that jested.

And when the morning arose, the angels hastened Lot, 15 saying, "Arise, take thy wife, and thy two daughters, who are here, lest thou be destroyed in the punishment of the city." And while he lingered, the men took hold of his 16 hand, and of the hand of his wife, and of the hand of his two daughters, Jehovah being merciful to him; and they brought him forth, and placed him without the city. And it came to pass when they had brought them forth abroad, that he said, "Escape for thy life; look not behind thee, neither stay in any part of the plain; escape to the mountains, lest thou be destroyed." But Lot said to them, "Oh, not so, my lord: lo now, thy servant hath found favour in thy sight, and thou hast magnified thy mercy, which thou hast shewed to me in saving my life; but I cannot escape to the mountains, lest some evil overtake me, and I die. Lo now, this city is near to flee unto, and it is but a small one: oh, let me escape thither, (is it not a small one?) that my life may be preserved." And he said to him, "Lo, I have accepted thee concerning this thing also, that I will not overthrow this city, for which thou hast spoken. Haste thee, escape thither; for I cannot do any thing till thou art come thither." Therefore the name of the city was called Zoar [SMALL].

The sun had now risen upon the earth when Lot entered into Zoar. Then Jehovah rained upon Sodom, and upon Gomorrah, brimstone and fire from Jehovah out of heaven; and he overthrew those cities, and all the plain, and all the inhabitants of the cities, and that which grew upon the ground. But *Lot's* wife looked back from behind him, and she became a pillar of salt. And Abraham went early in the morning to the place where he had stood before Jehovah, and he looked towards Sodom and Gomorrah, and towards all the country of the plain, and beheld, and, lo, the smoke of the country went up as the smoke of a furnace. And it came to pass when God destroyed the cities of the plain, that God remembered Abraham, and sent Lot out of the midst of the overthrow, when he overthrew the cities in which Lot dwelt.

And Lot went up out of Zoar, and dwelt amongst the mountains, and his two daughters with him; for he feared to dwell in Zoar: and he dwelt in a cave, he and his two daughters. And the first-born said to the younger, "Our father is old, and there is not a man in the earth to come in unto us according to the custom of all the earth: Come, let us make our father drink wine, and we will lie with him, that we may preserve seed of our father." And they made their father drink wine that night: and the first-born went in, and lay with her father; and he perceived not when she lay down, nor when she arose. And it came to pass on the morrow, that the first-born said unto the younger, "Lo, I lay yesternight with my father: let us make him drink wine this night also; and go thou in, *and* lie with him, that we may preserve seed of our father." And they made their father drink wine that night also: and the younger arose, and lay with him; and he perceived not when she lay down, nor when she arose. Thus were both the daughters of Lot with child by their father. And the first-born bare a son, and called his name Moab [FROM A FATHER]: he was the father of the Moabites unto this day. And the younger also bare a son, and called his name Benammi [SON OF MY OWN PEOPLE]: he was the father of the children of Ammon unto this day.

CHAP. XX.—And Abraham journeyed thence toward the south country, and dwelt between Kadesh and Shur, and sojourned in Gerar. And Abraham said of Sarah his wife, "She is my sister:" and Abimelech king of Gerar sent and took Sarah. But God came to Abimelech in a dream by night, and said to him, "Lo, thou art a dead man, on account of the woman whom thou hast taken; for she is a man's wife." But Abimelech had not come near her: and he said, "O Jehovah, wilt thou slay also a righteous nation? Said he not to me, 'She is my sister?' and she, even she herself, said, 'He is my brother:' in the integrity of my heart and innocency of my hands have I done this." And God said to him in a dream, "Yea, I know that thou didst this in the integrity of thy heart; therefore I withheld thee from sinning against me, and suffered thee not to touch her. Now therefore restore the man's wife; for he is a prophet, and he will pray for thee, and thou shalt live: but if thou restore her not, know that thou shalt surely die, thou, and all that are thine." And Abimelech rose early in the morning, and called all his servants, and told all these things in their hearing: and all the men were greatly afraid. Then Abimelech called Abraham, and said to him, "What hast thou done to us? and in what have I offended thee, that thou wouldst bring on me and on my kingdom a great sin? Deeds that ought not to be done, thou hast done to me." Abimelech said also to Abraham, "What sawest thou, that thou shouldst do this thing?" And Abraham said, "Because I

thought, 'Surely the fear of God is not in this place; and
12 they will slay me for my wife's sake.' And yet indeed she
is my sister; the daughter of my father, but not the daughter
13 of my mother; and she became my wife. And it came to
pass, when God caused me to wander from my father's house,
that I said to her, 'This is thy kindness which thou shalt
shew to me; at every place to which we shall come, say of
14 me, 'He is my brother.'" And Abimelech took flocks, and
herds, and men-servants, and women-servants, and gave them
15 to Abraham, and restored to him Sarah his wife. And Abimelech said, "Lo, my land is before thee: dwell where it
16 pleaseth thee." And to Sarah he said, "Lo, I have given
thy brother a thousand pieces of silver; lo! this is for a covering of the eyes of thyself, *and* of all who are with thee,
17 and of all *others*." Thus she was absolved. So Abraham
prayed to God: and God healed Abimelech, and his wife, and
18 his maid-servants; so that they might have children. For
Jehovah had fast closed up all the wombs of the house of
Abimelech, because of Sarah, Abraham's wife.

1 CHAP. XXI.—And Jehovah visited Sarah as he had said,
2 and Jehovah did to Sarah as he had spoken: for Sarah
conceived, and bare a son to Abraham in his old age, at the
3 appointed time of which God had spoken to him. And Abraham called the name of his son that was born to him, whom
4 Sarah bare to him, Isaac. And Abraham circumcised his
son Isaac, when eight days old, as God had commanded him.
5 Now Abraham was a hundred years old when his son Isaac
6 was born to him. And Sarah said, "God hath prepared
laughter for me; whosoever shall hear *of this* will laugh with
7 me." And she said, "Who would have said to Abraham,
'Sarah shall suckle children?' yet I have borne him a son
8 in his old age." And the child grew, and was weaned: and
Abraham made a great feast on the day that Isaac was
9 weaned. And Sarah saw the son of Hagar the Egyptian,
10 whom she had borne to Abraham, mocking: wherefore she
said to Abraham, "Cast out this bond-woman and her son:
for the son of this bond-woman shall not be heir with my
11 son, with Isaac." And the speech was very displeasing to
12 Abraham, because of his son. But God said to Abraham,
"Let it not be displeasing to thee because of the lad, and
because of thy bond-woman: in all that Sarah hath said to
thee, hearken to her voice; for in Isaac shall thy seed be

called. Yet also of the son of the bond-woman will I make 13
a nation, because he is thy seed."

Then Abraham rose up early in the morning, and took 14
bread and a bottle of water, and gave them to Hagar, putting
them on her shoulder, and sent her away with the lad: and
she departed, and wandered in the desert of Beer-sheba.
And the water was spent in the bottle, and she placed the 15
lad under one of the shrubs. And she went, and sat down 16
over against *him* a good way off, about the distance of a bow-
shot: for she said, "Let me not see the death of the lad."
So she sat down over against *him*, and lifted up her voice
and wept. And God heard the voice of the youth: and the 17
angel of God called to Hagar out of heaven, and said to her,
"What aileth thee, Hagar? fear not; for God hath heard
the voice of the youth where he *lieth*. Arise, lift up the 18
youth, and hold him in thy hand; for I will make him a
great nation." And God opened her eyes, and she saw a 19
well of water; and she went, and filled the bottle with
water, and gave drink to the youth. And God was with the 20
youth; and he grew, and dwelt in the desert, and became
an archer. And he dwelt in the desert of Paran: and 21
his mother took a wife to him out of the land of Egypt.

And it came to pass at that time that Abimelech, and 22
Phicol the chief of his host, spake to Abraham, saying,
"God is with thee in all that thou doest. Now therefore 23
swear to me here by God, that thou wilt not deal falsely
with me, nor with my posterity; according to the kindness that I have done to thee, thou shalt do to me, and
to the land in which thou hast sojourned." And Abraham 24
said, "I swear." Then Abraham reproved Abimelech 25
because of a well of water, which Abimelech's servants had
violently seized. And Abimelech said, "I know not who 26
hath done this thing; for neither didst thou tell me, nor
did I hear of it till this day." And Abraham took sheep 27
and oxen, and gave them to Abimelech; and both of them
made a covenant. Then Abraham set seven ewe-lambs of 28
the flock by themselves. And Abimelech said to Abraham, 29
"What mean these seven ewe-lambs, which thou hast set by
themselves?" And he said, "That thou mayest take these 30
seven ewe-lambs from my hand, that they may be a testimony for me that I digged this well." Wherefore that 31
place was called Beer-sheba [THE WELL OF THE OATH];
because there they both sware. Thus they made a covenant 32

at Beer-sheba. Then Abimelech rose up, and Phicol the chief of his host, and they returned to the land of the Philistines. And *Abraham* planted a tamarisk *grove* at Beer-sheba, and called there on the name of Jehovah, the everlasting God. And Abraham sojourned in the land of the Philistines many days.

CHAP. XXII.—And it came to pass after these things, that God proved Abraham, and said to him, "Abraham:" and he said, "Here I am." And he said, "Take now thy son, thine only *son* Isaac, whom thou lovest, and go into the land of Moriah; and offer him there for a burnt-offering upon one of the mountains of which I will tell thee." And Abraham arose early in the morning, and saddled his ass, and took two of his young men with him, and Isaac his son, and clave the wood for the burnt-offering, and set out to go to the place of which God had told him. And on the third day Abraham lifted up his eyes, and saw the place afar off. Then Abraham said to his young men, "Abide ye here with the ass; and I and the youth will go yonder and worship and come again to you." And Abraham took the wood of the burnt-offering, and laid it upon Isaac his son; and he took the fire in his hand, and a knife: and they went both of them together. And Isaac spake to Abraham his father, and said, "My father:" and he said, "Here I am, my son." And he said, "Lo, the fire and the wood; but where is the lamb for a burnt-offering?" And Abraham said, "My son, God will provide himself a lamb for a burnt-offering:" so they went both of them together, till they came to the place of which God had told him: and Abraham built an altar there, and laid the wood in order; and bound Isaac his son, and laid him on the altar upon the wood. And Abraham stretched forth his hand, and took the knife to slay his son. But an angel of Jehovah called to him out of heaven, and said, "Abraham, Abraham:" and he said "Here I am." And he said, "Lay not thy hand upon the youth, nor do any thing to him: for now I know that thou fearest God, seeing thou hast not withheld thy son, thine only *son*, from me." And Abraham lifted up his eyes, and looked, and lo, behind *him* a ram caught in a thicket by his horns; and Abraham went and took the ram, and offered it for a burnt-offering in stead of his son. And Abraham called the name of that place Jehovah-jireh [JEHOVAH WILL PROVIDE:] as it is said to this day, "In the mountain Jehovah will provide." And the angel of Jehovah called to Abraham out of heaven the second time, and said, "By myself I swear, saith Jehovah, that because thou hast done this thing, and hast not withheld thy son, thine only *son*, I will greatly bless thee, and I will exceedingly multiply thy seed, as the stars of heaven, and as the sand which is upon the sea-shore; and thy seed shall possess the gate of their enemies: and in thy seed shall all the nations of the earth be blessed, because thou hast obeyed my voice." Then Abraham returned to his young men; and they rose up, and went together to Beer-sheba: and Abraham dwelt at Beer-sheba.

And it came to pass after these things that it was told to Abraham, saying, "Lo, Milcah hath also borne children to thy brother Nahor; Huz his first-born, and Buz his brother, and Kemuel the father of Aram, and Chesed, and Hazo, and Pildash, and Jidlaph, and Bethuel." (Now Bethuel was the father of Rebekah:) these eight Milcah did bear to Nahor, Abraham's brother. His concubine also, whose name *was* Reumah, bare Tebah, and Gaham, and Thahash, and Maachah.

CHAP. XXIII.—And Sarah was a hundred and twenty-seven years old; *these were* the years of the life of Sarah; and Sarah died in Kirjath-arba, which is Hebron in the land of Canaan: and Abraham went to mourn for Sarah, and to weep for her. And Abraham stood up from before his dead, and spake to the sons of Heth, saying, "I am a stranger and a sojourner with you: give me a possession of a burying-place with you, that I may bury my dead out of my sight." And the sons of Heth answered Abraham, saying to him, "Hear us, my lord: thou art a mighty prince amongst us: in the choicest of our sepulchres bury thy dead: not one of us will withhold from thee his sepulchre, but that thou mayest bury thy dead." And Abraham stood up, and bowed himself to the people of the land, to the sons of Heth. And he spake to them, saying, "If it be your mind that I should bury my dead out of my sight, hear me, and intercede for me with Ephron the son of Zohar, that he may give me the cave of Machpelah which he hath, which is at the end of his field: at its full price let him give it

me, for a possession of a burying-place amongst you."
10 Now Ephron was sitting amongst the sons of Heth; and Ephron the Hittite answered Abraham in the hearing of the sons of Heth, of all that went in at the gate of his city,
11 saying, "Nay, my lord, hear me: the field I give thee, and the cave also that is in it, I give thee; in the presence of the sons of my people I give it thee: bury thy dead."
12 And Abraham bowed down himself before the people of
13 the land; and he spake to Ephron, in the hearing of the people of the land, saying, "Since thou *art favourable* to me, hear me: I will give thee money for the field;
14 take it from me, and I will bury my dead there." And
15 Ephron answered Abraham, saying, "My lord, hearken to me: the land *is worth* four hundred shekels of silver; what is that between me and thee? bury therefore thy dead."
16 And Abraham hearkened to Ephron; and Abraham weighed to Ephron the silver, which he had named in the hearing of the sons of Heth, four hundred shekels of silver, current
17 with the merchant. So the field of Ephron, in Machpelah, which was opposite to Mamre, the field, and the cave which was in it, and all the trees, which were in all the
18 borders round about, were made sure to Abraham for a possession, in the presence of the sons of Heth, before all that
19 went in at the gate of their city. And after this Abraham buried Sarah his wife in the cave of the field of Machpelah, opposite to Mamre, which is Hebron, in the land of Canaan.
20 Thus the field, and the cave that is in it, were made sure to Abraham, for a possession of a burying-place, by the sons of Heth.

1 CHAP. XXIV.—Abraham was now old, and far advanced in years: and Jehovah had blessed Abraham in all things.
2 And Abraham said to his servant, the eldest of his house, who ruled over all that he had, "Put thy hand, I pray thee,
3 under my thigh; and I will make thee to swear by Jehovah, the God of the heavens, and the God of the earth, that thou wilt not take a wife for my son of the daughters of the
4 Canaanites, amongst whom I dwell: but that thou wilt go to my country, and to my kindred, and take a wife for my
5 son Isaac." And the servant said to him, "Peradventure the woman will not be willing to follow me to this land: must I then take back thy son to the land whence thou
6 camest?" And Abraham said to him, "Beware, that thou

D

take not my son thither again. Jehovah, God of the heavens, who brought me from my father's house, and from the land of my kindred, and who spake to me, and who sware to me, saying, 'To thy seed will I give this land,' he will send his angel before thee, that thou mayest take thence a wife for my son. But if the woman be not willing to follow thee, then thou shalt be free from this my oath; only take not my son thither again." And the servant put his hand under the thigh of Abraham his master, and sware to him to that purport.

Then the servant took ten camels, of the camels of his master, and departed, *taking* all the best things of his master with him. And he arose and went to Mesopotamia, to the city of Nahor. And he made his camels kneel down without the city by a well of water, at the time of the evening, the time that women go out to draw *water*. And he said, "O Jehovah, God of my master Abraham, I pray thee give me success this day, and shew kindness to my master Abraham. Lo, I stand by the well of water; and the daughters of the men of the city are coming out to draw water: and let it come to pass that the damsel to whom I shall say, 'Let down thy pitcher, I pray thee, that I may drink;' and she shall say, 'Drink; and I will give thy camels drink also,' be she whom thou hast appointed for thy servant Isaac. By this shall I know that thou hast shewed kindness to my master."

And it came to pass before he had done speaking that lo, Rebekah, who was born to Bethuel, son of Milcah, the wife of Nahor, Abraham's brother, came out with her pitcher upon her shoulder. And the damsel was very beautiful, a virgin whom no man had known: and she went down to the well, and filled her pitcher, and came up; and the servant ran to meet her, and said, "Let me, I pray thee, drink a little water out of thy pitcher." And she said, "Drink, my lord:" and she made haste, and let down her pitcher upon her hand, and gave him drink. And, when she had done giving him drink, she said, "I will draw *water* for thy camels also, until they have done drinking." And she made haste, and emptied her pitcher into the trough, and ran again to the well to draw *water*, and drew for all his camels. And the man gazed upon her in silence, *anxious* to know whether Jehovah had made his journey prosperous or not. And it came to pass when the camels had done drinking,

that the man took a golden ring of half a shekel weight, and
two bracelets for her hands of ten *shekels* weight of gold,
23 and said, " Whose daughter art thou ? tell me I pray thee:
24 is there room in thy father's house for us to lodge in ?" And
she said to him, "I am the daughter of Bethuel the son of
25 Milcah, whom she bare to Nahor." She said moreover to
him, "We have both straw and provender in abundance, and
26 also room to lodge in." And the man bowed his head, and
27 worshipped Jehovah, and said, " Blessed be Jehovah, God of
my master Abraham, who hath not withdrawn from my
master his mercy and his truth : I am in the *right* way ;
Jehovah hath led me to the house of my master's brother."
28 And the damsel ran, and told these things to her mother's
29 household. Now Rebekah had a brother, whose name was
30 Laban: and Laban ran out to the man to the well. And it
came to pass when he saw the ring, and the bracelets upon
his sister's hands, and when he heard the words of Rebekah
his sister saying, "Thus spake the man to me," that he
went to the man : and lo, he was standing by the camels at
31 the well. And he said, " Come in, thou blessed of Jehovah ;
wherefore standest thou without ? for I have prepared the
32 house, and a place for the camels." So the man came into
the house: and *Laban* ungirded his camels, and gave straw
and provender for the camels, and water to wash his feet, and
33 the feet of the men that were with him. And meat was set
before him to eat: but he said, "I will not eat until I have
34 told mine errand." And *Laban* said " Tell *it*." And he
35 said, " I am Abraham's servant. And Jehovah hath blessed
my master exceedingly, so that he is become great : and he
hath given him flocks and herds, and silver and gold, and
36 men-servants and maid-servants, and camels and asses. And
Sarah, my master's wife, bare a son to my master when she
37 was old : and to him hath he given all that he hath. Now
my master made me to swear saying, ' Thou shalt not take a
wife for my son of the daughters of the Canaanites, in whose
38 land I dwell : but thou shalt go to my father's house, and to
39 my kindred, and take a wife for my son.' And I said to my
40 master, ' Peradventure the woman will not follow me.' And
he said to me, ' Jehovah, before whom I walk, will send his
angel with thee, and prosper thy way; that thou mayest
take a wife for my son of my kindred, and of my father's
41 house. Thou shalt be free from my oath, when thou comest
to my kindred ; if they will not give thee *one*, thou shalt
42 be free from my oath.' Now when I came this day to the

well, I said, 'O Jehovah, God of my master
thou prosper my way which I go, lo, I st
of water; and when the maiden cometh fort
and I say to her, Give me, I pray thee, a li
pitcher to drink; and she say to me, Both
I will also draw for thy camels; let the san
whom Jehovah hath appointed for my master'
yet done speaking with myself, when, lo, Reb
with her pitcher on her shoulder; and she w
well, and drew *water :* and I said to her, '
thee, a little water of thy pitcher to drink.'
haste, and let down her pitcher from her *sh*
'Drink;. and I will give thy camels dri
drank, and she gave the camels drink
asked her, and said, ' Whose daughter art th
said, 'The daughter of Bethuel, Nahor's son
bare to him:' and I put the ring upon h
bracelets upon her hands. And I bowed my
shipped Jehovah, and blessed Jehovah, Go
Abraham, who had led me in the right w
daughter of my master's brother for his son
ye will deal kindly and truly with my master
not, tell me; that I may turn to the right han

Then Laban and Bethuel answered and sa
proceedeth from Jehovah; we cannot say to t.
Lo, Rebekah is before thee; take her and go
the wife of thy master's son, as Jehovah hath
it came to pass that when Abraham's serv
words, he bowed himself to the ground
And the servant brought forth jewels of sil
of gold, and raiment, and gave them to Reb
also to her brother and to her mother preciou
both he and the men that were with him, ate
tarried all night.

When they arose in the morning, *the serva*
me away to my master." But her brother a
said, "Let the damsel abide with us *a few* da
ten; and after that she shall go." And he s
"Hinder me not, seeing Jehovah hath pros
send me away, that I may go to my maste
said, "We will call the damsel, and inqu
mouth." And they called Rebekah, and said
thou go with this man?" And she said, " I
they sent away Rebekah their sister, and l

60 Abraham's servant, and his men. And they blessed Rebekah, and said to her, "Thou art our sister, mayest thou be *the mother of* thousands of millions, and may thy seed possess
61 the gate of those who hate them." And Rebekah arose, and her damsels, and they rode upon the camels, and followed the man. Thus the servant took Rebekah, and departed.
62 And Isaac had returned from Beer-lahai-roi; for he dwelt
63 in the south country. And Isaac went out to meditate in the field towards the evening; and he lifted up his eyes, and
64 saw, and lo, the camels were coming. And Rebekah lifted up her eyes; and when she saw Isaac, she alighted off the
65 camel, and said to the servant, "What man is this that walketh in the field to meet us?" And the servant said, "It is my master:" so she took a veil and covered herself.
67 And the servant told Isaac all that he had done. Then Isaac brought Rebekah into his mother Sarah's tent, and he took her to be his wife, and loved her: and Isaac was comforted for the loss of his mother.

1 CHAP. XXV. — And Abraham took another wife,
2 whose name was Keturah. And she bare to him Zimran, and Jokshan, and Medan, and Midian, and Ishbak, and
3 Shuah. And Jokshan begat Sheba and Dedan. And the sons of Dedan were the Ashurites, and the Letushites, and
4 the Leumites. And the sons of Midian; Ephah, and Epher, and Hanoch, and Abidah, and Eldaah. All these were the
5 children of Keturah. Now Abraham gave all that he had
6 to Isaac. But to the sons whom Abraham had by his concubines, Abraham, while he was yet living, gave gifts, and sent them away from Isaac his son eastward, into the land of Kedem.
7 And these are the days of the years of Abraham's life,
8 which he lived, a hundred and seventy-five years. Then Abraham expired, and died in a good old age, an old man
9 and full *of days;* and was gathered to his people. And his sons Isaac and Ishmael buried him in the cave of Machpelah, in the field of Ephron, the son of Zohar the Hittite, which is
10 opposite to Mamre; the field which Abraham had purchased of the sons of Heth: there was Abraham buried, with Sarah
11 his wife. And it came to pass after the death of Abraham, that God blessed his son Isaac: and Isaac dwelt at Beer-lahai-roi.

Now this is the account of the descendants of Ishmael, Abraham's son, whom Hagar the Egyptian, Sarah's handmaid, bare to Abraham. And these are the names of the sons of Ishmael, according to their names in their genealogies. Nebaioth the first-born of Ishmael; and Kedar, and Adbeel, and Mibsham, and Mishma, and Dumah, and Massa, Hadad, and Tema, Jetur, Naphish, and Kedemah. These were the sons of Ishmael, and these their names, according to their villages and their strongholds; twelve princes according to their nations. And these are the years of the life of Ishmael, a hundred and thirty-seven years: and he expired, and died, and was gathered to his people. And they dwelt from Havilah unto Shur, on the borders of Egypt, in the way to Assyria. In the presence of all his brethren *his lot* fell.

Now this is the account of the descendants of Isaac the son of Abraham.

Abraham begat Isaac. And Isaac was forty years old when he took for his wife Rebekah, the daughter of Bethuel the Syrian, of Padan-aram, the sister to Laban the Syrian. And Isaac entreated Jehovah for his wife, because she was barren: and Jehovah heard his request, and Rebekah his wife conceived. But the children struggled together within her: and she said, "If it be so, why am I thus?" so she went to inquire of Jehovah. And Jehovah said to her,

"Two nations are in thy womb,
And two peoples shall be separated from thy bowels:
And *one* people shall be stronger than *the other* people:
And the elder shall be subject to the younger."

And when the time of her being delivered was come, lo, twins were in her womb. And the first came out red, all over like a hairy garment; so they called his name Esau [COVERED, or HAIRY]. And after that came out his brother, and his hand took hold on Esau's heel, so his name was called Jacob [HE HOLDS THE HEEL]: and Isaac was sixty years old when they were born. And the boys grew: and Esau became a skilful hunter, a man of the field; but Jacob was a quiet man, dwelling in tents. And Isaac loved Esau, because he ate of his venison; but Rebekah loved Jacob.

And Jacob was seething pottage: and Esau came from the field, and he was faint. And Esau said to Jacob, "Let me eat, I pray thee, of that red, red *pottage;* for I am faint:" hence

31 was his name called Edom [RED]. And Jacob said, "Sell 32 me this day thy birth-right." And Esau said, "Lo, I am about to die; and what will this birth-right profit me?" 33 And Jacob said, "Swear to me this day;" so he sware to 34 him; and sold his birth-right to Jacob. Then Jacob gave Esau bread and pottage of lentiles; and he ate and drank, and rose up, and went his way. Thus Esau despised the birth-right.

1 CHAP. XXVI.—And there was a famine in the land, beside the former famine in the days of Abraham. And Isaac went to Gerar, to Abimelech, king of the Philistines. 2 For Jehovah had appeared to him, and said, "Go not down 3 into Egypt; dwell in the land of which I tell thee. Sojourn in this land, and I will be with thee, and will bless thee: for to thee, and to thy seed, I will give all these lands; and I will perform the oath which I sware to Abraham thy father. 4 And I will make thy seed as numerous as the stars of heaven, and will give to thy seed all these lands; and in 5 thy seed shall all the nations of the earth be blessed: because Abraham obeyed my voice, and kept my charge, my commandments, my statutes, and my laws."

7 So Isaac dwelt in Gerar. And the men of the place asked him concerning his wife: and he said, "She is my sister:" for he was afraid to say, "She is my wife;" "lest," *said he*, "the men of the place should kill me on account of Re-8 bekah;" because she was a beautiful woman. But it came to pass, when he had been there a long time, that Abimelech, king of the Philistines, looked out at a window and saw, and 9 lo, Isaac was sporting with Rebekah his wife. And Abimelech called Isaac, and said, "Lo, surely she is thy wife: and how saidst thou, 'She is my sister?'" And Isaac said to him, 10 "Because I said, 'Lest I die for her.'" And Abimelech said, "What is this thou hast done to us? one of the people might readily have lain with thy wife, and thou wouldst have 11 brought guilt upon us." Then Abimelech charged all his people, saying, "He that toucheth this man, or his wife, shall surely be put to death."

12 And Isaac sowed in that land, and received in the same 13 year a hundred-fold; for Jehovah blessed him. And the man throve, and went on thriving until he became very 14 great: for he had possession of flocks, and possession of herds, and a great number of servants; so that the Philis-

tines were jealous of him. And all the wells which his 15 father's servants had digged, in the days of Abraham his father, the Philistines stopped up, and filled them with earth. Abimelech therefore said to Isaac, "Go from us; for thou 16 art much mightier than we." So Isaac departed thence, and 17 pitched his tent in the valley of Gerar, and dwelt there.

And Isaac digged again the wells of water which they had 18 digged in the days of Abraham his father (for the Philistines had stopped them up after the death of Abraham): and he called them by the names by which his father had called them. And Isaac's servants digged in the valley, and found 19 there a well of springing water. And the herdmen of Gerar 20 strove with Isaac's herdmen, saying, "The water is ours:" so he called the name of the well Esek [STRIFE]; because they strove with him. And they digged another well, and 21 strove for that also: so he called the name of it Sitnah [ENMITY]. And he removed thence, and digged another 22 well; and for that they strove not; therefore he called the name of it Rehoboth [ROOM]; "For now," said he, "Jehovah hath made room for us, and we shall be fruitful in the land." And he went up thence to Beer-sheba. And 24 Jehovah appeared to him the same night, and said, "I am the God of Abraham thy father; fear not, for I am with thee, and will bless thee, and multiply thy seed, for the sake of my servant Abraham." So he built an altar there, and 25 called upon the name of Jehovah, and pitched his tent there: and there Isaac's servants digged a well.

Then Abimelech went to him from Gerar, and Ahuzzath 26 one of his friends, and Phicol the captain of his army. And 27 Isaac said to them, "Wherefore come ye to me, seeing ye hate me, and have sent me away from you?" And they 28 said, "We have clearly seen that Jehovah is with thee: we say therefore, 'Let there be now an oath between us, between us and thee, and let us make a covenant with thee; that as we have not touched thee, and as we have done to 29 thee nothing but good, and have sent thee away in peace; so thou wilt do us no hurt now that thou art blessed by Jehovah.'" And he made them a feast, and they ate and 30 drank. And they arose early in the morning, and sware 31 one to another: and Isaac sent them away, and they departed from him in peace. Now it came to pass that day, 32 that Isaac's servants came and told him concerning the well which they had digged, and said to him, "We have found

33 water." So he called it Shebah [AN OATH]: therefore the name of the city is Beer-sheba [THE WELL OF AN OATH] to this day.
34 And Esau was forty years old when he took for wives Judith the daughter of Beeri the Hittite, and Bashemath the
35 daughter of Elon the Hittite: who were a grief of mind to Isaac and to Rebekah.

1 CHAP. XXVII.—Now it came to pass that when Isaac was become old, and his eyes were dim, so that he could not see, he called Esau his eldest son, and said to him, "My
2 son!" and he said to him, "Lo, here I am." And he said, "Lo now, I am old, I know not the day of my death: now therefore take, I pray thee, thy weapons, thy quiver
3 and thy bow, and go out to the field, and take for me
4 venison: and make me savoury meat, such as I love, and bring it to me, that I may eat; that I may bless thee before I die."
5 And Rebekah heard Isaac when he spake to Esau his son. And Esau went to the field to take venison, to bring *to his*
6 *father*. Then Rebekah spake to Jacob her son, saying, "Lo,
7 I heard thy father speak to Esau thy brother, saying, 'Bring me venison, and make me savoury meat, that I may eat, and bless thee in the presence of Jehovah before my death.'
8 Now therefore, my son, obey my voice, according to that
9 which I command thee: go now to the flock, and fetch me thence two kids of the goats; and I will make of them
10 savoury meat for thy father, such as he loveth: and thou shalt take it to thy father, that he may eat, to the end that
11 he may bless thee before his death." But Jacob said to Rebekah his mother, "Lo, Esau my brother is a hairy man,
12 and I am a smooth man: my father will perhaps feel me, and I shall seem to him as a deceiver; so shall I bring upon
13 myself a curse, and not a blessing." And his mother said to him, "Upon me be thy curse, my son; only obey my
14 voice, and go fetch me *the kids*." And he went, and fetched and brought them to his mother: and his mother made savoury meat, such as his father loved.
15 Then Rebekah took the choicest of the raiment of her eldest son Esau, which she had by her in the house, and put
16 it upon Jacob her youngest son: and she put the skins of the kids upon his hands, and upon the smooth part
17 of his neck: she then gave the savoury meat and the

bread, which she had prepared, into the hand of her son Jacob. And he went to his father, and said, "My father!" 18 And he said, "Here I am; who art thou, my son?" And 19 Jacob said to his father, "I am Esau thy first-born; I have done according as thou badest me: arise, I pray thee, sit up and eat of my venison, that thy soul may bless me." And 20 Isaac said to his son, "How is it that thou hast found it so quickly, my son?" And he said, "Because Jehovah thy God put it in my way." And Isaac said to Jacob, "Come 21 near, I pray thee, that I may feel thee, my son, whether thou be my son Esau himself or not." Then Jacob went near to Isaac 22 his father; and he felt him, and said, "The voice is the voice of Jacob, but the hands are the hands of Esau." And he dis- 23 cerned him not, because his hands were hairy, as the hands of his brother Esau: so he blessed him. And he said, 24 "Art thou my very son Esau?" and he said, "I am." And he said, "Bring it near to me, and let me eat of my 25 son's venison, that my soul may bless thee." And he brought it near to him, and he ate: and he brought him wine, and he drank. And his father Isaac said to him, "Come near now, 26 and kiss me, my son." And he came near, and kissed him: 27 and he smelled the fragrance of his raiment, and blessed him, and said,

"See! the fragrance of my son is as the fragrance of a field
Which Jehovah hath blessed:
So may God give thee of the dew of heaven, 28
And of the fatness of the earth,
And abundance of corn and wine:
May peoples serve thee, 29
And nations bow down to thee:
Mayest thou be lord over thy brethren,
And may thy mother's sons bow down to thee
Cursed be every one that curseth thee,
And blessed be he that blesseth thee."

Now when Isaac had made an end of blessing Jacob, and 30 Jacob was yet scarcely gone out from the presence of Isaac his father, Esau his brother came in from his hunting. And 31 he also made savoury meat, and brought it to his father, and said to his father, "Let my father arise, and eat of his son's venison, that thy soul may bless me." And Isaac his father 32 said to him, "Who art thou?" And he said, "I am thy son, thy first-born, Esau." And Isaac trembled very ex- 33

ceedingly, and said, "Who then is he that hath taken venison, and brought it to me, of all which I have eaten before thou camest? for I have blessed him, and blessed he
34 must be." And when Esau heard the words of his father, he uttered a loud and exceedingly bitter cry, and said to his
35 father, "Bless me, me also, O my father!" And *Isaac* said, "Thy brother came with subtilty, and hath taken away thy
36 blessing." And *Esau* said, "Is he not rightly named Jacob [SUPPLANTER]? for twice hath he supplanted me: he took away my birth-right; and, behold, now he hath taken away my blessing." And he said, "Hast thou not reserved a
37 blessing for me?" And Isaac answered and said to Esau, "Lo, I have made him thy lord, and all his brethren have I given to him for servants; corn also and wine have I given to him for his support: and what can I do now for thee, my
38 son?" And Esau said to his father, "Hast thou but one blessing, my father? bless me, me also, O my father!" And
39 Esau lifted up his voice and wept. And Isaac his father answered and said to him,

"Lo, thy dwelling shall be without the fatness of the earth,
And without the dew of heaven from above;
40 And by thy sword shalt thou live,
And shalt serve thy brother:
But a time shall come, when thou wilt have dominion,
And break his yoke from off thy neck."

41 And Esau hated Jacob, because of the blessing with which his father had blessed him: and Esau said within himself, "The days of mourning for my father are at hand, then will
42 I slay my brother Jacob." And these words of Esau, her elder son, were told to Rebekah. And she sent and called Jacob her younger son, and said to him, "Lo, thy brother Esau
43 threatens to kill thee. Now, therefore, my son, obey my
44 voice. Arise, flee to Haran, to Laban my brother; and tarry
45 with him a few days, until thy brother's fury turn away; until thy brother's anger turn away from thee, and he forget that which thou hast done to him: then I will send and fetch thee thence. Why should I be deprived of you both in one day?"
46 Then Rebekah said to Isaac, "I am weary of my life because of the daughters of Heth: if Jacob were to take a wife from among the daughters of Heth, such as these *who are* of the daughters of the land, what would life be to me?"

CHAP. XXVIII.—So Isaac called Jacob, and blessed him, 1 and charged him, and said to him, "Thou shalt not take a wife from among the daughters of Canaan. Arise, go to Pa- 2 dan-aram, to the house of Bethuel thy mother's father, and take thee a wife thence from among the daughters of Laban, thy mother's brother. And may God Almighty bless thee, 3 and make thee fruitful, and multiply thee, that thou mayest become an assembly of peoples; and may he give to thee the 4 blessing of Abraham, to thee, and to thy seed with thee; that thou mayest inherit the land in which thou sojournest, which God gave to Abraham." Thus Isaac sent away Jacob: and 5 he went to Padan-aram, to Laban, son of Bethuel the Syrian, the brother of Rebekah, the mother of Jacob and of Esau.

And when Esau saw that Isaac had blessed Jacob, and sent 6 him away to Padan-aram, to take thence a wife for himself; and that, as he blessed him, he gave him a charge, saying, "Thou shalt not take a wife from among the daughters of Canaan;" and that Jacob obeyed his father and his mother, 7 and was gone to Padan-aram; also when Esau saw that the 8 daughters of Canaan pleased not Isaac his father; then Esau 9 went to Ishmael, and took for his wife (besides the wives which he had) Mahalah the daughter of Ishmael, Abraham's son, the sister of Nebajoth.

And Jacob departed from Beer-sheba, and went towards 10 Haran. And he arrived at a certain place, and tarried there 11 all night, because the sun was set: and he took one of the stones of that place, and put it for his pillow, and lay down in that place to sleep. And he dreamed, and lo, a ladder set 12 up on the earth, and the top of it reached to heaven: and, lo, the angels of God were ascending and descending on it. And lo, Jehovah stood above it, and said, "I am Jeho- 13 vah, the God of Abraham thy father, and the God of Isaac: the land on which thou liest, to thee will I give it, and to thy seed; and thy seed shall be as the dust of the earth; and 14 thou shalt spread abroad to the west, and to the east, and to the north, and to the south: and in thee and in thy seed shall all the families of the earth be blessed. And lo, I am 15 with thee, and will keep thee whithersoever thou goest, and will bring thee again into this land: for I will not leave thee, until I have done that of which I have spoken to thee." And 16 Jacob awaked out of his sleep, and said, "Surely Jehovah

17 is in this place, though I knew it not." And he was afraid, and said, "How dreadful is this place! this is nothing else than the house of God, and this is the gate of heaven."
18 And Jacob arose early in the morning, and took the stone that he had put for his pillow, and set it up as a pillar, and
19 poured oil upon the top of it. And he called the name of that place Beth-el [HOUSE OF GOD]: but the name of
20 that city before, was Luz. And Jacob made a vow, saying, "If God will be with me, and will keep me in this way that I go, and will give me bread to eat, and raiment to put on,
21 so that I return to my father's house in peace; then Jehovah
22 shall be my God, and this stone, which I have set up as a pillar, shall be God's house: and of all that thou shalt give me, I will surely give the tenth to thee."

1 CHAP. XXIX.—Then Jacob went on his journey, and
2 came into the land of the people of the east. And he looked, and, lo, a well in the field, and, lo, three flocks of sheep were lying by it; for out of that well they watered the flocks. Now there was a great stone upon the mouth of
3 the well. And when all the flocks were assembled, they rolled the stone from the mouth of the well, and watered the sheep, and put the stone again upon the mouth of the well, in its place.
4 And Jacob said to them, "My brethren, whence are ye?"
5 And they said, "Of Haran are we." And he said to them, "Know ye Laban the son of Nahor?" And they said,
6 "We know him." And he said to them, "Is it well with him?" And they said, "It is well; and, lo, Rachel his
7 daughter cometh with the sheep." And he said to them "Lo, it is yet full day, nor is it time that the cattle should be gathered together: water ye the sheep, and go *and* feed
8 them." And they said, "We cannot until all the flocks are assembled, and they have rolled the stone from the mouth of the well; then we water the sheep."
9 And while he was yet speaking to them, Rachel came
10 with her father's sheep; for she kept them. Now when Jacob saw Rachel the daughter of Laban his mother's brother, and the sheep of Laban his mother's brother, Jacob went near, and rolled the stone from the mouth of the well,
11 and watered the flock of Laban his mother's brother. And Jacob kissed Rachel, and lifted up his voice, and wept.
12 And Jacob told Rachel that he was her father's kinsman,

and that he was Rebekah's son: and she ran and told her father. And when Laban heard the tidings of Jacob his 13 sister's son, he ran to meet him, and embraced him, and kissed him, and brought him to his house. And he told Laban all these things. And Laban said to him, "Surely 14 thou art my own bone and my own flesh."

And when he had remained with him the space of a month, Laban said to Jacob, "Although thou be my kins- 15 man, shouldest thou therefore serve me for nothing? tell me, what shall be thy wages?" Now Laban had two 16 daughters: the name of the elder was Leah, and the name of the younger was Rachel. Leah was tender-eyed; but 17 Rachel was beautiful and well-favoured. And Jacob loved 18 Rachel; and said, "I will serve thee seven years for Rachel thy younger daughter." And Laban said, "It is better 19 that I should give her to thee, than that I should give her to any other man: abide with me." And Jacob served 20 seven years for Rachel; and they seemed to him but single days, from the love he had for her.

And Jacob said to Laban, "Give me my wife, for my 21 time is completed, that I may go in unto her." So Laban 22 gathered together all the men of the place, and made a feast. But in the evening, he took Leah his daughter, and 23 brought her to him: and he went in unto her. And Laban 24 gave Zilpah his handmaid, to his daughter Leah, for a handmaid. And it came to pass in the morning that, lo, it was 25 Leah; and he said to Laban, "What is this thou hast done to me? Did I not serve thee for Rachel? Why then hast thou deceived me?" And Laban said, "It must not be 26 so done in our country, to give the younger before the firstborn. Complete her week, and I will give thee this one 27 also, for the service which thou shalt serve with me yet seven other years." And Jacob did so, and completed 28 her week: and *Laban* gave him Rachel also his daughter for a wife. And Laban gave to Rachel his daughter, Bilhah 29 his handmaid, to be her handmaid. And *Jacob* went in 30 also unto Rachel, and he loved Rachel more than Leah, and served with him yet seven other years.

And when Jehovah saw that Leah was hated, he opened 31 her womb: but Rachel was barren. And Leah conceived, 32 and bare a son, and she called his name Reuben [BEHOLD A SON:] for she said, "Surely Jehovah hath beheld my affliction; now, therefore, my husband will love me." And 33

she conceived again, and bare a son; and said, "Because Jehovah hath heard that I was hated, he hath therefore given me this *son* also:" and she called his name Simeon
34 [HE HATH HEARD THE AFFLICTION]. And she conceived again, and bare a son; and said, "Now this time will my husband be bound to me, because I have borne to him three sons:" therefore his name was called Levi [A BOND].
35 And she conceived again, and bare a son: and she said, "Now will I praise Jehovah:" therefore she called his name Judah [PRAISE]. She then ceased to bear.

1 CHAP. XXX.—And when Rachel saw that she bare no children to Jacob, Rachel envied her sister, and said to
2 Jacob, "Give me children, or else I die." And Jacob's anger was kindled against Rachel; and he said, "Am I in the place of God, who hath withheld from thee the fruit of
3 the womb?" And she said, "Behold my maid Bilhah, go in unto her; and let her bear upon my knees, that I may
4 also have children by her." So she gave him Bilhah her
5 handmaid for a wife; and Jacob went in unto her. And
6 Bilhah conceived, and bare to Jacob a son. And Rachel said, "God hath decided for me, and hath also heard my voice, and hath given me a son:" therefore she called his name Dan [HE HATH DECIDED]. And Bilhah, Rachel's
7 handmaid, conceived again, and bare to Jacob a second son.
8 And Rachel said, "With great wrestlings have I wrestled with my sister, and I have prevailed:" and she called his name Naphtali [MY WRESTLING].
9 When Leah saw that she had ceased to bear, she took Zilpah her handmaid, and gave her to Jacob for a wife.
10 And Zilpah, Leah's handmaid, bare to Jacob a son. And Leah said, "A troop cometh:" and she called his name
12 Gad [A TROOP]. And Zilpah, Leah's handmaid, bare to
13 Jacob a second son. And Leah said, "Happy am I, for women will call me happy:" so she called his name Asher [HAPPY].
14 And Reuben went, in the days of wheat-harvest, and found mandrakes in the field, and brought them to his mother Leah. Then Rachel said to Leah, "Give me, I
15 pray thee, of thy son's mandrakes." But she said to her, "Is it a small matter that thou hast taken my husband? and wouldest thou take away my son's mandrakes also?" And Rachel said, "Therefore he shall lie with thee to night

for thy son's mandrakes." And Jacob came out of the field 16
in the evening, and Leah went out to meet him, and said,
"Thou must come in unto me; for surely I have hired thee
with my son's mandrakes." So he lay with her that night.
And God hearkened to Leah, and she conceived, and bare 17
to Jacob a fifth son. And Leah said, "God hath given me 18
my reward, because I gave my handmaid to my husband:"
so she called his name Issachar [A REWARD IS HE]. And 19
Leah conceived again, and bare to Jacob a sixth son. And 20
Leah said, "God hath given me a good gift: now will my
husband dwell with me, because I have borne him six
sons:" so she called his name Zebulun [A DWELLING].
And afterwards she bare a daughter, and called her name 21
Dinah [JUDGEMENT].

And God remembered Rachel, and God hearkened to her, 22
and opened her womb. And she conceived, and bare a son; 23
and said, "God hath taken away my reproach:" and she 24
called his name Joseph [MAY HE ADD]; saying; "May
Jehovah add to me another son!"

Now it came to pass when Rachel had borne Joseph, that 25
Jacob said to Laban, "Send me away, that I may go to my
own place, and to my own country. Give me my wives for 26
whom I have served thee, and my children, and let me go:
for thou knowest what service I have done thee." And 27
Laban said to him, "If I have found favour in thine eyes,
tarry: for I have learned by experience that Jehovah hath
blessed me for thy sake." He also said, "Fix thine hire 28
with me, and I will give it." And *Jacob* said to him, 29
"Thou knowest how I have served thee, and what thy cattle
has become with me. For it was little which thou hadst 30
before I *came*, but it is *now* greatly increased; and Jehovah
hath blessed thee since my coming: and now, when shall I
provide for my own house also?" And he said, "What 31
shall I give thee?" And Jacob said, "Thou shalt not give
me any thing. If thou wilt do this thing for me, I will
again feed *and* keep thy flock: Let me pass through all 32
thy flock to-day, removing thence all the speckled and
spotted and all the brown among the sheep, and the
spotted and speckled among the goats; and *such* shall
be my hire. So shall my integrity answer for me on a 33
future day, when thou shalt come to inspect my hire:
every one that is not speckled and spotted amongst
the goats, and brown amongst the sheep, that shall be

34 counted stolen with me." And Laban said, "Lo! be it according to thy word."
35 And he removed that day the he-goats, that were ringstreaked and spotted, and all the she-goats that were speckled and spotted, (all that had any white in them,) and all the brown amongst the sheep, and gave them into the
36 hand of his sons. And he set three days' journey between himself and Jacob: and Jacob fed the rest of Laban's
37 flocks. And Jacob took rods of fresh poplar, and of the almond and plane-tree; and peeled white streaks in them,
38 and made bare the white which was in the rods. And he set the rods which he had peeled before the flocks in the troughs at the watering places, when the flocks came to
39 drink: for they coupled when they came to drink. And the flocks coupled before the rods, and brought forth ring-
40 streaked, speckled, and spotted. And Jacob separated the lambs, and set the faces of the flocks towards the ringstreaked and all the brown in the flock of Laban; and he put his own flocks by themselves, and put them not to Laban's cattle.
41 And whenever the stronger flocks were coupling, Jacob laid the rods before the eyes of the flocks in the troughs,
42 that they might couple among the rods: but when the flocks were feeble he put them not in: so the feebler were
43 Laban's, and the stronger Jacob's. And the man increased exceedingly, and had large flocks, and maid-servants, and men-servants, and camels, and asses.

1 CHAP. XXXI.—But *Jacob* heard the words of Laban's sons, saying, ".Jacob hath taken away all that was our father's; and of that which was our father's hath he gotten
2 all this wealth." And Jacob beheld the countenance of
3 Laban, and, lo! it was not towards him as before. And Jehovah said to Jacob, "Return to the land of thy fathers,
4 and to thy kindred; and I will be with thee." And Jacob sent and called Rachel and Leah to the field, unto his flock,
5 and said to them, "I see your father's countenance, that it is not towards me as before: but the God of my father hath
6 been with me. Now ye know, that with all my power I
7 have served your father. Yet your father hath deceived me, and changed my wages ten times: but God suffered him
8 not to hurt me. If he said thus, 'The speckled shall be thy wages;' then all the flocks bare speckled: and if he

E

said thus, 'The ring-streaked shall be thy hire;' then all the flocks bare ring-streaked. Thus God hath taken away 9 the substance of your father, and given it to me. For it 10 came to pass at the time that the flocks were coupling, that I lifted up mine eyes, and saw in a dream, and, lo, the he-goats which leaped upon the flocks were ring-streaked, speckled, and spotted. And the angel of God spake to me 11 in a dream, *saying*, 'Jacob:' and I said, 'Here I *am*.' And 12 he said, 'Lift up now thine eyes, and see, all the he-goats which leap upon the flocks are ring-streaked, speckled, and spotted: for I have seen all that Laban doeth to thee. I 13 am the God of Beth-el, where thou anointedst a pillar, and where thou vowedst a vow to me: now therefore arise, go from this land, and return to the land of thy kindred.'" And Rachel and Leah answered and said to him, 14 " Have we yet had any portion or inheritance in our father's house? Have we not been accounted by him as aliens? 15 for he hath sold us, and hath also quite devoured our price. Since all the riches which God hath taken from our father, 16 are ours, and our children's, do now whatsoever God hath said to thee."

Then Jacob arose, and set his sons and his wives upon 17 camels; and he carried away all his cattle, and all his sub- 18 stance which he had acquired, the cattle which he possessed, which he had acquired in Padan-aram, to go to Isaac his father in the land of Canaan. Now Laban had gone to 19 shear his sheep: and Rachel stole her father's images. And 20 Jacob stole away unawares to Laban the Syrian, for he told him not that he fled. So he fled with all that he had; and 21 passed over the river and set his face towards mount Gilead. And it was told Laban on the third day, that Jacob had 22 fled. And he took his brethren with him, and pursued 23 him a journey of seven days, and they overtook him on mount Gilead. Now God had come to Laban the Syrian in 24 a dream by night, and had said to him, " Take heed that thou speak not to Jacob either good or bad."

When Laban overtook Jacob, Jacob had pitched his tent 25 on the mount; and Laban with his brethren pitched on mount Gilead. And Laban said to Jacob, " What hast 26 thou done, that thou hast stolen away unawares to me, and carried away my daughters as captives *taken* with the sword? Wherefore didst thou flee away secretly, and steal 27 away from me; and didst not tell me, that I might have

sent thee away with mirth and with songs, and with tabret
28 and with harp? Thou hast not even suffered me to kiss
my sons and my daughters. Thou hast now done foolishly
29 in so doing. It is in my power to do you hurt: but the
God of your father spake to me yesternight, saying, 'Take
heed that thou speak not to Jacob either good or bad.'
30 And now, though thou wast resolved to go, because thou
greatly longedst after thy father's house, yet wherefore hast
31 thou stolen my gods?" And Jacob answered and said to
Laban, "Because I was afraid: for I said that peradventure
32 thou wouldest take by force thy daughters from me. With
whomsoever thou findest thy gods, let him not live: before
our brethren, discern thou what is thine with me, and take
it to thee." For Jacob knew not that Rachel had stolen
them.
33 And Laban went into Jacob's tent, and into Leah's tent,
and into the tents of both the handmaids; but he found
them not. Then went he out of Leah's tent, and entered
34 into the tent of Rachel. Now Rachel had taken the
images, and put them in the camel's furniture, and sat upon
them. And Laban searched all the tent, but found them
35 not. And she said to her father, "Let it not displease my
lord that I cannot rise up before thee; for the custom of
women is upon me." Thus he searched, but found not the
images.
36 And Jacob was wroth, and chode with Laban: and Jacob
answered and said to Laban, "What is my trespass, what is
37 my sin, that thou hast so hotly pursued after me? Now
that thou hast searched all my furniture, what hast thou
found of all the furniture of thy house? set it here before
my brethren and thy brethren, and let them judge between
38 us both. These twenty years have I been with thee; thy
ewes and thy goats have not cast their young, nor have
39 I eaten the rams of thy flock. That which was torn
I brought not to thee; I bare the loss of it: of my
hand didst thou require it, *whether* stolen by day, or
40 stolen by night. *Thus* I was; by day the drought consumed me, and the frost by night; and my sleep departed
41 from mine eyes. Thus have I been twenty years in thy
house: I served thee fourteen years for thy two daughters,
and six years for thy cattle: and ten times thou hast
42 changed my wages. Unless the God of my father, the God
of Abraham, and he whom Isaac feareth, had been with me,

surely thou hadst sent me away now empty. My afflictions and the labours of my hands God hath seen; therefore he rebuked thee yesternight."

And Laban answered and said to Jacob, "These 43 daughters are my daughters, and these children are my children, and these flocks are my flocks, and all that thou seest is mine: and what can I do this day to these my daughters, or to their children which they have borne? Now, therefore, come thou, and let us make a covenant, I 44 and thou; and let it be for a witness between me and thee." And Jacob took a stone, and set it up *for* a pillar. And 46 Jacob said to his brethren, "Gather stones:" so they took stones, and made a heap; and they did eat there upon the heap. And Laban called it Jegar-sahadutha; but Jacob 47 called it Galeed. For Laban had said, "Let this heap be a 48 witness between me and thee this day." Therefore was the name of it called Galeed [WITNESS-HEAP]; and Mizpah 49 [WATCH-TOWER]: for he said, "Jehovah watch between me and thee, when we are absent one from another. If 50 thou shalt afflict my daughters, or if thou shalt take wives beside my daughters, no man is with us; see, God is witness between me and thee." And Laban said to Jacob, 51 "Lo, this heap, and lo, the pillar, which I have raised between me and thee; let this heap be a witness, and the 52 pillar be a witness, that I will not pass over this heap to thee, and that thou wilt not pass over this heap and this pillar to me, for harm. The God of Abraham, and the God 53 of Nahor, the God of their father, judge between us." And Jacob sware by *Him* whom his father Isaac feared.

Then Jacob offered sacrifice on the mount, and called his 54 brethren to eat bread: and they did eat bread, and tarried all night on the mount. And early in the morning Laban 55 arose, and kissed his sons and his daughters, and blessed them: and Laban departed, and returned to his own place.

CHAP. XXXII.—And Jacob went on his way, and 1 angels of God met him. And when Jacob saw them, he 2 said, "This is the camp of God:" and he called the name of that place Mahanaim [THE TWO CAMPS].

And Jacob sent messengers before him to Esau his 3 brother, unto the land of Seir, the country of Edom, and 4 commanded them, saying, "Thus shall ye speak to my lord Esau; 'Thy servant Jacob saith thus, I have sojourned

5 with Laban, and stayed there until now: and I have oxen, and asses, and flocks, and men-servants, and women-servants: and I have sent to tell my lord, that I may find favour 6 in thy sight.'" And the messengers returned to Jacob, saying, "We went to thy brother Esau, and, lo! he is now coming to meet thee, and four hundred men with him."

7 Then Jacob was greatly afraid and distressed: and he divided the people that were with him, and the flocks, and the 8 herds, and the camels, into two companies; for he said, "If Esau come to one company and smite it, then the other 9 company which is left may escape." And Jacob said, "O God of my father Abraham, and God of my father Isaac, O Jehovah, who saidst to me, 'Return to thy own land, and 10 to thy own kindred, and I will deal well with thee:' I am not worthy of the least of all the mercies, and of all the faithfulness which thou hast shewn to thy servant; for with my staff I passed over this Jordan, and now I am be-11 come two companies. Deliver me, I pray thee, from the hand of my brother, from the hand of Esau: for I fear him, lest he come and smite me, the mother with the 12 children. Yet thou hast said, 'I will surely do thee good, and make thy seed as the sand of the sea, which cannot be numbered for multitude.'"

13 And he lodged there that night; and took of that which 14 he had with him a present for Esau his brother; two hundred she-goats and twenty he-goats; two hundred ewes and 15 twenty rams; thirty milch-camels with their colts; forty heifers, and ten steers; twenty she-asses, and ten foals. 16 And he gave them in charge to his servants, each drove by itself; and he said to his servants, "Pass over before me, 17 and put a space between drove and drove." And he commanded the foremost, saying, "When Esau my brother shall meet thee, and shall ask thee, saying, 'Whose art thou? and whither goest thou? and whose are these before 18 thee?' then thou shalt say, 'They are thy servant Jacob's; it is a present sent to my lord Esau: and, lo, he also is 19 behind us.'" And so commanded he the second, and the third, and all who followed the droves, saying, "After this 20 manner shall ye speak to Esau, when ye meet him. And ye shall moreover, say, 'Lo, thy servant Jacob is behind us.'" For he said, "I will appease him with the present that goeth before me, and afterward I will see his face;

peradventure he will receive me kindly." So the present 21
passed over before him; but he himself lodged that night
in the company.

And he arose that night, and took his two wives, and his 22
two handmaids, and his eleven sons, and passed over the ford
of the Jabbok. And he took them, and sent them over the 23
brook, he also sent over *all* that he had. And Jacob was 24
left alone; and there wrestled a man with him until the
breaking of the day: and when *the man* saw that he pre- 25
vailed not against him, he touched the hollow of his thigh;
and the hollow of Jacob's thigh was strained, as he wrestled
with him. And *the man* said, "Let me go, for the day 26
breaketh." But *Jacob* said, "I will not let thee go, except
thou bless me." And he said to him, "What is thy 27
name?" And he said, "Jacob." And he said, "Thy 28
name shall be called no more Jacob, but Israel [HE CON-
TENDETH WITH GOD]: for thou hast contended with God
and with men, and hast prevailed. Then Jacob asked, and 29
said, "Tell me, I pray thee, thy name." And he said,
"Wherefore dost thou ask after my name?" And he
blessed him there. And Jacob called the name of the 30
place Peniel [THE FACE OF GOD]: "for I have seen God
face to face, yet my life is preserved."

And as he passed over Peniel the sun rose upon him, and 31
he halted upon his thigh. Therefore the children of Israel 32
eat not *of* the sinew which shrank, which is upon the hollow
of the thigh unto this day: because he touched the hollow
of Jacob's thigh in the sinew that shrank.

CHAP. XXXIII.—And Jacob lifted up his eyes, and 1
looked, and, lo, Esau was coming, and with him four hundred men. And he distributed the children to Leah, and to
Rachel, and to the two handmaids. And he put the hand- 2
maids and their children foremost, and Leah and her children after them, and Rachel and Joseph after these. He 3
then passed on before them, and bowed himself to the
ground seven times, till he came near to his brother. But 4
Esau ran to meet him, and embraced him, and fell on his
neck, and kissed him: and they wept. And *Esau* lifted up 5
his eyes, and saw the women and the children, and said,
"Who are these with thee?" And he said, "The children
whom God hath graciously given to thy servant." Then 6
the handmaids came near, they and their children, and they

7 bowed themselves. And Leah also with her children came near, and bowed themselves: and afterwards Joseph with
8 Rachel, and they bowed themselves. And *Esau* said, "What meanest thou by all that drove which I met?" And he said,
9 "To obtain favour in the sight of my lord." And Esau said, "I have enough, my brother; keep to thyself that
10 which thou hast." And Jacob said, "Nay, I pray thee; if now I have found favour in thy sight, receive my present from my hand: since I have appeared before thee, as though I had appeared before God, that thou mightest be
11 favourable to me. Take, I pray thee, my blessing which is brought to thee; because God hath dealt graciously with me, and because I have every thing." Thus he urged him, and he took it.
12 Then *Esau* said, "Let us proceed on our journey, and I will
13 go with thee." But *Jacob* said to him, "My lord knoweth that the children are tender, and flocks and herds with *their* young are with me; and if they should overdrive
14 them one day, the whole flock would die. Let my lord, I pray thee, pass on before his servant; and I will lead on gently at the pace of the cattle before me and at the pace of the
15 children, until I come to my lord unto Seir." And Esau said, "Let me then leave with thee some of the men who are with me." And he said, "Wherefore this? let me find favour in
16 the sight of my lord." So Esau returned that day on his way to Seir.
17 And Jacob journeyed to Succoth, and built for himself a house, and made booths for his cattle: therefore the name of
18 the place is called Succoth [BOOTHS]. And Jacob came in safety, on his return from Padan-aram to the city of Shechem, in the land of Canaan; and pitched his tent near the city.
19 And he bought that part of the field, where he had pitched his tent, of the children of Hamor, the father of Shechem,
20 for a hundred pieces of money. And he set up there an altar, and called it El-elohe-Israel [GOD THE GOD OF ISRAEL].

1 CHAP. XXXIV.—Now Dinah the daughter of Leah, whom she bare to Jacob, went out to see the daughters of
2 the land. And when Shechem the son of Hamor the Hivite, prince of the country, saw her, he took her, and lay
3 with her, and humbled her. And his soul clave to Dinah the daughter of Jacob; and he loved the damsel, and spake
4 kindly to the damsel. And Shechem spake to his father

Hamor, saying, "Get me this damsel for a wife." Now 5 Jacob heard that he had defiled Dinah his daughter: but his sons were with his cattle in the fields, so Jacob was silent until they should come.

Then Hamor the father of Shechem went out to Jacob 6 to commune with him. And the sons of Jacob came out of 7 the field when they heard *what had happened:* and the men were grieved, and were greatly enraged, because he had done wickedly against Israel by lying with Jacob's daughter; which thing ought not to have been done. And Hamor 8 communed with them, saying, "The soul of my son Shechem longeth for your daughter: I pray you give her to him for a wife. And make ye marriages with us; give your 9 daughters to us, and take our daughters to you. So ye shall 10 dwell with us, and the land shall be before you: dwell and trade ye therein, and get therein possessions for yourselves." And Shechem said to her father, and to her brethren, "Let 11 me find favour in your eyes, and what ye shall say to me I will give. Ask of me the largest dowry and gifts, and I 12 will give according as ye shall say to me: only give me the damsel for a wife."

But the sons of Jacob answered Shechem and Hamor his 13 father deceitfully, because *Shechem* had defiled Dinah their sister; and they spake and said to them, "We cannot do 14 this thing, to give our sister to one who is uncircumcised; for that would be a reproach to us: but on this *condition* 15 we will assent to you: If ye will be as we are, so that every male of you be circumcised, then will we give our daughters 16 to you, and we will take your daughters to us, and we will dwell with you, and become one people. But if ye will not 17 hearken to us, to be circumcised; then will we take our daughter, and be gone." And their words pleased Hamor, 18 and Shechem Hamor's son. And the young man delayed 19 not to do the thing, because he had delight in Jacob's daughter: and he was the most honourable of all the house of his father. Then Hamor and Shechem his son went to the gate 20 of their city, and communed with the men of their city, saying, "These men are peaceable with us; therefore let them 21 dwell in the land, and trade therein; for, lo! the land is large enough for them: let us take their daughters to us for wives, and let us give to them our daughters. But on this 22 *condition* only will the men consent to dwell with us, so as to be one people, that every male among us be circumcised,

23 as they are circumcised. Shall not their cattle, and their substance, and every beast of theirs, be ours? only let us assent
24 to them, that they may dwell with us." And to Hamor and to Shechem his son all that went out of the gate of the city hearkened: and every male was circumcised, all that went
25 out of the gate of the city. But on the third day, when they were sore, two of the sons of Jacob, Simeon and Levi, Dinah's brethren, took each man his sword, and came without fear
26 upon the city, and slew all the males. And they slew Hamor and Shechem his son with the edge of the sword, and
27 took Dinah out of Shechem's house, and went away. The sons of Jacob then came upon the slain, and plundered the
28 city, because they had defiled their sister. They took their sheep, and their oxen, and their asses, both those that were in
29 the city, and those that were in the field, and all their wealth; and all their little ones, and their wives, they took captive, and plundered even all that was in their houses.
30 And Jacob said to Simeon and Levi, "Ye have troubled me, by making me abominable among the inhabitants of the land, amongst the Canaanites and the Perizzites: and I being few in number, they will gather themselves together against me, and slay me; thus I shall be destroyed, I and my
31 house." And they said, "Should he have treated our sister as a harlot?"

1 CHAP. XXXV.—And God said to Jacob, "Arise, go up to Beth-el, and dwell there; and make there an altar to God, who appeared to thee when thou fleddest from the face of
2 Esau thy brother." Then Jacob said to his household, and to all who were with him, " Put away the strange gods that are among you, and purify yourselves, and change your
3 garments: and let us arise, and go up to Beth-el; that I may make there an altar to God, who answered me in the day of my distress, and was with me in the way which I
4 went." So they gave to Jacob all the strange gods which they had, and the rings which were in their ears; and Jacob
5 hid them under the terebinth-tree by Shechem. And they journeyed: and a great terror was upon the cities around them, so that they did not pursue the sons of Jacob.
6 So Jacob came to Luz (that is, Beth-el), in the land of
7 Canaan, he, and all the people that were with him. And he built there an altar, and called the place Beth-el [HOUSE OF GOD]; because there God had appeared to him, when he

fled from the face of his brother. Now Deborah, Rebekah's 8
nurse, died, and was buried below Beth-el, under a terebinth-
tree: and the name of it was called Alon-bachuth [TERE-
BINTH-TREE OF MOURNING].

And God appeared to Jacob again, when he had come out 9
of Padan-aram, and blessed him. And God said to him, 10
"Thy name is Jacob: thy name shall no more be called
Jacob, but Israel shall be thy name:" so he called his name
Israel. And God said to him, "I am God Almighty; be 11
fruitful and multiply: a nation, and a company of nations,
shall come from thee; and kings shall proceed from thy
loins: and the land which I gave to Abraham and Isaac, to 12
thee I will give it; and to thy seed after thee will I give the
land." And God went up from him at the place where he 13
had talked with him. And Jacob set up a pillar in the 14
place where he had talked with him, a pillar of stone; and
he poured upon it a drink-offering, and he poured upon it
oil. And Jacob called the name of the place, where God 15
spake with him, Beth-el.

And they journeyed from Beth-el; and when there was 16
but a little way to come to Ephrath, Rachel fell in labour,
and had hard labour. And it came to pass whilst she was in 17
hard labour, that the midwife said to her, "Fear not; for
this also is a son for thee." And when her soul was depart- 18
ing (for she died), she called his name Ben-oni [SON OF MY
SORROW]; but his father called him Ben-jamin [SON OF THE
RIGHT HAND]. Thus Rachel died, and was buried in the 19
way to Ephrath, which is now Bethlehem. And Jacob set a 20
pillar upon her grave, which *is called* The Pillar of Rachel's
grave, to this day. And Israel journeyed, and pitched his 21
tent beyond Migdol Eder. And it came to pass whilst Israel 22
dwelt in that land, that Reuben went and lay with Bilhah
his father's concubine: and Israel heard it.

Now the sons of Jacob were twelve: the sons of Leah; 23
Reuben, Jacob's first-born, and Simeon, and Levi, and Judah,
and Issachar, and Zebulun: the sons of Rachel; Joseph, and 24
Benjamin: and the sons of Bilhah, Rachel's handmaid; 25
Dan, and Naphtali: and the sons of Zilpah, Leah's hand- 26
maid; Gad, and Asher. These are the sons of Jacob, who
were born to him in Padan-aram.

And Jacob came to Isaac his father unto Mamre, unto 27
Kirjath-Arbah (which is Hebron) where Abraham and Isaac
had sojourned. And the days of Isaac were a hundred 28

29 and eighty years. And Isaac expired and died, and was gathered unto his people, when old and full of days: and his sons Esau and Jacob buried him.

1 CHAP. XXXVI.—Now this is the account of the descendants of Esau, who is *also called* Edom.
2 Esau took his wives of the daughters of Canaan; Adah the daughter of Elon the Hittite, and Aholibamah the
3 daughter of Anah, the daughter of Zibeon the Hivite; and
4 Basemath, Ishmael's daughter, sister of Nebajoth. And Adah bare to Esau, Eliphaz; and Basemath bare Reuel.
5 And Aholibamah bare Jeush, and Jaalam, and Korah. These are the sons of Esau, who were born to him in the land of Canaan.
6 And Esau took his wives, and his sons, and his daughters, and all the persons of his house, and his flocks, and all his herds, and all his substance, which he had gotten in the land of Canaan, and went into *another* land from the face of his
7 brother Jacob: for their riches were more than that they might dwell together; and the land wherein they were
8 strangers could not bear them because of their cattle. Thus dwelt Esau in mount Seir. Esau is *also called* Edom.
9 This is the account of the descendants of Esau the father of the Edomites, in mount Seir.
10 These are the names of Esau's sons; Eliphaz the son of Adah the wife of Esau; Reuel the son of Basemath the
11 wife of Esau. And the sons of Eliphaz were Teman, Omar,
12 Zepho, Gatam, and Kenaz. And Timna was concubine to Eliphaz, Esau's son; and she bare to Eliphaz, Amalek:
13 these were the sons of Adah, Esau's wife. And these were the sons of Reuel; Nahath, Zerah, Shammah, and Mizzah:
14 these were the sons of Basemath, Esau's wife. And these were the sons of Aholibamah, the daughter of Anah, daughter of Zibeon, Esau's wife; and she bare to Esau, Jeush, and Jaalam, and Korah.
15 These were princes of the sons of Esau: the sons of Eliphaz, the first-born *son* of Esau; prince Teman, prince
16 Omar, prince Zepho, prince Kenaz, prince Korah, prince Gatam, *and* prince Amalek. These were the princes *who sprung* from Eliphaz in the land of Edom: these were the sons of Adah.
17 And these were the sons of Reuel, Esau's son; prince Nahath, prince Zerah, prince Shammah, prince Mizzah.

These were the princes *who sprung* from Reuel in the land of Edom: these were the sons of Basemath, Esau's wife.

And these were the sons of Aholibamah, Esau's wife; 18 prince Jeush, prince Jaalam, prince Korah: these were the princes *who sprung* from Aholibamah, the daughter of Anah, Esau's wife. These were the sons of Esau, who is *also* 19 *called* Edom, and these were their princes.

These were the sons of Seir the Horite, who *first* inha- 20 bited the land; Lotan, and Shobal, and Zibeon, and Anah, and Dishon, and Ezer, and Dishan. These were the princes 21 of the Horites, the sons of Seir in the land of Edom. And 22 the sons of Lotan were Hori and Heman: and Lotan's sister was Timna. And the sons of Shobal were these; 23 Alvan, and Manahath, and Ebal, Shepho, and Onam. And 24 these were the sons of Zibeon; Ajah and Anah: this was that Anah who found the hot springs in the wilderness, as he fed the asses of Zibeon his father. And the children of 25 Anah were these; Dishon, and Aholibamah the daughter of Anah. And these were the sons of Dishon; Hemdan, and 26 Eshban, and Ithran, and Cheran. The sons of Ezer were 27 these; Bilhan, and Zaavan, and Akan. The sons of Dishan 28 were these; Uz, and Aran. These were the princes of 29 the Horites; prince Lotan, prince Shobal, prince Zibeon, prince Anah, prince Dishon, prince Ezer, prince Dishan. 30 These were the princes of the Horites, among their princes in the land of Seir.

Now these were the kings who reigned in the land of 31 Edom, before there reigned any king over the children of Israel. Bela, the son of Beor, reigned in Edom: and 32 the name of his city was Dinhabah. And Bela died; and 33 Jobab, the son of Zerah of Bozrah, reigned in his stead. And Jobab died; and Husham of the land of the Temanites 34 reigned in his stead. And Husham died; and Hadad, the 35 son of Bedad, who smote the Midianites in the field of Moab, reigned in his stead; and the name of his city was Avith. And Hadad died; and Samlah of Masrekah reigned 36 in his stead. And Samlah died; and Saul of Rehoboth on 37 the river reigned in his stead. And Saul died; and Baal- 38 hanan, the son of Achbor, reigned in his stead. And Baal- 39 hanan, the son of Achbor, died; and Hadar reigned in his stead: and the name of his city was Pau; and his wife's name was Mehetabel, the daughter of Matred, the daughter of Mezahab.

40 And these were the names of the princes *who sprung* from Esau, according to their families, after their places, by their
41 names; prince Timnah, prince Alvah, prince Jetheth, prince
42 Aholibamah, prince Elah, prince Pinon, prince Kenaz, prince
43 Teman, prince Mibzar, prince Magdiel, prince Iram: these were the princes of Edom, according to their habitations in the land of their possession: *Edom is also called* Esau, the father of the Edomites.

1 CHAP. XXXVII.—And Jacob dwelt in the land in which his father had sojourned, in the land of Canaan.
2 This is the account of the family of Jacob.
Joseph, when seventeen years old, was feeding the flocks with his brethren; and being a youth, he was with the sons of Bilhah, and with the sons of Zilpah, his father's wives: and Joseph brought unto his father an evil report of them.
3 For Israel loved Joseph more than all his children, because he was the son of *his* old age: and he made him a coat of
4 many colours. So when his brethren saw that their father loved him more than all his brethren, they hated him, and could not speak peaceably to him.
5 And Joseph dreamed a dream, and he told it to his breth-
6 ren; and they hated him yet the more. And he said to them, "Hear, I pray you, this dream which I have dreamed:
7 for, lo, we were binding sheaves in the field, when, lo! my sheaf arose, and also stood upright; and, lo, your sheaves
8 stood round about, and made obeisance to my sheaf." And his brethren said to him, "Shalt thou indeed reign over us? or shalt thou indeed have dominion over us?" And they hated him yet the more for his dreams, and for his sayings.
9 And he dreamed yet another dream, and told it to his brethren, and said, "Lo, I have dreamed another dream; for, lo, the sun, and the moon, and eleven stars, made obeisance
10 to me." And he told it to his father, and to his brethren: and his father rebuked him, and said to him, "What is this dream that thou hast dreamed? Shall we indeed come, I, and thy mother, and thy brethren, to bow ourselves down to
11 the earth to thee?" And his brethren were jealous of him; but his father observed the saying.
12 Now his brethren went to feed their father's flock in
13 Shechem; and Israel said to Joseph, "Do not thy brethren feed *the flocks* in Shechem? come, and I will send thee to
14 them." And he said to him, "Here *am I.*" And he said

to him, "Go, I pray thee, see whether it be well with thy brethren, and well with the flocks; and bring me word again." So he sent him from the vale of Hebron, and he went to Shechem. And a man found him, and lo, he was wandering in the fields: and the man asked him, saying, "What seekest thou?" And he said, "I seek my brethren: tell me, I pray thee, where they feed *their flocks*." And the man answered, "They are departed hence; for I heard them say, 'Let us go to Dothan.'" Then Joseph went after his brethren, and found them in Dothan. And they saw him afar off; and before he came near unto them, they conspired against him to slay him, and said one to another, "Lo, this dreamer cometh. Come now, therefore, and let us slay him, and cast him into some pit; and let us say, 'Some evil beast hath devoured him:' we shall then see what will become of his dreams." But Reuben heard this, and delivered him out of their hands, and said, "Let us not kill him." Again Reuben said to them, "Shed no blood, *but* cast him into this pit which is in the wilderness, and lay no hand upon him," that he might deliver him out of their hands, and send him back to his father. And it came to pass when Joseph was come to his brethren, that they stripped Joseph of his coat, the coat of many colours that was on him, and they took him, and cast him into a pit; and the pit was empty; there was no water in it.

And they sat down to eat bread, and they lifted up their eyes, and looked, and, lo, a company of Ishmaelites came from Gilead, with their camels bearing storax and balm and ladanum, which they were going to carry down to Egypt. And Judah said to his brethren, "What profit would it be if we should slay our brother, and conceal his blood? Come, and let us sell him to the Ishmaelites, and let not our hand be upon him; for he is our brother, our flesh." And his brethren assented; and as the Midianite merchants were then passing by, they drew up Joseph out of the pit, and sold Joseph for twenty pieces of silver to the Ishmaelites; and they brought Joseph into Egypt.

And Reuben returned to the pit; and, lo, Joseph was not in the pit; and he rent his clothes, and returned to his brethren, and said, "The child is not; and I, whither shall I go?" Then they took Joseph's coat, and killed a kid, and dipped the coat in the blood; and they sent the coat of many

colours, and brought it to their father, and said, "This have we found: know now whether it be thy son's coat or not."
33 And he knew it, and said, "My son's coat! a wild beast
34 hath devoured him: torn, torn in pieces, is Joseph!" And Jacob rent his clothes, and put sackcloth upon his loins, and
35 mourned for his son many days. And all his sons and all his daughters rose up to comfort him; but he refused to be comforted; and he said, "For I will go down to my son mourning, to the grave." Thus his father wept for him.
36 And the Midianites sold him into Egypt, to Potiphar, an officer of Pharaoh's, captain of the guard.

1 CHAP. XXXVIII.—Now it came to pass at that time, that Judah went down from his brethren, and turned in to
2 a certain Adullamite, whose name was Hirah. And Judah saw there a daughter of a Canaanite, whose name was
3 Shuah; and he took her, and went in to her. And she conceived, and bare a son; and she called his name Er.
4 And she conceived again, and bare a son, and she called his
5 name Onan. And she yet again conceived, and bare a son; and called his name Shelah: now *Judah* was at Chezib when she bare him.
6 And Judah took a wife for Er his first-born, whose name
7 was Tamar. But Er, Judah's first-born, was wicked in the
8 sight of Jehovah; and Jehovah slew him. Judah therefore said to Onan, "Go in to thy brother's wife and do the duty of a husband's brother to her, and raise up seed to thy bro-
9 ther." But Onan knowing that the seed would not be his own, whenever he went in to his brother's wife, spilled it on
10 the ground, lest he should give seed to his brother. And the thing which he did displeased Jehovah; wherefore he
11 slew him also. Then said Judah to Tamar his daughter-in-law, "Remain a widow at thy father's house till Shelah my son be grown:" for he said, "Lest peradventure he also die, as his brethren *died*." So Tamar went and dwelt in her father's house.
12 And after many days the daughter of Shuah, Judah's wife, died; and Judah having consoled himself went up to his sheepshearers to Timnath, he and his friend Hirah the Adul-
13 lamite. And one told Tamar, saying, "Lo, thy father-in-
14 law goeth up to Timnath to shear his sheep." So she put off the garments of her widowhood, and covered herself with a veil, and wrapped herself up, and sat near the entrance of

Enaim, which is on the way to Timnath: for she saw that though Shelah was grown, she was not given to him for a wife. When Judah saw her, he thought her to be a harlot; because she had covered her face. And he turned aside to her by the way, and said, "Let me, I pray thee, come in unto thee;" for he knew not that she was his daughter-in-law. And she said, "What wilt thou give me, that thou mayest come in unto me?" And he said, "I will send *thee* a kid from the flock." And she said, "Wilt thou give *me* a pledge till thou send *it*?" And he said, "What pledge shall I give thee?" And she said, "Thy signet, and thy ribband and the staff which is in thy hand." So he gave them to her, and went in unto her; and she conceived by him. Then she arose and went away, and laid aside her veil, and put on the garments of her widowhood. And Judah sent the kid by the hand of his friend the Adullamite, to receive the pledge from the woman; but he found her not. Then he asked the men of that place, saying, "Where is the harlot, who was at Enaim by the way-side?" And they said, "There was no harlot here." And he returned to Judah, and said, "I cannot find her; and also the men of the place said, that there had been no harlot there." And Judah said, "Let her keep *what she hath gotten*, lest we be shamed: lo, I sent this kid, and thou hast not found her."

Now it came to pass about three months after, that one told Judah, saying, "Tamar thy daughter-in-law hath played the harlot; and moreover, lo, she is with child through harlotry. And Judah said, "Bring her forth, and let her be burnt." When she was brought forth, she sent to her father-in-law, saying, "By the man whose these are, am I with child: Discern," said she, "I pray thee, whose are these, the signet, and ribband, and staff." And Judah acknowledged them, and said, "She hath been more righteous than I; since I gave her not to Shelah my son." But he knew her again no more.

And it came to pass in the time of her labour that, lo, twins were in her womb. And while she was in labour, *one of them* put out his hand; and the midwife took and bound upon his hand a scarlet thread, saying, "This came out first." And it came to pass as he drew back his hand, lo, his brother came out; and she said, "How hast thou broken forth? *this* breach be upon thee:" therefore his name was called Pharez [BREACH]. And afterward came out his brother, who had the scarlet thread about his hand; and his name was called Zarah [RISING].

1 CHAP. XXXIX.—And Joseph was brought down to Egypt; and Potiphar, an officer of Pharaoh, captain of the guard, an Egyptian, bought him of the Ishmaelites, who had 2 brought him down thither. And Jehovah was with Joseph, so that he was a prosperous man; and he was in the house of his 3 master the Egyptian. For his master saw that Jehovah was with him, and that Jehovah made all that he did to prosper in his 4 hand. And Joseph found favour in his sight, and he served him, and he made him the overseer of his house, and all that 5 he had he put into his hand. And from the time *that* he had made him the overseer of his house, and of all that he had, Jehovah blessed the house of the Egyptian for Joseph's sake; and the blessing of Jehovah was upon all that he had 6 in the house, and in the field. So he left all that he had in Joseph's hand; and knew not anything which was under his care, except the food which he ate.

Now Joseph was beautiful in form, and beautiful in coun-
7 tenance. And it came to pass after these things, that his master's wife cast her eyes upon Joseph; and she said, "Lie 8 with me." But he refused; and said to his master's wife, "Lo, my master knoweth not that which is under my care in the house, but he hath committed all that he hath to my 9 hand: he is not greater in this house than I; nor hath he kept back any thing from me but thee, because thou art his wife. How then can I do this great wickedness, and sin 10 against God?" And though she spake to Joseph day by day, he hearkened not to her, to lie by her, *or* to be with her. 11 And it came to pass about this time that *Joseph* went into the house to do his business; and none of the men of 12 the house were within; and she caught him by his garment, saying, "Lie with me:" but he left his garment in her 13 hand, and fled, and went away. And when she saw that he had left his garment in her hand, and had fled and gone 14 away, she called to the men of her house, and spake to them, saying, "See, he hath brought in a Hebrew to us to insult us; he came in unto me to lie with me, but I cried 15 with a loud voice: and when he heard that I lifted up my voice and cried, he left his garment with me, and fled, and 16 went away." And she laid up his garment by her, until his 17 master came home. And she spake to him according to

these words, saying, "The Hebrew servant, whom thou hast brought unto us, came in to me to insult me; but when I 18 lifted up my voice and cried, he left his garment with me, and fled and went away." And it came to pass when his 19 master had heard the words of his wife, which she spake to him, saying, "After this manner did thy servant to me," that his wrath was kindled; and Joseph's master took him, 20 and put him into the prison, the place where the king's prisoners were bound; and he was there in the prison. But 21 Jehovah was with Joseph, and shewed him kindness, and gave him favour in the sight of the keeper of the prison, so 22 that the keeper of the prison committed to Joseph's care all the prisoners who were in the prison; and of all that they did there, he was the doer. The keeper of the prison 23 looked not to any thing that was under his care; because Jehovah was with him; and all that he did, Jehovah made to prosper.

CHAP. XL.—And it came to pass after these things, that 1 the butler of the king of Egypt, and the baker offended their lord the king of Egypt. And Pharaoh was wroth 2 against his two officers, against the chief of the butlers, and against the chief of the bakers. And he put them into 3 custody in the house of the captain of the guard, into the prison, the place where Joseph was bound; and the captain 4 of the guard charged Joseph with them, and he served them. Now when they had been some time in custody, they both 5 dreamed a dream, each his dream in one night, each according to the interpretation of his dream, the butler and the baker of the king of Egypt, who were bound in the prison. And Joseph came in unto them in the morning, and saw that 6 they were troubled. And he asked the officers of Pharaoh 7 who were with him in custody in his master's house, saying, "Why are your countenances sad to-day?" And they said 8 to him, "We have dreamed a dream, and there is no interpreter of it." And Joseph said to them, "Do not interpretations belong to God? Tell me *your dreams*, I pray you."

Then the chief butler told his dream to Joseph, and said 9 to him, "In my dream, lo, a vine *was* before me; and on 10 the vine were three branches, and it seemed to bud; its blossoms shot forth, and its clusters ripened into grapes. And the cup of Pharaoh was in my hand; and I took the 11 grapes, and pressed them into the cup of Pharaoh, and I

12 gave the cup into Pharaoh's hand." Then Joseph said to him, "This is the interpretation of it: The three branches
13 are three days. Three days hence Pharaoh will lift up thy head, and restore thee to thy place; and thou shalt deliver the cup of Pharaoh into his hand, as thou didst formerly
14 when thou wast his butler. But think on me when it shall be well with thyself, and shew kindness, I pray thee, to me; and make mention of me to Pharaoh, and bring me out of
15 this house: for I was secretly stolen away out of the land of the Hebrews; and here also I have done nothing for which
16 they should put me into a dungeon." When the chief baker saw that the interpretation was favourable, he said to Joseph, "I also had my dream, and, lo, three wicker baskets
17 *were* on my head, and in the uppermost basket were all sorts of pastry work for Pharaoh's eating; and the birds ate them
18 out of the basket upon my head." And Joseph answered and said, "This is the interpretation of it: The three baskets
19 are three days. Three days hence Pharaoh will lift up thy head from off thee, and will hang thee on a tree; and the birds will eat thy flesh from off thee."
20 And it came to pass on the third day, the birth-day of Pharaoh, that he made a feast for all his servants; and he lifted up the head of the chief butler and of the chief baker
21 among his servants. And he restored the chief butler to his
22 butlership, and he gave the cup into Pharaoh's hand; but the chief baker he hanged, as Joseph had interpreted to
23 them. Yet the chief butler did not remember Joseph, but forgot him.

1 CHAP. XLI.—And it came to pass at the end of two full years, that Pharaoh dreamed; and, lo, he was standing by
2 the River; when, lo, there came up out of the River seven
3 heifers, beautiful and fat; and they fed on the sedge. And, lo, seven other heifers came up after them out of the River, ugly, and lean; and stood by the *other* heifers on the bank
4 of the River. And the ugly and lean heifers devoured the
5 seven beautiful and fat heifers. Then Pharaoh awoke. And he slept, and dreamed a second time: and, lo, seven ears of
6 corn came up upon one stalk, large and good. And, lo, seven *other* ears, thin and blasted by the east wind, sprung
7 up after them. And the seven thin ears devoured the seven large and full ears. And Pharaoh awoke, and, lo, it was a dream.

And it came to pass in the morning that his spirit was 8 troubled; and he sent and called for all the magicians, and all the wise men of Egypt; and Pharaoh told them his dreams, but no one could interpret them to Pharaoh. Then spake 9 the chief butler to Pharaoh, saying, "I remember my fault this day. Pharaoh was wroth with his servants, and put me 10 into custody in the captain of the guard's house, and the chief baker with me. And we dreamed a dream in one night, 11 I and he; we dreamed each of us according to the interpretation of his dream. Now *there was* with us there a young 12 man, a Hebrew, servant to the captain of the guard; and we told our dreams to him, and he interpreted them to us: to each man according to his dream he interpreted. And it 13 came to pass that as he interpreted to us so it was: me he restored to my office, and him he hanged."

Then Pharaoh sent and called for Joseph, and they brought 14 him hastily out of the dungeon: and he shaved himself, and changed his raiment, and went in to Pharaoh. And Pha- 15 raoh said to Joseph, "I have dreamed a dream, and no one can interpret it: but I have heard it said of thee, that on hearing a dream thou canst interpret it:" and Joseph an- 16 swered Pharaoh, saying, "No one without God can give to Pharaoh an answer of peace." Then Pharaoh said to Joseph, 17 "In my dream, lo, I was standing on the bank of the River. When, lo, there came up out of the River seven heifers, fat 18 and beautiful; and they fed on the sedge. And, lo, seven 19 other heifers came up after them, poor, and very ugly, and lean, such as I had never seen in all the land of Egypt for badness: and the lean and ugly heifers devoured the first 20 seven fat heifers; and when they had swallowed them, it 21 could not be known that they had swallowed them; but they were still ugly, as at the first. So I awoke. Again I 22 saw in my dream, that, lo, seven ears came up on one stalk, full and good: and, lo, seven ears, withered, thin, *and* blasted 23 by the east wind, sprang up after them: and the thin ears 24 devoured the seven good ears. And I told this to the magicians; but no one could explain it to me."

Then Joseph said to Pharaoh, "The dream of Pharaoh is 25 one; what God is about to do, he maketh known to Pharaoh. The seven good heifers are seven years; and the 26 seven good ears are seven years; the dream is one. And 27 the seven lean and ugly heifers, that came up after them, are seven years; and the seven empty ears blasted by the

28 east wind, will be seven years of famine. This is what I said to Pharaoh: what God is about to do he sheweth to
29 Pharaoh. Lo, seven years of great plenty throughout all
30 the land of Egypt are coming; and seven years of famine will arise after them; and all the plenty shall be forgotten in the land of Egypt; for the famine will consume the
31 land; and the plenty will be no more remembered in the land on account of the succeeding famine; for it will be
32 very grievous. And as to the dream being doubled to Pharaoh; it is because the thing is determined by God, and God
33 is hastening to do it. Now, therefore, let Pharaoh look out for a man intelligent and wise, and set him over the land of
34 Egypt. Let Pharaoh do *this*, and let him *also* appoint officers over the land, and take up the fifth part *of the produce* of the land of Egypt during the seven years of plenty.
35 And let them gather all the food of those good years which are coming, and lay up corn under the hand of Pharaoh, for
36 food in the cities, and preserve it, that the food may be in store for the land against the seven years of famine, which shall be in the land of Egypt; that the land perish not through the famine."
37 And the speech pleased Pharaoh, and all his servants.
38 And Pharaoh said to his servants, "Can we find such *a one*
39 as this, a man in whom is the spirit of God?" Then Pharaoh said to Joseph, "Since God hath shewed thee all this, no
40 one is so intelligent and wise as thyself: thou shalt be over my house, and according to thy word shall all my people be ruled; in the throne only will I be greater than thou."
41 And Pharaoh said to Joseph, "See, I have set thee over all
42 the land of Egypt." And Pharaoh took his ring from off his own hand, and put it on the hand of Joseph, and arrayed him in robes of fine linen, and put a chain of gold about
43 his neck, and made him to ride in the second chariot which he had; whilst one cried before him, ABREK [BOW THE KNEE]: thus he made him ruler over all the land of Egypt.
44 And Pharaoh said to Joseph, "I am Pharaoh, and without thee shall no man lift up his hand or foot in all the land of
45 Egypt." And Pharaoh called Joseph's name Zaphnath-paaneah; and he gave him for a wife Asenath, the daughter of Poti-pherah priest of On. And Joseph went out over
46 *all* the land of Egypt, and Joseph was thirty years old when he stood before Pharaoh king of Egypt. And Joseph went out from the presence of Pharaoh, and went through all the

land of Egypt. And during the seven years of plenty the 47
earth brought forth by handfuls. And he gathered together 48
all the food of the seven years, which were in the land of
Egypt, and laid up the food in the cities: the food of the
fields around every city he laid up in that *city*. Thus Joseph 49
gathered corn as the sand of the sea, so very much, that he
ceased to number it; for it was without number.

Now to Joseph, before the years of famine came, were 50
born two sons, which Asenath, the daughter of Poti-pherah
priest of On, bare to him. And Joseph called the name of 51
the first-born Manasseh [causing to forget] : " For God,
said he, hath made me forget all my trouble, and all my
father's house." And the name of the second he called 52
Ephraim [fruitful] : " For God, *said he,* hath caused me
to be fruitful in the land of my affliction."

The seven years of plenty that was in the land of Egypt 53
were now ended, and the seven years of famine had begun 54
to come, as Joseph had said, and the famine was in all *other*
lands; but in all the land of Egypt there was food. And 55
when all the land of Egypt was famished, the people cried
to Pharaoh for food; and Pharaoh said to all the Egyptians,
" Go to Joseph; what he saith to you, do." And when the 56
famine was over the whole land, Joseph opened all the storehouses, and sold to the Egyptians; for the famine prevailed
in the land of Egypt. And all the countries *around* came 57
into Egypt to Joseph to buy *corn;* because the famine prevailed in all lands.

CHAP. XLII.—Now when Jacob saw that there was a 1
sale *of corn* in Egypt, Jacob said to his sons, "Why do ye
look one at another?" And he said, " Lo, I have heard 2
that there is a sale *of corn* in Egypt: go down thither,
and buy for us thence, that we may live, and not die." So 3
ten of Joseph's brethren went to buy corn in Egypt.
But Benjamin, Joseph's *own* brother, Jacob sent not with 4
his brethren: for he said, " Lest peradventure mischief befall him."

And the sons of Israel came to buy *corn* among those who 5
came; for the famine was in the land of Canaan. Now Jo- 6
seph was the governor over the land, and he it was that sold
to all the people of the land. And Joseph's brethren came
and bowed down themselves before him *with* their faces to
the ground. And when Joseph saw his brethren, he knew 7

them, but he made himself strange to them, and spake to them harshly, and said to them, "Whence come ye?" And
8 they said, "From the land of Canaan, to buy food." For though Joseph knew his brethren, they knew not him.
9 Then Joseph remembered the dreams which he had dreamed of them, and said to them, "Ye are spies: to see
10 the nakedness of the land ye are come." And they said to him, "Nay, my lord, but to buy food are thy servants come.
11 We are all the sons of one man; we are true men; thy ser-
12 vants are no spies." And he said to them, "Nay, but to
13 see the nakedness of the land ye are come." And they said, "Thy servants *were* twelve brethren, the sons of one man in the land of Canaan; and, lo, the youngest is this day with
14 our father, and one is not." And Joseph said to them, "This is what I have spoken to you, saying, 'Ye are spies;'
15 hereby ye shall be proved; by the life of Pharaoh ye shall not go hence, unless your youngest brother come hither.
16 Send one of you and let him fetch your brother, and ye shall be kept in prison, that your words may be proved, whether *there be* truth in you; or else, by the life of Pharaoh, surely ye are spies."
17 And he put them all together into custody three days.
18 And Joseph said to them the third day, "This do, and live;
19 *for* I fear God. If ye be true men, let one of your brethren be bound in the house of your prison; and go ye, carry corn
20 for the famine of your households, but bring your youngest brother to me; so shall your words be verified, and ye shall
21 not die." And they did so. Then they said one to another, "We are indeed guilty on account of our brother, because we saw the anguish of his soul, when he besought us, yet we would not hear; therefore is this distress come on our-
22 selves." And Reuben answered them, saying, "Spake I not to you, saying, 'Do not sin against the child?' but ye would not hear; therefore, lo, his blood is demanded *from*
23 *us.*" Now they knew not that Joseph understood *them;*
24 for he spake to them by an interpreter. And he turned away from them, and wept; then having returned to them again, and talked with them, he took from them Simeon, and bound him before their eyes.
25 Then Joseph commanded that their sacks should be filled with corn, and that every man's money should be restored into his sack, and that provision should be given to them
26 for the way. This being done to them, they laded their

asses with corn, and departed thence. But as one of them 27 opened his sack at the lodging place, to give his ass provender, he spied his money; for, lo, it was in the mouth of his sack. And he said to his brethren, "My money is restored; 28 and, lo, it is even in my sack;" and their hearts failed them, and they were afraid, saying one to another, "What is this which God hath done to us?"

And they came to Jacob their father into the land of Ca- 29 naan, and told him all that had happened to them, saying, "The man, the lord of the land, spake harshly to us, and 30 took us for spies of the country. And we said to him, 'We 31 are true men; we are no spies; we *were* twelve brethren, 32 sons of our father: one is not, and the youngest is this day with our father in the land of Canaan.' And the man, the 33 lord of the land, said to us, 'Hereby shall I know that ye are true men: leave one of your brethren with me, and take *food for* the famine of your households, and depart; and 34 bring your youngest brother to me; then shall I know that ye are no spies, but that ye are true men; and I will deliver to you your brother, and ye shall traffic in the land.'"

And when they emptied their sacks, lo, every man's 35 bundle of money was in his sack; and when they and their father saw the bundles of money, they were afraid. Then 36 Jacob their father said to them, "Me have ye bereaved *of my children:* Joseph is not, and Simeon is not, and ye would take Benjamin away: all these things are against me." And Reuben spake to his father, saying, "Slay my 37 two sons if I bring him not back to thee: deliver him into my hand, and I will bring him to thee again." But he said, 38 "My son shall not go down with you; for his brother is dead, and he only remaineth: if mischief befall him by the way in which ye go, then will ye bring down my grey hairs in sorrow to the grave."

CHAP. XLIII.—And the famine was grievous in the land. 1 And it came to pass when they had eaten up the corn which 2 they had brought out of Egypt, that their father said to them, "Go again, buy for us a little food." And Judah spake to 3 him, saying, "The man did solemnly protest to us, saying, 'Ye shall not see my face, unless your brother be with you.' If thou wilt send our brother with us, we will go down and 4 buy thee food; but if thou wilt not send him, we will not 5 go down: for the man said to us, 'Ye shall not see my face,

GENESIS XLIII.

6 unless your brother be with you.'" And Israel said, "Why did ye deal so ill with me, as to tell the man that ye had yet 7 a brother?" And they said, "The man questioned us strictly about ourselves, and about our kindred, saying, 'Is your father yet alive? have ye a brother?' and we told him according to the tenor of those words. Could we at all know 8 that he would say, 'Bring your brother down?'" And Judah said to Israel his father, "Send the youth with me, and we will arise and go, that we may live, and not die, both 9 we, and thou, and also our little ones. I will be surety for him; of my hand thou mayest require him; if I bring him not to thee, and set him before thee, then let me bear the 10 blame for ever. Surely if we had not lingered, we might now 11 have returned a second time." Then Israel their father said to them, "If now *it must be so*, do this; Take of the best fruits of the land in your vessels, and carry down to the man a present, a little balsam, and a little honey, spices and lada- 12 num, nuts and almonds; and take double money in your hands, and carry back with you the money that was returned in the mouth of your sacks; peradventure it was an over- 13 sight. Take also your brother, and arise, go again to the 14 man; and may God Almighty give you favour before the man, that he may send back your other brother, and Benjamin. But if I be bereaved *of my children*, I am bereaved." 15 So the men took that present; they took also double money in their hands, and Benjamin, and arose, and went down to 16 Egypt, and stood before Joseph. And when Joseph saw Benjamin with them, he said to the ruler of his house, "Take these men home, and slay, and make ready; for the men shall 17 eat with me at noon." And the man did as Joseph ordered, 18 and brought the men into Joseph's house. And the men were afraid, because they were brought into Joseph's house; and they said, "Because of the money that was returned in our sacks at the first time are we brought in, that he may seek occasion against us, and fall upon us, and take us for 19 slaves and our asses." So they came near to the ruler of Joseph's house, and they talked with him at the door of the 20 house, and said, "Oh, my lord! we came indeed down before 21 to buy food; and it came to pass when we came to the lodging place, that we opened our sacks, and, lo, every man's money was in the mouth of his sack, our money in full 22 weight: we have now brought it again in our hands; and other money have we brought down in our hands to buy food:

we cannot tell who put our money in our sacks." And he said, " Peace be to you, fear not: your God, and the God of your father, gave you treasure in your sacks: your money came to me." Then he brought Simeon out to them. He then took the men into Joseph's house, and gave them water, that they might wash their feet; and he gave their asses provender.

And they made ready the present against Joseph came at noon: for they had heard that they were to eat bread there. So when Joseph came home, they brought him the present which was in their hands into the house, and bowed themselves to him to the ground. And he asked them of *their* welfare, and said, "Is your father well? the old man of whom ye spake? Is he yet alive?" And they answered, "Thy servant our father is well, he is yet alive." And they bowed down their heads, and made obeisance. And he lifted up his eyes, and saw his brother Benjamin, his own mother's son, and said, " Is this your youngest brother, of whom ye spake to me?" And he said, "God be gracious to thee, my son!" And Joseph made haste; for his bowels yearned towards his brother; and sought where to weep; and he entered into his chamber, and wept there. Then he washed his face, and went out, and restrained himself, and said, " Set on food." And they set on for him by himself, and for them by themselves, and for the Egyptians who ate with him by themselves: because the Egyptians might not eat with the Hebrews; for that would be an abomination to the Egyptians. Now *his brethren* sat before him, the first-born according to his birthright, and the youngest according to his youth: and the men looked with astonishment at each other. And he sent portions to them from what was before himself; but the portion of Benjamin was five times as much as any of their portions. And they drank, and were merry with him.

CHAP. XLIV. — Then he commanded the ruler of his house, saying, "Fill the men's sacks with food, as much as they can carry, and put the money of each in the mouth of the sack. But put my cup, the silver cup, in the mouth of the sack of the youngest, together with his purchase-money." And he did according to the order that Joseph had given.

As soon as the morning was light, the men were sent away, they and their asses. They were not yet gone far from the city, when Joseph said to the ruler of his house, "Arise,

follow the men; and when thou overtakest them, say to them,
5 'Wherefore have ye requited evil for good? Is not this it in which my lord drinketh, and by which indeed he divineth?
6 Ye have done evil in so doing.'" And he overtook them,
7 and spake to them these same words. And they said to him, "Wherefore saith my lord these words? Far be it
8 from thy servants to do after this manner. Lo, the money which we found in the mouths of our sacks we brought again to thee out of the land of Canaan: how then should we steal
9 out of thy lord's house silver or gold? With whomsoever of thy servants it shall be found, let him die, and let us also
10 be the slaves of my lord." And he said, "Be it now according to your words: he with whom it shall be found shall be
11 my slave; but ye shall be blameless." Then they speedily took down every man his sack to the ground, and opened every
12 man his sack. And he searched, beginning at the eldest, and ending at the youngest: and the cup was found in the
13 sack of Benjamin. Then they rent their clothes, and laded every man his ass, and returned to the city.
14 And Judah and his brethren came to Joseph's house; for he was yet there; and they fell before him on the ground.
15 And Joseph said to them, "What deed is this that ye have done? Knew ye not that such a man as I can with certainty
16 divine?" And Judah said, "What shall we say to my lord? what shall we speak? or how shall we clear ourselves? God hath found out the iniquity of thy servants: lo, we are my lord's slaves, both we, and he also with whom the cup was
17 found." And he said, "Far be it from me to do so: the man with whom the cup was found, he shall be my slave;
18 but as for you, go ye up in peace to your father." Then Judah came near to him, and said, "Oh, my lord, let thy servant, I pray thee, speak a word in my lord's ears, and let not thine anger burn against thy servant: for thou art even
19 as Pharaoh. My lord asked his servants, saying, 'Have ye
20 a father, or a brother?' And we said to my lord, 'We have a father, an old man, and *he has* a younger *son*, the child of his old age, whose brother is dead; and he alone is left of his
21 mother, and his father loveth him.' And thou saidst to thy servants, 'Bring him down to me, that I may set mine eyes
22 upon him.' And we said to my lord, 'The lad cannot leave his father: for if he should leave his father, he would die.'
23 And thou saidst to thy servants, 'Unless your youngest brother come down with you, ye shall see my face no more.'

And it came to pass when we came up to thy servant our 24 father, that we told him the words of my lord. And our 25 father said, 'Go again, and buy for us a little food.' But 26 we said, 'We cannot go down: if our youngest brother be with us, then will we go down; for we may not see the man's face, unless our youngest brother be with us.' And thy ser- 27 vant our father said to us, 'Ye know that my wife bare me two *sons;* and one went out from me, and I said, Surely 28 he is torn in pieces; and I have not seen him since: now 29 if ye take this also from me, and mischief befall him, ye will bring down my grey hairs in sorrow to the grave.' Now, 30 therefore, when I come to thy servant our father, and the lad be not with us, seeing that his life is bound up in the lad's life, it shall come to pass, when he seeth that the lad is not, 31 he will die: thus thy servants will bring down the grey hairs of thy servant our father in sorrow to the grave. Now thy 32 servant became surety for the lad to my father, saying, 'If I bring him not again to thee, then let me bear the blame to my father for ever.' Now, therefore, I pray thee, let thy 33 servant remain instead of the lad, a slave to my lord; and let the lad go up with his brethren. For how can I go up to 34 my father, and the lad be not with me? lest peradventure I see the evil that will come on my father?"

CHAP. XLV.—Then Joseph could not refrain himself be- 1 fore all those who stood by him; so he cried, "Cause every man to go out from me." And there stood no man with him, while Joseph made himself known to his brethren. And he 2 wept aloud; and the Egyptians and the house of Pharaoh heard. And Joseph said to his brethren, "I am Joseph: 3 doth my father yet live?" And his brethren could not answer him; for they were troubled at his presence. And 4 Joseph said to his brethren, "Come near to me, I pray you:" And they came near. And he said, "I am Joseph your brother, whom ye sold into Egypt. But be not now grieved, 5 nor angry with yourselves, that ye sold me hither; for God sent me before you to preserve life. For these two years hath 6 the famine been in the land; and there will yet be five years, in which there will be neither plowing nor harvest. So God 7 sent me before you to preserve you a remnant on the earth, and to save your lives by a great deliverance. Now then it 8 was not you who sent me hither, but God; and he hath made me a father to Pharaoh, and lord of all his house, and a ruler

9 over all the land of Egypt. Haste ye, and go up to my father, and say to him, 'Thus saith thy son Joseph, God hath made me lord of all Egypt: come down to me, delay 10 not. And thou shalt dwell in the land of Goshen, that thou mayest be near to me, thou, and thy children, and thy children's children, and thy flocks, and thy herds, and all that 11 thou hast. And there will I nourish thee, (for there will yet be five years of famine,) lest thou, and thy household, and 12 all that thou hast, come to poverty.' And, lo, your eyes and the eyes of my brother Benjamin see, that it is my mouth 13 that speaketh to you. And ye shall tell my father of all my glory in Egypt, and of all that ye have seen; and ye shall 14 haste, and bring down my father hither." Then he fell upon the neck of his brother Benjamin, and wept; and Benjamin 15 wept upon his neck. And he kissed all his brethren, and wept upon them: and after that his brethren talked with him.

16 And a report was heard in the house of Pharaoh, saying, "Joseph's brethren are come;" and it pleased Pharaoh well, 17 and his servants. And Pharaoh said to Joseph, "Say unto thy brethren, 'This do ye; lade your beasts, and depart, go 18 ye unto the land of Canaan, and take your father, and your households, and come unto me, and I will give you the best of all the land of Egypt, and ye shall eat the fat of the 19 land.' Command them also, *saying*, 'This do ye; take ye wagons out of the land of Egypt for your little ones, and 20 for your wives, and bring your father, and come. And have no regard for your goods: for the best of all the land of Egypt shall be yours.'"

21 And the sons of Israel did so: and Joseph gave them wagons, according to the commandment of Pharaoh. He 22 also gave them provision for the way. To every one of them he gave changes of raiment; but to Benjamin he gave three 23 hundred *pieces* of silver, and five changes of raiment. And to his father he sent these things; ten asses laden with the best things of Egypt, and ten she-asses laden with corn and 24 bread and meat for his father by the way. So he sent his brethren away; and when they were departing, he said to them, "See that ye fall not out by the way."

25 And they went up out of Egypt, and came into the land 26 of Canaan to Jacob their father, and told him, saying, "Joseph is yet alive, and he is ruler over all the land of Egypt." And Jacob's heart fainted, for he believed them

not. But when they told him all the words of Joseph, 27 which he had said to them: and when he saw the wagons which Joseph had sent to carry him, the spirit of Jacob their father revived. And Israel said, "It is enough: Joseph my 28 son is yet alive: I will go and see him before I die."

CHAP. XLVI.—So Israel took his journey with all that 1 he had, and came to Beer-sheba, and offered sacrifices to the God of his father Isaac. And God spake to Israel in the 2 visions of the night, and said, "Jacob, Jacob!" And he said, "Here am I." And he said, "I am God, the God of 3 thy father: fear not to go down into Egypt; for I will there make of thee a great nation. I will go down with thee into 4 Egypt, and I will also surely bring thee up again; and Joseph shall put his hand upon thine eyes."

And Jacob moved on from Beer-sheba: and the sons of 5 Israel carried Jacob their father, and their little ones, and their wives, in the wagons which Pharaoh had sent to carry him. And they took their cattle, and their substance which 6 they had gathered in the land of Canaan, and came into Egypt, Jacob, and all his seed with him; his sons, and his 7 sons' sons with him, his daughters, and his sons' daughters, and all his seed he brought with him into Egypt.

Now these are the names of the children of Israel who 8 went into Egypt; Jacob and his sons:

Reuben, Jacob's first-born. And the sons of Reuben; 9 Hanoch, and Phallu, and Hezron, and Carmi.

And the sons of Simeon; Jemuel, and Jamin, and Ohad, 10 and Jachin, and Zohar; and Saul, the son of a Canaanite woman.

And the sons of Levi; Gershon, Kohath, and Merari. 11

And the sons of Judah; Er, and Onan, and Shelah, and 12 Pharez, and Zarah: but Er and Onan had died in the land of Canaan. And the sons of Pharez were Hezron and Hamul.

And the sons of Issachar; Tola, and Phuah, and Job, 13 and Shimron.

And the sons of Zebulun; Sered, and Elon, and Jahleel. 14

These were the sons of Leah, whom she bare to Jacob in 15 Padan-aram, with his daughter Dinah: all his sons and his daughters were thirty-three persons.

And the sons of Gad; Ziphion, and Haggi, Shuni, and 16 Ezbon, Eri, and Arodi, and Areli.

GENESIS XLVI.

17 And the sons of Asher; Jimnah, and Ishuah, and Ishui, and Beriah, and Serah their sister: And the sons of Beriah; Heber, and Malchiel.
18 These were the sons of Zilpah, whom Laban gave to Leah his daughter: and these she bare to Jacob, sixteen persons.
19 The sons of Rachel, Jacob's wife; Joseph and Benjamin.
20 And to Joseph, in the land of Egypt, were born Manasseh and Ephraim, whom Asenath, the daughter of Poti-pherah priest of On, bare to him.
21 And the sons of Benjamin were Belah, and Becher, and Ashbel, Gera, and Naaman, Ehi, and Rosh, Muppim, and Huppim, and Ared.
22 These were the sons of Rachel, who were born to Jacob: in all, fourteen persons.
23 And the sons of Dan; Hushim.
24 And the sons of Naphtali; Jahzeel, and Guni, and Jezer, and Shillem.
25 These were the sons of Bilhah, whom Laban gave to Rachel his daughter; and she bare these to Jacob: in all, seven persons.
26 All the persons who went with Jacob into Egypt, who came out of his loins, besides the wives of Jacob's sons, all
27 the persons were sixty-six. And the sons of Joseph, who were born to him in Egypt, were two persons: all of the house of Jacob, who went into Egypt, were seventy persons.
28 Now *Jacob* sent Judah before him to Joseph, to direct him unto Goshen; and they came into the land of Goshen.
29 And Joseph made ready his chariot, and went up to Goshen to meet Israel his father, and he presented himself to him, and fell on his neck, and wept on his neck a long while.
30 And Israel said to Joseph, "Now let me die, since.I have
31 seen thy face; for thou art yet alive." And Joseph said to his brethren and to his father's house, "I will go up, and tell Pharaoh, and say to him, ' My brethren and my father's house, who were in the land of Canaan, are come to
32 me; and the men are shepherds, for their occupation hath been to feed cattle, and they have brought their flocks, and
33 their herds, and all that they have.' And it shall come to pass when Pharaoh shall call for you, and shall say, ' What
34 is your occupation?' that ye shall answer, ' Thy servants have been keepers of cattle from our youth even until now, both we and our fathers;' that ye may dwell in the land of Go-

shen: for every shepherd is an abomination to the Egyptians."

CHAP. XLVII.—Then Joseph went and told Pharaoh, and said, "My father, and my brethren, and their flocks, and their herds, and all that they have, are come out of the land of Canaan; and, lo, they are in the land of Goshen." And he took from among his brethren, five men, and presented them to Pharaoh. And Pharaoh said to his brethren, "What is your occupation?" And they said to Pharaoh, "Thy servants are shepherds, both we, and our fathers." They also said to Pharaoh, "To sojourn in the land are we come; for thy servants have no pasture for their flocks; for the famine is grievous in the land of Canaan: now therefore, we pray thee, let thy servants dwell in the land of Goshen." Then Pharaoh spake to Joseph, saying, "Thy father and thy brethren are come to thee; the land of Egypt is before thee: in the best of the land make thy father and brethren to dwell; in the land of Goshen let them dwell; and if thou knowest *any* men of ability among them, make them rulers over my own cattle."

And Joseph brought in Jacob his father, and presented him to Pharaoh; and Jacob blessed Pharaoh. And Pharaoh said to Jacob, "How many are the days of the years of thy life?" And Jacob said to Pharaoh, "The days of the years of my pilgrimage are a hundred and thirty years: few and evil have the days of the years of my life been, and have not attained to the days of the years of the life of my fathers, in the days of their pilgrimage." And Jacob blessed Pharaoh, and went out from before Pharaoh.

And Joseph settled his father and his brethren, and gave them a possession in the land of Egypt, in the best of the land, in the land of Rameses, as Pharaoh had commanded. And Joseph nourished his father, and his brethren, and all his father's household with bread, according to their families.

Now there was no bread in all the land; for the famine was very grievous, so that the land of Egypt and the land of Canaan, were distressed by the famine. And Joseph gathered up all the money that was found in the land of Egypt, and in the land of Canaan, for the corn which they bought: and Joseph brought the money into Pharaoh's house. And when money failed in the land of Egypt, and in the land of Canaan, all the Egyptians came to Joseph, and

said, "Give us bread: for why should we die in thy presence?
16 although money faileth." And Joseph said, "Give *me* your cattle; and I will give you bread *in exchange* for your cattle,
17 since money faileth." And they brought their cattle to Joseph: and Joseph gave them bread *in exchange* for the horses, and for the flocks, and for the herds, and for the asses; and he supplied them with bread *in exchange* for all their cattle during that year.
18 When that year was ended, they came to him the second year, and said to him, "It is not hidden from my lord, that our money is spent; my lord also hath our herds of cattle: there is nothing left in the sight of my lord, but our bodies
19 and our lands: why should we die before thine eyes, both we and our land? buy us and our land for bread, and we and our land will be servants to Pharaoh; and give us seed, that we may live and not die, and that the land be not desolate."
20 Thus Joseph bought all the land of Egypt for Pharaoh; for the Egyptians sold every man his field, because the famine
21 prevailed over them: so the land became Pharaoh's. And as for the people he removed them to cities from one extre-
22 mity of Egypt to the other. The land of the priests only he bought not; for the priests had a portion *assigned them* by Pharaoh, and lived on the portion which Pharaoh gave them; wherefore they sold not their lands.
23 Then Joseph said to the people, "Lo, I have this day bought you, and your land, for Pharaoh: lo, here is seed for you,
24 that ye may sow the land. But of the produce, ye shall give a fifth part to Pharaoh, and four parts shall be your own, for seed of the field, and for food for yourselves, and
25 for your households, and for food for your little ones." And they said, "Thou hast saved our lives; let us find favour in the sight of my lord, and we will be the servants of Pha-
26 raoh." So Joseph made it a law over the land of Egypt to this day, that Pharaoh should have the fifth part, except the land of the priests only, which became not Pharaoh's.
27 And the Israelites dwelled in the land of Egypt, in the land of Goshen; and they had possessions therein, and were
28 fruitful and multiplied exceedingly. And Jacob lived in the land of Egypt seventeen years: so all the days of the years
29 of Jacob were a hundred and forty-seven years. And when the time drew nigh that Israel must die, he called his son Joseph, and said to him, "If now I have found favour in thy sight, put thy hand, I pray thee, under my thigh, and

deal kindly and truly with me; bury me not, I pray thee, in
Egypt, for I would lie with my fathers; carry me therefore 30
out of Egypt, and bury me in their burying-place." And
he answered, "I will do as thou hast said." Then *Israel* 31
said, "Swear to me." And he sware to him. And Israel
bowed himself *leaning* on the head of his staff.

CHAP. XLVIII.—And it came to pass after these things, 1
that one told Joseph, "Lo, thy father is sick:" so he took
with him his two sons, Manasseh and Ephraim. And *one* 2
told Jacob, and said, "Lo, thy son Joseph is come to thee:"
and Israel strengthened himself, and sat upon the bed. And 3
Jacob said to Joseph, "God Almighty appeared to me at
Luz in the land of Canaan, and blessed me, and said to me, 4
'Lo, I will make thee fruitful, and multiply thee, and I will
make of thee a multitude of people, and will give this land
to thy seed after thee, for an everlasting possession.' And 5
now thy two sons, Ephraim and Manasseh, who were born
to thee in the land of Egypt before I came to thee into
Egypt, are mine; as Reuben and Simeon, they shall be
mine. And thy progeny, which thou mayest beget after 6
them, shall be thine; they shall be called after the name of
their brethren in their inheritance. For when I had come 7
from Padan, Rachel died by me in the land of Canaan, in
the way, at a short distance from Ephrath, and I buried her
there on the way to Ephrath;" which is *now* Bethlehem.

And when Israel saw Joseph's sons, he said, "Who are 8
these?" And Joseph said to his father, "They are my sons, 9
whom God hath given me in this *land*." And he said,
"Bring them, I pray thee, to me, that I may bless them."
Now the eyes of Israel were dim from age, so that he could 10
not see. And he brought them near to him; and he kissed
them, and embraced them. And Israel said to Joseph, "I 11
had not thought to see thy face; and, lo, God hath shewed
me also thy seed." Then Joseph took them out from be- 12
tween his knees, and he bowed himself with his face to the
ground. Again Joseph took them both, Ephraim in his 13
right hand, toward Israel's left hand, and Manasseh in his
left hand, toward Israel's right hand, and brought them near
to him. But Israel stretched out his right hand, and laid 14
it upon Ephraim's head, who was the younger, and his left
hand upon Manasseh's head, though Manasseh was the first-
born, guiding his hands wittingly. And he blessed Joseph, 15

and said, " May the God, before whom my fathers Abraham and Isaac walked, the God who fed me from my birth unto 16 this day, the Angel who redeemed me from all evil, bless the youths: and let my name, and the name of my fathers Abraham and Isaac be called upon them; and may they grow 17 into a multitude in the midst of the earth." But when Joseph saw that his father had laid his right hand upon the head of Ephraim, it displeased him, and he held up his father's hand, to remove it from the head of Ephraim to the 18 head of Manasseh. And Joseph said to his father, "Not so, my father: for this is the first-born; put thy right hand 19 upon his head." But his father refused, and said, "I know it my son, I know it: he also shall become a people, and he also shall be great: but yet his younger brother shall be greater than he, and his seed shall become a multitude of 20 nations." Thus he blessed them that day, saying, "In thee shall Israel bless, saying, 'God make thee as Ephraim and as Manasseh.'" And he set Ephraim before Manasseh.
21 And Israel said to Joseph, "Lo, I die; but God shall be with you, and bring you again into the land of your fathers. 22 And I give to thee one portion above thy brethren, which I took out of the hand of the Amorites with my sword and with my bow."

1 CHAP. XLIX.—And Jacob called to his sons, and said, " Gather yourselves together, that I may tell you that which shall befall you in after times.

2 Gather yourselves together and hear, ye sons of Jacob;
And hearken to Israel, your father.
3 Reuben, my first-born art thou;
My might and the beginning of my strength:
The excellence of dignity and the excellence of power.
4 Swelling as water, thou shalt not excel;
Because thou ascendedst thy father's bed:
Then didst thou profane my couch, by ascending *it*.
5 Simeon and Levi are brethren:
Instruments of violence are their swords.
6 Into their council enter not, my soul!
To their assembly, my honour! be not thou united.
For in their anger they slew men;
In their wilfulness, they rooted out princes.
7 Cursed be their anger! for it was fierce;
And their wrath! for it was cruel.

I will divide them in Jacob,
And I will scatter them in Israel.
  Judah! thee thy brethren shall praise;
Thy hand shall be on the neck of thine enemies;
To thee the sons of thy father shall bow down.
A lion's whelp is Judah;
From the prey, my son, thou comest up.
He coucheth, he lieth down,
As a lion, and as a lioness;
Who shall rouse him up?
The sceptre shall not depart from Judah,
Nor a lawgiver, from between his feet,
Until Shiloh come;
And to him shall peoples be obedient.
Binding to the vine his foal,
And to the choice vine, his ass's colt,
He shall wash his garments in wine,
And his raiment in the blood of grapes.
His eyes shall be red with wine,
And his teeth white with milk.
  Zebulun shall dwell on the sea coast;
And he shall be a coast for ships:
And his boundary shall reach to Zidon.
  Issachar is a strong ass;
Lying down between the bars.
And he saw that the resting-place is good,
And that the land is pleasant,
So he bowed the shoulder to the burden,
And became a servant to task-work.
  Dan shall judge his people
Like one of the tribes of Israel.
Dan shall be a serpent in the way,
A horned viper in the path,
Which biteth the heels of the horse,
So that his rider falleth backward.
  For thy salvation I wait, O Jehovah!
  Gad, a troop shall attack him,
But he shall attack their rear.
  Out of Asher *cometh* rich food;
And he shall yield royal dainties.
  Naphtali is a spreading terebinth,
Which sendeth forth beautiful branches.
  A fruitful stem is Joseph,

A fruitful stem by a fountain,
Whose boughs spread over the wall.
23 The archers sorely grieved him,
And shot *at* him, and hated him:
24 But his bow remained in strength,
And the arms of his hands were vigorous;
By the power of the Mighty One of Jacob;
By the name of the Shepherd, the rock of Israel;
25 By the God of thy father, who helped thee,
By the Almighty, who blessed thee.
May the blessings of the heavens above,
May the blessings of the deep lying beneath,
May the blessings of the breast, and of the womb,
26 May the blessings of thy father,
Surpass the blessings of the eternal mountains,
The desirable things of the everlasting hills!
May they be on the head of Joseph!
On the crown-of-the-head of the chief of his brethren!
27 Benjamin is a wolf that teareth:
In the morning he devoureth *his* prey,
In the evening he divideth the spoil.

28 All these were the twelve *chiefs* of the tribes of Israel, and this is what their father spake to them, when he blessed them; every one of them he blessed according to his blessing.
29 And he charged them, and said to them, "I am about to be gathered to my people: bury me with my fathers in the
30 cave that is in the field of Ephron the Hittite, in the cave that is in the field of Machpelah, which is opposite to Mamre, in the land of Canaan, which Abraham bought with the field of Ephron the Hittite, a possession for a bury-
31 ing-place. There they buried Abraham and Sarah his wife; there they buried Isaac and Rebekah his wife; and there I
32 buried Leah. Both the field, and the cave that is in it, were a purchase from the sons of Heth."
33 And when Jacob had made an end of commanding his sons, he drew up his feet into the bed, and expired, and was gathered to his people.

1 CHAP. L.—And Joseph fell upon his father's face, and wept over him, and kissed him.
2 Then Joseph commanded his servants the physicians to embalm his father: so the physicians embalmed Israel.
3 And when forty days were fulfilled for him; for so are ful-

filled the days of those who are embalmed; the Egyptians mourned for him seventy days.

And when the days of his mourning were past, Joseph 4 spake to the household of Pharaoh, saying, "If now I have found favour in your eyes, speak, I pray you, in the ears of Pharaoh, saying, 'My father adjured me, saying, Lo, I die: 5 in my grave which I digged for myself in the land of Canaan, there shalt thou bury me. Now, therefore, let me go up, I pray thee, and bury my father, and I will return.'" And Pharaoh said, "Go up and bury thy father, as he ad- 6 jured thee." So Joseph went up to bury his father: and 7 with him went up all the servants of Pharaoh, the elders of his house, and all the elders of the land of Egypt, and all 8 the house of Joseph, and his brethren, and his father's house: only their little ones, and their flocks, and their herds, they left in the land of Goshen. And there went up 9 with him both chariots and horsemen, so that the camp was very great. And they came to the threshing-floor of Atad, 10 which is beyond Jordan; and there they mourned with a great and very grievous lamentation: and he made a mourning for his father seven days. And when the inhabitants of 11 the land, the Canaanites, saw the mourning at the threshing-floor of Atad, they said, "This is a grievous mourning to the Egyptians;" wherefore the name of *the place* was called Abel-mizraim [THE MOURNING OF THE EGYPTIANS]; which is beyond Jordan. And the sons *of Jacob* did to him accord- 12 ing as he commanded them; for his sons carried him into the 13 land of Canaan, and buried him in the cave of the field of Machpelah, which Abraham bought with the field, a possession for a burying-place, of Ephron the Hittite, opposite to Mamre. And after he had buried his father, Joseph re- 14 turned into Egypt, he, and his brethren, and all who had gone up with him to bury his father.

Now when the brethren of Joseph saw that their father 15 was dead, they said, "Joseph will peradventure hate us, and will fully requite us all the evil which we did to him." And 16 they sent a messenger to Joseph, saying, "Thy father charged us before he died, saying, Thus shall ye say to Joseph, 'For- 17 give, I pray thee, the transgression of thy brethren, and their sin; although they did evil to thee:' and now, we pray thee, forgive the transgression of the servants of the God of thy father." And Joseph wept when they spake to him. And his brethren also went and fell down before his 18

19 face; and they said, "Lo, we are thy servants." And Joseph said to them, "Fear not; for am I in the place of
20 God? Ye indeed devised evil against me; but God devised it for good, to be the means, as it is this day, of saving much
21 people alive. Now, therefore, fear ye not; I will nourish you, and your little ones." Thus he comforted them, and spake kindly to them.
22 So Joseph dwelt in Egypt, he and his father's house; and
23 Joseph lived a hundred and ten years. And Joseph saw Ephraim's children of the third *generation:* the children also of Machir, the son of Manasseh, were born on Joseph's knees.
24 And Joseph said to his brethren, "I die: but God will surely visit you, and bring you out of this land into the land
25 which he sware to Abraham, to Isaac, and to Jacob." And Joseph adjured the children of Israel, saying, "God will surely visit you: then ye shall carry up hence my bones with you."
26 So Joseph died, being a hundred and ten years old: and when they had embalmed him, he was put in a coffin in Egypt.

THE BOOK OF EXODUS.

CHAP. I.—Now these are the names of the sons of Is- 1 rael, who went into Egypt with Jacob; every one went with his family. Reuben, Simeon, Levi, and Judah, Issachar, 3 Zebulun, and Benjamin, Dan, and Naphtali, Gad, and 4 Asher. And all the persons that came out of the loins of 5 Jacob were seventy persons. And Joseph was *already* in Egypt. And Joseph died, and all his brethren, and all that 6 generation. And the children of Israel were fruitful, and in- 7 creased abundantly, and multiplied, and became very mighty, so that the land was filled with them.

And there arose a new king over Egypt, who knew not 8 Joseph; and he said to his people, "Lo, the people of 9 the children of Israel are numerous and stronger than we. Come, let us deal wisely with them, lest they multiply, and it 10 come to pass that when there falleth out any war, they also join themselves to our enemies, and fight against us, and so go up out of the land." Therefore they set over them 11 task-masters, to afflict them with their burdens. And they built for Pharaoh treasure-cities, Pithom and Rameses: but 12 the more they afflicted them, the more they multiplied and grew. And *the Egyptians* were grieved because of the children of Israel. So the Egyptians made the children of 13 Israel serve with rigour, and made their lives bitter with 14 hard service, in mortar, and in brick, and with all manner of service in the field: all their service, in which they made them serve, was with rigour.

And the king of Egypt spake to the Hebrew midwives, of 15 whom the name of one was Siphrah, and the name of the other Phuah, and said, "When ye do the office of a mid- 16 wife to the Hebrew women, and inspect the troughs, if it be a son, ye shall kill him; but if it be a daughter, let her live." But the midwives feared God, and did not as the 17 king of Egypt commanded them, but saved the male-children alive. And the king of Egypt called for the midwives, and said to them, "Why have ye done this thing, and saved the male-children alive?" And the midwives said to Pharaoh, "The Hebrew women are not as the Egyptian women; for they are strong, and are delivered before the midwives come in unto them." Therefore God dealt well with the midwives; and the people multiplied, and became very mighty. And because the midwives feared God, he made them families. Then Pharaoh charged all his people, saying, "Every son that is born ye shall cast into the River, but every daughter ye shall save alive."

CHAP. II.—And a man of the house of Levi went and took *for a wife* a daughter of Levi. And the woman conceived and bare a son; and when she saw that he was beautiful, she hid him three months. And when she could no longer hide him, she took for him an ark of reeds, and covered it with bitumen and with pitch, and put the child in it, and laid it amongst the flags on the brink of the River. And his sister stood afar off, to know what would be done to him. And the daughter of Pharaoh came down to bathe in the River; and her maidens walked along by the River side; and when she saw the ark among the flags, she sent her maid to fetch it. And when she had opened it, she saw the child, and, lo, the babe wept. And she had compassion on him, and said, "This is one of the children of the Hebrews." Then said his sister to the daughter of Pharaoh, "Shall I go and call to thee a nurse of the Hebrew women, that she may suckle the child for thee?" And the daughter of Pharaoh said to her, "Go;" and the maid went and called the child's mother. And the daughter of Pharaoh said to her, "Take this child away, and suckle it for me, and I will give *thee* thy wages; and the woman took the child, and suckled it. And the child grew, and she brought him unto the daughter of Pharaoh, and he became her son. And she called his name Moses [DRAWN OUT]: for she said, "Because I drew him out of the water."

And it came to pass in those days, when Moses was grown, that he went out unto his brethren, and looked on their burdens; and he saw an Egyptian smiting a Hebrew, one of his brethren. And he looked this way and that way, and when he saw that there was no man, he smote the Egyptian, and

hid him in the sand. And he went out the next day, and 13
lo, two men of the Hebrews were striving together; and he
said to him who did the wrong, "Wherefore smitest thou thy
neighbour?" And he said, "Who made thee a prince and 14
a judge over us? Intendest thou to slay me, as thou slewest the Egyptian?" And Moses was afraid, and said,
"Surely the thing is known." And when Pharaoh heard 15
this thing, he sought to slay Moses; but Moses fled from
the face of Pharaoh, and dwelt in the land of Midian; and
he sat near a well. Now the priest of Midian had seven 16
daughters; and they came and drew *water*, and filled the
troughs to water their father's flock. And the shepherds 17
came and drove them away; but Moses stood up and helped
them, and watered their flock. And when they came to 18
Reuel their father, he said, "How is it that ye are come so
soon to-day?" And they said, "An Egyptian delivered us 19
out of the hand of the shepherds, and also drew *water*
enough for us, and watered the flock." And he said to his 20
daughters, "And where is he? why have ye left the man?
call him, that he may eat bread." And Moses consented to 21
dwell with the man; and he gave to Moses Zipporah his
daughter. And she bare to him a son, and he called his 22
name Gershom [A STRANGER THERE]; for he said, "I have
been a stranger in a strange land."

And it came to pass during those many days, that the king 23
of Egypt died, and the children of Israel sighed on account
of the bondage. And they cried, and their cry on account
of the bondage went up unto God. And God heard their 24
groaning, and God remembered his covenant with Abraham,
and with Isaac, and with Jacob. And God looked upon the 25
children of Israel, and God manifested himself *to them*.

CHAP. III.—Now while Moses was feeding the flock of 1
Jethro his father-in-law, the priest of Midian, he led the
flock to the furthest part of the desert, and came to the
mountain of God, to Horeb. And an angel of Jehovah ap- 2
peared to him in a flame of fire, out of the midst of a bush;
and he looked, and, lo, the bush burned with fire, yet the
bush was not consumed. And Moses said, "Let me now 3
turn aside, and see this great sight, why the bush is not
burnt." And when Jehovah saw that he turned aside to see, 4
God called to him out of the midst of the bush, and said,
"Moses, Moses." And he said, "Here I am." And he 5

said, "Draw not nigh hither: put thy shoes from off thy feet; for the place on which thou standest is holy ground."
6 Moreover he said, "I am the God of thy fathers, the God of Abraham, and the God of Isaac, and the God of Jacob." And Moses hid his face; for he was afraid to look upon God.
7 And Jehovah said, "I have clearly seen the affliction of my people that are in Egypt, and have heard their cry on ac-
8 count of their task-masters; for I know their sorrows, and I am come down to deliver them out of the hand of the Egyptians, and to bring them up out of that land unto a land good and large, unto a land flowing with milk and honey; unto the place of the Canaanites, and the Hittites, and the Amorites, and the Perizzites, and the Hivites, and
9 the Jebusites. Now therefore, lo, the cry of the children of Israel is come unto me, and I have also seen the oppression
10 with which the Egyptians oppress them. Come now, therefore, and I will send thee to Pharaoh, that thou mayest bring
11 forth my people, the children of Israel, out of Egypt." And Moses said to God, "Who am I, that I should go unto Pharaoh, and that I should bring forth the children of Israel
12 out of Egypt?" And he said, "I will assuredly be with thee, and this shall be a token to thee that I have sent thee: when thou hast brought forth the people out of Egypt, ye
13 shall serve God upon this mountain." And Moses said to God, "Lo, when I come unto the children of Israel, and say to them, 'The God of your fathers hath sent me unto you;' if they say to me, 'What is his name?' what shall
14 I say to them?" And God said to Moses, "I WILL BE WHAT I WILL BE:" and he said, "Thus shalt thou say to the children of Israel, 'I WILL BE hath sent me unto you.'"
15 And God said again to Moses, "Thus shalt thou say to the children of Israel, 'Jehovah, the God of your fathers, the God of Abraham, and the God of Isaac, and the God of Jacob, hath sent me unto you.' This is my name for ever,
16 and this my memorial to all generations. Go and gather the elders of Israel together, and say to them, 'JEHOVAH, the God of your fathers, the God of Abraham, and of Isaac, and of Jacob, hath appeared to me, saying, 'I have attentively observed you, and that which hath been done to
17 you in Egypt; and I have said, I will bring you up out of the affliction of Egypt into the land of the Canaanites, and the Hittites, and the Amorites, and the Perizzites, and the

Hivites, and the Jebusites, into a land flowing with milk and honey.' And they shall hearken to thy voice; and thou 18 shalt go, thou and the elders of Israel, to the king of Egypt, and ye shall say to him, 'Jehovah, the God of the Hebrews, is our God; and now let us go, we pray thee, three days' journey into the desert, that we may sacrifice to Jehovah our God.' And I know that the king of Egypt will not let you 19 go; no not by a mighty hand. I will therefore stretch out 20 my hand, and smite Egypt with all my wonders which I will do in the midst of it; and after that he will let you go. And I will give this people favour in the sight of the Egyp- 21 tians, so that when ye go, ye shall not go empty; but every 22 woman shall ask of her neighbour, and of her that sojourneth in her house, jewels of silver, and jewels of gold, and raiment, and ye shall put them upon your sons, and upon your daughters; and ye shall spoil the Egyptians."

CHAP. IV.—And Moses answered and said, "But, lo, 1 they will not believe me, nor hearken to my voice; for they will say, 'Jehovah hath not appeared to thee.'" And Jeho- 2 vah said to him, "What is that in thy hand?" And he said, "A rod." And he said, "Cast it on the ground." 3 And he cast it on the ground, and it became a serpent; and Moses fled from before it. And Jehovah said to Moses, 4 "Put forth thy hand, and take it by the tail;" (and he put forth his hand and caught it, and it became a rod in his hand;) "that they may believe that Jehovah, the God of 5 their fathers, the God of Abraham, and the God of Isaac, and the God of Jacob, hath appeared to thee." And again Je- 6 hovah said to him, "Put now thy hand into thy bosom." And he put his hand into his bosom; and when he took it out, lo, his hand was leprous as snow. And he said, "Put thy 7 hand into thy bosom again." And he put his hand into his bosom again, and took it out of his bosom; and, lo, it was turned again like *the rest of* his flesh. "And it shall come 8 to pass that if they will not believe thee, nor hearken to the voice of the first sign, they will believe the voice of the latter sign. And if they will not believe even these two signs, nor 9 hearken to thy voice, thou shalt take some of the water of the River and pour it upon the dry land; and the water which thou takest out of the River shall become blood upon the dry land." And Moses said to Jehovah, "O my lord, I am not 10 eloquent, neither before, nor since thou hast spoken to thy

servant; but I am slow of speech, and of a slow tongue."
11 And Jehovah said to him, "Who hath made man's mouth? or who maketh the dumb, or deaf, or the seeing, or the
12 blind? Is it not I, Jehovah? Now therefore go, and I will be with thy mouth, and teach thee what thou shalt say."
13 And he said, "O my lord, send, I pray thee, by him whom
14 thou wilt send." And the anger of Jehovah was kindled against Moses; and he said, "Is not Aaron the Levite thy brother? I know that he can speak well. And also, lo, he cometh forth to meet thee; and when he seeth thee, he will
15 be glad in his heart. And thou shalt speak to him, and put the words in his mouth; and I will be with thy mouth, and
16 with his mouth, and will teach you what ye shall do. And he shall speak, for thee, to the people: so he shall be, *even* he shall be to thee a mouth, and thou shalt be to him a God.
17 And thou shalt take this rod in thy hand, with which thou shalt do the signs."

18 And Moses went, and returned to Jethro his father-in-law, and said to him, "Let me go, I pray thee, and return unto my brethren who are in Egypt, and see whether they be yet
19 alive." And Jethro said to Moses, "Go in peace." And Jehovah said to Moses in Midian, "Go, 'return into Egypt;
20 for all the men are dead who sought thy life." And Moses took his wife and his sons, and set them upon asses, and he returned to the land of Egypt; and Moses took the rod of
21 God in his hand. And Jehovah had said to Moses, "When thou shalt have returned into Egypt, see that thou do all those wonders before Pharaoh which I have put in thy hand; but I will harden his heart, that he will not let the people
22 go. And thou shalt say to Pharaoh, 'Thus saith Jehovah,
23 Israel is my son, my first-born, and I say to thee, Let my son go, that he may serve me; and if thou refuse to let him
24 go, lo, I will slay thy son, thy first-born.'" And it came to pass, at a lodging place on the way, that Jehovah met him,
25 and sought to kill him. Then Zipporah took a sharp stone, and cut off the foreskin of her son. She then threw *herself* at his feet, and said, "Surely a bloody husband art thou to
26 me." So he let him go: then she said, "A bloody husband *art thou*," because of the circumcision.

27 And Jehovah had said to Aaron, "Go into the desert to meet Moses." And he went, and met him at the mountain
28 of God, and kissed him. Then Moses told Aaron all the words of Jehovah who had sent him, and all the signs which

he had commanded him *to do*. And Moses and Aaron went, 29 and gathered together all the elders of the children of Israel; and Aaron spake all the words which Jehovah had 30 spoken to Moses, and did the signs in the sight of the people. And the people believed: and when they heard that 31 Jehovah had visited the children of Israel, and that he had looked upon their affliction, they bowed their heads and worshipped.

CHAP. V.—And afterward Moses and Aaron went, and 1 said to Pharaoh, "Thus saith Jehovah the God of Israel, 'Let my people go, that they may keep a feast to me in the desert.'" And Pharaoh said, "Who is Jehovah, that I 2 should obey his voice to let Israel go? I know not Jehovah, neither will I let Israel go." And they said, "The God of 3 the Hebrews is our God: let us go, we pray thee, three days' journey into the desert, and sacrifice to Jehovah our God, lest he fall upon us with pestilence, or with the sword." And the king of Egypt said to them, "Wherefore do ye, 4 Moses and Aaron, call off the people from their works? go to your burdens." Pharaoh also said, "Lo, the people are 5 now numerous in the land, yet ye would make them rest from their burdens." That same day Pharaoh commanded 6 the task-masters of the people, and their officers, saying, "Ye shall no more give the people straw to make bricks, as 7 heretofore; let them go and gather straw for themselves. Yet the stated number of bricks, which they have made 8 heretofore, ye shall lay upon them; ye shall not diminish it; for they are idle; therefore they cry, saying, 'Let us go that we may sacrifice to our God.' Let more work be laid 9 upon the men, that they may labour therein, and let them not regard vain words." So the task-masters of the people 10 went out with their officers and spake to the people, saying, "Thus saith Pharaoh, 'I will not give you straw. Go ye, 11 get for yourselves straw where ye can find it; yet not aught of your work shall be diminished.'" So the people were 12 scattered abroad throughout all the land of Egypt, to gather stubble instead of straw. And the task-masters hastened 13 them, saying, "Fulfil your works, *your* daily tasks, as when there was straw." And the officers of the children of Israel, 14 whom Pharaoh's task-masters had set over them, were beaten, *and* asked, "Why have ye not fulfilled your task in making bricks, both yesterday and to-day, as heretofore?" Then 15

the officers of the children of Israel came and cried to Pharaoh, saying, "Wherefore dealest thou thus with thy ser-
16 vants? There is no straw given to thy servants, yet they say to us, 'Make bricks;' and, lo, thy servants are beaten; but
17 the fault is in thine own people." But he said, "Ye are altogether idle, therefore ye say, 'Let us go and sacrifice to
18 Jehovah.' Go therefore now, and work; for no straw shall be given to you, yet shall ye deliver the stated number of
19 bricks." Then the officers of the children of Israel saw that they were in evil case, after it was said, " Ye shall not dimi-
20 nish your bricks of your daily task." And they met Moses and Aaron, who were standing in the way, as they came forth
21 from Pharaoh, and they said to them, " Jehovah look upon you, and judge; because ye have made us abominable in the eyes of Pharaoh, and in the eyes of his servants, to put
22 a sword in their hand to slay us." And Moses returned to Jehovah, and said, "Lord, why hast thou brought evil
23 upon this people? why hast thou sent me? For since I came to Pharaoh to speak in thy name, he hath done evil to this people; neither hast thou at all delivered thy people."

1 CHAP. VI.—Then Jehovah said to Moses, "Now shalt thou see what I will do to Pharaoh; for through a strong hand shall he let them go, and through a strong hand shall he drive them out of his land."
2 And God spake to Moses, and said to him, "I am Jeho-
3 vah, and I appeared to Abraham, to Isaac, and to Jacob, as God Almighty; but by my name JEHOVAH was I not
4 known to them. And I also established my covenant with them, to give them the land of Canaan, the land of their so-
5 journings, in which they sojourned. And I have also heard the groaning of the children of Israel, whom the Egyptians keep in bondage; and I have remembered my covenant.
6 Wherefore say to the children of Israel, 'I am Jehovah, and I will bring you out from under the burdens of the Egyptians, and I will deliver you from their bondage, and I will redeem you with an out-stretched arm, and with great judg-
7 ments, and I will take you to be my people, and I will be your God; and ye shall know that I, Jehovah, am your God, who bringeth you out from under the burdens of the Egyp-
8 tians. And I will bring you in unto the land, concerning which I sware to give it, to Abraham, to Isaac, and to Jacob;

and I will give it to you for a heritage: I am Jehovah."
And Moses spake thus to the children of Israel; but they 9
hearkened not to Moses, for anguish of spirit, and for cruel
bondage. And Jehovah spake to Moses, saying, "Go in, 11
speak to Pharaoh king of Egypt, that he let the children of
Israel go out of his land." And Moses spake before Jeho- 12
vah, saying, "Lo, the children of Israel have not hearkened
to me; how then shall Pharaoh hear me, who am of uncircumcised lips?" And Jehovah spake to Moses and to Aaron, 13
and gave them a charge to the children of Israel, and to
Pharaoh king of Egypt, to bring the children of Israel out
of the land of Egypt.

These were the heads of the houses of their fathers: The 14
sons of Reuben, the first-born of Israel; Hanoch, and
Phallu, Hezron, and Carmi: these were the families of Reuben. And the sons of Simeon; Jemuel, and Jamin, and 15
Ohad, and Jachin, and Zohar, and Shaul, the son of a Ca-
naanitish woman: these were the families of Simeon. And 16
these were the names of the sons of Levi, according
to their generations; Gershon, and Kohath, and Merari.
And the years of the life of Levi were a hundred and thirty-
seven years. The sons of Gershon; Libni, and Shimi, 17
according to their families. And the sons of Kohath; 18
Amram, and Izhar, and Hebron, and Uzziel. And the years
of the life of Kohath were a hundred and thirty-three
years. And the sons of Merari; Mahali, and Mushi: 19
these were the families of Levi, according to their generations. And Amram took to himself Jochabed, his father's 20
sister, for a wife; and she bare to him Aaron and Moses.
And the years of the life of Amram were a hundred and
thirty-seven years. And the sons of Izhar; Korah, and 21
Nepheg, and Zichri. And the sons of Uzziel; Mishael, 22
and Elzaphan, and Sithri. And Aaron took to himself 23
Elisheba, daughter of Aminadab, sister of Naashon, for a
wife; and she bare to him Nadab and Abihu, Eleazar and
Ithamar. And the sons of Korah; Assir, and Elkanah, 24
and Abiasaph: these were the families of the Korahites.
And Eleazar, Aaron's son, took to himself one of the daugh- 25
ters of Putiel for a wife; and she bare to him Phineas: these
were the heads of the fathers of the Levites, according to
their families.

These were that Aaron and Moses, to whom Jehovah said, 26
"Bring out the children of Israel from the land of Egypt,

27 according to their hosts." These were they who spake to Pharaoh king of Egypt, to bring out the children of Israel from Egypt: these were that Moses and Aaron.
28 Now it came to pass on the day *when* Jehovah spake to
29 Moses in the land of Egypt, that Jehovah spake to Moses, saying, "I am Jehovah: speak thou to Pharaoh king of
30 Egypt all that I say to thee." And Moses said before Jehovah, "Lo, I am of uncircumcised lips, and how shall Pharaoh
1 hearken to me?" CHAP. VII.—And Jehovah said to Moses, "See, I have made thee a God to Pharaoh, and Aaron thy
2 brother shall be thy prophet. Thou shalt speak all that I command thee, and Aaron thy brother shall speak to Pharaoh,
3 that he may send the children of Israel out of his land. But I will harden Pharaoh's heart, and multiply my signs and my
4 wonders in the land of Egypt. For Pharaoh will not hearken to you, that I may lay my hand upon Egypt, and bring my hosts, my people the children of Israel, out of the land of
5 Egypt by great judgments. And the Egyptians shall know that I am Jehovah, when I stretch forth my hand upon Egypt, and bring out the children of Israel from among
6 them." And Moses and Aaron did as Jehovah commanded
7 them; so they did. Now Moses was eighty years old, and Aaron eighty-three years old, when they spake to Pharaoh.
8 And Jehovah spake to Moses and to Aaron, saying,
9 "When Pharaoh shall speak to you, saying, 'Shew a miracle for yourselves;' then thou shalt say to Aaron, 'Take thy rod, and cast it before Pharaoh;' *and* it shall become a serpent."
10 And Moses and Aaron went in unto Pharaoh, and they did as Jehovah had commanded; for Aaron cast down his rod before Pharaoh, and before his servants, and it became a ser-
11 pent. Then Pharaoh called also the wise men and the sorcerers: and the magicians of Egypt did in like manner by
12 their enchantments; for they cast down every man his rod, and they became serpents; but Aaron's rod swallowed up
13 their rods. And the heart of Pharaoh was hardened, so that he hearkened not to them; as Jehovah had said.
14 And Jehovah said to Moses, "Pharaoh's heart is hardened,
15 he refuseth to let the people go. Go to Pharaoh in the morning; lo, he goeth out unto the water; and thou shalt stand on the bank of the River to meet him; and the rod which
16 was turned into a serpent thou shalt take in thy hand. And thou shalt say to him, 'Jehovah, God of the Hebrews, hath

sent me unto thee, saying, 'Let my people go, that they may serve me in the desert:' and, lo, hitherto thou hast not hearkened. Thus saith Jehovah, 'By this thou shalt know 17 that I am Jehovah :' lo, I will smite with the rod which is in my hand the waters which are in the River, and they shall be turned into blood. And the fish that is in the River shall 18 die, and the River shall stink; so that the Egyptians shall loath to drink of the water of the River." And Jehovah said 19 to Moses, "Say to Aaron, 'Take thy rod, and stretch out thy hand over the waters of Egypt, over their streams, over their canals, and over their pools, and over every cistern of water, that they may become blood; and that there may be blood throughout all the land of Egypt, both in *vessels of wood*, and in *vessels of* stone.'" And Moses and Aaron did 20 so, as Jehovah commanded; for *Aaron* lifted up his rod, and smote the waters that were in the River, in the sight of Pharaoh, and in the sight of his servants; and all the waters that were in the River were turned into blood; and the fish that were in the River died; and the River stank, so that the Egyptians could not drink of the water of the River; and there was blood throughout all the land of Egypt. And the 22 magicians of Egypt did so with their enchantments; and Pharaoh's heart was hardened, so that he hearkened not to them, as Jehovah had said. But Pharaoh turned, and went 23 into his house, and did not set his heart even to this. And 24 all the Egyptians digged round about the River for water to drink; for they could not drink of the water of the River.

And when seven days were fulfilled, and after that Jeho- 25 vah had smitten the river, CHAP. VIII.—Jehovah said 1 to Moses, "Go unto Pharaoh, and say to him, 'Thus saith Jehovah, Let my people go, that they may serve me. For 2 if thou refuse to let them go, lo, I will smite all thy borders with frogs; and the River shall swarm with frogs, which 3 shall go up and come into thy house, and into thy bedchamber, and upon thy bed, and into the houses of thy servants, and upon thy people, and into thy ovens, and into thy **kneading-bowls**; and the frogs shall come up, 4 both upon thee, and upon thy people, and upon all thy servants.'" And Jehovah said to Moses, "Say to Aaron, 5 'Stretch forth thy hand with thy rod over the streams, and over the canals, and over the pools, and cause frogs to come up upon

6 the land of Egypt.'" And Aaron stretched out his hand over the waters of Egypt; and the frogs came up, and covered
7 the land of Egypt. And the magicians did so with their enchantments, and brought up frogs upon the land of Egypt.
8 Then Pharaoh called for Moses and Aaron, and said, "Entreat Jehovah, that he may take away the frogs from me, and from my people, and I will let the people go, that they may
9 sacrifice to Jehovah." And Moses said to Pharaoh, "Appoint me at what time I shall entreat for thee, and for thy servants, and for thy people, that the frogs may be removed from thee, and from thy houses, *and* may remain in the River
10 only." And he said, "To-morrow." And *Moses* said, "*Be it* according to thy word, that thou mayest know that there
11 is none like Jehovah our God. And the frogs shall depart from thee, and from thy houses, and from thy servants, and from thy people; they shall remain in the River only."
12 Then Moses and Aaron went out from Pharaoh; and Moses cried to Jehovah, because of the frogs which he had brought
13 against Pharaoh. And Jehovah did according to the word of Moses; for the frogs died out of the houses, and out of
14 the villages, and out of the fields. And they gathered them
15 together in heaps, and the land stank. But when Pharaoh saw that there was respite, he hardened his heart, and hearkened not to them; as Jehovah had said.

16 And Jehovah said to Moses, "Say to Aaron, ' Stretch forth thy rod, and smite the dust of the earth, that it may become
17 gnats throughout all the land of Egypt.'" And they did so; for Aaron stretched out his hand with his rod, and smote the dust of the earth, and it became gnats on man and on beast; and all the dust of the land became gnats
18 throughout all the land of Egypt. And the magicians did so with their enchantments to bring forth gnats, but they could
19 not. And there were gnats on man and on beast. Then the magicians said to Pharaoh, "This is the finger of God:" yet Pharaoh's heart was hardened, and he hearkened not to them; as Jehovah had said.

20 And Jehovah said to Moses, "Rise up early in the morning, and stand before Pharaoh; (lo, he cometh forth to the water) and say to him, ' Thus saith Jehovah, Let my people
21 go, that they may serve me: for, if thou wilt not let my people go, lo, I will send beetles upon thee, and upon thy servants, and upon thy people, and into thy houses; and the houses of the Egyptians shall be full of beetles, and also

the ground on which they are. But I will distinguish, on 22 that day, the land of Goshen, in which my people dwell, so that no beetles shall be there; in order that thou mayest know that I am Jehovah in the midst of the land; and I 23 will make a distinction between my people and thy people. To-morrow shall this sign be.'" And Jehovah did so: for 24 there came a grievous *swarm of* beetles into the house of Pharaoh, and *into* the houses of his servants, and into all the land of Egypt; the land was corrupted by reason of the beetles. Then Pharaoh called for Moses and for Aaron, and 25 said, "Go ye sacrifice to your God in the land." And Moses 26 said, "It is not right so to do; for we shall sacrifice the abomination of the Egyptians to Jehovah our God: lo, if we should sacrifice the abomination of the Egyptians before 27 their eyes, would they not stone us? We will go three' days' journey into the wilderness, and sacrifice to Jehovah our God, as he shall command us." And Pharaoh said, "I 23 will let you go, that ye may sacrifice to Jehovah your God in the wilderness; only ye shall not go very far away: entreat for me." And Moses said, " Lo, I go out from thee, and I 29 will entreat Jehovah that the beetles may depart from Pharaoh, from his servants, and from his people, to-morrow; but let not Pharaoh deal deceitfully any more in not letting the people go to sacrifice to Jehovah." Then Moses went out 30 from Pharaoh, and entreated Jehovah. And Jehovah did ac- 31 cording to the word of Moses; for he removed the beetles from Pharaoh, from his servants, and from his people: there remained not one. Yet Pharaoh hardened his heart at this 32 time also, and would not let the people go.

CHAP. IX.—Then Jehovah said to Moses, "Go unto 1 Pharaoh, and say to him, 'Thus saith Jehovah, God of the Hebrews, Let my people go, that they may serve me. For 2 if thou refuse to let *them* go, and wilt detain them still, lo, 3 the hand of Jehovah shall be upon thy cattle which is in the field, upon the horses, upon the asses, upon the camels, upon the oxen, and upon the sheep; a very grievous pestilence. But Jehovah will distinguish between the cattle of the 4 Israelites and the cattle of the Egyptians, so that nothing shall die of all that belongeth to the children of Israel.'" And 5 Jehovah appointed a fixed time, saying, "To-morrow Jehovah will do this thing in the land." And Jehovah did that thing 6 on the morrow; for all the cattle of the Egyptians died,

EXODUS IX.

7 but of the cattle of the children of Israel died not one. And Pharaoh sent, and, lo, there was not one of the cattle of the Israelites dead. Yet the heart of Pharaoh was hardened, and he did not let the people go.

8 Then Jehovah said to Moses and to Aaron, "Take to you handfuls of ashes of the furnace, and let Moses sprinkle it
9 towards heaven in the sight of Pharaoh; and it shall become small dust in all the land of Egypt, and shall be an ulcerous inflammation upon man and beast, throughout all the land
10 of Egypt." And they took ashes of the furnace, and stood before Pharaoh; and Moses sprinkled it up towards heaven; and it became an ulcerous inflammation upon man and upon
11 beast. And the magicians could not stand before Moses because of the inflammation; for the inflammation was upon
12 the magicians and upon all the Egyptians. But Jehovah hardened the heart of Pharaoh, so that he hearkened not to them, as Jehovah had spoken to Moses.
13 And Jehovah said to Moses, "Rise up early in the morning, and stand before Pharaoh, and say to him, 'Thus saith Jehovah, God of the Hebrews, Let my people go, that they
14 may serve me. For I will at this time send all my plagues upon thyself, and upon thy servants, and upon thy people, that thou mayest know that there is none like me in all the
15 earth. For now I could stretch out my hand and smite thee and thy people with pestilence, so that thou shouldst be cut
16 off from the earth. But for this cause indeed have I preserved thee, to shew in thee my power, and that my name
17 may be declared in all the earth. As thou yet exaltest thy-
18 self against my people, so that thou wilt not let them go, lo, to-morrow about this time I will cause it to rain a very grievous hail, such as hath not been in Egypt since the day
19 of its foundation even until now. Now therefore send, and gather in thy cattle, and all that thou hast in the field; every man and beast which shall be found in the field, and shall not have been brought home, the hail shall come down
20 upon them, and they shall die.'" He among the servants of Pharaoh who feared the word of Jehovah, made his
21 servants and his cattle flee into the houses; but he who regarded not the word of Jehovah left his servants and his
22 cattle in the field. Then Jehovah said to Moses, "Stretch forth thy hand towards heaven, that there may be hail in all the land of Egypt, upon man, and upon beast, and upon every herb of the field, throughout the land of Egypt."

And Moses stretched forth his rod towards heaven; and 23 Jehovah sent thunder and hail, and the fire ran along upon the ground; and Jehovah rained hail upon the land of Egypt. So there was hail, and fire mingled with the hail, 24 very grievous, such as there had not been in all the land of Egypt since it became a nation. And the hail smote through- 25 out all the land of Egypt all that was in the field, both man and beast; and the hail smote every herb of the field, and brake every tree of the field. Only in the land of Goshen, 26 where the children of Israel were, there was no hail. And 27 Pharaoh sent, and called for Moses and Aaron, and said to them, "I have sinned this time: Jehovah is righteous, but I and my people are wicked. Entreat Jehovah that there may 28 be an end of this mighty thunder and hail; and I will let you go, and ye shall stay no longer." And Moses said to 29 him, "As soon as I am gone out of the city, I will spread abroad my hands to Jehovah, and the thunder shall cease, and there shall be no more hail; in order that thou mayest know that the land is Jehovah's. But as for thee and thy 30 servants, I know that ye will not yet fear Jehovah God." Now the flax and the barley was smitten; for the barley was 31 in the ear, and the flax was in flower. But the wheat and 32 the spelt were not smitten; for they were not grown up. And 33 Moses went out of the city from Pharaoh, and spread abroad his hands to Jehovah; and the thunders and the hail ceased, and the rain was not poured upon the earth. And when Pha- 34 raoh saw that the rain and the hail and the thunders had ceased he sinned yet more and hardened his heart, he and his servants. So the heart of Pharaoh was hardened, nor would he 35 let the children of Israel go; as Jehovah had spoken by Moses.

CHAP. X.—And Jehovah said to Moses, "Go in unto 1 Pharaoh; for I have hardened his heart, and the heart of his servants, in order that I might shew these my signs among them, and that thou mightest tell in the ears of thy 2 son, and of thy son's son, what things I have wrought in Egypt, and my signs which I have done amongst them; that ye may know that I am Jehovah your God." And Moses 3 and Aaron went in unto Pharaoh, and said to him, "Thus saith Jehovah the God of the Hebrews, 'How long wilt thou refuse to humble thyself before me? Let my people go, that they may serve me. For if thou refuse to let my 4

people go, lo, to-morrow I will bring the locusts into thy bor-
5 ders; and they shall cover the face of the earth, that it will
not be possible to see the earth: and they shall eat the
residue of that which has escaped, which remaineth to you
from the hail, and they shall eat every tree which groweth
6 for you out of the field; and they shall fill thy houses, and
the houses of all thy servants, and the houses of all the
Egyptians: such neither thy fathers, nor thy fathers' fathers
saw, since the day they were upon the land unto this day.'"
7 And he turned himself, and went out from Pharaoh. And
Pharaoh's servants said to him, "How long shall this *man*
be a snare to us? Let the men go, that they may serve
Jehovah their God. Wouldst thou first know that Egypt is
8 destroyed?" And Moses and Aaron were brought again
unto Pharaoh, and he said to them, "Go, serve Jehovah your
9 God; *but* who are they that are to go?" And Moses said,
"We will go with our young and with our old, with our
sons and with our daughters, with our flocks and with our
herds will we go; for we *must keep* a feast to Jehovah our
10 God." And *Pharaoh* said to them, "May Jehovah be so
with you, as I will let you go, with your little ones! See!
11 what evil designs ye have! Not so: go now, ye men and
serve Jehovah; for that ye desired." And they were driven
12 out from the presence of Pharaoh. Then Jehovah said to
Moses, "Stretch out thy hand over the land of Egypt for
the locusts, that they may come up upon the land of Egypt,
and eat every herb of the land, all that the hail hath left."
13 And Moses stretched forth his rod over the land of Egypt,
and Jehovah brought an east wind upon the land all that
day, and all *that* night; *and* when it was morning, the east
14 wind brought the locusts. And the locusts went up over
all the land of Egypt, and rested in great numbers in all the
borders of Egypt: before them there were no such locusts
15 as they, neither after them shall there be such; for they
covered the face of the whole land, so that the land was
darkened; and they ate every herb of the land, and all the
fruit of the trees which the hail had left; and there remained
not any green thing in the trees, or in the herbs of the field,
16 through all the land of Egypt. Then Pharaoh called for
Moses and Aaron in haste; and he said, "I have sinned
17 against Jehovah your God, and against you. Now, therefore, forgive, I pray thee, my sin only this once, and entreat Jehovah your God, that he may take away from me this

death only." And he went out from Pharaoh, and en- 18 treated Jehovah, and Jehovah turned a very strong west 19 wind, which took away the locusts, and cast them into the Red Sea: there remained not one locust in all the borders of Egypt. But Jehovah hardened Pharaoh's heart, so that he 20 would not let the children of Israel go.

And Jehovah said to Moses, "Stretch out thy hand to- 21 wards heaven, that there may be darkness over the land of Egypt, even darkness which may be felt." And Moses 22 stretched forth his hand towards heaven; and there was a thick darkness in all the land of Egypt for three days: they saw not one another, neither rose any from his place 23 for three days; but all the children of Israel had light in their dwellings. Then Pharaoh called to Moses, and said, 24 "Go ye, serve Jehovah; only let your flocks and your herds remain: "let your little ones also go with you." And Mo- 25 ses said, "Thou must give us also sacrifices and burnt-offerings, that we may sacrifice to Jehovah our God. Our cattle 26 also shall go with us; there shall not a hoof be left behind; for of them we must take to serve Jehovah our God, and we know not with which we must serve Jehovah until we come thither." But Jehovah hardened the heart of Pharaoh, 27 so that he would not let them go. And Pharaoh said to 28 *Moses,* "Be gone from me. Take heed to thyself; see my face no more; for in the day thou seest my face thou shalt die." And Moses said, "Thou hast spoken well; I will see 29 thy face again no more."

CHAP. XI.—Now Jehovah had said to Moses, "Yet will 1 I bring one plague upon Pharaoh and upon Egypt, and afterwards he will let you go hence: when he shall let *you* go, he will surely thrust you out hence altogether. Speak 2 now in the ears of the people, and let every man ask of his neighbour, and every woman of her neighbour, jewels of silver, and jewels of gold." And Jehovah gave the people 3 favour in the sight of the Egyptians. The man Moses also was very great in the land of Egypt, in the sight of Pharaoh's servants, and in the sight of the people. And Moses 4 said, "Thus saith Jehovah, 'About midnight will I go through the midst of Egypt, and every first-born in the land 5 of Egypt shall die, from the first-born of Pharaoh who sitteth upon his throne, to the first-born of the maid-servant who is behind the mill; and to the first-born of every beast.'

6 And there shall be a great cry throughout all the land of Egypt, such as never hath been, and such as shall not be
7 again. But against all the children of Israel not a dog shall move his tongue, against either man or beast; that ye may know that Jehovah doth put a difference between the Egyp-
8 tians and the Israelites. And all these thy servants shall come down to me, and bow down themselves to me, saying, 'Go out, thou and all the people that follow thee:' and after that I will go out." And he went out from Pharaoh in
9 great anger. Now Jehovah had said to Moses, "Pharaoh will not hearken to you, that my wonders may be multiplied
10 in the land of Egypt." And Moses and Aaron did all these wonders before Pharaoh; and Jehovah hardened Pharaoh's heart, so that he would not let the children of Israel go out of his land.

1 CHAP. XII.—And Jehovah spake to Moses and Aaron in
2 the land of Egypt, saying, "This month shall be to you the beginning of months: it shall be the first month of the year
3 to you. Speak ye to all the congregation of the children of Israel, saying, 'In the tenth day of this month let them take to themselves every man a lamb, according to the house of
4 their fathers; a lamb for a house. But if the household be too small for the lamb, let him and his neighbour next to his house take *one*, according to the number of the persons: every man, according to his own eating, shall reckon for the
5 lamb. Your lamb shall be without blemish, a male of the first year: ye shall take it from the sheep, or from the goats;
6 and ye shall keep it until the fourteenth day of the same month; and the whole assembly of the congregation of
7 Israel shall kill it in the evening. And they shall take some of the blood, and sprinkle it on the two side-posts and on the
8 lintel of the houses in which they shall eat it. And they shall eat the flesh in that night, roasted by fire: with un-
9 leavened bread, and with bitter herbs they shall eat it. Ye shall not eat of it raw, nor boiled in water, but roasted by
10 fire; its head with its legs, and with its entrails. And ye shall let none of it remain until the morning; or that which remaineth of it until the morning ye shall burn with fire.
11 And thus shall ye eat it; your loins girded, your shoes on your feet, and your staff in your hand; and ye shall eat it in
12 haste: it is the passover of Jehovah. For I will pass through the land of Egypt this night, and will smite all the first-born

in the land of Egypt, both man and beast; and against all the gods of Egypt I will execute judgment: I am Jehovah. And the blood shall be to you for a token upon the houses where ye are; and when I see the blood, I will pass over you, and the plague shall not be upon you to destroy you, when I smite the land of Egypt. And this day shall be to you for a memorial, and ye shall keep it a feast to Jehovah throughout your generations; ye shall keep it a feast by a perpetual ordinance. Seven days shall ye eat unleavened bread; even on the first day ye shall put away leaven out of your houses; for whosoever eateth leavened bread from the first day until the seventh day, that person shall be cut off from Israel. And on the first day ye shall have a holy convocation, and on the seventh day a holy convocation; no manner of work shall be done in them, except what every man must eat; that only may be done by you. And ye shall observe *the feast of* unleavened bread; for in this very day I brought your hosts out of the land of Egypt: therefore shall ye observe this day throughout your generations by a perpetual ordinance. In the first month, from the evening of the fourteenth day of the month, ye shall eat unleavened bread, until the evening of the twenty-first day of the month. Seven days there shall be no leaven found in your houses; for whosoever eateth that which is leavened, even that person shall be cut off from the congregation of Israel, whether he be a stranger, or one born in the land. Ye shall eat nothing leavened; in all your habitations shall ye eat unleavened bread.'"

Then Moses called for the elders of Israel, and said to them, "Choose out and take for yourselves a lamb, according to your families, and kill the passover: then take a bunch of hyssop, and dip it in the blood that is in the bason, and strike the lintel and the two side-posts with the blood that is in the bason; and let none of you go out at the door of his house until the morning. For Jehovah will pass through to smite the Egyptians; and when he seeth the blood upon the lintel, and on the two side-posts, Jehovah will pass over the door, and will not suffer the destroyer to come in to your houses to smite *you*. And ye shall observe this thing as a perpetual ordinance to thee and to thy children. And it shall come to pass when ye are come into the land which Jehovah will give you, according as he hath promised, that ye shall keep this service; and it shall come to pass when your children shall

EXODUS XII.

27 say to you, 'What mean ye by this service?' that ye shall say, 'It is the sacrifice of the passover of Jehovah, who passed over the houses of the children of Israel in Egypt, when he smote the Egyptians, and delivered our houses.'"
28 And the people bowed the head, and made obeisance. And the children of Israel went away, and did as Jehovah had commanded Moses and Aaron; so they did.
29 And it came to pass that at midnight, Jehovah smote all the first-born in the land of Egypt, from the first-born of Pharaoh that sat on his throne, to the first-born of the captive that was in the dungeon; and all the first-born of cattle.
30 And Pharaoh rose up in the night, he, and all his servants, and all the Egyptians; and there was a great cry in Egypt; for there was not a house in which there was not one dead.
31 And he called for Moses and Aaron by night, and said, "Rise, depart from among my people, both you and the children of Israel, and go, serve Jehovah as ye have said.
32 Take your flocks also, and your herds, as ye have said, and
33 go; and bless me also." And the Egyptians were urgent upon the people, that they might send them out of the land
34 in haste; for they said, "We shall all be dead!" And the people took their dough being not yet leavened, their kneading-bowls being bound up in their clothes upon their shoul-
35 ders. And the children of Israel had done as Moses had commanded them; and they had asked of the Egyptians
36 jewels of silver and jewels of gold, and raiment; and Jehovah had given the people favour in the sight of the Egyptians, so that they gave to them *such things as they required;* and they spoiled the Egyptians.
37 And the children of Israel journeyed from Rameses to Succoth, about six hundred thousand on foot *that were* men,
38 beside children. And a mixed multitude went up also with
39 them; and flocks and herds, *even* very much cattle. And they baked unleavened cakes of the dough which they brought forth out of Egypt; for it had not been leavened, because they were thrust out of Egypt, and could not tarry, nor had
40 they prepared for themselves any food. Now the sojournment of the children of Israel who dwelt in Egypt, was four
41 hundred and thirty years. And it came to pass at the end of the four hundred and thirty years, even on that very day it came to pass that all the hosts of Jehovah went out from
42 the land of Egypt. It is a night to be much observed to Jehovah for bringing them out from the land of Egypt: this is

that night of Jehovah to be observed by all the children of Israel in their generations.

And Jehovah said to Moses and Aaron, "This is the ordinance of the passover. No alien shall eat of it, but every man's servant that is bought with money, when thou hast circumcised him, then shall he eat of it. A sojourner and a hired servant shall not eat of it. In one house shall it be eaten; thou shalt not carry forth out of the house any part of the flesh, nor shall ye break a bone thereof. All the congregation of the children of Israel shall keep it. And when a stranger shall sojourn with thee, and will keep the passover to Jehovah, let all his males be circumcised, and then let him come near and keep it; and he shall be as one that is born in the land; for no uncircumcised person shall eat of it. One law shall be for the native, and for the stranger that sojourneth among you." And all the children of Israel did as Jehovah commanded Moses and Aaron; so they did. And it came to pass that very day, that Jehovah brought the children of Israel out of the land of Egypt by their hosts.

CHAP. XIII.—And Jehovah spake to Moses, saying, "Sanctify to me every male first-born, which openeth every womb among the children of Israel, whether of man or of beast; it is mine." And Moses said to the people, "Remember this day, in which ye came out of Egypt, out of the house of bondage; for by strength of hand Jehovah brought you out thence: nothing leavened shall be eaten on the day in which ye came out, in the month Abib. And it shall be when Jehovah shall have brought thee into the land of the Canaanites, and the Hittites, and the Amorites, and the Hivites, and the Jebusites, which he sware to thy fathers to give thee, a land flowing with milk and honey, that thou shalt keep this service in this month. Seven days thou shalt eat unleavened bread, and in the seventh day *shall be* a feast to Jehovah. Unleavened bread shall be eaten seven days, and there shall no leavened bread be seen with thee, neither shall there be leaven seen with thee in all thy borders. And thou shalt shew thy son in that day, saying, '*It is* on account of that which Jehovah did to me when I came forth out of Egypt.' And it shall be for a sign to thee upon thy hand, and for a memorial between thine eyes; that the law of Jehovah may be in thy mouth; for with a strong

10 hand hath Jehovah brought thee out of Egypt. Thou shalt therefore keep this ordinance in its season every year.

11 "And it shall be when Jehovah shall have brought thee into the land of the Canaanites, as he sware to thee and thy
12 fathers, and shall have given it to thee, that thou shalt set apart to Jehovah every thing that openeth the womb and every firstling the issue of a beast which thou mayest have;
13 the males *shall be* Jehovah's. And every firstling of an ass thou shalt redeem with a lamb; and if thou wilt not redeem it, then thou shalt break its neck; but every male first-born
14 among thy children thou shalt redeem. And it shall be, when thy son asketh thee in time to come, saying, 'What is this?' that thou shalt say to him, 'By strength of hand Jehovah brought us out of Egypt, out of the house of bond-
15 age; for, it came to pass when Pharaoh obstinately refused to let us go, that Jehovah slew all the first-born in the land of Egypt, both the first-born of man, and the first-born of beast: therefore I sacrifice to Jehovah all that openeth the womb, being males; but all the first-born of my children I
16 redeem.' And it shall be for a token upon thy hand, and for frontlets between thine eyes: for by strength of hand Jehovah brought us forth out of Egypt."
17 And it came to pass when Pharaoh had let the people go, that God led them not by the way of the land of the Philistines, although that was the nearest; for God said, "Lest the people repent when they see war, and return to Egypt;"
18 but God led the people about, by the way of the desert of the Red Sea. And the children of Israel went up in array
19 out of the land of Egypt. And Moses took with him the bones of Joseph; for he had solemnly adjured the children of Israel, saying, "God will surely visit you, and ye shall
20 carry up my bones away hence with you." And they took their journey from Succoth, and encamped in Etham, at
21 the extremity of the desert. And Jehovah went before them, by day in a pillar of a cloud, to lead them on the way, and by night in a pillar of fire, to give them light; that
22 they might go by day and by night. He took not away the pillar of the cloud by day, nor the pillar of fire by night, *from* before the people.

1 CHAP. XIV.—And Jehovah spake to Moses, saying,
2 "Speak to the children of Israel, that they turn and encamp before Pi-hahiroth, between Migdol and the sea, over against

Baal-zephon: before it shall ye encamp, by the sea. For Pharaoh will say of the children of Israel, 'They are entangled in the land, the desert hath shut them in.' And I will harden Pharaoh's heart so that he shall follow after them; and I will be honoured upon Pharaoh, and upon all his host; that the Egyptians may know that I am Jehovah." And they did so. And it was told to the king of Egypt that the people had fled; and the heart of Pharaoh and of his servants was changed towards the people, and they said, "What is this that we have done, to let Israel go from serving us?" And he made ready his chariot, and took with him his people; and he took six hundred chosen chariots, and all the cavalry of Egypt, and officers over the whole. And Jehovah hardened the heart of Pharaoh king of Egypt, and he pursued after the children of Israel; though the children of Israel had gone out with a high hand. But the Egyptians pursued after them, all the horses *and* chariots of Pharaoh, and his horsemen, even his whole force, and overtook them encamping by the sea, beside Pi-hahiroth, before Baal-zephon. And when Pharaoh drew nigh, the children of Israel lifted up their eyes, and, lo, the Egyptians were marching after them; and the children of Israel were exceedingly afraid, and cried to Jehovah. And they said to Moses, "Because there were no graves in Egypt, hast thou brought us away to die in the desert? what is this thou hast done to us, by bringing us out of Egypt? Is not this what we told thee in Egypt, saying, 'Let us alone, that we may serve the Egyptians?' for it would have been better for us to serve the Egyptians, than to die in the desert." And Moses said to the people, "Fear ye not, stand still, and see the salvation of Jehovah, which he will work for you this day; for the Egyptians whom ye see to-day, ye shall see again no more for ever: Jehovah will fight for you, while ye are silent." And Jehovah said to Moses, "Wherefore criest thou to me? Tell the children of Israel to go forward; but lift thou up thy rod, and stretch out thy hand over the sea, and divide it, that the children of Israel may go through the midst of the sea on the dry ground. And, lo, I will harden the hearts of the Egyptians, and they shall follow them; and I will get me honour upon Pharaoh, and upon all his host, upon his chariots, and upon his horsemen. And the Egyptians shall know that I am Jehovah, when I have gotten me honour upon Pharaoh, upon his chariots, and upon his horse-

19 men." And the angel of God which had gone before the camp of the Israelites, removed, and went behind them, and the pillar of the cloud went from before them, and stood
20 behind them; and it came between the camp of the Egyptians, and the camp of the Israelites; and it was a cloud and darkness *to the Egyptians,* but it gave light by night *to the Israelites;* so that the one came not near to the other all the
21 night. Then Moses stretched out his hand over the sea; and Jehovah by a strong east wind caused the sea to go *back* all that night, and he turned the sea into dry ground, and
22 the waters were divided. And the children of Israel went into the midst of the sea on the dry ground: and the waters *were* a wall to them on their right hand and on their left.
23 And the Egyptians pursued, and went in after them to the midst of the sea, all the horses of Pharaoh, his chariots, and his horsemen.
24 And it came to pass that in the morning-watch Jehovah looked upon the host of the Egyptians through the pillar of fire, and of the cloud, and troubled the host of the Egyp-
25 tians, and turned aside their chariot-wheels, so that they drove them heavily: the Egyptians therefore said, "Let us flee from the face of the Israelites; for Jehovah fighteth for
26 them against the Egyptians." Then Jehovah said to Moses, "Stretch out thy hand over the sea, that the waters may come again upon the Egyptians, and upon their chariots,
27 and upon their horsemen." And Moses stretched forth his hand over the sea, and when the morning appeared the sea returned to its strength, and the Egyptians met it as they fled. Thus Jehovah overthrew the Egyptians in the midst
28 of the sea. For the waters returned, and covered the chariots, and the horsemen; all the host of Pharaoh that had gone into the sea after *the Israelites:* there remained not
29 even one of them. But the children of Israel walked upon dry ground in the midst of the sea; and the waters were a
30 wall to them on their right hand, and on their left. Thus Jehovah saved the Israelites that day out of the hand of the Egyptians; and the Israelites saw the Egyptians dead upon
31 the sea-shore. And when the Israelites saw that great work which Jehovah did upon the Egyptians, the people feared Jehovah, and trusted in Jehovah and in his servant Moses.

1 CHAP. XV.—Then sang Moses and the children of Israel this song to Jehovah, and spake, saying,

"I will sing unto Jehovah, for he hath highly exalted himself:
The horse and his rider he hath thrown into the sea.
Jehovah is my strength and my song, 2
And he is become my salvation:
He is my God, and I will glorify him;
My father's God, and I will exalt him.
Jehovah is mighty in war: 3
Jehovah is his name.
The chariots of Pharaoh and his host he hath cast into 4 the sea:
His chosen captains are drowned in the Red Sea.
The depths have covered them: 5
They went down to the bottom like a stone.
Thy right hand, O Jehovah, hath been glorious in power: 6
Thy right hand, O Jehovah, hath dashed in pieces the enemy.
In the greatness of thine excellency thou hast overthrown 7 them who rose up against thee:
Thou sentest forth thy wrath, it consumed them like stubble.
By the blast of thy nostrils the waters were heaped up; 8
The floods stood upright as a heap;
The depths were congealed in the midst of the sea.
The enemy said, 'I will pursue, I will overtake, 9
I will divide the spoil;
My desire shall be satisfied upon them;
I will draw my sword, my hand shall repossess them.'
Thou didst blow with thy breath, the sea covered them; 10
They sank like lead in the mighty waters.
Who among the gods is like thee, O Jehovah! 11
Who, like thee, is glorious in holiness,
Fearful in praises, doing wonders!
Thou stretchedst out thy right hand, 12
The earth swallowed them.
Thou hast led forth in thy mercy the people whom thou 13 hast redeemed:
Thou art guiding them in thy strength to thy holy habitation.
Peoples shall hear, and tremble: 14
Pangs shall seize the inhabitants of Philistia.
Then shall the princes of Edom be amazed: 15
Trembling shall seize the mighty men of Moab:

EXODUS XVI.

      All the inhabitants of Canaan shall melt away.
16 Fear and dread shall fall upon them:
      Through the greatness of thine arm they shall be still as a stone;
      Till thy people pass over, O Jehovah,
      Till the people pass over whom thou hast purchased.
17 Thou wilt bring them in, and plant them in the mountain of thine inheritance,
      The place, O Jehovah, *which* thou hast made for thyself to dwell in,
      The sanctuary, O Jehovah, *which* thine hands have established.
18 Jehovah shall reign for ever and ever."
19 For the horses of Pharaoh, with his chariots and with his horsemen, went into the sea, and Jehovah brought again the waters of the sea upon them; but the children of Israel went on dry ground in the midst of the sea.
20 And Miriam the prophetess, the sister of Aaron, took a timbrel in her hand; and all the women went out after
21 her with timbrels and with dances. And Miriam answered them,
      " Sing ye to Jehovah, for he hath highly exalted himself;
      The horse and his rider hath he thrown into the sea."
22 Then Moses led the Israelites away from the Red Sea; and they went out into the desert of Shur; and they jour-
23 neyed three days in the desert, and found no water. And when they came to Marah, they could not drink of the waters of Marah, for they were bitter; therefore the name
24 of *that place* was called Marah [BITTERNESS]. And the people murmured against Moses, saying, "What shall we
25 drink?" And he cried to Jehovah; and Jehovah shewed him a wood, which he cast into the waters, and the waters became sweet. There *Jehovah* made a statute and an ordi-
26 nance, and there he proved them, and said, "If thou wilt diligently hearken to the voice of Jehovah thy God, and wilt do that which is right in his sight, and wilt give ear to his commandments, and keep all his statutes, I will bring none of the diseases upon thee, which I brought upon the Egyptians: for I am Jehovah who healeth thee."
27 And they came to Elim, where were twelve wells of water, and seventy palm-trees; and they encamped there by the waters.
1 CHAP. XVI.—And they journeyed from Elim; and all the congregation of the children of Israel came unto the desert

I

of Sin, which is between Elim and Sinai, on the fifteenth day of the second month after their departure from the land of Egypt. And the whole congregation of the children of Israel murmured against Moses and Aaron in the desert; and the children of Israel said to them, "Oh that we had died by the hand of Jehovah in the land of Egypt, when we sat by the flesh-pots, when we ate bread to the full! for ye have brought us forth into this desert, to kill this whole assembly by famine." Then Jehovah said to Moses, "Lo, I will rain bread for you from the heavens; and the people shall go out and gather a certain portion every day, that I may prove them, whether they will walk in my law or not. And on the sixth day they shall prepare what they bring in, and it shall be twice as much as they gather daily." And Moses and Aaron said to all the children of Israel, "In the evening ye shall know that Jehovah hath brought you out from the land of Egypt, and in the morning ye shall see the glory of Jehovah; since he hath heard your murmurings against Jehovah: for what are we that ye murmur against us?" And Moses said, "*This shall be*, when Jehovah shall give you in the evening flesh to eat, and in the morning bread to the full; since Jehovah hath heard your murmurings which ye murmur against him. For what are we? your murmurings are not against us, but against Jehovah." And Moses said to Aaron, "Say to all the congregation of the children of Israel, 'Come near before Jehovah; for he hath heard your murmurings.'" And it came to pass while Aaron was speaking to the whole congregation of the children of Israel, that they looked toward the desert, and, lo, the glory of Jehovah appeared in the cloud. Now Jehovah had spoken to Moses, saying, "I have heard the murmurings of the children of Israel: speak to them saying, 'In the evening ye shall eat flesh, and in the morning ye shall be filled with bread; and ye shall know that I Jehovah am your God.'" And it came to pass that in the evening the quails came up, and covered the camp; and in the morning there was a fall of dew round about the camp. And when the fall of dew had gone off, lo, upon the face of the desert *there lay* something small and shining; small as the hoar frost on the earth. And when the children of Israel saw it, they said one to another, "What is it?" for they knew not what it was. And Moses said to them, "This is the bread which Jehovah giveth you to eat. This is what Jehovah hath

commanded. Gather of it, every one according to his eating; an omer for every man, according to the number of your persons; take ye every one for those who are in his tent."
17 And the children of Israel did so, and gathered, some more,
18 some less. And when they measured it with an omer, he that had gathered much had nothing over, and he that had gathered little had no want: they gathered every one ac-
19 cording to his eating. And Moses said, "Let no one leave
20 of it until the morning." Yet they hearkened not to Moses; but some of them left of it until the morning, and it bred
21 worms, and stank; and Moses was angry with them. So they gathered it every morning, every one according to his
22 eating; and when the sun grew hot, it melted away. But it came to pass that on the sixth day they gathered twice as much food, two omers for each person. And all the rulers
23 of the congregation came and told Moses, and he said to them, "This is what Jehovah hath said, 'To-morrow is the rest of the holy sabbath to Jehovah: bake what ye will bake, and boil what ye will boil; and that which remaineth over
24 lay up for yourselves, to be kept until the morning.'" And they laid it up until the morning, as Moses commanded;
25 and it did not stink, nor was there any worm in it. And Moses said, "Eat that to-day; for to-day is a sabbath to
26 Jehovah: to-day ye shall not find it in the field. Six days ye shall gather it; but on the seventh day, *which is* the sab-
27 bath, there shall be none." And it came to pass that some of the people went out on the seventh day to gather, but
28 they found none. And Jehovah said to Moses, "How long
29 refuse ye to keep my commandments and my laws? See, because Jehovah hath appointed to you the sabbath, therefore he giveth you on the sixth day the bread of two days: abide ye every man in his place; let no man go out of his
30 place on the seventh day." So the people rested on the
31 seventh day. And the house of Israel called the name of this *food* Manna: and it was like coriander-seed, white, and
32 its taste like a cake *made* with honey. And Moses said, "This is what Jehovah hath commanded, 'Fill an omer of it, to be kept throughout your generations, that they may see the bread with which I fed you in the desert, when I brought
33 you forth from the land of Egypt.'" And Moses said to Aaron, "Take a pot, and put in it a full omer of manna, and lay it up before Jehovah, to be kept throughout your
34 generations." So Aaron laid it up before the testimonials,

to be kept as Jehovah commanded Moses. And the children ²⁵ of Israel ate manna forty years, until they came to an inhabited land: they ate manna until they came to the borders of the land of Canaan.—Now an omer is the tenth part of ³⁶ an ephah.

CHAP. XVII.—And all the congregation of the children ¹ of Israel journeyed from the desert of Sin, ordering their journies according to the commandment of Jehovah; and they pitched in Rephidim, where there was no water for the people to drink. Wherefore the people contended with Mo- ² ses, and said, "Give us water that we may drink." And Moses said to them, "Why do ye contend with me? Why do ye try Jehovah?" And the people thirsted there for ³ water; and the people murmured against Moses, and said, "Wherefore hast thou thus brought us up out of Egypt, to kill us and our children and our cattle with thirst?" And ⁴ Moses cried to Jehovah, saying, "What shall I do to this people? they are almost ready to stone me." And Jehovah ⁵ said to Moses, "Go on before the people, and take with thee some of the elders of Israel, and thy rod, with which thou smotest the river, take in thy hand, and go. Lo, I will ⁶ stand before thee there by the rock in Horeb; and thou shalt smite the rock, and water shall come out of it, that the people may drink." And Moses did so in the sight of the elders of Israel. And he called the name of the place Mas- ⁷ sah [TRIAL], and Meribah [CONTENTION], because of the contention of the children of Israel, and because they tried Jehovah, saying, "Is Jehovah among us, or not?"

Then came the Amalekites and fought with the Israelites ⁸ in Rephidim. And Moses said to Joshua, "Choose out men ⁹ for us, and go out to fight with the Amalekites: to-morrow I will stand on the top of the hill, with the rod of God in my hand." So Joshua did as Moses had said to him, and ¹⁰ fought with the Amalekites, and Moses, Aaron, and Hur went up to the top of the hill. And it came to pass that ¹¹ when Moses held up his hand, the Israelites prevailed; and when he let down his hand, the Amalekites prevailed. But ¹² the hands of Moses were heavy; and they took a stone, and put *it* under him, and he sat on it, and Aaron and Hur held up his hands, the one on the one side, and the other on the other side; and his hands were steady until the going down of the sun. And Joshua discomfited the people of ¹³

14 Amalek and smote them with the edge of the sword. Then Jehovah said to Moses, "Write this for a memorial in a book, and rehearse it in the ears of Joshua, that I will utterly blot out the remembrance of the Amalekites from under
15 the heavens." And Moses built an altar, and called the
16 name of it Jehovah-nissi [JEHOVAH MY SIGNAL]: for he said, "It shall be known as a signal of the war which Jehovah will have with the Amalekites from generation to generation."

1 CHAP. XVIII.—When Jethro the priest of Midian, the father-in-law of Moses, heard of all that God had done for Moses, and for his people, the Israelites, how Jehovah had
2 brought the Israelites out of Egypt, then Jethro, the father-in-law of Moses, took Zipporah, the wife of Moses, after he
3 had sent her back, and her two sons (of whom the name of the one was Gershom [A STRANGER THERE]; for *Moses* said,
4 "I have been a stranger in a foreign land;" and the name of the other was Eliezer [GOD WILL HELP]; "For the God of my father, *said he*, has been my helper, and delivered me
5 from the sword of Pharaoh"); and Jethro, the father-in-law of Moses, came with his sons and his wife to Moses into the desert, where he was encamped by the mountain of God.
6 And he said to Moses, "I, thy father-in-law Jethro, am come to thee, and thy wife, and her two sons with her."
7 And Moses went out to meet his father-in-law, and he bowed himself, and kissed him; and when they had asked each other
8 of their welfare they went into the tent. And Moses told his father-in-law all that Jehovah had done to Pharaoh and to the Egyptians for the sake of the Israelites, and all the travail that had come upon them by the way, and how Je-
9 hovah had delivered them. And Jethro rejoiced for all the good which Jehovah had done to the Israelites, whom he
10 had delivered out of the hand of the Egyptians. And Jethro said, "Blessed be Jehovah, who hath delivered you out of the hand of the Egyptians, and out of the hand of Pharaoh; who hath delivered the people from under the hand of the
11 Egyptians. Now I know that Jehovah is greater than all gods, for in the matter in which they had dealt proudly *he*
12 *was* above them." And Jethro, the father-in-law of Moses, brought a burnt-offering and sacrifices to God, and Aaron came, and all the elders of Israel, to eat bread with the father-in-law of Moses before God.

Now it came to pass on the next day that Moses sat to 13 judge the people, and the people stood by Moses from the morning until the evening. And when the father-in-law of 14 Moses saw all that he did to the people, he said, "What is this that thou doest to the people? why sittest thou alone, and all the people stand by thee from the morning until the evening?" And Moses said to his father-in-law, "Because 15 the people come to me to inquire of God. When they have 16 any cause they come to me, and I judge between one and another, and make known to them the statutes of God and his laws." And the father-in-law of Moses said to him, 17 "The thing that thou doest is not good. Thou wilt surely 18 wear out both thyself and this people that is with thee; for this thing is too heavy for thee; thou art not able to perform it alone. Hearken now to my voice, I will give thee counsel, 19 and God will be with thee. Be thou before God for the people, and bring thou the causes to God, and teach them 20 ordinances and laws, and show them the way wherein they must walk, and the work that they must do. But provide 21 thou out of all the people able men, such as fear God, men of truth, hating unjust gain; and place these over them, rulers of thousands, rulers of hundreds, rulers of fifties, and rulers of tens; and let them judge the people at all seasons: but every 22 great matter *that arises* let them bring to thee, and every small matter let them judge: so shall it be easier for thyself, and they shall bear *the burden* with thee. If thou wilt do this 23 thing, and God command thee *so,* then thou wilt be able to endure, and all this people will also go to their place in peace." So Moses hearkened to the voice of his father-in-law, and 24 did all that he had said. And Moses chose able men out of 25 all Israel, and made them chiefs over the people, rulers of thousands, rulers of hundreds, rulers of fifties, and rulers of tens. And they judged the people at all seasons: the 26 cause that was hard they brought to Moses, but every small matter they judged themselves. And Moses let his father- 27 in-law depart; and he went his way into his own land.

CHAP. XIX.—In the third month from the going out of 1 the children of Israel from the land of Egypt, on that day they came to the desert of Sinai. For when they departed 2 from Rephidim, they came to the desert of Sinai, and pitched in the desert; and there the Israelites encamped before the mountain.

3 And Moses went up to God, and Jehovah called to him out of the mountain, saying, "Thus shalt thou say to
4 the house of Jacob, and tell the children of Israel; 'Ye have seen what I did to the Egyptians, and how I bare you
5 on eagles' wings, and brought you unto myself. Now therefore, if ye will attentively hearken to my voice, and keep my covenant, then ye shall be a peculiar treasure to me
6 above all peoples; for all the earth is mine, but ye shall be to me a kingdom of priests, and a holy nation.' These are the words which thou shalt speak to the children of Israel."
7 Then Moses went, and called for the elders of the people, and laid before them all these words which Jehovah had
8 commanded him. And all the people answered with one accord and said, "All that Jehovah hath spoken we will do." And Moses reported the words of the people to Jehovah.
9 And Jehovah said to Moses, "Lo, I come unto thee in a thick cloud, that the people may hear when I speak with thee, and believe in thee for ever." And Moses told the
10 words of the people to Jehovah. And Jehovah said to Moses, "Go unto the people, and sanctify them to-day and
11 to-morrow, and let them wash their clothes, and be ready against the third day; for the third day Jehovah will come down upon mount Sinai in the sight of all the people.
12 And thou shalt set a boundary to the people round about, saying, 'Take heed to yourselves *that ye go not* up to the mountain, nor touch the border of it; whosoever toucheth
13 the mountain shall be surely put to death. There shall not a hand touch him, but he shall surely be stoned, or shot through; whether *it be* beast or man, it shall not live.' When the trumpet soundeth long, they may come up to the
14 mountain." And Moses went down from the mountain to the people, and sanctified the people; and they washed their
15 clothes. And he said to the people, "Be ready against the
16 third day: approach not your wives." And it came to pass on the third day, in the morning, that there were thunders and lightnings, and a thick cloud upon the mountain, and the sound of a trumpet exceedingly loud; so that all the
17 people who were in the camp trembled. And Moses brought forth the people out of the camp to meet God; and they
18 stood at the lower part of the mountain. And mount Sinai was altogether in a smoke, because Jehovah had descended upon it in fire; and the smoke thereof ascended as the smoke of a furnace, and the whole mountain trembled ex-

ceedingly. And when the voice of the trumpet sounded ¹⁹ long, and became louder and louder, Moses spake, and God answered him by a voice. For Jehovah had descended on ²⁰ mount Sinai, on the top of the mountain: and Jehovah called Moses up to the top of the mountain, and Moses went up. And Jehovah said to Moses, "Go down, charge ²¹ the people, not to break through unto Jehovah to gaze, lest many of them perish. And let the priests also, who come ²² near to Jehovah, sanctify themselves, lest Jehovah break forth upon them." And Moses said to Jehovah, "The ²³ people cannot come up to mount Sinai; for thou chargedst us, saying, 'Set a boundary about the mountain, and sanctify it.'" And Jehovah said to him, "Go thou down; and ²⁴ come up *again*, thou, and Aaron with thee; but let not the priests and the people break through to come up unto Jehovah, lest he break forth upon them." So Moses went down ²⁵ to the people and spake to them.

CHAP. XX.—And God spake all these words, saying, ¹ "I am Jehovah thy God, who brought thee out of the land ² of Egypt, out of the house of bondage. Thou shalt not have ³ other gods before me.

Thou shalt not make for thyself a graven image, nor any ⁴ likeness of what is in heaven above, or what is in the earth beneath, or what is in the water under the earth: thou ⁵ shalt not bow down thyself to them, nor shalt thou serve them; for I Jehovah thy God am a jealous God, visiting the iniquity of the fathers upon the children to the third and fourth *generation* of them that hate me, but shewing ⁶ mercy to the thousandth of them that love me, and keep my commandments.

Thou shalt not utter the name of Jehovah thy God to ⁷ a falsehood; for Jehovah will not hold him guiltless who uttereth his name to a falsehood.

Remember the sabbath-day to keep it holy. Six days ⁹ mayest thou labour, and do all thy work, but the seventh ¹⁰ day is the sabbath of Jehovah thy God: in it thou shalt not do any work, thou, nor thy son, nor thy daughter, nor thy man-servant, nor thy maid-servant, nor thy cattle, nor thy stranger that is within thy gates. For in six days Jeho- ¹¹ vah made the heavens and the earth, and the sea, and all that is in them, and rested on the seventh day; wherefore Jehovah blessed the sabbath-day, and hallowed it.

12 Honour thy father and thy mother, that thy days may be long in the land which Jehovah thy God giveth thee.
13 Thou shalt not commit murder.
14 Thou shalt not commit adultery.
15 Thou shalt not steal.
16 Thou shalt not bear false witness against thy neighbour.
17 Thou shalt not covet thy neighbour's house, thou shalt not covet thy neighbour's wife, nor his man-servant, nor his maid-servant, nor his ox, nor his ass, nor any thing which is thy neighbour's."
18 And all the people saw the thunderings and the lightnings, and the sound of the trumpet and the mountain smoking; and when the people saw *it* they removed and
19 stood afar off. And they said to Moses, "Speak thou with us, and we will hear: but let not God speak with us, lest we
20 die." And Moses said to the people, "Fear not; for God is come to prove you, and that his fear may be before you, that
21 ye sin not." And the people stood afar off; and Moses drew near unto the thick darkness where God was.
22 And Jehovah said to Moses, "Thus thou shalt say to the children of Israel, 'Ye have seen that I have talked with
23 you from heaven. Ye shall not make with me gods of silver; and gods of gold ye shall not make for yourselves.
24 An altar of earth thou shalt make to me, and shalt sacrifice on it thy burnt-offerings, and thy peace-offerings, thy sheep, and thine oxen: in every place in which I record my name,
25 I will come unto thee, and I will bless thee. But if thou wilt make to me an altar of stone, thou shalt not build it of hewn stone; for if thou lift up thy tool upon it, thou hast
26 polluted it. Neither shalt thou go up by steps unto mine altar, that thy nakedness be not discovered at it.'

1 CHAP. XXI.—Now these are the ordinances which thou shalt set before them.
2 When thou buyest a Hebrew servant, six years he shall serve, and in the seventh he shall go out free for nothing.
3 If he came in single, single shall he go out: if he were
4 married, then his wife shall go out with him. If his master have given him a wife, and she have borne to him sons or daughters, the wife and her children shall be his master's,
5 and he shall go out single. But if the servant shall plainly say, 'I love my master, my wife, and my children; I will
6 not go out free;' then his master shall bring him to the

judges; he shall also bring him to the door, or the doorpost, and his master shall bore his ear through with an awl, and he shall serve him for ever. But when a man hath 7 sold his daughter to be a maid-servant, she shall not go out as men-servants go out. If she please not her master, who 8 had destined her for himself, then shall he let her be redeemed; he shall not have power to sell her to a strange nation, because he hath deceived her. And if he have 9 destined her for his son, he shall act towards her, according to the rights of daughters. If *the son* take for himself 10 another *wife*, her food, her raiment, and her duty of marriage, he shall not diminish. And if he do not these three 11 things to her, then shall she go out free without money.

He who smiteth a man, so that he die, shall be surely put 12 to death. Yet if a man lie not in wait, but God let *the other* 13 fall into his hand, then I will appoint thee a place whither he may flee. But if a man come maliciously upon his 14 neighbour, and slay him with guile; thou shalt take him *even* from my altar, that he may be put to death. And 15 he who smiteth his father or his mother shall surely be put to death. And he who stealeth a man, and selleth him, 16 or if he be found in his hand, he shall surely be put to death. And he who curseth his father, or his mother, shall surely 17 be put to death. And when men strive together, and one 18 smite another with a stone, or with *his* fist, and he die not, but keep his bed; if he rise again, and walk abroad *leaning* 19 upon his staff, then shall he that smote him be acquitted: only he shall pay for the loss of his time, and shall cause him to be thoroughly healed. And when a man smiteth 20 his man-servant, or his maid-servant with a rod, so that either die under his hand, it shall surely be avenged: but if 21 *his servant* continue a day or two, he shall not be punished; for he is his money. And when men are fighting to- 22 gether and strike a woman with child, so that her fruit depart *from her*, but no mischief follow, he *who struck* shall be surely fined, according as the woman's husband shall lay upon him; and he shall pay before the judges. But if mis- 23 chief follow, then shalt thou give life for life, eye for eye, 24 tooth for tooth, hand for hand, foot for foot, burning for burn- 25 ing, wound for wound, stripe for stripe. And when a man 26 smiteth the eye of his servant or the eye of his maid, so that it perish, he shall let him go free for the sake of his eye. 27 And if he smite out his man-servant's tooth, or his maid-servant's tooth, he shall let him go free for the sake of his tooth.

28 And when an ox goreth a man or a woman, that they die, then the ox shall be surely stoned, and his flesh shall not be 29 eaten; but the owner of the ox shall be acquitted. But if the ox were wont to gore in time past, and it hath been made known to his owner, and he hath not kept him in, and he kill a man or a woman, the ox shall be stoned, and his 30 owner also shall be put to death. If there be laid on him a sum of money, then shall he give, for the ransom of his 31 life, whatsoever is laid upon him. Whether *his ox* have gored a son, or have gored a daughter, according to this or-32 dinance, it shall be done to him. If the ox gore a manservant, or a maid-servant; *the owner* shall give to their master 33 thirty shekels of silver, and the ox shall be stoned. And when a man openeth a pit, or when a man diggeth a pit, 34 but doth not cover it, and an ox or an ass fall into it, the owner of the pit shall make compensation by giving money to the owner of them, and the dead *beast* shall be his. 35 And when one man's ox hurteth the ox of another so that it die, then they shall sell the live ox, and divide the price of 36 it, and the dead *ox* also they shall divide. Or if it be known that the ox was wont to gore in time past, and his owner hath not kept him in, he shall surely repay ox for ox, and the dead *ox* shall be his own.

1 CHAP. XXII.—When a man stealeth an ox, or a sheep, and killeth it, or selleth it, he shall repay five oxen for an 2 ox, and four sheep for a sheep. If the thief be found breaking in, and be smitten so that he die, he *who smiteth* 3 *him* shall not be guilty of bloodshed. If the sun be risen upon him he shall be guilty of bloodshed; he shall make compensation. If *the thief* have nothing *to repay*, then he 4 shall be sold for his theft. If what he stole be actually found in his possession alive, whether it be ox, or ass, or sheep, he 5 shall repay double. When a man causeth a field or a vineyard to be eaten, by putting in his beast, and feeding in another man's field, of the best of his own field, and of the 6 best of his own vineyard, he shall make restitution. When a fire breaketh out, and catcheth in thorns, so that the stacks of corn, or the standing corn, or the field, are consumed, he that kindled the fire shall make full restitution.

7 When a man delivereth to his neighbour money or furni-

ture to keep, and it is stolen out of the man's house, if the thief be found he shall pay double. But if the thief be not 8 found, then the master of the house shall be brought to the judges, *that he may swear* that he hath not put his hand to his neighbour's goods. For all manner of wrong doing 9 concerning either ox, or ass, or sheep, or raiment, or any manner of lost thing, which *another* challengeth to be his, the cause of both parties shall come before the judges; *and* he whom the judges shall condemn, shall pay double to his neighbour. When a man delivereth to his neighbour an ass, 10 or an ox, or a sheep, or any beast, to keep, and it die, or be hurt, or driven away, no man seeing it, *then* shall an oath of 11 Jehovah be between them both, that he hath not put his hand to his neighbour's goods; and the owner of it shall accept *the oath*, and he shall not make restitution. But if it have 12 been certainly stolen from him, he shall make restitution to the owner of it. If it have been torn in pieces, let 13 him bring it *as* a proof of the tearing, *and* he shall not make restitution. And when a man borroweth *a beast* 14 of his neighbour, and it be hurt or die, the owner thereof not being with it, he shall make full restitution. But if the 15 owner thereof be with it, he shall not make restitution. If it were hired, it came for its hire.

And when a man seduceth a virgin who is not betrothed, 16 and lieth with her, he shall surely pay her dowry, *and take her* to be his wife. But if her father utterly refuse to give 17 her to him, he shall pay money according to the dowry of virgins.

Thou shalt not suffer a sorceress to live. Whosoever 19 lieth with a beast shall surely be put to death. He that 20 sacrificeth to any god, save to Jehovah only, shall be devoted to death.

Thou shalt not injure a stranger, nor oppress him: for 21 ye were strangers in the land of Egypt. Ye shall not 22 afflict any widow or fatherless child. If thou afflict them in 23 any manner, and they cry aloud to me, I will surely hear their cry; and my wrath shall be kindled, and I will kill 24 you with the sword; so that your wives may be widows, and your children fatherless. If thou lend money to a poor 25 neighbour, one of my people, thou shalt not be to him as a usurer, neither shalt thou lay upon him usury. If thou at 26 all take in pledge thy neighbour's raiment, at the going down of the sun thou shalt deliver it to him; for that is his 27 only covering; it is his raiment for his skin; in it he must sleep: and when he crieth to me, I will hear; for I am gracious.

28 Thou shalt not revile the judges, nor curse the ruler of thy people.

29 The first of thy ripe fruits, and of thy liquors, thou shalt not delay to offer. The first-born of thy sons shalt thou

30 give to me. Thus thou shalt do with thy oxen, and with thy sheep: seven days it shall be with its dam; on the eighth day thou shalt give it to me.

31 And ye shall be holy men to me; and flesh which hath been torn in the field ye shall not eat: ye shall cast it to the dogs.

1 CHAP. XXIII.—Thou shalt not raise a false report: thou shalt not join thy hands with a wicked man to be an

2 injurious witness. Thou shalt not follow the great to do evil; nor shalt thou incline towards the great, so as to per-

3 vert *judgment*; nor shalt thou be partial to a poor man in his cause.

4 When thou meetest the ox or the ass of thine enemy

5 going astray, thou shalt surely bring it back to him. When thou seest the ass of him who hateth thee lying under his burden, and wouldst forbear to help him, thou shalt surely help him.

6 Thou shalt not pervert the judgment of thy poor in his

7 cause. Keep far from a false matter; and the innocent and righteous slay thou not; for I will not acquit the wicked.

8 And thou shalt not take a bribe; for a bribe blindeth the eyes of the clear-sighted, and perverteth the words of the

9 just. A stranger also thou shalt not oppress: for ye know the heart of a stranger, since ye were strangers in the land of Egypt.

10 And six years thou shalt sow thy land, and shalt gather

11 in its produce, but the seventh *year* thou shalt let it rest and be free, that the poor of thy people may eat; and what they leave, let the beasts of the field eat. So shalt thou do

12 with thy vineyard, and with thy olive-yard. Six days mayest thou do thy work, but on the seventh day thou shalt rest; in order that thine ox and thine ass may rest, and the son of thy handmaid and the stranger may be refreshed.

13 And all that I have said to you, ye shall observe; but of

the name of other gods thou shalt make no mention: let it not be heard from thy mouth.

Three times in the year thou shalt keep a feast to me. 14 Thou shalt keep the feast of unleavened bread. Thou shalt 15 eat unleavened bread seven days, as I commanded thee, at the time appointed in the month Abib; for in it thou camest out from Egypt, and none shall appear before me empty-handed; and the feast of harvest, of the first-fruits 16 of thy labours, which thou hast sown in the field; and the feast of in-gathering, at the end of the year, when thou hast gathered in thy labours out of the field. Three times in the 17 year all thy males shall appear before the Lord Jehovah. Thou shalt not offer the blood of my sacrifice with leavened 18 bread; nor shall the fat of my sacrifice remain until the morning. The first of the first-fruits of thy land thou 19 shalt bring into the house of Jehovah thy God. Thou shalt not seethe a kid in its mother's milk.

Lo, I send an Angel before thee, to keep thee in the way, 20 and to bring thee into the place which I have prepared. Give heed to him, and obey his voice, provoke him not; 21 for he will not pardon your transgressions, since my name is in him. But if thou wilt attentively hearken to his voice, 22 and do all that I speak, then I will be an enemy to thine enemies, and an adversary to thine adversaries. For my 23 Angel shall go before thee, and bring thee in unto the Amorites, and the Hittites, and the Perizzites, and the Canaanites, the Hivites, and the Jebusites; and I will cut them off. Thou shalt not bow down to their gods, nor 24 serve them, nor do after their works; but thou shalt utterly overthrow them, and break in pieces their images. And ye 25 shall serve Jehovah your God, and he will bless thy bread and thy water, and I will take sickness away from the midst of thee. And there shall be none that casteth her young 26 nor any barren one in thy land; the number of thy days I will fill up. I will send my terror before thee, and will 27 trouble all the people to whom thou shalt come; and I will make all thine enemies turn the back of their necks to thee. And I will send hornets before thee, which shall drive out 28 the Hivite, the Canaanite, and the Hittite, from before thee. I will not drive them out from before thee in one year, lest 29 the land become desolate, and the beasts of the field multiply against thee: by little and little I will drive them out 30 from before thee, until thou be increased, and inherit the

31 land. And I will set thy boundaries from the Red Sea even unto the sea of the Philistines, and from the desert unto the river; for I will deliver the inhabitants of the land into your hand, and thou shalt drive them out from before thee.
32 Thou shalt make no covenant with them, nor with their
33 gods. They shall not dwell in thy land, lest they make thee sin against me; for if thou serve their gods it will surely be a snare to thee."

1 CHAP. XXIV.—And he said to Moses, "Come up unto Jehovah, thou, and Aaron, Nadab, and Abihu, and seventy
2 of the elders of Israel, and worship ye afar off. And Moses alone shall come near Jehovah; but they shall not come near, nor shall the people come up with him."
3 And Moses came, and told the people all the words and all the ordinances of Jehovah; and all the people answered with one voice, and said, "All the words which Jehovah hath
4 spoken we will do." And Moses wrote all the words of Jehovah, and rose up early in the morning, and built an altar at the foot of the mountain, and set up twelve upright
5 stones, according to the twelve tribes of Israel. And he sent young men of the children of Israel, who offered burnt-offerings, and sacrificed peace-offerings of oxen to Jehovah.
6 And Moses took half of the blood, and put it in basons, and
7 half of the blood he sprinkled on the altar. Then he took the book of the covenant, and read in the hearing of the people, and they said, "All that Jehovah hath spoken we
8 will do, and be obedient." And Moses took the blood, and sprinkled it on the people, and said, "Lo, the blood of the covenant, which Jehovah hath made with you concerning all these words."
9 Then went up Moses and Aaron, Nadab, and Abihu, and
10 seventy of the elders of Israel, and they saw the God of Israel; and under his feet as it were a pavement of sapphire,
11 and in brightness like the heavens themselves. And upon the nobles of the children of Israel he laid not his hand: also
12 they saw God, and did eat and drink. And Jehovah said to Moses, "Come up to me to the mountain, and be there, and I will give thee the tables of stone, the law, and the commandments which I have written, that thou mayest teach
13 them." And Moses rose up, and his attendant Joshua;
14 and Moses went up to the mountain of God. And he said to the elders, "Tarry ye here for us, until we come again

unto you; and, lo, Aaron and Hur are with you; whosoever hath any matter of dispute, let him apply to them." And Moses went up to the mountain, and a cloud covered the mountain. And the glory of Jehovah abode upon mount Sinai, and the cloud covered it six days; and the seventh day he called to Moses out of the midst of the cloud. And the sight of the glory of Jehovah was like devouring fire on the top of the mountain, in the sight of the children of Israel. And Moses went into the midst of the cloud, and ascended into the mountain; and Moses was on the mountain forty days and forty nights.

CHAP. XXV.—And Jehovah spake to Moses, saying, "Speak to the children of Israel, that they bring me an offering: from every one whose heart maketh him willing ye shall take my offering. And this is the offering which ye shall take of them; gold, and silver, and brass, and blue, and purple, and scarlet, and linen, and goats' *hair*, and rams' skins dyed red, and seals' skins, and setim-wood; oil for the light, spices for the anointing oil, and for the sweet-smelling incense, onyx-stones, and stones to be set in the ephod, and in the breast-plate. And let them make for me a sanctuary, that I may dwell amongst them. According to all that I shew thee, *according to* the pattern of the tabernacle, and the pattern of all its utensils, even so shall ye make it.

And they shall make an ark of setim-wood: two cubits and a half *shall be* its length, and a cubit and a half its breadth, and a cubit and a half its height. And thou shalt overlay it with pure gold; within and without thou shalt overlay it, and shalt make upon it a moulding of gold round about. And thou shalt cast four rings of gold for it, and put them in the four corners of it; two rings on the one side of it, and two rings on the other side. And thou shalt make poles of setim-wood, and overlay them with gold. And thou shalt put the poles into the rings, by the sides of the ark, that the ark may be carried by them. The poles shall be in the rings of the ark; they shall not be taken from it. And thou shalt put into the ark the testimonials, which I shall give thee. And thou shalt make a lid of pure gold: two cubits and a half *shall be* its length, and a cubit and a half its breadth. And thou shalt make two cherubim of gold, of solid work shalt thou make them, at the two ends of the lid. And make one cherub on the one end, and the other cherub on the other end of the mercy-seat; thou shalt make the cherubim at the two ends of it.

20 And the cherubim shall spread out their wings above, covering the lid with their wings, with their faces one toward another; toward the lid shall the faces of the cherubim be.

21 And thou shalt put the lid above upon the ark, and in the ark thou shalt put the testimonials that I shall give thee.

22 And there I will meet with thee, and I will commune with thee from above the lid, from between the two cherubim which are upon the ark of the testimonials, concerning all the things which I shall give thee in charge to the children of Israel.

23 Thou shalt also make a table of setim-wood: two cubits *shall be* its length, and a cubit its breadth, and a cubit and 24 a half its height. And thou shalt overlay it with pure gold, 25 and make for it a moulding of gold round about. And thou shalt make for it a border of a hand-breadth round about, and thou shalt make a moulding of gold to its border 26 round about. And thou shalt make for it four rings of gold, and put the rings in the four corners by its four feet. 27 Near the border shall the rings be, for places for the poles, 28 that the table may be carried. And thou shalt make the poles of setim-wood, and overlay them with gold, that the 29 table may be carried by them. And thou shalt make its dishes, and its incense-pots, and its cups, and its flagons, with which to pour *the drink offerings;* of pure gold shalt 30 thou make them. And thou shalt set upon the table shewbread before me continually.

31 And thou shalt make a lamp-stand of pure gold; of solid work shall the lamp-stand be made: its shaft, and its branches, its cups, its knops, and its flowers shall be of the 32 same. And six branches shall come out of the sides of it; three branches of the lamp-stand out of the one side, and three branches of the lamp-stand out of the other side: 33 three cups made like almonds, with a knop and a flower, in one branch; and three cups made like almonds with a knop and a flower in the other branch; so in the six branches 34 that come out of the lamp-stand. And in the lamp-stand *shall be* four cups made like almonds, *with* their knops and 35 their flowers; so *that there may be* a knop under two branches of the same, and a knop under two branches of the same, according to the six branches that come out of the 36 lamp-stand. Their knops and their branches shall be of the

K

same, all of it one solid work of pure gold. And thou 37 shalt make its seven lamps, and place its lamps, so that they may give light forwards. And its snuffers and its snuff- 38 dishes *shall be of* pure gold; of a talent of pure gold shalt 39 thou make it, with all these utensils. And see that thou make 40 them after their pattern, which was shown to thee on the mountain.

CHAP. XXVI.—Thou shalt also make the tabernacle of 1 ten curtains of twisted linen, blue, and purple, and scarlet; with cherubim curiously inwoven shalt thou make them. The length of each curtain shall be twenty-eight cubits, and 2 the breadth of each curtain four cubits; all the curtains shall have the same measure. Five curtains shall be joined one to another, and five *other* curtains shall be joined 3 one to another. And thou shalt make loops of blue on the 4 edge of the outmost curtain of one of the joined pieces; and thou shalt do the same on the edge of the outmost curtain in the second joined piece. Fifty loops shalt thou make on 5 one curtain, and fifty loops shalt thou make on the edge of the outmost curtain of the second joined piece, the loops answering one to another. And thou shalt make fifty hooks 6 of gold, and join the curtains together by the hooks, so that it may be one tabernacle.

And thou shalt make curtains of goats' *hair*, to be a tent 7 over the tabernacle: eleven curtains shalt thou make. The 8 length of each curtain *shall be* thirty cubits, and the breadth of each curtain four cubits; and the eleven curtains shall have the same measure. And thou shall join together five 9 curtains by themselves, and six curtains by themselves, and shalt double down the sixth curtain at the front of the tent. And thou shalt make fifty loops on the edge of the outmost 10 curtain of the joined piece, and fifty loops on the edge of the *outmost* curtain of the second joined piece. And thou 11 shalt make fifty hooks of brass, and put the hooks into the loops, and join the tent together, that it may be one. And 12 the excess of the tent curtains, the half of the exceeding curtain, shall hang over the back part of the tabernacle. And a cubit on the one side, and a cubit on the other side, 13 of the excess in the length of the curtains of the tent, shall hang over the sides of the tabernacle on this side and on that side, to cover it. And thou shalt make a covering for the tent 14 of rams' skins dyed red, and a covering above of seals' skins.

15 And thou shalt make for the tabernacle boards of setim-
16 wood, standing upright. Ten cubits *shall be* the length of
each board, and a cubit and a half *shall be* the breadth of
17 each board. Each board shall have two tenons, answering
one to the other: thus shalt thou make all the boards of the
18 tabernacle. And thou shalt make the boards for the
tabernacle, twenty boards on the south side, southward.
19 And thou shalt make forty sockets of silver under the twenty
boards; two sockets under one board for its two tenons, and
20 two sockets under another board for its two tenons. And
for the other side of the tabernacle, northward, *thou shalt*
21 *make* twenty boards, and their forty sockets of silver; two
sockets under one board, and two sockets under another
22 board. And for the side of the tabernacle westward thou
23 shalt make six boards. And two boards thou shalt make for
24 the corners of the tabernacle in the two sides. And they
shall be coupled together at the bottom, and they shall be
coupled together at the top of it by one ring: thus shall it
be done with them both; they shall be for the two corners.
25 Thus there shall be eight boards, and their sockets of silver,
sixteen sockets; two sockets under one board, and two
26 sockets under another board. And thou shalt make bars of
setim-wood; five for the boards of the one side of the
27 tabernacle, and five bars for the boards of the other side of
the tabernacle, and five bars for the boards of the side of the
28 tabernacle, westward. And the middle bar at the middle of
29 the boards shall reach from end to end. And thou shalt
overlay the boards with gold, and make their rings of gold
to be places for the bars; and thou shalt overlay the bars
30 with gold. And thou shalt set up the tabernacle according
to the plan of it shown to thee on the mountain.
31 And thou shalt make a veil of blue, and purple, and
scarlet, and twisted linen; with cherubim of curious work
32 it shall be made. And thou shall hang it upon four pillars
of setim-wood overlaid with gold, having their hooks of gold,
33 upon the four bases of silver. And thou shalt hang up the
veil under the hooks *of the curtains*, that thou mayest bring
in thither, within the veil, the ark of the testimonials; and
the veil shall divide for you between the holy and the
34 most holy *place*. And thou shalt put the lid upon the ark
35 of the testimonials in the most holy *place*. And thou shalt
set the table without the veil, and the lamp-stand over against
the table on the side of the tabernacle towards the south;

and thou shalt put the table on the side towards the north. And thou shalt make a hanging for the entrance of the tabernacle, of blue, and purple, and scarlet, and twisted linen of needle-work; and thou shalt make for the hanging five pillars of setim-wood, and overlay them with gold, *and* their hooks *shall be of* gold: and thou shalt cast five sockets of brass for them.

CHAP. XXVII.—And thou shalt make an altar of setim-wood, five cubits long, and five cubits broad; the altar shall be square, and its height shall be three cubits. And thou shalt make the horns of it at its four corners: its horns shall be of the same piece; and thou shalt overlay it with brass. And thou shalt make its pans to move its ashes, and its shovels, and its basons, and its flesh hooks, and its fire pans, all its utensils thou shalt make of brass. And thou shalt make for it a grate of brazen lattice-work; and at the four corners of the lattice-work thou shalt make four brazen rings. And thou shalt put it below the band of the altar, that the lattice-work may be at the middle of the altar. And thou shalt make the poles for the altar, poles of setim-wood, and overlay them with brass. And the poles shall be put into the rings, and the poles shall be upon the two sides of the altar when it is carried. Hollow with boards shalt thou make it: as it was shown to thee on the mountain, so shall it be made.

And thou shalt make the court of the tabernacle: for the south side, southward, *there shall be* hangings for the court of twisted linen, a hundred cubits long for one side. And its twenty pillars, and their twenty sockets, *shall be* of brass: the hooks of the pillars and their rods *shall be of* silver. And likewise for the north side in length *there shall be* hangings of a hundred *cubits* long, and its twenty pillars, and their twenty sockets of brass; the hooks of the pillars and their rods of silver. And *for* the breadth of the court on the west side *shall be* hangings of fifty cubits; their pillars ten, and their sockets ten. And the breadth of the court on the east side eastward *shall be* fifty cubits. The hangings on one side *shall be* fifteen cubits; their pillars three, and their sockets three. And on the other side *shall be* hangings, fifteen cubits; their pillars three, and their sockets three. And for the gate of the court *shall be* a hanging of twenty cubits, of blue, and purple, and scarlet,

and twisted linen, wrought with needle-work; and their
17 pillars *shall be* four, and their sockets four. All the pillars
round about the court *shall be* joined by rods of silver;
their hooks *shall be* of silver, and their sockets of brass.
18 The length of the court *shall be* a hundred cubits, and the
breadth fifty cubits, and the height five cubits, of fine
19 twisted linen, and their sockets of brass. *And thou shalt
make* all the vessels of the tabernacle for the whole of its
service, and all its pins, and all the pins of the court, of
brass.
20 And thou shalt command the children of Israel, that they
bring to thee pure olive-oil beaten for the light, to set up the
21 lamp continually. In the tent of meeting, without the veil,
which is before the testimonial-*ark*, Aaron and his sons shall
set it in order from evening to morning before Jehovah. By
a perpetual statute throughout their generations it *shall be
required* from the children of Israel.

1 CHAP. XXVIII. — And take thou to thee Aaron thy
brother, and his sons with him, from among the children
of Israel, that he may minister to me in the priest's office;
Aaron; Nadab, and Abihu, Eleazar, and Ithamar, Aaron's
2 sons. And thou shalt make holy garments for Aaron thy
3 brother, for honour and for beauty. And thou shalt speak
to all wise-hearted men, whom I have filled with the spirit
of wisdom, that they may make Aaron's garments to sanctify
4 him, that he may minister to me in the priest's office. And
these are the garments which they shall make; a breastplate,
and an ephod, and a robe, and an embroidered inner garment, a mitre, and a girdle; and they shall make holy garments for Aaron thy brother, and his sons, that he may
5 minister to me in the priest's office. And they shall take
6 gold, and blue, and purple, and scarlet, and linen. And
they shall make the ephod of gold, of blue, and of purple,
7 and of scarlet, and twisted linen, curiously woven. Its two
shoulder-pieces shall be joined to it; at its two edges shall
8 the joining be. And the curiously wrought girdle of the
ephod, which is upon it, shall be of like work; *it shall proceed* from it, of gold, of blue, and purple, and scarlet, and
9 twisted linen. And thou shalt take two onyx-stones, and
10 engrave on them the names of the sons of Israel, six of
their names on one stone, and the six remaining names on
11 the other stone, according to their birth. With the work

of an engraver in stone, *like* the engravings of a signet, shalt thou engrave the two stones with the names of the children of Israel: thou shalt make for them sockets of gold. And 12 thou shalt put the two stones upon the shoulders of the ephod, as stones of memorial for the children of Israel; and Aaron shall bear their names before Jehovah upon his two shoulders for a memorial. And thou shalt make sockets of 13 gold, and two chains of pure gold of equal length; of 14 wreathed work shalt thou make them, and fasten the wreathed chains to the sockets.

And thou shalt make the breastplate of judgment of 15 curiously woven work; like the work of the ephod thou shalt make it; of gold, of blue, and of purple, and of scarlet, and of twisted linen shalt thou make it. It shall be square, 16 doubled; a span in length, and a span in breadth. And 17 thou shalt set in it settings of stones, four rows of stones: a row of a carnelian, a topaz, and a carbuncle *shall be* the first row. And the second row *shall be* an emerald, a sap- 18 phire, and a diamond. And the third row a ligure, an 19 agate, and an amethyst. And the fourth row a beryl, and an 20 onyx, and a jasper: they shall be inclosed in sockets of gold. And the stones shall be according to the names of the sons 21 of Israel, twelve, according to their names, *like* the engravings of a signet; each shall have its own name according to the twelve tribes. And thou shalt make upon the breast- 22 plate chains of wreathed work of pure gold. And thou 23 shalt make upon the breastplate two rings of gold, and shalt put the two rings on the two ends of the breastplate; and 24 thou shalt put the two wreathed chains of gold in the two rings on the ends of the breastplate. And the *other* two 25 ends of the two wreathed chains thou shalt fasten in the two sockets, and put *them* on the shoulder-pieces of the ephod in the front of it. And thou shalt make two rings of gold, 26 and thou shalt put them on the two ends of the breastplate, on the border of it, which is upon the side of the ephod inward. And two rings of gold thou shalt make, and 27 shalt put them on the two shoulder-pieces of the ephod underneath, toward the front of it over against the *other* coupling thereof, above the curiously wrought girdle of the ephod. And they shall bind the breastplate by its rings to 28 the rings of the ephod with a ribband of blue, that it may be above the curiously wrought girdle of the ephod, and that the breastplate be not loosed from the ephod. And Aaron 29 shall bear the names of the sons of Israel in the breastplate of judgment upon his heart, when he goeth into the holy 30 *place*, for a memorial before Jehovah continually. And thou shalt put on the breastplate of judgment the Urim and the Thummim; and they shall be upon Aaron's heart, when he goeth in before Jehovah; and Aaron shall bear the judgment of the children of Israel upon his heart before Jehovah continually.

31 And thou shalt make the robe of the ephod all of blue; 32 and there shall be a hole in the top of it, in the middle of it; it shall have a binding of woven work round about the hole of it, like the hole of a coat of mail, that it may not 33 be rent. And *below*, upon the hem of it, thou shalt make pomegranates of blue, and of purple, and of scarlet, round about the hem of it, and bells of gold between them round 34 about: a golden bell and a pomegranate, a golden bell and a pomegranate, upon the hem of the robe round about. 35 And it shall be upon Aaron when he ministereth; and his sound shall be heard when he goeth into the holy *place* before Jehovah, and when he cometh out, that he die not.

36 And thou shalt make a petal of pure gold, and grave upon 37 it, *like* the engravings of a signet, HOLY TO JEHOVAH. And thou shalt put it on a blue ribband, that it may be upon the 38 mitre: upon the front of the mitre it shall be. And it shall be upon Aaron's forehead, that Aaron may bear the iniquity of the holy things which the children of Israel shall sanctify in all their holy gifts; and it shall be always upon his forehead, to make them acceptable before Jehovah.

39 And thou shalt embroider the inner garment of linen, and thou shalt make the mitre of linen, but the girdle thou shalt 40 make of needle-work. And for the sons of Aaron thou shalt make inner garments, and thou shalt make for them girdles, and turbans shalt thou make for them, for honour and for 41 beauty. And thou shalt put them upon Aaron thy brother, and his sons with him; and shalt anoint them, and consecrate them, and sanctify them, that they may minister to me 42 in the priest's office. And thou shalt make them linen drawers to cover their nakedness; from the loins to the 43 thighs they shall reach. And they shall be upon Aaron, and upon his sons, when they come into the tent of meeting, or when they come near to the altar to minister in the holy place; that they bear not iniquity, and die. *This shall be* a perpetual statute to him, and to his seed after him.

CHAP. XXIX.—And this is what thou shalt do to them, to sanctify them, to minister to me in the priest's office: Take one young bullock, and two rams without blemish, and unleavened bread, and unleavened cakes tempered with oil, and unleavened wafers anointed with oil; of wheaten flour shalt thou make them. And thou shalt put them into one basket, and bring them in the basket, with the bullock and the two rams. And Aaron and his sons thou shalt bring to the door of the tent of meeting, and shalt wash them with water. And thou shalt take the garments, and clothe Aaron with the inner garment, and the robe of the ephod, and the ephod, and the breastplate, and gird on him the ephod, with the curiously wrought girdle of the ephod; and thou shalt put the mitre on his head, and put the holy crown on the mitre. Then shalt thou take the anointing oil, and pour it upon his head, and anoint him. And thou shalt cause his sons to approach, and put inner garments on them; and thou shalt gird them with girdles, Aaron and his sons, and bind the turbans on them, and the priest's office shall be theirs by a perpetual statute. And thou shalt consecrate Aaron and his sons. And thou shalt bring the bullock before the tent of meeting; and Aaron and his sons shall lay their hands upon the head of the bullock. And thou shalt slay the bullock before Jehovah at the door of the tent of meeting. And thou shalt take some of the blood of the bullock, and put it upon the horns of the altar with thy finger, and pour all *the rest of* the blood at the bottom of the altar. And thou shalt take all the fat that covereth the entrails, and the caul above the liver, and the two kidnies, and the fat that is upon them, and burn them upon the altar. But the flesh of the bullock, and his skin, and his dung thou shalt burn with fire without the camp: it is a sin-offering. Thou shalt also take the one ram; and Aaron and his sons shall lay their hands upon the head of the ram. And thou shalt slay the ram, and thou shalt take his blood, and sprinkle it round about upon the altar. And thou shalt cut the ram in pieces, and wash his entrails, and his legs, and put them upon his pieces, and upon his head. And thou shalt burn the whole ram upon the altar: it is a burnt-offering to Jehovah; an acceptable odour, an offering made by fire to Jehovah. And thou shalt take the other ram; and Aaron and his sons shall lay their hands upon the head of the ram. Then shalt thou slay the ram, and take some of his blood, and put it upon the tip of the right ear of Aaron, and upon the tip of the right ear of his sons, and upon the thumb of their right hand, and upon the great toe of their right foot, and sprinkle the *rest of the* blood round 21 about upon the altar. And thou shalt take some of the blood that is upon the altar, and some of the anointing oil, and sprinkle it upon Aaron, and upon his garments, and upon his sons, and upon the garments of his sons with him; and he shall be sanctified, and his garments, and his sons, and the garments of his sons with him. Thou 22 shalt also take from the ram the fat and the fat tail, and the fat that covereth the entrails, and the caul above the liver, and the two kidnies, and the fat that is upon them, and the right shoulder, (for it is a ram of consecra- 23 tion,) and one loaf of bread, and one cake of oiled bread, and one wafer out of the basket of the unleavened bread that is 24 before Jehovah; and thou shalt put all in the hands of Aaron, and in the hands of his sons, and shalt wave them 25 *for* a wave-offering before Jehovah. Then thou shalt take them from their hands, and burn them upon the altar with the burnt-offering, for an acceptable odour before Jehovah; 26 it is an offering made by fire to Jehovah. And thou shalt take the breast of the ram of Aaron's consecration, and wave it *for* a wave-offering before Jehovah; and it shall be thy 27 portion. Thus thou shalt sanctify the breast of the wave-offering, which hath been waved and the shoulder of the heave-offering, which hath been heaved, of the ram of the 28 consecration of Aaron, and of his sons; and it shall be for Aaron and his sons by a perpetual statute, from the children of Israel; for it is a heave-offering; and it shall be a heave-offering from the children of Israel of the sacrifice of their 29 peace-offerings, *even* their heave-offering to Jehovah. And the holy garments of Aaron shall be for his sons after him, that they may be anointed in them, and consecrated in 30 them. During seven days shall that son who is priest in his stead, who goes into the tent of meeting, to minister in 31 the sanctuary, put them on. And thou shalt take the ram of the consecration, and seethe his flesh in the holy place. 32 And Aaron and his sons shall eat the flesh of the ram, and the bread that is in the basket, at the door of the tent of 33 meeting, and they shall eat them, because by these an atonement was made to consecrate *and* to sanctify them; but a 34 stranger shall not eat of them, because they are holy. And if aught of the flesh of the *ram* of consecration, or of the bread, remain until the morning, then thou shalt burn the remainder with fire: it shall not be eaten, because it is holy. And thus shalt thou do to Aaron, and to his sons, according 35 to all that I have commanded thee: during seven days thou shalt consecrate them.

Thou shalt also offer every day a bullock *for* a sin-offering 36 for atonement; and thou shalt cleanse the altar, by making an atonement for it; and thou shalt anoint it, to sanctify it. During seven days thou shalt make an atonement for the 37 altar, and sanctify it; then the altar shall be most holy: whatsoever toucheth the altar must be holy. Now this *is* 38 what thou shalt offer upon the altar; two lambs of the first year every day continually. The one lamb thou shalt offer 39 in the morning, and the other lamb thou shalt offer in the evening; and with the one lamb a tenth part *of a measure* 40 of flour mingled with the fourth part of a hin of beaten oil; and the fourth part of a hin of wine for a drink-offering. And the other lamb thou shalt offer in the evening, and 41 with it thou shalt offer the same meal-offering as in the morning, and the same drink-offering, for an acceptable odour, an offering made by fire to Jehovah, a perpetual 42 burnt-offering throughout your generations, at the door of the tent of meeting, before Jehovah; where I will meet you, to speak to thee there. And there I will meet with the chil- 43 dren of Israel, and it shall be sanctified by my glory. And I 44 will sanctify the tent of meeting, and the altar: I will sanctify also both Aaron and his sons, to minister to me in the priest's office. And I will dwell amongst the children of Israel, and 45 will be their God. And they shall know that I Jehovah am 46 their God, who brought them out from the land of Egypt, that I may dwell amongst them: I Jehovah am their God.

CHAP. XXX.—And thou shalt make an altar to burn 1 incense upon; of setim-wood thou shalt make it. Its length 2 *shall be* a cubit, and its breadth a cubit; square shall it be; and its height *shall be* two cubits: its horns *shall be* of one piece with it. And thou shalt overlay it with pure gold, its 3 top, and its sides round about, and its horns; and thou shalt make for it a moulding of gold round about. And two rings 4 of gold shalt thou make for it under the moulding, by its two corners; on both its sides shalt thou make *them*; and they shall be for places for the poles by which it may be

EXODUS XXX.

5 carried. And thou shalt make the poles of setim-wood, and
6 overlay them with gold. And thou shalt put it before the veil that is by the ark of the testimonials, before the lid that
7 is over the testimonials, where I will meet with thee. And Aaron shall burn upon it sweet incense every morning: when he dresseth the lamps, he shall burn incense upon
8 it. And when Aaron lighteth the lamps in the evening, he shall burn incense upon it; a perpetual incense before
9 Jehovah throughout your generations. Ye shall offer on it no strange incense, or burnt-sacrifice, or meat-offering; nor
10 shall ye pour upon it a drink-offering. And Aaron shall make an atonement upon the horns of it once in a year with the blood of the sin-offering of atonements: once in a year shall he make atonement upon it, throughout your generations: it is most holy to Jehovah."

11 And Jehovah spake to Moses, saying, "When thou takest the sum of the children of Israel, after their number, then shall they give every man a ransom for his soul to Jehovah, when thou numberest them, that there be no plague amongst
13 them when they are numbered. This they shall give, every one that passeth among them that are numbered, half a shekel according to the shekel of the sanctuary: (the shekel is twenty gerahs:) a half shekel *shall be* the offering of
14 Jehovah. Every one that passeth among them that are numbered, from twenty years old and upward, shall give an
15 offering to Jehovah. The rich shall not give more, and the poor shall not give less, than half a shekel, when *ye* give an
16 offering to Jehovah, for the ransom of your souls. And thou shalt take the ransom-money of the children of Israel, and shalt appoint it for the service of the tent of meeting, that it may be a memorial unto the children of Israel before Jehovah, for the ransom of your souls."

17 And Jehovah spake to Moses, saying, "Thou shalt also make a laver of brass, and its foot of brass, to wash in; and thou shalt put it between the tent of meeting and the altar,
19 and thou shalt put water in it, that Aaron and his sons may
20 there wash their hands and their feet. When they go into the tent of meeting, or when they come near to the altar to minister, to burn *any* offering made by fire to Jehovah, they
21 shall wash with water and shall not die; they shall wash their hands and their feet, and shall not die; and this shall be a perpetual statute to them, to him and to his seed, throughout their generations."

And Jehovah spake to Moses, saying, "Take thou also 22 to thee most excellent spices; of purest myrrh five hundred *shekels*, and of sweet cinnamon half so much, *namely*, two hundred and fifty *shekels*, and of sweet cane two hundred and fifty *shekels*, and of cassia five hundred *shekels*, according 24 to the shekel of the sanctuary, and of olive-oil a hin; and 25 thou shalt make it a holy anointing-oil, compounded according to the art of the compounder: it shall be a holy anointing-oil. And with it thou shalt anoint the tent of meeting, 26 and the ark of the testimonials, and the table and all its 27 utensils, and the lamp-stand and its utensils, and the altar of incense, and the altar of burnt-offering with all its uten- 28 sils, and the laver and its foot. And thou shalt sanctify 29 them, that they may be most holy: whatsoever toucheth them shall be holy. Thou shalt anoint Aaron also and his 30 sons, and sanctify them, that they may minister to me in the priest's office. And thou shalt speak to the children 31 of Israel, saying, 'This shall be a holy anointing-oil to me throughout your generations. Upon the flesh of men it 32 shall not be poured; nor shall ye make *any other* like it, according to the composition of it: it is holy, *and* it shall be holy to you. Whosoever compoundeth *any* like it, or who- 33 soever putteth any of it upon a stranger, shall be cut off from his people.'"

Again Jehovah said to Moses, "Take to thee sweet-smell- 34 ing spices, stacte, and onycha, and galbanum, with pure frankincense; of each an equal quantity. And thou shalt 35 make it a perfume, compounded according to the art of the compounder, tempered together, pure *and* holy; and thou 36 shalt beat some of it very small, and put some of it before the testimonials in the tent of meeting, where I am to meet with thee: it shall be to you most holy. And ye shall not 37 make to yourselves any according to the composition of the perfume which thou shalt thus make: it shall be holy for Jehovah. He who shall make such as that, to smell to it, 38 shall be cut off from his people."

CHAP. XXXI.—And Jehovah spake to Moses, saying, 1 "See, I have called by name Bezaleel the son of Uri, the 2 son of Hur, of the tribe of Judah; and I have filled him 3 with the spirit of God, in wisdom, and in understanding, and in knowledge, and in all manner of workmanship, to 4 embroider, to work in gold, and in silver, and in brass, and 5

in engraving of stones, for setting, and in carving of wood,
6 for making any kind of work. And lo, I have appointed
with him Aholiab the son of Ahisamach, of the tribe of
Dan; and in the hearts of all that are wise-hearted I have
put wisdom, that they may make all that I have commanded
7 thee; the tent of meeting, and the ark of the testimonials,
and the lid that is upon it, and all the utensils of the tent,
8 and the table and its utensils, and the lamp-stand of pure
9 *gold* with all its utensils, and the altar of incense, and the altar
10 of burnt-offering with all its utensils, and the laver and its
foot, and the garments of service, and the holy garments for
Aaron the priest, and the garments of his sons, to minister
11 in the priests's office, and the anointing-oil, and sweet-
smelling incense for the sanctuary: according to all that I
have commanded thee they shall do."

12 And Jehovah spake to Moses, saying, "Speak thou also
to the children of Israel, saying, 'Verily my sabbaths ye
shall keep; for it is a sign between me and you throughout
your generations, that ye may know that I Jehovah am he
14 who sanctifieth you. Ye shall keep the sabbath therefore;
for it is holy to you; every one that defileth it shall surely
be put to death; for whosoever doeth *any* work on it, that
15 soul shall be cut off from amongst his people. Six days
may work be done; but on the seventh is the sabbath of
rest, holy to Jehovah: whosoever doeth *any* work on the
16 sabbath-day, he shall surely be put to death.' Wherefore
the children of Israel shall keep the sabbath, to observe the
sabbath throughout their generations, *for* a perpetual cove-
17 nant. It is a sign between me and the children of Israel for
ever." For in six days Jehovah made the heavens and the
earth, and on the seventh day he rested, and was refreshed.

18 And he gave to Moses, when he had made an end of
speaking with him upon mount Sinai, two testimonial-tables,
tables of stone, written by the finger of God.

1 CHAP. XXXII.—And when the people saw that Moses
delayed to come down from the mountain, the people gathered themselves together to Aaron, and said to him,
"Come, make us gods, who may go before us; for as to
that Moses, the man who brought us up out of the land of
2 Egypt, we know not what hath happened to him." And
Aaron said to them, "Pluck out the golden rings, which
are in the ears of your wives, of your sons, and of your

daughters, and bring them to me." And all the people 3 plucked out the golden rings which were in their ears, and brought them to Aaron. And he received *the gold* at their 4 hand, and fashioned it with a graving tool, and made of it a molten calf; and they said, "These are thy gods, O Israel, who have brought thee up out of the land of Egypt." And when Aaron saw it, he built an altar before it; and 5 Aaron made proclamation, and said, "To-morrow is a feast to Jehovah." And they rose up early on the morrow, and 6 offered burnt-offerings, and brought peace-offerings; and the people sat down to eat and to drink, and rose up to play.

And Jehovah said to Moses, "Go, go down; for thy 7 people, whom thou broughtest up out of the land of Egypt, have corrupted themselves: they have turned aside quickly 8 out of the way *in* which I commanded them *to go*: they have made for themselves a molten calf, and have worshipped it, and have sacrificed to it, and said, 'These are thy gods, O Israel, who have brought thee up out of the land of Egypt.'" And Jehovah said to Moses, "I have 9 seen this people, and, lo, it is a stiff-necked people. Now 10 therefore let me alone, that my wrath may be kindled against them, and that I may consume them; and I will make of thee a great nation." And Moses besought Jehovah, 11 his God, and said, "O Jehovah, why should thy wrath be kindled against thy people, whom thou hast brought forth out of the land of Egypt with great power, and with a mighty hand? Why should the Egyptians speak saying, 'For 12 evil he brought them out, to slay them in the mountains, and to consume them from the face of the earth?' Turn from the heat of thine anger, and repent of this evil against thy people. Remember Abraham, Isaac, and Israel, thy 13 servants, to whom thou swarest by thy own self, and saidst to them, 'I will multiply your seed as the stars of heaven, and all this land that I have spoken of will I give to your seed, and they shall inherit it for ever.'" Then Jehovah 14 repented of the evil which he had spoken of doing to his people. And Moses turned, and went down from the moun- 15 tain, with the two testimonial-tables in his hand: the tables were written on both their sides: on the one side and on the the other were they written. And the tables were the work 16 of God, and the writing was the writing of God, graven upon the tables.

And when Joshua heard the voice of the people as they 17

shouted, he said to Moses, "The sound of war is in the
18 camp." But *Moses* said, "It is not the sound of a shout
for victory, not the sound of a cry for being overcome; *but*
19 the sound of singing do I hear." And it came to pass when
he came nigh to the camp, and saw the calf, and the dancing,
that the anger of Moses was kindled, and he cast the tables
out of his hands, and brake them at the bottom of the
20 mountain. And he took the calf which they had made, and
burnt it in the fire, and ground it to powder, and strewed *it*
upon the water, and made the children of Israel drink *of it.*
And Moses said to Aaron, "What did this people to thee,
22 that thou hast brought upon them so great a sin?" And
Aaron said, "Let not the anger of my lord be kindled: thou
23 knowest the people, that they are prone to evil. For they
said to me, 'Make us gods who may go before us; for as to
that man Moses, who brought us up out of the land of
24 Egypt, we know not what hath happened to him.' And I
said to them, 'Whosoever hath any gold, let them pluck it
out.' So they gave it to me: then I cast it into the fire,
25 and there came out this calf." And when Moses saw that
the people were in disarray, (for Aaron had put them in disarray,) so that they might be slain by those who should rise
26 up against them, Moses stood in the gate of the camp, and
said, "Who is for Jehovah? *let him come* to me." And all
the sons of Levi gathered themselves together to him.
27 And he said to them, "Thus saith Jehovah God of Israel,
'Put every man his sword by his side; go in and out from
gate to gate throughout the camp, and slay every man his
brother, and every man his companion, and every man his
28 neighbour.'" And the children of Levi did according to
the command of Moses; and there fell of the people that
29 day about three thousand men. And Moses said, "Consecrate yourselves to-day to Jehovah, even every man upon his
son, and upon his brother, so as to obtain for yourselves a
blessing this day."
30 And it came to pass on the morrow, that Moses said to
the people, "Ye have committed a great sin; and now I
will go up to Jehovah: peradventure I may make an atone-
31 ment for your sin." And Moses returned to Jehovah, and
said, "Oh, this people have committed a great sin, and have
32 made them a god of gold; yet now, if thou wilt forgive
their sin—: but if not, blot me, I pray thee, out of thy book
33 which thou hast written." And Jehovah said to Moses,

"Whosoever hath sinned against me, him will I blot out of my book. Therefore now go, lead the people to *the place* 34 of which I have spoken to thee: lo, mine Angel shall go before thee: nevertheless, in the day when I visit, I will visit their sin upon them." And Jehovah sent a plague 35 amongst the people, because they made the calf, which Aaron made.

CHAP. XXXIII.—And Jehovah said to Moses, "De- 1 part, go up hence, thou and the people whom thou hast brought up out of the land of Egypt, unto the land which I sware to Abraham, to Isaac, and to Jacob, saying, 'To thy seed will I give it:' and I will send an Angel before thee; 2 and I will drive out the Canaanites, and the Amorites, and the Hittites, and the Perizzites and the Hivites, and the Jebusites, *and bring thee* into a land flowing with milk and 3 honey; but I will not go up in the midst of thee; for thou art a stiff-necked people; lest I consume thee in the way." And when the people heard these evil tidings, they mourned, 4 and no man put on him his ornaments. For Jehovah had 5 said to Moses, "Say to the children of Israel, Ye are a stiff-necked people: were I to go up in the midst of thee but for a moment, I should consume thee: therefore now put off thine ornaments from thee, that I may know what to do to thee." So the children of Israel stripped themselves of their 6 ornaments by the mountain Horeb.

And Moses took the tent, and pitched it without the camp, 7 afar off from the camp, and called it The Tent of Meeting. And all who would consult Jehovah went out to the tent of meeting, which was without the camp. And it came to pass 8 when Moses went out to the tent, that all the people rose up, and stood every man at his tent-door, and looked after Moses, until he was gone into the tent. And as Moses 9 entered into the tent, the pillar of cloud descended, and stood at the door of the tent, and Jehovah talked with Moses. And all the people saw the pillar of cloud stand- 10 ing at the door of the tent; and all the people rose up and worshipped, every man at his tent-door. And Jehovah 11 spake to Moses face to face, as a man speaketh to his friend. And he turned again into the camp; but his servant Joshua, the son of Nun, a young man, departed not out of the tent.

And Moses said to Jehovah, "See, thou sayest to me, 12

'Bring up this people;' but thou hast not let me know whom thou wilt send with me. Yet thou hast said, 'I know thee by name, and thou hast also found favour in my sight.' 13 Now therefore, I pray thee, if I have found favour in thy sight, shew me now thy way, that I may know thee, that I may find favour in thy sight; and consider that this nation 14 is thy people." And he said, "My presence shall go *with* 15 *thee*, and I will give thee rest." And he said to him, "If 16 thy presence go not with me, bring us not up hence. For by what now, shall it be known that I and thy people have found favour in thy sight? Is it not by thy going with us, that we may be distinguished, I and thy people, from all the 17 people that are upon the face of the earth?" And Jehovah said to Moses, "I will do this thing also that thou hast spoken; for thou hast found favour in my sight, and I know 18 thee by name." And *Moses* said, "Shew me, I beseech thee, 19 thy glory." And he said, "I will make all my goodness pass before thee, and I will proclaim the name of Jehovah before thee; for I will be gracious to whom I will be gracious, and 20 will shew mercy to whom I will shew mercy." And he said, "Thou canst not see my face; for no man can see me and 21 live." And Jehovah said, "Lo, there is a place by me, and 22 thou shalt stand upon a rock; and while my glory passeth by, I will put thee in a cleft of the rock, and will cover thee 23 with my hand while I pass by; and I will take away my hand, and thou shalt see my back; but my face may not be seen."

1 CHAP. XXXIV.—And Jehovah said to Moses, "Hew thee two tables of stone like the first; and I will write upon these tables the words that were in the first tables, which 2 thou brakest. And be ready in the morning, and come up in the morning unto mount Sinai, and present thyself there 3 to me on the top of the mountain. But let no one come up with thee, nor let any one be seen throughout all the mountain; let not even the flocks or herds feed about that moun- 4 tain." Then he hewed two tables of stone, like the first. And Moses rose up early in the morning, and went up unto mount Sinai, as Jehovah had commanded him, and took in 5 his hand the two tables of stone. And Jehovah descended in the cloud, and stood with him there, and proclaimed the 6 name of Jehovah. And Jehovah passed by before him and proclaimed "Jehovah! Jehovah! a God merciful and gra-

cious, slow to anger, but abundant in goodness and truth, keeping mercy for thousands, forgiving iniquity and trans- 7 gression and sin, acquitting even him who is not innocent, visiting the iniquity of the fathers upon the children, and upon the children's children, to the third and to the fourth generation." And Moses made haste, and bowed himself 8 toward the ground, and worshipped. And he said, "If now 9 I have found favour in thy sight, O Lord, let my Lord, I pray thee, go amongst us, although it is a stiff-necked people; and pardon our iniquities and our sins, and take us for thy possession." And *Jehovah* said, "Lo, I make a cove- 10 nant: before all thy people I will do wonders, such as have not been done in all the earth, nor in any nation; and all the people amongst whom thou art, shall see the work of Jehovah; for it is a terrible thing that I will do by thee. Observe thou that which I command thee this day; lo, I 11 drive out before thee the Amorites, and the Canaanites, and the Hittites, and the Perizzites, and the Hivites, and the Jebusites. Take heed to thyself, that thou make not a 12 covenant with the inhabitants of the land whither thou goest, lest it be a snare in the midst of thee; but ye shall destroy 13 their altars, break their images, and cut down their groves; for thou shalt worship no other god; for Jehovah, whose 14 name is Jealous, is a jealous God. *Take heed* that thou 15 make not a covenant with the inhabitants of the land, and when they go astray after their gods, and sacrifice to their gods, and any one inviteth thee, that thou eat not of his sacrifice; and that thou take not of their daughters for thy 16 sons, lest their daughters go astray after their gods, and make thy sons go astray after their gods. Molten gods 17 thou shalt not make for thyself. The feast of unleavened 18 bread thou shalt keep. Seven days, as I commanded thee, thou shalt eat unleavened bread, in the time of the month Abib: for in the month Abib thou camest out from Egypt. All that openeth the womb is mine; and every *male*-firstling 19 among thy cattle, *whether* ox or sheep. But the firstling 20 of an ass thou shalt redeem with a lamb; and if thou redeem him not, then shalt thou break his neck; but every first-born of thy sons thou shalt redeem. And let none appear before me empty-handed. Six days thou mayest work, 21 but on the seventh day thou shalt rest: *even* in seed-time and in harvest thou shalt rest. And thou shalt observe 22 the feast of weeks, of the first-fruits of wheat-harvest, and

23 the feast of in-gathering at the year's end. Three times in the year shall all thy males appear before the Lord Jehovah,
24 the God of Israel. For I will cast out the nations before thee, and enlarge thy borders: neither shall any man desire thy land, when thou shalt go up to appear before Jehovah
25 thy God three times in the year. Thou shalt not offer the blood of my sacrifice with leaven; nor shall the sacrifice
26 of the feast of passover be left until the morning. The first of the first-fruits of thy land thou shalt bring unto the house of Jehovah thy God. Thou shalt not seethe a kid in its mother's milk."
27 And Jehovah said to Moses, "Write thou these words; for after the tenor of these words I make a covenant with
28 thee and with Israel." And he was there with Jehovah forty days and forty nights; he did neither eat bread nor drink water. And he wrote upon the tables the words of
29 the covenant, the ten commandments. And it came to pass when Moses came down from mount Sinai with the two tables of testimony in the hand of Moses, when he came down from the mountain, that Moses knew not that the skin of his face had become shining from *Jehovah* having talked
30 with him. And when Aaron and all the children of Israel saw Moses, lo, the skin of his face was shining, and they
31 were afraid to come near him. And Moses called to them; and Aaron and all the rulers of the congregation returned
32 to him; and Moses talked with them. And afterward all the children of Israel came near; and he gave them in commandment all that Jehovah had spoken to him on mount Sinai.
33 And when Moses had done speaking with them, he put a
34 veil on his face. But when Moses went in before Jehovah to speak with him, he took off the veil until he came out. And he came out, and spake to the children of Israel that
35 which *Jehovah* commanded him. And the children of Israel saw the face of Moses, that the skin of the face of Moses shone; and Moses put the veil upon his face again, until he went in to speak with him.

1 CHAP. XXXV.—And Moses gathered all the congregation of the children of Israel together, and said to them, "These are the things which Jehovah hath commanded you
2 to do. Six days may work be done; but on the seventh day there shall be to you a holy-day, a sabbath of rest to Jehovah: whosoever doeth work on it shall be put to death.

Ye shall kindle no fire throughout your habitations upon ³ the sabbath-day."

And Moses spake to all the congregation of the children ⁴ of Israel, saying, "This is the thing which Jehovah hath commanded, saying, 'Take ye from amongst you an offering ⁵ to Jehovah: let every one whose heart is willing bring an offering to Jehovah, gold, and silver, and brass, and blue, ⁶ and purple, and scarlet, and linen, and goats' *hair*, and ⁷ rams' skins dyed red, and seals' skins, and setim-wood, and oil for the light, and spices for the anointing-oil, and ⁸ for the sweet-smelling incense, and onyx-stones, and stones ⁹ to be set in the ephod, and in the breastplate. And let ¹⁰ every one who is wise-hearted among you come, and make all that Jehovah hath commanded; the tabernacle, its tent, ¹¹ and its covering, its hooks, and its boards, its bars, its pillars, and its bases; the ark and its poles, *with* the lid, ¹² and the veil of the covering; the table and its poles, and all ¹³ its utensils, and the shew-bread; the lamp-stand also for ¹⁴ the light, and its utensils, and its lamps, with the oil for the light; and the incense-altar, and its poles, and the anointing- ¹⁵ oil, and the sweet-smelling incense, and the hanging for the entrance of the tabernacle; the altar of burnt-offering, with ¹⁶ its brazen grate, its poles, and all its vessels; the laver and its foot; the hangings of the court, its pillars, and their ¹⁷ bases, and the hanging for the gate of the court; the pins ¹⁸ of the tabernacle, and the pins of the court, and their cords; the garments of service, to be used in the sanctuary, and the ¹⁹ holy garments for Aaron the priest, and the garments of his sons, when they minister in the priest's office.'" And all the ²⁰ congregation of the children of Israel departed from the presence of Moses. And they came, every one whose heart ²¹ inclined him, and every one whose spirit made him willing, *and* they brought an offering to Jehovah for the work of the tent of meeting, and for all its service, and for the holy garments. And they came, both men and women, every ²² one whose heart was willing, *and* brought clasps, and ear-rings, and rings, and beads, all *kinds of* jewels of gold: and every man who would offer an offering of gold to Jehovah *brought it*. And every one who possessed blue, ²³ and purple, and scarlet, and linen, and goats' *hair*, and rams' skins dyed red, and seals' skins, brought them. Every one who would offer an offering of silver or of brass, ²⁴ brought it an offering to Jehovah: and every one who pos-

sessed setim-wood, for any work of the service, brought it.
25 And all the women who were wise-hearted spun with their own hands, and brought that which they had spun, of blue,
26 and of purple, and of scarlet, and of linen. And all the women whose heart inclined them spun skilfully goats' hair.
27 And the chiefs brought onyx-stones, and stones to be set in
28 the ephod, and in the breastplate: and spices, and oil for the light, and for the anointing-oil, and for the sweet-
29 smelling incense. *Thus* the children of Israel brought a willing offering to Jehovah, every man and woman, whose heart made them willing to bring, for all the work which
30 Jehovah by Moses had commanded to be done. And Moses said to the children of Israel, " See, Jehovah hath called by name Bezaleel the son of Uri, the son of Hur, of the tribe
31 of Judah; and he hath filled him with the spirit of God, in wisdom, and in understanding, and in knowledge, and in
32 all manner of workmanship; and curiously to inweave; to
33 work in gold, and in silver, and in brass, and in the engraving of stones for setting, and in carving of wood, for
34 making any sort of curious work. And he hath made him willing to teach *others;* him and Aholiab the son of Ahisa-
35 mach of the tribe of Dan. Them hath he filled with wisdom of heart, to do every kind of work, of the engraver, and of him who curiously inweaves, and of the embroiderer, in blue, and in purple, in scarlet, and in linen, and of the weaver; of them who do any work, and of them who curiously inweave."

1 CHAP. XXXVI.—Then Bezaleel and Aholiab, and every wise-hearted man, in whom Jehovah had put wisdom and understanding, to know how to do every kind of work for the service of the sanctuary, did according to all that Je-
2 hovah hath commanded. And Moses called Bezaleel and Aholiab, and every wise-hearted man, in whose heart Jehovah had put wisdom, every one whose heart inclined him
3 to come to the work to do it; and they received of Moses the whole offering which the children of Israel had brought for the work for the service of the sanctuary. And as they
4 yet brought to him free-will-offerings every morning, all the wise men who wrought all the work of the sanctuary, came
5 every one from his work which they were making, and spake to Moses, saying, "The people bring much more than enough for the service of the work which Jehovah hath commanded

to be done." Then Moses ordered that it should be pro- 6
claimed throughout the camp, saying, "Let neither man nor
woman do any more work for the offering of the sanctuary."
So the people were restrained from bringing. For the ma- 7
terials they had were more than sufficient for the making of
all the work.

And every wise-hearted man, among them that wrought 8
the work of the tabernacle, made ten curtains of twisted
linen, and blue, and purple, and scarlet: *with* cherubim
curiously inwoven he made them. The length of each 9
curtain was twenty-eight cubits, and the breadth of each
curtain four cubits: the curtains had the same measure.
Five curtains he joined one to another; and five curtains 10
he joined one to another. And he made loops of blue on 11
the edge of the outmost curtain of one of the joined pieces:
and he did the same on the edge of the outmost curtain in
the second joined piece. Fifty loops he made on one curtain, 12
and fifty loops he made on the edge of the outmost curtain
of the second joined piece: the loops answering one to
another. And he made fifty hooks of gold, and joined the 13
curtains together by the hooks: so that it might be one
tabernacle. And he made curtains of goats' *hair* for a 14
tent over the tabernacle: eleven *such* curtains he made.
The length of each curtain *was* thirty cubits, and four 15
cubits was the breadth of each curtain: the eleven curtains
had the same measure. And he joined together five curtains 16
by themselves, and six curtains by themselves. And he made 17
fifty loops on the edge of the outmost curtain of the joined
piece, and fifty loops he made on the edge of the *outmost*
curtain of the second joined piece. And he made fifty 18
hooks of brass to join the tent together, that it might be
one. And he made a covering for the tent, of rams' 19
skins dyed red, and a covering above of seals' skins.
And he made for the tabernacle boards of setim-wood, to 20
stand upright, ten cubits *was* the length of each board, and 21
a cubit and a half the breadth of each board. Each board 22
had two tenons, answering one to the other: thus he made
all the boards of the tabernacle. And he made the boards 23
for the tabernacle, twenty boards for the south side, southward. And forty sockets of silver he made under the twenty 24
boards: two sockets under one board for its two tenons, and
two sockets under another board for its two tenons. And for 25
the other side of the tabernacle, northward, he made twenty

26 boards, and their forty sockets of silver: two sockets under
27 one board and two sockets under another board. And for
the side of the tabernacle westward he made six boards.
28 And two boards he made for the corners of the tabernacle
29 in the two sides. And they were coupled together at the
bottom, and they were coupled together at the top by one
30 ring: thus he did to both of them at the two corners. Thus
there were eight boards; and their sockets of silver were
31 sixteen, under every board two sockets. And he made bars
of setim-wood: five for the boards of the one side of the
32 tabernacle, and five bars for the boards of the other side of
the tabernacle, and five bars for the boards of the tabernacle
33 for the side westward. And he made the middle bar, to pass
34 along the middle of the boards, from end to end. And he
overlaid the boards with gold, and made their rings of gold
to be places for the bars, and overlaid the bars with gold.
35 And he made a veil of blue, and purple, and scarlet, and
twisted linen: *with* cherubim of curious work he made it.
36 And he made for it four pillars of setim-wood, and overlaid
them with gold: their hooks were of gold; and he cast for
37 them four sockets of silver. And he made a hanging for
the entrance of the tabernacle, of blue, and purple, and
38 scarlet, and twisted linen, of needle-work; and its five
pillars, with their hooks: and he overlaid their capitals and
their rods with gold; but their five sockets were of brass.

1 CHAP. XXXVII.—And Bezaleel made the ark of setim-
wood: two cubits and a half *was* its length, and a cubit and
2 a half its breadth, and a cubit and a half its height. And
he overlaid it with pure gold within and without, and made
3 for it a moulding of gold round about. And he cast for it
four rings of gold, for the four corners of it; two rings on
the one side of it, and two rings on the other side of it.
4 And he made poles of setim-wood, and overlaid them with
5 gold. And he put the poles into the rings by the sides of
6 the ark, that the ark might be carried *by them*. And he
made the lid of pure gold: two cubits and a half *was* its
7 length, and a cubit and a half its breadth. And he made
two cherubim of gold, of solid work he made them, at the
8 two ends of the lid: one cherub on the one end, and another
cherub on the other end of the lid; he made the cherubim
9 at the two ends of it. And the cherubim spread out their
wings above, covering the lid with their wings, with their

faces one toward another; toward the lid were the faces of the cherubim. And he made the table of setim wood: two cubits *was* its length, and a cubit its breadth, and a cubit and a half its height. And he overlaid it with pure gold, and made for it a moulding of gold round about. He also made for it a border of a hand-breadth round about; and he made a moulding of gold to its border round about. And he cast for it four rings of gold, and put the rings in the four corners by its four feet. Near the border were the rings, the places for the poles, that the table might be carried. And he made the poles of setim-wood, and overlaid them with gold, that the table might be carried *by them*. And he made the vessels which were upon the table, its dishes, and its incense-pots, and its flagons, and its cups, with which to pour *the drink-offerings*, of pure gold. And he made the lamp-stand of pure gold: of solid work he made the lamp-stand; its shaft, and its branches, its cups, its knops, and its flowers, were of the same: and six branches came out of the sides of it; three branches of the lamp-stand out of the one side, and three branches of the lamp-stand out of the other side: three cups made like almonds, with a knop and a flower in one branch; and three cups made like almonds, with a knop and a flower in the other branch; so in the six branches that came out of the lamp-stand. And in the lamp-stand *were* four cups made like almonds, with its knops, and its flowers; so that there was a knop under two branches of the same, and a knop under two branches of the same, and a knop under two branches of the same, according to the six branches that proceeded out of it. Their knops and their branches were of the same: all of it one solid work of pure gold. And he made its seven lamps, and its snuffers, and its snuff-dishes, of pure gold. Of a talent of pure gold he made it, with all its utensils. And he made the incense altar of setim-wood. The length of it *was* a cubit, and the breadth of it a cubit; *so that it was* square; and two cubits *was* the height of it; its horns were of the same. And he overlaid it with pure gold, its top, and its sides round about, and its horns: and he made for it a moulding of gold round about. And two rings of gold he made for it under the moulding, by its two corners on both its sides, to be places for the poles, by which it might be carried. And he made the poles of setim-wood, and overlaid them with gold.

29 And he made the holy anointing-oil, and the pure incense of sweet spices, according to the work of the compounder.

1 CHAP. XXXVIII.—And he made the altar of burnt-offering of setim-wood: five cubits *was* its length, and five cubits its breadth, *so that it was* square, and its height *was*
2 three cubits. And he made the horns of it at its four corners: its horns were of one piece with it: and he over-
3 laid it with brass. And he made all the utensils of the altar, its pans, and its shovels, and its basons, and its flesh-hooks,
4 and its fire-pans: all its utensils he made of brass. And he made for the altar a grate of brazen lattice-work, below the
5 band down to the middle of *the altar*. And he cast four rings for the four ends of the grate of brass, to be places for
6 the poles. And he made the poles of setim-wood, and over-
7 laid them with brass. And he put the poles into the rings on the sides of the altar, that it might be carried by them:
8 he made the altar hollow with boards. And he made the laver of brass, and the foot of it of brass, of the mirrors of *the women* assembling, who assembled *at* the door of the tent of meeting.
9 And he made the court: on the south side southward, the hangings of the court *were* of twisted linen a hundred
10 cubits: their pillars *were* twenty, and their sockets of brass twenty: the hooks of the pillars and their rods *were* of
11 silver. And for the north side *the hangings were* a hundred cubits, their pillars *were* twenty, and their sockets of brass twenty: the hooks of the pillars and their rods of silver.
12 And for the west side *were* hangings of fifty cubits, their pillars ten, and their sockets ten; the hooks of the pillars
13 and their rods of silver. And for the east side eastward,
14 *the breadth of which was* fifty cubits, the hangings of one side *of the gate were* fifteen cubits; their pillars three, and
15 their sockets three. And for the other side of the court-gate, on this hand and that hand, *were* hangings of fifteen
16 cubits; their pillars three, and their sockets three. All the hangings of the court round about *were* of twisted linen.
17 And the sockets for the pillars *were* of brass; the hooks of the pillars and their rods of silver; and the overlaying of their capitals of silver: and all the pillars of the court
18 had rods of silver. And the hanging for the gate of the court *was* needle-work, of blue, and purple, and scarlet, and twisted linen; and twenty cubits *was* the length, and the

breadth *was* five cubits, answerable to the hangings of the court. And their pillars *were* four, and their sockets of brass four; their hooks of silver, and the overlaying of their capitals and their rods of silver. And all the pins of the tabernacle, and of the court round about, *were* of brass.

This is the sum of the tabernacle, the tabernacle of meeting, as it was counted, according to the commandment of Moses,*for* the service of the Levites, by Ithamar, son to Aaron the priest. And Bezaleel the son of Uri, the son of Hur, of the tribe of Judah, made all that Jehovah commanded Moses. And with him *was* Aholiab, son of Ahisamach, of the tribe of Dan, an engraver, and a weaver of curious work, and an embroiderer in blue, and in purple, and in scarlet, and in fine linen. All the gold that was employed for the work, in all the work of the sanctuary (which was the gold of the offering), was twenty-nine talents, and seven hundred and thirty shekels, according to the shekel of the sanctuary. And the silver of those who were numbered of the congregation, *was* a hundred talents, and a thousand seven hundred and seventy-five shekels, according to the shekel of the sanctuary: a bekah, *that is*, half a shekel, according to the shekel of the sanctuary, for every man, for every one that went to be numbered, from twenty years old and upward, being six hundred and three thousand, five hundred and fifty. And of the hundred talents of silver were cast the sockets of the sanctuary, and the sockets of the veil; a hundred sockets of the hundred talents, a talent for a socket. And of the thousand seven hundred and seventy-five *shekels* he made hooks for the pillars, and overlaid their capitals, and made rods for them. And the brass of the offering *was* seventy talents, and two thousand and four hundred shekels. And of this he made the sockets for the door of the tent of meeting, and the brazen altar, and the brazen gate for it, and all the vessels of the altar, and the sockets of the court round about, and the sockets of the court gate, and all the pins of the tabernacle, and all the pins of the court round about.

CHAP. XXXIX.—And of the blue, and purple, and scarlet, they made garments of service, to do service in the sanctuary, and they made the holy garments for Aaron; as Jehovah had commanded Moses. And he made the ephod

EXODUS XXXIX.

of gold, and blue, and purple, and scarlet, and twisted linen.
3 And they beat the gold into thin plates, and cut *it into* wires, to work *it* in the blue, and in the purple, and in the scarlet, and in the linen, with curiously inwoven work.
4 They made shoulder-pieces for *the ephod* to join *it* together:
5 at the two edges it was joined together. And the curiously wrought girdle of the ephod, which was upon it, *was* of the same, according to its work of gold, blue, and purple, and scarlet, and twisted linen; as Jehovah had commanded
6 Moses. And they wrought onyx-stones set in sockets of gold, engraven, as signets are engraven, with the names of
7 the children of Israel. And he put them on the shoulders of the ephod, *that they might be* stones of memorial for the children of Israel; as Jehovah had commanded Moses.
8 And he made the breastplate of curiously inwoven work, like the work of the ephod; of gold, of blue, and purple,
9 and scarlet, and twisted linen. It was square; they made the breastplate double: a span in length, and a span in
10 breadth, *when* doubled. And they set in it four rows of stones: a row of a carnelian, a topaz, and a carbuncle was the
11 first row. And the second row, an emerald, a sapphire,
12 and a diamond. And the third row, a ligure, an agate, and
13 an amethyst. And the fourth row, a beryl, an onyx, and a
14 jasper: *they were* inclosed in sockets of gold. And the stones *were* according to the names of the children of Israel, twelve, according to their names, *like* the engravings of a signet; each *had* its own name, according to the twelve
15 tribes. And they made upon the breastplate chains of
16 equal length, *of* wreathed work of pure gold. And they made two sockets of gold, and two rings of gold; and put
17 the two rings on the two ends of the breastplate. And they put the two wreathed chains of gold in the two rings
18 on the ends of the breastplate. And the *other* two ends of the two wreathed chains they fastened in the two sockets, and put them on the shoulder-pieces of the ephod in the
19 front of it. And they made two rings of gold, and put *them* on the two ends of the breastplate, on the border of
20 it, which was upon the joining of the ephod inward. And they made two *other* rings of gold, and put them on the two shoulder-pieces of the ephod underneath, toward the front of it, over against the *other* coupling above the girdle
21 of the ephod. And they bound the breastplate by its rings to the rings of the ephod with a ribband of blue, that it might

be above the curiously wrought girdle of the ephod, and that the breastplate might not be loosed from the ephod: as Jehovah had commanded Moses. And he made the robe of the ²² ephod of woven work, all of blue. And *there was* a hole in ²³ the robe, in the middle of it, as the hole of a coat of mail, *with* a binding round about the hole, that it might not be rent. And they made upon the hems of the robe pome- ²⁴ granates of blue, and purple, and scarlet, and twisted linen. And they made bells of pure gold, and put the bells upon ²⁵ the hem of the robe, between the pomegranates round about; a bell and a pomegranate, a bell and a pomegranate, ²⁶ upon the hem of the robe round about to minister *in;* as Jehovah had commanded Moses. And they made tunics ²⁷ of linen, of woven work, for Aaron and for his sons; and a ²⁸ mitre of linen, and beautiful turbans of linen, and linen drawers of twisted linen; and a girdle of twisted linen, ²⁹ and blue, and purple, and scarlet, of needle-work; as Jehovah had commanded Moses. And they made the petal ³⁰ of the holy crown of pure gold, and wrote upon it a writing, *like* the engravings of a signet, HOLY TO JEHOVAH. And ³¹ they fastened to it a ribband of blue, to fasten it above upon the mitre; as Jehovah had commanded Moses.

Thus was all the work of the tabernacle, the tent of ³² meeting, finished: for the children of Israel did according to all that Jehovah had commanded Moses; so they did. And they brought the tabernacle to Moses, the tent and all ³³ its furniture, its hooks, its boards, its bars, its pillars, and its sockets. And the covering of rams' skins dyed red, ³⁴ and the covering of seals' skins, and the veil of the covering, the ark of the testimonials, and its poles, and the ³⁵ lid, the table and all its furniture, and the shew-bread, ³⁶ the lamp-stand of pure *gold,* its lamps, *its* lamps to be ³⁷ set in order, and all its furniture, and the oil for light, and the golden altar, and the anointing-oil, and the sweet- ³⁸ smelling incense, and the hanging for the door of the tabernacle; the brazen altar, and its grate of brass, its ³⁹ poles, and all its utensils, the laver and its foot; the hang- ⁴⁰ ings of the court, and its pillars, and its sockets; and the hanging for the court gate, its cords, and its pins, and all the furniture for the service of the tabernacle, for the tent of meeting; the garments of service to be used in the ⁴¹ sanctuary, and the holy garments for Aaron the priest, and the garments of his sons to minister in the priest's

42 office. According to all that Jehovah had commanded
43 Moses, so the children of Israel made all the work. And
Moses looked upon all the work, and, lo, they had done it
as Jehovah had commanded, even so had they done it: and
Moses blessed them.

1 CHAP. XL.—Then Jehovah spake to Moses, saying,
2 "On the first day of the first month shalt thou set up the
3 tabernacle, the tent of meeting. And in it thou shalt put
the ark of the testimonials, and screen the ark with the
4 veil. And thou shalt bring in the table, and set in order
the things that are to be set in order upon it; and thou
5 shalt bring in the lamp-stand, and put on its lamps. And
thou shalt set the golden altar of incense before the ark of
the testimonials, and put up the hanging of the entrance
6 of the tabernacle. And thou shalt set the altar of the
burnt-offering before the entrance of the tabernacle, the
7 tent of meeting. And thou shalt set the laver between the
tent of meeting and the altar, and shalt put water into it.
8 And thou shalt set up the court round about, and hang up
9 the hanging at the gate of the court. Then thou shalt take
the anointing-oil, and anoint the tabernacle, and all that is
in it, and shalt sanctify it, and all its furniture: and it shall
10 be holy. And thou shalt anoint the altar of the burnt-offering, and all its furniture, and sanctify the altar: and it shall
11 be an altar most holy. And thou shalt anoint the laver and
12 its foot, and sanctify it. Thou shalt then bring Aaron and
his sons to the door of the tent of meeting, and wash them
13 with water. And thou shalt put upon Aaron the holy
garments, and anoint him, and sanctify him; that he may
14 minister to me in the priest's office. And thou shalt bring
15 his sons, and clothe them with tunics: and thou shalt anoint
them, as thou didst anoint their father, that they may
minister to me in the priest's office: and this shall be done
that their anointing may be to them for a perpetual priest-
16 hood, throughout their generations." Thus did Moses: according to all that Jehovah commanded him, so he did.
17 Now it came to pass in the first month, in the second
year, on the first day of the month, the tabernacle was
18 erected. And Moses set up the tabernacle, and fixed its
sockets, and placed its boards, and put in its bars, and set
19 up its pillars. And he spread the tent over the tabernacle,
and over this he put the covering of the tent, as Jehovah

had commanded Moses. And he took the testimonials and ²⁰ put them into the ark, and set the poles to the ark, and put the lid above upon the ark. And he brought the ark into ²¹ the tabernacle, and hung up the veil of the covering, and concealed the ark of the testimonials; as Jehovah had commanded Moses. And he placed the table in the tent of ²² meeting, upon the side of the tabernacle northward, without the veil. And he set the bread in order upon it before ²³ Jehovah; as Jehovah had commanded Moses. And he put ²⁴ the lamp-stand in the tent of meeting, opposite to the table, on the side of the tabernacle southward. And he ²⁵ put on the lamps before Jehovah; as Jehovah had commanded Moses. And he put the golden altar in the tent ²⁶ of meeting, before the veil: and he burnt sweet-smelling ²⁷ incense on it; as Jehovah had commanded Moses. And ²⁸ he put up the hanging at the entrance of the tabernacle. And he put the altar of burnt-offering *before* the entrance ²⁹ of the tabernacle, the tent of meeting, and offered upon it the burnt-offering and the meal-offering; as Jehovah had commanded Moses. And he set the laver between the tent ³⁰ of meeting and the altar, and put water there, to wash with; and Moses and Aaron and his sons there washed their hands ³¹ and their feet. When they went into the tent of meeting, ³² and when they came near the altar, they washed, as Jehovah had commanded Moses. And he set up the court round ³³ about the tabernacle and the altar, and set up the hanging of the gate of the court.

When Moses had finished the work, a cloud covered the ³⁴ tent of meeting, and the glory of Jehovah filled the tabernacle. So that Moses was not able to enter into the tent ³⁵ of meeting, because the cloud rested on it, and the glory of Jehovah filled the tabernacle. When the cloud was taken ³⁶ up from over the tabernacle, the children of Israel went onward in all their journeys; but when the cloud was not ³⁷ taken up, then they journeyed not till the day in which it was taken up. For the cloud of Jehovah *was* upon the ³⁸ tabernacle by day, and fire was on it by night, in the sight of all the house of Israel, throughout all their journeys.

THE BOOK OF LEVITICUS.

CHAP. I.—¹And Jehovah called to Moses, and spake to ²him from the tent of meeting, saying, "Speak to the children of Israel, and say to them, 'If any of you will bring an offering to Jehovah from the cattle; from the herd or ³from the flock ye shall bring your offering. If his offering be a burnt-offering from the herd, let him offer a male without blemish: he shall offer it at the door of the tent of ⁴meeting, for his acceptance before Jehovah. And he shall lay his hand upon the head of the burnt-offering; and it ⁵shall be accepted for him, to make atonement for him. And he shall slay the bullock before Jehovah: and the priests, the sons of Aaron, shall bring the blood, and sprinkle the blood round about upon the altar which *is* by the door of the tent ⁶of meeting. And he shall flay the burnt-offering, and cut it ⁷in pieces. Then the sons of Aaron the priest shall put fire ⁸upon the altar, and lay the wood in order upon the fire; and the priests, the sons of Aaron, shall lay the pieces, the head, and the fat, in order upon the wood that is on the fire upon ⁹the altar; but its entrails and its legs shall he wash in water; and the priest shall burn all on the altar, *as* a burnt-offering, an offering made by fire, an acceptable odour to Jehovah.

¹⁰And if his offering be a burnt-offering from the flocks, from the sheep or from the goats he shall bring it, a male ¹¹without blemish. And he shall slay it on the side of the altar northward before Jehovah: and the priests, the sons of Aaron, shall sprinkle its blood round about upon the altar: ¹²and he shall cut it in pieces, and these, with its head and its fat, the priest shall lay in order on the wood that is on the fire ¹³upon the altar. But he shall wash the entrails and the legs with water; and the priest shall bring the whole, and burn it upon the altar: it is a burnt-offering, an offering made by fire, an acceptable odour to Jehovah.

But if his burnt-offering to Jehovah be an offering from 14
the birds, then he shall bring his offering of turtle-doves, or
of young pigeons. And the priest shall bring it to the altar, 15
and pinch off its head, and burn it on the altar; and its
blood shall be wrung out at the side of the altar; and he 16
shall pluck out its crop with its contents, and cast it beside
the altar, on the eastern part, by the place of the ashes; and 17
he shall cleave it with its wings, but shall not divide it asunder; and the priest shall burn it upon the altar, upon the
wood that is on the fire: it is a burnt-offering, an offering
made by fire, an acceptable odour to Jehovah.

CHAP. II.—And if any one will offer a meal-offering to 1
Jehovah, his offering shall be of fine flour; and he shall
pour upon it oil, and put upon it frankincense. And he 2
shall bring it to the priests, the sons of Aaron; and he shall
take from it his handful of the flour, and of the oil, with all
the frankincense, and the priest shall burn *them as* a memorial of it upon the altar, an offering made by fire, an acceptable odour to Jehovah; and the remainder of the meal- 3
offering shall be for Aaron and his sons: the most holy of
the offerings made by fire to Jehovah. And if thou bring 4
an offering of a meal-offering baked in an oven, it shall be
unleavened cakes of fine flour mingled with oil, or unleavened
wafers anointed with oil. And if a meal-offering on a pan 5
be thy offering, it shall be of fine flour unleavened, mingled
with oil. Thou shalt part it in pieces, and pour upon it oil: 6
it is a meal-offering. And if a meal-offering baked on a 7
plate be thy offering, it shall be made of fine flour with oil.
And thou shalt bring the meal-offering which is made of 8
these things to Jehovah; and when it is presented to the
priest, he shall bring it to the altar. And the priest shall 9
take from the meal-offering a memorial of it, and shall burn
it upon the altar, as an offering made by fire, an acceptable
odour to Jehovah; and the remainder of the meal-offering 10
shall be for Aaron and his sons: the most holy of the offerings made by fire to Jehovah. No meal-offering, which ye 11
shall bring to Jehovah, shall be made with leaven: for ye
shall burn no leaven, or honey, in any offering made by fire
to Jehovah. As first-fruit-offerings, ye may offer them to 12
Jehovah; but they shall not be burnt on the altar for an acceptable odour. And every offering of thy meal-offering 13
thou shalt season with salt; neither shalt thou withhold the

salt of the covenant of thy God from thy meal-offerings:
14 with all thine offerings thou shalt offer salt. And if thou offer a meal-offering of first-fruits to Jehovah, thou shalt offer, for the meal-offering of thy first-fruits, green ears of
15 corn roasted at the fire, or corn rubbed out of full ears. And thou shalt put oil upon it, and lay upon it frankincense: it
16 is a meal-offering. And the priest shall burn, as a memorial of it, some of the corn rubbed out *of the ear*, and some of the oil, with all its frankincense: it is an offering made by fire to Jehovah.

1   CHAP. III.—And if a sacrifice of peace-offering be the offering of any one, if he offer it from the herd, whether male or female, he shall offer it without blemish before Jeho-
2 vah. And he shall lay his hand upon the head of his offering, and slay it at the door of the tent of meeting; and the priests, the sons of Aaron, shall sprinkle the blood round
3 about upon the altar. And he shall offer of the sacrifice of the peace-offering, *as* an offering made by fire to Jehovah: the fat that covereth the entrails, and all the fat that is upon
4 the entrails, and the two kidneys, and the fat that is on them, which is by the loins, and the caul above the liver, to-
5 gether with the kidneys, he shall take away; and the sons of Aaron shall burn it on the altar upon the burnt sacrifice, which is upon the wood that is on the fire, *as* an offering made by fire, an acceptable odour to Jehovah.
6   And if his offering for a sacrifice of peace-offering to Jehovah be from the flock, male or female, he shall offer it
7 without blemish. If he offer a lamb for his offering, then
8 shall he offer it before Jehovah. And he shall lay his hand upon the head of his offering, and slay it before the tent of meeting; and the sons of Aaron shall sprinkle the blood of
9 it round about upon the altar. And he shall offer of the sacrifice of the peace-offering, as an offering made by fire to Jehovah: its fat, and the whole of the fat tail, which he shall take off close to the rump, and the fat that covereth the
10 entrails, and all the fat that is upon the entrails, and the two kidneys, and the fat that is upon them, which is by the loins, and the caul above the liver, together with the kidneys,
11 he shall take away; and the priest shall burn *them* upon the altar, *as* the food of the offering made by fire to Jehovah.
12   And if his offering be a goat, then he shall offer it before
13 Jehovah. And he shall lay his hand upon the head of it,

and slay it before the tent of meeting; and the sons of
Aaron shall sprinkle its blood round about upon the altar.
And of it he shall offer his offering, an offering made by fire 14
to Jehovah : the fat that covereth the entrails, and all the fat
that is upon the entrails, and the two kidneys, and the fat 15
that is upon them, which is by the loins, and the caul above
the liver, together with the kidneys, he shall take away, and 16
the priest shall burn them upon the altar, *as* the food of the
offering made by fire, for an acceptable odour. All the fat is
Jehovah's. *This shall be* a perpetual statute for your genera- 17
tions, throughout all your dwellings, that ye eat neither fat
nor blood.'"

CHAP. IV.—And Jehovah spake to Moses, saying, " Speak 2
to the children of Israel, saying, 'If any one have sinned
through ignorance and done any one of those things which
Jehovah hath commanded not to be done: if the anointed 3
priest have sinned so as to bring guilt upon the people, he
shall bring to Jehovah, for his sin which he hath committed,
a young bullock without blemish for a sin-offering. And he 4
shall bring the bullock to the door of the tent of meeting
before Jehovah; and shall lay his hand upon the head of
the bullock, and slay the bullock before Jehovah. And the 5
anointed priest shall take some of the blood of the bullock,
and bring it to the tent of meeting; and the priest shall dip 6
his finger in the blood, and sprinkle some of the blood with
his finger seven times before Jehovah, before the veil of the
sanctuary. Then the priest shall put some of the blood 7
upon the horns of the altar of sweet-incense before Jehovah,
which is in the tent of meeting; and shall pour all the *rest
of the* blood of the bullock at the bottom of the altar of
the burnt-offering, which is at the door of the tent of meeting. And he shall take off from the bullock all the fat, for 8
the sin-offering; the fat that covereth the entrails, and all
the fat that is upon the entrails, and the two kidneys, and 9
the fat that is upon them, which is by the loins, and the caul
above the liver, together with the kidneys, he shall take
away, as it was taken off from the bullock of the sacrifice of 10
peace-offerings; and the priest shall burn them upon the
altar of the burnt-offering. And the skin of the bullock, 11
and all his flesh, with his head, and with his legs, and his
entrails, and his dung, even the whole bullock shall he carry 12
forth without the camp to a clean place, where the ashes are

poured out, and burn him on the wood with fire: where the ashes are poured out shall he be burnt.

13 And if the whole congregation of Israel sin through ignorance, and the thing be hidden from the eyes of the assembly, and they have done any thing which Jehovah hath com-
14 manded not to be done, and are guilty; and the sin, which they have committed, becomes known, the congregation shall offer a young bullock for the sin, and bring him before the
15 tent of meeting. And the elders of the congregation shall lay their hands upon the head of the bullock before Jeho-
16 vah; and the bullock shall be slain before Jehovah. And the anointed priest shall bring some of the blood of the bullock
17 to the tent of meeting; and the priest shall dip his finger in some of the blood, and sprinkle *it* seven times before Jeho-
18 vah, before the veil. And he shall put some of the blood upon the horns of the altar which is before Jehovah in the tent of meeting, and shall pour out all the *rest of the* blood at the bottom of the altar of the burnt-offering, which is at
19 the door of the tent of meeting. And he shall take all his fat
20 from him, and burn it upon the altar. And he shall do with the bullock as he did with the *other* bullock for a sin-offering, so shall he do with this; thus the priest shall make an atone-
21 ment for them, and it shall be forgiven them. And he shall carry forth the bullock without the camp, and burn it as he burned the first bullock: it is a sin-offering for the congregation.

22 When a ruler hath sinned, and, through ignorance, hath done any thing which Jehovah his God hath commanded not
23 to be done, and is guilty; when his sin, which he hath committed, cometh to his knowledge, he shall bring for his offer-
24 ing, a kid of the goats, a male without blemish; and he shall lay his hand upon the head of the goat, and slay it in the place where they slay the burnt-offering before Jehovah:
25 it is a sin-offering. And the priest shall take some of the blood of the sin-offering with his finger, and put it upon the horns of the altar of burnt-offering, and shall pour out *the rest of* his blood at the bottom of the altar of burnt-offering.
26 And he shall burn all his fat upon the altar, as the fat of the sacrifice of peace-offerings: thus the priest shall make an atonement for him concerning his sin, and it shall be forgiven him.

27 And if any one of the people of the land sin through ignorance, by doing any one of those things which Jehovah

hath commanded not to be done, and be guilty; when his 28
sin, which he hath committed, cometh to his knowledge, he
shall bring his offering, a kid of the goats, a female without
blemish, for his sin, which he hath committed. And he shall 29
lay his hand upon the head of the sin-offering, and slay the
sin-offering in the place of the burnt-offering. And the 30
priest shall take some of the blood of it with his finger, and
put it upon the horns of the altar of burnt-offering, and
shall pour out all *the rest of* the blood at the bottom of the
altar. And he shall take away all the fat of it, as the fat is taken 31
away from off the sacrifice of peace-offerings; and the priest
shall burn it upon the altar, for an acceptable odour to Jehovah: thus the priest shall make an atonement for him, and
it shall be forgiven him. And if he bring a lamb for a sin- 32
offering, he shall bring it a female without blemish. And 33
he shall lay his hand upon the head of the sin-offering, and
it shall be slain for a sin-offering, in the place where they
slay the burnt-offering. And the priest shall take some of 34
the blood of the sin-offering with his finger, and put it upon
the horns of the altar of burnt-offering, and shall pour out
all *the rest of* the blood of it at the bottom of the altar.
And he shall take away all the fat of it, as the fat of the 35
lamb is taken away from the sacrifice of the peace-offerings;
and the priest shall burn them upon the altar, according to
the offerings made by fire to Jehovah: thus the priest shall
make an atonement for his sin that he hath committed, and
it shall be forgiven him.

CHAP. V.—And if any one having heard the voice of 1
adjuration, shall not bear witness concerning what he hath
seen or known, *and thus* commit sin, he shall bear his
iniquity; or if any one have touched any unclean thing, 2
whether *it be* the carcase of an unclean wild beast, or the
carcase of unclean cattle, or the carcase of an unclean reptile, and it be hidden from him; and he become unclean,
and guilty: or if he have touched uncleanness in man, any 3
uncleanness by which a man may be defiled, and it be
hidden from him; when he knoweth it, he shall be guilty:
or if any one have rashly sworn with his lips to do evil, or 4
to do good, with regard to any thing that a man may rashly
swear, and it be hidden from him; when he knoweth it, he
shall be guilty in one of these. When he shall have be- 5
come guilty in one of these things, he shall confess that he

6 hath sinned in that thing. And he shall bring his trespass-offering to Jehovah, for his sin which he hath committed, a female from the flock, a lamb or a kid of the goats, for a sin-offering: thus the priest shall make an atonement for
7 him concerning his sin. And if he cannot afford a lamb, then he shall bring, for his trespass which he hath committed, two turtle-doves, or two young pigeons, to Jehovah; one for a sin-offering, and the other for a burnt-offering.
8 And he shall bring them to the priest, who shall offer that which is for the sin-offering first, and pinch off its head
9 from its neck, but shall not divide *the bird* asunder. And he shall sprinkle some of the blood of the sin-offering upon the side of the altar; and the rest of the blood shall be wrung out at the bottom of the altar: it is a sin-offering.
10 And he shall offer the second for a burnt-offering, according to the ordinance: thus the priest shall make an atonement for him, for his sin which he hath committed, and it shall be
11 forgiven him. But if he cannot afford two turtle-doves, or two young pigeons, then he who sinned shall bring for his offering the tenth part of an ephah of fine flour, for a sin-offering: he shall put no oil upon it, nor shall he put *any*
12 frankincense upon it, for it is a sin-offering. Then he shall bring it to the priest, and the priest shall take from it his handful, *as* a memorial of it, and burn it on the altar, according to the offerings made by fire to Jehovah: it is a sin-
13 offering. Thus the priest shall make an atonement for the sin of any one who may have been guilty in one of these things, and it shall be forgiven him: and *the remainder* shall be the priest's, as a meal-offering.'"

15 And Jehovah spake to Moses, saying, "If any one have transgressed, and sinned through ignorance in *any of* the holy things of Jehovah; then he shall bring to Jehovah his trespass-offering, a ram without blemish from the flock, by thy valuation in shekels of silver, according to the shekel of
16 the sanctuary, for a trespass-offering. And he shall restore that with respect to which he had sinned, in the holy things, and shall add to it the fifth part and give it to the priest: and the priest shall make an atonement for him with the ram of the trespass-offering, and it shall be forgiven him.
17 And if any one sin, and commit any of these things which are forbidden to be done by the commandments of Jehovah; though he knew it not, yet is he guilty, and shall bear his
18 iniquity. And he shall bring a ram without blemish from

the flock, by thy valuation, for a trespass-offering, to the priest; and the priest shall make an atonement for him concerning his ignorance in which he erred, and knew it not; and it shall be forgiven him. It is a trespass-offering: he 19 hath certainly trespassed against Jehovah."

CHAP. VI.—And Jehovah spake to Moses, saying, "If 2 any one have sinned and transgressed against Jehovah, by denying to his neighbour a trust or a deposit, or by any thing taken away by violence, or have defrauded his neighbour; or have found that which was lost, and denieth it, 3 and sweareth falsely concerning any one of those things in respect of which men may sin; then because he hath sinned, 4 and is guilty, he shall restore that which he took violently away, or the thing which he hath deceitfully gotten, or that which was entrusted to him to keep, or the lost thing which he found, or whatever it be concerning which he hath sworn 5 falsely; he shall even restore it in its original state, and shall add to it a fifth part more, and give it to him to whom it appertaineth, in the day *when he offereth* his trespass-offering. And he shall bring his trespass-offering to Jehovah, a 6 ram without blemish from the flock, by thy valuation, for a trespass-offering, to the priest: thus the priest shall make 7 an atonement for him before Jehovah; and it shall be forgiven him in respect of whatever he had done, so as to be guilty therein."

And Jehovah spake to Moses, saying, "Command Aaron 9 and his sons, saying, 'This is the law concerning the *daily* burnt-offering: The burnt-offering shall be on the fire-place of the altar during the whole night until the morning, and the fire of the altar shall be burning on it. Then the priest 10 shall put on his linen garment, and his linen drawers he shall put upon his flesh, and shall take up the ashes of the burnt-offering which the fire hath consumed on the altar, and he shall put them beside the altar. He shall then put 11 off his garments, and put on other garments, and carry forth the ashes without the camp, to a clean place. But the 12 fire upon the altar shall be burning on it, it shall not be put out; and the priest shall burn wood on it every morning, and lay the burnt-offering in order upon it; he shall also burn upon it the fat of the peace-offerings. The fire shall 13 be continually burning upon the altar: it shall never go out.

And this is the law concerning the *daily* meal-offering: 14

The sons of Aaron shall offer it before Jehovah, before the
15 altar. And he shall take from it his handful of the fine flour
of the meal-offering, and of its oil, and all the frankincense
which is upon the meal-offering, and shall burn them upon
the altar, an acceptable odour, a memorial of it to Jehovah.
16 And the remainder of it Aaron and his sons shall eat: unleavened shall it be eaten in the holy place; in the court of
17 the tent of meeting they shall eat it. It shall not be baked
with leaven: I have given it *to them* as their portion of my
offerings made by fire; it is most holy, as the sin-offering,
18 and as the trespass-offering. All the males among the children of Aaron may eat of it. *This shall be* a perpetual
statute in your generations, concerning the offerings of Jehovah made by fire: every one that toucheth them must be
holy.'"
20 And Jehovah spake to Moses, saying, "This is the offering of Aaron and of his sons, which they shall offer to
Jehovah on the day in which he shall be anointed; the tenth
part of an ephah of fine flour for a continual meal-offering,
half of it in the morning, and half of it in the evening.
21 In a pan it shall be prepared with oil; *and when it* hath
been fried, thou shalt bring it cut in pieces, and offer it, a
22 meal-offering, an acceptable odour to Jehovah. And the
priest who shall be anointed in his stead from among his
sons shall offer it, according to a perpetual statute to Jeho-
23 vah; it shall be wholly burnt. And every meal-offering of
the priest shall be wholly burnt: it shall not be eaten."
25 And Jehovah spake to Moses, saying, "Speak to Aaron
and to his sons, saying, 'This is the law concerning the sin-
offering: In the place where the burnt-offering is slain shall
the sin-offering be slain before Jehovah: it is most holy.
26 The priest that offereth the sin-offering shall eat it; in a
holy place shall it be eaten, in the court of the tent of
27 meeting. Every one who toucheth its flesh must be holy;
and when any of its blood is sprinkled upon any garment,
that on which it hath been sprinkled shall be washed in a
28 holy place. And the earthen vessel in which it hath been
seethed shall be broken; but if it be seethed in a brazen
29 vessel, it shall be scoured, and rinsed in water. All the
males among the priests may eat of it: it is most holy.
30 But no sin-offering, of which part of the blood is brought
into the tent of meeting, as an atonement in the sanctuary,
shall be eaten: it shall be burnt in the fire.

CHAP. VII.—And this is the law concerning the trespass-offering: it is most holy. In the place where they slay the burnt-offering shall they slay the trespass-offering: and the blood of it he shall sprinkle round about upon the altar. And *the priest* shall offer of it all its fat; the fat tail, and the fat that covereth the entrails, and the two kidneys, and the fat that is on them, which is by the loins, and the caul above the liver, together with the kidneys, shall he take away; and the priest shall burn them upon the altar, an offering made by fire to Jehovah: it is a trespass-offering. Every male among the priests may eat of it: it shall be eaten in the holy place: it is most holy. For the sin-offering and for the trespass-offering, there is one law: the priest that maketh atonement by them shall have *them*. And the priest that offereth the burnt-offering of any one, that priest shall have for himself the skin of the burnt-offering which he hath offered. And every meal-offering that is baked in an oven, and every one that is prepared on a hearth, or in a pan, shall belong to the priest that offereth it. And every meal-offering, mingled with oil or dry, shall belong to all the sons of Aaron, to one *as much* as to another.

And this is the law concerning the sacrifice of peace-offerings, which *any one* shall offer to Jehovah. If he offer it for a thanksgiving, then he shall offer with the sacrifice of thanksgiving unleavened cakes mingled with oil, and unleavened wafers anointed with oil, and cakes of fine flour, fried, mingled with oil. With the cakes, he shall offer for his offering leavened bread with the sacrifice of thanksgiving of his peace-offerings. And of it he shall offer one out of the whole offering for a heave-offering to Jehovah; it shall be for the priest that sprinkleth the blood of the peace-offerings. And the flesh of the sacrifice of his peace-offerings for thanksgiving shall be eaten on the same day in which it is offered; no part of it shall be left until the morning. But if the sacrifice of his offering be for a vow, or for a voluntary offering, it shall be eaten the same day that he offereth his sacrifice; and on the morrow also the remainder of it may be eaten; but the remainder of the flesh of the sacrifice on the third day shall be burnt with fire. And if any of the flesh of the sacrifice of his peace-offerings be eaten at all on the third day, it shall not be accepted, nor shall it be reckoned to him that offereth it: it shall be abominable, and the soul that eateth of it shall bear

LEVITICUS VII.

19 his iniquity. And if the flesh have touched any *thing* unclean, it shall not be eaten; it shall be burnt with fire.
20 Every one who is clean may eat the flesh; but the soul that eateth *any* of the flesh of the sacrifice of peace-offerings which *are offered* to Jehovah, having his uncleanness upon
21 him, even that soul shall be cut off from his people. The soul also that shall touch any unclean *thing, as* the uncleanness of man, or *any* unclean beast, or any unclean reptile, and eat of the flesh of the sacrifice of peace-offerings which *are offered* to Jehovah, even that soul shall be cut off from his people.'"
23 And Jehovah spake to Moses, saying, "Speak to the children of Israel, saying, 'Ye shall eat no fat, of ox, or
24 of sheep, or of goat. The fat of the beast that hath died of itself, and the fat of that which hath been torn by beasts, may be applied to any other use; but ye shall on no account
25 eat it. For whosoever eateth the fat of the beast, of which men offer an offering made by fire to Jehovah, even the soul
26 that eateth it shall be cut off from his people. Nor shall ye eat any blood, of bird, or of beast, in any of your dwellings.
27 Whosoever shall eat any blood, even that soul shall be cut off from his people.'"
29 And Jehovah spake to Moses, saying, "Speak to the children of Israel, saying, 'He that offereth the sacrifice of his peace-offerings to Jehovah, shall bring his offering to
30 Jehovah of the sacrifice of his peace-offerings. His own hands shall bring the offerings of Jehovah made by fire; the fat with the breast shall he bring, that the breast
31 may be waved a wave-offering before Jehovah. And the priest shall burn the fat upon the altar; but the breast shall
32 be for Aaron and his sons. The right shoulder also ye shall give to the priest, a heave-offering of the sacrifices of your
33 peace-offerings. He among the sons of Aaron, who offereth the blood of the peace-offerings, and the fat, shall have the
34 right shoulder for *his* portion. For the wave-breast and the heave-shoulder have I taken of the children of Israel from the sacrifices of their peace-offerings, and have given them from the children of Israel, to Aaron the priest and to his
35 sons, by a perpetual statute.'" This is the portion of Aaron, and the portion of his sons, out of the offerings of Jehovah made by fire, *appointed* on the day in which *Moses* presented them to minister to] Jehovah in the priest's
36 office; which Jehovah commanded to be given to them by

the children of Israel, in the day in which *Moses* anointed them, *by* a perpetual statute throughout their generations.

This is the law concerning the burnt-offering, and the 37 meal-offering, and the sin-offering, and the trespass-offering, and the consecration-*offerings*, and the sacrifice of the peace-offerings, which Jehovah commanded Moses on Mount Sinai, 38 in the day that he commanded the children of Israel to offer their offerings to Jehovah, in the desert of Sinai.

CHAP. VIII.—And Jehovah spake to Moses, saying, 1 "Take Aaron, and his sons with him, and the garments, and 2 the anointing-oil, and the bullock for a sin-offering, and the two rams, and the basket of unleavened bread; and gather 3 thou all the congregation together to the door of the tent of meeting." And Moses did as Jehovah commanded him; 4 and the congregation was gathered together to the door of the tent of meeting. And Moses said to the congregation, 5 "This is what Jehovah hath commanded to be done." Then 6 Moses brought Aaron and his sons, and washed them with water. And he put upon him the tunic, and girded him 7 with the girdle, and clothed him with the robe, and put on him the ephod, and girded him with the curiously wrought girdle of the ephod, and with it bound it upon him. And 8 he put the breastplate upon him; and on the breastplate he put the Urim and the Thummim. And he put the mitre on 9 his head; and on the mitre, on his forehead, he put the golden petal, the holy crown, as Jehovah had commanded Moses. And Moses took the anointing-oil, and anointed the taber- 10 nacle, and all that was in it; so he sanctified them. And he 11 sprinkled some of *the oil* upon the altar seven times, and anointed the altar, and all its vessels, both the laver and its foot, to sanctify them. And he poured some of the anoint- 12 ing-oil upon the head of Aaron, and anointed him, in order to sanctify him. Moses also brought the sons of Aaron, and 13 clothed them with tunics, and girded them with girdles, and put turbans upon them, as Jehovah had commanded Moses. He then brought the bullock for the sin-offering; and Aaron 14 and his sons laid their hands upon the head of the bullock for the sin-offering. And he slew it; and Moses took the 15 blood, and put *some of* it upon the horns of the altar round about with his finger, and purified the altar, and poured *the rest of* the blood at the bottom of the altar, and sanctified

LEVITICUS VIII.

16 it, to make atonement for it. And he took all the fat that was upon the entrails, and the caul above the liver, and the two kidneys, and their fat, and Moses burned them upon the
17 altar. But the bullock and his skin, his flesh and his dung, he burnt with fire without the camp, as Jehovah had com-
18 manded Moses. He then brought the ram for the burnt-offering: and Aaron and his sons laid their hands upon the
19 head of the ram. And he slew it; and Moses sprinkled the
20 blood round about upon the altar. And he cut the ram in pieces, and Moses burnt the head, and the pieces, and the
21 fat. And he washed the entrails and the legs in water; and Moses burnt the whole ram upon the altar: it was a burnt-offering for an acceptable odour, an offering made by fire to
22 Jehovah, as Jehovah had commanded Moses. He then brought the other ram, the ram of consecration: and Aaron
23 and his sons laid their hands upon the ram. And he slew *it*; and Moses took some of the blood of it, and put it upon the tip of Aaron's right ear, and upon the thumb of his right
24 hand, and upon the great toe of his right foot. And he brought Aaron's sons, and Moses put some of the blood upon the tip of their right ear, and upon the thumbs of their right hands, and upon the great toes of their right feet; and Moses sprinkled *the rest of* the blood round about upon the altar.
25 And he took the fat, and the fat tail, and all the fat that was upon the entrails, and the caul above the liver, and the two
26 kidneys, and their fat, and the right shoulder; and out of the basket of unleavened bread, which was before Jehovah, he took one unleavened cake, and one cake of oiled bread, and one wafer, and put them upon the fat, and upon the
27 right shoulder; and he placed all in the hands of Aaron, and in the hands of his sons, and waved them *for* a wave-offer-
28 ing before Jehovah. Then Moses took them from their hands and burnt them on the altar upon the burnt-offering: they were consecration-*offerings* for an acceptable odour, an offer-
29 ing made by fire to Jehovah. And Moses took the breast, and waved it *for* a wave-offering before Jehovah; *for* of the ram of consecration it was the portion of Moses; as Jehovah
30 had commanded Moses. And Moses took some of the anointing-oil, and some of the blood which was upon the altar, and sprinkled it upon Aaron, and upon his garments, and upon his sons, and upon the garments of his sons with him, and sanctified Aaron, and his garments, and his sons, and
31 the garments of his sons with him. And Moses said to

Aaron, and to his sons, "Seethe the flesh at the door of the tent of meeting, and there eat it with the bread that is in the basket of consecration, as I commanded, saying, 'Aaron and his sons shall eat it.' And that which remaineth of the 32 flesh and of the bread ye shall burn with fire. And ye shall 33 not go from the door of the tent of meeting during seven days, until the days of your consecration be ended; for during seven days must ye be consecrated. According to what hath 34 been done this day, so Jehovah hath commanded to be done, to make an atonement for you. Therefore shall ye abide at 35 the door of the tent of meeting day and night, during seven days, and observe the ordinance of Jehovah, that ye die not; for so I am commanded." So Aaron and his sons did all 36 things which Jehovah had commanded by Moses.

CHAP. IX.—And on the eighth day, Moses called Aaron 1 and his sons, and the elders of Israel, and said to Aaron, 2 "Take thee a calf for a sin-offering, and a ram for a burnt-offering, without blemish, and offer them before Jehovah. And to the children of Israel thou shalt speak, saying, 3 'Take ye a kid of the goats for a sin-offering, and a calf, and a lamb, *both* of the first year, without blemish, for a burnt-offering; also a bullock and a ram for peace-offerings, 4 to be sacrificed before Jehovah, and a meal-offering mingled with oil: for to-day Jehovah will appear to you.'" And 5 they brought that which Moses commanded before the tent of meeting; and all the congregation drew near, and stood before Jehovah. And Moses said, "This is what Jehovah 6 hath commanded you to do, that the glory of Jehovah may appear to you." And Moses said to Aaron, "Go to the 7 altar, and offer thy sin-offering, and thy burnt-offering, and make an atonement for thyself and for the people: then offer the offering of the people, and make an atonement for them, as Jehovah hath commanded." Aaron therefore 8 went to the altar, and slew the calf of the sin-offering, which was for himself. And the sons of Aaron brought 9 the blood to him, and he dipped his finger in the blood, and put *some of* it upon the horns of the altar, and poured out *the rest of* the blood at the bottom of the altar. But the fat, and the kidneys, and the caul above the liver of 10 the sin-offering, he burnt upon the altar, as Jehovah had commanded Moses. And the flesh and the hide he burnt 11 with fire without the camp. Then he slew the burnt-offer- 12

ing, and the sons of Aaron presented to him the blood,
13 which he sprinkled round about upon the altar. And they presented the burnt-offering to him, with its pieces, and the
14 head; and he burnt these upon the altar. And he washed the entrails and the legs, and burnt them upon the burnt-
15 offering on the altar. And he brought the people's offering, and took the goat, which was the sin-offering for the people, and he slew it, and offered it for a sin-offering, as the first.
16 And he brought the burnt-offering, and offered it according
17 to the ordinance. And he brought the meal-offering, and took a handful from it, and burnt it upon the altar, together
18 with the burnt sacrifice of the morning. He slew also the bullock and the ram, *for* the sacrifice of peace-offerings, for the people; and the sons of Aaron presented to him the
19 blood, which he sprinkled round about upon the altar, and the fat of the bullock and of the ram, the fat tail, and that which covereth *the entrails*, and the kidneys, and the caul
20 above the liver; and they put the fat upon the breasts, and
21 burnt the fat upon the altar; and the breasts and the right shoulder Aaron waved *for* a wave-offering before Jehovah, as
22 Jehovah had commanded Moses. And Aaron lifted up his hands towards the people, and blessed them, and came down from offering the sin-offering, and the burnt-offering, and the peace-offerings.
23 And Moses and Aaron went into the tent of meeting, and when they had come out, and blessed the people, the
24 glory of Jehovah appeared to all the people. And fire came out from before Jehovah, and consumed upon the altar the burnt-offering and the fat; and all the people saw it, and shouted for joy, and fell on their faces.

1 CHAP. X.—And Nadab and Abihu, the sons of Aaron, took each his censer, and put in them fire, and on that placed incense, and offered strange fire before Jehovah, which he
2 had not commanded them *to offer*. And there went out fire from before Jehovah, and devoured them; and they died be-
3 fore Jehovah. Then Moses said to Aaron, "This is what Jehovah spake, saying, 'I will be sanctified by them who come nigh me, and before all the people I will be glorified.'"
4 And Aaron was silent. And Moses called to Mishael and to Elzaphan, the sons of Uzziel the uncle of Aaron, and said to them, "Come hither, carry your brethren from before the
5 sanctuary out of the camp." So they went near, and carried

them in their tunics out of the camp, as Moses had said.
And Moses said to Aaron, and to Eleazar and to Ithamar, 6
his sons, "Uncover not your heads, nor rend your clothes,
lest ye die, and lest wrath come upon all the people; but
let your brethren, the whole house of Israel, bewail the burning which Jehovah hath kindled. But ye shall not go out 7
from the door of the tabernacle of the congregation, lest ye
die; for the anointing-oil of Jehovah is upon you." And
they did according to the word of Moses.

And Jehovah spake to Aaron, saying, "Wine or strong 9
liquor neither thou nor thy sons shall drink, when ye are
going into the tent of meeting, lest ye die: this shall be a
perpetual statute throughout your generations; so that ye 10
may be able to distinguish between what is holy and what is
unholy, and between what is unclean and what is clean, and 11
to teach the children of Israel all the statutes which Jehovah
hath spoken to them by Moses."

And Moses said to Aaron, and to Eleazar and to Ithamar, 12
his remaining sons, "Take the meal-offering which remaineth
of the offerings of Jehovah made by fire, and eat it without
leaven beside the altar; for it is most holy. And ye shall 13
eat it in the holy place, because it is thy portion, and the
portion of thy sons, of the sacrifices of Jehovah made by
fire; for so I am commanded. And the wave-breast and 14
heave-shoulder ye may eat in a clean place, thou, and thy
sons, and thy daughters with thee; for they are thy portion,
and the portion of thy sons, *which* are given to you from
the sacrifice of peace-offerings of the children of Israel.
The heave-shoulder, and the wave-breast they shall bring, 15
together with the offerings of fat, made by fire, to wave as a
wave-offering before Jehovah; and it shall be thine, and thy
sons', by a perpetual statute, as Jehovah hath commanded."

And Moses diligently sought the goat of the sin-offering, 16
and, lo, it was burnt; and he was angry with Eleazar and
Ithamar, the remaining sons of Aaron, saying, "Why have 17
ye not eaten the sin-offering in the holy place, seeing it is
most holy, and *Jehovah* hath given it you that ye may bear
the iniquity of the congregation, that ye may make atonement for them before Jehovah? Lo, the blood of it was 18
not brought into the sanctuary: ye should indeed have eaten
it in the holy place, as I commanded." And Aaron said to 19
Moses, "Lo, this day have *my sons* offered their sin-offering
and their burnt-offering before Jehovah, and such things

have befallen me; and if I had eaten the sin-offering to-day,
20 would it have been pleasing in the sight of Jehovah?" And
when Moses heard that, he was satisfied.

1 CHAP. XI.—And Jehovah spake to Moses, and to Aaron,
2 saying to them, "Speak to the children of Israel, saying,
'These are the animals which ye may eat of all the beasts
3 that are on the earth. Every beast whose hoof is divided,
and whose foot is cloven into two parts, and which cheweth
4 the cud, ye may eat. But ye may not eat of those which
only chew the cud, or of those which only have a divided
hoof; *as* the camel, because he cheweth the cud, but hath
5 not the hoof divided; he shall be unclean to you. And the
cavy, because he cheweth the cud, but hath not the hoof di-
6 vided; he shall be unclean to you. And the hare, because
he cheweth the cud, but hath not the hoof divided; he shall
7 be unclean to you. And the swine, because he hath a divided
hoof, and is cloven-footed, yet cheweth not the cud, shall
8 be unclean to you. Of their flesh ye shall not eat, and their
carcase ye shall not touch: they shall be unclean to you.
9 These also may ye eat, of all that are in the waters: every
thing in the waters which hath fins and scales, in the seas,
10 or in the rivers, ye may eat. But of all that move in the
waters, and of every living thing which is in the waters, in
the seas, or in the rivers, every thing which hath not fins and
11 scales, shall be abominable to you. They shall be even
abominable to you; ye shall not eat of their flesh, and even
12 their carcases ye shall hold in abomination. Every thing in
the waters which hath not fins or scales, *shall be* abominable
to you.
13 And these among birds shall ye hold in abomination; they
shall not be eaten; they shall be abominable: the eagle,
14 and the ossifrage, and the osprey, and the vulture, and the
15 kite after his kind; every raven after his kind; and the
ostrich, and the techemes, and the falcon, and the hawk after
18 his kind, and the cus, and the cormorant, and the ibis, and
19 the swan, and the pelican, and the rechem, and the stork, the
heron after her kind, and the hoopoe, and the bat.
20 And every creeping thing with wings which goeth upon four
21 feet, shall be abominable to you. Yet of all creeping things
with wings which go upon four feet, ye may eat those which
have hinder legs jointed, for the purpose of leaping upon the
22 ground. These of them ye may eat; the arba-locust according

to its kind, and the solam-locust according to its kind, and the hargol-locust according to its kind, and the hagab-locust according to its kind. But all *other* creeping things with ²³ wings, which have four feet, shall be abominable to you.

And by these ye shall become unclean: whosoever touch- ²⁴ eth their carcase shall be unclean until the evening. And ²⁵ whosoever carrieth any part of their carcase, shall wash his clothes, and be unclean until the evening. All beasts whose ²⁶ hoof is divided, but whose foot is not cloven, and which cheweth not the cud, *are* unclean to you: every one that toucheth their carcases shall be unclean. And whatsoever ²⁷ goeth upon its paws, of all animals that go on four feet, those shall be unclean to you: whosoever toucheth their carcase shall be unclean until the evening. And he that ²⁸ carrieth their carcase shall wash his clothes, and be unclean until the evening: they shall be unclean to you.

These also shall be unclean to you among the creeping ²⁹ things that creep upon the earth: the mole, and the mouse, and the tzeb-lizard, according to its kind, and the gecko- ³⁰ lizard, and the warrel-lizard, and the lethaë-lizard, and the chemeth-lizard, and the chamæleon. These shall be unclean ³¹ to you among all creeping things: whosoever toucheth them, when they are dead, shall be unclean until the evening. And every thing upon which *any* of them, when dead, shall ³² fall, shall be unclean; whether it be any vessel of wood, or raiment, or skin, or sack: whatever vessel it be, that is employed in any use, it must be put into water, and it shall be unclean until the evening: so shall it be cleansed. And ³³ if any of them shall fall into any earthen vessel, whatsoever is in it shall be unclean; and ye shall break *the vessel*. Of all meat which may be eaten, that on which ³⁴ water *from such a vessel* cometh shall be unclean: and all drink that may be drunken out of every *such* vessel shall be unclean. And every vessel upon which *any part* ³⁵ of their carcase falleth shall be unclean; *whether* oven, or kettles, they shall be broken: they are unclean, and shall be unclean to you. Yet a fountain, or a pit, the receptacle ³⁶ of water, shall be clean: but he who toucheth the carcases of such shall be unclean. And if *any part* of their carcase ³⁷ fall upon any sowing seed which is to be sown, it shall be clean. But if water have been put upon the seed, and *any* ³⁸ *part* of their carcase fall upon it, it shall be unclean to you. And if any beast, of which ye may eat, die; he that touch- ³⁹

40 eth its carcase shall be unclean until the evening. And he that eateth of the carcase of it shall wash his clothes, and be unclean until the evening: he also that carrieth the carcase of it shall wash his clothes, and be unclean until the evening.
41 And every creeping thing that creepeth upon the earth
42 shall be abominable; it shall not be eaten. Whatsoever goeth upon the belly, and whatsoever goeth upon four feet, or whatsoever hath more feet among all creeping things that creep upon the earth, them ye shall not eat; for they are
43 abominable. Ye shall not make yourselves abominable with any creeping thing that creepeth, nor shall ye make yourselves unclean with them, that ye should be defiled thereby.
44 For I Jehovah am your God: ye shall therefore sanctify yourselves, and ye shall be holy; for I am holy: neither shall ye defile yourselves with any manner of creeping thing that
45 creepeth upon the earth. For I am Jehovah that bringeth you up out of the land of Egypt, to be your God: ye shall therefore be holy, for I am holy.
46 This is the law concerning beasts, and fowls, and every living creature that moveth in the waters, and every creature
47 that creepeth upon the earth; to make a distinction between the unclean and the clean, and between the animal that may be eaten and the animal that may not be eaten.'"

1 CHAP. XII.—And Jehovah spake to Moses, saying,
2 "Speak to the children of Israel, saying, 'If a woman have conceived, and borne a male-child, she shall be unclean seven days; as in the time of the impurity of her sickness
3 shall she be unclean. And on the eighth day the flesh of the
4 foreskin *of the child* shall be circumcised. And she shall then continue in the blood of her purification thirty-three days: she shall touch no holy thing, nor come into the sanctuary, until the days of her purification be completed.
5 But if she bear a female child, then she shall be unclean two weeks, as in her impurity; and she shall continue in the
6 blood of her purification sixty-six days. And when the days of her purification for a son, or for a daughter, are completed, she shall bring a lamb of the first year for a burnt-offering, and a young pigeon, or a turtle-dove, for a sin-offering, to the door of the tent of meeting, to the priest;
7 and he shall offer it before Jehovah, and make an atonement for her, and she shall be cleansed from the issue of her

N

blood. This is the law for her who hath borne a child, whether a male or a female. But if she cannot afford a 8 lamb, then she shall bring two turtle-doves or two young pigeons, the one for a burnt offering, and the other for a sin-offering; and the priest shall make an atonement for her, and she shall be clean.'"

CHAP. XIII.—And Jehovah spake to Moses and Aaron, 1 saying, "When a man shall have in the skin of his flesh a 2 pimple, a scurf, or a white spot, and it be in the skin of his flesh *like* the disease of leprosy; then he shall be brought to Aaron the priest, or to one of his sons, the priests; and the 3 priest shall look on the disease in the skin of the flesh. And if the hair in the diseased part be turned white, and the disease appear to be deeper than the skin of his flesh, it is the disease of leprosy; and the priest shall look on him and shall pronounce him unclean. But if the spot in the 4 skin of his flesh be white and appear not deeper than the skin, and the hair in it be not turned white; then the priest shall shut him up *that hath* the disease seven days; and 5 the priest shall look on him the seventh day; and, lo, *if* the disease appear to him to remain as it was, *if* the disease have not spread in the skin, then the priest shall shut him up seven days more: and the priest shall look on him again 6 the seventh day; and, lo, *if* the diseased part be grown faint, *and* the disease have not spread in the skin, the priest shall pronounce him clean; it is *but* a scurf: and he shall wash his clothes, and be clean. But if the scurf spread much 7 abroad in the skin, after he hath been seen by the priest for the purpose of being declared clean, he shall be seen by the priest again: and *if* the priest see that, lo, the scurf is 8 spreading in the skin, then the priest shall pronounce him unclean: it is leprosy. When the disease of leprosy is in 9 a man, and he is brought to the priest, and the priest 10 seeth that, lo, the pimple is white in the skin, and that the hair is turned white, and there is the mark of raw flesh in the pimple; it is an old leprosy in the skin of his flesh; 11 and the priest shall pronounce him unclean, and shall not shut him up; for he is unclean. But if the leprosy have 12 spread itself throughout the skin, so that the leprosy covers all the skin of the diseased person from his head even to his foot, wheresoever the priest looketh; and the priest see, 13 that, lo, the leprosy hath covered all his flesh, he shall pro-

LEVITICUS XIII.

nounce the diseased person clean : being all turned white,
14 he is clean. But whenever raw flesh appeareth in *the*
15 *diseased part,* he shall be unclean. And when the priest
seeth the raw flesh, he shall pronounce him to be unclean:
16 for the raw flesh is unclean: it is leprosy. Yet if the raw
flesh turn again, and be changed into white, he shall go to
17 the priest; and when the priest seeth him, and, lo, the dis‑
eased part is changed into white, then the priest shall pro‑
18 nounce the diseased person clean: he is clean. And if
there have been an ulcer in the skin, which has been healed,
19 but in the place of the ulcer there be a white pimple, or a
20 white and red spot, it shall be shewn to the priest; and if
the priest see that, lo, it appeareth deeper than the skin,
and the hair in it is turned white; the priest shall pro‑
nounce him unclean: it is the disease of leprosy broken out
21 of the ulcer. But if the priest look on it, and, lo, there
are no white hairs in it, and it is not deeper than the
skin, and it is faint, then the priest shall shut him up
22 seven days; and if it spread much abroad in the skin, then
the priest shall pronounce him unclean: it is the disease of
23 leprosy. But if the spot remain in its place, and spread not, it
is an inflamed ulcer; and the priest shall pronounce him clean.
24 Or if there have been a burning by fire in the skin, and
the mark of the burn have a spot, white and red, or white,
25 then the priest shall look upon it; and, lo, if the hair in the
spot be turned white, and it appear to be deeper than the
skin, it is a leprosy broken out of the burning: wherefore
the priest shall pronounce him unclean: it is the disease of
26 leprosy. But if when the priest looketh on it, lo, there be
no white hair in the spot, and it be no deeper than the skin,
and it be faint, then the priest shall shut him up seven days;
27 and the priest shall look upon him the seventh day; *and*
if it be spread much abroad in the skin, then the priest shall
28 pronounce him unclean; it is the disease of leprosy. But
if the white spot remain in its place, and spread not in the
skin, but be grown faint, it is a pimple of the burning, and
the priest shall pronounce him clean; for it is an inflam‑
mation of the burning.
29 If a man or woman have a disease on the head or the
30 beard, then the priest shall look upon the disease; and, lo,
if it appear deeper than the skin, and there be in it yellow
thin hair, then the priest shall pronounce him unclean: it is
31 a scall, a leprosy upon the head or beard. And when the

priest looketh on the disease of the scall, and, lo, it appeareth not deeper than the skin, and there is no black hair in it, then the priest shall shut up *him that hath* the disease seven days; and on the seventh day the priest shall 32 look on the diseased part; and, lo, *if* the scall appear not, and there be in it no yellow hair, and the scall appear not deeper than the skin, he shall be shaven, but the scall he 33 shall not shave; and the priest shall shut up *him that hath* the scall seven days more; and on the seventh day the priest 34 shall look on the scall; and, lo, *if* the scall be not spread in the skin, nor appear deeper than the skin, then the priest shall pronounce him clean; and he shall wash his clothes, and be clean. But if the scall spread much in the skin 35 after his cleansing, then the priest shall look on him: and, 36 lo, if the scall be spread in the skin, let not the priest seek for yellow hair; he is unclean. But if the scall appear to 37 him to remain as it was, and there be black hairs grown up in it, the scall is healed, he is clean; and the priest shall pronounce him clean.

If also a man or a woman have spots in the skin of their 38 flesh, white spots, then the priest shall look; and, lo, *if* the 39 spots in the skin of their flesh be of an obscure white, it is a dandriff, spreading in the skin; he is clean.

And the man whose hair is fallen off from his head *behind*, 40 he is bald, *but* he is clean. And he that hath his hair fallen 41 off from the part of his head toward his face, he is foreheadbald, but he is clean. But if there be in the bald head, or 42 bald forehead, a white and red sore, it is leprosy breaking forth in his bald head, or his bald forehead; then the priest 43 shall look upon it; and, lo, *if* the pimple of the sore be white and red in his bald head, or in his bald forehead, as the leprosy appeareth in the skin of the flesh, he is a leprous 44 man, he is unclean: the priest shall pronounce him utterly unclean; his disease *of leprosy* is in his head.

And the clothes of the leper, who hath the disease, shall 45 be rent, and his head bared, and he shall put a covering upon his chin, and shall cry, "Unclean, unclean." As long 46 as the disease is in him he shall be considered unclean; he is unclean: he shall dwell alone; without the camp shall be his habitation.

The garment also in which is the disease of leprosy, 47 *whether it be* a woollen garment or a linen garment, whether 48 *it be* in the warp or woof, of linen, or of woollen; whether

49 in a skin, or in any thing made of skin; if the diseased part be green or red in the garment, or in the skin, either in the warp or in the woof, or in any apparel made of skin; it is the disease of leprosy, and shall be shewn to the priest:
50 and the priest shall look upon the diseased place, and shut
51 up *that which hath* the disease seven days; and he shall look on the diseased place on the seventh day: if the disease be spread in the garment, either in the warp or in the woof, or in a skin, *or* in any thing made of skin, the disease is a
52 fretting leprosy; *the garment* is unclean. He shall therefore burn that garment, whether the disease be in the warp or in the woof, in woollen or in linen, or in any apparel made of skin: for it is a fretting leprosy; it shalt be burnt in the
53 fire. And if the priest look, and, lo, the disease be not spread in the garment, either in the warp or in the woof, or
54 in any apparel of skin; then the priest shall command that they wash *the thing* in which the disease is; and he shall
55 shut it up seven days more: and the priest shall look on the diseased place after it is washed: and, lo, *if* the disease have not changed its colour, and the disease be not spread, it is unclean: thou shalt burn it with fire; it is a corroding
56 *leprosy*, on the wrong or on the right side *of the cloth*. And if the priest look, and, lo, the diseased place is become faint after the washing of it, then he shall rend it out of the garment, or out of the skin, whether from the warp or from
57 the woof: and if it appear still in the garment, either in the warp or in the woof, or in any apparel of skin, it is a spreading *leprosy;* thou shalt burn that in which the disease
58 is with fire. And the garment, either warp or woof, or whatsoever apparel of skin it be which thou shalt wash, if the disease be departed from them, then it shall be washed a
59 second time, and shall be clean." This is the law concerning the disease of leprosy in a garment of woollen or linen, either in the warp or in the woof, or any apparel of skin, to pronounce it clean, or to pronounce it unclean.

1 CHAP. XIV.—And Jehovah spake to Moses, saying,
2 "This shall be the law for the leper in the day of his
3 cleansing: He shall be brought to the priest, and the priest shall go forth out of the camp, and the priest shall look, and,
4 lo, if the disease of leprosy be healed in the leper, then the priest shall command that there be taken for him who is to be cleansed two small birds alive *and* clean, and cedar-wood,

and scarlet *thread*, and hyssop; and the priest shall com- 5
mand that one of the birds be slain over spring water in an
earthen vessel. Then he shall take the living bird, and the cedar- 6
wood, and the scarlet *thread*, and the hyssop, and shall dip
them and the living bird in the blood of the bird which hath
been slain over the spring water; and he shall sprinkle upon 7
him who is to be cleansed from the leprosy seven times, and
shall pronounce him clean, and shall let the living bird loose
into the open field. Then he who is to be cleansed shall 8
wash his clothes, and shave off all his hair, and wash himself
in water, that he may be clean; and after that he shall come
into the camp; but he shall dwell without his tent seven
days. But on the seventh day, he shall shave all his hair 9
off his head, and his beard, and his eyebrows, even all his
hair he shall shave off: he shall then wash his clothes, and
bathe his body in water, and shall be clean. And on the 10
eighth day he shall take two male lambs without blemish,
and one ewe lamb of the first year without blemish, and
three-tenths *of an ephah* of fine flour for a meal-offering,
mingled with oil, and one log of oil. And the priest who 11
pronounceth him clean shall present the man who is to be
cleansed, and these things, before Jehovah, at the door of
the tent of meeting; and the priest shall take one male 12
lamb, and offer him for a trespass-offering, together with the
log of oil, and he shall wave them for a wave-offering before
Jehovah; and he shall slay the lamb in the place where the 13
sin-offering and the burnt-offering are slain, in the holy
place: for as the sin-offering is the priest's, so is the trespass-offering; it is most holy; and the priest shall take 14
some of the blood of the trespass-offering, and shall put it
upon the tip of the right ear of him who is to be cleansed,
and upon the thumb of his right hand, and upon the great
toe of his right foot. And the priest shall take some of the 15
log of oil, and pour it into the palm of his own left hand;
and the priest shall dip his right finger in the oil that is in 16
his left hand, and shall sprinkle some of the oil with his
finger, seven times before Jehovah; and some of the oil that 17
is in his hand shall the priest put upon the tip of the right
ear of him who is to be cleansed, and upon the thumb of his
right hand, and upon the great toe of his right foot, upon
the place of the blood of the trespass-offering: and the re- 18
mainder of the oil that is in the priest's hand he shall pour
upon the head of him who is to be cleansed; and the priest

19 shall thus make an atonement for him before Jehovah. And the priest shall offer the sin-offering, and make an atonement for him who is to be cleansed from his uncleanness; and
20 afterward he shall kill the burnt-offering. And the priest shall offer the burnt-offering, and the meal-offering, upon the altar: thus the priest shall make an atonement for him, and he shall be clean.
21 But if he be poor, and cannot afford so much; then he shall take one lamb for a trespass-offering to be waved, to make an atonement for him, and a tenth *of an ephah* of fine flour mingled with oil, for a meal-offering, and a log of oil;
22 and two turtle-doves, or two young pigeons, such as he can afford; and the one shall be a sin-offering, and the other
23 a burnt-offering. And he shall bring them on the eighth day, for his cleansing, to the priest, to the door of the
24 tent of meeting, before Jehovah; and the priest shall take the lamb for the trespass-offering, and the log of oil, and the priest shall wave them for a wave-offering before
25 Jehovah. And he shall slay the lamb for the trespass-offering, and the priest shall take some of the blood of the trespass-offering, and put it upon the tip of the right ear of him who is to be cleansed, and upon the thumb of his right hand, and upon the great toe of his right foot:
26 and the priest shall pour some of the oil into the palm of
27 his own left hand: and the priest shall sprinkle with his right finger some of the oil that is in his left hand, seven
28 times before Jehovah: and the priest shall put some of the oil that is in his hand upon the tip of the right ear of him that is to be cleansed, and upon the thumb of his right hand, and upon the great toe of his right foot, upon the place of
29 the blood of the trespass-offering; and the rest of the oil that is in the priest's hand he shall put upon the head of him who is to be cleansed, to make an atonement for him
30 before Jehovah. And he shall offer one of the turtle-doves,
31 or of the young pigeons, whichever he can afford; such as he can afford, *he shall offer*; the one *for* a sin-offering, and the other *for* a burnt-offering, with the meal-offering: thus the priest shall make an atonement for him who is to be
32 cleansed, before Jehovah." This is the law for him in whom is the disease of leprosy, who cannot afford *more* for his cleansing.
33 And Jehovah spake to Moses and to Aaron, saying,
34 "When ye come into the land of Canaan, which I give to

you for a possession, and I put the disease of leprosy in a house of the land of your possession; and the owner of the ³⁵ house shall go, and tell the priest, saying, 'It seemeth to me *there is* as it were a disease in the house;' then the priest ³⁶ shall command that they empty the house, before the priest go *into it* to see the diseased place, that all that is in the house be not made unclean; and afterward the priest shall go in to see the house. And he shall look on the diseased ³⁷ place, and, lo, if the disease be in the walls of the house, with hollow streaks, green or red, which appear deeper than the wall; then the priest shall go out of the house, to the ³⁸ door of the house, and shut up the house seven days; and ³⁹ the priest shall come again the seventh day, and shall look: and, lo, if the disease be spread in the walls of the house, the priest shall command that they take away the stones in ⁴⁰ which the disease is, and that they cast them into an unclean place without the city. He shall then cause the house to be ⁴¹ scraped within round about, and they shall pour out the dust that they scrape off without the city, into an unclean place; and they shall take other stones, and shall put them in the ⁴² place of those stones; and he shall take other mortar, and shall plaster the house. And if the disease return, and ⁴³ break out in the house, after he hath taken away the stones, and after he hath scraped the house, and after it hath been plastered; then the priest shall come and look, and, lo, if ⁴⁴ the disease be spread in the house, it is a fretting leprosy in the house: it is unclean. And he shall break down the ⁴⁵ house, the stones of it, and the timber of it, and all the mortar of the house; and he shall carry them forth out of the city, into an unclean place. Moreover he that goeth into ⁴⁶ the house, during all the time that it is shut up, shall be unclean until the evening. And he that lieth in the house ⁴⁷ shall wash his clothes; and he that eateth in the house shall wash his clothes. But if the priest come in, and look *upon* ⁴⁸ *it*, and, lo, the disease hath not spread in the house, after the house was plastered; then the priest shall pronounce the house clean, because the disease is healed. And he shall ⁴⁹ take to cleanse the house two small birds, and cedar-wood, and scarlet *thread*, and hyssop; and he shall kill one of the ⁵⁰ birds over spring water in an earthen vessel; and he shall ⁵¹ take the cedar-wood, and the hyssop, and the scarlet *thread*, and the living bird, and dip them in the blood of the slain bird, and in the spring water, and sprinkle the house seven

52 times; and he shall cleanse the house with the blood of the bird, and with the spring water, and with the living bird, and with the cedar-wood, and with the scarlet *thread*, and with
53 the hyssop; but he shall let go the living bird out of the city into the open field: thus he shall make an atonement for the house: and it shall be clean."
55 This is the law for every disease of leprosy, and scall, and
56 for the leprosy of a garment, and of a house, and for a pim-
57 ple, and for a scurf, and for a spot; to teach when it is unclean, and when it is clean: this is the law of leprosy.

1 CHAP. XV.—And Jehovah spake to Moses and to Aaron,
2 saying, "Speak to the children of Israel, and say to them, 'When any man hath an issue from his flesh, *because of* his
3 issue he is unclean. And this shall be his uncleanness in his issue: whether his flesh run with his issue, or his flesh be stopped from running with his issue, it is his uncleanness.
4 Every bed on which he who hath the issue lieth shall be unclean; and every thing on which he sitteth shall be unclean.
5 And whosoever toucheth his bed shall wash his clothes, and
6 bathe in water, and be unclean until the evening. And he that sitteth on *any* thing on which he who hath the issue hath sitten, shall wash his clothes, and bathe in water, and be unclean until
7 the evening. And he that toucheth the flesh of him who hath the issue shall wash his clothes, and bathe in water, and be
8 unclean until the evening. And if he who hath the issue spit upon him that is clean, *the latter* shall wash his clothes,
9 and bathe in water, and be unclean until the evening. And every thing on which he who hath the issue rideth shall be
10 unclean. And whosoever toucheth any thing that hath been under him shall be unclean until the evening: and he that carrieth *any of* those things shall wash his clothes, and bathe
11 in water, and be unclean until the evening. And every one whom he that hath the issue toucheth, not having thoroughly washed his hands in water, shall wash his clothes, and bathe
12 in water, and be unclean until the evening. And the earthen vessel which he who hath the issue toucheth shall be broken;
13 and every vessel of wood shall be rinsed in water. And when he who hath an issue is cleansed of his issue, then he shall reckon to himself seven days for his cleansing, and wash his clothes, and bathe his body in spring water, and be clean.
14 And on the eighth day he shall take two turtle-doves, or two young pigeons, and go before Jehovah to the door of the tent

of meeting, and give them to the priest; and the priest shall 15 offer them, the one for a sin-offering, and the other for a burnt-offering: thus the priest shall make an atonement for him before Jehovah for his issue. And if any man's seed go 16 out from him, then he shall bathe his body in water, and be unclean until the evening. And every garment, and every 17 skin, on which the seed is, shall be washed with water, and be unclean until the evening.

The woman also with whom a man shall carnally con- 18 verse, they shall both bathe in water, and be unclean until the evening.

And when a woman hath an issue, *and* her issue in her 19 flesh is blood, she shall be in her impurity seven days; and whosoever toucheth her shall be unclean until the evening. And every thing on which she lieth during her impurity 20 shall be unclean: every thing also on which she sitteth shall be unclean. And every one who toucheth her bed shall wash 21 his clothes, and bathe in water, and be unclean until the evening. And every one who toucheth any thing on which 22 she hath sitten, shall wash his clothes, and bathe in water, and be unclean until the evening. Whether it be her bed, 23 or any thing on which she sitteth, when he toucheth it, he shall be unclean until the evening. And if a man lie by her 24 at all, and her impurity be upon him, he shall be unclean seven days; and every bed on which he lieth shall be unclean. And when a woman hath an issue of her blood many 25 days out of the time of her impurity, or if it run beyond the time of her impurity; all the days of the issue of her uncleanness shall be as the days of her impurity: she shall be unclean. Every bed on which she lieth all the days of 26 her issue shall be to her as the bed of her impurity; and whatsoever she sitteth upon shall be unclean, as the uncleanness of her impurity. And whosoever toucheth those things 27 shall be unclean, and shall wash his clothes, and bathe in water, and be unclean until the evening. But when she is 28 cleansed of her issue, then she shall reckon to herself seven days, and after that she shall be clean. And on the eighth 29 day she shall take two turtle-doves, or two young pigeons, and bring them to the priest, to the door of the tent of meeting. And the priest shall offer one for a sin-offering, and the 30 other for a burnt-offering; thus the priest shall make an atonement for her before Jehovah for the issue of her uncleanness. Thus shall ye separate the children of Israel from 31

their uncleanness, that they die not in their uncleanness, when they defile my tabernacle that is among them.
32 This is the law for him who hath an issue, and whose seed
33 goeth from him, and who is defiled by it; and for her who is sick in her impurity, and for one who hath an issue, whether male or female, and for him who lieth by her who is unclean.'"

1 CHAP. XVI.—And Jehovah spake to Moses after the two sons of Aaron had died, when they had approached the
2 presence of Jehovah, and died; and Jehovah said to Moses, "Speak to Aaron thy brother, that he come not at all times into the sanctuary within the veil, before the lid which is upon the ark, that he die not: for I will appear in the cloud
3 upon the lid *of the ark*. Thus shall Aaron come into the sanctuary: with a young bullock for a sin-offering, and a
4 ram for a burnt-offering. And he shall put on the holy linen tunic, and he shall have the linen drawers upon his flesh, and he shall be girded with a linen girdle, and with the linen mitre shall he be attired: these are holy garments; therefore he shall bathe his body in water, and put them on.
5 He shall then receive from the congregation of the children of Israel two kids of the goats for a sin-offering, and one
6 ram for a burnt-offering. And Aaron shall bring his bullock of the sin-offering which is for himself, that he may make
7 an atonement for himself, and for his household. He shall then take the two goats, and present them before Jehovah at
8 the door of the tent of meeting. And Aaron shall cast lots upon the two goats, one lot for Jehovah, and the other lot
9 for the scape-goat. And Aaron shall bring the goat upon which the lot for Jehovah fell, and offer him for a sin-offer-
10 ing; but the goat, on which the lot fell to be the scape-goat, shall be presented alive before Jehovah, to make an atonement with him, to let him go for a scape-goat into the wil-
11 derness. And Aaron shall bring the bullock of the sin-offering which is for himself, and shall make an atonement for himself, and for his household, and shall kill the bullock
12 of the sin-offering which is for himself. And he shall take a censer full of burning coals of fire from off the altar before Jehovah, and his hands-full of sweet incense beaten small,
13 and bring it within the veil. And he shall put the incense upon the fire before Jehovah, that the cloud of the incense may cover the lid that is upon the testimonial-*ark*, that he
14 die not. And he shall take some of the blood of the bul-

lock, and sprinkle it with his finger upon the lid eastward; and before the lid shall he sprinkle some of the blood with his finger seven times. Then he shall kill the goat of the 15 sin-offering, which is for the people, and bring his blood within the veil, and do with that blood as he did with the blood of the bullock, sprinkling it upon the lid, and before the lid *of the ark*. Thus he shall make an atonement for 16 the sanctuary, because of the uncleanness of the children of Israel, and because of their transgressions in all their sins; and so shall he do for the tent of meeting that is placed among them in the midst of their uncleanness. And no 17 one shall be in the tent of meeting when he goeth in to make an atonement in the sanctuary, until he come out, and have made an atonement for himself, and for his household, and for all the congregation of Israel. Then he shall go out 18 to the altar that is before Jehovah, and make an atonement for it; and shall take some of the blood of the bullock, and some of the blood of the goat, and put it upon the horns of the altar round about. And he shall sprinkle some of the 19 blood upon it with his finger seven times, and cleanse it, and sanctify it from the uncleanness of the children of Israel. And when he hath made an end of atoning for the sanc- 20 tuary, and the tent of meeting, and the altar, he shall bring the live goat; and Aaron shall lay both his hands upon the 21 head of the live goat, and confess over him all the iniquities of the children of Israel, and all their transgressions in all their sins, and he shall put them upon the head of the goat, and send him away, by a man chosen for this purpose, into the desert. And the goat shall bear upon him all their 22 iniquities unto a land not inhabited; and he shall let go the goat in the desert. Then Aaron shall go into the tent of 23 meeting, and shall put off the linen garments which he had put on when he went into the sanctuary, and shall leave them there; and he shall bathe his body in water in the holy 24 place, and put on his garments, and come forth, and offer his burnt-offering, and the burnt-offering of the people, and make an atonement for himself, and for his household, and for the people. And the fat of the sin-offering he shall burn 25 upon the altar. And he that let go the goat for the scape- 26 goat shall wash his clothes, and bathe his body in water, and afterward come into the camp. And the bullock for the sin- 27 offering, and the goat for the sin-offering, the blood of which was brought into the sanctuary to made atonement, shall be

carried forth without the camp; and their skins, and their
28 flesh, and their dung, shall be burned with fire. And he
that burneth them shall wash his clothes, and bathe his body
in water, and afterward he shall come into the camp.
29 And this shall be a perpetual statute to you: In the
seventh month, on the tenth day of the month, ye shall
afflict yourselves, and ye shall do no work, neither a native
30 nor a stranger that sojourneth among you. For on that
day shall atonement be made for you, to cleanse you, that ye
31 may be clean from all your sins before Jehovah. It shall be
a sabbath of rest to you, and ye shall afflict yourselves, by a
32 perpetual statute. And the priest, who shall be anointed,
and who shall be consecrated to minister in the priest's office
in his father's stead, shall make the atonement and shall put
33 on the linen garments, the holy garments; and he shall
make an atonement for the holy sanctuary, and he shall
make an atonement for the tent of meeting, and for the
altar; and he shall make an atonement for the priests, and
34 for all the people of the congregation. And this shall be
a perpetual statute to you; that an atonement may be made
for the children of Israel, for all their sins, once a year."
And *Aaron* did as Jehovah commanded Moses.

1 CHAP. XVII.—And Jehovah spake to Moses, saying,
2 "Speak to Aaron, and to his sons, and to all the children of
Israel, and say to them, 'This is what Jehovah hath com-
3 manded, saying, Whosoever of the house of Israel shall
slay an ox, or a lamb, or a goat, in the camp, or shall slay it
4 out of the camp, and shall not bring it to the door of the
tent of meeting, to offer *it* an offering to Jehovah, before the
tabernacle of Jehovah, blood shall be imputed to that man;
he hath shed blood; and that man shall be cut off from
5 among his people; in order that the children of Israel may
bring their sacrifices, which they offer in the open field, even
that they may bring them to Jehovah, to the door of the
tent of meeting to the priest, and offer them for peace-offer-
6 ings to Jehovah. And the priest shall sprinkle the blood
upon the altar of Jehovah at the door of the tent of meeting; and burn the fat for an acceptable odour to Jehovah.
7 And they shall no more offer their sacrifices to demons, after
whom they have gone astray.' This shall be a perpetual
8 statute to them throughout their generations. And thou
shalt say to them, 'Whosoever of the house of Israel, or of

the strangers who sojourn among you, shall offer a burnt-offering or sacrifice, and not bring it to the door of the tent of meeting, to offer it to Jehovah, that man shall be cut off from among his people.

And whosoever of the house of Israel, or of the strangers that sojourn among you, shall eat any blood, I will even set my face against that soul who shall eat blood, and will cut him off from among his people. For the life of *the* flesh is in the blood; and I have appointed it to you for the altar, to make an atonement for your lives; for it is the blood that maketh an atonement for the life. Therefore I said to the children of Israel, No soul of you shall eat blood, nor shall any stranger that sojourneth among you eat blood. And whosoever of the children of Israel, or of the strangers that sojourn among you, shall hunt and catch any beast or fowl that may be eaten; he shall pour out its blood, and cover it with dust. For it is the life of all flesh; the blood of it is for its life: therefore I said to the children of Israel, Ye shall eat the blood of no flesh: for the life of all flesh is its blood; whosoever eateth it shall be cut off. And every one who eateth that which hath died *of itself,* or that which hath been torn *by beasts, whether it be* one of your own country, or a stranger, shall both wash his clothes, and bathe in water, and be unclean until the evening; then shall he be clean. But if he wash *them* not, nor bathe his body, then he shall bear his iniquity.'"

CHAP. XVIII.—And Jehovah spake to Moses, saying, "Speak to the children of Israel, and say to them, 'I am Jehovah your God. According to the doings of the land of Egypt, wherein ye dwelt, ye shall not do: and according to the doings of the land of Canaan, into which I bring you, ye shall not do; nor shall ye walk in their statutes. Ye shall do my judgments, and observe my statutes, to walk in them: I am Jehovah your God. Ye shall therefore observe my statutes and my judgments; which if a man do, he shall live by them: I am Jehovah.

No one of you shall approach to any near kinswoman, to uncover *her* nakedness: I am Jehovah. The nakedness of thy father, that is, the nakedness of thy mother, thou shalt not uncover: she is thy mother; thou shalt not uncover her nakedness. The nakedness of thy step-mother thou shalt not uncover: it is thy father's nakedness. The nakedness

of thy sister, the daughter of thy father, or the daughter of thy mother, *whether* born at home, or born abroad, their
10 nakedness thou shalt not uncover. The nakedness of thy son's daughter, or of thy daughter's daughter, their nakedness thou shalt not uncover: for it is thy own nakedness.
11 The nakedness of thy stepmother's daughter, begotten by thy father (she is thy sister), thou shalt not uncover her
12 nakedness. Thou shalt not uncover the nakedness of thy
13 father's sister: she is thy father's near kinswoman. Thou shall not uncover the nakedness of thy mother's sister: for
14 she is thy mother's near kinswoman. Thou shalt not uncover the nakedness of thy father's brother, thou shalt not
15 approach to his wife; she is thy aunt. Thou shalt not uncover the nakedness of thy daughter-in-law: she is thy
16 son's wife; thou shalt not uncover her nakedness. Thou shalt not uncover the nakedness of thy brother's wife; it is
17 thy brother's nakedness. Thou shalt not uncover the nakedness of a woman and her daughter, neither shalt thou take her son's daughter, or her daughter's daughter, to uncover her nakedness; they are her near kinswomen: it is
18 wickedness. Nor shalt thou take a wife to her sister, to cause her jealousy, to uncover her nakedness, besides the
19 other, in her life-time. Nor shalt thou approach a woman during the impurity of her uncleanness, to uncover her naked-
20 ness. And with thy neighbour's wife thou shalt not lie
21 carnally, to defile thyself with her. And thou shalt not cause any of thy offspring to pass through *the fire* to Molech, nor shalt thou profane the name of thy God: I am
22 Jehovah. Thou shalt not lie with mankind, as with
23 womankind: it is an abomination. Nor shalt thou lie with any beast, to defile thyself with it; nor shall any woman stand before a beast to lie down to it: it is confusion.
24 Defile not yourselves by any of these things: for by all these the nations are defiled which I cast out before you,
25 and the land is defiled: therefore I will visit its iniquity upon it, and the land itself shall vomit out her inhabitants.
26 Ye shall therefore observe my statutes and my judgments, and shall not commit any of these abominations; *neither* any of your own nation, nor any stranger that sojourneth among
27 you; (for all these abominations have the men of the land done, which were before you, so that the land is defiled;) that
28 the land vomit you not out also, when ye defile it, as it hath
29 vomited out the nations that were before you. For whoso-

ever shall commit any of these abominations, even the souls that commit them shall be cut off from among their people. Therefore ye shall observe my ordinances, so as not to commit 30 any of these abominable customs, which have been committed before you, and not to defile yourselves by them: I am Jehovah your God.'"

CHAP. XIX.—And Jehovah spake to Moses, saying, 1 "Speak to all the congregation of the children of Israel, and 2 say to them, 'Ye shall be holy: for I Jehovah your God am holy.

Every one of you shall revere his mother, and his father, 3 and keep my sabbaths: I am Jehovah your God.

Turn ye not to idols, nor make for yourself molten gods: 4 I am Jehovah your God.

And when ye sacrifice a sacrifice of peace-offerings to Je- 5 hovah, ye shall sacrifice it for your acceptance. It shall be 6 eaten on the same day in which ye sacrifice it; or on the morrow: and if any part remain until the third day, it shall be burnt with fire. And if it be eaten at all on the third 7 day, it is abominable; it shall not be accepted. And he who 8 eateth it shall bear his iniquity, because he hath profaned that which had been consecrated to Jehovah; that soul, therefore, shall be cut off from among his people.

And when ye reap the harvest of your land, thou shalt 9 not wholly reap the corners of thy field, neither shalt thou gather the gleanings of thy harvest. And thou shalt not 10 glean thy vineyard, neither shalt thou gather *every* grape of thy vineyard; thou shalt leave them for the poor and stranger: I am Jehovah your God.

Ye shall not steal, nor deal falsely, nor lie one to another. 11 And ye shall not swear by my name to a falsehood, and pro- 12 fane the name of thy God: I am Jehovah. Thou shalt not 13 oppress thy neighbour, nor rob *him;* nor shall the wages of a hired servant abide with thee all night until the morning.

Thou shalt not curse the deaf, nor put a stumbling- 14 block before the blind, but shalt fear thy God: I am Jehovah.

Ye shall do no injustice in judgment: thou shalt not 15 respect the person of the poor, nor honour the person of the mighty: in righteousness shalt thou judge thy neighbour.

Thou shalt not go about, a tale-bearer among thy people; 16 nor shalt thou stand up against the blood of thy neighbour:

17 I am Jehovah. Thou shalt not hate thy brother in thy heart: thou shalt freely reprove thy neighbour, and not 18 suffer sin upon him. Thou shalt not avenge, nor bear any malice against the children of thy people, but thou shalt 19 love thy neighbour as thyself: I am Jehovah. Ye shall keep my statutes.

Thou shalt not let thy cattle gender with a diverse kind: nor shalt thou sow thy field with mingled seed: nor shall a garment mingled of linen and woollen come upon thee.

20 And when a man lieth carnally with a woman who is a bond-maid, a concubine, but who hath not been redeemed, nor is free, scourging shall be *inflicted:* they shall not be 21 put to death, because she was not free. And *the man* shall bring his trespass-offering to Jehovah, to the door of the tent 22 of meeting, a ram for a trespass-offering. And the priest shall make an atonement for him with the ram of the trespass-offering, before Jehovah, for his sin which he hath committed; and the sin which he hath committed shall be forgiven him.

23 And when ye shall have come into the land, and shall have planted any kind of food-bearing trees, ye shall account its fruit a foreskin: three years shall it be as a foreskin to you; 24 it shall not be eaten. And in the fourth year all the fruit of 25 it shall be holy, *for* the praises of Jehovah. But in the fifth year ye may eat of the fruit of it, that it may yield to you its increase: I am Jehovah your God.

26 Ye shall not eat *any thing* with the blood; nor shall ye 27 use divination, or observe times.—Ye shall not round the corners of your heads, nor shalt thou mar the corners of 28 thy beard.—Ye shall not make any cuttings in your flesh for the dead, nor print any marks upon you: I am Jehovah.

29 Do not prostitute thy daughter, to cause her to be a harlot; lest the land fall to harlotry, and the land become full of wickedness.

30 Ye shall observe my sabbaths, and reverence my sanctuary; I am Jehovah.

31 Apply not to necromancers nor seek after wizards, to be defiled by them: I am Jehovah your God.

32 In the presence of the hoary head thou shalt rise up, and honour the face of the old man, and fear thy God: I am Jehovah.

33 And when a stranger sojourneth with thee in your land, 34 ye shall not vex him. As one born amongst you, shall be the stranger that dwelleth with you, and thou shalt love him

as thyself; for ye were strangers in the land of Egypt: I am Jehovah your God.

35 Ye shall do no injustice in judgment, in meting, in weight, or in measure. 36 Just balances, just weights, a just ephah, and a just hin, shall ye have.

37 I am Jehovah your God, who brought you out of the land of Egypt. Therefore ye shall observe all my statutes, and all my judgments, and do them: I am Jehovah.'"

CHAP. XX.—1 And Jehovah spake to Moses, saying, 2 "Again, thou shalt say to the children of Israel, 'Whoever of the children of Israel, or of the strangers who sojourn in Israel, shall give any of his seed to Molech, he shall surely be put to death; the people of the land shall stone him with stones. 3 And I will set my face against that man, and will cut him off from among his people; because he hath given of his seed to Molech, so as to defile my sanctuary, and to profane my holy name. 4 And if the people of the land do wilfully hide their eyes from the man, when he giveth of his seed to Molech, and put him not to death; 5 then I will set my face against that man, and against his family, and will cut him off, and all that go astray after him, to commit harlotry with Molech, from among their people. 6 And the person that shall apply to necromancers, and to wizards, to go astray after them, I will even set my face against that person, and will cut him off from among his people. 7 Sanctify yourselves, therefore, and be ye holy; for I am Jehovah your God. 8 And ye shall observe my statutes, and do them; I am Jehovah who sanctify you.

9 When any one curseth his father or his mother he shall surely be put to death: he hath cursed his father or his mother; his blood shall be upon him.

10 And if any man commit adultery with *another* man's wife, if any man commit adultery with his neighbour's wife, the adulterer and the adultress shall surely be put to death. 11 And if a man lie with his father's wife, he hath uncovered his father's nakedness: both of them shall surely be put to death; their blood shall be upon them. 12 And if a man lie with his daughter-in-law, both of them shall surely be put to death: they have wrought confusion; their blood shall be upon them. 13 If a man also lie with a male as he lieth with a woman, both of them have committed an abomination: they shall both surely be put to death; their blood

14 shall be upon them. And if a man take a wife and her mother, it is wickedness; they shall be burnt with fire, both he and they; that there be no wickedness among you.
15 And if a man lie with a beast, he shall surely be put to
16 death; and ye shall slay the beast. And if a woman approach any beast, and lie down to it, thou shalt kill the woman and the beast; they shall surely be put to death;
17 their blood shall be upon them. And if a man take his sister, his father's daughter, or his mother's daughter, and see her nakedness, and she see his nakedness, it is a wicked thing; and they shall both be cut off in the sight of their people: he hath uncovered his sister's nakedness; he shall
18 bear his iniquity. And if a man lie with a woman during her sickness, and uncover her nakedness, he hath discovered her fountain, and she hath uncovered the fountain of her blood; and both of them shall be cut off from among their
19 people. And thou shalt not uncover the nakedness of thy father's sister, nor of thy mother's sister; for it is uncovering the nakedness of a near kinswoman: they shall bear
20 their iniquity. And if a man lie with his uncle's wife, he hath uncovered his uncle's nakedness; they shall bear
21 their sin; they shall die childless. And if a man shall take his brother's wife, it is an unclean thing; he hath uncovered his brother's nakedness: they shall be childless.
22 Ye shall therefore observe all my statutes, and all my judgments, and do them; that the land, to which I am about to bring you that ye may dwell in it, vomit you not
23 out. And ye shall not walk in the statutes of the nations which I cast out before you; for they committed all these
24 things, and therefore I abhorred them. But I have said to you, Ye shall inherit their land, and I will give it to you to possess, a land that floweth with milk and honey: I am Jehovah your God, who have separated you from the peoples.
25 Ye shall therefore make a distinction between beasts clean and unclean, and between birds unclean and clean; and ye shall not make yourselves abominable by beast, or by fowl, or by any thing that creepeth on the ground, which I have
26 separated from you as unclean. But ye shall be holy to me; for I Jehovah am holy, and have distinguished you from the peoples, that ye should be mine.
27 A man also, or a woman, that is a necromancer, or that is a wizard, shall surely be put to death: they shall stone them with stones; their blood shall be upon them.'"

CHAP. XXI.—And Jehovah said to Moses, "Speak to 1 the priests, the sons of Aaron, and say to them, 'None *of you* shall be defiled for the dead among his people, except for 2 his near kindred, for his mother, and for his father, and for his son, and for his daughter, and for his brother, and for 3 his sister a virgin, who resideth with him, who hath no husband, for her he may be defiled. But he shall not defile himself *for* a chief among his people, to pollute himself. They 5 shall not make baldness upon their head; nor shall they shave off the corners of their beard, or make any cuttings in their flesh. They shall be holy to their God, and not 6 pollute the name of their God; for the offerings of Jehovah made by fire, the food of their God, they must offer; therefore they shall be holy. They shall not marry a woman 7 *who is* a harlot, or one polluted; nor shall they marry a woman divorced from her husband; for *every priest* is holy to his God. Thou shalt sanctify him therefore; for he 8 offereth the food of thy God : he shall be holy to thee; for I Jehovah, who sanctify you, am holy. And if the daugh- 9 ter of any priest pollute herself by harlotry, she polluteth her father: she shall be burnt with fire. And he who is 10 the high priest among his brethren, upon whose head the anointing-oil hath been poured, and who is consecrated to put on the garments, shall not uncover his head, or rend his garments; nor shall he go in to any dead body, or defile 11 himself for his father, or for his mother; nor shall he go 12 out of the sanctuary, or pollute the sanctuary of his God; for the crown *and* the anointing-oil of his God are upon him: I am Jehovah.—And he shall marry a woman in her 13 virginity. A widow, or a divorced woman, or one polluted, 14 or a harlot, he shall not marry; but he shall marry a virgin of his own people. So shall he not pollute his seed among 15 his people; for I Jehovah sanctify him.'"

And Jehovah spake to Moses, saying, "Speak to Aaron, 16 saying, 'Whosoever of thy seed in their generations shall have *any* blemish, let him not approach to offer the food of his God; for no one who hath a blemish shall approach : a 18 man blind, or lame, or maimed, or who hath any thing superfluous, or a man who is broken-footed, or broken- 19 handed, or crook-backed, or a dwarf, or who hath a blemish 20 in his eye, or hath scurvy, or is scabbed, or hath his testicles broken: no one of the seed of Aaron the priest 21 who hath a blemish shall come nigh to offer the offerings of

Jehovah made by fire: he hath a blemish; he shall not 22 come nigh to offer the food of his God. He may eat the food of his God, *both* of the most holy, and of the holy; 23 only he may not go in to the veil, nor come nigh to the altar, because he hath a blemish; that he profane not my 24 holy things; for I Jehovah sanctify them.'" And Moses told *this* to Aaron, and to his sons, and to all the children of Israel.

1 CHAP. XXII.—And Jehovah spake to Moses, saying, 2 "Speak to Aaron and to his sons, that they abstain from the holy things of the children of Israel, and that they pollute not my holy name *in those things* which they consecrate to 3 me: I am Jehovah. Say to them, 'Whosoever of all your seed, throughout your generations, shall approach the holy things which the children of Israel consecrate to Jehovah, having his uncleanness upon him, that soul shall be cut off 4 from my presence: I am Jehovah. Whosoever of the seed of Aaron is a leper, or hath a running issue, he shall not eat of the holy things until he be clean. And whosoever hath touched any thing *that hath been made* unclean by a dead 5 body; or whose seed hath gone from him; or who hath touched any creeping thing, by which he may be made unclean, or a man by whom he may be made unclean, whatso-6 ever uncleanness he may have; the soul who hath touched any such shall be unclean until evening, and shall not eat 7 of the holy things, unless he bathe his body in water. And when the sun is down he shall be clean, and may afterward eat of the holy things, because they are his food. 8 That which dieth of itself, or is torn *by beasts*, he shall not 9 eat, to defile himself with it: I am Jehovah. They shall therefore observe my ordinance, lest they bear sin and die for having profaned it: I Jehovah sanctify them.

10 Nor shall any stranger eat of that which is holy: a sojourner of the priest, or a hired servant, shall not eat of that 11 which is holy. But if the priest buy *any* soul with his money, he may eat of it, and he that is born in his house; 12 they may eat of his food. If the priest's daughter also be married to a stranger, she may not eat of an offering of the 13 holy things. But if the priest's daughter be a widow, or divorced, and have no child, and have returned to her father's house, as in her youth, she may eat of her father's food; but 14 no stranger shall eat of it. And if any one eat of that which is holy through error, then he shall add the fifth

part of *the whole* to it, and shall give it to the priest with that which is holy. Thus they shall not profane the holy things of the children of Israel, which they offer to Jehovah; or cause them to bear the iniquity of trespass, by eating their holy things; for I Jehovah sanctify them.'"

And Jehovah spake to Moses, saying, "Speak to Aaron, and to his sons, and to all the children of Israel, and say to them, 'Whosoever of the house of Israel, or of the strangers who sojourn in Israel, will offer his oblation for any vow, or for any free-will-offering, which they would offer to Jehovah for a burnt-offering, for your acceptance *it must be* a male without blemish, from the herd, from the sheep, or from the goats. Whatsoever hath a blemish, ye shall not offer; for it will not be acceptable for you. And whosoever offereth a sacrifice of peace-offerings to Jehovah to accomplish a vow, or a free-will-offering from the herd or from the flock, it must be perfect, to be accepted; no blemish must be in it. Blind, or broken, or maimed, or having the rot, or having scurvy, or being scabbed, ye shall not offer these to Jehovah, nor make an offering by fire of them upon the altar to Jehovah. Either a bullock or a lamb that hath any thing superfluous or deficient in his parts, thou mayest offer *for* a free-will-offering; but for a vow it will not be accepted. But that which hath had its testicles torn out, bruised, or crushed, or cut out, ye shall not offer to Jehovah; nor shall ye make such in your land. Nor from the hand of an alien shall ye offer the food of your God of any of these: because their corruption is in them, blemishes are in them; they will not be accepted for you.'"

And Jehovah spake to Moses, saying, "When a calf, or a lamb, or a kid is brought forth, it shall be seven days under the dam; but on the eighth day, and thenceforth, it shall be accepted for an offering made by fire to Jehovah. And neither cow nor ewe shall ye slay on the same day with her young. And when ye offer a sacrifice of thanksgiving to Jehovah, if ye would offer it for your acceptance, it must be eaten on the same day; ye shall leave none of it until the morrow: I am Jehovah. Thus shall ye observe my commandments, and do them: I am Jehovah. And ye shall not profane my holy name; but I will be sanctified amongst the children of Israel: I am Jehovah who sanctify you, who brought you out of the land of Egypt, to be your God: I am Jehovah."

1 CHAP. XXIII.—And Jehovah spake to Moses, saying,
2 "Speak to the children of Israel, and say to them, 'The feasts of Jehovah, which ye shall proclaim to be holy convo-
3 cations, these are my feasts. Six days may work be done; but the seventh day is the sabbath of rest, a holy convocation; *on it* ye shall do no work: it is the sabbath of Jehovah in
4 all your dwellings. These are also the feasts of Jehovah, holy convocations, which ye shall proclaim in their seasons.
5 On the fourteenth day of the first month in the evening, is
6 the passover of Jehovah. And on the fifteenth day of the same month, is the feast of unleavened bread to Jehovah:
7 seven days ye shall eat unleavened bread. On the first day ye shall have a holy convocation: *on it* ye shall do no servile
8 work. But ye shall offer an offering made by fire to Jehovah seven days: on the seventh day shall be a holy convocation; *on it* ye shall do no servile work.'"
9 And Jehovah spake to Moses, saying, "Speak to the children of Israel, and say to them, 'When ye come into the land which I give to you, and shall reap its harvest, then ye shall bring a sheaf of the first-fruits of your harvest to the
11 priest; and he shall wave the sheaf before Jehovah for your acceptance: on the morrow after the sabbath the priest shall
12 wave it. And on the day in which ye wave the sheaf, ye shall offer a male-lamb without blemish of the first year, for
13 a burnt-offering to Jehovah. With its meal-offering of two-tenths *of an ephah* of fine flour mingled with oil, an offering made by fire to Jehovah, an acceptable odour; and its drink-
14 offering of wine, the fourth *part* of a hin. And ye shall eat neither bread, nor parched corn, nor full *ripe* ears, until the very day in which ye bring an offering to your God: this shall be a perpetual statute throughout your generations, in all your dwellings.
15 And ye shall reckon from the morrow after the sabbath, from the day on which ye brought the sheaf of the wave-
16 offering, seven complete weeks: to the morrow after the seventh sabbath ye shall number fifty days; when ye shall
17 offer a new meal-offering to Jehovah. Ye shall bring from your dwellings two wave-loaves, of two tenths *of an ephah:* they shall be of fine flour: they shall be baked with leaven:
18 they are the first-fruits to Jehovah. And ye shall offer with the loaves seven lambs without blemish, of the first year, and one young bullock, and two rams: they shall be *for* a burnt-offering to Jehovah, with their meal-offering, and their

drink-offerings, an offering made by fire, an acceptable odour to Jehovah. Ye shall then sacrifice one kid of the goats for a sin-offering, and two lambs of the first year for a sacrifice of peace-offerings. And the priest shall wave them with the loaves of the first-fruits, a wave-offering before Jehovah, with the two lambs: they shall be holy to Jehovah for the priest. And ye shall proclaim on that very day, a holy convocation; *on it* ye shall do no servile work: this shall be a perpetual statute in all your dwellings, throughout your generations.

And when ye reap the harvest of your land, thou shalt not completely reap the corners of the field, nor shalt thou gather any gleanings of thy harvest; thou shalt leave them to the poor, and to the stranger: I am Jehovah your God.'"

And Jehovah spake to Moses, saying, "Speak to the children of Israel, saying, 'In the seventh month, on the first day of the month, ye shall have a sabbath, a memorial of blowing of trumpets, a holy convocation: *on it* ye shall do no servile work; but ye shall offer an offering made by fire to Jehovah.'"

And Jehovah spake to Moses, saying, "Moreover the tenth day of this seventh month shall be a day of atonement: it shall be a holy convocation to you, and ye shall afflict your souls, and offer an offering made by fire to Jehovah. And ye shall do no work on that same day; for it is a day of atonement, to make an atonement for you before Jehovah your God. For every soul who shall not be afflicted on that same day, shall be cut off from among his people. And every soul who doeth any work on that same day, that soul I will destroy from among his people. Therefore ye shall do no manner of work *on it :* this shall be a perpetual statute throughout your generations, in all your dwellings. It shall be to you a sabbath of rest, and ye shall afflict your souls: on the ninth day of the month in the evening, from evening until evening, ye shall celebrate your sabbath."

And Jehovah spake to Moses, saying, "Speak to the children of Israel, saying, 'The fifteenth day of this seventh month shall be the feast of tabernacles *to be kept during* seven days to Jehovah. On the first day shall be a holy convocation; on it ye shall do no servile work. Seven days ye shall offer an offering made by fire to Jehovah: on the eighth day shall be a holy convocation to you, and ye shall

offer an offering made by fire to Jehovah: it is a solemn
37 assembly: *on it* ye shall do no manner of work. These
are the feasts of Jehovah, which ye shall proclaim to be holy
convocations, to offer an offering made by fire to Jehovah, a
burnt-offering, and a meal-offering, a sacrifice, and drink-
38 offerings, each on its proper day; beside the sabbaths of
Jehovah, and beside your gifts, and beside all your vows, and
beside all your free-will-offerings, which ye give to Jehovah.
39 Also on the fifteenth day of the seventh month, when ye
have gathered in the fruit of the land, ye shall keep a feast
to Jehovah during seven days: on the first day shall be a
40 sabbath, and on the eighth day shall be a sabbath. And ye
shall take on the first day the shoots of beautiful trees,
branches of palm-trees, and the boughs of thick-leaved trees,
and willows of the brook; and ye shall rejoice before Jehovah
41 your God seven days. And ye shall keep it a feast to
Jehovah seven days in the year: *this shall be* a perpetual
statute in your generations: ye shall celebrate it in the
42 seventh month. Ye shall dwell in booths seven days: all
43 Israelites born shall dwell in booths; that your generations
may know that I made the children of Israel to dwell in
booths, when I brought them out of the land of Egypt: I
am Jehovah your God.'"
44 And Moses declared to the children of Israel the feasts
of Jehovah.

1 CHAP. XXIV.—And Jehovah spake to Moses, saying,
2 "Command the children of Israel, that they bring to thee
pure olive-oil, beaten, for the light, to cause the lamp to burn
3 continually. Without the veil of the testimonial-*ark* in the
tent of meeting, shall Aaron order it from the evening until
the morning, before Jehovah continually: *this shall be* a per-
4 petual statute in your generations. He shall order the lamps
5 upon the pure lamp-stand before Jehovah continually. And
thou shalt take fine flour, and bake of it twelve cakes: two
6 tenths *of an ephah* shall be in one cake. And thou shalt
set them in two piles, six in a pile, upon the pure table
7 before Jehovah. And thou shalt put pure frankincense upon
each pile, that it may be on the bread for a memorial, an
8 offering made by fire to Jehovah. Every sabbath he shall
set it in order before Jehovah continually, *being taken* from
9 the children of Israel by an everlasting covenant. And it
shall be for Aaron and for his sons; and they shall eat it in

the holy place: for it belongs to him, by a perpetual statute, as most holy of the offerings of Jehovah made by fire."

10 Now the son of an Israelitish woman, whose father was an Egyptian, had come out among the children of Israel; and 11 this son of the Israelitish woman and a man of Israel strove together in the camp; and the son of the Israelitish woman blasphemed the name *of Jehovah*, and cursed. And they 12 brought him to Moses. Now his mother's name was Shelomith, the daughter of Dibri, of the tribe of Dan; and they put him in custody, until the will of Jehovah should be made 13 known to them. And Jehovah spake to Moses, saying, 14 "Take forth him who hath cursed without the camp; and let all that heard him lay their hands upon his head, and let 15 all the congregation stone him. And thou shalt speak to the children of Israel, saying, 'Whosoever curseth his God shall 16 bear his sin. And he who blasphemeth the name of Jehovah, shall surely be put to death; all the congregation shall certainly stone him: the stranger as well as the native, when he blasphemeth the name *of Jehovah*, shall be put to death.

17 And he who killeth any man shall surely be put to death. 18 But he who killeth a beast shall make restitution; beast for 19 beast. And if a man cause a blemish in his neighbour, as 20 he hath done, so shall it be done to him; breach for breach, eye for eye, tooth for tooth; as he hath caused a blemish in 21 a man, so shall it be caused in him. And he who killeth a beast, shall make restitution: but he who killeth a man, 22 shall be put to death. Ye shall have one manner of law, as well for the stranger as for one of your own country: for I 23 am Jehovah your God.'"—Then Moses ordered the children of Israel to bring forth him who had cursed out of the camp, and to stone him with stones. And the children of Israel did as Jehovah had commanded Moses.

CHAP. XXV.—And Jehovah spake to Moses in mount 1 Sinai, saying, "Speak to the children of Israel, and say to 2 them, 'When ye shall have come into the land which I give to you, the land shall keep a sabbath to Jehovah. Six years 3 thou shalt sow thy field, and six years thou shalt prune thy vineyard, and gather in its produce; but in the seventh year 4 the land shall have a sabbath of rest, a sabbath to Jehovah: thy field thou shalt not sow, and thy vineyard thou shalt not prune. The crop from the scattered seeds of thy *former* 5

harvest thou shalt not reap, nor gather the grapes of thy
6 unpruned vine: it is a year of rest to the land. But *that
which groweth during* the sabbath of the land shall be food
for you; for thee, and for thy man-servant, and for thy maid-
servant, and for thy hired servant, and for the stranger who
7 sojourneth with thee, and for thy cattle, and for the wild
beasts which are in thy land, shall all its produce be food.

8 And thou shalt reckon seven sabbaths of years, seven times
seven years; so that the space of the seven sabbaths of years
9 shall be to thee forty-nine years. Then thou shalt cause the
trumpet of the jubilee to be sounded, on the tenth day of
the seventh month: on the day of atonement shall ye cause
10 the trumpet to be sounded throughout all your land. And
ye shall sanctify the fiftieth year, and proclaim liberty throughout the land to all its inhabitants: it shall be a jubilee to
you; and ye shall return every man to his possession, and ye
11 shall return every man to his family. A jubilee shall that
fiftieth year be to you, in which ye shall not sow, nor reap
the crop from the scattered seed, nor gather in it *the grapes
12 of thy unpruned vine.* For it is the jubilee; it shall be
holy to you: from the field ye shall eat the produce *of the
year.*

13 In this year of jubilee ye shall return every man to his pos-
14 session. And if thou sell any *possession* to thy neighbour, or
buy *any* of thy neighbour, ye shall not oppress one another:
15 according to the number of years after the jubilee thou shalt
buy of thy neighbour, *and* according to the number of years
16 of the produce he shall sell to thee: as the years be many
thou shalt increase the price, and as the years be few thou
shalt diminish the price: for *according* to the number of its
17 crops he shall sell to thee. Ye shall not therefore oppress
one another; but thou shalt fear thy God: for I am Jehovah
18 your God. Wherefore ye shall do my statutes, and keep my
judgments, and do them; that ye may dwell in the land in
19 security. And the land shall yield her fruit, and ye shall eat
your fill, and dwell therein in security.
20 And if ye shall say, What shall we eat in the seventh
21 year? lo, we shall not sow, nor gather in our produce! Then
I will command my blessing upon you in the sixth year, and it
22 shall bring forth fruit for three years. And ye may sow in
the eighth year, but eat of the old produce until the ninth
year; until the produce *of the eighth year* come in ye shall
eat *of* the old.

The land shall not be sold for ever: for the land is mine; 23
for ye are strangers and sojourners with me. Therefore 24
throughout the land of your possession ye shall allow the
land to be redeemed. And if thy brother have become poor, 25
and have sold *some part* of his possession, and if his nearest
relation come to redeem it, then may he redeem that which
his kinsman had sold. And if the man have none to redeem 26
it, but acquire himself sufficient to redeem it; then let him 27
count the years of its sale, and return the overplus to the
man to whom he had sold it, that he may return to his possession. But if he be not able to return *the overplus* to him, 28
then that which hath been sold shall remain in the hand of
him who hath bought it until the year of jubilee; and in
the jubilee it shall be quitted, and *the owner* shall return to
his possession.

And if a man sell a dwelling-house in a walled city, then 29
he may redeem it within the space of a full year after it hath
been sold; *within* a full year may he redeem it. But if it 30
be not redeemed within the space of a full year, then the
house that is in the walled city shall be established for ever
to him who bought it, throughout his generations: it shall
not be quitted at the jubilee. But the houses of villages 31
which have no walls round about them shall be accounted as
the fields of the country; they may be redeemed, and they
shall be quitted at the jubilee. As to the cities of the Le- 32
vites, the Levites may redeem, at any time, the houses of the
cities of their possession. And if he who hath redeemed *it* 33
be a Levite, he shall quit the house which he hath bought
in the city of his possession, at the jubilee; for the houses
of the cities of the Levites are their possession among the
children of Israel. But the field of the suburbs of their 34
cities may not be sold; for it is their perpetual possession.

And if thy brother have become poor, and fallen into 35
decay with thee, then thou shalt succour him; *as* a stranger,
or a sojourner, he shall live with thee. Take thou no usury 36
of him, or produce: but fear thy God; that thy brother may
live with thee. Thy money thou shalt not give to him for 37
usury, nor for produce shalt thou give to him thy victuals.
I am Jehovah your God, who brought you forth out of the 38
land of Egypt, to give to you the land of Canaan, *and* to be
your God. And when thy brother who is with thee hath 39
become poor, and been sold to thee, thou shalt not compel
him to serve as a bond-servant: as a hired servant, as 40

LEVITICUS XXV.

a sojourner, he shall be with thee; until the year of jubilee
41 he shall serve thee: then he shall depart from thee, he and his children with him, and shall return to his own family, and to the possession of his fathers he shall return.
42 For they are my servants, whom I brought forth out of the land of Egypt: they shall not be sold as bondmen.
43 Thou shalt not rule over him with rigour, but shalt fear
44 thy God. Both thy bondmen and thy bondmaidens, whom thou shalt have, shall be of the nations that are round about you; of them ye may buy bondmen and bondmaidens.
45 And of the children of the strangers also who sojourn among you, of them ye may buy, and of their families that are with you, which they may have begotten in your
46 land; and they shall be your possession. And ye may leave these as an inheritance to your children after you, a perpetual possession; these may be your bondmen: but over your brethren, the children of Israel, ye shall not rule one over another with rigour.
47 And if a sojourner or stranger become rich by thee, and thy brother *who dwelleth* by him become poor, and sell himself to the stranger or sojourner by thee, or to one sprung
48 from a stranger's family, after he is sold he may be redeemed
49 again; one of his brethren may redeem him: either his uncle, or his uncle's son, may redeem him, or any near kinsman of his family may redeem him; or, if he be able, he
50 may redeem himself. And he shall reckon with him who bought him, from the year that he was sold to him to the year of jubilee; and the price of his sale shall be according to the number of years; according to the time of a hired ser-
51 vant shall it be with him. If there be yet many years *remaining*, according to them he shall give again the price of his redemption out of the money for which he had been bought.
52 And if there remain but few years to the year of jubilee, then he shall reckon with him, *and* according to his years
53 shall he give to him again the price of his redemption. As a yearly hired servant may he be with him: *and the other*
54 shall not rule with rigour over him in thy sight. But if he be not redeemed in these *years*, then he shall go out in the
55 year of jubilee, he, and his children with him. For the children of Israel are my servants; they are my servants, whom I brought out of the land of Egypt: I am Jehovah your God.

CHAP. XXVI.—Ye shall not make for yourselves idols ¹ nor a graven image, nor shall ye raise up for yourselves a statue, nor shall ye place in your land a stone inscribed with figures, to bow down at it: for I am Jehovah your God. Ye shall keep my sabbaths, and reverence my sanctuary: I am Jehovah. ²

If ye walk in my statutes, and observe my commandments, and do them; then I will give you rain in due season, ⁴ and the land shall yield its produce, and the trees of the field shall yield their fruit. And your threshing shall reach ⁵ to the vintage, and the vintage shall reach to the seed time; and ye shall eat your bread to the full, and dwell in your land securely. And I will give peace in the land, and ye ⁶ shall lie down, and none shall make *you* afraid; and I will drive away wild beasts out of the land, and the sword shall not pass through your land. And ye shall pursue your ⁷ enemies, and they shall fall before you by the sword. And ⁸ five of you shall pursue a hundred, and a hundred of you shall pursue ten thousand: thus shall your enemies fall before you by the sword. For I will be favourable to you, ⁹ and make you fruitful, and multiply you, and establish my covenant with you. And ye shall eat old store, and bring ¹⁰ forth the old to make room for the new. And I will set my ¹¹ tabernacle amongst you: and I will not abhor you; but I ¹² will walk among you, and will be your God, and ye shall be my people. I am Jehovah your God, who brought you forth ¹³ out of the land of Egypt, that ye should not be their bondmen; and I have broken the bands of your yoke, and made you to walk upright.

But if ye will not hearken to me, and will not do all ¹⁴ these commandments; and if ye despise my statutes, ¹⁵ and if ye abhor my judgments, so as not to do all my commandments, *but* to break my covenant, I also will ¹⁶ do this to you; I will even appoint over you terror, consumption, and fever which shall consume the eyes, and cause sorrow of heart: and in vain shall ye sow your seed, for your enemies shall eat it. And I will set my face ¹⁷ against you, and ye shall be slain before your enemies: they who hate you shall reign over you; and ye shall flee when no one pursueth you. And if for all this ye will not yet ¹⁸ hearken to me, then I will punish you seven times more for your sins, and I will break the pride of your stubbornness; ¹⁹

and I will make your heavens as iron, and your earth as
20 brass. And your strength shall be spent in vain : for your
land shall not yield its produce, nor shall the trees of the
21 field yield their fruits. And if ye still walk contrary to me,
and will not hearken to me, I will bring seven times more
22 plagues upon you, according to your sins. For I will send
wild beasts among you, which shall rob you of your children, and destroy your cattle, and make you few in number,
so that your high-ways shall be desolate.
23 And if by these things ye will not be reclaimed, but will
24 walk contrary to me; then will I also walk contrary to you,
25 and will punish you yet seven-fold for your sins. For I will
bring a sword upon you, that shall avenge the cause of *my*
covenant : and, when ye are gathered together within your
cities, I will send the pestilence among you; and ye shall be
26 delivered into the hand of the enemy, while I break under
you the staff of your bread, so that ten women shall bake
your bread in one oven, and shall return *to you* your bread
27 by weight; which ye shall eat, and not be satisfied. And if
for all this ye will not hearken to me, but will walk contrary
28 to me; then I will walk contrary to you also, in fury; and
29 I, even I, will chastise you seven-fold for your sins. And
ye shall eat the flesh of your sons, and the flesh of your
30 daughters ye shall eat. And I will destroy your high places,
and cut down your solar-images, and cast your carcases upon
31 the carcases of your idols, and I will abhor you. And I
will make your cities waste, and bring your sanctuary to
desolation, and I will not smell the savour of your acceptable
32 odours. And I will make the land desolate; so that your
33 enemies who dwell in it shall be astonished. And I will
scatter you among the nations, and will draw out a sword
after you; and your land shall be desolate, and your cities
34 shall be waste. Then shall the land enjoy its sabbaths, as
long as it lieth desolate, and ye are in the land of your
enemies; then shall the land rest, and enjoy its sabbaths.
35 As long as it lieth desolate it shall rest; because it did not
36 rest in your sabbaths, when ye dwelt upon it. And as to
those of you who shall remain I will send such a faintness
into their hearts in the lands of their enemies, that the
sound of a shaking leaf shall put them to flight; and they
shall flee, as if fleeing from a sword; and they shall fall
37 when no one pursueth. And they shall stumble one over
another, as it were before a sword, when no one pursueth:

and ye shall have no power to stand before your enemies. And ye shall perish among the nations, and the land of your 38 enemies shall consume you. And those of you who remain 39 shall pine away in their iniquity in the lands of their enemies; and in the iniquities of their fathers also shall they pine away.

If they shall confess their iniquity, and the iniquity of their 40 fathers, in their transgression which they have committed against me, and also that they have walked contrary to me (for which cause I also have walked contrary to them, and 41 have brought them into the land of their enemies); if then their uncircumcised hearts shall be humbled, and they shall accept of the punishment of their iniquity; then will I re- 42 member my covenant with Jacob, and also my covenant with Isaac, and also my covenant with Abraham will I remember; and I will remember the land. For the land shall be left by 43 them, and shall enjoy its sabbaths, while it lieth desolate without them; and they shall accept the punishment of their iniquity; because, even because they despised my judgments, and because their soul abhorred my statutes. And 44 yet notwithstanding that, when they are in the land of their enemies, I will not cast them away, neither will I abhor them, to destroy them utterly, and to break my covenant with them: for I am Jehovah their God. But I will for 45 their sakes remember the covenant of their ancestors, whom I brought forth out of the land of Egypt in the sight of the nations, that I might be their God: I am Jehovah.'"

These *are* the statutes and judgments and laws which 46 Jehovah made between him and the children of Israel on mount Sinai, by Moses.

CHAP. XXVII.—And Jehovah spake to Moses, saying, 1 "Speak to the children of Israel, and say to them, 'When 2 any one will make a personal vow, thy valuation of persons shall be for Jehovah. And thy valuation shall be, of a male 3 from twenty years old to sixty years old, *of such* thy valuation shall be fifty shekels of silver, according to the shekel of the sanctuary. But if it be a female, then thy valuation 4 shall be thirty shekels. And if it be from five years old to 5 twenty years old, then thy valuation shall be for a male twenty shekels, and for a female ten shekels. And if it be 6 from a month old to five years old, then thy valuation for a male shall be five shekels of silver, and for a female thy

7 valuation shall be three shekels of silver. And if it be from sixty years old and above; if it be a male, then thy valuation shall be fifteen shekels, and for a female ten 8 shekels. But if he be too poor for thy valuation, then he shall present himself before the priest, and the priest shall value him; according to the ability of him who made the vow shall the priest value him.

9 And if *any one vow* a beast, of a kind of which an offering is brought to Jehovah, all that *any one* giveth of such 10 to Jehovah shall be holy. He shall not alter it, or change it, a good for a bad, or a bad for a good: but if he shall at all change beast for beast, then it and that for which it hath 11 been changed shall be holy. And if *it be* any unclean beast, of which an offering is not brought to Jehovah, then 12 he shall present the beast before the priest, and the priest shall value it, whether it be good or bad: as thou the 13 priest valuest it, so shall it be. But if he will indeed redeem it, then he shall add a fifth part to thy valuation.

14 And if any one will sanctify his house, to be holy to Jehovah, then the priest shall value it, whether it be good or 15 bad: as the priest shall value it, so shall it stand. But if he that sanctified it will redeem his house, then he shall add the fifth *part* of the money of thy valuation to it, and it shall be his.

16 And if any one will sanctify to Jehovah *some part* of a field of his possession, then thy valuation shall be according to its seed: a homer of barley seed *being valued* at fifty 17 shekels of silver. And if he sanctify his field from the year of jubilee, according to thy valuation it shall stand. 18 But if he sanctify his field after the jubilee, then the priest shall reckon to him the money according to the years that remain, to the year of the jubilee, and there shall be an 19 abatement in thy valuation. And if he who sanctified the field will indeed redeem it, then he shall add the fifth *part* of the money of thy valuation to it, and it shall be assured 20 to him. But if he will not redeem the field, or if he have sold the field to another man, it shall not be redeemed any 21 more; but the field, when it is quitted in the jubilee, shall be holy to Jehovah, as a field devoted; the possession there-22 of shall be the priest's. And if *any one* sanctify to Jehovah a field which he hath bought, which is not of the fields of 23 his possession; then the priest shall reckon to him the sum of thy valuation, to the year of the jubilee: and he shall

give thy valuation in that day, *as* a holy thing to Jehovah. And in the year of the jubilee the field shall return to him 24 of whom it had been bought, to him to whom the possession of the land *did belong*. And all thy valuations shall be ac- 25 cording to the shekel of the sanctuary: twenty gerahs shall be the shekel.

Only the firstling of the beasts, which should be the first- 26 ling of Jehovah, no man shall sanctify it; whether ox or sheep, it is Jehovah's. But if it be of an unclean beast, 27 then he may redeem it according to thy valuation, and shall add a fifth *part* to it: or if it be not redeemed, then it shall be sold according to thy valuation.

Yet, no devoted thing that any one shall devote to Jeho- 28 vah of all that he hath, of man or beast, or of the field of his possession, shall be sold or redeemed: every devoted thing is most holy to Jehovah. None devoted, which shall 29 be devoted by men, shall be redeemed; *but* shall surely be put to death.

And all the tithe of the land, *whether* of the seed of the 30 land or of the fruit of the tree, is Jehovah's: it is holy to Jehovah. And if a man will indeed redeem any part of his 31 tithes, oe shall add the fifth *part* of it. And every tithe of the 32 herd, or of the flock, whatsoever passeth under the rod, the tenth shall be holy to Jehovah. No search shall be made 33 whether it be good or bad, nor shall it be changed: and if it be changed at all, then both it and that for which it hath been changed shall be holy: it shall not be redeemed.'"

These are the commandments which Jehovah delivered to 34 Moses for the children of Israel, in mount Sinai.

THE BOOK OF NUMBERS.

1 CHAP. I.—And Jehovah spake to Moses in the desert of Sinai, in the tent of meeting, on the first day of the second month, in the second year after they had come out of the 2 land of Egypt, saying, "Take ye the sum of all the congregation of the children of Israel, according to their families, according to the house of their fathers, by registering the 3 names of all the males, one by one, from the age of twenty years and upward, all who are able to go forth to war in Israel: thou and Aaron shall muster them by their hosts. 4 And with you there shall be a man out of every tribe; each 5 a chief of the house of his fathers. And these are the names of the men who shall stand with you: Of *the tribe of* Reuben; 6 Elizur the son of Shedeur. Of *the tribe of* Simeon; Shelu-7 miel the son of Zurishaddai. Of *the tribe of* Judah; Nahshon 8 the son of Amminadab. Of *the tribe of* Issachar; Nethaneel 9 the son of Zuar. Of *the tribe of* Zebulun; Eliab the son of 10 Helon. Of the children of Joseph—of *the tribe of* Ephraim; Elishama the son of Ammihud: of *the tribe of* Manasseh; 11 Gamaliel the son of Pedahzur. Of *the tribe of* Benjamin; 12 Abidan the son of Gideoni. Of *the tribe of* Dan; Ahiezer 13 the son of Ammishaddai. Of *the tribe of* Asher; Pagiel the 14 son of Ocran. Of *the tribe of* Gad; Eliasaph the son of 15 Deuel. Of *the tribe of* Naphtali; Ahira the son of Enan." 16 —These were the called of the congregation, princes of the tribes of their fathers, heads of thousands in Israel. 17 And Moses and Aaron took these men who were expressly 18 named; and they assembled all the congregation together on the first day of the second month, who declared their genealogies according to their families, according to the house of their fathers, *their* names being registered from the age of 19 twenty years and upward, one by one. As Jehovah had commanded Moses, so he mustered them in the desert of Sinai.

And the children of Reuben, the first-born of Israel, by 20 their genealogies, according to their families, according to the house of their fathers, the names of all the males being registered, one by one, from the age of twenty years and upward, all that were able to go forth to war;—those that were mus- 21 tered of them, of the tribe of Reuben, were forty-six thousand and five hundred.

Of the children of Simeon, by their genealogies, accord- 22 ing to their families, according to the house of their fathers, the names of all the males being registered, one by one, from the age of twenty years and upward, all that were able to go forth to war;—those that were mustered of them, of the 23 tribe of Simeon, were fifty-nine thousand and three hundred.

Of the children of Gad, by their genealogies, according 24 to families, according to the house of their fathers, the names being registered, from the age of twenty years and upward, all that were able to go forth to war;—those that were mus- 25 tered of them, of the tribe of Gad, were forty-five thousand six hundred and fifty.

Of the children of Judah, by their genealogies, according 26 to their families, according to the house of their fathers, the names being registered, from the age of twenty years and upward, all that were able to go forth to war;—those 27 that were mustered of them, of the tribe of Judah, were seventy-four thousand and six hundred.

Of the children of Issachar, by their genealogies, accord- 28 ing to their families, according to the house of their fathers, the names being registered, from the age of twenty years and upward, all that were able to go forth to war;—those 29 that were mustered of them, of the tribe of Issachar, were fifty-four thousand and four hundred.

Of the children of Zebulun, by their genealogies, accord- 30 ing to their families, according to the house of their fathers, the names being registered, from the age of twenty years and upward, all that were able to go forth to war;—those 31 that were mustered of them, of the tribe of Zebulun, were fifty-seven thousand and four hundred.

Of the children of Joseph;—of the children of Ephraim, 32 by their genealogies, according to their families, according to the house of their fathers, the names being registered, from the age of twenty years and upward, all that were able to go forth to war;—those that were mustered of them, of the 33 tribe of Ephraim, were forty thousand and five hundred.

NUMBERS I. 213

34 Of the children of Manasseh, by their genealogies, according to their families, according to the house of their fathers, the names being registered, from the age of twenty years and
35 upward, all that were able to go forth to war;—those that were mustered of them, of the tribe of Manasseh, were thirty-two thousand and two hundred.
36 Of the children of Benjamin, by their genealogies, according to their families, according to the house of their fathers, the names being registered, from the age of twenty years
37 and upward, all that were able to go forth to war;—those that were mustered of them, of the tribe of Benjamin, were thirty-five thousand and four hundred.
38 Of the children of Dan, by their genealogies, according to their families, according to the house of their fathers, the names being registered, from the age of twenty years and
39 upward, all that were able to go forth to war;—those that were mustered of them, of the tribe of Dan, were sixty-two thousand and seven hundred.
40 Of the children of Asher, by their genealogies, according to their families, according to the house of their fathers, the names being registered, from the age of twenty years and
41 upward, all that were able to go forth to war;—those that were mustered of them, of the tribe of Asher, were forty-one thousand and five hundred.
42 Of the children of Naphtali, by their genealogies, according to their families, according to the house of their fathers, the names being registered, from the age of twenty years and
43 upward, all that were able to go forth to war;—those that were mustered of them, of the tribe of Naphtali, were fifty-three thousand and four hundred.
44 These are they who were mustered, whom Moses and Aaron mustered, with the princes of Israel, twelve men;
45 *according to* the house of his fathers. Now all they who were mustered of the children of Israel, according to the house of their fathers, from the age of twenty years and
46 upward, all who were able to go forth to war in Israel;—all they who were mustered were six hundred and three thousand and five hundred and fifty.
47 But the Levites, according to the tribe of their fathers,
48 were not mustered among them. For Jehovah had spoken
49 to Moses, saying, "Only thou shalt not muster the tribe of Levi, nor take the sum of them among the children of Is-
50 rael; but thou shalt appoint the Levites over the tabernacle of

the testimonials, and over all its utensils, and over every thing which belongeth to it: they shall carry the tabernacle, and all its utensils; and they shall minister at it, and shall encamp round about the tabernacle. And when the tabernacle 51 is to be removed, the Levites shall take it down; and when the tabernacle is to be pitched, the Levites shall set it up; and the stranger who approacheth shall be put to death. And *the rest of* the children of Israel shall encamp, every 52 man in his own camp, and every man by his own standard, according to their hosts. But the Levites shall encamp 53 round about the tabernacle of the testimonials, that there be no wrath upon the congregation of the children of Israel: and the Levites shall keep the charge of the tabernacle of the testimonials." And the children of Israel did according 54 to all that Jehovah commanded Moses, so they did.

CHAP. II.—Then Jehovah spake to Moses and to Aaron, 1 saying, "Every man of the children of Israel shall encamp 2 by his own standard, under the ensign of their father's house: over against the tent of meeting shall they encamp around.

Thus on the east side, toward the rising of the sun, shall 3 they of the standard of the camp of Judah encamp, according to their hosts: and the captain of the children of Judah shall be Nahshon, the son of Amminadab; whose host being 4 mustered are seventy-four thousand and six hundred.—And 5 they who encamp next to him shall be the tribe of Issachar: and the captain of the children of Issachar shall be Nethaneel, the son of Zuar; whose host, being mustered, are fifty-four 6 thousand and four hundred.—Then the tribe of Zebulun: 7 and the captain of the children of Zebulun shall be Eliab, the son of Helon; whose host, being mustered, are fifty-seven 8 thousand and four hundred. All they who were mustered 9 in the camp of Judah are a hundred and eighty-six thousand and four hundred, according to their hosts. These shall march the first.

On the south side shall be the standard of the camp of 10 Reuben, according to their hosts: and the captain of the children of Reuben shall be Elizur, the son of Shedeur; whose host, being mustered, are forty-six thousand and five 11 hundred.—And they who encamp by him shall be the tribe of 12 Simeon: and the captain of the children of Simeon shall be Shelumiel, the son of Zurishaddai; whose host, being mustered, 13

14 are fifty-nine thousand and three hundred.—Then the tribe of Gad: and the captain of the children of Gad shall be
15 Eliasaph, the son of Deuel; whose host, being mustered, are
16 forty-five thousand and six hundred and fifty. All they who were mustered in the camp of Reuben are a hundred and fifty-one thousand, and four hundred and fifty, according to their hosts. And these shall march in the second rank.

17 Then the tent of meeting shall march, with the camp of the Levites in the midst of the camp: as they encamp so shall they march, every man in his place by their standard.

18 On the west side shall be the standard of the camp of Ephraim, according to their hosts: and the captain of the children of Ephraim shall be Elishama, the son of Ammihud;
19 whose host, being mustered, are forty thousand and five
20 hundred.—And by him shall be the tribe of Manasseh: and the captain of the children of Manasseh shall be Gamaliel,
21 the son of Pedazhur; whose host, being mustered, are
22 thirty-two thousand and two hundred.—Then the tribe of Benjamin: and the captain of the children of Benjamin shall
23 be Abidan, the son of Gideoni; whose host, being mustered,
24 are thirty-five thousand and four hundred. All they who were mustered of the camp of Ephraim are a hundred and eight thousand and one hundred, according to their hosts. And these shall march in the third rank.

25 The standard of the camp of Dan shall be on the north side according to their hosts: and the captain of the children
26 of Dan shall be Ahiezer, the son of Ammishaddai; whose host, being mustered, are sixty-two thousand and seven hundred.—
27 And they who encamp by him shall be the tribe of Asher: and the captain of the children of Asher shall be Pagiel, the son
28 of Ocran; whose host, being mustered, are forty-one thou-
29 sand and five hundred.—Then the tribe of Naphtali: and the captain of the children of Naphtali shall be Ahira, the son
30 of Enan; whose host, being mustered, are fifty-three thousand
31 and four hundred. All they who were mustered in the camp of Dan, are a hundred and fifty-seven thousand, and six hundred. These shall march the hindmost according to
32 their standards." These are they who were mustered of the children of Israel according to the house of their fathers: all they who were mustered of the camps, according to their hosts, were six hundred and three thousand, and five hundred
33 and fifty. But the Levites were not mustered among the

children of Israel; as Jehovah commanded Moses. And the 34 children of Israel did according to all that Jehovah commanded Moses: so they encamped by their standards, and so they marched, every one according to their families, according to the house of their fathers.

CHAP. III.—These also are the generations of Aaron 1 and of Moses, at the time when Jehovah spake with Moses in mount Sinai. And these are the names of the sons of 2 Aaron; Nadab the first-born, and Abihu, and Eleazar, and Ithamar. These are the names of the sons of Aaron, the 3 priests who were anointed, whom he had consecrated to minister in the priest's office. But Nadab and Abihu died 4 before Jehovah, when they offered strange fire before Jehovah in the desert of Sinai, and they had no sons: so Eleazar and Ithamar ministered in the priest's office in the sight of Aaron their father.

And Jehovah spake to Moses, saying, "Bring the tribe of 5 Levi near, and present them before Aaron the priest, that they may minister to him. And they shall keep his charge, 7 and the charge of the whole congregation before the tent of meeting, to do the service of the tabernacle. And they shall 8 keep all the utensils of the tent of meeting, and the charge of the children of Israel, to do the service of the tabernacle. And thou shalt give the Levites to Aaron, and to his sons: 9 they are wholly given to him from among the children of Israel. And thou shalt appoint Aaron and his sons, and 10 they shall attend to their priestly office; and the stranger who approacheth shall be put to death."

And Jehovah spake to Moses, saying, "And I, lo I have 11 taken the Levites from among the children of Israel instead of all the *male* first-born that open the womb among the children of Israel; therefore the Levites shall be mine; be- 13 cause all the first-born are mine: on the day that I smote all the first-born in the land of Egypt I sanctified to myself all the first-born in Israel, both man and beast; mine they shall be: I am Jehovah."

And Jehovah spake to Moses in the wilderness of Sinai, 14 saying, "Muster the children of Levi, according to the house 15 of their fathers, according to their families: every male from the age of a month and upward shalt thou muster them." Then Moses mustered them, according to the word of 16 Jehovah, as he was commanded.

NUMBERS III.

17 And these were the sons of Levi by their names; Gershon, and Kohath, and Merari.
18 And these are the names of the sons of Gershon, according to their families; Libni, and Shimei.
19 And the sons of Kohath, according to their families; Amram, and Izhar, Hebron, and Uzziel.
20 And the sons of Merari, according to their families; Mahali, and Mushi.

These are the families of the Levites according to the
21 house of their fathers. Of Gershon was the family of the Libnites, and the family of the Shimeites: these are the
22 families of the Gershonites. They who were mustered of them, according to the number of all the males from the age of a month and upward, they who were mustered of them,
23 were seven thousand and five hundred.—The families of the Gershonites were to encamp behind the tabernacle westward.
24 And the chief of the house of *his* father among the Ger-
25 shonites was Eliasaph, the son of Lael. And the charge of the sons of Gershon, in the tent of meeting, was the tabernacle, and the tent, its covering, and the curtain for the door
26 of the tent of meeting, and the hangings of the court, and the curtain for the door of the court, which surrounded the tabernacle, and the altar, and the cords of it, for all its service.
27 And of Kohath was the family of the Amramites, and the family of the Izharites, and the family of the Hebronites, and the family of the Uzzielites: these were the families
28 of the Kohathites. In the numbering of all the males, from the age of a month and upward, were eight thousand and six hundred, keeping the charge of the sanctuary.
29 The families of the sons of Kohath were to encamp on the
30 side of the tabernacle southward. And the chief of the house of *his* father among the families of the Kohathites was
31 Elizaphan, the son of Uzziel. And their charge was the ark, and the table, and the lamp-stand, and the altars, and the vessels of the sanctuary with which they ministered, and
32 the hanging, and all its service. And Eleazar the son of Aaron the priest, chief of the chief of the Levites, had the oversight of those who attended to the charge of the sanctuary.
33 Of Merari was the family of the Mahalites, and the family of the Mushites: these were the families of Merari.
34 And they who were mustered of them, according to the

number of all the males, from the age of a month and upward, were six thousand and two hundred. And the chief 35 of the house of *his* father among the families of Merari was Zuriel the son of Abihail: these were to encamp on the side of the tabernacle northwards. And the charge under the 36 care of the sons of Merari was the boards of the tabernacle, and its bars, and its pillars, and its sockets, and all its utensils, and all its service; and the pillars of the surround- 37 ing court, and their sockets, and their pins, and their cords.

But they who encamped before the tabernacle toward the 38 east, before the tent of meeting eastward, were Moses, and Aaron and his sons, keeping the charge of the sanctuary for the charge of the children of Israel; and the stranger who should approach was to be put to death. All they who were 39 mustered of the Levites, whom Moses and Aaron mustered at the commandment of Jehovah, according to their families, all the males from the age of a month and upward, were twenty-two thousand.

And Jehovah said to Moses, "Muster all the first-born of 40 the males of the children of Israel, from the age of a month and upward, and take the number of their names. And take 41 the Levites for me (I am Jehovah) instead of all the first-born among the children of Israel; and the cattle of the Levites instead of all the firstlings among the cattle of the children of Israel." And Moses mustered, as Jehovah com- 42 manded him, all the first-born among the children of Israel. And all the first-born males, according to the number of 43 *their* names, from the age of a month and upward, on their being mustered, were twenty-two thousand two hundred and seventy-three.

And Jehovah spake to Moses, saying, "Take the Levites 44 instead of all the first-born among the children of Israel, and the cattle of the Levites instead of their cattle; and the Levites shall be mine: I am Jehovah. And for those who 46 are to be redeemed of the two hundred and seventy-three of the first-born of the children of Israel, who exceed *the number* of the Levites; thou shalt take five shekels for every 47 one; according to the shekel of the sanctuary shalt thou take *them*; twenty gerahs to the shekel. And thou shalt 48 give to Aaron and his sons the redemption-money of those of them who exceeded *the number of the Levites.*" So Moses 49 took the redemption-money of those who exceeded the number of those who were redeemed by the Levites: of the 50

first-born of the children of Israel he took the money; a thousand three hundred and sixty-five *shekels,* according to
51 the shekel of the sanctuary: and Moses gave the money of those who were redeemed to Aaron and to his sons, according to the word of Jehovah, as Jehovah commanded Moses.

1 CHAP. IV.—And Jehovah spake to Moses and to Aaron,
2 saying, "Take the sum of the sons of Kohath from among the sons of Levi, according to their families, according to
3 the house of their fathers; from the age of thirty years and upward, to the age of fifty years, all that are included in the
4 host, to do the work in the tent of meeting. This service of the sons of Kohath, in the tent of meeting, *shall be* about
5 the most holy things. And when the camp is about to move, Aaron and his sons shall come, and shall take down the covering veil, and cover the ark of the testimonials with
6 it; and they shall put over it a covering of seals' skins, and shall spread over *that* a cloth entirely of blue, and shall put
7 in its poles. And upon the table of shew-bread they shall spread a cloth of blue, and put on it the dishes, and the incense-pots, and the cans, and cups for pouring: and the con-
8 tinual *shew*-bread shall be upon it. And they shall spread over them a cloth of scarlet, and cover that with a covering
9 of seals' skins, and shall put in its poles. And they shall take a cloth of blue, and cover the lamp-stand for the light, and its lamps, and its snuffers, and its snuff-dishes, and all
10 its oil-vessels, with which they minister at it: and they shall put it, and all its utensils, within a covering of seals'
11 skins, and shall put *it* on a bearer. And upon the golden altar they shall spread a cloth of blue, and cover it with a
12 covering of seals' skins, and shall put in its poles. And they shall take all the utensils which are used in the service of the sanctuary, and put them in a cloth of blue, and cover them with a covering of seals' skins, and put them on a bearer.
13 And they shall take away the ashes from the altar, and spread
14 on it a purple cloth: and they shall put upon it all the utensils which are used in its service, the censers, the forks, and the shovels, and the basons, all the utensils of the altar: and they shall spread over it a covering of seals' skins, and put
15 in its poles. And when Aaron and his sons have made an end of covering the sanctuary, and all the utensils of the sanctuary, when the camp is to move; then the sons of Kohath shall come to carry them; but they shall not touch the

sanctuary, lest they die. These *things are* the burden of the sons of Kohath in the tent of meeting. And Eleazar, the 16 son of Aaron the priest, shall have the charge of the oil for the light, and the sweet incense, and the daily meal-offering, and the anointing-oil; the charge of all the tabernacle, and of every thing in it, relating to the sanctuary, and its utensils." And Jehovah spake to Moses and to Aaron, saying, 17 "Cut ye not off the tribe of the families of the Kohathites 18 from among the Levites; but do thus to them, that they may 19 live, and not die, when they approach to the most holy things: Aaron and his sons shall go in, and appoint them every one to his service and to his burden; but these shall not go in 20 to see when the holy things are covered, lest they die."

And Jehovah spake to Moses, saying, "Take also the 21 sum of the sons of Gershon, according to the house of their fathers, according to their families; from the age of 23 thirty years and upward, to the age of fifty years, thou shalt muster them; all that are included in the host to do the work in the tent of meeting. This is the service of the 24 families of the Gershonites, in serving and bearing burdens. And they shall carry the curtains of the tabernacle, and 25 the tent of meeting, its *inner* covering, and the covering of the seals' skins which is *placed* above it, and the hanging for the door of the tent of meeting, and the hangings of the 26 court, and the hanging for the door of the gate of the court which surrounds the tabernacle and the altar, and their cords, and all the utensils of their service, and all that is made for them; and they shall serve. At the appointment 27 of Aaron and his sons shall be all the service of the sons of the Gershonites, as to all their burdens, and all their service: so shall ye appoint to them the charge of all their burdens. This is the service of the families of the sons 28 of Gershon in the tent of meeting: and their charge *shall be* under the direction of Ithamar, the son of Aaron the priest.

The sons of Merari thou shalt muster according to their 29 families, according to the house of their fathers: from the age of thirty years and upward, to the age of fifty years, thou shalt 30 muster them; all that are included in the host to do the work of the tent of meeting. And this is the charge of their 31 burden, according to all their service in the tent of meeting; the boards of the tabernacle, and its bars, and its pillars, and its sockets, and the pillars of the surrounding court, and their 32 sockets, and their pins, and their cords, with all their utensils,

NUMBERS IV.

and with all their service: and by name ye shall appoint the
33 utensils of the charge of their burden. This is the service of the families of the sons of Merari, according to all their service in the tent of meeting, under the direction of Ithamar, the son of Aaron the priest."

34 So Moses and Aaron, and the chiefs of the congregation, mustered the sons of the Kohathites, according to their
35 families, and according to the house of their fathers, from the age of thirty years and upward, to the age of fifty years, all that were included in the host for the work of the tent
36 of meeting: and they who were mustered of them, according to their families, were two thousand seven hundred and
37 fifty. These were they who were mustered of the families of the Kohathites, all who could do service in the tent of meeting, whom Moses and Aaron mustered, according to the commandment of Jehovah by Moses.

38 And they who were mustered of the sons of Gershon, according to their families, and according to the house of their
39 fathers, from the age of thirty years and upward, to the age of fifty years, all that were included in the host for the work in
40 the tent of meeting,—they who were mustered of them, according to their families, according to the house of their fathers,
41 were two thousand and six hundred and thirty. These were they who were mustered of the families of the sons of Gershon, of all that could do service in the tent of meeting, whom Moses and Aaron mustered according to the commandment of Jehovah.

42 And they who were mustered of the families of the sons of Merari, according to their families, according to the house
43 of their fathers, from the age of thirty years and upward, to the age of fifty years, all that were included in the host for
44 the work in the tent of meeting,—they who were mustered of them, according to their families, were three thousand and
45 two hundred. These were they who were mustered of the families of the sons of Merari, whom Moses and Aaron mustered, according to the word of Jehovah by Moses.

46 All they who were mustered of the Levites, whom Moses and Aaron and the chiefs of Israel mustered, according to their families, and according to the house of their fathers,
47 from the age of thirty years and upward, to the age of fifty years, every one that came to do the service of the ministry,
48 and the service of the burden in the tent of meeting, even they who were mustered of them, were eight thousand five

hundred and eighty. According to the commandment of Jehovah they were mustered by Moses, every one according to his service, and according to his burden: thus were they mustered by him, as Jehovah commanded Moses.

CHAP. V.—And Jehovah spake to Moses, saying, "Command the children of Israel, that they put out of the camp every leper, and every one who hath an issue, and every one who is defiled on account of the dead: both male and female ye shall put out, without the camp shall ye put them; that they defile not their camps, in the midst of which I dwell." And the children of Israel did so, and put them out without the camp: as Jehovah spake to Moses, so did the children of Israel.

And Jehovah spake to Moses, saying, "Speak to the children of Israel, saying, 'When a man or a woman shall have committed any sin that men commit, transgressing against Jehovah, and that person be guilty; then they shall confess their sin which they have committed; and he shall restore that in which he hath trespassed in its original state, and add to it a fifth part more, and give it to him against whom he hath trespassed. But if the man have no kinsman to whom the trespass can be restored, let the trespass be restored to Jehovah, to the priest; beside the ram of the atonement, by which an atonement shall be made for him.

And every heave-offering of all the holy things of the children of Israel, which they bring to the priest, shall be his. And every man's hallowed things shall be his: whatsoever any man giveth the priest, it shall be his.'"

And Jehovah spake to Moses, saying, "Speak to the children of Israel, and say to them, 'If any man's wife go astray, and be guilty of a transgression against him, and a man lie carnally with her, and it be hidden from the eyes of her husband, and be kept secret, and she be defiled, and there be no witness against her, and she be not taken *in the fact;* but the spirit of jealousy come upon him, and he be jealous of his wife, who hath been defiled: or if the spirit of jealousy come upon him, and he be jealous of his wife, although she hath not been defiled; then shall the man bring his wife to the priest; he shall also bring her offering for her, the tenth *part* of an ephah of barley meal; he shall not pour oil upon it, nor put frankincense on it; for it is

an offering of jealousy, an offering of memorial, bringing
16 iniquity to remembrance. And the priest shall bring her
17 near, and place her before Jehovah; and the priest shall
take holy water in an earthen vessel, and some of the dust
that is on the floor of the tabernacle the priest shall take,
18 and put it into the water: then the priest shall place the
woman before Jehovah, and uncover the woman's head, and
put the offering of memorial in her hands, which is the
offering of jealousy: and in the hand of the priest shall be
19 the bitter water that causeth the curse. And the priest
shall adjure her, and say to the woman, If no man have
lain with thee, and if thou have not gone astray to uncleanness *with another* instead of thy husband, be thou unhurt
20 by this bitter water that causeth the curse: but if thou
have gone astray *to another* instead of thy husband, and if
thou be defiled, and some man have lain with thee beside
21 thy husband;—then the priest shall adjure the woman;
and the priest shall say to the woman,—" May Jehovah
make thee an execration and an oath among thy people, by
Jehovah's making thy thigh to rot, and thy belly to swell;
22 and may this water that causeth the curse go into thy
bowels, to make *thy* belly to swell, and *thy* thigh to rot.
23 And the woman shall say, Amen, amen. Then the priest
shall write these execrations in a book, and he shall blot
24 them out with the bitter water; and he shall cause the
woman to drink the bitter water that causeth the curse; and
the water that causeth the curse shall enter into her, *and be*
25 bitter. Then the priest shall take the offering of jealousy
out of the woman's hand, and shall wave the offering before
26 Jehovah, and offer it upon the altar: and the priest shall
take a handful of the offering, the memorial of it, and burn
it upon the altar, and afterward shall cause the woman to
27 drink the water. And when he hath made her to drink the
water, if she be defiled, and have been guilty of a transgression against her husband, the water that causeth the
curse shall enter into her, *and be* bitter, and her belly shall
swell, and her thigh shall rot: and the woman shall be an
28 execration among her people. But if the woman be not
defiled, but be clean; then she shall be unhurt, and shall
29 conceive seed. This is the law of jealousies. When a wife
goeth astray *to another* instead of her husband, and is de-
30 filed; or when the spirit of jealousy cometh upon him, and
he is jealous of his wife, and he shall place the woman be-

fore Jehovah, and the priest shall execute upon her all this law; then shall the man be guiltless from iniquity, but the woman shall bear her iniquity.'"

CHAP. VI.—And Jehovah spake to Moses, saying, "Speak to the children of Israel, and say to them, 'When a man or a woman will distinguish *themselves* by vowing the vow of a Nazarite, to separate *themselves* to Jehovah; he shall abstain from wine, and strong drink; no vinegar of wine, or vinegar of strong drink, shall he drink, no liquor of grapes shall he drink, nor shall he eat grapes, moist or dried. All the days of his separation he shall eat nothing that is produced from the vine, from the stones of the grapes even to the husk. All the days of the vow of his separation no razor shall come upon his head: until the days in which he separateth himself to Jehovah be completed he shall be holy, *and* shall let the locks of the hair of his head grow. All the days that he separateth himself to Jehovah he shall not come near a dead body. He shall not make himself unclean for his father, or for his mother, for his brother, or for his sister, when they die; because the consecration of his God is upon his head. All the days of his separation he is holy to Jehovah. And if any one die very suddenly near him, and he hath defiled the head of his consecration; then he shall shave his head in the day of his cleansing; on the seventh day he shall shave it. And on the eighth day he shall bring two turtle-doves, or two young pigeons, to the priest, to the door of the tent of meeting; and the priest shall offer the one for a sin-offering, and the other for a burnt-offering, and make an atonement for him, for having sinned respecting the dead, and he shall hallow his head *again* on that day. And he shall separate to Jehovah the days of his separation, and shall bring a lamb of the first year for a trespass-offering: but the days that were before shall be lost, because his separation was defiled.

This also is the law of the Nazarite. When the days of his separation are completed, he shall be brought to the door of the tent of meeting; and he shall offer his offering to Jehovah, one he-lamb of the first year without blemish for a burnt-offering, and one ewe-lamb of the first year without blemish for a sin-offering, and one ram without blemish for a peace-offering, and a basket of unleavened bread, cakes of fine flour mingled with oil, and wafers of unleavened bread anointed with oil, and their meal-offering, 16 and their drink-offerings. And the priest shall bring them before Jehovah, and shall offer his sin-offering, and his 17 burnt-offering. And he shall offer the ram for a sacrifice of peace-offerings to Jehovah, with the basket of unleavened bread: the priest shall offer also his meal-offering, and his 18 drink-offering. And the Nazarite shall shave the head of his separation at the door of the tent of meeting; and shall take the hair of the head of his separation, and put it on the fire which is under the sacrifice of the peace-offerings. 19 And the priest shall take the boiled shoulder of the ram, and one unleavened cake out of the basket, and one unleavened wafer, and shall put them upon the hands of the 20 Nazarite, after *the hair of his* separation is shaven; and the priest shall wave them for a wave-offering before Jehovah: this is holy for the priest, with the wave-breast and heave-shoulder. And after that the Nazarite may drink wine.— 21 This is the law of the Nazarite who hath vowed his offering to Jehovah for his separation, besides what *else* he can afford: according to the vow which he vowed, so he must do after the law of his separation.'"

23 And Jehovah spake to Moses, saying, "Speak to Aaron, and to his sons, saying, 'Thus shall ye bless the children of Israel, saying to them,
24 May Jehovah bless thee, and keep thee!
25 May Jehovah make his face to shine upon thee, and be gracious to thee!
26 May Jehovah lift up his countenance upon thee, and give thee peace!'
27 Thus they shall put my name on the children of Israel, and I will bless them."

1 CHAP. VII.—And it came to pass on the day in which Moses had fully set up the tabernacle, and had anointed it, and sanctified it, with all its utensils, and had also anointed 2 and sanctified the altar with all its utensils, that the chiefs of Israel, heads of the house of their fathers, who were the chiefs of the tribes, and had the command of them who 3 were mustered, offered. And they brought their offering before Jehovah; six covered wagons, and twelve oxen; a wagon for two of the chiefs, and for every one an ox: and 4 they brought them before the tabernacle. And Jehovah

spake to Moses, saying, "Take *these* from them, that they ⁵ may be employed in the service of the tent of meeting; and give them to the Levites, to every one according to his service." So Moses took the wagons and the oxen, and ⁶ gave them to the Levites. Two wagons and four oxen he ⁷ gave to the sons of Gershon, according to their service: And four wagons and eight oxen he gave to the sons of ⁸ Merari, according to their service, under the direction of Ithamar, the son of Aaron the priest. But to the sons of ⁹ Kohath he gave none; because to them belonged the service of the sanctuary, which they were to carry upon their shoulders.

And the chiefs offered for the dedication of the altar, on ¹⁰ the day in which it was anointed; the chiefs offered their offering before the altar. For Jehovah had said to Moses, "They ¹¹ shall offer their offering, each chief on his day, for the dedication of the altar."

And he who offered his offering on the first day was ¹² Nahshon, the son of Amminadab, of the tribe of Judah: and his offering was one silver dish, of the weight of a hun- ¹³ dred and thirty *shekels*, one silver bowl of seventy shekels, according to the shekel of the sanctuary; both of them full of fine flour mingled with oil, for a meal-offering: one ¹⁴ golden incense-pot of ten *shekels*, full of incense: one young ¹⁵ bullock, one ram, one lamb of the first year, for a burnt-offering: one kid of the goats for a sin-offering: and for a ¹⁷ sacrifice of peace-offerings, two oxen, five rams, five he-goats, five lambs of the first year. This was the offering of Nahshon, the son of Amminadab.

On the second day Nethaneel, the son of Zuar, chief of ¹⁸ Issachar, offered. He offered for his offering one silver dish, ¹⁹ of the weight of a hundred and thirty *shekels*, one silver bowl of seventy shekels, according to the shekel of the sanctuary; both of them full of fine flour mingled with oil, for a meal-offering: one golden incense-pot of ten *shekels*, ²⁰ full of incense: one young bullock, one ram, one lamb of ²¹ the first year, for a burnt-offering: one kid of the goats for ²² a sin-offering: and for a sacrifice of peace-offerings, two ²³ oxen, five rams, five he-goats, five lambs of the first year. This was the offering of Nethaneel, the son of Zuar.

On the third day Eliab, the son of Helon, chief of the ²⁴ children of Zebulun, offered. His offering was one silver ²⁵ dish, of the weight of a hundred and thirty *shekels*, one

silver bowl of seventy shekels, according to the shekel of the sanctuary; both of them full of fine flour mingled with oil,
26 for a meal-offering: one golden incense-pot of ten *shekels*,
27 full of incense: one young bullock, one ram, one lamb of
28 the first year, for a burnt-offering: one kid of the goats for
29 a sin-offering: and for a sacrifice of peace-offerings, two oxen, five rams, five he-goats, five lambs of the first year. This was the offering of Eliab, the son of Helon.

30 On the fourth day Elizur, the son of Shedeur, chief of
31 the children of Reuben, *offered*. His offering was one silver dish, of a hundred and thirty *shekels*, one silver bowl of seventy shekels, according to the shekel of the sanctuary; both of them full of fine flour mingled with oil, for a meal-
32 offering: one golden incense pot of ten *shekels*, full of
33 incense: one young bullock, one ram, one lamb of the first
34 year, for a burnt offering: one kid of the goats for a sin-
35 offering: and for a sacrifice of peace-offerings, two oxen, five rams, five he-goats, five lambs of the first year. This was the offering of Elizur, the son of Shedeur.

36 On the fifth day Shelumiel, the son of Zurishaddai, chief
37 of the children of Simeon, *offered*. His offering was one silver dish, of the weight of a hundred and thirty *shekels*, one silver bowl of seventy shekels, according to the shekel of the sanctuary; both of them full of fine flour mingled
38 with oil, for a meal-offering: one golden incense-pot of ten
39 *shekels*, full of incense: one young bullock, one ram, one
40 lamb of the first year, for a burnt-offering: one kid of the
41 goats for a sin-offering: and for a sacrifice of peace-offerings, two oxen, five rams, five he-goats, five lambs of the first year. This was the offering of Shelumiel, the son of Zurishaddai.

42 On the sixth day Eliasaph, the son of Deuel, chief of the
43 children of Gad, *offered*. His offering was one silver dish, of the weight of a hundred and thirty *shekels*, a silver bowl of seventy shekels, according to the shekel of the sanctuary; both of them full of fine flour mingled with oil, for a meal-
44 offering: one golden incense-pot of ten *shekels*, full of incense:
45 one young bullock, one ram, one lamb of the first year,
46 for a burnt-offering: one kid of the goats for a sin-offering:
47 and for a sacrifice of peace-offerings, two oxen, five rams, five he-goats, five lambs of the first year. This was the offering of Eliasaph, the son of Deuel.
48 On the seventh day Elishama, the son of Ammihud, chief

of the children of Ephraim, *offered*. His offering was one 49
silver dish, of the weight of a hundred and thirty *shekels*, one
silver bowl of seventy shekels, according to the shekel of the
sanctuary; both of them full of fine flour mingled with oil,
for a meal-offering: one golden incense-pot of ten *shekels*, 50
full of incense: one young bullock, one ram, one lamb of 51
the first year, for a burnt-offering: one kid of the goats for 52
a sin-offering: and for a sacrifice of peace-offerings, two 53
oxen, five rams, five he-goats, five lambs of the first year.
This was the offering of Elishama, the son of Ammihud.

On the eighth day Gamaliel, the son of Pedahzur, chief of 54
the children of Manasseh, *offered*. His offering was one 55
silver dish, of a hundred and thirty *shekels*, one silver bowl of
seventy shekels, according to the shekel of the sanctuary;
both of them full of fine flour mingled with oil, for a meal-
offering: one golden incense-pot of ten *shekels*, full of 56
incense: one young bullock, one ram, one lamb of the first 57
year, for a burnt-offering: one kid of the goats for a sin- 58
offering: and for a sacrifice of peace-offerings, two oxen, five 59
rams, five he-goats, five lambs of the first year. This was
the offering of Gamaliel, the son of Pedahzur.

On the ninth day Abidan, the son of Gideoni, chief of the 60
children of Benjamin, *offered*. His offering was one silver 61
dish, of the weight of a hundred and thirty *shekels*, one
silver bowl of seventy shekels, according to the shekel of the
sanctuary; both of them full of fine flour mingled with oil,
for a meal-offering: one golden incense-pot of ten *shekels*, 62
full of incense: one young bullock, one ram, one lamb of 63
the first year, for a burnt-offering: one kid of the goats for 64
a sin-offering: and for a sacrifice of peace-offerings, two 65
oxen, five rams, five he-goats, five lambs of the first year.
This was the offering of Abidan, the son of Gideoni.

On the tenth day Ahiezer, the son of Ammishaddai, chief 66
of the children of Dan, *offered*. His offering was one silver 67
dish, of the weight of a hundred and thirty *shekels*, one silver
bowl of seventy shekels, according to the shekel of the
sanctuary; both of them full of fine flour mingled with
oil, for a meal-offering: one golden incense-pot of ten 68
shekels, full of incense: one young bullock, one ram, one 69
lamb of the first year, for a burnt-offering: one kid of the 70
goats for a sin-offering: and for a sacrifice of peace-offerings, 71
two oxen, five rams, five he-goats, five lambs of the first

NUMBERS VII. 229

year. This was the offering of Ahiezer, the son of Ammishaddai.

72 On the eleventh day Pagiel, the son of Ocran, chief of
73 the children of Asher, *offered*. His offering was one silver dish, of the weight of a hundred and thirty *shekels*, one silver bowl of seventy shekels, according to the shekel of the sanctuary; both of them full of fine flour mingled with oil,
74 for a meal-offering: one golden incense-pot of ten *shekels*,
75 full of incense: one bullock, one ram, one lamb of the first
76 year, for a burnt-offering: one kid of the goats for a sin-
77 offering: and for a sacrifice of peace-offerings, two oxen, five rams, five he-goats, five lambs of the first year. This was the offering of Pagiel, the son of Ocran.

78 On the twelfth day Ahira, the son of Enan, chief of the
79 children of Naphtali, *offered*. His offering was one silver dish, of the weight of a hundred and thirty *shekels*, one silver bowl of seventy shekels, according to the shekel of the sanctuary; both of them full of fine flour mingled with
80 oil, for a meal-offering: one golden incense-pot of ten
81 *shekels*, full of incense: one young bullock, one ram, one lamb
82 of the first year, for a burnt-offering: one kid of the goats for
83 a sin-offering: and for a sacrifice of peace-offerings, two oxen, five rams, five he-goats, five lambs of the first year. This was the offering of Ahira, the son of Enan.

84 This was the dedication of the altar, on the day in which it was anointed, by the chiefs of Israel: twelve dishes of
85 silver, twelve silver bowls, twelve incense-pots of gold: each dish of silver *weighing* a hundred and thirty *shekels*, each bowl seventy: all the silver vessels two thousand and four hundred *shekels*, according to the shekel of the sanctuary:
86 the golden incense-pots *were* twelve, full of incense, *weighing* ten *shekels* each, according to the shekel of the sanctuary: all the gold of the incense-pots *was* a hundred and twenty
87 *shekels*. All the bullocks for the burnt-offering *were* twelve, the rams twelve, the lambs of the first year twelve, with their meal-offering: and the kids of the goats for sin-offering,
88 twelve. And all the bullocks for the sacrifice of the peace-offerings *were* twenty-four, the rams sixty, the he-goats sixty, the lambs of the first year sixty. This was the dedication of the altar, after it was anointed.

89 Now when Moses went into the tent of meeting to speak with *Jehovah*, he heard the voice of one speaking to him from off the lid that was upon the ark of the testimo-

nials, from between the two cherubim: and he spake to him.

CHAP. VIII.—And Jehovah spake to Moses, saying, 1 "Speak to Aaron, and say to him, 'When thou settest up 2 the lamps, the seven lamps shall give light in front of the lamp-stand.'" And Aaron did so: in front of the lamp- 3 stand he set up its lamps as Jehovah commanded Moses. Now this was the work of the lamp-stand; it was of solid 4 gold; both its shaft and its flowers were solid work: according to the pattern which Jehovah had shewn to Moses, so he had made the lamp-stand.

And Jehovah spake to Moses, saying, "Take the Levites 6 from among the children of Israel, and purify them. And 7 thus shalt thou do to them, to purify them: Sprinkle water of cleansing upon them, and let them pass a razor over their whole body, and let them wash their clothes, and *so* purify themselves. Then let them take a young bullock with his 8 meal-offering, fine flour mingled with oil, and another young bullock take thou for a sin-offering. And thou shalt bring 9 the Levites before the tent of meeting: and thou shalt gather the whole assembly of the children of Israel together: and thou shalt bring the Levites before Jehovah; and the 10 children of Israel shall lay their hands upon the Levites: and Aaron shall offer the Levites before Jehovah for an 11 offering of the children of Israel, that they may execute the service of Jehovah. And the Levites shall lay their hands 12 upon the heads of the bullocks: and thou shalt offer one for a sin-offering, and the other for a burnt-offering, to Jehovah, to make an atonement for the Levites. And thou 13 shalt set the Levites before Aaron, and before his sons, and offer them for an offering to Jehovah. Thus shalt thou 14 separate the Levites from among the children of Israel: and the Levites shall be mine. And after that the Levites shall 15 go in to do the service of the tent of meeting, when thou shalt have purified them, and offered them for an offering. For they are wholly given to me from among the children 16 of Israel; instead of that which openeth every womb, the first-born of all the children of Israel, have I taken them for myself. For all the first-born of the children of Israel are 17 mine, *both* man and beast: on the day that I smote every first-born in the land of Egypt I sanctified them for myself. And I have taken the Levites for all the first-born of the 18

19 children of Israel. And I have given the Levites *as* a gift to Aaron and to his sons from among the children of Israel, to do the service of the children of Israel in the tent of meeting, and to make an atonement for the children of Israel; that there may be no plague among the children of Israel, when the children of Israel come nigh to the sanctuary."
20 And Moses, and Aaron, and all the congregation of the children of Israel, did to the Levites according to all that Jehovah commanded Moses concerning the Levites, so the
21 children of Israel did to them. And the Levites purified themselves, and washed their clothes; and Aaron offered them *as* an offering before Jehovah; and Aaron made an
22 atonement for them to purify them. And after that the Levites went in to do their service in the tent of meeting before Aaron, and before his sons: as Jehovah had commanded Moses concerning the Levites, so they did to them.
24 And Jehovah spake to Moses, saying, "This it is that belongeth to the Levites: from the age of twenty-five years and upward they shall enter in to perform the service of the
25 tent of meeting; and from the age of fifty years they shall cease from performing the service *of it*, and shall serve no
26 more: they shall minister with their brethren in the tent of meeting, to keep the charge, but shall do no service. Thus shalt thou do to the Levites concerning their charge."

1 CHAP. IX.—Now Jehovah had spoken to Moses in the wilderness of Sinai, in the first month of the second year after they had come out of the land of Egypt, saying,
2 "Let the children of Israel keep the passover at its ap-
3 pointed season. In the fourteenth day of this month, at evening, ye shall keep it at its appointed season: according to all its statutes, and according to all its ordinances, ye
4 shall keep it." And Moses spake to the children of Israel,
5 that they should keep the passover. So they kept the passover on the fourteenth day of the first month, at evening, in the wilderness of Sinai: according to all that Jehovah had commanded Moses, so did the children of Israel.
6 But there were certain men who were defiled by the dead body of a man, so that they could not keep the passover on that day: and they came before Moses and before Aaron on
7 that day: and these men said to him, "We are defiled by the dead body of a man: why should we be kept back, from offering the offering of Jehovah at its appointed

season among the children of Israel?" And Moses said 8
to them, "Wait ye till I hear what Jehovah will command
concerning you." And Jehovah spake to Moses, saying, 9
"Speak to the children of Israel, saying, 'If any one of 10
you or of your posterity shall be defiled by a dead body, or
be on a journey afar off, yet he must keep the passover to
Jehovah. On the fourteenth day of the second month, at 11
evening, they shall keep it, *and* eat it with unleavened bread
and bitter *herbs*. They shall leave none of it until the 12
morning, nor break any bone of it: according to all the
statutes of the passover they shall keep it. But the man 13
who is clean and not on a journey, yet forbeareth to keep
the passover, that soul shall be cut off from his people,
because he offered not the offering of Jehovah at its appointed season: that man shall bear his sin. And if a 14
stranger shall sojourn among you, and will keep the passover to Jehovah; according to the statute of the passover,
and according to its ordinances, so shall he do: ye shall
have one statute, both for the stranger, and for him who
was born in the land.'"

And on the day in which the tabernacle was set up, the 15
cloud covered the tabernacle, the tent of the testimonials:
and at evening there was upon the tabernacle the appearance
of fire, until the morning. So it was continually: the cloud 16
covered it *by day*, and the appearance of fire by night.
Now whenever the cloud was taken up from the tabernacle, 17
then after that the children of Israel journeyed: and in the
place where the cloud abode, there the children of Israel encamped. At the command of Jehovah the children of Israel 18
journeyed, and at the command of Jehovah they encamped:
as long as the cloud abode upon the tabernacle they remained encamped. And when the cloud tarried upon the 19
tabernacle many days, then the children of Israel kept the
charge of Jehovah, and journeyed not. And whenever the 20
cloud was a few days upon the tabernacle, at the command
of Jehovah they remained encamped, and at the command
of Jehovah they journeyed. And whenever the cloud abode 21
from evening till morning, and the cloud was taken up in
the morning, then they journeyed; whether it were by day
or by night, when the cloud was taken up they journeyed.
But were it for days, or a month, or a year, that the cloud 22
tarried upon the tabernacle, abiding upon it, the children
of Israel remained encamped, and journeyed not: but when

23 it was taken up, they journeyed. At the command of Jehovah they remained encamped, and at the command of Jehovah they journeyed: they kept the charge of Jehovah, at the command of Jehovah *given* by Moses.

1 CHAP. X.—And Jehovah spake to Moses, saying, " Make thee two trumpets of silver : of solid *silver* thou shalt make them ; and thou shalt use them for the calling of the as-
3 sembly, and for the journeying of the camps. And when both are blown the whole assembly shall assemble themselves
4 to thee at the door of the tent of meeting. But when only one is blown, the chiefs, the heads of the families of Israel,
5 shall gather themselves to thee.—When ye blow an alarm,
6 then the camps that lie on the east side shall march. When ye blow an alarm the second time, then the camps that lie on the south side shall take their march : they shall blow an
7 alarm for their marches. But when the congregation is to be gathered together, ye shall blow, but ye shall not sound
8 an alarm. And the sons of Aaron, the priests, shall blow with the trumpets ; and they shall be to you a perpetual
9 statute throughout your generations.—And if ye go to war in your land against the enemy that oppresseth you, then ye shall blow an alarm with the trumpets ; and ye shall be remembered before Jehovah your God, and ye shall be saved
10 from your enemies.—Also on the day of your gladness, and on your solemn days, and at the beginnings of your months, ye shall blow with the trumpets over your burnt-offerings, and over the sacrifices of your peace-offerings ; that they may be to you for a memorial before your God : I am Jehovah your God."
11 And it came to pass on the twentieth day of the second month, of the second year, that the cloud was taken up from
12 off the tabernacle of the testimonials. And the children of Israel took their journeys from the desert of Sinai ; and
13 the cloud rested in the desert of Paran. Then first they took their journey at the command of Jehovah *given* by
14 Moses.—In the front went the standard of the camp of the children of Judah according to their hosts : and over his
15 host was Nahshon the son of Amminadab. And over the host of the tribe of the children of Issachar was Nethaneel
16 the son of Zuar. And over the host of the tribe of the
17 children of Zebulun was Eliab the son of Helon.—Then the tabernacle was taken down ; and the sons of Gershon

and the sons of Merari journeyed, carrying the tabernacle.
—Next went the standard of the camp of Reuben accord- 18
ing to their hosts: and over his host was Elizur the son of
Shedeur. And over the host of the tribe of the children of 19
Simeon was Shelumiel the son of Zurishaddai. And over 20
the host of the tribe of the children of Gad was Eliasaph
the son of Deuel.—Then the Kohathites journeyed, carrying 21
the sanctuary: and *the others* set up the tabernacle against
they came.—Next went the standard of the camp of the 22
children of Ephraim according to their hosts: and over
his host was Elishama the son of Ammihud. And over 23
the host of the tribe of the children of Manasseh was
Gamaliel the son of Pedahzur. And over the host of the 24
tribe of the children of Benjamin was Abidan the son of
Gideoni.—Next went the standard of the camp of the chil- 25
dren of Dan in the rear of all the camps according to their
hosts: and over his host was Ahiezer the son of Ammishaddai. And over the host of the tribe of the children of 26
Asher was Pagiel the son of Ocran. And over the host of 27
the tribe of the children of Naphtali was Ahira the son of
Enan. Such were the journeys of the children of Israel 28
according to their hosts, when they journeyed.

And Moses said to Hobab, the son of Reuel the Midian- 29
ite, the father-in-law of Moses, "We are journeying to the
place of which Jehovah hath said, 'I give it to you:' come
thou with us, and we will do thee good: for Jehovah hath
spoken good concerning Israel." And he said to him, "I 30
will not go; but I will depart to my own land, and to my
kindred."—But *Moses* said, "Leave us not, I pray thee: 31
since thou knowest our encampments in the wilderness, and
thou mayest be to us instead of eyes. And it shall be, if 32
thou go with us, and the good which Jehovah is about to
do to us, happens, we will do good to thee."

And they departed from the mountain of Jehovah three 33
days' journey: and the ark of the covenant of Jehovah
went before them during the three days' journey, to search
out a place for their encampment. And the cloud of Jeho- 34
vah was upon them by day, when they journeyed from *their*
encampment. And it came to pass when the ark set forward, 35
Moses said, "Arise, O Jehovah, and let thine enemies be
scattered, and let those who hate thee flee before thee."
And when it rested, he said, "Return, O Jehovah, to the 36
myriads of Israel!"

NUMBERS XI.

1 CHAP. XI.—And the people complained wickedly in the hearing of Jehovah: and Jehovah heard it; and his anger was kindled; and the fire of Jehovah burnt among them,
2 and consumed in the uttermost parts of the camp. And the people cried to Moses; and when Moses prayed to Jehovah,
3 the fire ceased. And he called the name of the place Taberah [BURNING]; because the fire of Jehovah had burnt
4 among them. And the mixed multitude that was among them eagerly longed *for other food*: and the children of Israel also wept again, and said, "Who will give us flesh to
5 eat? We remember the fish which we ate in Egypt for nothing; the cucumbers, and the melons, and the leeks, and
6 the onions, and the garlick: but now we are withering away, there being nothing at all, besides this manna, before
7 our eyes." (Now the manna was as coriander-seed, and its
8 colour as the colour of bdellium. The people went about, and gathered it, and ground it in mills, or beat it in a mortar, and baked it in pans, or made hearth-cakes of it; and
9 the taste of it was as the taste of oiled cake. And when the dew fell upon the camp in the night, the manna fell with
10 it.) Then Moses heard the people weep throughout their families, every man at the door of his tent: and the anger of Jehovah was kindled greatly; Moses also was displeased.
11 And Moses said to Jehovah, "Why hast thou afflicted thy servant? and why have I not found favour in thy sight, that
12 thou layest the burden of all this people upon me? Have I conceived all this people? have I begotten them, that thou shouldest say to me, 'Carry them in thy bosom, as a nursing father beareth the sucking child, unto the land
13 which thou swarest *to give* to their fathers?' Whence should I have flesh to give to all this people? when they weep about me, saying, 'Give us flesh, that we may eat.'
14 I am not able alone to bear all this people, because it is too
15 heavy for me. And if thou wilt deal thus with me, kill me, I pray thee, instantly, if I have found favour in thy sight, and let me not see my wretchedness."
16 And Jehovah said to Moses, "Call together seventy of the elders of Israel, whom thou knowest to be the elders and officers of the people; and bring them to the tent of meet-
17 ing, that they may stand there with thee. And I will come down and talk with thee there; and I will take of the spirit which is upon thee, and will put it upon them, and they shall bear the burden of the people with thee, that thou bear

it not thyself alone. And say thou to the people, 'Sanctify ¹⁸ yourselves against to-morrow, and ye shall eat flesh: since ye have wept in the ears of Jehovah, saying, Who will give us flesh to eat! it was well with us in Egypt: therefore Jehovah will give you flesh, and ye shall eat. Not one day ¹⁹ shall ye eat, nor two days, nor five days, nor ten days, nor twenty days, but a whole month, until it come out at your ²⁰ nostrils, and it be loathsome to you: because ye have despised Jehovah who is among you, and have wept before him, saying, Why came we out of Egypt?'" And Moses ²¹ said, "The people, in the midst of whom I am, are six hundred thousand footmen; and yet thou sayest, I will give them flesh, that they may eat a whole month. Were the ²² flocks and herds to be slain for them, would it suffice them? or were all the fish of the sea to be gathered together for them, would it suffice them?" And Jehovah said to ²³ Moses, "Is the hand of Jehovah shortened? thou shalt see now whether my word shall come to pass unto thee or not."

And Moses went out, and told the people the words of ²⁴ Jehovah, and gathered together seventy of the elders of the people, and placed them around the tent. And Jehovah ²⁵ came down in the cloud, and spake to him, and took of the spirit that was upon him, and gave it to the seventy elders: and when the spirit rested upon them, they prophesied. But two men remained in the camp, the name of the one ²⁶ was Eldad, and the name of the other Medad: and the spirit rested upon them: (for they were amongst those who were enrolled, but they had not gone to the tent;) and they prophesied in the camp. And a young man ran and told ²⁷ Moses, and said, "Eldad and Medad are prophesying in the camp." And Joshua the son of Nun, the chosen attendant ²⁸ on Moses, answered and said, "My lord Moses, forbid them." And Moses said to him, "Art thou jealous on my ²⁹ account? Oh that all the people of Jehovah were prophets, that Jehovah would put his spirit upon them!"

And Moses returned into the camp, together with the ³⁰ elders of Israel. Then there went forth a wind from Jehovah ³¹ and brought quails from the sea, and scattered them about the camp, about a day's journey on one side, and about a day's journey on the other side around the camp, and about two cubits above the ground. And the people stood up all ³² that day, and all the night, and all the next day, and gathered the quails: he who gathered the least gathered ten omers: and they spread them all abroad for themselves 33 around the camp. The flesh was yet between their teeth, unchewed, when the wrath of Jehovah was kindled against the people, and Jehovah smote the people with a very great 34 plague. So the name of that place was called Kibroth-hattaavah [THE GRAVES OF LONGING]: because there they buried the people who had longed.

35 From Kibroth-hattaavah the people journeyed unto Hazeroth. Now while they abode at Hazeroth, CHAP. XII.
1 Miriam and Aaron spake against Moses because of the Cushite woman whom he had married; for he had married 2 a Cushite woman; and said, "Hath Jehovah indeed spoken by Moses only? hath he not spoken also by us?" And 3 Jehovah heard *it*. (Now this man, Moses, was the meekest 4 of all men who were upon the face of all the earth.) And Jehovah said suddenly to Moses, and to Aaron, and to Miriam, "Come out ye three to the tent of meeting." And they 5 three went out. And Jehovah came down in the pillar of the cloud, and stood at the door of the tent, and called Aaron 6 and Miriam: and they both came forth. And he said, "Hear now my words: If there be a prophet of Jehovah among you, I make myself known to him in a vision, and 7 speak to him in a dream. Not so my servant Moses, who 8 is intrusted with all my house. With him I speak mouth to mouth, plainly, and not obscurely; and the similitude of Jehovah he beholds: wherefore then were ye not afraid to 9 speak against my servant Moses?" And the anger of Je-10 hovah was kindled against them; and he departed. And the cloud departed from off the tent; when lo, Miriam *became* leprous, like snow: and Aaron looked upon Miriam, 11 and, lo, she was leprous. And Aaron said to Moses, "Alas, my lord, I beseech thee, lay not the sin upon us, wherein 12 we have done foolishly and wherein we have sinned. Let her not be as one dead, whose flesh is half consumed 13 when he cometh out of his mother's womb!" And Moses cried to Jehovah, saying, "Heal her now, O God, I beseech 14 thee!" And Jehovah said to Moses, "If her father had but spit before her face, should she not be ashamed seven days? Let her be shut out from the camp seven days, and 15 after that let her be taken in again." And Miriam was shut out from the camp seven days: and the people journeyed 16 not till Miriam was taken in again. And afterward the

people removed from Hazeroth, and encamped in the desert of Paran.

CHAP. XIII.—And Jehovah spake to Moses, saying, 1 " Send thou men, that they may search the land of Canaan, 2 which I give to the children of Israel: of every tribe of their fathers ye shall send one man, every one a ruler among them. And Moses at the command of Jehovah sent them 3 from the desert of Paran: all those men were chiefs of the children of Israel. And these were their names: Of the 4 tribe of Reuben, Shammua the son of Zaccur. Of the tribe 5 of Simeon, Shaphat the son of Hori. Of the tribe of Judah, 6 Caleb the son of Jephunneh. Of the tribe of Issachar, 7 Igal the son of Joseph. Of the tribe of Ephraim, Oshua 8 the son of Nun. Of the tribe of Benjamin, Palti the son 9 of Raphu. Of the tribe of Zebulun, Gadiel the son of 10 Sodi. Of the tribe of Joseph (that is, of the tribe of Ma- 11 nasseh), Gadi the son of Susi. Of the tribe of Dan, Amiel 12 the son of Gemali. Of the tribe of Asher, Sethur the son of 13 Michael. Of the tribe of Naphtali, Nahbi the son of Vophsi. 14 Of the tribe of Gad, Geuel the son of Machi. These were 16 the names of the men whom Moses sent to spy out the land. Now Moses had named Oshua the son of Nun, Joshua.

And Moses sent them to spy out the land of Canaan, and 17 said to them, " Go up this *way*, the south, and go up into the mountainous country; and see the land what it is; 18 and the people who dwell in it, whether they be strong or weak, few or many; and whether the land in which they 19 dwell, be good or bad; and what cities they be in which they dwell, whether in camps, or in fortified cities; and 20 whether the land be rich or poor, whether there be wood in it or not: and be ye of good courage, and bring some of the fruit of the land, since it is the season of the first ripe grapes. So they went up, and searched the land, from the 21 desert of Zin to Rehob, in the way to Hamath. And 22 they went up by the south, and came to Hebron, and there were Ahiman, Sheshai, and Talmai, the children of Anak. Now Hebron was built seven years before Zoan in Egypt. And they came to the valley of Eshcol, and cut down thence 23 a branch with one cluster of grapes, and they carried it upon a pole, between two, with some pomegranates, and some figs. That place was called the valley of Eshcol [A CLUSTER 24 OF GRAPES], because of the cluster of grapes which the

25 children of Israel cut down thence. And they returned
26 from searching the land after forty days; and they went and came to Moses, and to Aaron, and to all the congregation of the children of Israel, to the desert of Paran, to Kadesh; and made report to them, and to all the congre-
27 gation, and shewed them the fruit of the land. And they told him, and said, " We went to the land whither thou sentest us, and truly it floweth with milk and honey; and
28 this is the fruit of it. But the people who dwell in the land are strong, and the cities are walled, *and* very great:
29 the children of Anak also we saw there. The Amalekites dwell in the southern part of the land; and the Hittites, and the Jebusites, and the Amorites, dwell among the mountains; and the Canaanites dwell by the sea, and by the
30 side of Jordan."—And Caleb stilled the people towards Moses, and said, "Let us go up at once and possess it; for
31 we are well able to subdue it." But the men who had gone up with him said, " We are not able to go up against the
32 people; for they are stronger than we." They also spread among the children of Israel an evil report of the land which they had searched, saying, "The land, through which we passed, to search it, is a land that devoureth its inhabitants: and all the people that we saw in it are men of a
33 great stature; and there we saw the giants, the sons of Anak, of the race of the giants; and we were in our own sight as locusts, and so we were in their sight."

1 CHAP. XIV.—And all the congregation lifted up their voices, and cried; and the people wept during that night.
2 And all the children of Israel murmured against Moses and against Aaron: and the whole congregation said to them, "Oh that we had died in the land of Egypt! or that in
3 this desert we might die! For why hath Jehovah brought us into this land, to fall by the sword, and our wives and our children to become a prey? would it not be better for us to
4 return into Egypt?" And they said to one another, "Let us
5 appoint a chief, and let us return into Egypt." Then Moses and Aaron fell on their faces before all the assembly of the
6 congregation of the children of Israel. And Joshua the son of Nun, and Caleb the son of Jephunneh, *who were* of
7 those that had searched the land, rent their clothes, and spake to all the congregation of the children of Israel, saying, " The land, through which we passed to search it, is an

exceeding good land. If Jehovah delight in us, he will bring us into this land, and give it to us; a land which floweth with milk and honey. Only rebel not ye against 9 Jehovah, nor fear ye the people of the land; for they will be bread for us: their defence is departed from them, and Jehovah is with us: fear them not." Then all the congre- 10 gation spake of stoning them with stones: but the glory of Jehovah appeared on the tent of meeting, before all the children of Israel. And Jehovah said to Moses, "How long 11 will this people provoke me? and how long will they distrust me, after all the signs which I have shewed among them? I will smite them with pestilence, and disinherit them, and 12 will make thee a nation greater and mightier than they." But Moses said to Jehovah, "Since the Egyptians have 13 heard that thou broughtest up this people in thy might from among them; and have told it to the inhabitants of this 14 land; *and these* have heard that thou, Jehovah, art among this people; that thou, Jehovah, art seen face to face; and thy cloud remaineth over them; and *that* thou goest before them, by day in a pillar of cloud, and in a pillar of fire by night.—Now, if thou kill all this people as one man, the 15 nations who have heard their report of thee will speak, saying, 'Because Jehovah was not able to bring this people 16 into the land which he sware to them, therefore he hath slain them in the desert.' And now, I beseech thee, let 17 thy power, O Jehovah, be magnified, according as thou hast spoken, saying, 'Jehovah is slow to anger, but abundant in 18 mercy, forgiving iniquity and trangression, acquitting even him who is not innocent; visiting the iniquity of the fathers upon the children to the third and to the fourth generation.' Pardon, I beseech thee, the iniquity of this 19 people, according to the greatness of thy mercy, and as thou hast forgiven this people from *their leaving* Egypt even until now." And Jehovah said, "I pardon *them*, according to thy 20 word: yet truly as I live, and *as* all the earth is filled with 21 the glory of Jehovah, none of those men, who have seen my 22 glory, and my miracles which I have done in Egypt and in the desert, and have tried me now these ten times, and have not hearkened to my voice, shall see the land which 23 I sware to their fathers; none of those who have despised me shall see it. But my servant Caleb, because he had 24 another spirit in him, and hath followed me fully, I will bring him into the land into which he hath been, and his

25 seed shall possess it. Since the Amalekites and the Canaanites are stationed in the valley, turn about to-morrow and journey towards the desert by the way of the Red Sea."

26 Again Jehovah spake to Moses and to Aaron, saying,
27 "How long *shall I bear with* this evil congregation, who murmur against me? I have heard the murmurings of the
28 children of Israel, which they utter against me. Say to them, 'As I live, saith Jehovah, as ye have spoken in my
29 hearing, so will I do to you: in this desert, your carcases shall fall; and none of you who were mustered, according to your whole number, from the age of twenty years and
30 upward, who have murmured against me, shall go into the land in which I sware that ye should dwell, except Caleb the
31 son of Jephunneh, and Joshua the son of Nun. But your little ones, who ye said would be a prey, I will bring in, and
32 they shall know the land which ye have despised. But
33 as for you, your carcases shall fall in this desert. And your children shall wander in the desert forty years, and bear your transgressions, until your carcases are wasted in the
34 desert. According to the number of the days in which ye were searching the land, forty days, each day for a year, shall ye bear your iniquities, *even* forty years; and ye shall
35 know my estrangement *from you*. I Jehovah have said, I will surely do it to all this evil congregation, who have gathered together against me; in this desert they shall be
36 consumed, and there they shall die.'" Now the men whom Moses had sent to search the land, who returned, and made all the congregation to murmur against him, by bringing up
37 an evil report concerning the land, even those men, who brought up the evil report concerning the land, died by the
38 plague before Jehovah. But Joshua the son of Nun, and Caleb the son of Jephunneh, survived of the men who went to search the land.

39 Then Moses told these things to all the children of Israel:
40 and the people mourned greatly. And they rose early in the morning, that they might go up to the hill-top, saying, "Lo, we are here, and will go up to the place which Jehovah
41 hath promised: for we have sinned." And Moses said, "Why will ye now transgress the command of Jehovah?
42 but it will not prosper. Go not up, for Jehovah is not
43 among you; lest ye be smitten before your enemies. For the Amalekites and the Canaanites are there before you, and

R

ye shall fall by the sword: because ye have turned away from Jehovah, Jehovah will not be with you." But they presumed to go up to the hill-top; although the ark of the covenant of Jehovah, and Moses, moved not from the midst of the camp. Then the Amalekites, and the Canaanites who were stationed on that hill, came down to meet them, and smote them, and discomfited them unto Hormah. 44 45

CHAP. XV.—And Jehovah spake to Moses, saying, "Speak to the children of Israel, and say to them, 'When ye come into the land of your habitation, which I give to you, and will make an offering by fire to Jehovah, a burnt-offering, or a sacrifice, to accomplish a vow, or as a free-will-offering, or in your solemn feasts, to make an acceptable odour to Jehovah, from the herd, or from the flock; then shall he who offereth his offering to Jehovah bring a meal-offering of a tenth *part of an ephah* of fine flour, mingled with the fourth *part* of a hin of oil. And the fourth *part* of a hin of wine for a drink-offering shalt thou prepare, with the burnt-offering or sacrifice, for every lamb. But for a ram, thou shalt prepare for a meal-offering two-tenths *of an ephah* of fine flour mingled with the third *part* of a hin of oil. And for a drink-offering thou shalt offer the third *part* of a hin of wine, an acceptable odour to Jehovah. And when thou preparest a bullock as a burnt-offering, or as a sacrifice to accomplish a vow, or as a peace-offering to Jehovah; then shall be brought with a bullock a meal-offering of three-tenths *of an ephah* of fine flour mingled with half a hin of oil. And thou shalt bring for a drink-offering half a hin of wine, for an offering made by fire, an acceptable odour to Jehovah. Thus shall it be done for a bullock, or for a ram, or for a lamb, or for a kid. According to the number that ye shall prepare, thus shall ye offer for every one, according to their number. Every one born in the land shall do these things in this manner, in offering an offering made by fire, an acceptable odour to Jehovah. And if a stranger sojourning with you, or whoso-ever *be living* among you throughout your generations, will offer an offering made by fire, an acceptable odour to Jehovah; as ye do, so he shall do. There shall be one statute for you of the congregation, and for the stranger that sojourneth *with you*, a perpetual statute throughout your generations: as ye are, so shall the stranger be before

16 Jehovah: one law and one ordinance shall be for you, and for the stranger that sojourneth with you.'"

18 And Jehovah spake to Moses, saying, "Speak to the children of Israel, and say to them, 'When ye come into 19 the land into which I am bringing you, and ye are about to eat of the bread of the land, ye shall offer up a heave-20 offering to Jehovah. Ye shall offer up a cake of the first of your dough for a heave-offering; as the heave-offering 21 of the threshing-floor, so shall ye heave it. Of the first of your dough ye shall give to Jehovah a heave-offering throughout your generations.

22 And if ye have erred, and not observed all these com-23 mandments which Jehovah hath spoken to Moses, all that Jehovah hath commanded you by Moses, from the day in which Jehovah commanded *Moses*, and thenceforward 24 throughout your generations; if a sin have been committed through ignorance, without the knowledge of the congregation, then the whole congregation shall offer one young bullock for a burnt-offering, for an acceptable odour to Jehovah, with its meal-offering, and its drink-offering, according to the ordinance, and one kid of the goats for a 25 sin-offering. Thus the priest shall make an atonement for all the congregation of the children of Israel, and they shall be forgiven: for it was *done through* ignorance, and they have brought their offering, a sacrifice made by fire to Jehovah, and their sin-offering before Jehovah, for their *sin* 26 *of* ignorance. And all the congregation of the children of Israel, and the stranger who sojourneth among them, shall be forgiven; since all the people *sinned* through ignorance. 27 And if any soul sin through ignorance, he shall bring a 28 she-goat of the first year for a sin-offering. And the priest shall make an atonement for the soul who hath sinned through ignorance, when he hath sinned through ignorance before Jehovah, to make an atonement for him; and he 29 shall be forgiven. Ye shall have one law for him who sinneth through ignorance, *both* for him who is born among the children of Israel, and for the stranger who sojourneth 30 among them. But the soul who doeth any thing presumptuously, *whether* born in the land, or a stranger, he insulteth Jehovah; that soul therefore shall be cut off from 31 among his people. Because he has despised the word of Jehovah, and hath broken his commandment, that soul shall be utterly cut off; his iniquity shall be upon him.'"

Now while the children of Israel were in the desert, they ³² found a man gathering sticks on the sabbath-day. And ³³ they who had found him gathering sticks brought him to Moses and Aaron, and to all the congregation; and they ³⁴ put him in custody, because it had not been declared what should be done to him. And Jehovah said to Moses, "The ³⁵ man shall be surely put to death: the whole congregation shall stone him with stones without the camp." So the whole ³⁶ congregation brought him without the camp, and stoned him with stones, and he died; as Jehovah commanded Moses.

And Jehovah spake to Moses, saying, "Speak to the ³⁸ children of Israel, and bid them to make, throughout their generations, fringes on the borders of their garments, and to put upon the fringe of the borders a riband of blue; and ye shall have this fringe, that when ye look upon it, ye ³⁹ may remember all the commandments of Jehovah, and do them; and not wander after your own heart, and your own eyes, after which ye have gone astray; that ye may re- ⁴⁰ member, and do all my commandments, and be holy to your God. I am Jehovah your God, who brought you out of ⁴¹ the land of Egypt, to be your God: I am Jehovah your God."

CHAP. XVI.—Now Korah the son of Izhar, the son of ¹ Kohath, the son of Levi; and Dathan and Abiram the sons of Eliab, and On the son of Peleth, sons of Reuben, murmured; and they rose up before Moses, with two hundred ² and fifty men of the children of Israel, princes of the assembly, the called of the congregation, men of renown; and ³ they gathered themselves together against Moses and against Aaron, and said to them, "*Ye take* too much upon you, since all the congregation are holy, every one of them, and Jehovah is among them: why then do ye exalt yourselves above the congregation of Jehovah?" And when Moses ⁴ heard this, he fell upon his face; and he spake to Korah, ⁵ and to all his company, saying, "In the morning Jehovah will shew who is his, and who is holy, and will cause him to come near to him; him whom he hath chosen will he cause to come near to him. This do: Take ye censers, Korah, ⁶ and all his company, and put fire in them, and put incense ⁷ on them before Jehovah to-morrow; and that man whom Jehovah shall choose, shall be holy: *ye take* too much upon you, ye sons of Levi." And Moses also said to Korah, ⁸

9 "Hear, I pray you, ye sons of Levi: Is it a small thing with you, that the God of Israel hath separated you from the congregation of Israel, to bring you near to himself, to do the service of the tabernacle of Jehovah, and to stand 10 before the congregation, to minister to them? And he hath brought thee, and all thy brethren the sons of Levi, near 11 to himself; and ye seek the priesthood also. For which cause *both* thou and all thy company are gathered together against Jehovah: for what is Aaron, that ye murmur against 12 him?" Then Moses sent to call Dathan and Abiram, the 13 sons of Eliab; but they said, "We will not come up. Is it a small thing that thou hast brought us up out of a land flowing with milk and honey, to kill us in the desert, that 14 thou wouldst make thyself a prince over us? Moreover, thou hast not brought us into a land flowing with milk and honey, or given us inheritance of fields and vineyards. Wilt thou put out the eyes of these men? We will not 15 come up." And Moses was very angry, and said to Jehovah, "Respect not thou their offering! Not one ass have I taken away from them, nor have I injured one of them." 16 And Moses said to Korah, "Be thou and all thy company 17 before Jehovah, thou, and they, and Aaron, to-morrow; and take every man his censer, and put incense on them, and bring ye before Jehovah every man his censer, two hundred and fifty censers; thou also, and Aaron, each *of you* his 18 censer." And they took every man his censer, and put fire in them, and laid incense on them, and stood at the door of 19 the tent of meeting with Moses and Aaron. And Korah gathered all the congregation against them, to the door of the tent of meeting; and the glory of Jehovah appeared to 20 all the congregation. And Jehovah spake to Moses, and to 21 Aaron, saying, "Separate yourselves from among this con-22 gregation, that I may consume them in a moment." And they fell upon their faces, and said, "O God, the God of the spirits of all flesh, shall one man sin, and wilt thou be wroth 23 with all the congregation?" Again Jehovah spake to Moses, 24 saying, "Speak to the congregation, saying, 'Go ye up from about the tabernacle of Korah, Dathan, and Abiram.'" 25 And Moses rose up, and went to Dathan and Abiram; 26 and the elders of Israel followed him. And he spake to the congregation, saying, "Depart, I pray you, from the tents of these wicked men, and touch nothing of 27 theirs lest ye be consumed in all their sins." So they

went up from the tabernacle of Korah, Dathan, and Abiram, on every side; and Dathan and Abiram came out, and stood in the door of their tents, and their wives, and their sons, and their little children. And Moses said, "By this ye 28 shall know that Jehovah hath sent me to do all these works; that *I have* not *done them* of my own mind. If these men 29 die as all *other* men die, or if they be punished as all *other* men are punished; *then* Jehovah hath not sent me: but if 30 Jehovah make a new thing, and the ground open her mouth, and swallow them up, with all that belong to them, and they go down alive into the grave; then ye shall know that these men have despised Jehovah." And it came to pass when 31 he had made an end of speaking all these words, that the ground clave asunder that *was* under them; and the earth 32 opened her mouth, and swallowed them, and their families, and all the men who *were* joined with Korah, and all *their* goods. They, and all that *belonged* to them, went down alive into 33 the grave, and the earth closed upon them; and they perished from among the congregation. And all the Israelites 34 who were round about them fled at their cry: for they said, "Lest the earth swallow us up *also*." And there came out 35 a fire from Jehovah, and consumed the two hundred and fifty men that offered incense.

And Jehovah spake to Moses, saying, "Speak to Eleazar 37 the son of Aaron the priest, that he take up the censers out of the burning, and scatter thou the fire abroad; for these 38 sinners have hallowed the censers by their deaths. And make them into broad plates for a covering of the altar; for they offered them before Jehovah, therefore they are hallowed; and they shall be a sign to the children of Israel." So Eleazar the priest took the brazen censers, with which 39 they who were burnt had offered; and they were made into broad *plates* for a covering to the altar, *to be* a memorial to 40 the children of Israel, that no stranger, who is not of the seed of Aaron should approach to offer incense before Jehovah; that he be not as Korah, and as his company: as Jehovah had said to him by Moses.

Yet, on the morrow, all the congregation of the children 41 of Israel murmured against Moses and against Aaron, saying, "Ye have killed the people of Jehovah." And it came to 42 pass when the congregation was gathered together against Moses and against Aaron, that they turned toward the tent of meeting: and, lo, the cloud covered it, and the glory of

43 Jehovah appeared. And Moses and Aaron came before the
44 tent of meeting. And Jehovah spake to Moses, saying,
45 "Go ye up from the midst of this congregation, and I will
consume them in a moment." And they fell on their faces.
46 And Moses said to Aaron, "Take a censer, and put in
it fire from off the altar, and put on incense, and go quickly
to the congregation, and make an atonement for them: for
wrath is gone forth from Jehovah; the plague is begun."
47 And Aaron took *a censer,* as Moses commanded, and ran
into the midst of the congregation; and, lo, the plague was
begun among the people; so he put on incense, and made
48 an atonement for the people. And he stood between the
49 dead and the living; and the plague was stayed. Now they
who died of the plague were fourteen thousand and seven
50 hundred, beside those who died in the affair of Korah. And
Aaron returned to Moses, to the door of the tent of meeting,
when the plague was stayed.

1   CHAP. XVII.—And Jehovah spake to Moses, saying,
2 "Speak to the children of Israel, and take from every one of
them a staff, according to the house of their fathers, from all
their princes, according to the house of their fathers, twelve
3 staves: write thou every man's name upon his staff. And
the name of Aaron thou shalt write upon the staff of Levi:
for each staff shall be for the head of the house of their
4 fathers. And thou shalt lay them up in the tent of meeting,
5 before the testimonials, where I meet with you. And it shall
come to pass that the staff of that man, whom I choose,
shall blossom, that I may cause to cease from me the murmurings of the children of Israel, which they murmur against
6 you." And Moses spake to the children of Israel; and all
their princes gave him a staff, a staff for each prince, according to their fathers' houses, twelve staves: and the staff of
7 Aaron was among their staves. Then Moses laid up the
8 staves before Jehovah in the tent of the testimonials. And
it came to pass that on the morrow, Moses went into the
tent of the testimonials; and, lo, the staff of Aaron, for the
house of Levi, had budded, and brought forth buds, and
9 produced blossoms, and yielded almonds. And Moses
brought out all the staves from before Jehovah to all the
children of Israel: and they looked, and took every man his
10 staff. Then Jehovah said to Moses, "Bring Aaron's staff
again before the testimonials, to be kept for a sign to the

rebels; that thou mayest entirely take away their murmurings from me, that they die not." And Moses did as Jehovah commanded him; so he did.

And the children of Israel spake to Moses, saying, "Lo, we expire, we perish, we all perish! Every one who cometh even near to the tabernacle of Jehovah dies! Must we all expire?" CHAP. XVIII.—Then Jehovah said to Aaron, "Thou, and thy sons, and thy father's house with thee, shall bear the iniquity of the sanctuary; and thou and thy sons with thee shall bear the iniquity of your priesthood. And thy brethren also, the tribe of Levi, the tribe of thy father, thou shalt take with thee, that they may be joined to thee, and minister to thee. Thou indeed, and thy sons with thee *shall minister* before the tent of the testimonials; and they shall keep thy charge, and the charge of all the tent: but they shall not come nigh the utensils of the sanctuary and the altar, that neither they nor ye die. And they shall be joined to thee, and keep the charge of the tent of meeting, for all the service of the tabernacle: and a stranger shall not come nigh to you. But ye shall keep the charge of the sanctuary, and the charge of the altar; that there be no more wrath against the children of Israel. For, lo, I have taken your brethren the Levites from among the children of Israel, a gift to you, given to Jehovah, to do the service of the tent of meeting. But thou and thy sons with thee shall keep your priesthood for every thing about the altar, and within the veil; and ye shall serve: the priesthood I give *to you as* a gift; and the stranger that cometh nigh shall be put to death."

And Jehovah spake to Aaron, "Lo, I also give to thee the charge of my heave-offerings of all the hallowed things of the children of Israel; to thee I give them, the portion of thyself and thy sons, by a perpetual statute. This shall be thine of the most holy things, *reserved* from the fire: Every offering of theirs, every meal-offering of theirs, and every sin-offering of theirs, and every trespass-offering of theirs, which they shall render to me, shall be most holy for thee and for thy sons. In the most holy *place* thou shalt eat it; every male may eat of it: it shall be holy to thee. And this is thine: the heave-offering of their gift, with all the wave-offerings of the children of Israel: I give them to thee, and to thy sons, and to thy daughters with thee, by a perpetual statute: every one who is clean in thy house may eat

NUMBERS XVIII.

2 of it. All the best of the oil, and all the best of the wine, and of the wheat, the first-fruits of them, which they shall 13 offer to Jehovah, these I give to thee. Whatsoever is first ripe in the land, which they shall bring to Jehovah, shall be thine: 14 every one who is clean in thy house may eat of it. Every 15 thing devoted in Israel shall be thine. Every thing that openeth the womb of all flesh, which they offer to Jehovah, both of men and of beasts, shall be thine: but the first-born of man thou shalt surely redeem, and the first-born of un-
16 clean beasts thou shalt redeem. And those that are redeemed from the age of one month, thou shalt redeem according to thy valuation, at five shekels, according to the shekel of the
17 sanctuary, which is twenty gerahs. But the firstling of a cow, or the firstling of a sheep, or the firstling of a goat, thou shalt not redeem; they are holy: thou shalt sprinkle their blood upon the altar, and shalt burn their fat an offer-
18 ing made by fire, an acceptable odour to Jehovah. And the flesh of them shall be thine, as the wave-breast and as the
19 right shoulder it shall be thine. All the heave-offerings of the holy things, which the children of Israel offer to Jehovah, I give to thee and thy sons, and thy daughters with thee, by a perpetual statute; a perpetual covenant of salt before Jehovah to thee, and to thy seed with thee."

20 And Jehovah said to Aaron, "Thou shalt have no inheritance in their land, nor shalt thou have any portion among them: I am thy portion, and thine inheritance, among the 21 children of Israel. And, lo, I give to the children of Levi all the tithes in Israel as an inheritance, for their service 22 which they serve, the service of the tent of meeting. For the children of Israel must not henceforth come nigh the 23 tent of meeting, lest they bear sin and die. But the Levites shall do the service of the tent of meeting, and they shall bear their iniquity. *It shall* be a perpetual statute throughout your generations, that among the children of Israel they 24 shall have no inheritance. But the tithes of the children of Israel, which they offer *as* a heave-offering to Jehovah, I give to the Levites to inherit: therefore I have said of them, 'Among the children of Israel they shall have no inheri-
26 tance.'" And Jehovah spake to Moses, saying, "Speak to the Levites, and say to them, 'When ye take of the children of Israel the tithes, which I give to you from them for your inheritance, then ye shall offer up a heave-offering of it to 27 Jehovah, a tithe of the tithe. And *this* your heave-offering

shall be reckoned to you as the corn from the threshing-floor, and as the fulness of the wine-press. Thus ye also shall 28 offer a heave-offering to Jehovah of all your tithes which ye receive of the children of Israel; and of them ye shall give the heave-offering of Jehovah to Aaron the priest. Of all 29 your gifts ye shall offer every heave-offering of Jehovah, of all the best of them, the part of them which is hallowed. Therefore thou shalt say to them, 'When ye have heaved 30 the best *part* of it, then it shall be counted to the Levites as the produce of the threshing-floor, and as the produce of the wine-press. And ye may eat it in any place, ye and your 31 households: for it is your reward for your service in the tent of meeting. And ye shall bear no sin on account of it, when 32 ye have heaved from it the best of it; nor shall ye pollute the holy things of the children of Israel, and die.'"

CHAP. XIX.—And Jehovah spake to Moses, and to 1 Aaron, saying, "This is an ordinance of the law which Je- 2 hovah hath commanded, saying, 'Speak to the children of Israel, that they bring to thee a red heifer, in which is no spot, without blemish, upon which a yoke never came. And ye shall give her to Eleazar the priest, who 3 shall take her forth without the camp, and *one* shall slay her before his face. Then Eleazar the priest shall take 4 some of her blood with his finger, and sprinkle some of her blood directly before the tent of meeting seven times. And 5 *one* shall burn the heifer in his sight; her skin, and her flesh, and her blood, with her dung, shall he burn. And the 6 priest shall take cedar-wood, and hyssop, and scarlet *thread*, and cast them into the midst of the fire in which the heifer is burning. Then the priest shall wash his clothes, and he 7 shall bathe his body in water, and after that he shall come into the camp, and the priest shall be unclean until the evening. He also who burneth *the heifer* shall wash his clothes 8 in water, and bathe his body in water, and shall be unclean until the evening. Then one who is clean shall gather up 9 the ashes of the heifer, and lay *them* up without the camp in a clean place, and they shall be kept for the congregation of the children of Israel, for a water of impurity: it is a purification from sin. And he who gathereth up the ashes 10 of the heifer shall wash his clothes, and be unclean until the evening. Now this shall be to the children of Israel, and to the stranger that sojourneth among them, a perpetual

11 statute. He that toucheth the dead body of any one shall
12 be unclean seven days. He shall purify himself with it on the third day, and on the seventh day he shall be clean: but if he purify not himself on the third day, and on the seventh
13 day, he shall not be clean. Whosoever toucheth the dead body of any one that is dead, and purifieth not himself, defileth the tabernacle of Jehovah; and that person shall be cut off from Israel: because the water of impurity was not sprinkled upon him, he shall be unclean: his uncleanness is yet upon him.
14 And this is the law when any one dieth in a tent: All who come into the tent, and all who are in the tent, shall be un-
15 clean seven days. And every open vessel, which hath no
16 covering bound upon it, shall be unclean. And whosoever toucheth one that is slain with a sword in the open fields, or a dead body, or a bone of a man, or a grave, shall be unclean
17 seven days. And for *the purification of* an unclean person, let them take some of the ashes of the burnt heifer of purification from sin, and let running water be put to them in a
18 vessel; then let a clean person take hyssop, and dip it in the water, and sprinkle *it* upon the tent, and upon all the utensils, and upon all the persons that were there, and upon him that touched a bone, or one slain, or one dead, or a
19 grave. And the clean person shall sprinkle upon the unclean on the third day, and on the seventh day; and on the seventh day he shall purify himself, and wash his clothes, and bathe
20 himself in water, and in the evening he shall be clean. But the man that shall be unclean, and shall not purify himself, that soul shall be cut off from among the congregation, because he hath defiled the sanctuary of Jehovah: the water of impurity hath not been sprinkled upon him; he is un-
21 clean. And it shall be a perpetual statute to you, that he who sprinkleth the water of impurity, shall wash his clothes; and he who toucheth the water of impurity shall be unclean
22 until evening. And whatsoever the unclean *person* toucheth shall be unclean; and the soul that toucheth it shall be unclean until evening.'"

1 CHAP. XX.—And the children of Israel, the whole congregation, came into the desert of Zin, in the first month, and the people abode in Kadesh; and there Miriam died,
2 and there she was buried. But there was no water for the congregation; so they gathered themselves together against

Moses and against Aaron. And the people contended with 3 Moses, and spake, saying, "Oh that we had expired when our brethren expired before Jehovah! And why have ye brought 4 up the congregation of Jehovah into this desert, that we and our cattle should die here? And why have ye made us to come 5 up out of Egypt, to bring us into this evil place? it is not a place of seed, or of figs, or of vines, or of pomegranates; and there is no water to drink." And Moses and Aaron went 6 from the presence of the assembly to the door of the tent of meeting, and they fell upon their faces; and the glory of Jehovah appeared to them. And Jehovah spake to Moses, 7 saying, "Take the rod, and gather thou the congregation 8 together, thou and Aaron thy brother, and speak ye to the rock in their presence, that it give forth its water, and that thou mayest bring forth to them water out of the rock: so thou shalt give drink to the congregation and their beasts." Then Moses took the rod from before Jehovah, as he com- 9 manded him. And Moses and Aaron gathered the assembly 10 together before the rock, and *Moses* said to them, "Hear now, ye rebels, must we bring forth water for you out of this rock?" And Moses lifted up his hand, and with his rod he 11 smote the rock twice; and the water came out abundantly: and the congregation and their beasts drank. But Jehovah 12 said to Moses and Aaron, "Because ye believed me not, to sanctify me in the presence of the children of Israel, ye shall not bring this congregation into the land which I give to them." This is the water of Meribah [CONTENTION]; be- 13 cause the children of Israel contended with Jehovah, and he was sanctified in them.

And Moses sent messengers from Kadesh to the king of 14 Edom, "Thus say thy brethren the Israelites; 'Thou knowest all the labours that have befallen us; how our fathers went 15 down into Egypt, how we dwelt in Egypt a long time, and how the Egyptians afflicted us and our fathers: but when we 16 cried to Jehovah, he heard our voice, and sent an angel, and brought us forth out of Egypt; and, lo, we are in Kadesh, a city in the extremity of thy border: let us pass, we pray 17 thee, through thy land: we will not pass through the fields, or through the vineyards, nor will we drink the water of the wells: by the king's way we will go; we will not turn to the right hand or to the left, until we have passed thy borders.'" But the Edomite said to him, "Thou shalt not 18 pass by me, lest I come out against thee with the sword."

19 And the children of Israel said to him, "By the highway we will go; and if I and my cattle drink of thy water, then I will pay for it: I will only, without *doing* any thing *else*, go
20 through on my feet." But he said, "Thou shalt not go through." Then the Edomite came out against him with
21 much people, and with a strong hand. Thus the Edomite refused to give the Israelites a passage through his border: wherefore the Israelites turned away from him.
22 And the children of Israel, the whole congregation,
23 journeyed from Kadesh, and came to mount Hor. And Jehovah spake to Moses and Aaron in mount Hor, on the
24 border of the land of Edom, saying, "Aaron must be gathered to his people; for he shall not enter into the land which I give to the children of Israel, because ye rebelled
25 against my word at the waters of Meribah. Take Aaron
26 and Eleazar his son, and bring them up to mount Hor; and strip Aaron of his garments, and put them upon Eleazar his son; and Aaron shall be gathered *to his people*, and shall
27 die there." And Moses did as Jehovah commanded; and they went up to mount Hor, in the sight of all the congre-
28 gation. And Moses stripped Aaron of his garments, and put them upon Eleazar his son; and Aaron died there on the top of the mountain; and Moses and Eleazar came
29 down from the mountain. And when all the congregation saw that Aaron had expired, all the house of Israel mourned for Aaron thirty days.

1 CHAP. XXI.—Now the Canaanite, the king of Arad, who dwelt in the south, heard that the Israelites were coming by the way of Atharim; and he fought against the Israelites,
2 and took some of them prisoners. And the Israelites vowed a vow to Jehovah, and said, "If thou wilt indeed deliver this people into my hand, then I will devote their
3 cities." And Jehovah hearkened to the voice of the Israelites, and delivered the Canaanites *into their hand;* and they devoted them and their cities: so the name of the place was called Hormah [THE DEVOTED PLACE].
4 Then they journeyed from mount Hor, by the way of the Red Sea, to go round the land of Edom: and the soul of the
5 people was dispirited because of the way. And the people spake against God, and against Moses, "Why have ye brought us up out of Egypt, to die in the desert? for there is no bread, and there is no water; and our soul loatheth

this very light bread." And Jehovah sent fiery serpents 6
among the people, and they bit the people; so that much
people of the Israelites died. Therefore the people came to 7
Moses, and said, "We have sinned, for we have spoken
against Jehovah, and against thee; pray to Jehovah, that he
may take away the serpents from us." And Moses prayed
for the people. And Jehovah said to Moses, "Make thee a 8
fiery serpent, and set it upon a pole; and it shall come to
pass that every one who is bitten, when he looketh upon it,
shall live." So Moses made a serpent of brass, and put it 9
upon a pole: and it came to pass that if a serpent had
bitten any man, when he beheld the serpent of brass, he
lived.

And the children of Israel journeyed, and encamped in 10
Oboth. And they journeyed from Oboth, and encamped at 11
Ije-abarim, in the desert which is before Moab, toward
the sun-rising. Thence they journeyed, and encamped in 12
the valley of Zared. Thence they journeyed, and encamped 13
by the side of Arnon, which *flows* through the desert
coming out of the coasts of the Amorites: for Arnon is the
boundary of the Moabites, between the Moabites and the
Amorites. Wherefore it is said in the Book of the Wars of 14
Jehovah,

"He showed himself in a tempest,
  And the torrents of Arnon;
  And he poured forth the torrents that turn to Shebeth-ar, 15
  And lean on the border of Moab."

And thence *they journeyed* to Beer: that is the well 16
where Jehovah spake to Moses, "Gather the people
together, and I will give them water." Then the Israelites 17
sang this song;

"Spring up, O well; sing ye to it:
  Well, which the princes digged,
  Which the nobles of the people digged,
  Digging with their staves."

And from the desert *they journeyed* to Mattanah; and 19
from Mattanah to Nahaliel; and from Nahaliel to Bamoth;
and from Bamoth *in* the valley, that is in the country of 20
Moab, to the top of Pisgah, which looketh towards Jeshimon.

And Israel sent messengers to Sihon, king of the 21
Amorites, saying, "Let me pass through thy land; we will 22
not turn into the fields, or the vineyards; we will not drink

of the water of the well: we will go along by the king's
23 highway, until we be past thy borders." But Sihon would
not suffer the Israelites to pass through his border. So Sihon
gathered all his people together, and went out against the
Israelites into the desert; and he came to Jahaz, and fought
24 against the Israelites. And the Israelites smote him with
the edge of the sword, and took possession of his land from
the Arnon to the Jabbok, even to the children of Ammon:
25 for the border of the children of Ammon *was* strong. And
the Israelites took all these cities; and the Israelites dwelt
in all the cities of the Amorites, in Heshbon, and in all its
26 villages. For Heshbon was the city of Sihon, the king of
the Amorites, who had fought against the former king of
Moab, and taken all his land out of his hand, even to the
27 Arnon. Wherefore the poets have said,
"Come to Heshbon, let it be rebuilt,
Let the city of Sihon be repaired:
28 For a fire went forth from Heshbon,
A flame from the city of Sihon:
It consumed Ar of Moab,
The lords of Bamoth-Arnon.
Alas for thee, Moab!
Thou art undone, O people of Chemosh:
He gave up his sons to flight,
And his daughters to captivity,
To Sihon king of the Amorites.
30 And their sown fields Heshbon destroyed unto Dibon,
Their fallow fields unto Nophah, which *reacheth* to Medeba."
31 Thus the Israelites dwelt in the land of the Amorites.
32 And Moses sent men to spy out Jazer; and they took its
33 villages, and drove out the Amorites who were there. And
they turned, and went up by the way to Bashan: and Og
the king of Bashan went out against them, he and all his
34 people, to battle at Edrei. And Jehovah said to Moses,
"Fear him not: for I have delivered him into thy hand,
and all his people, and his land; and thou shalt do to
him as thou didst to Sihon king of the Amorites, who
35 dwelt at Heshbon." So they smote him, and his sons
and all his people, until there was none left to him alive,
1 and they took possession of his land. CHAP. XXII.—
And the children of Israel journeyed, and encamped in the
plains of Moab, on the side of the Jordan *opposite to* Jericho.

And Balak, the son of Zippor, saw all that the Israelites 2 had done to the Amorites. And the Moabites were greatly 3 afraid of the people, because they were numerous: and the Moabites were distressed because of the children of Israel. And the Moabites said to the elders of Midian, "This mul- 4 titude will now lick up all around us, as the ox licketh up the grass of the field." Now Balak, the son of Zippor, was king of the Moabites at that time. And he sent messengers 5 to Balaam, the son of Beor, to Pethor, which is by the river of the land of the children of Ammon, to invite him, saying, "Lo, there is a people come out from Egypt; and, lo, they cover the face of the land, and they are set down over against me. Come now, therefore, I pray thee, curse for 6 me this people, for they are too mighty for me: perhaps I shall be able to smite them, and to drive them out of the land: for I know that he whom thou blessest is blessed, and he whom thou cursest is cursed." And the elders of Moab, 7 and the elders of Midian departed, with the rewards of divination in their hands; and they came to Balaam, and spake to him the words of Balak. And he said to them, "Lodge 8 here this night, and I will bring you an answer, as Jehovah shall speak to me." So the princes of Moab abode with Balaam.

And God came to Balaam, and said, "Who are these men 9 that are with thee?" And Balaam said to God, "Balak, the 10 son of Zippor, king of Moab, hath sent to me, *saying*, 'Lo, 11 a people is come out of Egypt, who cover the face of the land: now then come, curse them for me; perhaps I shall be able to overcome them, and to drive them out.'" And God 12 said to Balaam, "Thou shalt not go with them; thou shalt not curse the people: for they are blessed." And Balaam 13 rose up in the morning, and said to the princes of Balak, "Go ye to your own land: for Jehovah refuseth to permit me to go with you." And the princes of Moab rose up, and 14 they went to Balak, and said, "Balaam refuseth to come with us."

And Balak sent yet again princes, more, and more hon- 15 ourable than they. And they came to Balaam, and said to 16 him, "Thus saith Balak, the son of Zippor, 'Refrain not, I pray thee, from coming to me: For I will greatly honour 17 thee, and I will do whatsoever thou sayest to me. Come, therefore, I pray thee, curse for me this people.'" And 18 Balaam answered and said to the servants of Balak, "If

Balak would give me his house full of silver and gold, I cannot go beyond the word of Jehovah my God, by doing 19 what is little or great. Yet, now, I pray you, remain ye also here this night, that I may know what more Jehovah 20 will say to me." And God came to Balaam at night, and said to him, "Since the men have come to invite thee, rise up, *and* go with them; but yet the word which I shall say 21 to thee, that shalt thou do." And Balaam rose up in the morning, and saddled his ass, and went with the princes of 22 Moab. And the anger of God was kindled because he went; and an angel of Jehovah stood in the way to oppose him. Now he was riding upon his ass, and his two servants were 23 with him. And the ass saw the angel of Jehovah standing in the way, and his sword drawn in his hand; and the ass turned aside out of the way, and went into the field; and 24 Balaam smote the ass, to turn her into the way. But the angel of Jehovah stood in a narrow path between two vineyards, a wall being on this side and a wall on that side. 25 And when the ass saw the angel of Jehovah, she pressed against the wall, and crushed Balaam's foot against the wall; 26 and he smote her again. And the angel of Jehovah went further, and stood in a place so narrow that there was no 27 room to turn, either to the right hand or to the left. And when the ass saw the angel of Jehovah, she fell down under Balaam; and Balaam's anger was kindled, and he smote the 28 ass with a staff. And Jehovah opened the mouth of the ass; and she said to Balaam, "What have I done to thee, 29 that thou hast smitten me these three times?" And Balaam said to the ass, "Because thou hast mocked me: I would there were a sword in my hand, for now would I kill thee." 30 And the ass said to Balaam, "Am I not thine ass, upon which thou hast ridden ever since I was thine to this day? Have I ever been accustomed to do so to thee?" And he 31 said, "No." Then Jehovah opened the eyes of Balaam, and he saw the angel of Jehovah standing in the way, and his sword drawn in his hand; and he bowed his head, and 32 fell down on his face. And the angel of Jehovah said to him, "Wherefore hast thou smitten thine ass these three times? lo, I went out to oppose thee, because thy way is 33 perverse before me: and the ass saw me, and turned from me these three times; unless she had turned from me, surely now I had slain thee indeed, and saved her alive." 34 And Balaam said to the angel of Jehovah, "I have sinned;

for I knew not that thou stoodest in the way against me: now, therefore, if it displease thee, I will return." And the angel of Jehovah said to Balaam, "Go with the men: but speak only the word that I shall speak to thee." So Balaam went with the princes of Balak.

And when Balak heard that Balaam was come, he went out to meet him, to a city of Moab, which is near the boundary of Arnon, in the extreme boundary of the land of Moab. And Balak said to Balaam, "Did I not earnestly send to thee to invite thee? wherefore camest thou not to me? am I not able indeed to honour thee?" And Balaam said to Balak, " Lo, I am come to thee: have I now any power at all to say any thing? the word that God putteth into my mouth, that I must speak."

And Balaam went with Balak, and they came to Kirjath-huzoth. And Balak slew oxen and sheep, and sent portions to Balaam, and to the princes that were with him. And on the morrow, Balak took Balaam, and brought him up to the high places of Baal, that thence he might see the extreme part of the people. CHAP. XXIII. And Balaam said to Balak, "Build me here seven altars, and prepare me here seven oxen and seven rams." And Balak did as Balaam had spoken; and Balak and Balaam offered on *every* altar a bullock and a ram. And Balaam said to Balak, "Stand by thy burnt-offerings, and I will go; perhaps Jehovah will come t meet me: and whatsoever he sheweth me I will tell thee." Then he went to a high place. And God met Balaam; and he said to him, "I have prepared seven altars, and I have offered upon *every* altar a bullock and a ram." And Jehovah put a word in Balaam's mouth, and said, "Return to Balak, and thus thou shalt speak." And he returned to him; and, lo, he was standing by his burnt-offerings, he, and all the princes of Moab. And he took up his parable and said,

"From Aram hath Balak brought me,
The king of Moab, from the mountains of the East;
saying,
'Come, curse for me Jacob,
And come, execrate Israel.'
How shall I curse, whom God hath not cursed?
Or how shall I execrate, whom Jehovah hath not execrated?
When from the top of the rocks I see them,

And from the hills I look at them :
Lo ! a people who shall dwell alone,
And who shall not be reckoned among the nations !
10   Who can count the dust of Jacob,
And the number of the fourth part of Israel ?
May I die the death of the righteous,
And may my end be like theirs ! "

11 Then Balak said to Balaam, "What hast thou done to me ? I brought thee to curse my enemies, and, lo, thou hast
12 greatly blessed them." And he answered and said, " Must I not be careful to speak that which Jehovah hath put into
13 my mouth ? " And Balak said to him, " Come, I pray thee, with me to another place, whence thou mayest see them ; thou canst see but the extreme part of them, and canst not
14 see them all ; and curse them for me thence." So he brought him to the field of Zophim, to the top of Pisgah, and built seven altars, and offered a bullock and a ram on
15 every altar. Then *Balaam* said to Balak, "Stand here by thy burnt-offerings, while I go yonder to meet *Jehovah*."
16 And Jehovah met Balaam, and put a word into his mouth
17 and said, "Go again to Balak, and thus speak." And when he came to him, lo, he was standing by his burnt-offerings, and the princes of Moab with him. And Balak said to him,
18 "What hath Jehovah spoken ?." And he took up his parable, and said,

" Rise up, Balak, and hear ;
Hearken to me, thou son of Zippor.
19   God is not a man, that he should lie ;
Or the son of man, that he should repent.
Hath he said, and shall he not do *it* ?
Hath he spoken, and shall he not perform *it* ?
20   Lo, I am commanded to bless ;
And he hath blessed, and I cannot reverse it.
21   He beholdeth no sorrow in Jacob,
Neither doth he see trouble in Israel.
Jehovah their God is with them,
And the shout of a king is among them,
22   God brought them out of Egypt :
As the strength of the buffalo is he to them.
23   Surely there is no enchantment in Jacob,
Nor is there any divination in Israel :
At the *appointed* time it shall be told to Jacob,
And to Israel, what God is about to do !

<blockquote>
Lo! the people shall rise up as a lioness,   24
And as a young lion shall lift themselves up:
He shall not lie down until he eat of the prey,
And drink the blood of the slain."
</blockquote>

And Balak said to Balaam, "Neither curse them at all, 25 nor bless them at all." But Balaam answered and said to 26 Balak, "Spake I not to thee, saying, 'All that Jehovah speaketh that I must do?'"

And Balak said to Balaam, "Come, I pray thee, let me 27 take thee to another place: peradventure it will please God that thou mayest curse them for me thence." So Balak 28 brought Balaam to the top of Peor, that looketh toward Jeshimon. And Balaam said to Balak, "Build for me here 29 seven altars, and prepare for me here seven bullocks and seven rams." And Balak did as Balaam had said, and 30 offered a bullock and a ram on *every* altar.

CHAP. XXIV.

And when Balaam saw that it pleased Jehovah to bless 1 Israel, he went not, as at other times, to seek for enchantments, but he set his face toward the desert. And Balaam 2 lifted up his eyes, and saw the Israelites encamped according to their tribes; and the spirit of God came upon him. And he took up his parable, and said,   3

<blockquote>
"Balaam the son of Beor saith,
And the man whose eyes are open saith,
He saith who hath heard the words of God,   4
Who hath seen the vision of the Almighty,
Falling *into a trance*, but having his eyes open:
'How beautiful are thy tents, O Jacob!   5
And thy tabernacles, O Israel!
As the valleys are they spread forth,   6
As gardens by the river's side,
As lign-aloes which Jehovah hath planted,
As cedars beside the waters.
Waters shall flow from his urn,   7
And his seed shall be in many waters,
And his king shall be higher than Agag,
And his kingdom shall be exalted.
God brought him out of Egypt;   8
As the strength of the buffalo is he to him.
He shall eat up the nations his enemies,
And shall break their bones,
And pierce them through with his arrows.
He coucheth, he lieth down as a lion,   9
</blockquote>

And as a lioness: who shall rouse him?
Blessed is he that blesseth thee,
And cursed is he that curseth thee.'"

10 Then Balak's anger was kindled against Balaam, and he smote his hands together: and Balak said to Balaam, "I invited thee to curse my enemies, and, lo, thou hast greatly
11 blessed them these three times. Therefore now flee thou to thy own place: I said I would greatly honour thee; but,
12 lo, Jehovah hath kept thee back from honour." And Balaam said to Balak, "Spake I not also to thy messengers
13 whom thou sentest to me, saying, 'If Balak would give me his house full of silver and of gold, I cannot go beyond the commandment of Jehovah, to do *either* good or bad of my
14 own mind; what Jehovah saith, that must I speak?' And now, lo, I go to my own people: come, let me advise thee
15 of what this people will hereafter do to thy people." And he took up his parable and said,

"Balaam the son of Beor saith,
And the man whose eyes are open saith,
16 He saith who hath heard the words of God,
And hath known the knowledge of the Most High,
Who hath seen the vision of the Almighty,
Falling *into a trance*, but having his eyes open:
17 'I see him, but not now;
I behold him, but not nigh:
A star proceeding from Jacob,
And a sceptre rising out of Israel,
And it shall smite the corners of Moab,
And destroy all the sons of Sheth.
18 And Edom shall be a possession,
And Seir shall be a possession of his enemies,
And Israel shall do valiantly.
19 And one *sprung* from Jacob shall rule,
And he shall destroy him that remaineth of the city.'"

20 And he looked on Amalek, and took up his parable, and said,
"The first of the nations is Amalek;'
Yet its latter end will be utter destruction."
21 And he looked on the Kenites, and took up his parable, and said,
"Strong is thy dwelling-place,
And thou puttest in a rock thy nest.
22 Nevertheless the Kenite shall be destroyed,

Until Ashur shall carry thee away captive."
And he took up his parable, and said, 23
"Alas, who shall be preserved when he doeth this?
For ships *shall come* from the coast of Chittim, 24
And they will afflict Ashur, and they will afflict Eber,
And he also shall be utterly destroyed."
Then Balaam rose up, and went and returned to his place: 25
and Balak also went his way.

CHAP. XXV.—Now while the Israelites abode in Setim, 1
the people profaned themselves by committting fornication
with the daughters of Moab, who invited the people to the 2
sacrifices of their gods; and the people ate, and bowed down
to their gods. And the Israelites joined themselves to Baal- 3
Peor; and the anger of Jehovah was kindled against the
Israelites. And Jehovah said to Moses, "Take all the chiefs of 4
the people *with thee,* and order them to slay those men
who have joined themselves to Baal-Peor, and hang them up
before Jehovah against the sun, that the fierce anger of
Jehovah may be turned away from Israel." And Moses said 5
to the judges of Israel, "Slay ye every one his men who
have joined themselves to Baal-Peor." And, lo, one of the 6
children of Israel came, and brought to his brethren a Midianitish woman, in the sight of Moses, and in the sight of
all the congregation of the children of Israel, who were
weeping before the door of the tent of meeting. And when 7
Phinehas the son of Eleazar, the son of Aaron the priest, saw
it, he rose up from among the congregation, and took a
javelin in his hand; and he followed the man of Israel into 8
the tent, and thrust both of them through, the man of
Israel, and the woman, in her belly. So the plague was
stayed from the children of Israel. And those who died in 9
the plague were twenty-four thousand.
And Jehovah spake to Moses, saying, "Phinehas the son 11
of Eleazar, the son of Aaron the priest, hath turned my
wrath away from the children of Israel, by being jealous for
me among them, that I might not consume the children of
Israel in my jealousy. Wherefore, say, 'Lo, I make with him 12
a covenant of peace; and it shall be to him, and to his seed 13
after him, a covenant of a perpetual priesthood; because he
was jealous for his God, and made an atonement for the
children of Israel.'" Now the name of the Israelite who was 14
slain, (who was slain with the Midianitish woman,) was

Zimri, the son of Salu, a prince of a family among the
15 Simeonites. And the name of the Midianitish woman who
was slain was Cozbi, the daughter of Zur; chief of a people,
of a family in Midian.
17 And Jehovah spake to Moses, saying, "Distress the
18 Midianites, and smite them; for they have distressed you
by their wiles, with which they have beguiled you, in the
affair of Peor, and in the affair of Cozbi, their sister, the
daughter of a prince of Midian, who was slain in the day
of the plague, on account of Peor."

1 CHAP. XXVI.—Now after the plague, Jehovah spake to
Moses, and to Eleazar the son of Aaron the priest, saying,
2 "Take ye the sum of all the congregation of the children of
Israel, from the age of twenty years and upward, according to
the house of their fathers, all who are able to go forth to war
3 in Israel." So Moses and Eleazar the priest spake to them in
the plains of Moab, by the Jordan *opposite* to Jericho,
4 saying, *Take the sum of the people* from the age of twenty
years and upward, as Jehovah commanded Moses.

Now the children of Israel, who had come forth out of the
5 land of Egypt, *were:* Reuben, the eldest son of Israel:
and the children of Reuben; Hanoch, of whom was the
family of the Hanochites: Pallu, of whom was the family
6 of the Palluites: Hezron, of whom was the family of the
Hezronites: Carmi, of whom was the family of the
7 Carmiites. These were the families of the Reubenites:
and they who were mustered of them were forty-three thou-
8 sand and seven hundred and thirty.—And the son of Pallu;
9 Eliab. And the sons of Eliab; Nemuel, Dathan, and
Abiram. These were the Dathan and Abiram who were
called of the congregation, who strove against Moses and
against Aaron in the company of Korah, when they strove
10 against Jehovah: and the earth opened her mouth, and
swallowed them up together with Korah, when that company died, the fire devouring two hundred and fifty men;
11 and they became an example. But the children of Korah
died not.
12 The sons of Simeon, according to their families: Nemuel,
of whom was the family of the Nemuelites: Jamin, of whom
was the family of the Jaminites: Jachin, of whom was the
13 family of the Jachinites: Zerah, of whom was the family of
the Zerahites: Shaul, of whom was the family of the

Shaulites. These were the families of the Simeonites, 14 twenty-two thousand and two hundred.

The children of Gad, according to their families: Zephon, 15 of whom was the family of the Zephonites: Haggi, of whom was the family of the Haggites: Shuni, of whom was the family of the Shunites: Ozni, of whom was the family of 16 the Oznites: Eri, of whom was the family of the Erites: Arod, of whom was the family of the Arodites: Areli, of 17 whom was the family of the Arelites. These were the 18 families of the children of Gad, of whom were mustered forty thousand and five hundred.

The sons of Judah were Er and Onan: but Er and Onan 19 died in the land of Canaan. And the other sons of Judah 20 according to their families were; Shelah, of whom was the family of the Shelahites: Pharez, of whom was the family of the Pharezites: Zerah, of whom was the family of the Zerahites.—And the sons of Pharez were; Hezron, of whom 21 was the family of the Hezronites: Hamul, of whom was the family of the Hamulites. These were the families of Judah, 22 of whom were mustered seventy-six thousand and five hundred.

The sons of Issachar, according to their families were; 23 Tola, of whom was the family of the Tolaites: Pua, of whom was the family of the Punites: Jashub, of whom was the 24 family of the Jashubites: Shimron, of whom was the family of the Shimronites. These were the families of Issachar, 25 of whom were mustered sixty-four thousand and three hundred.

The sons of Zebulun, according to their families were; 26 Sered, of whom was the family of the Seredites: Elon, of whom was the family of the Elonites: Jahleel, of whom was the family of the Jahleelites. These were the families of 27 the Zebulunites, of whom were mustered sixty thousand and five hundred.

The sons of Joseph, according to their families, were 28 Manasseh and Ephraim. The sons of Manasseh were; 29 Machir, of whom was the family of the Machirites; and Machir begat Gilead: of Gilead was the family of the Gileadites.—These were the sons of Gilead: Jeezer, of 30 whom was the family of the Jeezerites: Helek, of whom was the family of the Helekites: and Asriel, of whom was 31 the family of the Asrielites: and Shechem, of whom was the family of the Shechemites: and Shemida, of whom was the 32

family of the Shemidaites: and Hepher, of whom was the
33 family of the Hepherites. And Zelophehad the son of
Hepher had no sons, but daughters: and the names of the
daughters of Zelophehad were Mahala, and Noa, Hogla,
34 Milca, and Tirza. These were the families of Manasseh, of
whom were mustered fifty-two thousand and seven hundred.
35 These were the sons of Ephraim, according to their
families: Shuthelah, of whom was the family of the Shuthe-
lahites: Becher, of whom was the family of the Becherites:
36 Tahan, of whom was the family of the Tahanites.—These
were the sons of Shuthelah: Eran, of whom was the family
37 of the Eranites. These were the families of the sons of
Ephraim, of whom were mustered thirty-two thousand and
five hundred. These were the sons of Joseph according to
their families.
38 The sons of Benjamin, according to their families were;
Bela, of whom was the family of the Belaites: Ashbel, of
whom was the family of the Ashbelites: Ahiram, of whom
39 was the family of the Ahiramites: Shupham, of whom was
the family of the Shuphamites: Hupham, of whom was the
40 family of the Huphamites.—And the sons of Bela were
Ared and Naaman: Ared, of whom was the family of the
Aredites: and Naaman, of whom was the family of the
41 Naamites. These were the sons of Benjamin, according to
their families: of whom were mustered forty-five thousand
and six hundred.
42 These were the sons of Dan, according to their families:
Shuham, of whom was the family of the Shuhamites. These
43 were the families of Dan, according to their families. All the
families of the Shuhamites, according to those who were
mustered of them, were sixty-four thousand and four
hundred.
44 The sons of Asher, according to their families were;
Jimni, of whom was the family of the Jimniites: Jesui, of
whom was the family of the Jesuiites: Beriah, of whom
45 was the family of the Beriahites.—Of the sons of Beriah:
Heber, of whom was the family of the Heberites: Malchiel,
46 of whom was the family of the Malchielites. And the
47 name of the daughter of Asher was Sarah. These were the
families of the sons of Asher, of whom were mustered fifty-
three thousand and four hundred.
48 The sons of Naphtali, according to their families were;
Jahzeel, of whom was the family of the Jahzeelites: Guni,

of whom was the family of the Guniites: Jezer, of whom ⁴⁹ was the family of the Jezerites: Shillem, of whom was the family of the Shillemites. These were the families of ⁵⁰ Naphtali, according to their families: and of them were mustered forty-five thousand and four hundred. These were ⁵¹ mustered of the children of Israel, six hundred and one thousand, and seven hundred and thirty.

And Jehovah spake to Moses, saying, "Among these the ⁵³ land shall be divided for an inheritance, according to the number of names. To many thou shalt give the greater ⁵⁴ inheritance, and to few thou shalt give the less inheritance: to every one shall his inheritance be given, according to those who were mustered of him. Yet the land shall be divided ⁵⁵ by lot: according to the names of the tribes of their fathers they shall inherit. According to the lot shall the inheri- ⁵⁶ tance be divided between many and few."

And these were mustered of the Levites, according to ⁵⁷ their families: Gershon, of whom was the family of the Gershonites: Kohath, of whom was the family of the Kohathites: Merari, of whom was the family of the Merarites. These were the families of the Levites: the ⁵⁸ family of the Libnites, the family of the Hebronites, the family of the Mahlites, the family of the Mushites, the family of the Korathites.—And Kohath begat Amram. And ⁵⁹ the name of Amram's wife was Jochabed, a daughter of Levi, whom *his wife* bare to Levi in Egypt: and she bare to Amram, Aaron, and Moses, and Miriam their sister. And ⁶⁰ to Aaron was born Nadab, and Abihu, and Eleazar, and Ithamar: but Nadab and Abihu died, when they offered ⁶¹ strange fire before Jehovah. And those who were mustered ⁶² of them were twenty-three thousand, all males, from the age of a month and upward: for they were not mustered among the children of Israel, because there was no inheritance given to them among the children of Israel. These were ⁶³ mustered by Moses and Eleazar the priest, who mustered the children of Israel in the plains of Moab, by the Jordan *opposite to* Jericho. And among these there was not a man ⁶⁴ of those whom Moses and Aaron the priest had mustered, when they mustered the children of Israel in the desert of Sinai: for Jehovah had said of them, "They shall surely ⁶⁵ die in the desert." And there was not left a man of them, except Caleb the son of Jephunneh, and Joshua the son of Nun.

1 CHAP. XXVII.—Then came the daughters of Zelophehad, the son of Hepher, the son of Gilead, the son of Machir, the son of Manasseh, of the family of Manasseh, the son of Joseph, and these were the names of his daughters; Mahala, and Noa, Hogla, Milca, and Tirza.
2 And they stood before Moses, and before Eleazar the priest, and before the princes and all the assembly, at the door of
3 the tent of meeting, saying, " Our father died in the desert, although he was not in the company of those who gathered themselves together against Jehovah in the company of Korah; but died in his own sin, and had no sons.
4 Why should the name of our father be taken away from among his family, because he hath no son? Give to us, *therefore,* a possession among the brethren of our father."
6 And Moses brought their cause before Jehovah. And Je-
7 hovah spake to Moses, saying, "The daughters of Zelophehad speak rightly: thou shalt surely give them a possession of inheritance among their father's brethren; and thou shalt
8 cause the inheritance of their father to pass to them. And thou shalt speak to the children of Israel, saying, 'If a man die, and have no son, then ye shall cause his inheritance to
9 pass to his daughter. And if he have no daughter, then ye
10 shall give his inheritance to his brethren. And if he have no brethren, then ye shall give his inheritance to his father's
11 brethren. And if his father have no brethren, then ye shall give his inheritance to the nearest kinsman of his family, and he shall possess it:'"—So this became a statute of law to the children of Israel, as Jehovah had commanded Moses.
12 And Jehovah said to Moses, " Go up this mountain Abarim, and view the land which I give to the children of
13 Israel. And when thou hast viewed it thou also shalt be gathered to thy people, as Aaron thy brother hath been
14 gathered: because, in the desert of Zin, in the strife of the congregation, ye rebelled against my commandment, to sanctify me at the waters before their eyes. (These were the waters of Meribah, at Kadesh, in the desert of Zin.)
16 Then Moses spake to Jehovah, saying, "May Jehovah, the God of the spirits of all flesh, set a man over the assembly,
17 who may go out before them, and who may go in before them, and who may lead them out, and who may bring them in; that the assembly of Jehovah be not as sheep which
18 have no shepherd!" And Jehovah said to Moses, "Take

Joshua the son of Nun, a man in whom is the spirit, and lay thy hand upon him; and set him before Eleazar the 19 priest, and before all the assembly: and give him a charge in their sight. And impart to him some of thy honour, 20 that all the assembly of the children of Israel may be obedient. And he shall stand before Eleazar the priest, who 21 shall consult for him, according to the judgment of Urim, before Jehovah: at his word they shall go out, and at his word they shall come in, *both* he, and all the children of Israel with him, even all the assembly." And Moses did as 22 Jehovah commanded him: and took Joshua, and set him before Eleazar the priest, and before all the assembly: and 23 he laid his hands upon him, and gave him a charge, as Jehovah had commanded by Moses.

CHAP. XXVIII.—And Jehovah spake to Moses, saying, 1 "Command the children of Israel, and say to them, ' My 2 offering, my food of the offerings made by fire, an acceptable odour, ye shall observe to offer to me in their season.'

And thou shalt say to them, ' This is the offering made by 3 fire, which ye shall offer to Jehovah; two lambs of the first year without blemish, daily, a perpetual burnt-offering. One lamb thou shalt offer in the morning, and the other 4 lamb thou shalt offer in the evening, with a tenth part of 5 an ephah of fine flour for a meal-offering, mingled with the fourth part of a hin of beaten oil: a perpetual burnt-offering 6 which was ordained in mount Sinai, an acceptable odour, a sacrifice made by fire to Jehovah. And its drink-offering 7 shall be the fourth part of a hin *of wine* for each lamb: in the holy place thou shalt cause the strong wine to be poured out to Jehovah for a drink-offering. And the other lamb 8 thou shalt offer in the evening: with the same meal-offering as in the morning, and with the same drink-offering, thou shalt offer it, a sacrifice made by fire, an acceptable odour to Jehovah.

But on the sabbath day *thou shalt offer* two lambs of the 9 first year without blemish, and two-tenths *of an ephah* of fine flour for a meal-offering, mingled with oil, and its drink-offering; the burnt-offering of every sabbath, beside the 10 perpetual burnt-offering, and its drink-offering.

And in the beginning of your months, ye shall offer a 11 burnt-offering to Jehovah; two young bullocks, and one ram, seven lambs of the first year without blemish; and 12

three-tenths *of an ephah* of fine flour, mingled with oil, a meal-offering for one bullock, and two-tenths *of an ephah*
13 of fine flour, mingled with oil, a meal-offering for one ram; and one-tenth *of an ephah* of fine flour, mingled with oil, a meal-offering for each lamb, for a burnt-offering, an
14 acceptable odour, a sacrifice made by fire to Jehovah. And their drink-offerings shall be half a hin of wine for a bullock, and the third *part* of a hin for a ram, and the fourth *part* of a hin for a lamb. This is the burnt-offering
15 of every month throughout the months of the year. And one kid of the goats for a sin-offering to Jehovah shall be offered, besides the perpetual burnt-offering, and its drink-offering.
16 And in the first month, on the fourteenth day of the month, is the passover of Jehovah.
17 And on the fifteenth day of this month is a feast: seven
18 days shall unleavened bread be eaten. On the first day ye shall have a holy convocation; no servile work shall ye do;
19 but ye shall offer a sacrifice made by fire, a burnt-offering to Jehovah; two young bullocks, and one ram, and seven lambs
20 of the first year: they shall be to you without blemish; and their meal-offering *shall be* fine flour mingled with oil: three-tenths *of an ephah* shall ye offer for a bullock, and
21 two-tenths for a ram; and one-tenth shalt thou offer for
22 every lamb of the seven lambs; and one goat for a sin-offer-
23 ing, to make an atonement for you. Beside the burnt-offering in the morning, which is for a perpetual burnt-offering,
24 ye shall offer these. Thus ye shall offer daily, throughout the seven days, the food of the sacrifice made by fire, an acceptable odour to Jehovah: it shall be offered beside the
25 perpetual burnt-offering, and its drink-offering. And on the seventh day ye shall have a holy convocation; ye shall do no servile work.
26 Also on the day of the first-fruits, when ye bring a new meal-offering to Jehovah, after your weeks, ye shall have a
27 holy convocation; ye shall do no servile work: but ye shall offer a burnt-offering, an acceptable odour to Jehovah; two
28 young bullocks, one ram, seven lambs of the first year; and their meal-offering of fine flour mingled with oil, three-tenths
29 *of an ephah* for one bullock, two-tenths for one ram, and
30 one-tenth for every lamb, of the seven lambs; and one kid of the goats, for a sin-offering to make an atonement for
31 you. Beside the perpetual burnt-offering, and its meal-offer-

ing, ye shall offer these, which shall be without blemish, with their drink-offerings.

CHAP. XXIX.—And in the seventh month, on the first day of the month, ye shall have a holy convocation: ye shall do no servile work; it is a day of blowing trumpets to you. And ye shall offer a burnt-offering, an acceptable odour to Jehovah, one young bullock, and one ram, and seven lambs of the first year without blemish; and their meal-offering shall be fine flour mingled with oil, three-tenths *of an ephah* for a bullock, and two-tenths for a ram, and one-tenth for every lamb, of the seven lambs; and one kid of the goats for a sin-offering, to make an atonement for you; beside the burnt-offering of the month, and its meal-offering, and the daily burnt-offering, and its meal-offering, and their drink-offerings, according to their rite, for an acceptable odour, a sacrifice made by fire to Jehovah.

And on the tenth day of this seventh month ye shall have a holy convocation; and ye shall afflict your souls: ye shall do no servile work; but ye shall offer a burnt-offering to Jehovah, an acceptable odour: one young bullock, and one ram, and seven lambs of the first year, which shall be without blemish: and their meal-offering shall be fine flour mingled with oil, three-tenths *of an ephah* to one bullock, and two-tenths to one ram, and one-tenth for every lamb, of the seven lambs; and one kid of the goats for a sin-offering, beside the sin-offering of atonement, and the perpetual burnt-offering, and their meal-offering, and their drink-offerings.

And on the fifteenth day of the seventh month ye shall have a holy convocation; no servile work shall ye do, and ye shall keep a feast to Jehovah seven days: and ye shall offer a burnt-offering, a sacrifice made by fire, an acceptable odour to Jehovah; thirteen young bullocks, two rams, *and* fourteen lambs of the first year; they shall be without blemish: and their meal-offering shall be fine flour mingled with oil, three-tenths *of an ephah* for every bullock of the thirteen bullocks, and two-tenths for each ram of the two rams, and one-tenth for every lamb of the fourteen lambs; and one kid of the goats for a sin-offering, beside the continual burnt-offering, and its meal-offering, and its drink-offering. And on the second day *ye shall offer* twelve young bullocks, two rams, fourteen lambs of the first year, without blemish; and

their meal-offering, and their drink-offerings, for the bullocks, for the rams, and for the lambs, shall be according to
19 their number, according to the rite; and one kid of the goats for a sin-offering; beside the perpetual burnt-offering,
20 and its meal-offering, and its drink-offering. And on the third day *ye shall offer* eleven bullocks, two rams, fourteen
21 lambs of the first year without blemish; and their meal-offering, and their drink-offerings, for the bullocks, for the rams, and for the lambs, shall be according to their number,
22 according to the rite; and one kid of the goats for a sin-offering; beside the perpetual burnt-offering, and its meal-
23 offering, and its drink-offering. And on the fourth day *ye shall offer* ten bullocks, two rams, fourteen lambs of the
24 first year without blemish; and their meal-offering, and their drink-offerings, for the bullocks, for the rams, and for the lambs, shall be according to their number, according to
25 the rite; and one kid of the goats for a sin-offering, beside the perpetual burnt-offering, and its meal-offering, and its
26 drink-offering. And on the fifth day *ye shall offer* nine bullocks, two rams, fourteen lambs of the first year, without
27 blemish: and their meal-offering, and their drink-offerings, for the bullocks, for the rams, and for the lambs, shall be
28 according to their number, according to the rite; and one goat for a sin-offering; beside the perpetual burnt-offering,
29 and its meal-offering, and its drink-offering. And on the sixth day *ye shall offer* eight bullocks, two rams, fourteen
30 lambs of the first year without blemish: and their meal-offering, and their drink-offerings, for the bullocks, for the rams, and for the lambs, shall be according to their number,
31 according to the rite; and one goat for a sin-offering; beside the perpetual burnt-offering, and its meal-offering, and
32 its drink-offering. And on the seventh day *ye shall offer* seven bullocks, two rams, fourteen lambs of the first year
33 without blemish: and their meal-offering, and their drink-offerings, for the bullocks, for the rams, and for the lambs, shall be according to their number, according to the rite;
34 and one goat for a sin-offering; beside the perpetual burnt-
35 offering, and its meal-offering, and its drink-offering. But on the eighth day ye shall have a solemn assembly; no ser-
36 vile work shall ye do; but ye shall offer a burnt-offering, a sacrifice made by fire, an acceptable odour to Jehovah; one bullock, one ram, seven lambs of the first year without
37 blemish: their meal-offering, and their drink-offerings, for

the bullock, for the ram, and for the lambs, shall be according to their number, according to the rite; and one goat for 38 a sin-offering; beside the perpetual burnt-offering, and its meal-offering, and its drink-offering.

These ye shall offer to Jehovah in your set feasts, besides 39 your vows, and your freewill-offerings, for your burnt-offerings, and for your meal-offerings, and for your drink-offerings, and for your peace-offerings.'" And Moses told the 40 children of Israel, according to all that Jehovah commanded Moses.

CHAP. XXX.—And Moses spake to the chiefs of the 1 tribes of the children of Israel, saying, "This is what Jehovah hath commanded. 'If a man make a vow to Jehovah, 2 or swear an oath to bind his soul with a bond; he shall not break his word, he shall do according to all that hath proceeded out of his mouth. If a woman also make a vow to 3 Jehovah, and bind *herself* by a bond, while she is yet in her father's house, in her youth; and her father hear of her 4 vow, and her bond with which she hath bound her soul, and her father be silent to her; then all her vows shall stand, and every bond with which she hath bound her soul shall stand. But if her father disallow her in the day that he 5 heareth of it; not any of her vows, or of her bonds, with which she hath bound her soul, shall stand: and Jehovah will forgive her, because her father disallowed her. And if 6 she had a husband, when she vowed, or uttered anything rashly with her lips, by which she bound her soul; and her 7 husband heard of it, and was silent to her in the day that he heard of it; then all her vows shall stand, and her bonds with which she bound her soul shall stand. But if her hus- 8 band disallowed her on the day that he heard of it; then he shall make her vow which she vowed, and that which she uttered rashly with her lips, with which she bound her soul, of no effect: and Jehovah will forgive her. But every vow 9 of a widow, and of her that is divorced, with which they have bound their souls, shall stand against them.— And if *a* 10 *woman* vow in her husband's house, or bind her soul by a bond with an oath; and her husband hear of it, and be 11 silent to her, and disallow her not; then all her vows shall stand, and every bond with which she bound her soul shall stand. But if her husband hath made them entirely of no 12 effect on the day he heard of them; *then* whatsoever pro-

ceedeth out of her lips concerning her vows, or concerning the bond of her soul, shall not stand; her husband hath made them of no effect, and Jehovah will forgive her.
13 Every vow, and every binding oath to afflict her soul, her husband may establish it, or her husband may make it of
14 no effect. But if her husband be altogether silent to her, from day to day; then he establisheth all her vows, or all her bonds, which are upon her: he confirmeth them, because
15 he was silent to her in the day that he heard of them. But if he shall make them entirely of no effect, after that he hath heard of them; then he shall bear her iniquity.'"
16 These are the statutes which Jehovah commanded Moses, between a man and his wife; and between the father and his daughter, while yet in her youth, in her father's house.

1 CHAP. XXXI.—And Jehovah spake to Moses, saying,
2 "Avenge the children of Israel of the Midianites: after
3 that thou shalt be gathered to thy people." And Moses spake to the people, saying, "Arm some of yourselves for war, and let them go against the Midianites, and avenge Je-
4 hovah of the Midianites. Out of every tribe, of all the
5 tribes of Israel, ye shall send a thousand to the war." So there were delivered out of the thousands of Israel, a thousand out of every tribe, twelve thousand armed for war.
6 And Moses sent them to the war, a thousand out of *every* tribe; them and Phinehas the son of Eleazar the priest, with the holy instruments, and the trumpets to blow, in his
7 hand, *he sent* to the war. And they warred against the Midianites, as Jehovah had commanded Moses; and they
8 slew all the males. And they slew the kings of Midian, beside their *forces that were* slain, Evi, and Rekem, and Zur, and Hur, and Reba, five kings of Midian: Balaam also, the
9 son of Beor, they slew with the sword. And the children of Israel took the women of Midian captives, and their little ones, and made spoil of all their cattle, and all their flocks,
10 and all their goods. And all their cities in which they
11 dwelt, and all their strongholds they burnt with fire. But they took all the spoil, and all the prey, *both* of men and of
12 beasts. And they brought the captives, and the prey, and the spoil, to Moses and Eleazar the priest, and to all the assembly of the children of Israel, to the camp in the plains of Moab, which are by the Jordan *opposite to* Jericho.

T

And Moses, and Eleazar the priest, and all the princes of 13 the assembly, went forth to meet them without the camp. And Moses was angry with the officers of the host, the 14 captains over thousands, and captains over hundreds, who came from the battle. And Moses said to them, 15 "Have ye saved all the women alive? Lo, these caused the 16 children of Israel, through the counsel of Balaam, to commit trespass against Jehovah in the affair of Peor, so that there was a plague in the assembly of Jehovah. Now therefore 17 kill every male among the little ones, and kill every woman that hath known man by lying with him. But all 18 the female children that have not known a man, by lying with him, keep alive for yourselves. And abide ye without 19 the camp seven days: whosoever hath killed any person, and whosoever hath touched any slain, must purify himself on the third day, and on the seventh day. Yourselves and your 20 captives, and all raiment, and every thing made of skins, and all work of goats' *hair*, and all vessels made of wood, ye must purify." And Eleazar the priest said to the men of 21 war who had gone to the battle, "This is the ordinance of the law which Jehovah commanded Moses; 'Only the gold, 22 and the silver, and the copper, and the iron, and the tin, and the lead, every thing that can abide the fire, ye shall cause 23 to pass through fire, that it may be clean; it must also be purified with the water of impurity: but all that cannot abide the fire, ye shall cause to pass through water. And 24 ye shall wash your clothes on the seventh day, and be clean, and after that ye may come into the camp.'"

And Jehovah spake to Moses, saying, "Take, thou and 26 Eleazar the priest and the chiefs of the fathers of the assembly, the sum of the prey that hath been taken, both of men and of beasts; and divide the prey into two parts, between 27 them that carried on the war, who went out to battle, and between all the assembly: and levy a tribute to Jehovah of 28 the men of war who went out to battle: one out of every hundred of the persons, and of the beeves, and of the asses, and of the sheep. Take this from their half, and give 29 it to Eleazar the priest, for a heave-offering of Jehovah, and 30 from the half *which belongs to* the children of Israel, thou shalt take one portion of every fifty, of the persons, and of the beeves, and of the asses, and of the sheep, of the cattle, and of all beasts, and give them to the Levites, who have the charge of the tabernacle of Jehovah." And Moses and 31

NUMBERS XXXI.

32 Eleazar the priest did as Jehovah commanded Moses. And the booty, the residue of the prey which the men of war had
33 taken, was six hundred and seventy-five thousand sheep, and
34 seventy-two thousand beeves, and sixty-one thousand asses,
35 and of persons, in all, thirty-two thousand women who had
36 not known a man by lying with him. So the half, the portion of those who had gone out to war, was in number three hundred and thirty-seven thousand and five hundred sheep:
37 and the tribute to Jehovah of the sheep was six hundred and
38 seventy-five. And the beeves were thirty-six thousand; of
39 which the tribute to Jehovah was seventy-two. And the asses were thirty thousand.five hundred; of which the tri-
40 bute to Jehovah was sixty-one. And the persons were sixteen thousand; of which the tribute to Jehovah was thirty-
41 two persons. And Moses gave the tribute, the heave-offering of Jehovah, to Eleazar the priest; as Jehovah commanded
42 Moses. And out of the half which belonged to the children of Israel, which Moses had separated from the portion of the
43 men who had gone out to war; which half, that was assigned to the assembly, was three hundred and thirty-seven thou-
44 sand and five hundred sheep, and thirty-six thousand beeves,
46 and thirty thousand and five hundred asses, and sixteen
47 thousand persons; out of this half which belonged to the children of Israel, Moses took one portion of fifty, *both* of man and of beast, and gave them to the Levites, who kept the charge of the tabernacle of Jehovah; as Jehovah commanded Moses.

48 Then the officers who were commanders of the host, the captains of thousands, and the captains of hundreds, came
49 near to Moses; and they said to Moses, "Thy servants have taken the sum of the men of war under our charge, and
50 there is not missing of us a single man. We have therefore brought an offering to Jehovah, each what he hath found, jewels of gold, chains, and bracelets, rings, collars, and beads, to make an atonement for our souls before Jeho-
51 vah." And Moses and Eleazar the priest took the gold
52 of them, all the wrought jewels. And all the gold of the heave-offering that they offered up to Jehovah, from the captains of thousands, and from the captains of hundreds, was sixteen thousand and seven hundred and fifty shekels.
53 (*For* the warriors had taken spoil, every man for himself.)
54 And Moses and Eleazar the priest took the gold of the captains of thousands and of hundreds, and brought it into the

tent of meeting, a memorial for the children of Israel before Jehovah.

CHAP. XXXII.—Now the children of Reuben, and the children of Gad had a very great multitude of cattle. So when they saw the land of Jazer, and the land of Gilead, that the place was a place for cattle; the children of Gad, and the children of Reuben came and spake to Moses, and to Eleazar the priest, and to the princes of the assembly, saying, "Ataroth, and Dibon, and Jazer, and Nimrah, and Heshbon, and Elealeh, and Shebam, and Nebo, and Beon, the country which Jehovah hath smitten before the assembly of Israel, is a land *fit* for cattle, and thy servants have cattle; wherefore," said they, "if we have found favour in thy sight, let this land be given to thy servants for a possession; make us not pass over the Jordan." And Moses said to the children of Gad and to the children of Reuben, "Shall your brethren go to war, while ye rest here? and why would ye discourage the children of Israel from going over into the land which Jehovah hath given them? Thus did your fathers, when I sent them from Kadesh-barnea to view the land. For when they had gone up to the vale of Eshcol, and had viewed the land, they so discouraged the children of Israel, that they would not go into the land which Jehovah had given them. And the anger of Jehovah was kindled at that time, and he sware, saying, 'None of the men who came up out of Egypt, from the age of twenty years and upward, shall see the land which I sware to Abraham, to Isaac, and to Jacob; because they have not wholly followed me; except Caleb the son of Jephunneh the Kenezite, and Joshua the son of Nun; for they have wholly followed Jehovah.' Thus the anger of Jehovah was kindled against the Israelites, and he made them wander in the desert forty years, until all the generation that had done evil in the sight of Jehovah was consumed. And, lo, ye are risen up in your fathers' stead, a progeny of sinful men, to increase the fierce anger of Jehovah toward the Israelites. For if ye turn away from following him, he will yet longer detain them in the desert, and ye will destroy all this people." And they came near to him *again*, and said, "We will build sheep-folds here for our cattle, and cities for our little ones; but we ourselves will go ready armed before the children of Israel, until we have brought

them to their place; and our little ones shall dwell in the
18 fenced cities, because of the inhabitants of the land. We
will not return to our houses, until the children of Israel be
19 every man in possession of his portion: for we will not
possess with them on the other side of Jordan, because our
portion will have fallen to us on this side of the Jordan east-
20 ward." And Moses said to them, "If ye will do this thing,
21 if ye will go armed before Jehovah to war, and will go all of
you armed over the Jordan before Jehovah, until he hath
22 driven out his enemies from before him, and the land be
subdued before Jehovah; then afterward ye shall return, and
be guiltless before Jehovah, and before *the rest of* the Israelites; and this land shall be your possession before Jehovah.
23 But if ye will not do so, lo, ye have sinned against Jehovah;
24 and be sure your sin will find you out. Build ye cities for
your little ones, and folds for your sheep; and that which
25 ye have promised, perform." And the children of Gad, and
the children of Reuben spake to Moses, saying, "Thy ser-
26 vants will do as my lord commandeth. Our little ones, our
wives, our flocks, and all our cattle, shall be there in the
27 cities of Gilead; but thy servants will pass over, every man
armed for war, before Jehovah to battle, as my lord hath
said."
28 So concerning them, Moses commanded Eleazar the priest,
and Joshua the son of Nun, and the chief fathers of the
29 tribes of the children of Israel; and Moses said to them,
"If the children of Gad, and the children of Reuben will
pass with you over the Jordan, every man armed for battle
before Jehovah, and the land shall be subdued before you,
then ye shall give to them the land of Gilead for a posses-
30 sion; but if they will not pass over with you armed, they
shall have possessions among you in the land of Canaan."
31 And the children of Gad, and the children of Reuben
answered, saying, "As Jehovah hath said to thy servants, so
32 will we do. We will pass over armed before Jehovah into
the land of Canaan, that the possession of our inheritance
33 beyond Jordan may be ours." And Moses gave to them,
to the children of Gad, and to the children of Reuben, and
to the half of the tribe of Manasseh the son of Joseph, the
kingdom of Sihon king of the Amorites, and the kingdom
of Og king of Bashan, the land, with its cities within its
34 boundaries, the cities of the land on all sides. And the
35 children of Gad built Dibon, and Ataroth, and Aroer, and

Atroth, Shophan, and Jazer, and Jogbehah, and Beth-nim- 36 rah, and Beth-haran, fenced cities; and sheep-folds. And 37 the children of Reuben built Heshbon, and Elealeh, and Kirjathaim, and Nebo, and Baal-meon (their names being 38 changed), and Shibmah; and gave names to the cities which they builded. And the children of Machir, the 39 son of Manasseh, went to Gilead, and took it, and dispossessed the Amorites who were in it. And Moses gave 40 Gilead to Machir the son of Manasseh; and he dwelt in it. And Jair, the son of Manasseh, went and took their hamlets 41 and called them Havoth-Jair [THE HAMLETS OF JAIR]. And 42 Nobah went and took Kenath, with its villages, and called it Nobah, after his own name.

CHAP. XXXIII.—These are the journeys of the chil- 1 dren of Israel, who went forth out of the land of Egypt with their armies, under the command of Moses and Aaron. For Moses wrote their goings out according to their jour- 2 neys, at the command of Jehovah: and these were their journeys according to their goings out.

In the first month, on the fifteenth day of the first month, 3 they departed from Rameses: on the morrow after the passover, the children of Israel went out with a high hand in the sight of all the Egyptians. (For the Egyptians were 4 burying all their firstborn, whom Jehovah had smitten among them: on their gods also Jehovah had executed judgments.) So the children of Israel removed from Rameses, 5 and encamped in Succoth. And they removed from Suc- 6 coth, and encamped in Etham, which is in the edge of the desert. And they removed from Etham, and turned 7 again to Pi-hahiroth, which is before Baal-zephon: and they encamped before Migdol. And they removed from Pi- 8 hahiroth, and passed through the midst of the sea into the desert, and went three days' journey in the desert of Etham, and encamped at Marah. And they removed 9 from Marah, and came to Elim: and at Elim were twelve fountains of water, and seventy palm-trees; and they encamped there. And they removed from Elim, and en- 10 camped by the Red Sea. And they removed from the 11 Red Sea, and encamped in the desert of Sin. And 12 they removed from the desert of Sin, and encamped in Dophkah. And they removed from Dophkah, and en- 13 camped in Alush. And they removed from Alush, and 14

NUMBERS XXXIII.

encamped at Rephidim, where was no water for the peo-
15 ple to drink. And they removed from Rephidim, and
16 encamped in the desert of Sinai. And they removed
from the desert of Sinai, and encamped at Kibroth-hat-
17 taavah. And they removed from Kibroth-hattaavah, and
18 encamped at Hazeroth. And they removed from Haze-
19 roth, and encamped at Rithmah. And they removed from
20 Rithmah, and encamped at Rimmon-parez. And they removed from Rimmon-parez, and encamped at Libnah.
21 And they removed from Libnah, and encamped at Rissah.
22 And they removed from Rissah, and encamped at Kehela-
23 thah. And they removed from Kehelathah, and en-
24 camped in mount Shapher. And they removed from
25 mount Shapher, and encamped at Haradah. And they
26 removed from Haradah, and encamped at Makheloth. And
they removed from Makheloth, and encamped at Tahath.
27 And they removed from Tahath, and encamped at Tarah.
28 And they removed from Tarah, and encamped at Mithcah.
29 And they removed from Mithcah, and encamped at Hasmo-
30 nah. And they removed from Hasmonah, and encamped
31 at Moseroth. And they removed from Moseroth, and en-
32 camped at Bene-jaakan. And they removed from Bene-
33 jaakan, and encamped at mount Gidgad. And they removed from mount Gidgad, and encamped at Jotbathah.
34 And they removed from Jotbathah, and encamped at
35 Ebronah. And they removed from Ebronah, and en-
36 camped at Ezion-gaber. And they removed from Ezion-
gaber, and encamped in the desert of Zin, which is
37 Kadesh. And they removed from Kadesh, and encamped
38 in mount Hor, in the edge of the land of Edom. And
Aaron the priest went up to mount Hor, at the command of
Jehovah, and died there, in the fortieth year after the children of Israel had come out of the land of Egypt, in the
39 first day of the fifth month. And Aaron was a hundred
and twenty-three years old when he died in mount Hor.
40 And king Arad the Canaanite, who dwelt in the south, in
the land of Canaan, heard of the coming of the children
41 of Israel. And they removed from mount Hor, and en-
42 camped at Zalmonah. And they removed from Zalmonah,
43 and encamped at Punon. And they removed from Punon,
44 and encamped at Oboth. And they removed from Oboth,
45 and encamped at Ije-abarim, in the border of Moab. And
they removed from Ije-*abarim*, and encamped at Dibon-gad.

And they removed from Dibon-gad, and encamped at Al- 46
mon-diblathaim. And they removed from Almon-dibla- 47
thaim, and encamped in the mountains of Abarim, before
Nebo. And they removed from the mountains of 48
Abarim, and encamped in the plains of Moab, by the
Jordan *opposite to* Jericho. And they encamped by the 49
Jordan from Beth-jesimoth, to Abel-setim, in the plains
of Moab.

And Jehovah spake to Moses in the plains of Moab, by 50
Jordan *opposite to* Jericho, saying, "Speak to the children 51
of Israel, and say to them, 'When ye shall have passed over
the Jordan, into the land of Canaan, ye shall drive out all 52
the inhabitants of the land from before you, and destroy all
their *stones* inscribed with figures, and all their molten
images ye shall destroy, and all their high places ye shall
lay waste. And ye shall take possession of the land, and 53
dwell in it; for I have given to you the land that ye may
possess it. And ye shall divide the land by lot among your 54
families; to the more ye shall give a greater portion, and to
the fewer ye shall give a less portion: every man's *inheritance* shall be in the place where his lot falleth; according
to the tribes of your fathers ye shall divide. But if ye will 55
not drive out the inhabitants of the land from before you,
then it shall come to pass that those of them whom ye suffer
to remain will be prickles in your eyes, and thorns in your
sides, and will distress you in the land in which ye dwell.
And it shall come to pass that as I purposed to do to them, 56
I will do to you.'"

CHAP. XXXIV.—And Jehovah spake to Moses, saying, 1
"Command the children of Israel, and say to them, 'When 2
ye come into the land of Canaan, this shall be the land
which shall fall to you for an inheritance, the land of Canaan, according to its boundaries. Your south side shall be 3
by the desert of Zin, along by the border of Edom; and
your southern boundary shall be from the extreme point of
the salt sea eastward; and your boundary shall turn from 4
the south to the ascent of Akrabim, and pass on to Zin; and
its direction shall be from the south to Kadesh-barnea, and
it shall go on to Hazar-Adar, and pass on to Azmon. And the 5
boundary shall turn from Azmon unto the torrent of Egypt,
and its termination shall be at the sea. And for the western 6
boundary, ye shall even have the great sea for a boundary:

7 this shall be your western boundary. And this shall be your northern boundary; from the great sea ye shall draw a line
8 to mount Hor; and from mount Hor ye shall draw a line to the entrance of Hamath; and the extent of the boundary
9 shall be to Zedad. And the boundary shall pass on to Ziphron, and its termination shall be at Hazar-enan: this shall be
10 your northern boundary. And ye shall draw a line for your
11 eastern boundary from Hazar-enan to Shepham; and the boundary shall go down from Shepham to Riblah, on the east side of Ain; and the boundary shall descend, until it
12 reach the side of the sea of Chinnereth eastward. The boundary shall then go down to the Jordan, and its termination shall be at the salt sea. Such shall be your land, with its boundaries round about.'"

13 And Moses commanded the children of Israel, saying, "This is the land which ye shall divide by lot, which Jehovah hath commanded to be given to the nine tribes, and to
14 the half-tribe. For the tribe of the children of Reuben according to the house of their fathers, and the tribe of the children of Gad according to the house of their fathers, have received *their portion*, and the half of the tribe of
15 Manasseh have received their portion: the two tribes and the half-tribe have received their portion on this side of the Jordan *opposite to* Jericho, eastward, toward the sunrising."

16 And Jehovah spake to Moses, saying, "These are the
17 names of the men who shall divide the land to you; Eleazar
18 the priest, and Joshua the son of Nun. And ye shall take
19 one prince of every tribe, to divide the land. And the names of the men are these. Of the tribe of Judah, Caleb
20 the son of Jephunneh. Of the tribe of Simeon, Shemuel
21 the son of Ammihud. Of the tribe of Benjamin, Elidad
22 the son of Chislon. And the prince of the tribe of the
23 children of Dan, Bukki the son of Jogli. The prince of the children of Joseph, for the tribe of the children of Manas-
24 seh, Hanniel the son of Ephod. And the prince of the tribe of the children of Ephraim, Kemuel the son of Shiph-
25 tan. And the prince of the tribe of the children of Zebu-
26 lun, Elizaphan the son of Parnach. And the prince of the tribe of the children of Issachar, Paltiel the son of Azzan.
27 And the prince of the tribe of the children of Asher, Ahi-
28 hud the son of Shelomi. And the prince of the tribe of the children of Naphtali, Pedahel the son of Ammihud."

These were they whom Jehovah commanded to divide the ²⁹ land of Canaan to the children of Israel.

CHAP. XXXV.—And Jehovah spake to Moses in the ¹ plains of Moab, by Jordan *opposite to* Jericho, saying, "Command the children of Israel, that they give to the ² Levites, out of the portion of their possessions, cities to dwell in; and suburbs also around the cities ye shall give to the Levites. And the cities they shall have to dwell in; ³ and their suburbs shall be for their cattle, and for their substance, and for all their beasts. And the suburbs of the ⁴ cities, which ye shall give to the Levites, *shall reach* from the wall of the city and outward, a thousand cubits every way. So that ye shall measure from without the city on ⁵ the east side two thousand cubits, and on the south side two thousand cubits, and on the west side two thousand cubits, and on the north side two thousand cubits; and the city shall be in the midst. These shall be to them the suburbs of their cities. And the cities which ye shall give to ⁶ the Levites, shall be six cities for refuge, which ye shall appoint for the manslayer, that he may flee thither; and beside these ye shall give forty-two cities. So all the cities ⁷ which ye shall give to the Levites shall be forty-eight cities; these with their suburbs. And the cities which ye shall ⁸ give out of the possessions of the children of Israel, ye shall give many from those that have many; but from those that have few ye shall give few: every one shall give of his cities to the Levites, according to his portion which he possesseth."

And Jehovah spake to Moses, saying, "Speak to the chil- ⁹ dren of Israel, and say to them, 'When ye shall have ¹⁰ passed over the Jordan into the land of Canaan, then ye ¹¹ shall appoint for yourselves cities; cities of refuge they shall be for you; that the manslayer may flee thither, who hath killed any person unawares. And they shall be for you cities ¹² of refuge from the blood-avenger; that the manslayer die not, until he have stood before the assembly to be judged. And of these cities which ye shall give *to the Levites,* six ¹³ cities shall ye have for refuge. Three cities ye shall give ¹⁴ beyond the Jordan, and three cities ye shall give in the land of Canaan; cities of refuge shall they be. For the ¹⁵ children of Israel, and for the stranger, and for the sojourner among them, these six cities shall be a refuge, that

every one who killeth any person unawares may flee thither.
16 And if he have smitten him with an instrument of iron, so that he die, he is a murderer: the murderer shall surely be
17 put to death. And if he have smitten him by throwing a stone, by means of which he may die, and he die, he is a
18 murderer: the murderer shall surely be put to death. Or *if* he have smitten him with a hand-weapon of wood, by means of which he may die, and he die, he is a murderer:
19 the murderer shall surely be put to death. The avenger of blood himself may slay the murderer: when he meeteth
20 him, he may slay him. And if he hath thrust at him through hatred, or thrown *any thing* at him, lying in wait,
21 so that he die; or through enmity, have smitten him with his hand, so that he die; he that smote *him* shall surely be put to death; he is a murderer: the avenger of blood may
22 slay the murderer when he meeteth him. But if suddenly, without enmity, he have thrust at him, or have cast upon
23 him any weapon without lying in wait, or with any stone, by means of which a man may die, seeing *him* not, and have cast it upon him so that he die, not being his enemy, nor
24 seeking to injure him; then the assembly shall judge between the slayer and the avenger of blood, according to
25 these ordinances; and the assembly shall deliver the manslayer out of the hand of the avenger of blood, and the assembly shall restore him to the city of his refuge, whither he had fled; and he shall abide in it until the death of the
26 high-priest, who hath been anointed with the holy oil. But if the manslayer shall at any time come without the boun-
27 dary of the city of his refuge, whither he had fled, and the avenger of blood find him without the boundary of the city of his refuge, and the avenger of blood kill the manslayer;
28 he shall not be guilty of blood; because *the manslayer* should have remained in the city of his refuge until the death of the high-priest; but after the death of the high-priest, the manslayer may return to the land of his posses-
29 sion. So these shall be statutes of law to you, throughout
30 your generations, in all your dwellings. Whoever killeth any person, on the testimony of witnesses the murderer shall be put to death; but one witness shall not testify
31 against any person, *to cause him* to die. Moreover, ye shall take no atonement for the life of a murderer, of one who is
32 guilty of death; but he shall be surely put to death. And ye shall take no atonement for him who hath fled to the

city of his refuge, that he may come again to dwell in the land, until the death of the *high*-priest. So ye shall not ³³ profane the land in which ye are; for blood profaneth the land: and no atonement can be made for the blood that is shed in it, but by the blood of him who shed it. Defile ³⁴ not therefore the land in which ye abide, in which I dwell: for I, Jehovah, dwell among the children of Israel.'"

CHAP. XXXVI.—And the chief fathers of the families of ¹ the children of Gilead, the son of Machir, the son of Manasseh, of the families of the sons of Joseph, came near, and spake before Moses, and before the princes, the chief fathers of the children of Israel; and they said, "Jehovah commanded my ² lord to give the land for an inheritance by lot to the children of Israel: and my lord was commanded by Jehovah to give the inheritance of Zelophehad our brother to his daughters. Now, if they become wives to any of the sons ³ of the *other* tribes of the children of Israel, then will their inheritance be taken from the inheritance of our fathers, and be put to the inheritance of the tribe into which they shall be *received*: so shall it be taken from the lot of our inheritance. Even when the jubilee of the children of Israel ⁴ shall come, then will their inheritance be added to the inheritance of the tribe into which they shall be *received*: so shall their inheritance be taken away from the inheritance of the tribe of our fathers." And Moses commanded the chil- ⁵ dren of Israel, according to the word of Jehovah, saying, "The tribe of the sons of Joseph hath rightly spoken. This is the thing which Jehovah commandeth concerning ⁶ the daughters of Zelophehad, saying, 'Let them become wives to whomsoever they please; only into a family of the tribe of their fathers they must marry: so shall not the ⁷ inheritance of the children of Israel remove from tribe to tribe; for every one of the children of Israel must keep himself to the inheritance of the tribe of his fathers. And ⁸ every daughter, who possesseth an inheritance in any tribe of the children of Israel, must be wife to one of the family of the tribe of her father, that the children of Israel may enjoy, every man the inheritance of his fathers. For the ⁹ inheritance must not remove from *one* tribe to another tribe; but every one of the tribes of the children of Israel must keep to their own inheritance.'"

As Jehovah commanded Moses, so did the daughters of ¹⁰

11 Zelophehad; for Mahla, and Tirza, and Hogla, and Milca, and Noa, the daughters of Zelophehad, became wives to the
12 sons of their uncles. They were married into the families of the sons of Manasseh, the son of Joseph; and their inheritance remained in the tribe of the family of their father.
13 These are the commandments and the ordinances which Jehovah commanded, by Moses, to the children of Israel, in the plains of Moab, by the Jordan *opposite to* Jericho.

THE BOOK OF DEUTERONOMY.

CHAP. I.—These are the words which Moses spake to all Israel beyond the Jordan, in the desert, in the plain over against Suph, between Paran, and Tophel, and Laban, and Hazeroth, and Dizahab; eleven days' *journey* from Horeb, by the way of mount Seir, to Kadesh-barnea. Now it was in the fortieth year, in the eleventh month, on the first day of the month, that Moses spake to the children of Israel, according to all that Jehovah had charged him *to speak* to them; after he had slain Sihon the king of the Amorites, who dwelt in Heshbon; and, at Edrei, Og the king of Bashan, who dwelt at Astaroth: beyond the Jordan, in the land of Moab, it pleased Moses to declare this law, saying,

"Jehovah our God spake to us in Horeb, saying, 'Ye have dwelt long enough by this mountain. Turn you, and take your journey, and go to the mountainous country of the Amorites, and to all *the places* near unto it, in the plain *of Jordan,* in the mountainous country, and in the lowland, and in the south, and by the sea-shore, to the land of the Canaanites, and to Lebanon, as far as the great river, the river Euphrates. See, I place the land before you: go and possess the land which Jehovah sware to your fathers, Abraham, Isaac, and Jacob, to give to them, and to their seed after them.' And I spake to you at that time, saying, 'I am not able alone to bear *the charge of* you. Jehovah your God hath multiplied you, so that, lo, ye are at this day as the stars of the heavens for multitude. May Jehovah the God of your fathers make you a thousand times so many more, and may he bless you, as he hath promised you! How can I alone bear the burdensome charge of you and your contentions? Choose for yourselves men wise, and intelligent, and known among your tribes, whom I may appoint rulers over you.' And ye answered me, and said, 'That which thou hast spoken is good to be done.'

DEUTERONOMY I.

15 So I took the chiefs of your tribes, men wise, and known, and made them chiefs over you, rulers over thousands, and rulers over hundreds, rulers over fifties, and rulers over tens,
16 and officers among your tribes. And I charged your judges at that time, saying, 'Hear *causes* between your brethren, and judge justly between a man and his brother, and the stranger
17 that is with him. Ye shall not respect persons in judgment; ye shall hear the small as *ye hear* the great; ye shall not be afraid of the face of man; for the judgment is God's. But the cause which is too hard for you, ye shall bring to
18 me, and I will hear it.' And I gave you in charge at that time all the things which ye should do.
19 Now when we had departed from Horeb, we went, as Jehovah our God commanded us, through all that great and terrible desert, which ye saw on the way to the mountainous country of the Amorites, and we came to Kadesh-barnea.
20 Then I said to you, 'Ye are come to the mountainous country of the Amorites, which Jehovah our God giveth to us.
21 See, Jehovah thy God hath placed the land before thee: go up, take possession of it, as Jehovah the God of thy fathers
22 hath said to thee; fear not, nor be discouraged.' But ye came near to me every one of you, and said, 'Let us send men before us, who may explore the land for us, and report to us by what way we must go up, and into what cities we
23 shall come.' And the saying pleased me well: and I took
24 twelve men of you, one out of each tribe; and they turned, and went up into the mountainous country, and came to the
25 valley of Eshcol. And they searched out the land, and took some of the fruit of the land in their hands, and brought it down to us, and reported to us, and said, 'The land is good
26 which Jehovah our God giveth us.' Yet ye would not go up, but rebelled against the commandment of Jehovah your
27 God; and ye murmured in your tents, and said, 'Because Jehovah hateth us, he hath brought us out of the land of Egypt, to deliver us into the hand of the Amorites, to de-
28 stroy us. Whither shall we go up? our own brethren have discouraged our heart, saying, The people are greater and taller than we; the cities are large and walled up to the heavens; and the sons of the Anakites also we saw there.'
29 Then I said to you, 'Dread not, nor be afraid of them.
30 Jehovah your God, who goeth before you, will himself fight for you, according to all that he did for you in Egypt before
31 your eyes; and *as he hath done* in the desert, where

thou hast seen how that Jehovah thy God hath carried thee, as a man carrieth his son, through all the way that ye have gone, until ye came unto this place. Yet in this thing 32 ye confide not in Jehovah your God, who goeth in the way 33 before you, to search out for you a place for your encampment, in a fire by night, to show you the way in which ye should go, and in a cloud by day.' And Jehovah heard the 34 voice of your words, and was wroth, and sware, saying, 'Not one of these men of this evil generation shall see that 35 good land, which I sware to your fathers that I would give *them*, except Caleb the son of Jephunneh; he shall see it; 36 and to him will I give the land that he hath trodden upon, and to his children, because he hath wholly followed Jehovah.' Jehovah was angry even with me for your sakes, 37 saying, 'Thou also shalt not go in thither. *But* Joshua the 38 son of Nun, who standeth before thee, shall go in thither: encourage him; for he shall cause Israel to inherit it. Moreover, your little ones, who, ye said, should be a prey, 39 and your children, who as yet know not good or evil, they shall go in thither, and to them will I give it, and they shall possess it. But as for you, turn ye, and take your journey 40 into the desert, by the way of the Red Sea.'

Then ye answered and said to me, 'We have sinned 41 against Jehovah; we will go up, and fight, according to all that Jehovah our God commanded us.' And when ye had girded on every man his weapons of war, ye were ready to go up to the mountains. But Jehovah said to me, 42 'Say to them, Go not up, nor fight; for I am not among you; lest ye be smitten before your enemies.' So I spake to 43 you; and ye would not hear, but rebelled against the commandment of Jehovah, and went presumptuously up to the mountains. And the Amorites who dwelt in those moun- 44 tains, came out against you, and chased you as bees do, and smote you in Seir, *even* unto Hormah. Then ye returned 45 and wept before Jehovah; but Jehovah would not hearken to your voice, nor listen to you. So ye abode in Kadesh 46 many days, according to the days that ye abode *there*.

CHAP. II.—Then we turned, and took our journey 1 into the desert, by the way of the Red Sea, as Jehovah spake to me. And we had compassed mount Seir many days, when Jehovah spake to me saying, 'Ye have compassed 3 this mountain long enough: turn ye northward. And 4

charge the people, saying, Ye are to pass by the boundaries of your brethren the children of Esau, who dwell in Seir; and they will be afraid of you: take ye good heed to your-
5 selves therefore; contend not with them; for of their land I will not give you so much as a foot-breadth, because I have
6 given mount Seir to Esau for a possession. Ye shall buy food of them with money, that ye may eat; ye shall purchase
7 water also with money, that ye may drink. For Jehovah thy God hath blessed thee in all the works of thy hands; he knoweth thy journeying through this great desert: these forty years Jehovah thy God hath been with thee, thou hast
8 wanted nothing.' So we passed by our brethren the children of Esau, who dwelt in Seir, through the way of the plain from Elath, and from Eziongaber, and we turned, and passed
9 by the way of the desert of Moab. And Jehovah said to me, 'Distress not the Moabites, and contend not with them in battle; for I will not give thee any of their land for a possession, because I have given Ar to the children of Lot for
10 a possession.' (The Emites formerly dwelt there, a people
11 great, and numerous, and tall, as the Anakites, who also were accounted giants, as the Anakites; but the Moabites call
12 them Emites. The Horites also formerly dwelt in Seir; but the children of Esau dispossessed them, and dwelt in their stead; as the Israelites did to the land of their possession,
13 which Jehovah gave to them.) 'Now then, arise, and pass over the torrent Zered.' So we passed over the torrent Zered.
14 Now the time in which we were going from Kadesh-barnea, until we passed over the torrent Zered, was thirty-eight years; until all the generation of the men of war were consumed from among the host, as Jehovah had sworn to them.
15 For indeed the hand of Jehovah was against them, to destroy them from among the host, until they were consumed.
16 And it came to pass that when all the men of war were
17 consumed by death from among the people, Jehovah spake
18 to me, saying, 'Thou art, this day, to pass by Ar, the
19 boundary of Moab, and to come nigh the children of Ammon: distress them not, nor contend with them; for I will not give thee any of the land of the children of Ammon for a possession; because I have given it to the
20 children of Lot for a possession.' (That also was accounted a land of giants: giants dwelt in it formerly, and the
21 Ammonites call them Zamzumites; a people great, and numerous, and tall, as the Anakites; but Jehovah destroyed

U

these from before them; so they dispossessed them, and dwelt in their stead; as he did for the children of Esau, 22 who dwelt in Seir, when he destroyed the Horites from before them; and they dispossessed them, and dwelt in their stead even to this day; and the Caphtorites, who came out 23 of Caphtor, destroyed the Avites who dwelt in Hazerim, unto Gaza, and dwelt in their stead.) 'Arise, take your 24 journey, and pass over the torrent Arnon : lo, I have given into thy hand Sihon king of Heshbon, the Amorite, and his land: begin to possess it, and contend with him in battle. This day will I begin to put the dread of thee and 25 the fear of thee upon the nations under the whole heavens, who shall hear report of thee, and shall tremble, and be in anguish because of thee.' Yet I sent messengers from the 26 desert of Kedemoth, unto Sihon king of Heshbon, with words of peace, saying, 'Let me pass through thy land. I 27 will go along by the high-way; I will turn aside neither to the right nor to the left. Thou shalt sell me food for 28 money, that I may eat; and give me water for money, that I may drink : only let me pass through on my feet; as the 29 children of Esau who dwell in Seir, and the Moabites who dwell in Ar, did to me; until I shall pass over the Jordan, into the land which Jehovah our God giveth us.' But 30 Sihon king of Heshbon would not let us pass through his land; for Jehovah thy God hardened his mind, and made his heart obstinate, that he might deliver him into thy hand, as *it is* this day. And Jehovah said to me, 'Lo, I 31 begin to give Sihon and his land before thee: begin to possess it, that thou mayest inherit his land.' Then Sihon 32 came out against us, he and all his people, to fight at Jahaz. And Jehovah our God delivered him before us; and we 33 smote him, and his sons, and all his people. And we took 34 all his cities at that time, and utterly destroyed the men, the women, and the little ones, of every city; we left no remainder. Only the cattle we kept as a prey to ourselves, 35 and the spoil of the cities which we took. From Aroer, 36 which is on the brink of the torrent of Arnon, the city that is by the torrent, even unto Gilead, there was not one city too strong for us : the whole *of them* Jehovah our God delivered to us. Only into the land of the children of Ammon 37 thou camest not, the whole tract on the torrent Jabbok, nor into the cities among the mountains, nor into any place which Jehovah our God had forbidden us.

1 CHAP. III.—We then turned, and went up the way to Bashan; and Og the king of Bashan with all his people,
2 came out to meet us in battle at Edrei. And Jehovah said to me, 'Fear him not; for I will deliver him, and all his people, and his land, into thy hand, and thou shalt do to him as thou didst to Sihon king of the Amorites, who dwelt
3 at Heshbon.' So Jehovah our God delivered into our hands Og also, the king of Bashan, and all his people; and we
4 smote him, until no remainder of them was left. And we took all his cities at that time; there was not a city which we took not from them; sixty cities *we took*, all the
5 region of Argob, the kingdom of Og in Bashan. All these cities were fenced with high walls, gates, and bars; beside a
6 great number of unwalled towns. And we utterly destroyed them, as we did in respect to Sihon king of Heshbon, utterly destroying the men, women, and children, of every city.
7 But all the cattle, and the spoil of the cities, we kept as a
8 prey to ourselves. And we took at that time, from the hand of the two kings of the Amorites, the land beyond the Jordan, from the torrent Arnon even unto mount Hermon;
9 (The Sidonians call Hermon Sirion; and the Amorites call
10 it Senir;) all the cities of the plain, and all Gilead, and all Bashan, unto Salchah and Edrei, cities of the kingdom of
11 Og in Bashan. (For Og alone, king of Bashan, remained of the remnant of the giants; lo, his bed was a bed of iron: is it not in Rabbath of the children of Ammon? nine cubits is its length, and four cubits its breadth, according to the cubit of a man.)
12 Now this land, which we took possession of at that time, from Aroer, which is upon the banks of the torrent Arnon, with half mount Gilead, and its cities, I gave to the
13 Reubenites, and to the Gadites. And the rest of Gilead, and all Bashan, the kingdom of Og, I gave to the half of the tribe of Manasseh; all the region of Argob, with all
14 Bashan, which was called the land of the giants. (Jair the son of Manasseh took all the country of Argob, unto the boundary of Geshuri, and Maachathi, and called them after
15 his own name, Bashan-havoth-jair, unto this day.) And to
16 the Machirites I gave Gilead. And to the Reubenites, and to the Gadites, I gave from Gilead, even to the torrent Arnon, the middle of the torrent, and the boundary, unto the torrent Jabbok, the boundary of the children of Ammon;
17 the plain *of Jordan* also, and the Jordan, and *its* bank, from

Chinnereth to the sea of the plain, the salt sea, below Ashdoth-Pisgah eastward.

And I charged you at that time, saying, 'Jehovah your God hath given you this land to possess it: all of you who are fit for war, shall pass over armed before your brethren the children of Israel. But your wives, and your little ones, and your cattle, (*for* I know that ye have much cattle) shall abide in your cities which I have given to you, until Jehovah shall have given rest to your brethren, as well as to you, and they also possess the land which Jehovah your God hath given them beyond the Jordan: then shall ye return every man to his possession which I have given to you.' And I commanded Joshua at that time, saying, 'Thine eyes have seen all that Jehovah your God hath done to these two kings: so will Jehovah do to all the kingdoms into which thou art to pass. Fear them not; for Jehovah your God will himself fight for you.'

And I besought Jehovah at that time, saying, 'O Lord Jehovah, thou hast begun to show thy servant thy greatness, and thy mighty hand; for what God is there in heaven or on earth that can do according to thy deeds, and according to thy might? Let me, I pray thee, go over, and see that good land which is beyond the Jordan, those goodly mountains, and Lebanon.' But Jehovah was very angry with me on your account, and would not hear me; and Jehovah said to me, 'Let it suffice thee; speak no more to me of this matter. Go up to the top of Pisgah, and look westward, and northward, and southward, and eastward, and behold *the land* with thine eyes; for thou shalt not go over this Jordan. But charge Joshua, and encourage him, and strengthen him; for he shall go over before this people, and he shall cause them to inherit the land which thou shalt see.' So we abode in the valley opposite to Beth-peor.

CHAP. IV.—Now therefore hearken, O Israel, to the statutes and to the judgments which I teach you, so as to do them, that ye may live, and go in and possess the land which Jehovah the God of your fathers giveth you. Ye shall not add to the word which I command you, nor shall ye take away from it, that ye may keep the commandments of Jehovah your God which I command you. Your eyes have seen what Jehovah did because of Baal-peor: for all the men that followed Baal-peor, Jehovah your God hath destroyed from

4 among you. But ye who did cleave to Jehovah your God,
5 *are* all of you alive this day. See, I have taught you statutes, and judgments, even as Jehovah my God commanded me, that ye may do so in the land into which ye are going
6 to possess it. Keep, therefore, and do them; for this will be your wisdom and your understanding in the sight of the nations, who, when they hear of all these statutes, will say, 'Surely a wise and understanding people is this great nation.'
7 For what great nation is there that hath God so nigh to them, as Jehovah our God is to us in all things for
8 which we call upon him? And what great nation is there, that hath statutes and judgments so righteous as all this
9 law, which I set before you this day? Only take heed to thyself, and keep thy soul diligently, that thou forget not the things which thine eyes saw, and that they depart not from thy heart all the days of thy life; but teach them to
10 thy sons, and thy sons' sons; *what thou sawest* on the day when thou stoodest before Jehovah thy God in Horeb, when Jehovah said to me, 'Gather me the people together, and I will make them hear my words, that they may learn to fear me all the days that they shall live upon the earth, and *that*
11 they may teach *the same to* their children.' So ye came near, and stood under the mountain; and the mountain burned with fire unto the midst of the heavens, with dark-
12 ness, clouds, and thick darkness. And Jehovah spake to you from the midst of the fire: ye heard the sound of the words, but ye saw no similitude; only *ye heard* a voice.
13 And he declared to you his covenant, which he commanded you to perform, *even* ten commandments; and he wrote them
14 upon two tables of stone. And Jehovah commanded me, at that time, to teach you statutes and judgments, that ye might do them in the land into which ye are going over to
15 possess it. Take ye, therefore, good heed to yourselves, since ye saw no manner of similitude when Jehovah spake to
16 you at Horeb from the midst of the fire, that ye corrupt not yourselves, and make you a graven image, the similitude of
17 any figure, the likeness of male or female; the likeness of any beast that is upon the earth, the likeness of any winged
18 fowl that flieth in the air, the likeness of any thing that creepeth on the ground, the likeness of any fish that is in
19 the waters beneath the earth: and when thou liftest up thine eyes to the heavens, and when thou seest the sun, and the moon, and the stars, all the host of heaven, that thou be

not induced to worship them, and serve them, which Jehovah thy God hath distributed to all nations under the whole heavens. But Jehovah hath taken you, and brought you 20 forth out of the iron furnace, out of Egypt, to be to him a peculiar people, as *ye are* at this day. Yet Jehovah was 21 angry with me on your account, and sware that I should not pass over the Jordan, and that I should not go into that good land which Jehovah thy God giveth thee for an inheritance. So I must die in this land; I may not go over the 22 Jordan; but ye shall go over, and possess that good land. Take heed to yourselves, that ye forget not the covenant of 23 Jehovah your God, which he hath made with you, nor make to yourselves a graven image, the likeness of any thing, which Jehovah thy God hath forbidden thee. For Jehovah 24 thy God is a consuming fire, a jealous God.

If when thou shalt have begotten children, and children's 25 children, and shalt have remained long in the land, ye shall corrupt yourselves, and make a graven image, the likeness of any thing, and shall do evil in the sight of Jehovah thy God, to provoke him to anger; I this day call the heavens and 26 the earth to witness against you, that ye shall soon utterly perish from off the land to which ye are going over the Jordan to possess it: ye shall not prolong *your* days upon it, but shall utterly be destroyed. For Jehovah will scatter 27 you among the peoples, and ye shall be left few in number among the nations, whither Jehovah shall lead you. And 28 there ye shall serve gods, the work of men's hands, wood and stone, which neither see, nor hear, nor eat, nor smell. Yet if thence thou shalt seek Jehovah thy God, thou shalt 29 find him, if thou seek him with all thy heart and with all thy soul. When thou shalt be in tribulation, and all these 30 things shall have come upon thee, if thou turn to Jehovah thy God, and be obedient to his voice, since Jehovah thy God 31 is a merciful God, he will not forsake thee, nor destroy thee, nor forget the covenant of thy fathers, which he sware to them. For ask now of the former days, which were before 32 thee, from the day that God created man upon earth, and from the one end of heaven unto the other, whether *any thing* such as this great thing, or *any thing* like it hath been heard? Did a people ever hear the voice of God speaking from the 33 midst of fire, as thou hast heard, and live? Or hath God 34 essayed to take for himself a nation from the midst of *another* nation, by trials, by signs, and by wonders, and by war, and by a mighty hand, and by an out-stretched arm, and by great terrors, according to all that Jehovah your God did for you 35 in Egypt before your eyes? To thee it was shewn, that thou mightest know that Jehovah is God; that there is none else 36 besides him. From the heavens he made thee to hear his voice, that he might instruct thee; and upon the earth he shewed thee his great fire; and thou heardest his words from 37 the midst of the fire. And because he loved thy fathers, therefore he chose their seed after them, and brought thee 38 out from Egypt in his own sight by his mighty power, to drive out from before thee nations greater and mightier than thou art, to bring thee in, to give thee their land for 39 an inheritance, as at this day. Know therefore this day, and consider *it* in thy heart, that Jehovah he is God in the heavens above, and upon the earth beneath: there is none 40 else. Thou shalt, therefore, observe his statutes, and his commandments, which I command thee this day, that it may be well with thee, and with thy children after thee, and that thou mayest prolong *thy* days upon the land, which Jehovah thy God giveth thee for ever."

41 Then Moses set apart three cities on the eastern side of 42 the Jordan, whither the man-slayer, who should kill his neighbour unawares, whom he had not hated in times past, might flee; and that, fleeing unto one of these cities, he 43 might live: *namely,* Bezer in the desert, in the plain country of the Reubenites; and Ramoth in Gilead, *the land* of the Gadites; and Golan in Bashan, *the land* of the Manassites.

44 Now this is the law which Moses set before the children 45 of Israel; these are the testimonies, the statutes, and the decrees, which Moses spake to the children of Israel, after 46 they came forth out of Egypt, beyond the Jordan, in the valley opposite to Beth-peor, in the land of Sihon king of the Amorites, who dwelt at Heshbon, whom Moses and the children of Israel had smitten, after they were come forth 47 from Egypt, and of whose land they had taken possession, and of the land of Og king of Bashan, two kings of the Amorites, who were beyond the Jordan towards sun-rising; 48 from Aroer, which is on the banks of the torrent Arnon, 49 even to mount Sion, which is Hermon; and all the plain beyond the Jordan eastward, even to the sea of the plain, below Ashdoth-Pisgah.

CHAP. V.—And Moses called together all Israel, and said to them, " Hear, O Israel, the statutes and judgments which I speak in your ears this day, that ye may learn them, and observe, and do them. Jehovah our God made a cove- 2 nant with us at Horeb. Jehovah made not this covenant 3 with our fathers, but with us, *with* us, who are all of us here alive this day. Face to face Jehovah spake with you on 4 the mountain, from the midst of the fire (I stood between 5 Jehovah and you at that time, to show you the word of Jehovah; for ye were afraid of the fire, and went not up into the mountain); saying,

'I am Jehovah thy God, who brought thee out of the land 6 of Egypt, out of the house of bondage. Thou shalt not 7 have other gods before me.

Thou shalt not make for thyself a graven image, any like- 8 ness of what is in the heavens above, or of what is in the earth beneath, or of what is in the waters under the earth: thou shalt not bow down thyself to them, and thou shalt 9 not serve them; for I Jehovah thy God am a jealous God, visiting the iniquity of the fathers upon the children to the third and fourth *generation* of them who hate me; but 10 shewing mercy to the thousandth of them who love me, and keep my commandments.

Thou shalt not utter the name of Jehovah thy God to a 11 falsehood; for Jehovah will not hold him guiltless who uttereth his name to a falsehood.

Observe the sabbath day to sanctify it, as Jehovah thy 12 God hath commanded thee. Six days mayest thou labour, 13 and do all thy work; but the seventh day is the sabbath of 14 Jehovah thy God: *on it* thou shalt do no work, thou, nor thy son, nor thy daughter, nor thy man-servant, nor thy maid-servant, nor thine ox, nor thine ass, nor any of thy cattle, nor thy stranger that is within thy gates; that thy man-servant and thy maid-servant may rest as well as thou. For remember that thou wast a servant in the land of 15 Egypt, and *that* Jehovah thy God brought thee out thence, by a mighty hand, and by an out-stretched arm: therefore Jehovah thy God commanded thee to keep the sabbath day.

Honour thy father and thy mother, as Jehovah thy God 16 hath commanded thee; that thy days may be prolonged, and that it may be well with thee, in the land which Jehovah thy God giveth thee.

17 Thou shalt not commit murder.
18 Neither shalt thou commit adultery.
19 Neither shalt thou steal.
20 Neither shalt thou bear false witness against thy neighbour.
21 Neither shalt thou desire thy neighbour's wife, nor shalt thou covet thy neighbour's house, his field, or his man-servant, or his maid-servant, his ox, or his ass, or any thing which is thy neighbour's.'
22 These words Jehovah spake to all your assembly in the mount, out of the midst of the fire, of the cloud, and of the thick darkness, with a great voice; and he added no more: and he wrote them on two tables of stone, and de-
23 livered them to me. And it came to pass when ye heard the voice from the midst of the darkness, while the mountain burned with fire, that ye came near to me, *even* all the heads of your
24 tribes, and your elders; and ye said, ' Lo, Jehovah our God hath shewed us his great glory, and his voice we have heard from the midst of the fire. We have this day seen that God
25 may speak with man, and he may *yet* live. And now why should we die? For this great fire will consume us if we continue to hear the voice of Jehovah our God, and we shall
26 die. For who is there of all flesh who hath heard the voice of the living God speaking from the midst of the fire, as we
27 *have heard it*, and hath lived? Go thou near, and hear all that Jehovah our God shall say; and thou shalt speak to us all that Jehovah our God shall speak to thee, and we will
28 hear and do *it*.' And Jehovah heard the voice of your words, when ye spake to me; and Jehovah said to me, ' I have heard the voice of the words of this people, which they have spoken to thee. All that they have spoken is right.
29 O that they may have a heart to fear me, and keep my commandments all their days, that it may be well with them,
30 and with their children for ever! Go say to them, Return
31 to your tents. But as for thee, stand thou here by me, that I may tell thee all the commandments, the statutes, and the judgments, which thou shalt teach them, that they may do *them* in the land which I shall give them for a possession.'
32 Ye shall observe to do, therefore, as Jehovah your God hath commanded you: ye shall not turn aside to the right hand
33 or to the left. Ye shall walk in all the ways which Jehovah your God hath commanded you, that ye may live, and that it may be well with you, and that ye may prolong *your* days in the land which ye are to possess.

CHAP. VI.—Now these are the commandments, the 1
statutes, and the judgments, which Jehovah your God commanded you to be taught, that ye might do them in the
land whither ye are going over to possess it; that thou 2
mightest fear Jehovah thy God, to keep all his statutes and
his commandments which I command thee; thou and thy
son, and thy son's son, all the days of thy life; and that
thy days may be prolonged. Hear, therefore, O Israel, and 3
observe to do *it*, that it may be well with thee, and that ye
may increase greatly, as Jehovah the God of thy fathers hath
promised thee, in a land that floweth with milk and honey.

Hear, O Israel: Jehovah our God is one Jehovah, and 5
thou shalt love Jehovah thy God with all thy heart, and
with all thy soul, and with all thy might. And these words, 6
which I command thee this day, shall be in thy heart; and 7
thou shalt teach them diligently to thy children, and shalt
talk of them when thou sittest in thy house, and when thou
walkest by the way, when thou liest down, and when thou
risest up. And thou shalt bind them for a sign upon thy 8
hands, and they shall be as frontlets between thine eyes.
And thou shalt write them upon the posts of thy houses, 9
and on thy gates.

And when Jehovah thy God shall have brought thee 10
into the land which he sware to thy fathers, to Abraham,
to Isaac, and to Jacob, to give thee great and goodly
cities, which thou buildedst not, and houses full of all 11
good things, which thou filledst not, and wells digged, which
thou diggedst not, vineyards and olive-trees, which thou
plantedst not; when thou shalt have eaten, and be full; be- 12
ware lest thou forget Jehovah thy God, who brought thee
forth out of the land of Egypt, from the house of bondage.
Thou shalt fear Jehovah thy God, and serve him, and shalt 13
swear by his name. Ye shall not go after other gods, of the 14
gods of the peoples which are round about you; (for Jeho- 15
vah thy God is a jealous God among you;) lest the anger of
Jehovah thy God be kindled against thee, and destroy thee
from off the face of the land. Ye shall not try Jehovah 16
your God, as ye tried him in Massah. Ye shall diligently 17
keep the commandments of Jehovah your God, and his
testimonies, and his statutes, which he hath commanded
thee. And thou shalt do what is right and good in the 18
sight of Jehovah; that it may be well with thee, and that
thou mayest go in and possess the good land which Jehovah

19 sware to thy fathers; by driving out all thine enemies from
20 before thee, as Jehovah hath spoken. And when thy son asketh thee in time to come, saying, 'What *mean* the testimonies, the statutes, and the judgments, which Jehovah our
21 God hath commanded you?' then shalt thou say to thy son, 'We were Pharaoh's bondmen in Egypt; and Jehovah
22 brought us out of Egypt with a mighty hand; and Jehovah shewed signs and wonders, great and grievous, upon Egypt, upon Pharaoh, and upon all his household, before our eyes;
23 and he brought us out thence, that he might bring us hither, to give us the land which he sware to our fathers.
24 And Jehovah commanded us to do all these statutes, to fear Jehovah our God, for our good always, that he might pre-
25 serve us alive, as at this day. And it shall be our righteousness, if we observe to do all these commandments before Jehovah our God, as he hath commanded us.'

1 CHAP. VII.—When Jehovah thy God shall have brought thee into the land whither thou art going to possess it, and shall have cast out many nations before thee, the Hittites, and the Girgashites, and the Amorites, and the Canaanites, and the Perizzites, and the Hivites, and the Jebusites, seven
2 nations greater and mightier than thou; and when Jehovah thy God shall have delivered them before thee; thou shalt smite them, *and* utterly destroy them: thou shalt make no
3 covenant with them, nor shew mercy to them; nor shalt thou make marriages with them: thy daughter thou shalt not give to his son, nor his daughter shalt thou take to thy son.
4 For he will turn away thy son from following me, that they may serve other gods: so will the anger of Jehovah be kindled
5 against you, and destroy thee suddenly. But thus shall ye deal with them; ye shall destroy their altars, and break down their images, and cut down their groves, and burn
6 their graven images with fire. For thou art a people holy to Jehovah thy God; and Jehovah thy God hath chosen thee to be a peculiar people to himself, above all the peoples
7 that are upon the face of the earth. Not because ye were more numerous than all the peoples, did Jehovah set his love upon you, and choose you; for ye are the fewest of all
8 peoples; but because Jehovah loved you, and because he would keep the oath which he had sworn to your fathers, hath Jehovah brought you out with a mighty hand, and redeemed you out of the house of bondmen, from the hand

DEUTERONOMY VII.

of Pharaoh king of Egypt. Know therefore that Jehovah thy God, he is God, the faithful God, who keepeth covenant and mercy with them who love him and keep his commandments, to the thousandth generation; and repayeth them who hate him to their face, to destroy them: he will not delay in respect to him who hateth him, he will repay him to his face. Thou shalt therefore keep the commandments, and the statutes, and the judgments, which I command thee this day, to do them. For if ye hearken to these judgments, and keep and do them, then Jehovah thy God will keep with thee the covenant and the mercy which he sware to thy fathers; and he will love thee, and bless thee, and multiply thee: he will also bless the fruit of thy womb, and the fruit of thy land, thy corn, thy wine, and thine oil, the increase of thy kine, and the flocks of thy sheep, in the land which he sware to thy fathers to give thee. Thou shalt be blessed above all peoples, there shall not be male or female barren among you, or among your cattle. And Jehovah will take away from thee all sickness, and none of the evil diseases of Egypt, which thou knowest, will be put upon thee; but he will lay them upon all those who hate thee. And thou shalt consume all the peoples which Jehovah thy God shall deliver to thee; thine eye shall have no pity upon them, nor shalt thou serve their gods; for that would be a snare to thee. If thou shalt say in thy heart, 'These nations are more numerous than I; how can I dispossess them?' be not afraid of them; remember well what Jehovah thy God did to Pharaoh, and to all Egypt; the great trials which thine eyes saw, the signs, and the wonders, and the mighty hand, and the outstretched arm, with which Jehovah thy God brought thee out; so shall Jehovah thy God do to all the peoples of whom thou art afraid. Moreover, Jehovah thy God will send hornets among them, until they that are left, and hide themselves from thee, be destroyed. Be not terrified at them; for Jehovah thy God is among you, a God mighty and terrible. And Jehovah thy God will cast out those nations before thee by little and little: thou mayest not consume them at once, lest the beasts of the field increase upon thee. But Jehovah thy God shall deliver them to thee, and shall destroy them with a mighty destruction, until they be destroyed. And he shall deliver their kings into thy hand, and thou shalt destroy their name from under the

heavens: no man shall be able to stand before thee, until
25 thou shalt have destroyed them. The graven images of
their gods ye shall burn with fire; thou shalt not desire the
silver or gold that is on them, nor take it to thee, lest thou
be snared by it; for it is an abomination to Jehovah thy
26 God. Nor shalt thou bring an abomination into thy house,
lest thou be a devoted thing like it; but thou shalt utterly
detest it, and thou shalt utterly abhor it; for it is a devoted
thing.

1 CHAP. VIII.—All the commandments which I command thee this day, shall ye observe to do, that ye may live, and multiply, and go in and possess the land which
2 Jehovah sware to your fathers. And thou shalt remember all the way through which Jehovah thy God hath led thee these forty years in the desert, to humble thee, to prove thee, to know what was in thy heart, whether thou wouldest
3 keep his commandments, or not. And he humbled thee, and suffered thee to hunger, and fed thee with manna, which thou knewest not, neither did thy fathers know, that he might make thee know that man doth not live by bread alone, but by whatever proceedeth out of the mouth of Je-
4 hovah doth man live. Thy raiment wasted not from off
5 thee, nor did thy foot swell, these forty years. Thou shalt also consider in thy heart, that, as a man chasteneth his son,
6 so Jehovah thy God chasteneth thee. Therefore thou shalt keep the commandments of Jehovah thy God, to walk in his
7 ways, and to fear him. For Jehovah thy God bringeth thee into a good land; a land of brooks of water, of fountains, and lakes issuing out of valleys and hills; a land of wheat,
8 and barley, of vines, and fig-trees, and pomegranates; a
9 land of olive-oil, and honey; a land in which thou shalt eat bread without scarceness, where thou shalt not lack any thing; a land, the stones of which are iron, and out of the
10 mountains of which thou mayest dig copper. When thou hast eaten and art full, and hast blessed Jehovah thy God,
11 for the good land which he hath given thee, beware that thou forgot not Jehovah thy God, in not keeping his commandments, and his judgments, and his statutes, which I
12 command thee this day; lest, when thou hast eaten and art
13 full, and hast built goodly houses, and dwelt *therein*, and when thy herds and thy flocks are increased, and thy silver and thy gold are increased, and all that thou hast is in-

creased; thy heart be lifted up, and thou forget Jehovah 14
thy God, who brought thee forth out of the land of Egypt,
from the house of bondage; who led thee through that
great and terrible desert; in which were fiery serpents, and 15
scorpions, and drought; where was no water; who brought
thee forth water out of the rock of flint; who fed thee in 16
the desert with manna, which thy fathers knew not, that he
might humble thee, and that he might prove thee, to do
thee good at the last; and thou say in thy heart, ' My power, 17
and the might of my hand hath gotten me this wealth.'
But thou shalt remember Jehovah thy God; for it is he who 18
giveth thee power to get wealth, and that he may establish
his covenant, which he sware to thy fathers, as *it is* this day.
But if thou do at all forget Jehovah thy God, and walk 19
after other gods, and serve them, and worship them, I testify
against you this day, that ye shall utterly perish. As the 20
nations which Jehovah destroyeth before your face, so shall
ye perish, because ye would not be obedient to the voice of
Jehovah your God.

CHAP. IX.—Hear, O Israel; Thou art this day about 1
to pass over the Jordan, to go in to possess nations greater
and mightier than thou, cities great, and fenced up to
heaven; a people great and tall, the children of the Ana- 2
kites, whom thou knowest, and *of whom* thou hast heard *it
said*, ' Who can stand before the children of Anak?' Know 3
therefore this day, that Jehovah thy God is he who goeth
over before thee, a consuming fire: he will destroy them,
and he will bring them down before thy face: so shalt thou
drive them out, and destroy them quickly, as Jehovah hath
said to thee. Speak not thou in thy heart, after that Je- 4
hovah thy God hath cast them out from before thee, saying,
' For my righteousness Jehovah hath brought me to possess
this land;' but for the wickedness of these nations Jehovah
driveth them out from before thee. Not for thy righteous- 5
ness, or for the uprightness of thy heart, dost thou go to
possess their land; but for the wickedness of these nations
Jehovah thy God driveth them out from before thee, and
that he may perform the word which Jehovah sware to thy
fathers, Abraham, Isaac, and Jacob. Know therefore that 6
Jehovah thy God giveth thee not this good land to possess
it for thy righteousness; for thou art a stiff-necked people.
Remember and forget not, how thou provokedst Jehovah thy 7

God to wrath in the desert: from the day that thou didst depart from the land of Egypt, until ye came unto this 8 place, ye have been rebellious against Jehovah. Even at Horeb ye provoked Jehovah to wrath, so that Jehovah was 9 angry with you, and would have destroyed you. When I went up to the mountain, to receive the tables of stone, the tables of the covenant which Jehovah made with you, I remained on the mountain forty days and forty nights, neither 10 eating bread nor drinking water. And Jehovah delivered to me two tables of stone, written with the finger of God; and on them *was written* according to all the words which Jehovah spake with you on the mountain, out of the midst of 11 the fire, in the day of the assembly. And it came to pass at the end of forty days and forty nights, that Jehovah gave me the two tables of stone, the tables of the covenant. 12 And Jehovah said to me, 'Arise, go down quickly hence; for thy people whom thou hast brought forth out of Egypt have corrupted *themselves*: they have quickly turned aside out of the way which I commanded them; they have made 13 for themselves a molten image.' Jehovah also spake to me, saying, 'I have seen this people, and behold, it is a stiff-14 necked people: let me alone, that I may destroy them, and blot out their name from under the heavens; and I will make of thee a nation mightier and more numerous than 15 they.' So I turned, and came down from the mountain, and the mountain burned with fire; and the two tables of 16 the covenant were in my two hands. And I looked, and, lo, ye had sinned against Jehovah your God, ye had made for yourselves a molten calf: ye had turned aside quickly 17 out of the way which Jehovah had commanded you. And I took the two tables, and cast them out of my two hands, 18 and brake them before your eyes; and I fell down before Jehovah, as at the first, forty days and forty nights: I neither ate bread, nor drank water, on account of all your sins which ye had committed, in doing wickedly in the sight 19 of Jehovah, to provoke him to anger; for I was afraid of the anger and hot displeasure wherewith Jehovah was wroth against you to destroy you. But Jehovah hearkened to me 20 at that time also. With Aaron also, Jehovah was exceedingly angry, and would have destroyed him; but I prayed 21 for Aaron also at the same time. And your sin which ye had made, the calf, I took and burnt with fire, and beat it in pieces, and ground it very small, until it was as small as dust; and I cast the dust of it into the brook which ran down from the mountain. And at Taberah, and at Massah, and at Kibroth-hattaavah, ye provoked Jehovah to wrath. Likewise, when Jehovah sent you from Kadesh-barnea, saying, 'Go up and possess the land which I have given you;' then ye rebelled against the commandment of Jehovah your God, and ye believed him not, nor hearkened to his voice. Ye have been rebellious against Jehovah from the day that I knew you. Thus I fell down before Jehovah forty days and forty nights, as I had fallen down *before;* because Jehovah had said he would destroy you. I prayed therefore to Jehovah, and said, 'O Lord Jehovah, destroy not thy people, and thy inheritance, which thou hast redeemed through thy greatness, which thou hast brought forth out of Egypt with a mighty hand. Remember thy servants, Abraham, Isaac, and Jacob: regard not the stubbornness of this people, nor their wickedness, nor their sin; lest *the people of* the land whence thou broughtest us out say, Because Jehovah was not able to bring them into the land which he promised them, and because he hated them, he hath brought them out to slay them in the desert. Yet they are thy people, and thy inheritance, which thou broughtest out by thy mighty power, and by thy out-stretched arm.'

CHAP. X.—At that time Jehovah said to me, 'Hew thee two tables of stone like the former, and come up to me to the mountain, and make thee an ark of wood; and I will write on the tables the words that were in the former tables, which thou brakest, and thou shalt put them in the ark.' So I made an ark of setim wood, and hewed two tables of stone like the former, and went up to the mountain, having the two tables in my hand. And *Jehovah* wrote on the tables, according to the former writing, the ten commandments, which Jehovah spake to you in the mountain out of the midst of the fire, in the day of the assembly; and Jehovah gave them to me. And I turned, and came down from the mountain, and put the tables in the ark which I had made; that they may be there, as Jehovah commanded me. And the children of Israel took their journey from Beeroth, of the children of Jaakah to Mosera: there Aaron died, and there he was buried; and Eleazar his son ministered in the priest's office, in his stead. Thence they journeyed to Gudgodah; and from Gudgodah to Jotbath, a

8 land of rivers of water. At that time Jehovah separated the tribe of Levi, to bear the ark of the covenant of Jehovah, to stand before Jehovah, to minister to him, and to 9 bless in his name, until this day. Wherefore Levi hath no part nor inheritance with his brethren: Jehovah is his inheritance, according as Jehovah thy God promised him. 10 And I stayed on the mountain, as at the first time, forty days and forty nights; and Jehovah hearkened to me at that time also, and Jehovah would not destroy thee.

11 And Jehovah said to me, 'Arise, take thy journey before this people, that they may go in and possess the land, which 12 I sware to their fathers, to give to them.' And now, O Israel, what doth Jehovah thy God require of thee, but to fear Jehovah thy God, to walk in all his ways, and to love him, and to serve Jehovah thy God with all thy heart, and 13 with all thy soul, to keep the commandments of Jehovah, and his statutes which I command thee this day for thy 14 good? Behold, to Jehovah thy God belong the heavens, and the heaven of heavens, the earth, with all that is therein. 15 Yet Jehovah had a delight in thy fathers to love them, and he chose their seed after them, even you above all peoples, 16 as it is this day. Circumcise therefore the foreskin of your 17 heart, and be no more stiff-necked. For Jehovah your God is the God of gods, and the Lord of lords, a God, great, and mighty, and terrible, who regardeth not persons, nor 18 taketh a bribe. He executeth justice for the fatherless and the widow, and loveth the stranger, giving him food and 19 raiment. Love ye therefore the stranger; for ye were 20 strangers in the land of Egypt. Jehovah thy God thou shalt fear; and him thou shalt serve, and to him thou shalt 21 cleave, and by his name thou shalt swear. He is thy praise, and he is thy God, who hath done for thee these great and 22 terrible things, which thine eyes have seen. Thy fathers went down into Egypt with seventy persons, and now Jehovah thy God hath made thee as the stars of heaven 1 for multitude. CHAP. XI.—Therefore thou shalt love Jehovah thy God, and keep his charge, his statutes, and his 2 judgments, and his commandments, always. And ye yourselves this day know: for *I speak* not with your children who have not known, and who have not seen the chastisement of Jehovah your God, his greatness, and his mighty 3 hand, and his outstretched arm, his miracles, and his acts, which he did in the midst of Egypt, to Pharaoh the king

of Egypt, and to all his land; and what he did to the army 4 of Egypt, to their horses, and to their chariots; how he made the water of the Red Sea to overflow them as they pursued after you, and how Jehovah hath destroyed them to this day; and what he did to yourselves in the desert, until 5 ye came to this place; and what he did to Dathan and 6 Abiram, the sons of Eliab, the son of Reuben: how the earth opened her mouth, and swallowed them up, and their households, and their tents, and all the substance that was in their possession, in the midst of all the Israelites: but 7 your eyes have seen all the great deeds of Jehovah which he did. Ye shall therefore keep all the commandments which 8 I command you this day, that ye may be strong, and go in and possess the land whither ye are going to possess it; and 9 that ye may prolong your days in the land which Jehovah sware to your fathers to give to them and to their seed, a land flowing with milk and honey. For the land whither thou 10 art going to possess it, is not like the land of Egypt, out of which ye are come, where thou sowedst thy seed, and wateredst it with thy foot, as a garden of herbs; but 11 the land, whither ye are going over to possess it, is a land of hills and valleys; it drinketh water of the rain of heaven; a land which Jehovah thy God careth for: the 12 eyes of Jehovah thy God are always upon it, from the beginning of the year even to the end of the year. If then 13 ye will hearken diligently to my commandments which I command you this day, to love Jehovah your God, and to serve him with all your heart, and with all your soul, I will 14 give thee the rain of your land in its due season, the first rain and the latter rain, that thou mayest gather in thy corn, and thy wine, and thine oil. And I will send grass in thy fields 15 for thy cattle, that thou mayest eat and be satisfied. Take 16 heed to yourselves, that your heart be not deceived, and ye turn aside, and serve other gods, and worship them; so that 17 the wrath of Jehovah be kindled against you, and he shut up the heavens, that there be no rain, and that the land yield not its fruit; and ye perish quickly from off the good land which Jehovah giveth you. Therefore shall ye lay up these 18 my words in your heart, and in your soul, and bind them for a sign upon your hand, that they may be as frontlets between your eyes. And ye shall teach them your children, 19 speaking of them when thou sittest in thy house, and when thou walkest by the way, and when thou liest down, and

20 when thou risest up. And thou shalt write them upon the
21 door-posts of thy house, and upon thy gates; that your days, and the days of your children, may be multiplied in the land which Jehovah sware to your fathers, to give them, as the
22 days of the heavens over the earth. For if ye shall diligently keep all these commandments which I command you this day, to do them, to love Jehovah your God, to walk in
23 all his ways, and to cleave to him; then will Jehovah drive out all these nations from before you, and ye shall possess
24 nations greater and mightier than yourselves. Every place on which the soles of your feet shall tread shall be yours; from the desert to Lebanon, and from the river, the river Euphrates, even to the farther sea, shall your boundary be.
25 No man shall be able to stand before you; for Jehovah your God will put the fear of you, and the dread of you upon all the land on which ye shall tread, as he hath said to you.
27 See, I set before you this day a blessing and a curse: a blessing, if ye obey the commandments of Jehovah your
28 God, which I command you this day; and a curse, if ye will not obey the commandments of Jehovah your God, but turn aside out of the way which I command you this day,
29 to go after other gods, which ye have not known. And when Jehovah thy God shall have brought thee into the land which thou art going to possess, thou shalt put the blessing
30 upon mount Gerizim, and the curse upon mount Ebal. Are they not beyond the Jordan, towards the setting of the sun, in the land of the Canaanites, which dwell in the plain
31 opposite to Gilgal, near the terebinth-trees of Moreh? For ye shall pass over the Jordan, to go in to possess the land which Jehovah your God giveth you, and ye shall pos-
32 sess it, and dwell therein. And ye shall observe to do all the statutes and judgments which I set before you this day.

1 CHAP. XII.—These are the statutes and judgments which ye shall observe to do in the land which Jehovah the God of thy fathers giveth thee to possess, all the days that ye live
2 upon the land. Ye shall utterly destroy all the places where the nations which ye are to dispossess served their gods, on the high mountains, or on the hills, or under any green tree;
3 and ye shall overthrow their altars, and break their statues, and burn their groves with fire; and ye shall hew down the graven images of their gods, and destroy the names of them

out of that place. Ye shall not do so to Jehovah your God; 4
but to the place in which Jehovah your God shall choose out 5
of all your tribes, to put his name and to dwell there, ye
shall seek, and thither thou shalt go; and thither ye shall 6
carry your burnt-offerings, and your sacrifices, and your
tithes, and the heave-offerings of your hand, and your votive
and your free-will-offerings, and the firstlings of your herds
and of your flocks; and there ye shall eat before Jehovah 7
your God, and ye shall rejoice, ye and your families in all
that ye put your hand to, in which Jehovah thy God hath
blessed thee. Ye shall not do according to all that we do 8
here this day, every one whatsoever is right in his own eyes.
For ye are not yet come to the rest and to the inheritance, 9
which Jehovah your God giveth you. But when ye shall 10
have gone over the Jordan, and shall dwell in the land which
Jehovah your God giveth you to inherit, and when he shall
have given you rest from all your enemies round about, so
that ye dwell in safety; then there shall be a place which 11
Jehovah your God shall choose, to cause his name to dwell
there; thither shall ye carry all that I command you; your
burnt-offerings, and your sacrifices, your tithes, and the
heave-offerings of your hand, and all your choice votive-
offerings which ye vow to Jehovah; and ye shall rejoice 12
before Jehovah your God, ye, and your sons, and your
daughters, your men-servants, and your maid-servants, and
the Levite that is within your gates; forasmuch as he hath
no part or inheritance with you. Take heed to thyself that 13
thou offer not thy burnt-offerings in every place that thou
seest: but in that place only which Jehovah shall choose in 14
one of thy tribes, there thou shalt offer thy burnt-offerings,
and there thou shalt do all that I command thee. Never- 15
theless whenever thou desirest it, thou mayest kill and eat
flesh in any of thy gates, according to the blessing which
Jehovah thy God shall have given thee: the unclean and the
clean may eat of it, as of the antelope, and as of the hart.
Only ye shall not eat the blood; ye shall pour it upon the 16
ground as water. Thou mayest not eat within thy gates the 17
tithe of thy corn, or of thy wine, or of thy oil, or the firstlings of thy herds, or of thy flock, or any of thy votive-
offerings which thou vowest, or thy free-will-offerings, or
heave-offerings of thy hands; but thou must eat them be- 18
fore Jehovah thy God, in the place which Jehovah thy God
shall choose, thou, and thy son, and thy daughter, thy man-

servant, and thy maid-servant, and the Levite that is within
thy gates; and thou shalt rejoice before Jehovah thy God in
19 all that thou puttest thy hands to. Take heed to thyself
that thou forsake not the Levite as long as thou livest upon
thy land.
20 When Jehovah thy God shall have enlarged thy boundary,
as he hath promised thee, and thou shalt say, 'I will eat
flesh,' because thou hast a desire to eat flesh, thou mayest eat
21 flesh, whenever thou desirest it. If the place which Jehovah
thy God hath chosen to put his name there, be too far from
thee, then thou mayest kill of thy herd, and of thy flock,
which Jehovah hath given thee, as I have commanded thee,
and thou mayest eat in thy gates whenever thou desirest.
22 Only as the antelope and the hart is eaten, so thou shalt eat
them; and the unclean and the clean may eat of them alike.
23 Only be sure thou eat not the blood; for the blood is the
24 life; and thou mayest not eat the life with the flesh. Thou
shalt not eat it; thou shalt pour it upon the earth as water:
25 thou shalt not eat it, that it may be well with thee, and with
thy children after thee, when thou shalt do that which is
26 right in the sight of Jehovah. Only thy holy things which
thou hast, and thy vows, thou shalt take, and go to the place
27 which Jehovah shall choose; and thou shalt offer thy burnt-
offerings, the flesh and the blood, upon the altar of Jehovah
thy God; and the blood of thy sacrifices shall be poured out
upon the altar of Jehovah thy God, and thou shalt eat the
28 flesh. Observe, and hear all these words which I command
thee this day, that it may be well with thee, and with thy
children after thee for ever, when thou doest that which is
29 good and right in the sight of Jehovah thy God. When
Jehovah thy God shall have cut off the nations from before
thee, whither thou goest to dispossess them, and thou shalt
30 have dispossessed them, and shalt dwell in their land; take
heed to thyself, that thou be not ensnared by following them,
after they shall have been destroyed from before thee; and
that thou inquire not after their gods, saying, 'How did
these nations serve their gods? even so will I do likewise.'
31 Thou shalt not do so to Jehovah thy God; for every abomination to Jehovah, which he hateth, have they done to their
gods; for even their sons and their daughters they have
32 burnt in the fire to their gods. Everything that I command
you observe to do: thou shalt not add to it, nor take from
it.

CHAP. XIII.—If there arise among you a prophet, or a dreamer of dreams, and he give thee a sign or a wonder, and the sign or the wonder come to pass, of which he spake to thee, saying, 'Let us go after other gods, which thou hast not known, and let us serve them;' thou shalt not hearken to the words of that prophet, or that dreamer of dreams; for Jehovah your God proveth you, to know whether ye love Jehovah your God with all your heart, and with all your soul. Ye shall walk after Jehovah your God, and fear him, and keep his commandments, and obey his voice, and ye shall serve him, and cleave to him. And that prophet, or that dreamer of dreams, shall be put to death; because he hath proposed rebellion against Jehovah your God, who brought you out of the land of Egypt, and redeemed you from the house of bondage, to seduce thee from the way in which Jehovah thy God commanded thee to walk: so shalt thou put away the evil from the midst of thee. If thy brother, the son of thy mother, or thy son, or thy daughter, or the wife of thy bosom, or thy friend, who is as thy own soul, entice thee secretly, saying, 'Let us go and serve other gods,' which thou hast not known, thou, nor thy fathers; some of the gods of the peoples around you, whether near to thee, or far from thee, from one end of the earth even unto the other end of the earth; thou shalt not consent to him, nor hearken to him; neither shall thine eye pity him, thou shalt not spare, neither shalt thou conceal him; but thou shalt surely kill him; thy hand shall be first upon him to put him to death, and afterwards the hands of all the people. And thou shalt stone him with stones, that he die; because he hath sought to seduce thee from Jehovah thy God, who brought thee out of the land of Egypt, from the house of bondage. And all Israel shall hear, and fear, and shall do no more any such wickedness as this is among you. If thou shalt hear it said that in one of thy cities, which Jehovah thy God shall have given thee to dwell in, *certain* men, sons of Belial, are gone out from among you, and have withdrawn the inhabitants of their city, saying, 'Let us go and serve other gods;' which ye have not known; then shalt thou inquire, and make search, and ask diligently; and, behold, if it be true, and the thing certain, that such abomination hath been wrought among you; thou shalt surely smite the inhabitants of that city with the edge of the sword, devoting it, and all that is in it, and its cattle, *to be destroyed* by the edge of the sword.

16 And thou shalt gather all the spoil of it into the midst of its street, and shalt burn with fire the city, and all its spoil, a whole *burnt-offering* to Jehovah thy God; and it shall be a
17 ruin for ever; it shall not be built again. And nothing of what is devoted shall cleave to thy hand; that Jehovah may turn from the fierceness of his anger, and shew thee mercy, and have compassion upon thee, and increase thee, as he
18 hath sworn to thy fathers; when thou shalt hearken to the voice of Jehovah thy God, to keep all his commandments which I command thee this day, to do that which is right in the eyes of Jehovah thy God.

1 CHAP. XIV.—Ye are the children of Jehovah your God: ye shall not cut yourselves, nor make any baldness between
2 your eyes for the dead; for thou art a people holy to Jehovah thy God, and Jehovah hath chosen thee to be a people peculiar to himself, out of all the nations that are upon the earth.
4 Thou shalt not eat any abominable thing. These are the beasts which ye may eat; the ox, and the sheep, and the
5 goat, the hart, and the antelope, and the fallow-deer, and the wild goat, and the dishon, and the harte-beest, and the roe.
6 And every beast whose hoof is divided, and whose foot is cloven into two parts, and which cheweth the cud among the
7 beasts, ye may eat. But ye may not eat of those which only chew the cud, or of those which only have a divided hoof; as the camel, and the hare, and the cavy; for they chew the cud, but have not the hoof divided; they shall be unclean
8 to you. And the swine, he hath a divided hoof, yet he cheweth not the cud; he shall be unclean to you: ye shall
9 not eat of their flesh, nor touch their dead carcase. These ye may eat, of all that are in the waters: every thing
10 that hath fins and scales ye may eat. But every thing which hath not fins and scales, ye may not eat; it shall be
12 unclean to you. Of all clean birds ye may eat. But these are they which ye shall not eat: the eagle, and the
13 ossifrage, and the osprey, and the vulture, and the kite, after
15 his kind, and every raven after his kind, and the ostrich, and the techemes, and the saph, and the hawk after his
17 kind, and the cus, and the ibis, and the swan, and the
18 pelican, and the rechem, and the cormorant, and the stork, and the anapha after her kind, and the hoopoe, and the
19 bat. And every creeping thing that flieth is unclean unto
20 you: they shall not be eaten; but of all clean fowls ye may

eat. Ye shall not eat of any thing that dieth of itself: thou 21 mayest give it to the sojourner that is in thy gates, that he may eat it; or thou mayest sell it to an alien: for thou art a people holy to Jehovah thy God. Thou shalt not seethe a kid in its mother's milk.

Thou shalt truly tithe all the increase of thy seed, that 22 the field bringeth forth year by year. And thou shalt eat 23 before Jehovah thy God, in the place which he shall choose to cause his name to dwell there, the tithe of thy corn, of thy wine, and of thy oil, and the firstlings of thy herds, and of thy flocks; that thou mayest learn to fear Jehovah thy God always. But if the way be too long for thee, so that 24 thou shalt not be able to carry it; if the place be too far from thee which Jehovah thy God shall choose to place his name there, when Jehovah thy God shall have blessed thee; then shalt thou turn it into money, and bind up the money 25 in thy hand, and shalt go to the place which Jehovah thy God shall choose; and thou shalt bestow that money for 26 whatsoever thou desirest, for oxen, or for sheep, for wine, or for strong drink, or for whatsoever thou desirest; and thou shalt eat there before Jehovah thy God, and thou shalt rejoice, thou, and thy household, and the Levite that is within 27 thy gates; thou shalt not forsake him; for he hath no part or inheritance with thee. At the end of three years thou 28 shalt bring forth all the tithe of thy increase the same year, and shalt lay it up within thy gates; and the Levite, 29 because he hath no part or inheritance with thee, and the stranger, and the fatherless, and the widow, who are within thy gates, shall come, and shall eat, and be satisfied; that Jehovah thy God may bless thee in all the work of thy hand which thou doest.

CHAP. XV.—At the end of every seven years thou shalt 1 make a remission. And this is the nature of the remission: 2 Every creditor who hath lent to his neighbour, shall remit it; he shall not exact it of his neighbour, *and* of his brother, when the remission of Jehovah shall have been proclaimed. Of an alien thou mayest exact it; but what thy brother hath 3 of thine, thy hand shall remit, unless there shall be no poor 4 among you; for Jehovah thy God will greatly bless thee in the land which Jehovah thy God giveth thee for an inheritance to possess it, if only thou wilt carefully hearken to the 5 voice of Jehovah thy God, to observe and to do all these

6 commandments which I command thee this day. For Jehovah thy God will bless thee, as he promised thee; and thou shalt lend to many nations, but thou shalt not borrow; and thou shalt rule over many nations, but they shall not 7 rule over thee. If there be among you a poor man, one of thy brethren, within any of thy gates, in thy land which Jehovah thy God giveth thee, thou shalt not harden thy 8 heart, nor shut thy hand from thy poor brother; but thou shalt open thy hand wide to him, and shalt willingly lend to 9 him what he wanteth, sufficient for his need. Beware that there be not a wicked thought in thy heart, saying, 'The seventh year, the year of remission is at hand;' and thine eye be evil against thy poor brother, and thou give him nought; and he cry to Jehovah against thee, and it be sin 10 unto thee. Thou shalt freely give him, and thy heart shall not be grieved when thou givest to him; because for this thing Jehovah thy God will bless thee in all thy works, and 11 in all to which thou puttest thy hands. For the poor shall never cease out of the land: therefore I command thee, saying, 'Thou shalt open thy hands wide to thy brother, to thy poor, and to thy needy, in the land.'

12 When thy brother, a Hebrew man, or a Hebrew woman, hath been sold to thee, and served thee six years, then in the 13 seventh year thou shalt let him go free from thee. And when thou sendest him out free from thee, thou shalt not 14 let him go away empty: thou shalt furnish him liberally from thy flock, and from thy threshing-floor, and from thy wine-press: from that with which Jehovah thy God hath 15 blessed thee thou shalt give to him. And thou shalt remember that thou wast a bondman in the land of Egypt, and Jehovah thy God redeemed thee: therefore I command 16 thee this thing to-day. But if he say to thee, 'I will not go away from thee,' because he loveth thee and thy household, 17 because he is well with thee, then thou shalt take an awl, and thrust it through his ear into the door, and he shall be thy servant for ever. Thus also thou shalt do to thy maid-18 servant. It shall not seem hard to thee, when thou sendest him away free from thee; for he hath been doubly worth a hired servant in serving thee six years; and Jehovah thy God will bless thee in all that thou doest.

19 All the firstling males that are born of thy herd and of thy flock, thou shalt sanctify to Jehovah thy God: thou shalt do no work with the firstling of thy bullock, nor shear

the firstling of thy sheep: thou shalt eat it before Jehovah 20
thy God year by year, in the place which Jehovah shall
choose, thou and thy household. And if there be any 21
blemish therein, *if it be* lame, or blind, or *have* any ill
blemish, thou shalt not sacrifice it to Jehovah thy God.
Thou mayest eat it within thy gates: the unclean and the 22
clean person may eat it alike, as the antelope and as the
hart. Only thou shalt not eat its blood; thou shalt pour it 23
upon the ground as water.

CHAP. XVI.—Observe the month Abib, and keep the 1
passover to Jehovah thy God; for in the month Abib Jehovah thy God brought thee forth out of Egypt by night.
Thou shalt therefore sacrifice the passover to Jehovah thy 2
God, from the flock and the herd, in the place in which
Jehovah shall choose to place his name. Thou shalt eat 3
with it nothing leavened; seven days shalt thou eat with it
unleavened bread, bread of affliction; for thou camest forth
in haste from the land of Egypt; that thou mayest remember the day when thou camest forth from the land of Egypt
all the days of thy life. And there shall be no leavened 4
bread seen with thee within all thy borders seven days; nor
shall any of the flesh, which thou didst slay the first day in
the evening, remain all night until the morning. Thou 5
mayest not slay the passover within any of the gates, which Jehovah thy God giveth thee; but in the place which Jehovah 6
thy God shall choose to place his name there, thou shalt slay
the passover in the evening, at the going down of the sun,
at the season in which thou camest forth from Egypt. And 7
thou shalt cook and eat it in the place which Jehovah thy
God shall choose; and thou mayest turn in the morning, 8
and go to thy tents. Six days thou shalt eat unleavened
bread; and on the seventh day shall be a solemn assembly
to Jehovah thy God: thou shalt do no work. Seven 9
weeks shalt thou number to thee: begin to number seven
weeks from the time of beginning to put the sickle to
the corn. And thou shalt keep the feast of weeks to Jehovah 10
thy God with a tribute of a free-will-offering of thy
hand, which thou shalt give Jehovah according as Jehovah
thy God hath blessed thee; and thou shalt rejoice before 11
Jehovah thy God, thou, and thy son, and thy daughter, thy
man-servant, and thy maid-servant, and the Levite that is
within thy gates, and the stranger, and the fatherless,

and the widow, that are among you, in the place which Jehovah thy God hath chosen to place his name there.
12 And thou shalt remember that thou wast a bondman in the land of Egypt; and thou shalt observe and do these statutes.
13 Thou shalt observe the feast of tabernacles seven days, after that thou hast gathered in *the produce* of thy threshing-floor
14 and thy wine-press; and thou shalt rejoice in thy feast, thou, and thy son, and thy daughter, and thy man-servant, and thy maid-servant, and the Levite, the stranger, and the
15 fatherless, and the widow, that are within thy gates. Seven days shalt thou keep a solemn feast to Jehovah thy God, in the place which Jehovah shall choose: because Jehovah thy God shall bless thee in all thy increase, and in all the works
16 of thy hands, therefore thou shalt surely rejoice. Three times in the year shall all thy males appear before Jehovah thy God in the place which he shall choose; in the feast of unleavened bread, and in the feast of weeks, and in the feast of tabernacles; and they shall not appear before Jehovah
17 empty-handed. Every man shall give as he is able, according to the blessing of Jehovah thy God, which he hath given thee.
18 Judges and officers shalt thou make thee in all thy gates, which Jehovah thy God giveth thee, throughout thy tribes;
19 and they shall judge the people with just judgment. Thou shalt not wrest judgment; thou shalt not respect persons, neither take a gift; for a gift blindeth the eyes of the wise,
20 and perverteth the words of the just. That which is altogether just shalt thou follow, that thou mayest live, and inherit the land which Jehovah thy God giveth thee.
21 Thou shalt not plant thyself a grove of any trees near to the altar of Jehovah thy God, which thou shalt make for
22 thyself: neither shalt thou set thee up any image, which Jehovah thy God hateth.

1 CHAP. XVII.—Thou shalt not sacrifice to Jehovah thy God a bullock or a sheep which hath a blemish, any evil thing; for that is an abomination to Jehovah thy God.
2 When there is found among you, within any of thy gates which Jehovah thy God giveth thee, man or woman, that hath wrought wickedness in the sight of Jehovah thy God,
3 in transgressing his covenant, and hath gone and served other gods, and worshipped them, either the sun, or the moon, or any of the host of the heavens, which I have not

commanded *thee;* and it is told thee, and thou hast heard 4
of it, and inquired diligently, and, lo, it is true, and the
thing certain, that such abomination hath been wrought in
Israel; then thou shalt bring forth that man or that woman, 5
who have committed that wicked thing, to thy gates, even
that man or that woman, and shalt stone them with stones,
till they die. On the testimony of two witnesses, or of 6
three witnesses, shall he that is worthy of death, be put to
death; on the testimony of one witness, he shall not be put
to death. The hands of the witnesses shall be first upon 7
him to put him to death, and afterwards the hands of all the
people. So shalt thou put away the evil from among you.
When there arises a matter too hard for thee in judgment, 8
between blood and blood, between plea and plea, and between
stroke and stroke, matters of controversy within thy gates;
then shalt thou arise, and go up to the place which Jehovah
thy God shall choose; and thou shalt come to the priests 9
the Levites, and to the judge that shall be in those days, and inquire; and they shall declare to thee the sentence of judgment,
and thou shalt do according to the sentence, which they of 10
that place which Jehovah shall choose, shall declare to thee;
and thou shalt observe to do according to all that they shall
teach thee: according to the sentence of the law which they 11
shall teach thee, and according to the judgment which they
shall tell thee, thou shalt do: thou shalt not decline from the
sentence which they shall show thee, to the right hand or to
the left. And the man that will act presumptuously, and will 12
not hearken to the priest that standeth to minister there before
Jehovah thy God, or to the judge, even that man shall die:
and thou shalt put away the evil from Israel. And all the 13
people shall hear, and fear, and act no more presumptuously.

When thou shalt come to the land which Jehovah thy God 14
is about to give thee, and shalt possess it, and shalt dwell
therein, and shalt say, 'I will set a king over me, like all the
nations that are about me;' thou shalt be sure to set him king 15
over thee whom Jehovah thy God shall choose: one from among
thy brethren shalt thou set king over thee: thou mayest not
set an alien over thee, who is not thy brother. But he shall 16
not multiply horses to himself, nor cause the people to return
to Egypt, that he may multiply horses; forasmuch as Jehovah
hath said to you, 'Ye shall henceforth return no more that
way.' Nor shall he multiply wives to himself, that his heart 17
turn not away; nor shall he greatly multiply to himself

18 silver and gold. And when he sitteth upon the throne of his kingdom, he shall write for himself a copy of this law according to the book which is before the priests the
19 Levites; and it shall be with him, and he shall read therein all the days of his life; that he may learn to fear Jehovah his God, to keep all the words of this law and these statutes,
20 to do them; that his heart be not lifted up above his brethren, and that he turn not aside from the commandment to the right hand, or to the left; so that he may prolong his days in his kingdom, he, and his children, in the midst of Israel.

1 CHAP. XVIII.—The priests the Levites, the whole tribe of Levi, shall have no part or inheritance with Israel: they shall eat the offerings of Jehovah made by fire, and his in-
2 heritance. Therefore shall they have no inheritance among their brethren: Jehovah is their inheritance, as he hath said
3 to them. And this shall be the priest's due from the people, from them who offer a sacrifice, whether it be bullock or sheep; they shall give to the priest the shoulder, and the
4 two cheeks, and the maw. The first-fruit *also* of thy corn, of thy wine, and of thine oil, and the first of the fleece of thy
5 sheep, thou shalt give to him. For him Jehovah thy God hath chosen out of all thy tribes, to stand to minister in the
6 name of Jehovah, him and his sons for ever. And when a Levite cometh from any of thy gates out of all Israel, where he sojourned, and cometh with all the desire of his mind to
7 the place which Jehovah shall choose; then he shall minister in the name of Jehovah his God, as all his brethren the
8 Levites do, who stand there before Jehovah. They shall have equal portions to eat, besides that which cometh from the sale of his patrimony.
9 When thou art come into the land which Jehovah thy God is about to give thee, thou shalt not learn to do after
10 the abominations of those nations. There shall not be found among you any one that maketh his son or his daughter to pass through the fire, that useth divination, is an observer
11 of times, a diviner by serpents, a sorcerer, or a charmer, or a consulter with a spirit, or a wizard, or one who inquires of
12 the dead. For all that do these things are an abomination to Jehovah; and because of these abominations Jehovah thy
13 God is about to drive them out from before thee. Thou
14 shalt be perfect with Jehovah thy God. For these nations,

which thou shalt dispossess, hearkened to observers of times, and to diviners; but as for thee, Jehovah thy God hath not suffered thee so *to do*. A prophet from the midst of thee, of thy brethren, like me, Jehovah thy God will raise up for thee; to him ye shall hearken; according to all that thou desiredst of Jehovah thy God in Horeb in the day of the assembly, saying, 'Let me not hear again the voice of Jehovah my God, neither let me see this great fire any more, that I die not.' And Jehovah said to me, 'What they have spoken is right. I will raise up for them a prophet from among their brethren, like thee, and will put my words in his mouth; and he shall speak to them all that I shall command him. And whosoever will not hearken to my words which he shall speak in my name, I will require it of him. But the prophet who shall presume to speak a word in my name, which I have not commanded him to speak, or shall speak in the name of other gods, that prophet shall die.' And if thou say in thy heart, 'How shall we know the word which Jehovah hath not spoken?' When a prophet speaketh in the name of Jehovah, if the thing follow not, nor come to pass, that is the thing which Jehovah hath not spoken; the prophet hath spoken it presumptuously: thou shalt not be afraid of him.

CHAP. XIX.—When Jehovah thy God shall have cut off the nations, whose land Jehovah thy God is about to give thee, and thou shalt have dispossessed them, and shalt dwell in their cities, and in their houses; thou shalt set apart for thyself three cities in thy land, which Jehovah thy God is about to give thee to possess it. Thou shalt prepare the road *thither*, and divide the bounds of thy land, which Jehovah thy God is about to give thee to inherit, into three parts, that every man-slayer may flee thither. And this is the case of the man-slayer who shall flee thither, that he may live. Whoso killeth his neighbour without design, whom he hated not in time past; as when a man goeth into a wood with his neighbour to hew wood, and his hand aimeth a stroke with the axe to cut down the tree, and the head slippeth from the handle, and lighteth upon his neighbour, that he die; he shall flee unto one of those cities, and live; lest the avenger of blood pursue the man-slayer while his heart is hot, and overtake him, because the way is long, and slay him; although he was not deserving of death, inas-

7 much as he hated him not in time past. Wherefore I command thee, saying, Thou shalt set apart three cities for thy-
8 self. And when Jehovah thy God shall have enlarged thy boundary, as he hath sworn to thy fathers, and shall have given to thee all the land which he promised to thy fathers
9 to give, if thou shalt keep all these commandments, to do them, which I command thee this day, to love Jehovah thy God, to walk ever in his ways; then shalt thou add three
10 cities more for thyself, beside these three; that innocent blood be not shed in thy land which Jehovah thy God giveth
11 thee for an inheritance, and blood be upon thee. But when any man hateth his neighbour, and lieth in wait for him, and riseth up against him, and smiteth him mortally, that
12 he die, and fleeth into one of these cities; then the elders of his own city shall send and fetch him thence, and deliver him into the hand of the avenger of blood, that he may be
13 put to death. Thine eye shall not pity him, but thou shalt put away *the guilt of* innocent blood from Israel, that it may be well with thee.
14 Thou shalt not remove thy neighbour's land-mark, which they of old time have set in thine inheritance, which thou shalt inherit in the land that Jehovah thy God is about to give thee to possess it.
15 One witness shall not rise up against a man for any iniquity, or for any sin, in any sin that he committeth: on the testimony of two witnesses, or on the testimony of
16 three witnesses, shall the matter be established. And when a false witness riseth up against any man, to testify against
17 him some crime; then both the men, between whom the controversy is, shall stand before Jehovah, before the priests
18 and the judges, who shall be in those days; and the judges shall make diligent inquisition; and, lo, if the witness be a false witness, and have testified falsely against his brother;
19 then shall ye do to him as he had thought to do to his brother:
20 so shall ye put the evil away from among you. And they who remain shall hear and fear, and shall henceforth commit
21 no more any such evil among you. And thine eye shall not pity: life shall go for life, eye for eye, tooth for tooth, hand for hand, foot for foot.

1 CHAP. XX.—When thou goest out to battle against thine enemies, and seest horses and chariots, and a people more numerous than thou, be not afraid of them; for Jeho-

vah thy God is with thee, who brought thee up out of the land of Egypt. And when ye are come nigh to the battle, 2 the priest shall approach, and speak to the people, and shall 3 say to them, 'Hear, O Israel, ye approach this day to battle against your enemies: be not faint-hearted; fear not, and do not tremble, neither be ye terrified by them; for Jehovah 4 your God goeth with you, to fight for you against your enemies, and to save you.' And the officers shall speak to 5 the people, saying, 'What man is there that hath built a new house, and hath not dedicated it? let him go and return to his house, lest he die in the battle, and another man dedicate it. And what man is there that hath planted 6 a vineyard, and hath not eaten of it? let him go and return to his house, lest he die in the battle, and another man eat of it. And what man is there that hath betrothed a wife, 7 and hath not taken her? let him go and return to his house, lest he die in battle, and another man take her.' And the 8 officers shall speak further to the people, and they shall say, 'What man is there that is fearful and faint-hearted? let him go and return to his house, lest his brethren's heart faint as well as his heart.' And when the officers have made an end 9 of speaking to the people, they shall make captains of the armies to lead the people.

When thou comest nigh to a city to fight against it, 10 then proclaim peace to it. And if it make thee answer 11 of peace, and open *its gates* to thee, then all the people found therein shall be tributaries to thee, and shall serve thee. But if it will make no peace with thee, but will 12 make war with thee, then thou shalt besiege it. And when 13 Jehovah thy God hath delivered it into thy hands, thou shalt smite every male in it with the edge of the sword; but the 14 women, and the little ones, and the cattle, and all that is in the city, even all the spoil of it, thou shalt take to thyself; and thou shalt eat the spoil of thine enemies, which Jehovah thy God hath given thee. Thus shalt thou do to all the 15 cities which are very far off from thee, which are not of the cities of these nations. But of the cities of these people, 16 which Jehovah thy God doth give thee for an inheritance, thou shalt save alive nothing that breathed, but shalt utterly 17 devote them; *namely*, the Hittites, and the Amorites, the Canaanites, and the Perizzites, the Hivites, and the Jebusites, as Jehovah thy God hath commanded thee; that they 18 teach you not to do after all their abominations, which they

have done to their gods; so should ye sin against Jehovah
19 your God. When thou shalt besiege a city a long time, in making war against it to take it, thou shalt not destroy its trees, by forcing an axe against them; for thou mayest eat of them, and thou shalt not cut them down, to employ them in the siege; for the trees of the field are *the life of*
20 *man*. Only trees which thou knowest that they are not trees for food, thou mayest destroy and cut down, and build bulwarks against the city that maketh war with thee, until it be subdued.

1 CHAP. XXI.—When a person is found slain in the land which Jehovah thy God giveth thee to possess it, lying in
2 the field, *and* it is not known who hath slain him; then thine elders and thy judges shall go forth, and they shall measure unto the cities which are round about the person
3 who is slain; and the city which is nighest to the slain person, even the elders of that city, shall take a heifer which hath not been wrought with, and which hath not drawn in
4 the yoke; and the elders of that city shall bring down the heifer to a stony torrent-bed, which can neither be plowed nor sown, and shall there strike off the head of the heifer
5 into the torrent-bed: and the priests the sons of Levi shall come near; for them Jehovah thy God hath chosen to minister to him, and to bless in the name of Jehovah, and by their word shall every controversy and every assault be
6 *decided*; and all the elders of that city, who are nighest to the slain person, shall wash their hands over the heifer that
7 hath been beheaded over the torrent-bed; and shall declare and say, 'Our hands shed not this blood, nor did our eyes
8 see *it shed*. Forgive thy people Israel, whom thou hast redeemed, O Jehovah, and impute not innocent blood to thy people Israel.' And the blood shall be forgiven them.
9 So shalt thou put away the *guilt of* innocent blood from among you, when thou shalt do what is right in the sight of Jehovah.
10 When thou goest forth to war against thine enemies, and Jehovah thy God delivereth them into thy hands, and thou
11 takest them captive, and seest among the captives a beautiful woman, and hast a desire for her, and wouldst take her to
12 be thy wife; then thou shalt bring her home to thy house,
13 and she shall shave her head, and pare her nails, and she shall put the raiment of her captivity from off her, and shall

Y

remain in thy house, and bewail her father and her mother a full month; and after that thou mayest go in unto her, and be her husband, and she shall be thy wife. But if thou have 14 no delight in her, then thou shalt let her go whither she will; but thou shalt by no means sell her for money, thou shalt not make her thy slave, because thou hast humbled her. When a man hath two wives, one beloved, and the other 15 hated, and both the beloved and the hated have borne him children, and the first-born son is hers who is hated; when 16 he maketh his sons to inherit what he hath, he may not give the right of the first-born to the son of the beloved, before the son of the hated *who is* the first-born; but he 17 shall acknowledge the son of the hated for the first-born, by giving him a double portion of all that he hath; for he is the beginning of his strength, and the right of the first-born is his.

When a man hath a refractory and rebellious son, who 18 will not obey the voice of his father, or the voice of his mother, and when they have reproved him, will not hearken to them; then shall his father and his mother lay hold on 19 him, and bring him out to the elders of his city, and to the gate of his place; and they shall say to the elders of the 20 city, 'This our son is refractory and rebellious; he will not obey our voice; he is a profligate, and a drunkard.' Then 21 all the men of his city shall stone him with stones, that he die: so shalt thou put away evil from among you; and all Israel shall hear and fear.

When a man hath committed a crime worthy of death, 22 and he is put to death, and thou hangest him on a tree; his 23 body shall not remain all night upon the tree, but thou shalt certainly bury him that day; (for accursed of God is one who is hanged;) that thy land be not defiled, which Jehovah thy God giveth thee for an inheritance.

CHAP. XXII.—Thou shalt not see thy brother's ox or 1 his sheep go astray, and withdraw thyself from them: thou shalt by all means bring them back to thy brother. And 2 if thy brother be not nigh to thee, or if thou know him not, then thou shalt bring it to thine own house, and it shall be with thee until thy brother seek after it, and thou shalt restore it to him again. In like manner shalt thou do with 3 his ass; and so shalt thou do with his raiment; and so shalt thou do with every lost thing of thy brother's, which he

hath lost, and thou hast found; thou shalt not withdraw
4 thyself. Thou shalt not see thy brother's ass or his ox fall
down by the way, and withdraw thyself from them: thou
shalt surely help him to lift them up again.

5 The woman shall not wear the apparel of a man, nor shall
a man put on a woman's garment; for an abomination to
Jehovah thy God is every one who doeth these things.

6 When a bird's nest happeneth to be before thee in the
way in any tree, or on the ground, containing young ones or
eggs, and the dam is sitting upon the young or upon the
7 eggs, thou shalt not take the dam with the young: thou
shalt certainly let the dam go, but thou mayest take the
young for thyself; that it may be well with thee, and that
thou mayest prolong *thy* days.

8 When thou buildest a new house, then thou shalt make
a parapet for thy roof, that thou bring not blood upon thy
house, if any man fall from it.

9 Thou shalt not sow thy vineyard with mingled seed; lest
the fruit of thy seed which thou hast sown, and the fruit of
10 thy vineyard, be defiled. Thou shalt not plow with an ox
11 and an ass together. Thou shalt not wear garments of
12 divers sorts, of woollen and linen together. Thou shalt
make thee fringes upon the four quarters of thy vesture,
wherewith thou coverest thyself.

13 When a man taketh a wife, and goeth in unto her, and
14 hateth her, and layeth against her a shameful charge, and
bringeth upon her an evil name, and saith, 'I took this
woman, and, when I came to her, I found not in her *the*
15 *tokens of* virginity;' then shall the father of the damsel,
and her mother, take and bring forth *the tokens of* the
16 damsel's virginity to the elders of the city at the gate; and
the father of the damsel shall say to the elders, 'I gave my
17 daughter to this man for a wife, and he hateth her; and,
lo, he hath laid against her a shameful charge, saying, I
found not in thy daughter *the tokens of* virginity; and
yet these are *the tokens of* my daughter's virginity;' then
they shall spread the cloth before the elders of the city.
18 And the elders of that city shall take that man, and chastise
19 him, and they shall fine him a hundred *shekels* of silver, and
give them to the father of the damsel, because he hath
brought an evil name upon a virgin of Israel; and she shall
20 be his wife: he may not put her away all his days. But
if this thing be true, and *the tokens of* virginity be not

found for the damsel; then they shall bring out the damsel 21 to the door of her father's house, and the men of her city shall stone her with stones, that she die; because she hath done wickedly in Israel, by committing harlotry in her father's house: so shalt thou put away evil from among you. When a man is found lying with a woman married 22 to a husband, they shall both of them die, both the man that lay with the woman, and the woman: so shalt thou put away evil from Israel. When a damsel, who is a 23 virgin, is betrothed to a husband, and a man findeth her in the city, and lieth with her; then ye shall bring them both 24 out to the gate of that city, and ye shall stone them with stones that they die; the damsel, because she cried not, though in the city, and the man, because he hath humbled his neighbour's wife: so thou shalt put away evil from among you. But if a man find a betrothed damsel in the 25 field, and the man force her, and lie with her; then the man only that lay with her shall die; but to the damsel, 26 thou shalt do nothing; in the damsel there is no crime *deserving* of death: for as when a man riseth against his neighbour, and slayeth him, so is this case: for he found 27 her in the field, and the betrothed damsel cried, but there was none to save her. When a man findeth a damsel, a 28 virgin, who is not betrothed, and layeth hold on her, and lieth with her, and they are found; then the man that lay 29 with her shall give to the damsel's father fifty *shekels* of silver, and she shall be his wife: because he hath humbled her, he may not put her away all his days. A man shall 30 not take his father's wife, nor uncover his father's skirt.

CHAP. XXIII.—He who is mutilated by the bruising or 1 cutting out of the testicles, shall not enter into the congregation of Jehovah. The son of a harlot shall not enter into 2 the congregation of Jehovah; even his tenth generation shall not enter into the congregation of Jehovah. An Ammonite 3 or Moabite shall not enter into the congregation of Jehovah; even their tenth generation shall not enter into the congregation of Jehovah for ever; because they met you not with 4 bread and with water on the way, when ye came forth out of Egypt; and because they hired against thee Balaam the son of Beor, from Pethor of Mesopotamia, to curse thee. But 5 Jehovah thy God would not hearken to Balaam, and Jehovah thy God turned the curse into a blessing to thee, because

6 Jehovah thy God loved thee. Thou shalt not seek their
7 peace or their prosperity all thy days for ever. Thou shalt
not abhor an Edomite; for he is thy brother: nor shalt
thou abhor an Egyptian, because thou wast a sojourner in his
8 land. The children that are begotten of them may enter
into the congregation of Jehovah, in their third generation.
9 When the host goeth forth against thine enemies, then
10 keep thyself from every evil thing. When there is among
you any man that is not clean by reason of uncleanness that
may have happened to him by night, he shall go abroad out
11 of the camp, he shall not come within the camp, but, when
evening cometh on, he shall wash himself with water; and
when the sun is set, he shall come into the camp again.
12 Thou shalt have a place also without the camp, to which
13 thou mayest go forth abroad; and thou shalt have a paddle
amongst thy weapons; and when thou wilt ease thyself
abroad, thou shalt dig a hole with it, and shalt turn and
14 cover that which cometh from thee; for Jehovah thy God
walketh in the midst of thy camp, to deliver thee, and to
give up thine enemies before thee; therefore shall thy camp
be holy; that he see no unclean thing in thee, and turn
away from thee.
15 Thou shalt not deliver up to his master the slave who hath
16 escaped from his master unto thee: he shall dwell with thee,
in the midst of thee, in that place which he shall choose in
one of thy gates, wherever he pleases: thou shalt not oppress
him.
17 There shall be no prostitute among the daughters of
Israel, nor a male prostitute among the sons of Israel.
18 Thou shalt not bring the hire of a harlot, or the price of a
dog, into the house of Jehovah thy God for any vow; for an
abomination to Jehovah thy God are both these.
19 Thou shalt not take usury from thy brother; usury of
money, usury of victuals, usury of any thing from which
20 usury may be taken. From an alien thou mayest take
usury; but from thy brother, thou shalt not take usury,
that Jehovah thy God may bless thee in all to which thou
settest thy hand, in the land into which thou art going to
possess it.
21 When thou shalt vow a vow to Jehovah thy God, thou
shalt not delay to perform it; for Jehovah thy God will
22 surely require it of thee; and it would be sin in thee. But
if thou shalt forbear to vow, it shall be no sin in thee.

That which thou hast promised, thou shalt observe; and 23 thou shalt perform, according as thou hast vowed to Jehovah thy God, that which thou hast willingly pronounced with thy mouth.

When thou goest into thy neighbour's vineyard, thou 24 mayest eat grapes until thou art fully satisfied; but thou shalt not put any into thy vessel. When thou goest into the 25 standing corn of thy neighbour, thou mayest pluck the ears with thy hand; but thou shalt not move a sickle to thy neighbour's standing corn.

CHAP. XXIV.—When a man hath taken a wife, and 1 married her, and she findeth not favour in his eyes, because he hath found some uncleanness in her; then let him write her a bill of divorcement, and give it into her hand, and send her out of his house. And when she is departed out 2 of his house, she may go, and be the wife of another man. But if the latter husband dislike her, and write her a bill of 3 divorcement, and give it into her hand, and send her out of his house; or if the latter husband dieth, who took her to be his wife, her former husband, who sent her away, may 4 not take her again to be his wife, after she is defiled; for that would be an abomination before Jehovah; and thou shalt not bring guilt upon the land, which Jehovah thy God giveth thee for an inheritance. When a man hath taken 5 a new wife, he shall not go out to war, nor shall he be charged with any business: he shall be free at home one year, and shall cheer his wife whom he hath taken.

No man shall take for a pledge the mill or the upper 6 millstone: for he taketh *a man's* life to pledge.

When a man is found stealing any of his brethren of the 7 children of Israel, and making him his slave, or selling him; then that thief shall die: so shalt thou put away evil from among you.

Take heed, in the plague of leprosy, that thou observe 8 diligently, and do according to all that the priests the Levites shall teach you: as I commanded them, so ye shall observe to do. Remember what Jehovah thy God did to 9 Miriam by the way, after ye were come out of Egypt.

When thou lendest thy brother any thing, thou shalt not 10 go into his house to receive his pledge. Thou shalt stand 11 without, and the man to whom thou dost lend shall bring the pledge out to thee. And if the man be poor, thou 12

13 shalt not sleep with his pledge; thou shalt surely deliver him the pledge again when the sun goeth down, that he may sleep in his own raiment, and bless thee; and it shall
14 be righteousness to thee before Jehovah thy God. Thou shalt not oppress a hired servant who is poor and needy, *whether he be* one of thy own brethren, or of thy strangers
15 that are in thy land, within thy gates. In his day thou shalt give him his hire, and before the sun shall have gone down upon him; because he is poor, and setteth his heart upon it; lest he cry against thee to Jehovah, and it be sin to thee.
16 The fathers shall not be put to death for the children, nor shall the children be put to death for the fathers: every man
17 shall be put to death for his own sin. Thou shalt not pervert the judgment of the stranger, or of the fatherless,
18 nor take a widow's raiment to pledge; but thou shalt remember that thou wast a bondman in Egypt, and Jehovah thy God redeemed thee thence: therefore I command thee to do this thing.
19 When thou cuttest down thy harvest in thy field, and hast forgotten a sheaf in the field, thou shalt not go again to fetch it: it shall be for the stranger, for the fatherless, and for the widow, that Jehovah thy God may bless thee in all
20 the work of thy hands. When thou beatest thy olive-tree, thou shalt not go over the boughs again: it shall be for the
21 stranger, for the fatherless, and for the widow. When thou gatherest the grapes of thy vineyard, thou shalt not glean it afterward: it shall be for the stranger, for the fatherless,
22 and for the widow. And thou shalt remember that thou wast a bondman in the land of Egypt: therefore I command thee to do this thing.

1 CHAP. XXV.—When there is a controversy between *two* men, and they come into judgment, that the judges may decide between them; then they shall acquit the innocent,
2 and condemn the guilty. And, if the guilty man be worthy to be beaten, the judge shall cause him to lie down, and to be beaten before his face, with a certain number *of stripes,*
3 according to his fault. Forty stripes he may give him, but not exceed; lest, if he should exceed, and beat him with many stripes above these, thy brother should seem vile to thee.
4 Thou shalt not muzzle the ox when he is treading out the corn.

When two brothers dwell together, and one of them 5 dieth, and hath no child, the wife of the dead shall not marry without, to a stranger: her husband's brother shall go in unto her, and take her to himself for a wife, and perform the duty of a husband's brother to her. And the first-born 6 which she beareth, shall succeed in the name of his brother who is dead, that his name be not blotted out from Israel. And if the man be not willing to take his brother's wife, 7 then let his brother's wife go up to the gate to the elders, and say, 'My husband's brother refuseth to raise up to his brother a name in Israel; he will not perform the duty of my husband's brother.' Then the elders of his city shall 8 call him, and speak to him: and if he persist, and say, 'I am not willing to take her;' then his brother's wife shall 9 come to him in the presence of the elders, and loose his shoe from off his foot, and spit before his face, and shall address him, and say, 'So shall it be done to that man who will not build up his brother's house.' And the name *of his house* 10 shall be called in Israel, 'The house of him that hath had his shoe loosed.'

When two men strive together one with another, and the 11 wife of the one draweth near to deliver her husband out of the hand of him that smiteth him, and putteth forth her hand, and taketh him by the secrets; then thou shalt cut off 12 her hand, thine eye shall not pity her.

Thou shalt not have in thy bag different weights, a great 13 and a small. Thou shalt not have in thy house different 14 measures, a great and a small. A perfect and a just weight 15 thou shalt have, a perfect and a just measure thou shalt have, that thy days may be lengthened in the land which Jehovah thy God giveth thee. For all who do such things, 16 all who do unrighteously, are an abomination to Jehovah thy God.

Remember what the Amalekites did to thee by the 17 way, when ye were come forth out of Egypt; how they met 18 thee by the way, and smote the hindmost of thee, all that were feeble behind thee, when thou wast faint and weary; and he feared not God. Therefore, when Jehovah 19 thy God shall have given thee rest from all thy enemies round about, in the land which Jehovah thy God giveth thee for an inheritance to possess it, thou shalt blot out the remembrance of the Amalekites from under the heavens: forget it not.

1 CHAP. XXVI.—And when thou art come into the land which Jehovah thy God giveth thee for an inheritance, and
2 possessest it and dwellest in it, thou shalt take some of the first of all the fruits of the ground, which thou shalt raise from thy land that Jehovah thy God giveth thee, and shalt put it in a basket, and shalt go to the place which Jehovah thy God shall choose to place his name
3 there. And thou shalt go to the priest that shall be in those days, and say to him, 'I declare this day to Jehovah thy God, that I am come into the land which Jehovah
4 sware to our fathers that he would give to us.' And the priest shall take the basket out of thy hand, and set it
5 down before the altar of Jehovah thy God. Then thou shalt speak, and say before Jehovah thy God, 'A wandering Aramæan was my father; and he went down into Egypt, and sojourned there with a few, and became there a nation,
6 great, and mighty, and numerous; but the Egyptians ill-treated us, and afflicted us, and laid upon us hard service;
7 and when we cried to Jehovah the God of our fathers, Jehovah heard our voice, and looked on our affliction, and
8 our labour, and our oppression; and Jehovah brought us forth out of Egypt with a mighty hand, and with an outstretched arm, and with very terrible signs, and wonders;
9 and he hath brought us into this place, and hath given to
10 us this land, a land that floweth with milk and honey. And now, behold, I have brought the first-fruits of the land, which thou, O Jehovah, hast given to me.' And thou shalt set it before Jehovah thy God, and worship before Jehovah
11 thy God; and thou shalt rejoice in every good thing which Jehovah thy God hath given to thee, and to thy house, thou, and the Levite, and the stranger that is among you.
12 When thou hast completed the tithing of all thy produce in the third year, the year of tithing, and hast given it to the Levite, the stranger, the fatherless, and the widow, that they
13 may eat within thy gates, and be filled; then thou shalt say before Jehovah thy God, 'I have wholly carried away these hallowed things out of my house, and also have given them to the Levite, and to the stranger, to the fatherless, and to the widow, according to all thy commandments, which thou hast commanded me: I have not transgressed thy command-
14 ments, nor have I forgotten them: I have not eaten of those things in my mourning, nor have I taken away any part of them for an unclean use, nor given any part of them to the

dead: I have hearkened to the voice of Jehovah my God: I have done according to all that thou hast commanded me. Look down from thy holy habitation, from heaven, and bless thy people Israel, and the land which thou hast given us, as thou swarest to our fathers, a land that floweth with milk and honey.'

This day Jehovah thy God hath commanded thee to do these statutes and judgments: thou shalt therefore keep and do them with all thy heart, and with all thy soul. Thou hast declared Jehovah this day to be thy God, and that thou wilt walk in his ways, and keep his statutes, and his commandments, and his judgments, and hearken to his voice; and Jehovah hath declared thee this day, to be his peculiar people, as he hath promised thee, and that thou shouldest keep all his commandments; and that he will set thee on high above all the nations which he hath made, in praise, and in name, and in honour; and that thou shalt be a people holy to Jehovah thy God, as he hath spoken."

CHAP. XXVII.—And Moses, with the elders of Israel, commanded the people, saying, "Keep all the commandments which I command you this day. And on the day when ye shall pass over the Jordan, into the land which Jehovah thy God giveth thee, thou shalt set thee up great stones, and cover them with plaster; and thou shalt write upon them all the words of this law, when thou art passed over, that thou mayest go into the land which Jehovah thy God giveth thee, a land that floweth with milk and honey; as Jehovah the God of thy fathers hath promised thee. Therefore, when ye have passed over the Jordan, ye shall set up these stones, which I command you this day, on mount Ebal, and thou shalt cover them with plaster. And there shalt thou build an altar to Jehovah thy God, an altar of stones: thou shalt not lift up *any tool of* iron upon them. Thou shalt build the altar of Jehovah thy God of whole stones; and thou shalt offer on it burnt-offerings to Jehovah thy God; and thou shalt offer peace-offerings, and shalt eat there, and rejoice before Jehovah thy God. And thou shalt write upon the stones all the words of this law very plainly." And Moses, and the priests the Levites, spake to all Israel, saying, "Take heed, and hearken, O Israel: this day thou art become the people of Jehovah thy God. Thou shalt there-

fore obey the voice of Jehovah thy God, and do his commandments, and his statutes, which I command thee this day."
12 And Moses charged the people the same day, saying, "These shall stand upon Mount Gerizim to bless the people, when ye are come over Jordan; Simeon, and Levi, and Judah, and
13 Issachar, and Joseph, and Benjamin. And these shall stand upon mount Ebal to curse; Reuben, Gad, and Asher, and
14 Zebulon, Dan, and Naphtali. And the Levites shall speak, and say to all the men of Israel, with a loud voice,
15 'Cursed be the man that maketh any carved or molten image, an abomination to Jehovah, the work of the hands of the artificer, and setteth it up in secret.' And all the people
16 shall answer and say, 'Amen.' 'Cursed be he that despiseth his father or his mother.' And all the people shall
17 say, 'Amen.' 'Cursed be he that removeth his neighbour's land-mark.' And all the people shall say, 'Amen.'
18 'Cursed be he that maketh the blind to err in the way.'
19 And all the people shall say, 'Amen.' 'Cursed be he that perverteth the judgment of the stranger, the fatherless, and
20 the widow.' And all the people shall say, 'Amen.' 'Cursed be he that lieth with his father's wife; because he uncovereth his father's skirt.' And all the people shall say, 'Amen.'
21 'Cursed be he that lieth with any beast.' And all the people
22 shall say, 'Amen.' 'Cursed be he that lieth with his sister, the daughter of his father, or the daughter of his
23 mother.' And all the people shall say, 'Amen.' 'Cursed be he that lieth with his mother-in-law.' And all the people
24 shall say, 'Amen.' 'Cursed be he that smiteth his neighbour secretly.' And all the people shall say, 'Amen.'
25 Cursed be he that taketh a bribe to slay an innocent person.'
26 And all the people shall say, 'Amen.' 'Cursed be he that confirmeth not the words of this law to do them.' And all the people shall say, 'Amen.'

1 CHAP. XXVIII.—And it shall come to pass, if thou wilt hearken diligently to the voice of Jehovah thy God, to observe and to do all his commandments which I command thee this day, that Jehovah thy God will set thee on high above
2 the nations of the earth; and all these blessings shall come on thee, and overtake thee, when thou shalt hearken to the
3 voice of Jehovah thy God. Blessed shalt thou be in the
4 city, and blessed shalt thou be in the field. Blessed shall be the fruit of thy womb, and the fruit of thy ground, and

the fruit of thy cattle, the issue of thy kine, and the flocks of thy sheep. Blessed shall be thy basket and thy kneading-bowls. Blessed shalt thou be when thou comest in, and blessed shalt thou be when thou goest out. Jehovah will cause thine enemies that rise up against thee to be smitten before thy face: by one way shall they come out against thee, but by seven ways shall they flee before thee. Jehovah will command a blessing upon thee in thy store-houses, and in all to which thou puttest thy hands; and he will bless thee in the land which Jehovah thy God giveth thee. Jehovah will establish thee a people holy to himself, as he hath sworn to thee, if thou wilt keep the commandments of Jehovah thy God, and walk in his ways. And all the peoples of the earth shall see that thou art called by the name of Jehovah; and they shall be afraid of thee. And Jehovah will cause thee to abound in good things, in the fruit of thy womb, and in the fruit of thy cattle, and in the fruit of thy ground, in the land which Jehovah sware to thy fathers, to give thee. Jehovah will open to thee his good treasure, the heavens to give rain to thy land in its season, and to bless all the work of thy hands; and thou shalt lend to many nations, but thou shalt not borrow. And Jehovah will make thee the head, and not the tail; and thou shalt be above only, and thou shalt not be beneath, when thou shalt hearken to the commandments of Jehovah thy God, which I command thee this day, to observe and to do them, and shalt not turn aside from any of the words which I command thee this day, to the right hand or to the left, to go after other gods to serve them. But, if thou wilt not hearken to the voice of Jehovah thy God, to observe and to do all his commandments and his statutes, which I command thee this day, it shall come to pass that all these curses shall come upon thee, and overtake thee. Cursed shalt thou be in the city, and cursed shalt thou be in the field. Cursed shall be thy basket and thy kneading-bowls. Cursed shall be the fruit of thy womb, and the fruit of thy land, the issue of thy kine and the flocks of thy sheep. Cursed shalt thou be when thou comest in, and cursed shalt thou be when thou goest out. Jehovah will send upon thee cursing, terror, and rebuke, in all which thou puttest forth thy hand to do, until thou be destroyed, and until thou perish quickly; because of the wickedness of thy doings, by which thou hast forsaken me. Jehovah will make the pestilence cleave to thee, until

he have consumed thee from off the land, whither thou
22 goest to possess it. Jehovah will smite thee with consumption, and with fever, and with inflammation, and with extreme burning, and with drought, and with blasting, and with mil-
23 dew; and they shall pursue thee until thou perish. And thy heavens that are over thy head shall be brass, and the
24 earth that is under thee iron. Jehovah will make the rain of thy land powder and dust: from the heavens shall it come
25 down upon thee, until thou be destroyed. Jehovah will cause thee to be smitten before thine enemies: by one way shalt thou go out against them, but by seven ways shalt thou flee before them; and thou shalt wander through all the king-
26 doms of the earth. And thy carcase shall be food for all fowls of the air, and for the beasts of the earth; and no man
27 shall scare them away. Jehovah will smite thee with the ulcerous inflammation of Egypt, and with the piles, and with the scab, and with the itch, of which thou canst not be healed.
28 Jehovah will smite thee with distraction, and blindness, and
29 astonishment of heart; and thou shalt grope at noon-day, as the blind gropeth in darkness, and thou shalt not prosper in thy ways; and thou shalt be only oppressed and spoiled
30 continually, and no one shall save thee. Thou shalt betroth a wife, but another man shall lie with her: thou shalt build a house, but thou shalt not dwell therein: thou shalt plant
31 a vineyard, but shalt not gather its fruit. Thine ox shall be slaughtered before thine eyes, and thou shalt not eat of it: thine ass shall be violently taken away from before thy face, and shall not be restored to thee: thy sheep shall be given to thine enemies, and thou shalt have none to
32 rescue them. Thy sons and thy daughters shall be given to another people, and thine eyes shall look, and fail *with looking* for them all the day long; and there shall be no might
33 in thy hand. The fruit of thy land, and all thy labours, shall a nation which thou knowest not eat up; and thou shalt
34 be only oppressed and crushed continually; so that thou shalt be mad at the sight of thine eyes which thou shalt see.
35 Jehovah will smite thee in the knees, and in the legs, with a sore ulcerous inflammation that cannot be healed, from the
36 sole of thy foot, to the crown of thy head. Jehovah will bring thee, and thy king whom thou shalt set over thee, unto a nation which neither thou nor thy fathers have known; and there thou shalt serve other gods, of wood and stone.
37 And thou shalt be an astonishment, and a proverb, and a

taunt among all nations, whither Jehovah shall lead thee.
Much seed shalt thou carry out into the field, but little shalt 38
thou gather in; for the locust shall consume it. Vineyards 39
shalt thou plant, and dress, but shalt neither drink the wine,
nor gather the grapes; for the weevils shall eat them. Olive- 40
trees thou shalt have throughout all thy coasts, but thou
shalt not anoint thyself with the oil; for thine olive shall
cast its fruit. Sons and daughters thou shalt beget, but 41
they shall not be thine, for they shall go into captivity. All 42
thy trees and the fruit of thy land shall the locust consume.
The stranger who is among thee, shall rise very high above 43
thee; and thou shalt sink very low. He shall lend to thee, 44
but thou shalt not lend to him: he shall be the head, but
thou shalt be the tail. Now all these curses shall come upon 45
thee, and shall pursue thee, and overtake thee, till thou be
destroyed; because thou hearkenedst not to the voice of Jehovah thy God, to keep his commandments, and his statutes
which he commanded thee; and they shall be upon thee 46
for a sign and for a wonder, and upon thy seed for ever.
Because thou servedst not Jehovah thy God with joyfulness, 47
and with gladness of heart, for the abundance of all things;
therefore shalt thou serve thine enemies, whom Jehovah shall 48
send against thee, in hunger, and in thirst, and in nakedness,
and in want of all things; and he shall put a yoke of iron
upon thy neck, until he shall have destroyed thee. Jehovah 49
will raise up a nation against thee from afar, from the end
of the earth, as swiftly as the eagle flieth; a nation whose
language thou shalt not understand; a nation of a fierce 50
countenance, which shall not respect the person of the old,
nor shew favour to the young; and which will eat the fruit 51
of thy cattle, and the fruit of thy land, until thou be destroyed; which will not leave thee corn, or wine, or oil, the
issue of thy kine, or the flocks of thy sheep, until he have
destroyed thee. And he shall besiege thee in all thy gates, 52
until thy high and fenced walls, in which thou trustedst,
throughout all thy land, come down; and he shall besiege
thee in all thy gates throughout all thy land, which Jehovah
thy God hath given thee. And thou shalt eat the fruit of 53
thine own body, the flesh of thy sons and of thy daughters,
whom Jehovah thy God hath given thee, in the siege, and in
the straitness, with which thine enemies shall distress thee.
The eye of the tender and very delicate man among you shall 54
be evil towards his brother, and towards the wife of his bosom,

and towards the remnant of his children which he shall have
55 remaining; so that he will not give to any of them any portion of the flesh of his children whom he shall eat: because nothing is left him in the siege, and in the straitness with
56 which thine enemies shall distress thee in all thy gates. The eye of the tender and delicate woman among you, who would not venture to set the sole of her foot upon the ground for delicateness and tenderness, shall be evil towards the husband of her bosom, and towards her son, and towards her daughter,
57 and towards her after-birth that cometh out from between her feet, and towards her children which she shall bear: for she shall eat them for want of all things secretly in the siege and straitness, with which thine enemy shall distress thee in
58 thy gates. If thou wilt not observe to do all the words of this law, which are written in this book, and revere this
59 glorious and fearful name, JEHOVAH THY GOD; then Jehovah will make thy plagues wonderful, and the plagues of thy seed, great plagues, and of long continuance, and grievous
60 sicknesses, and of long continuance. For he will bring upon thee all the diseases of Egypt, of which thou wast afraid;
61 and they shall cleave to thee. Also every sickness, and every plague, which is not written in the book of this law, them
62 will Jehovah bring upon thee, until thou be destroyed. And ye shall be left few in number, whereas ye were as the stars of heaven for multitude; because thou wouldest not obey the
63 voice of Jehovah thy God. And as Jehovah rejoiced over you to do you good, and to multiply you; so will Jehovah rejoice over you to destroy you, and to bring you to nought; and ye shall be torn away from the land whither thou goest
64 to possess it. And Jehovah will scatter thee among all the peoples, from the one end of the earth, even unto the other; and there thou shalt serve other gods, which neither thou
65 nor thy fathers have known, of wood and stone. And among these nations thou shalt find no ease, neither shall the sole of thy foot have rest; but Jehovah will give thee there a trembling heart, and failing of eyes, and sorrow of mind;
66 and thy life shall hang in doubt before thee; and thou shalt fear day and night, and shalt have no assurance of thy life.
67 In the morning thou shalt say, 'Would that it were evening!' and in the evening thou shalt say, 'Would that it were morning!' for the fear of thy heart, with which thou shalt fear,
68 and for the sight of thine eyes which thou shalt see. For Jehovah will bring thee into Egypt again in ships, the way

of which I said to thee, 'Thou shalt see it no more again;' and there ye shall be sold to your enemies for bondmen and bondwomen, until there be no one to buy you." CHAP. XXIX.—These are the words of the covenant, which Jeho- 1 vah commanded Moses to make with the children of Israel in the land of Moab, besides the covenant which he had made with them in Horeb.

And Moses called to all the Israelites, and said to them, 2 " Ye have seen all that Jehovah did before your eyes in the land of Egypt to Pharaoh, and to all his servants, and to all his land; the great trials which thine eyes have seen, the 3 signs, and those great miracles; yet Jehovah hath not given 4 you a heart to perceive, and eyes to see, and ears to hear, unto this day. And I have led you forty years in the wilder- 5 ness: your clothes have not wasted from off you, and thy shoe hath not wasted from off thy foot. Ye have not eaten 6 bread, nor have ye drunk wine or strong drink; that ye might know that I am Jehovah your God. And when ye came 7 unto this place, Sihon the king of Heshbon, and Og, the king of Bashan, came out against us to battle, and we smote them, and we took their land, and gave it for 8 an inheritance to the Reubenites, and to the Gadites, and to the half of the tribe of Manasseh. Keep, there- 9 fore, the words of this covenant, and do them, that ye may prosper in all that ye do. Ye are standing this day all of 10 you before Jehovah your God; your chiefs of your tribes, your elders, and your officers, all the men of Israel, your 11 little ones, and your wives, and thy stranger that is in thy camp, from the hewer of thy wood to the drawer of thy water; that thou shouldest enter into covenant with Jehovah 12 thy God, and into his oath, which Jehovah thy God maketh with thee this day; that he may establish thee this day for 13 a people to himself, and that he may be to thee a God, as he hath said to thee, and as he hath sworn to thy fathers, to Abraham, to Isaac, and to Jacob. Nor with you alone do I 14 make this covenant and this oath; but with him that stand- 15 eth here with us this day before Jehovah our God, and also with him that is not here with us this day. For ye your- 16 selves know how we dwelt in the land of Egypt; and how we passed in the midst of the nations through which ye passed; and ye have seen their abominations, and their idols, of 17 wood and stone, of silver and gold, which were among them. Let there not *therefore* be among you man, or woman, or 18

family, or tribe, whose heart turneth away this day from Jehovah our God, to go and serve the gods of these nations; let there not be among you a root that beareth hemlock and
19 wormwood; any one who, when he heareth the words of this curse, shall bless himself in his heart, saying, 'I shall have peace, though I walk in the imagination of my heart, to add
20 drunkenness to thirst.' Jehovah will not spare him, but then the anger of Jehovah and his jealousy will smoke against that man, and all the curses that are written in this book shall lie upon him, and Jehovah will blot out his name
21 from under the heavens. And Jehovah will separate him for evil, out of all the tribes of Israel, according to all the curses of the covenant that are written in this book of
22 the law; so that the generation to come of your children, that shall rise up after you, and the stranger that shall come from a distant land, shall say, when they see the plagues of that land, and the sicknesses which Jehovah shall have laid
23 upon it; the whole land burnt up with sulphur and salt, not sown, nor bearing, nor any grass growing therein; like the overthrow of Sodom and Gomorrah, Admah and Zeboim,
24 which Jehovah overthrew in his anger, and in his wrath; even all the nations shall say, 'Wherefore hath Jehovah done thus to this land? what *meaneth* the heat of this great
25 anger?' Then it shall be said, 'Because they have forsaken the covenant of Jehovah, the God of their fathers, which he made with them when he brought them forth out of the
26 land of Egypt: for they went and served other gods, and worshipped them, gods whom they knew not, and whom he
27 had not given to them: so the anger of Jehovah was kindled against this land, to bring upon it all the curses that are
28 written in this book; and Jehovah rooted them out of their land in anger, and in wrath, and in great indignation, and
29 cast them into another land, as *it is seen* this day.' Secret things *belong to* Jehovah our God; but things revealed, to us and to our children for ever, that we may do all the words of this law.

1 CHAP. XXX.—Yet when all these things shall have come upon thee, the blessing and the curse, which I have set before thee, if thou shalt consider among all the nations
2 whither Jehovah thy God shall have driven thee, and shalt return to Jehovah thy God, and shalt obey his voice according to all that I command thee this day, thou, and thy chil-

dren, with all thy heart, and with all thy soul; then Jehovah 3
thy God will reverse thy captivity, and have compassion upon
thee, and will again gather thee from all the nations,
whither Jehovah thy God shall have scattered thee. If any 4
of thine be driven out unto the outmost parts of the heavens,
thence will Jehovah thy God gather thee, and thence will he
fetch thee. And Jehovah thy God will bring thee into the 5
land which thy fathers possessed, and thou shalt possess it;
and he will do thee good, and multiply thee more than thy
fathers. And Jehovah thy God will circumcise thy heart, 6
and the heart of thy seed, to love Jehovah thy God with all
thy heart, and with all thy soul, that thou mayest live. And 7
Jehovah thy God will lay all these curses upon thine enemies,
and on those who hate thee, who have persecuted thee. But 8
if thou return, and obey the voice of Jehovah, and do all his
commandments, which I command thee this day, then Je- 9
hovah thy God will make thee greatly to abound in every
work of thy hand, in the fruit of thy body, and in the fruit
of thy cattle, and in the fruit of thy land. For Jehovah will
again rejoice over thee for good, as he rejoiced over thy
fathers, if thou wilt hearken to the voice of Jehovah thy 10
God, to keep his commandments and his statutes, which are
written in this book of the law, and if thou wilt turn to
Jehovah thy God with all thy heart, and with all thy soul.
Now this commandment which I command thee this day, is 11
not hidden from thee, nor is it far off. It is not in the 12
heavens, that thou shouldest say, 'Who will go up for us to
the heavens, and bring it to us, that we may hear it, and do
it?' Nor is it beyond the sea, that thou shouldest say, 13
'Who will go over the sea for us, and bring it to us, that we
may hear it, and do it?' but the word is very nigh to thee, 14
in thy mouth, and in thy heart, that thou mayest do it.
See, I set before thee this day, life and good, and death and 15
evil; in that I command thee this day, to love Jehovah thy 16
God, to walk in his ways, and to keep his commandments
and his statutes and his judgments, that thou mayest live
and multiply; and that Jehovah thy God may bless thee in
the land whither thou goest to possess it. But if thy heart 17
turn away, so that thou wilt not hear, but thou be drawn
away and worship other gods, and serve them; I denounce 18
to you this day, that ye shall surely perish, and that ye shall
not prolong your days upon the land whither thou art passing over the Jordan to go to possess it. I call heaven and 19

earth to witness this day against you, that I have set before
you life and death, blessing and cursing: therefore choose
20 life, that both thou and thy seed may live; that thou mayest
love Jehovah thy God, and that thou mayest obey his voice,
and that thou mayest cleave to him; for he is thy life, and
the length of thy days; that thou mayest dwell in the land
which Jehovah sware to thy fathers, to Abraham, to Isaac,
and to Jacob, to give them."

1   CHAP. XXXI.—Then Moses went, and spake these
2 words to all the Israelites. And he said to them, "I am a
hundred and twenty years old this day: I can no more go
out and come in: and Jehovah hath said to me, 'Thou shalt
3 not go over this Jordan.' Jehovah thy God will himself go
over before thee; he will destroy these nations from before
thee, and thou shalt possess them; Joshua shall go over
4 before thee, as Jehovah hath said. And Jehovah will do to
them as he did to Sihon and to Og, kings of the Amorites,
5 and to their land, whom he destroyed. And Jehovah will give
them up before your face, that ye may do to them according
to all the commandments which I have commanded you.
6 Be strong and of good courage; fear them not, nor dread
them; for it is Jehovah thy God himself, who goeth with
7 thee; he will not fail thee, nor forsake thee." And Moses
called to Joshua, and said to him in the sight of all Israel,
"Be strong and of good courage; for thou must go with this
people into the land which Jehovah hath sworn to their
fathers to give them; and thou shalt cause them to inherit
8 it. And it is Jehovah himself who goeth before thee; he
will be with thee, he will not fail thee, neither forsake thee:
fear not, nor be dismayed."
9   And Moses wrote this law, and delivered it to the priests
the sons of Levi, who bare the ark of the covenant of Je-
10 hovah, and to all the elders of Israel. And Moses commanded
them, saying, "At the end of every seven years, in the
solemnity of the year of remission, in the feast of tabernacles,
11 when all the Israelites come to appear before Jehovah thy
God in the place which he shall choose, thou shalt read this
12 law before all the Israelites in their hearing. Gather the
people together, men, and women, and children, and thy
stranger that is within thy gates, that they may hear, and
that they may learn, and fear Jehovah your God, and ob-
13 serve to do all the words of this law; and that their children

who have not known *it* may hear, and learn to fear Jehovah your God, as long as ye live in the land whither ye are going over the Jordan to possess it."

And Jehovah said to Moses, "Lo, thy days approach that thou must die: call Joshua, and present yourselves in the tent of meeting, that I may give him a charge." Then Moses and Joshua went and presented themselves in the tent of meeting. And Jehovah appeared in the tent in a pillar of a cloud; and the pillar of the cloud stood over the door of the tent. And Jehovah said to Moses, "Lo, thou shalt lie with thy fathers; and this people will rise up, and go astray after the strange gods of the land whither they are going, and will forsake me, and break my covenant which I have made with them. Then my anger shall be kindled against them in that day, and I will forsake them, and I will hide my face from them, and they shall be devoured, and many evils and troubles shall befall them; so that they will say in that day, 'Are not these evils come upon us, because our God is not amongst us?' and I will surely hide my face in that day, for all the evil which they shall have done, by turning to other gods. Now therefore write for yourselves this song, and teach it to the children of Israel: put it in their mouths, that this song may be a witness for me against the children of Israel. For when I shall have brought them into the land which I sware to their fathers, that floweth with milk and honey; and they shall have eaten and filled themselves, and become fat; then will they turn to other gods, and serve them, and provoke me, and break my covenant. And when many evils and troubles shall have befallen them, this song shall testify against them as a witness; for it shall not be forgotten out of the mouths of their seed. For I know their imagination, what they are disposed to do, even now, before I have brought them into the land which I sware *to give them.*" Moses therefore wrote this song the same day, and taught it to the children of Israel. And he gave Joshua the son of Nun a charge, and said, "Be strong and of good courage: for thou shalt bring the children of Israel into the land which I sware to them: and I will be with thee."—And when Moses had made an end of writing the words of this law in a book, until they were finished, Moses commanded the Levites, who bare the ark of the covenant of Jehovah, saying, "Take this book of the law, and put it by the side of the ark of the covenant of

Jehovah your God, that it may be there for a witness against
27 thee. For I know thy rebellion, and thy stiff neck: behold,
while I am yet alive with you this day ye have been rebellious
against Jehovah; and how much more after my death?
28 Gather to me all the elders of your tribes, and your officers,
that I may speak these words in their ears, and call the
29 heavens and the earth to witness against them. For I know
that after my death ye will utterly corrupt yourselves, and
turn aside from the way which I have commanded you; and
evil will hereafter befall you because ye will do evil in the
sight of Jehovah to provoke him to anger through the work
30 of your hands." So Moses spake in the ears of all the
congregation of Israel, the words of this song, until they
were ended.

1   CHAP. XXXII.—" Give ear, O ye heavens! while I speak;
    And let the earth hear the words of my mouth.
2   Let my doctrine drop as the rain,
    And my speech distil as the dew,
    As showers on the tender herb,
    And as copious rain on the grass:
3   For I proclaim the name of Jehovah.
    Ascribe ye greatness unto our God.
4   *He is* the Rock, perfect is his work;
    For all his ways are just:
    A God of truth and without iniquity,
    Just and right is he.
5   They are corrupted—not his—children of pollution;
    A generation perverse and crooked.
6   Do ye thus requite Jehovah?
    O people foolish and unwise!
    Is he not thy father who bought thee?
    Hath he not made thee, and formed thee?
7   Remember the days of old,
    Consider the years of successive generations;
    Ask thy father, and he will declare to thee;
    Thine elders, and they will tell thee:
8   When the Most High divided to the nations their inheritance,
    When he separated the sons of Adam,
    He set the bounds of the peoples
    According to the number of the children of Israel.

For the portion of Jehovah is his people; 9
Jacob the lot of his inheritance.
   He found him in a desert land, 10
And in the waste, howling wilderness:
He surrounded him, he instructed him;
And he guarded him as the apple of his eye.
As an eagle stirreth up her nest, 11
Fluttereth over her young,
Spreadeth abroad her wings, taketh them up,
Beareth them on her pinions:
So Jehovah alone led him, 12
And no strange god was with him.
He made him ride over the heights of the earth, 13
And gave him to eat of the increase of the fields;
He nourished him with honey out of the crag,
And with oil out of the flinty rock;
Cream of kine, and milk of sheep; 14
With the fat of lambs,
And of rams of the breed of Bashan, and of he-goats;
With the fat of kidneys of wheat;
And thou didst drink the foaming blood of the grape.
But Jeshurun became fat, and kicked: 15
Thou art become fat, thou art grown thick, thou art
   covered *with fatness*:
Then he forsook God who made him,
And despised the Rock of his salvation.
They moved him to jealousy by strange *gods*, 16
By abominations they provoked him to anger.
They sacrificed to demons, not to God; 17
To gods whom they knew not;
To new *gods* that came newly up,
Whom your fathers feared not.
Of the Rock that begat thee thou wast unmindful, 18
And didst forget the God that gave thee birth.
   And Jehovah saw it, and was indignant, 19
At the provocation of his sons, and of his daughters.
And he said, 'I will hide my face from them, 20
And I will see what will be their end:
For a perverse generation are they,
Children in whom is no faithfulness.
They have moved me to jealousy by that which is not 21
   God;
They have provoked me to anger by their vanities:

I will therefore move them to jealousy by those who are
    not a people;
By a foolish nation I will provoke them to anger.
22   For a fire is kindled in mine anger,
And it shall burn to the lowest depths,
And it shall consume the earth with its increase,
And set on fire the foundations of the mountains.
23   I will heap upon them evils:
Mine arrows I will exhaust upon them.
24   They shall be wasted by famine, and devoured by burn-
    ing heat,
And by bitter destruction:
The teeth of wild beasts also I will send upon them,
With the poison of serpents of the dust.
25   Without, the sword shall bereave,
And within, terror,
Both the young man and the virgin,
The suckling, with the man of gray hairs.
26   I would say, I will cut them off,
I will make the remembrance of them to cease among
    men;
27   Were I not afraid of the wrath of the enemy,
Lest their adversaries should misunderstand,
Lest they should say, Our own high hand,
And not Jehovah hath done all this.
28   For a nation void of counsel are they,
And there is no understanding in them.
29   Neither are they wise, to understand this,
And to discern their end.
30   How should one chase a thousand,
And two put ten thousand to flight,
Unless their Rock had sold them,
And Jehovah had delivered them up?
31   For their Rock is not like our Rock,
Even our enemies themselves being judges.
32   For of the vines of Sodom are their vines,
And of the fields of Gomorrah:
Their grapes are grapes of poison,
Clusters of bitterness have they.
33   The poison of dragons is their wine,
And the cruel venom of asps.
34   Is not this laid up in store with me,
Sealed up among my treasures?

With me are vengeance and retribution,   35
For a time when their foot shall slip.
For near is the day of their calamity,
And that which is ready for them is hastening on.'
    For Jehovah will avenge his people,   36
And repent himself for his servants,
When he shall see that their power is gone,
And not *even* one shut up or left at large.
And he will say, ' Where are their gods,   37
The Rock in whom they trusted,
Who ate the fat of their sacrifices,   38
And drank the wine of their drink-offerings ?
Let them arise, and help you,
And let them be your protection.
See now that I, *even* I, am He,   39
And there is no god with me :
I kill, and I make alive ;
I wound, and I heal ;
And no one can deliver out of my hand.
For I lift up my hand to the heavens,   40
And I say, As I live for ever,
If I sharpen the lightning of my sword,   41
And my hand take hold on judgment,
I will render vengeance to mine enemies,
And those who hate me I will requite.
I will make mine arrows drunk with blood,   42
And my sword shall devour flesh ;
With the blood of the slain and of captives,
The flesh of the chiefs of the foe.'
    Rejoice, O ye nations, his people ;   43
For the blood of his servants he will avenge,
And he will render vengeance to his adversaries,
And expiate the land of his own people."

And Moses came and spake all the words of this song in 44 the hearing of the people, he, and Joshua the son of Nun. And when Moses had made an end of speaking all these 45 words to all the Israelites ; he said to them, "Apply your 46 hearts to all the words which I testify among you this day, which ye shall command your children to observe, and to do all the words of this law. For it is not a light thing for 47 you ; because it is your life ; and by this ye shall prolong your days in the land, whither ye are going over the Jordan to possess it."

49 And Jehovah spake to Moses that very day, saying, "Go up to this mount Abarim, mount Nebo, which is in the land of Moab, over against Jericho; and behold the land of Canaan,
50 which I give to the children of Israel for a possession; and die on the mount whither thou goest up, and be gathered to thy people, as Aaron thy brother died in mount Hor,
51 and was gathered to his people; because ye trespassed against me among the children of Israel, at the waters of Meribah-Kadesh, in the wilderness of Zin; because ye sanctified me
52 not in the midst of the children of Israel. Yet thou shalt see the land before thee; but thou shalt not go thither into the land which I give to the children of Israel."

1 CHAP. XXXIII.—Now this is the blessing, with which Moses the man of God, blessed the children of Israel before
2 his death. And he said,
"Jehovah came from Sinai,
And dawned upon them from Seir;
He shone forth from mount Paran,
And came with ten thousands from Kadesh.
From his right hand, streams *issued* for them.
3 Truly, he loveth the people:
All its saints are in thy hand:
And at thy feet they sat down,
That they might receive thy commands;
4 The law *which* Moses prescribed to us,
The inheritance of the congregation of Jacob.
5 And he was king in Jeshurun,
When the heads of the people were assembled,
Together with the tribes of Israel.

6 May Reuben live, and not die;
Though his men be few!"
7 And this *is the blessing* of Judah; and he said,
"Hear, O Jehovah, the voice of Judah,
And bring him *back* to his people:
Let his own hand contend for him;
And be thou a help against his enemies."
8 And of Levi he said,
"May thy Thummim and thy Urim be with thy holy one,·
Whom thou didst try at Massah,
With whom thou didst contend at the waters of Meribah;

Who said to his father and to his mother,   9
'I see him not;'
And his brethren he acknowledged not,
And his own children he knew not.
For they observed thy word,
And they kept thy covenant.
They shall teach Jacob thy judgments,   10
And Israel thy law:
They shall put incense before thee,
And whole burnt-sacrifices upon thine altar.
Bless, O Jehovah, his substance,   11
And accept the work of his hands:
Smite through the loins of them who rise up against him,
And of them who hate him, that they rise not up again."

Of Benjamin he said,   12
"The beloved of Jehovah! may he dwell in safety near him;
May he continually protect him;
And between his shoulders may he dwell!"

And of Joseph he said,   13
"Blessed by Jehovah be his land,
With the precious thing of the heavens, with the dew,
And with the deep that lieth beneath,
And with the precious productions of the sun,   14
And with the precious produce of the moons,
And with the chief things of the ancient mountains,   15
And with the precious things of the everlasting hills,
And with the precious things of the earth and its fulness.   16
And may the favour of Him who dwelt in the bush,
Come upon the head of Joseph,
And upon the crown-of-the-head of the chief of his brethren.
As of a first-born steer, be his beauty;   17
And *as* the horns of a buffalo, his horns:
With these may he push the people
Together, to the ends of the earth.
Such are the ten thousands of Ephraim,
And such the thousands of Manasseh."

And of Zebulun he said,   18
"Rejoice, Zebulun, in thy going out;
And, Issachar, in thy tents.
They shall call the people to the mountain: 19

There they shall offer sacrifices of righteousness;
For of the abundance of the seas they shall suck,
And of treasures hidden in the sand."

And of Gad he said,

20 "Blessed be he that enlargeth Gad!
As a lioness he dwelleth,
And teareth the arm with the crown-of-the-head.
21 So he seeth the first part *allotted* to himself,
For there a portion from the Lawgiver is secured.
Yet he goeth with the heads of the people,
And executeth the justice of Jehovah,
And his judgments with Israel."

22 And of Dan he said,
"Dan is a lion's whelp;
Which leapeth from Bashan."

23 And of Naphtali he said,
"Naphtali satisfied with favour,
And full of the blessing of Jehovah,
Shall possess the west and the south."

24 And of Asher he said,
"May Asher be blessed with children;
May he be acceptable to his brethren,
And may he dip his foot in oil!
25 Thy bars shall be iron and brass;
And as thy days, so shall be thy strength."

26 "No one is like the God of Jeshurun,
Who rideth upon the heavens in thine aid,
And in his majesty on the clouds.
27 *Thy* refuge *is the* eternal God,
And beneath *thee* the everlasting arms.
And he shall drive out the enemy from before thee;
And shall say, 'Destroy them.'
28 And Israel shall dwell in safety alone;
The eye of Jacob
Shall be on a land of corn and wine;
His heavens also shall drop down dew.
29 Happy thou, O Israel!
Who is like to thee, O people, saved by Jehovah,
The shield of thy help,
And the sword of thine excellency?
And thine enemies shall submit to thee;
And thou shalt tread upon their high places."

CHAP. XXXIV.—Then Moses went up from the plains 1 of Moab to mount Nebo, to the top of Pisgah, which is opposite to Jericho. And Jehovah showed him all the land of Gilead, unto Dan, and all Naphtali, and the land of Ephraim, 2 and Manasseh, and all the land of Judah, unto the farther sea, and the south, and the plain of the valley of Jericho, 3 the City of palm-trees, unto Zoar. And Jehovah said to 4 him, "This is the land which I sware to Abraham, to Isaac, and to Jacob, saying, 'I will give it to thy seed:' I have caused thee to see it with thine eyes, but thou shalt not go over thither." So Moses the servant of Jehovah died there 5 in the land of Moab, according to the word of Jehovah. And he was buried in a valley in the land of Moab, over 6 against Bethpeor; but no one knoweth of his sepulchre to this day. And Moses was a hundred and twenty years old 7 when he died: his eye was not dim, nor his natural force abated. And the children of Israel wept for Moses in the 8 plains of Moab thirty days, until the days of weeping and mourning for Moses were ended.

And Joshua the son of Nun was full of the spirit of 9 wisdom; for Moses had laid his hands upon him; and the children of Israel hearkened to him, and did as Jehovah commanded Moses. And there arose not a prophet since in 10 Israel, like to Moses, whom Jehovah knew face to face, in all 11 the signs and the wonders which Jehovah sent him to do in the land of Egypt, against Pharaoh, and all his servants, and all his land, and in all that mighty hand, and in all the 12 great terror which Moses shewed in the sight of all Israel.

THE BOOK OF JOSHUA.

1 CHAP. I.—It came to pass after the death of Moses the servant of Jehovah, that Jehovah spake to Joshua the son of 2 Nun, the minister of Moses, saying,—"Moses my servant is dead; now therefore arise, go over this Jordan, thou, and all this people, to the land which I give to them, *even* the children 3 of Israel. Every place that the sole of your foot shall tread 4 upon, I give to you, as I said to Moses. From the desert and this Lebanon, even unto the great river, the river Euphrates, all the land of the Hittites, and unto the great sea toward the going down of the sun, shall be your boundary. 5 No man shall be able to stand against thee all the days of thy life: as I was with Moses, so I will be with thee: I will 6 not fail thee, neither will I forsake thee. Be strong and of good courage; for thou shalt divide for an inheritance to this people the land, which I sware to their fathers to give them. 7 Only be thou strong and very courageous, that thou mayest observe to do according to all the law which Moses my servant commanded thee: turn not from it to the right hand or to the left, that thou mayest prosper whithersoever thou goest. 8 Let not this book of the law depart out of thy mouth; but meditate therein day and night, that thou mayest observe to do according to all that is written therein: for then thou shalt make thy way prosperous, and then thou shalt have 9 good success. Have not I commanded thee? Be strong and of good courage; be not afraid, neither be thou dismayed; for Jehovah thy God is with thee whithersoever thou goest."

10 Then Joshua commanded the officers of the people, saying, 11 "Pass through the camp, and command the people, saying, 'Prepare for yourselves victuals; for within three days ye shall pass over this Jordan, to go in to possess the land, 12 which Jehovah your God giveth you to possess.'" And to the Reubenites, and to the Gadites, and to the half of the

tribe of Manasseh, Joshua spake, saying, "Remember the 13 word which Moses the servant of Jehovah commanded you, saying, 'Jehovah your God hath given you rest, and hath given you this land. Your wives, your little ones, and your 14 cattle, shall remain in the land which Moses gave you on this side of the Jordan; but ye shall pass before your brethren armed, all the mighty men of valour, and help them, until 15 Jehovah shall have given rest to your brethren, as he hath given to you, and they also shall have possessed the land which Jehovah your God giveth to them: then ye shall return to the land of your possession, which Moses, the servant of Jehovah, gave you on this side of the Jordan, toward the rising of the sun; and enjoy it."

And they answered Joshua, saying, "All that thou com- 16 mandest us we will do, and whithersoever thou sendest us we will go. According as we hearkened to Moses in all 17 things, so will we hearken to thee: only Jehovah thy God be with thee, as he was with Moses. Every one who rebel- 18 leth against thy commandment, and who will not hearken to thy words in all that thou commandest him, shall be put to death: only be strong and of good courage."

CHAP. II.—And Joshua the son of Nun secretly sent 1 out of Setim two spies, saying, "Go view the land and Jericho." And they went, and came to the house of a harlot, whose name was Rahab, and lodged there.

And it was told the king of Jericho, saying, "Lo, there 2 came in hither to-night men of the children of Israel, to search out the country." Then the king of Jericho sent to 3 Rahab, saying, "Bring forth the men that are come to thee, who are entered into thy house: for they are come to search out the whole land." And the woman took the two men, 4 and hid them; and she said, "Truly the men came unto me, but I know not whence they *came;* and when it was dark 5 and the gate was about to be shut, the men went out: whither the men went I know not: pursue them quickly, for ye may overtake them." But she had taken them up to the roof of 6 the house, and hidden them with the stalks of flax, which she had laid in order upon the roof. And the men pursued 7 them on the way to the Jordan, unto the fords: and as soon as they who pursued them were gone out, the gate was shut. Now they had not yet lain down, when she came up to them 8 upon the roof, and said to the men, "I know that Jehovah 9

hath given you the land, and that the dread of you is fallen upon us, and that all the inhabitants of the land faint before
10 you. For we have heard how Jehovah dried up the waters of the Red Sea before you, when ye came out of Egypt; and what ye have done to the two kings of the Amorites, on the other side of the Jordan, Sihon and Og, whom ye utterly
11 destroyed. When we heard *these things,* our hearts melted, and there remained no more courage in any man, because of you; for Jehovah your God he is God in the heavens above,
12 and on the earth beneath. Now therefore, I pray you, swear to me by Jehovah, since I have shewed you kindness, that ye will also shew kindness to my father's house; and give
13 me a token of truth. . And ye shall save alive my father, and my mother, and my brethren, and my sisters, and all that
14 they have, and deliver our lives from death." And the men answered her, "Our life for yours, if thou tell not this our business. And it shall be, when Jehovah hath given us the
15 land, that we will deal kindly and truly with thee." Then she let them down by a cord through the window; for her house was upon the town wall, and she dwelt upon the wall;
16 and said to them, "Go ye to the mountains, lest the pursuers meet you, and hide yourselves there three days, until the pursuers have returned; and afterward ye may go your way."
17 And the men said to her, "We will be blameless in respect
18 of this thy oath which thou hast made us swear. Lo, *when* we come into the land, thou shalt bind this line of scarlet thread in the window by which thou didst let us down; and thou shalt bring unto thee into the house, thy father, and thy mother, and thy brethren, and all thy father's household.
19 And whosoever shall go out of the doors of thy house into the street, his blood shall be upon his head, and we will be guiltless; but whosoever shall be with thee in the house, his
20 blood shall be on our head, if any hand be upon him. But if thou tell this our business, then we will be blameless in
21 respect of thy oath which thou hast made us swear." And she said, "According to your words so be it." And she sent them away, and they departed; and she bound the scarlet
22 cord in the window. And they went and came to the mountains, and abode there three days, until the pursuers were returned. And the pursuers sought them throughout all
23 the way, but found them not. So the two men returned, and descended from the mountains, and passed over, and came to Joshua the son of Nun, and told him all that had

befallen them; and they said to Joshua, "Truly Jehovah 24 hath delivered into our hands all the land; for already all the inhabitants of the land faint before us."

CHAP. III.—And Joshua rose early in the morning; and 1 they removed from Setim, and came to the Jordan, he and all the children of Israel, and lodged there before they passed over. And at the end of three days, the officers went 2 through the camp, and commanded the people, saying, 3 "When ye see the ark of the covenant of Jehovah your God, and the priests, the Levites, bearing it, then ye shall remove from your place, and go after it; (yet there shall be a space 4 between you and it, about two thousand cubits by measure: come not near to it;) that ye may know the way by which ye must go; for ye have not passed this way before."

And Joshua said to the people, "Sanctify yourselves; for 5 to-morrow Jehovah will do wonders among you." And 6 Joshua spake to the priests, saying, "Take up the ark of the covenant, and pass over before the people." And they took up the ark of the covenant, and went before the people.

And Jehovah said to Joshua, "This day will I begin to 7 magnify thee in the sight of all Israel, that they may know that, as I was with Moses, so I will be with thee. And thou 8 shalt command the priests that bear the ark of the covenant, saying, 'When ye are come to the brink of the waters of the Jordan, ye shall stand still in Jordan.'" And Joshua said 9 to the children of Israel, "Come hither, and hear the words of Jehovah your God." And Joshua said, "Hereby shall 10 ye know that the living God is among you, and that he will, without fail, drive out from before you the Canaanites, and the Hittites, and the Hivites, and the Perizzites, and the Girgashites, and the Amorites, and the Jebusites. Lo, the 11 ark of the covenant of the Lord of all the earth passeth on before you into the Jordan. Now therefore take ye twelve 12 men out of the tribes of Israel, out of every tribe a man. And it shall come to pass, as soon as the soles of the feet of 13 the priests that bear the ark of Jehovah, the lord of all the earth, shall rest in the waters of the Jordan, that the waters of the Jordan, the waters that come down from above, shall be cut off, and they shall stand in one heap." And it came 14 to pass, when the people removed from their tents, to pass over the Jordan, and the priests bearing the ark of the covenant before the people, and when they who bare the ark were 15

come to the Jordan, and the feet of the priests who bare the ark were dipped in the brim of the water (for the Jordan
16 overfloweth all its banks at the time of harvest), that the waters which came down from above stood *and* rose up in one heap, very far off, at the city Adam, which is beside Zaretan; and those that went down toward the sea of the plain, the salt sea, failed, *and* were cut off; and the
17 people passed over opposite to Jericho. And the priests who bare the ark of the covenant of Jehovah stood firm on dry ground in the midst of the Jordan, while all the Israelites were passing over on dry ground; until the whole nation had passed completely over the Jordan.

1 CHAP. IV.—And it came to pass when the whole nation had completely passed over the Jordan, that Jehovah spake
2 to Joshua, saying, "Take for yourselves twelve men out of
3 the people, a man from every tribe, and command them, saying, 'Take for yourselves hence out of the midst of the Jordan, from the place where the feet of the priests stood firm, twelve stones; and carry them over with you, and leave them in the lodging-place where ye shall lodge this night.'"
4 Then Joshua called the twelve men whom he had appointed from among the children of Israel, a man out of every tribe.
5 And Joshua said to them, "Pass over before the ark of Jehovah your God into the midst of the Jordan, and take ye up every one of you a stone upon his shoulder, according to
6 the number of the tribes of the children of Israel, that this may be a sign among you. When your children shall ask in time to come, saying, 'What *mean* ye by these
7 stones?' then ye shall answer them, that the waters of the Jordan were cut off before the ark of the covenant of Jehovah; when it passed over the Jordan, the waters of the Jordan were cut off; and these stones shall be for a memo-
8 rial to the children of Israel for ever." And the children of Israel did so as Joshua commanded, and took up twelve stones out of the midst of the Jordan, as Jehovah spake to Joshua, according to the number of the tribes of the children of Israel, and carried them over with them to the place where
9 they lodged, and laid them down there. And Joshua set up twelve stones in the midst of the Jordan, in the place where the feet of the priests who bare the ark of the covenant had
10 stood; and they are there unto this day. And the priests who bare the ark stood in the midst of the Jordan, until

A A

every thing was finished that Jehovah had commanded Joshua to speak to the people, according to all that Moses commanded Joshua: and the people hastened and passed over. And when all the people had completely passed over, 11 the ark of Jehovah passed over, and the priests, in the presence of the people. And the children of Reuben, and the 12 children of Gad, and the half of the tribe of Manasseh, passed over armed before the children of Israel, as Moses had spoken to them. About forty thousand armed for war 13 passed over before Jehovah to battle, to the plains of Jericho. On that day Jehovah magnified Joshua in the sight of all 14 Israel; and they feared him, as they had feared Moses, all the days of his life.

And Jehovah spake to Joshua, saying, "Command the 15 priests that bear the ark of the testimony, to come up out of 16 the Jordan." Joshua therefore commanded the priests, say- 17 ing, "Come ye up out of the Jordan." And it came to 18 pass, when the priests that bare the ark of the covenant of Jehovah were come up out of the midst of the Jordan, *and* the soles of the priests' feet had reached the dry land, that the waters of the Jordan returned to their place, and flowed over all its banks as before. And the people came up out 19 of the Jordan on the tenth day of the first month, and encamped in Gilgal, on the eastern boundary of Jericho. And 20 those twelve stones, which they took out of the Jordan, Joshua set up at Gilgal. And he spake to the children of 21 Israel, saying, "When your children shall ask their fathers in time to come, saying, 'What *mean* these stones?' Then 22 ye shall let your children know, saying, 'Israel came over this Jordan on dry land.' For Jehovah your God dried up 23 the waters of the Jordan from before you, until ye had passed over, as Jehovah your God did to the Red Sea, which he dried up before us, until we had passed over; that all 24 the people of the earth might know the hand of Jehovah, that it is mighty; that ye might fear Jehovah your God for ever." CHAP. V.—Now it came to pass, when all the kings 1 of the Amorites, who were on the side of the Jordan westward, and all the kings of the Canaanites, who were by the sea, heard that Jehovah had dried up the waters of the Jordan from before the children of Israel, until they had passed over, their heart melted, neither was there spirit in them any more, because of the children of Israel.

At that time Jehovah said to Joshua, "Make thee knives 2

of stone, and circumcise again the children of Israel the
3 second time." And Joshua made him knives of stone, and
circumcised the children of Israel at the Hill of the fore-
4 skins. And this is the cause why Joshua circumcised *them*:
all the people that had come out of Egypt, the males, *even* all
the men of war, had died in the desert by the way, after they
5 had come out of Egypt. Now all the people that came out
had been circumcised; but all the people that had been born in
the desert on the way, after they had come forth out of Egypt,
6 they had not circumcised. For the children of Israel journeyed forty years in the desert, till all the people *that were*
men of war, who came out of Egypt, were consumed, because
they obeyed not the voice of Jehovah; to whom Jehovah
sware that he would not show them the land which Jehovah
had sworn to their fathers that he would give us, a land flow-
7 ing with milk and honey. And their children, whom he had
raised up in their stead, Joshua circumcised; for they were
uncircumcised, because they had not circumcised them by the
8 way. And when they had done circumcising all the people,
they abode in their places in the camp till they were healed.
9 And Jehovah said to Joshua, "This day have I rolled away
the reproach of Egypt from off you." Wherefore the name
of the place is called Gilgal [ROLLING AWAY] unto this
day.
10 And the children of Israel encamped in Gilgal, and kept
the passover on the fourteenth day of the first month, in the
11 evening, in the plains of Jericho. And they ate of the old
corn of the land, on the day after the passover, unleavened
12 cakes and parched *corn* on the same day. And the manna
ceased on the day after they had eaten of the old corn of the
land; neither had the children of Israel manna any more;
but they ate of the produce of the land of Canaan that
year.
13 And when Joshua was by Jericho, he lifted up his eyes
and looked, and, lo, there stood a man over against him with
his sword drawn in his hand: and Joshua went to him, and
14 said to him, "Art thou for us, or for our adversaries?" And
he said to him, "As captain of the host of Jehovah am I now
come." And Joshua fell on his face to the earth, and
worshipped, and said to him, "What saith my lord to his
15 servant?" And the captain of the host of Jehovah said
to Joshua, "Loose thy shoe from off thy foot; for the
place on which thou standest is holy." And Joshua did so.

CHAP. VI.—Now Jericho was closely shut up, because of 1 the children of Israel: no one went out, and no one came in. And Jehovah said to Joshua, " See, I have given into 2 thy hand Jericho, and its king, and the mighty men of valour. And ye shall compass the city, all ye men of war, 3 going round the city once. Thus shalt thou do six days. And seven priests shall bear before the ark seven jubilee 4 trumpets; and the seventh day ye shall compass the city seven times, and the priests shall blow with the trumpets. And it shall come to pass that when they make a long *blast* 5 with the jubilee horn, when ye hear the sound of the trumpet, all the people shall shout with a great shout; and the wall of the city shall fall down flat, and the people shall go up, every man straight before him." And Joshua the son of 6 Nun called the priests, and said to them, " Take up the ark of the covenant, and let seven priests bear seven jubilee trumpets before the ark of Jehovah." And he said to the 7 people, " Pass on, and compass the city, and let him that is armed pass on before the ark of Jehovah." And it came to 8 pass, when Joshua had spoken to the people, that the seven priests bearing the seven jubilee trumpets passed on before Jehovah, and blew with the trumpets; and the ark of the covenant of Jehovah followed them. And the armed men 9 went before the priests who blew with the trumpets, and the rear went after the ark, the trumpets sounding as they went on. Now Joshua had commanded the people, saying, "Ye 10 shall not shout nor let your voice be heard, neither shall a word proceed from your mouth, until the day when I say to you, ' Shout;' then shall ye shout." So the ark of Jehovah 11 compassed the city, going about it once; then they came into the camp, and lodged in the camp.

And Joshua rose early in the morning, and the priests 12 took up the ark of Jehovah; and the seven priests, bearing 13 seven jubilee trumpets before the ark of Jehovah, went on continually, and blew with the trumpets; and the armed men went before them; but the rear went after the ark of Jehovah, the trumpets sounding as they went on. And on 14 the second day they compassed the city once, and returned into the camp: so they did six days. But on the seventh 15 day, they rose early about the dawning of the day, and compassed the city after the same manner seven times; on that day only they compassed the city seven times. And it came 16 to pass at the seventh time, when the priests blew with the

trumpets, Joshua said to the people, "Shout; for Jehovah
17 hath given you the city. And the city shall be devoted, *even*
it and all that are therein, to Jehovah: only Rahab the harlot
shall live, she and all that are with her in the house, because
18 she hid the messengers that we sent. But do ye strictly keep
yourselves from the devoted thing, lest ye make *yourselves*
devoted, when ye take of the devoted thing, and make the
19 camp of Israel a devoted thing, and trouble it. But all the
silver, and gold, and vessels of brass and of iron, are consecrated
to Jehovah: they shall come into the treasury of Jehovah."
20 So the people shouted when *the priests* blew with the trumpets; and it came to pass, when the people heard the sound
of the trumpet, and the people shouted with a great shout,
that the wall fell down flat, so that the people went up into
the city, every man straight before him, and they took the
21 city: and they utterly destroyed, with the edge of the sword,
all that was in the city, both man and woman, young and
22 old, and ox, and sheep, and ass. But Joshua had said to the
two men that had spied out the country, "Go into the harlot's house, and bring out thence the woman, and all that
23 she hath, as ye sware to her." And the young men who had
been spies went in, and brought out Rahab, and her father,
and her mother, and her brethren, and all that she had; and
they brought out all her kindred, and left them without the
24 camp of Israel. And they burnt the city with fire, and all
that was therein: only the silver, and the gold, and the
vessels of brass and of iron, they put into the treasury of the
25 house of Jehovah. And Joshua saved Rahab the harlot
alive, and her father's household, and all that she had; and
she dwelleth in Israel *even* to this day; because she hid the
26 messengers whom Joshua sent to spy out Jericho. And
Joshua adjured *them* at that time, saying,
"Cursed be the man before Jehovah,
Who shall rise up and build this city Jericho:
In his first-born may he lay its foundations,
And in his youngest son may he set up its gates!"
27 Thus Jehovah was with Joshua; and his fame was spread
throughout all the land.

1 CHAP. VII.—But the children of Israel committed a
trespass in the devoted thing; for Achan, the son of Carmi,
the son of Zabdi, the son of Zerah, of the tribe of Judah,
had taken a part of that which had been devoted; and the

anger of Jehovah was kindled against the children of Israel. And Joshua sent men from Jericho to Ai, which is beside ² Beth-aven, on the east side of Bethel, and said to them, " Go up and explore the country." And the men went up and explored Ai. And they returned to Joshua, and said to him, ³ " Let not all the people go up; but let about two or three thousand men go up and smite Ai; weary not all the people *by sending them* thither; for they are few." So there went ⁴ up thither of the people about three thousand men: and they fled before the men of Ai. And the men of Ai smote of ⁵ them about thirty and six men; for they pursued them before the gate as far as to Shebarim, and smote them in the descent: wherefore the hearts of the people melted, and became *as* water. Then Joshua rent his clothes, and fell ⁶ upon his face to the ground before the ark of Jehovah until the evening, he and the elders of Israel, and they put dust upon their heads. And Joshua said, " Alas! O my Lord ⁷ Jehovah, wherefore hast thou at all brought this people over the Jordan, to deliver us into the hand of the Amorites, to destroy us? Oh, that we had been content, and dwelt on the other side of the Jordan! O my Lord, what shall I say, ⁸ when Israel turn their backs before their enemies? For the ⁹ Canaanites, and all the inhabitants of the land, will hear *of it*, and will encompass us, and cut off our name from the earth; and what wilt thou do for thy great name?" And ¹⁰ Jehovah said to Joshua, " Arise; why liest thou thus upon thy face? Israel hath sinned, and they have also trans- ¹¹ gressed my covenant which I enjoined upon them; for they have even taken of that which had been devoted, and have also stolen it, and dissembled also, and have even put *it* among their own baggage. Therefore the children of Israel ¹² could not stand before their enemies: they turned *their* backs before their enemies because they are devoted: I will not be with you any more, except ye destroy that which is devoted from among you. Arise, sanctify the people, and say, ¹³ 'Sanctify yourselves against to-morrow; for thus saith Jehovah God of Israel, A devoted thing is in the midst of thee, O Israel: thou canst not stand before thy enemies, until ye take away the devoted thing from among you.' In the ¹⁴ morning therefore ye shall be brought forward according to your tribes; and the tribe which Jehovah shall take shall come forward according to its families; and the family which Jehovah shall take shall come forward according to its

households; and the household which Jehovah shall take
15 shall come forward man by man. And he that is taken with the devoted thing shall be burnt with fire, he and all that he hath, because he hath transgressed the covenant of Jehovah, and because he hath done wickedly in Israel."
16 So Joshua rose up early in the morning, and brought forward the Israelites by their tribes; and the tribe of Judah
17 was taken; and he brought forward the family of Judah; and the family of the Zarhites was taken; and he brought forward the family of the Zarhites man by man; and Zabdi
18 was taken. And he brought forward his household man by man; and Achan, the son of Carmi, the son of Zabdi, the
19 son of Zerah, of the tribe of Judah, was taken. And Joshua said to Achan, "My son, give, I pray thee, glory to Jehovah God of Israel, and make confession to him; and tell me
20 now what thou hast done; hide it not from me." And Achan answered Joshua, and said, "I have sinned indeed against Jehovah God of Israel, and thus and thus have I
21 done: when I saw among the spoils a fine mantle of Shinaar, and two hundred shekels of silver, and a bar of gold of the weight of fifty shekels, I coveted them, and took them; and, behold, they are hidden in the earth within my
22 tent, and the silver undermost." So Joshua sent messengers, and they ran to the tent; and, lo, *the things* were hidden in
23 his tent, and the silver undermost. And they took them from within the tent, and brought them to Joshua, and to all the children of Israel, and spread them out before Jeho-
24 vah. And Joshua, and all Israel with him, took Achan the son of Zerah, and the silver, and the mantle, and the bar of gold, and his sons, and his daughters, and his oxen, and his asses, and his sheep, and his tent, and all that belonged to
25 him; and they brought them to the valley of Achor. And Joshua said, "Why hast thou troubled us? Jehovah will trouble thee this day." And all Israel stoned him with stones, and burned them with fire, and threw stones upon
26 them, and raised over him a great heap of stones, *which remaineth* to this day. So Jehovah turned from the fierceness of his anger. Wherefore the name of the place was called, "The valley of Achor" [TROUBLE], unto this day.

1 CHAP. VIII.—Then Jehovah said to Joshua, "Fear not, nor be dismayed: take with thee all the people of war, and arise, go up to Ai: see, I have given into thy hand the king

of Ai, and his people, and his city, and his land. And thou ² shalt do to Ai and its king as thou hast done to Jericho and its king: only its spoil, and its cattle ye shall take for a booty to yourselves: place thee an ambush for the city on its further side." So Joshua arose, and all the people of war, ³ to go up against Ai; and Joshua chose out thirty thousand mighty men of valour, and sent them away by night. And ⁴ he commanded them, saying, "Lo, ye shall lie in ambush against the city, on the further side of the city: go not very far from the city, but be ye all ready; and I, and all the ⁵ people that are with me, will approach to the city; and when they come out to meet us, we will flee before them as before. And they will come out after us, till we have drawn them ⁶ on from the city; for they will say, 'They flee before us, as before,' and we will flee before them. Then ye shall rise up ⁷ from the ambush, and take possession of the city; for Jehovah your God will deliver it into your hand. And when ⁸ ye have taken the city, ye shall set the city on fire: according to the commandment of Jehovah shall ye do. See, I have charged you." So Joshua sent them forth; and ⁹ they went to lie in ambush, and took their station between Beth-el and Ai, on the western side of Ai; but Joshua lodged that night among the people. And Joshua ¹⁰ rose up early in the morning, and mustered the people, and went up, he and the elders of Israel, before the people to Ai. And all the people of war that were with him, went up, ¹¹ and drew nigh, and came opposite to the city, and encamped on the north side of Ai: and there was a valley between them and Ai. Now he had taken about five thousand men, ¹² and set them to lie in ambush between Beth-el and Ai, on the western side of the city. And when they had set the ¹³ people, *even* all the host that *was* on the north of the city, and the ambush on the west of the city, Joshua went that night into the midst of the valley. And when the king of ¹⁴ Ai saw it, they made haste and rose up early, and the men of the city went out against the Israelites to battle, he and all his people, at an appointed time, before the plain; but he knew not that an ambush was laid for him on the further side of the city. And Joshua and all the Israelites feigned ¹⁵ to be beaten before them, and fled by the way of the desert. And all the people that were in Ai were called together to ¹⁶ pursue after them; and they pursued after Joshua, and were drawn away from the city. And there was not a man left ¹⁷

in Ai or Beth-el that went not out after the Israelites: and they left the city open, and pursued after the Israelites.
18 And Jehovah said to Joshua, "Stretch out the spear that is in thy hand toward Ai; for I will give it into thy hand." And Joshua stretched out the spear that was in his hand
19 toward the city. And the ambush arose quickly out of their place, and they ran as soon as he had stretched out his hand; and they entered into the city, and took it, and made haste,
20 and set the city on fire. And when the men of Ai looked behind them, they saw, and lo, the smoke of the city ascended up to the heavens, and they had no power to flee this way or that way; and the people that fled towards the
21 desert turned back upon the pursuers. For when Joshua and all the Israelites saw that the ambush had taken the city, and that the smoke of the city was ascending, then
22 they turned again, and slew the men of Ai; and the others issued out of the city against them; so they were in the midst of the Israelites, some on this side, and some on that side; and they smote them, so that they let none of them
23 remain or escape. But the king of Ai they took alive, and brought him to Joshua.
24 And it came to pass when the Israelites had made an end of slaying all the inhabitants of Ai in the field, in the desert whither they had pursued them, and when they were all fallen by the edge of the sword, until they were consumed, that all the Israelites returned to Ai, and smote it with the edge of the sword. And all that fell that day, both of
25 men and women, were twelve thousand; all the men of
26 Ai. For Joshua drew not his hand back, with which he stretched out the spear, until he had utterly destroyed all the
27 inhabitants of Ai. Only the cattle and the spoil of that city, the Israelites took for a booty to themselves, according
28 to the word of Jehovah, which he commanded Joshua. And Joshua burnt Ai, and made it a heap of ruins for ever, *even*
29 a desolation, unto this day. And the king of Ai he hanged on a tree until the evening: but as soon as the sun was down, Joshua commanded that they should take his carcase down from the tree, and cast it at the entrance of the gate of the city, and raise thereon a great heap of stones, which *remaineth* unto this day.
30 Then Joshua built an altar to Jehovah God of Israel on
31 mount Ebal, as Moses the servant of Jehovah had commanded the children of Israel, as it is written in the book of the law of

Moses, "An altar of whole stones, upon which no man hath lifted up *any* iron;" and they offered on it burnt-offerings to Jehovah, and sacrificed peace-offerings. And he wrote there 32 upon the stones a copy of the law of Moses, which he had written in the presence of the children of Israel. And all 33 Israel, and their elders, and officers, and their judges, stood on this side the ark and on that side, before the priests the Levites, who bare the ark of the covenant of Jehovah, as well the stranger as he that was born among them: half of them over against mount Gerizim, and half of them over against mount Ebal; as Moses the servant of Jehovah had before commanded, that they should bless the people of Israel. And 34 afterward he read all the words of the law, the blessings and cursings, according to all that is written in the book of the law. There was not a word of all that Moses had com- 35 manded which Joshua read not before all the congregation of Israel, with the women, and the little ones, and the strangers that were living among them.

CHAP. IX.—Now it came to pass, when all the kings 1 who were on this side of the Jordan, in the mountains, and in the plains, and in all the coasts of the great sea over against Lebanon, the Hittite, and the Amorite, the Canaanite, the Perizzite, the Hivite, and the Jebusite, heard *of these things*, that they gathered themselves together, to 2 fight with Joshua and with the Israelites, with one accord. But when the inhabitants of Gibeon heard what Joshua had 3 done to Jericho and to Ai, they acted craftily, and went 4 and prepared themselves provisions, and took old sacks upon their asses, and wine-skins old and rent and bound up, and shoes old and clouted upon their feet, and old 5 garments upon themselves; and all the bread of their provision was dry *and* mouldy. And they went to Joshua unto 6 the camp at Gilgal, and said to him, and to the men of Israel, "We are come from a far country: now therefore make ye a covenant with us." And the men of Israel said 7 to the Hivites, "Peradventure ye dwell among us; and how shall we make a covenant with you?" And they said to 8 Joshua, "We are thy servants." And Joshua said to them, "Who are ye? and whence come ye?" And they said to 9 him, "From a very far country thy servants are come, because of the name of Jehovah thy God: for we have heard the fame of him, and all that he did in Egypt, and all that 10

he did to the two kings of the Amorites that were beyond the Jordan, to Sihon king of Heshbon, and to Og king of
11 Bashan, who was at Ashtaroth. Wherefore our elders and all the inhabitants of our country spake to us, saying, 'Take victuals with you for the journey, and go to meet them, and say to them, We are your servants:' therefore now make ye
12 a covenant with us. This our bread we took hot for our provision out of our houses on the day we came forth to
13 come to you; but now, lo, it is dry, and it is mouldy: and these wine-skins, which we filled, were new; and, lo, they are rent: and these our garments and our shoes are become
14 old by reason of the very long journey." And the men took of their victuals, and asked not *counsel* at the mouth of Jehovah.
15 And Joshua made peace with them, and made a covenant with them, to let them live: and the princes of the congregation
16 sware to them. But it came to pass, at the end of three days, after they had made a covenant with them, that they heard that they were their neighbours, and that they dwelt among
17 them. And the children of Israel journeyed, and came to their cities on the third day. Now their cities were Gibeon,
18 and Chephirah, and Beeroth, *and* Kirjath-jearim. But the children of Israel smote them not, because the princes of the congregation had sworn to them by Jehovah God of Israel. And all the congregation murmured against the
19 princes. But all the princes said to all the congregation, "We have sworn unto them by Jehovah God of Israel:
20 now, therefore, we may not touch them. This we will do to them; we will even let them live, lest wrath be upon us, be-
21 cause of the oath which we sware to them." And the princes said to them, "Let them live; but let them be hewers of wood and drawers of water for the whole congregation, as
22 the princes had promised them." So Joshua called for them, and spake to them, saying, "Wherefore have ye beguiled us, saying, 'We are very far from you;' when ye dwell
23 among us? Now therefore ye are accursed; and there shall none of you be freed from being bondmen, and hewers of wood and drawers of water for the house of my God."
24 And they answered Joshua, and said, "Because it was certainly told thy servants, how that Jehovah thy God commanded his servant Moses to give you all the land, and to destroy all the inhabitants of the land from before you, therefore we were greatly afraid for our lives because of you, and

have done this thing. And now, lo, we are in thy hand: 25
as it seemeth good and right to thee to do to us, do."
And so did he to them, and delivered them out of the 26
hand of the children of Israel, that they slew them not. 27
But Joshua made them that day hewers of wood and
drawers of water, for the congregation and for the altar
of Jehovah, even unto this day, in the place which he shall
choose.

CHAP. X.—Now it came to pass when Adoni-zedek king 1
of Jerusalem had heard how Joshua had taken Ai, and had
utterly destroyed it; and had done to Ai and its king as he
had done to Jericho and its king, and how the inhabitants
of Gibeon had made peace with the Israelites, and were
among them; that they feared greatly, because Gibeon was 2
a great city, as one of the royal cities, and because it was
greater than Ai, and all the men in it were mighty.
Wherefore Adoni-zedek king of Jerusalem sent to Hoham 3
king of Hebron, and to Piram king of Jarmuth, and to
Japhia king of Lachish, and to Debir king of Eglon, saying,
"Come up to me, and help me, that we may smite Gibeon; 4
for it hath made peace with Joshua and with the children of
Israel." Then the five kings of the Amorites, the king of 5
Jerusalem, the king of Hebron, the king of Jarmuth, the king
of Lachish, the king of Eglon, gathered themselves together,
and went up, they and all their hosts, and encamped before
Gibeon, and made war against it. And the men of Gibeon 6
sent to Joshua to the camp at Gilgal, saying, "Stay not thy
hand from thy servants; come up to us quickly, and save us,
and help us; for all the kings of the Amorites that dwell in
the mountains are gathered together against us." So Joshua 7
went up from Gilgal, he, and all the people of war with
him, and all the mighty men of valour. And Jehovah said 8
to Joshua, "Fear them not; for I have delivered them into
thy hand: not a man of them shall stand before thee."
Joshua therefore came upon them suddenly, going up from 9
Gilgal all night. And Jehovah confounded them before the 10
Israelites, who slew them with a great slaughter at Gibeon,
and chased them along the way that goeth up to Beth-
horon, and smote them to Azekah, and to Makkedah. And 11
as they were fleeing from before the Israelites, *and* were in
the way going down to Beth-horon, Jehovah cast down great
stones from heaven upon them unto Azekah, and they died:

so that *they were* more who died by the hailstones than they
12 whom the children of Israel slew with the sword. Then spake Joshua to Jehovah in the day when Jehovah delivered up the Amorites before the children of Israel, and he said in the sight of Israel,

"Sun, stand thou still upon Gibeon ;
And thou, Moon, in the valley of Ajalon."

13 And the sun stood still, and the moon stayed,
Until the people had avenged themselves upon their enemies.

Is not this written in the book of Jasher? So the sun stood still in the midst of the heavens, and hastened not to
14 go down about a whole day. And there was no day like that before it or after it, that Jehovah hearkened to the voice
15 of a man; for Jehovah fought for Israel. And Joshua returned, and all Israel with him, to the camp, to Gilgal.
16 But these five kings fled, and hid themselves in a cave at
17 Makkedah. And it was told Joshua, saying, "The five
18 kings are found hidden in a cave at Makkedah." And Joshua said, "Roll great stones to the mouth of the cave,
19 and set men by it to watch them: and stay ye not, *but* pursue after your enemies, and smite the hindmost of them; suffer them not to enter into their cities; for Jehovah your
20 God hath delivered them into your hand." And it came to pass, when Joshua and the children of Israel had made an end of slaying them with a very great slaughter, till they were consumed, that the rest that remained of them entered
21 into fortified cities. And all the people returned to the camp to Joshua at Makkedah in peace: none moved his
22 tongue against any of the children of Israel. Then said Joshua, "Open the mouth of the cave, and bring out those
23 five kings to me out of the cave." And they did so, and brought forth those five kings to him out of the cave, the king of Jerusalem, the king of Hebron, the king of Jar-
24 muth, the king of Lachish, *and* the king of Eglon. And it came to pass, when they had brought those kings to Joshua, that Joshua called for all the men of Israel, and said to the captains of the men of war who went with him, "Come near, put your feet upon the necks of these kings." And they came near, and put their feet upon the necks of
25 them. And Joshua said to them, "Fear not, nor be dismayed, be strong and be of good courage: for thus shall Jehovah do to all your enemies against whom ye fight."

And afterwards Joshua smote them, and slew them, and 26
hanged them on five trees; and they were hanging upon
the trees until the evening. And it came to pass at the time 27
of the going down of the sun, that Joshua commanded,
and they took them down from the trees, and cast them into
the cave wherein they had been hidden, and laid great
stones on the mouth of the cave, *which remain* until this
very day. And that day Joshua took Makkedah, and smote 28
it with the edge of the sword, and its king he utterly
destroyed, them, and all the souls that were therein; he let
none remain: and he did to the king of Makkedah as he had
done to the king of Jericho.

Then Joshua passed from Makkedah, and all the Israelites 29
with him, to Libnah, and fought against Libnah: and Je- 30
hovah delivered it also, and its king, into the hand of the
Israelites, who smote it with the edge of the sword, and all
the souls who were therein; they let none remain in it; but
did to its king as they had done to the king of Jericho.
And Joshua passed from Libnah, and all the Israelites with 31
him, to Lachish, and encamped against it, and fought against
it: and Jehovah delivered Lachish into the hand of the 32
Israelites, who took it on the second day, and smote it with
the edge of the sword, and all the souls that were therein,
according to all that they had done to Libnah. Then Horam 33
king of Gezer came to help Lachish; and Joshua smote him
and his people, until he had left him none remaining.

And from Lachish Joshua passed to Eglon, and all the 34
Israelites with him; and they encamped against it, and
fought against it: and they took it on that day, and smote 35
it with the edge of the sword; and all the souls that were
therein he utterly destroyed that day, according to all that
he had done to Lachish. And Joshua went up from Eglon, 36
and all the Israelites with him, to Hebron; and they fought
against it; and they took it, and smote it with the edge of the 37
sword, and its king, and all its cities, and all the souls that
were therein; he left none remaining, according to all that he
had done to Eglon; but destroyed it utterly, and all the
souls that were therein. And Joshua returned, and all the 38
Israelites with him, to Debir, and fought against it, and 39
took it, and its king, and all its cities, and they smote them
with the edge of the sword, and devoted all the souls that
were therein; he left none remaining: as he had done to
Hebron, so he did to Debir, and to its king; as he had done

40 also to Libnah and to its king. So Joshua smote all the country of the hills, and of the south, and of the lowland, and of the hill sides, and all their kings: he left none remaining, but devoted all that breathed, as Jehovah God of
41 Israel had commanded. And Joshua smote them from Kadesh-barnea even to Gaza, and all the country of Goshen
42 even to Gibeon. And all these kings and their land did Joshua take at one time, because Jehovah God of Israel
43 fought for Israel. Then Joshua returned, and all the Israelites with him, to the camp, to Gilgal.

1 CHAP. XI.—Now it came to pass when Jabin king of Hazor had heard *these things*, that he sent to Jobab king of Madon, and to the king of Shimron, and to the king of
2 Achshaph, and to the kings that *were* on the north in the mountainous country; and in the plain *of Jordan* south of Chinneroth; and in the lowland, and in the region of Dor
3 on the west; *to* the Canaanites on the east and on the west, and to the Amorites, and the Hittites, and the Perizzites, and the Jebusites in the mountainous country, and *to* the
4 Hivites under Hermon, in the land of Mizpeh. And they went out, they and all their hosts with them, much people, even as the sand upon the sea-shore in multitude, with very
5 many horses and chariots. And when all these kings had appointed a meeting-place, they went and encamped together at the waters of Merom, to fight against the Israel-
6 ites. And Jehovah said to Joshua, "Be not afraid because of them: for to-morrow about this time will I deliver them up all slain before the Israelites: thou shalt hamstring their
7 horses, and burn their chariots with fire." So Joshua came, and all the people of war with him, against them by the waters of Merom suddenly; and they fell upon them,
8 and Jehovah delivered them into the hand of the Israelites, who smote them, and chased them to great Zidon, and to Misrephoth-maim, and to the valley of Mizpeh eastward; and they smote them, until they left them none re-
9 maining. And Joshua did to them as Jehovah bade him: he hamstrung their horses, and burnt their chariots with fire.
10 And Joshua at that time turned back, and took Hazor, and smote its king with the sword; (for Hazor was in
11 former time the head of all those kingdoms;) and they smote all the souls that were therein with the edge of the

sword, devoting *them;* there was not left any thing that breathed; and he burnt Hazor with fire. And all the cities 12 of those kings, and all their kings, Joshua took, and smote them with the edge of the sword; he devoted them, as Moses the servant of Jehovah had commanded. But the cities that 13 stood upon their heights, the Israelites burned none of them, save Hazor only; *that* did Joshua burn. And all the spoil 14 of these cities, and the cattle, the children of Israel took for a booty to themselves; but every man they smote with the edge of the sword, until they had destroyed them; they left not any thing that breathed. As Jehovah had commanded Moses 15 his servant, so did Moses command Joshua, and so did Joshua; he left nothing undone of all that Jehovah had commanded Moses. So Joshua took all that land, the 16 mountainous country, and all the south country, and all the land of Goshen, and the lowland, and the plain *of Jordan,* and the mountainous country of Israel, and its lowlands; even 17 from the bare mountain that goeth up towards Seir, to Baal-gad, in the valley of Lebanon, to mount Hermon: and all their kings he took, and smote them, and slew them. Joshua 18 made war a long time with all those kings. There was not 19 a city that made peace with the children of Israel, except the Hivites, the inhabitants of Gibeon: all *the rest* they took in battle. For it was of Jehovah to harden their 20 hearts, that they should come against the Israelites in battle, that they might devote them utterly, that they might have no favour, but that they might destroy them, as Jehovah had commanded Moses.

And at that time came Joshua, and cut off the Anakites 21 from the mountains, from Hebron, from Debir, from Anab, and from all the mountains of Judah, and from all the mountains of Israel: Joshua devoted them utterly with their cities. There was none of the Anakites left in the 22 land of the children of Israel: only in Gaza, in Gath, and in Ashdod, they remained. So Joshua took the whole 23 land, according to all that Jehovah had said to Moses; and Joshua gave it for an inheritance to the Israelites, according to their divisions by their tribes. And the land rested from war.

CHAP. XII.—Now these are the kings of the land, 1 whom the children of Israel smote, and possessed their land beyond the Jordan, toward the rising of the sun; from the

JOSHUA XII.

river Arnon to mount Hermon, and all the plain *of Jordan*
2 on the east: Sihon king of the Amorites, who dwelt in
Heshbon, *and* ruled from Aroer, which is upon the bank of
the torrent of Arnon, and from the middle of the torrent,
and from the half of Gilead, to the torrent Jabbok, the
3 boundary of the children of Ammon; and the plain *of
Jordan* to the sea of Chinneroth on the east, and unto the
sea of the plain *of Jordan*, the salt sea on the east, on the
way to Beth-jeshimoth; and from the south, on the side of
4 Ashdoth-pisgah: and the coast of Og king of Bashan, *who
was* of the remnant of the giants, that dwelt at Ashtaroth
5 and at Edrei, and reigned in mount Hermon, and in Salcah,
and in all Bashan, to the boundary of the Geshurites, and
the Maachathites, and the half of Gilead, the boundary of
6 Sihon king of Heshbon. These did Moses the servant of
Jehovah and the children of Israel smite; and Moses the
servant of Jehovah gave it *for* a possession to the Reubenites, and Gadites, and the half of the tribe of Manasseh.

7 And these are the kings of the country whom Joshua and
the children of Israel smote beyond the Jordan on the west,
from Baal-gad in the valley of Lebanon even to the bare
mountain, that goeth up towards Seir; which Joshua gave
to the tribes of Israel *for* a possession, according to their
8 divisions: in the mountainous country, and in the lowland,
and in the plain *of Jordan*, and in the hill-sides, and in the
desert, and in the south country; the Hittites, the Amorites,
and the Canaanites, the Perizzites, the Hivites, and the Je-
9 busites: The king of Jericho, one; the king of Ai, which
10 is beside Bethel, one; the king of Jerusalem, one; the king
11 of Hebron, one; the king of Jarmuth, one; the king of
12 Lachish, one; the king of Eglon, one; the king of Gezer,
14 one; the king of Debir, one; the king of Geder, one; the
15 king of Hormah, one; the king of Arad, one; the king of
16 Libnah, one; the king of Adullam, one; the king of Mak-
17 kedah, one; the king of Beth-el, one; the king of Tappuah,
18 one; the king of Hepher, one; the king of Aphek, one;
19 the king of Lasharon, one; the king of Madon, one; the
20 king of Hazor, one; the king of Shimron-meron, one; the
21 king of Achshaph, one; the king of Taanach, one; the
22 king of Megiddo, one; the king of Kedesh, one; the king
23 of Jokneam by Carmel, one; the king of Dor in the region
24 of Dor, one; the king of Goim by Gilgal, one; the king of
Tirzah, one; all the kings thirty and one.

JOSHUA XIII.

CHAP. XIII.—Now Joshua was old, far advanced in 1 years; and Jehovah said to him, "Thou art old, far advanced in years, and there remaineth yet very much land to be possessed. This *is* the land that yet remaineth: all the regions 2 of the Philistines, and all Geshuri, from Sihor, which is 3 before Egypt, even to the boundary of Ekron northward, *which* is counted to the Canaanite: five lords of the Philistines; the Gazathites, and the Ashdothites, the Eshkalonites, the Gittites, and the Ekronites; also the Avites towards the south; all the land of the Canaanites, and Mearah that 4 *is* beside the Sidonians, unto Aphek, to the boundary of the Amorites; and the land of the Giblites, and all Lebanon, 5 toward the sun-rising, from Baal-gad under mount Hermon to the entering into Hamath; all the inhabitants of the hill- 6 country, from Lebanon to Misrephoth-maim, *and* all the Sidonians, I will drive out from before the children of Israel: only divide thou it by lot to the Israelites for an inheritance, as I have commanded thee. Now therefore divide 7 this land for an inheritance to the nine tribes and the half of the tribe of Manasseh, with whom the Reubenites and 8 the Gadites have received their inheritance, which Moses gave them, beyond the Jordan eastward, as Moses the servant of Jehovah gave them; from Aroer, that is upon the 9 bank of the torrent Arnon, and the city that is in the midst of the torrent, and all the plain of Medeba to Dibon; and 10 all the cities of Sihon king of the Amorites, who reigned in Heshbon, to the boundary of the children of Ammon; and 11 Gilead, and the boundary of the Geshurites and Maachathites, and all mount Hermon, and all Bashan to Salcah: all 12 the kingdom of Og in Bashan, who reigned in Ashtaroth and in Edrei, who remained of the remnant of the giants: for these did Moses smite, and cast out. (Nevertheless the 13 children of Israel expelled not the Geshurites, nor the Maachathites; but the Geshurites and Maachathites dwell among the Israelites unto this day.) Only to the tribe of 14 Levi he gave no inheritance; the sacrifices of Jehovah God of Israel made by fire are their inheritance, as he said to them."
And Moses gave to the tribe of the children of Reuben 15 *inheritance* according to their families; and their boundary 16 was from Aroer on the bank of the torrent Arnon, and the city that *is* in the midst of the torrent, and all the plain by Madeba; Heshbon, and all her cities in the plain; Dibon, 17 and Bamoth-baal, and Beth-baal meon, and Jahaza, and 18

19 Kedemoth, and Mephaath, and Kirjathaim, and Sibmah, and
20 Zareth-shahar in the mount of the valley, and Beth-peor,
21 and Ashdoth-pisgah, and Beth-jeshimoth, and all the cities
of the plain *of Jordan*, and all the kingdom of Sihon king
of the Amorites, who reigned in Heshbon, whom Moses
smote with the princes of Midian, Evi, and Rekem, and Zur,
and Hur, and Reba, princes of Sihon, dwelling in the country.
22 Balaam also the son of Beor, the soothsayer, the children of
Israel slew with the sword among those who were slain by
23 them. And the boundary of the children of Reuben was
the Jordan and its boundary. This *was* the inheritance of
the children of Reuben after their families, the cities and
villages thereof.
24 And Moses gave *inheritance* to the tribe of Gad, to the chil-
25 dren of Gad, according to their families; and their boundary
was Jazer, and all the cities of Gilead, and half the land of
the children of Ammon, unto Aroer that is before Rabbah;
26 and from Heshbon unto Ramath-mizpeh, and Betonim; and
27 from Mahanaim unto the border of Debir; and in the valley,
Beth-aram, and Beth-nimrah, and Succoth, and Zaphon, the
rest of the kingdom of Sihon king of Heshbon, Jordan and *its*
border, unto the edge of the sea of Chinneroth, on the other
28 side Jordan eastward. This *is* the inheritance of the children
of Gad after their families, the cities and their villages.
29 And Moses gave *inheritance* unto the half of the tribe of
Manasseh: and *this* was the *possession* of the half of the tribe
30 of the children of Manasseh by their families: and their
boundary was from Mahanaim, all Bashan, all the kingdom
of Og king of Bashan, and all the towns of Jair, which are in
31 Bashan, sixty cities; and half of Gilead, and Ashtaroth, and
Edrei, cities of the kingdom of Og in Bashan, *were given* to
the children of Machir the son of Manasseh, to the one half
32 of the children of Machir by their families. These *are the
countries* which Moses distributed for inheritance in the plains
33 of Moab, beyond the Jordan, by Jericho, eastward. But to the
tribe of Levi, Moses gave not *any* inheritance: Jehovah God
of Israel was their inheritance, as he said to them.

1 CHAP. XIV.—And these *are the countries* which the
children of Israel inherited in the land of Canaan, which
Eleazar the priest, and Joshua the son of Nun, and the
heads of the fathers of the tribes of the children of Israel,
2 distributed for inheritance to them. By lot *was* their in-

heritance, as Jehovah commanded by the hand of Moses, for the nine tribes, and for the half tribe. For Moses had ³ given the inheritance of two tribes and a half tribe on the other side of the Jordan: but to the Levites he gave no inheritance among them. For the children of Joseph were ⁴ two tribes, Manasseh and Ephraim: therefore they gave no part to the Levites in the land, except cities to dwell in, with their suburbs for their cattle and for their substance. As ⁵ Jehovah commanded Moses, so the children of Israel did, and they divided the land.

Then the children of Judah came to Joshua in Gilgal; ⁶ and Caleb the son of Jephunneh the Kenezite said to him, "Thou knowest what Jehovah said to Moses the man of God concerning me and thee in Kadesh-barnea. Forty years ⁷ old was I when Moses the servant of Jehovah sent me from Kadesh-barnea to spy out the land; and I brought him word as it was in my heart. But my brethren who went up ⁸ with me made the heart of the people melt; but I wholly followed Jehovah my God. And Moses sware on that day, ⁹ saying, 'Surely the land whereon thy feet have trodden shall be thy inheritance, and thy children's for ever, because thou hast wholly followed Jehovah my God.' And now, ¹⁰ lo, Jehovah hath kept me alive, as he said, these forty and five years, even since Jehovah spake this word to Moses, while the Israelites wandered in the desert: and now, lo, I *am* this day fourscore and five years old; yet I am this day ¹¹ *as* strong as in the day that Moses sent me: as my strength was then, even so is my strength now for war, both to go out and to come in. Now therefore give me this mountainous ¹² land of which Jehovah spake in that day; for thou heardest in that day that the Anakites *were* there, and that the cities were great *and* fenced: if Jehovah be with me, I shall be able to drive them out, as Jehovah hath said." And Joshua ¹³ blessed him, and gave Hebron to Caleb, the son of Jephunneh, for an inheritance. Hebron therefore became the ¹⁴ inheritance of Caleb, the son of Jephunneh the Kenezite to this day, because that he wholly followed Jehovah God of Israel.

Now the name of Hebron before was Kirjath-arba [THE ¹⁵ CITY OF ARBA]; *which Arba was* a great man among the Anakites. And the land had rest from war.

CHAP. XV.—And the lot of the tribe of the children of ¹

Judah according to their families, was to the boundary of Edom; the desert of Zin southward was the uttermost 2 part of the south. And their southern boundary was from the shore of the salt sea, from the tongue *of land* 3 that looketh southward: and it went to the south side to Maaleh-acrabbim, and passed along to Zin, and went up on the south side unto Kadesh-barnea; and passed along to Hezron, and went up to Adar, and wound about to Karkaa: 4 *thence* it passed toward Azmon, and went on to the torrent of Egypt; and the extremities of that boundary were at the sea. This shall be your southern boundary.

5 And the eastern boundary *was* the salt sea, *even* unto the end of the Jordan. And *their* boundary in the north quarter was from the tongue *of land* of the sea at the termination of 6 the Jordan. And the boundary went up to Beth-hogla, and passed along by the north of Beth-arabah; and the boundary went up to the stone of Bohan the son of Reuben. 7 And the boundary went up toward Debir from the valley of Achor, and so northward, looking toward Gilgal, that *is* before the going up to Adummim, *which is* on the south side of the river; and the boundary passed toward the waters of 8 Enshemesh, and its extremities were at En-rogel; and the boundary went up by the valley of the son of Hinnom unto the south side of the Jebusite (the same *is* Jerusalem); and the boundary went up to the top of the mountain that *lieth* before the valley of Hinnom westward, which *is* at the end 9 of the valley of the giants northward; and the boundary was drawn from the top of the hill unto the fountain of the water of Nephtoah, and went on to the cities of mount Ephron; and the boundary was drawn to Baalah (which *is* 10 Kirjath-jearim); and the boundary wound about from Baalah westward unto mount Seir, and passed along unto the side of mount Jearim, which *is* Chesalon, on the north side, and 11 went down to Beth-shemesh, and passed on to Timnah; and the boundary went out unto the side of Ekron northwards; and the boundary was drawn to Shicron, and passed along to mount Baalah, and went on unto Jabneel; and the 12 extremities of the boundary were at the sea. And the western boundary *was* to the great sea, and its coast. This *is* the boundary of the children of Judah round about, according to their families.

13 And unto Caleb the son of Jephunneh he gave a part

among the children of Judah, according to the commandment of Jehovah to Joshua, *even* the city of Arba the father of Anak, which *city is* Hebron. And Caleb drove thence the ¹⁴ three sons of Anak, Sheshai, Ahiman, and Talmai, the children of Anak. And he went up thence to the inhabit- ¹⁵ ants of Debir: and the name of Debir before *was* Kirjath-sepher. And Caleb said, "He that smiteth Kirjath-sepher, ¹⁶ and taketh it, to him will I give Achsah my daughter to wife." And Othniel the son of Kenaz, the younger brother ¹⁷ of Caleb, took it; and he gave him Achsah his daughter to wife. And as she came *unto him*, it came to pass that she ¹⁸ moved him to ask of her father a field; and she lighted off *her* ass, and Caleb said unto her, "What wouldest thou?" who answered, "Give me a blessing; for thou hast given ¹⁹ me a south land; give me also springs of water." And he gave her the upper springs, and the lower springs.

This *is* the inheritance of the tribe of the children of ²⁰ Judah according to their families. And the cities at the ex- ²¹ tremity of the tribe of the children of Judah, toward the coast of Edom southward, were Kabzeel, and Eder, and Jagur, and Kinah, and Dimonah, and Adadah, and Kedesh, ²³ and Hazor, and Ithnan, Ziph, and Telem, and Bealoth, and ²⁵ Hazor, Hadattah, and Kerioth, *and* Hezron, which *is* Hazor, Amam, and Shema, and Moladah, and Hazar-gaddah, and ²⁷ Heshmon, and Beth-palet, and Hazar-shual, and Beersheba, ²⁸ and Bizjothjah, Baalah, and Iim, and Azem, and Eltolad, and ³⁰ Chesil, and Hormah, and Ziklag, and Madmannah, and San- ³¹ sannah, and Lebaoth, and Shilhim, and Ain, and Rimmon: ³² all the cities *are* twenty and nine, with their villages. *And* ³³ in the lowland, Eshtaol, and Zoreah, and Ashnah, and Zanoah, ³⁴ and En-gannim, Tappuah, and Enam, Jarmuth, and Adul- ³⁵ lam, Socoh, and Azekah, and Sharaim, and Adithaim, and ³⁶ Gederah, and Gederothaim; fourteen cities with their villages. Zenan, and Hadashah, and Migdalgad, and Dilean, ³⁸ and Mizpeh, and Joktheel, Lachish, and Bozkath, and Eglon, ³⁹ and Cabbon, and Lahmam, and Kithlish, and Gederoth, Beth- ⁴¹ dagon, and Naamah, and Makkedah; sixteen cities with their villages. Libnah, and Ether, and Ashan, and Jiphtah, and ⁴³ Ashnah and Nezib, and Keilah, and Achzib, and Mareshah; ⁴⁴ nine cities with their villages. Ekron with her towns and her villages: from Ekron even unto the sea, all that *lay* near ⁴⁶ Ashdod, with their villages: Ashdod with her towns and her ⁴⁷

villages, Gaza with her towns and her villages, unto the torrent of Egypt, and the great sea, and its coast; and in the moun-
49 tainous country, Shamir, and Jattir, and Socoh, and Dannah,
50 and Kirjath-sannah, which *is* Debir, and Anab, and Eshte-
51 moh, and Anim, and Goshen, and Holon, and Giloh; eleven
52 cities with their villages. Arab, and Dumah, and Eshean,
54 and Janum, and Beth-tappuah, Aphekah, and Humtah, and Kirjath-arba (which *is* Hebron), and Zior; nine cities
55 with their villages. Maon, Carmel, and Ziph, and Juttah,
57 and Jezreel, and Jokdeam, and Zanoah, Cain, Gibeah, and
58 Timnah; ten cities with their villages. Halhul, Bethzur,
59 and Gedor, and Maarath, and Beth-anoth, and Eltekon; six
60 cities with their villages. Kirjath-baal (which is Kirjath-
61 jearim), and Rabbah; two cities with their villages. In
62 the desert, Beth-arabah, Middin, and Lecacah, and Nibshan, and the city of Salt, and En-gedi; six cities with their villages.
63 As for the Jebusites, the inhabitants of Jerusalem, the children of Judah could not dispossess them; but the Jebusites dwell with the children of Judah at Jerusalem unto this day.

1 CHAP. XVI.—Then came forth the lot of the children of Joseph: from Jordan by Jericho, unto the water of Jericho on the east, to the desert that goeth up from Jericho
2 throughout mount Beth-el, and goeth out from Beth-el to Luz, and passeth along unto the boundary of Archi to
3 Ataroth, and goeth down westward to the boundary of Japhleti, unto the boundary of Beth-horon the lower, and to Gezer;
4 and its extremities are at the sea. So the children of Joseph, Manasseh and Ephraim, took their inheritance.
5 And the boundary of the children of Ephraim, according to their families, was *thus;* even the boundary of their inheritance on the east side was Ataroth-addar, unto Beth-
6 horon the upper; and the boundary went out toward the sea to Michmethah on the north side; and the boundary wound about eastward unto Taanath-shiloh, and passed by it
7 on the east to Janohah; and it went down from Janohah to Ataroth, and to Naarath, and came to Jericho, and termi-
8 nated at the Jordan. The boundary went out from Tappuah westward unto the river Kanah; and its termination was at the sea. This *is* the inheritance of the tribe of the children of Ephraim by their families.
9 And the separate cities for the children of Ephraim *were*

among the inheritance of the children of Manasseh, all the cities with their villages.

And they dispossessed not the Canaanites that dwelt in Gezer: but the Canaanites dwell among the Ephraimites unto this day, and serve under tribute.

CHAP. XVII.—There was also a lot for the tribe of Manasseh (for he *was* the first-born of Joseph), for Machir the first-born of Manasseh, the father of Gilead; because he was a man of war, therefore he had Gilead and Bashan. There was also *a lot* for the rest of the children of Manasseh according to their families; for the children of Abiezer, and for the children of Helek, and for the children of Asriel, and for the children of Shechem, and for the children of Hepher, and for the children of Shemida: these *were* the male children of Manasseh the son of Joseph, according to their families. But Zelophehad, the son of Hepher, the son of Gilead, the son of Machir, the son of Manasseh, had no sons, but daughters; and these are the names of his daughters, Mahlah, and Noah, Hoglah, Milcah, and Tirzah. And they came near before Eleazar the priest, and before Joshua the son of Nun, and before the princes, saying, "Jehovah commanded Moses to give us an inheritance among our brethren." Therefore, according to the commandment of Jehovah, he gave them an inheritance among the brethren of their father. And there fell ten portions to Manasseh, beside the land of Gilead and Bashan, which were on the other side of the Jordan; because the daughters of Manasseh had an inheritance among his sons; and the rest of Manasseh's sons had the land of Gilead. Now the boundary of Manasseh was from Asher to Michmethah, which is opposite to Shechem; and the boundary went along on the south unto the inhabitants of En-tappuah. (Manasseh had the land of Tappuah; but *the city of* Tappuah, on the boundary of Manasseh, *belonged* to the children of Ephraim.) And the boundary went down to the river Kanah, southward of the river: these cities of Ephraim *are* among the cities of Manasseh: the boundary of Manasseh also *was* on the north side of the river, and the extremities of it were at the sea. Southward *it was* Ephraim's, and northward *it was* Manasseh's, and the sea is his boundary; and they met together in Asher on the north, and in Issachar on the east. And Manasseh had in Issachar, and in Asher, Beth-shean

and her towns, and Ibleam and her towns, and the inhabitants of Dor and her towns, and the inhabitants of Endor and her towns, and the inhabitants of Taanach and her towns, and the inhabitants of Megiddo and her towns, three
12 districts. But the children of Manasseh were not able to dispossess *the inhabitants of* those cities; but the Canaanites
13 would dwell in that land. Yet it came to pass, when the children of Israel became strong, that they put the Canaanites under tribute; but they did not utterly dispossess them.
14 And the children of Joseph spake to Joshua, saying, "Why hast thou given me *but* one lot and one portion to inherit, seeing I *am* a great people, forasmuch as Jehovah
15 hath blessed me hitherto?" And Joshua answered them, "If thou be a great people, go up to the wood *country*, and clear for thyself there in the land of the Perizzites and of the giants, if mount Ephraim be too narrow for thee."
16 And the children of Joseph said, "The mountainous country is not enough for us; and all the Canaanites that dwell in the land of the valley have chariots of iron, *both they* who *are* of Beth-shean and her towns, and *they* who *are* of the
17 valley of Jezreel." And Joshua spake unto the house of Joseph, to Ephraim and to Manasseh, saying, "Thou *art* a great people, and hast great power; thou shalt not have one
18 lot *only*: but the mountainous country shall be thine; for it *is* a wood, and thou shalt clear it: and the extremities of it shall be thine: for thou shalt dispossess the Canaanites, though they have iron chariots, *and* though they *be* strong."

1 CHAP. XVIII.—And the whole congregation of the children of Israel assembled together at Shiloh, and set up the tent of meeting there. And the land was subdued before
2 them. Yet there remained among the children of Israel seven tribes which had not received their inheritance.
3 And Joshua said to the children of Israel, "How long *are* ye slack to go to possess the land which Jehovah God of your
4 fathers hath given you? Give out from among you three men for *each* tribe: and I will send them, and they shall arise and go through the land, and describe it, according to their in-
5 heritance; and they shall come *again* to me. And they shall divide it into seven parts: Judah shall abide in their boundary on the south, and the house of Joseph shall abide in their
6 boundaries on the north. Ye shall therefore describe the land *into* seven parts, and bring *the description* hither to me,

that I may cast lots for you here before Jehovah our God. But the Levites have no part among you; for the priesthood 7 of Jehovah *is* their inheritance; and Gad, and Reuben, and the half of the tribe of Manasseh, have received their inheritance beyond Jordan on the east, which Moses the servant of Jehovah gave them." And the men arose, and went away; 8 and Joshua charged them that went to describe the land, saying, "Go and walk through the land, and describe it, and come again to me, that I may here cast lots for you before Jehovah in Shiloh." And the men went, and passed through 9 the land, and described it by cities, into seven parts, in a book, and came *again* to Joshua to the encampment at Shiloh. And Joshua cast lots for them in Shiloh before Jehovah; 10 and there Joshua divided the land unto the children of Israel, according to their divisions.

And the lot of the tribe of the children of Benjamin 11 came up according to their families; and the boundary of their lot came forth between the children of Judah and the children of Joseph. And their boundary, on the 12 north side, was from the Jordan: and the boundary went up to the side of Jericho on the north side, and went up through the mountains westward; and the extremities thereof were at the desert of Beth-aven. And the boundary went 13 over from thence toward Luz to the side of Luz (which *is* Beth-el), southward; and the boundary descended to Ataroth-addar, near the hill that *lieth* on the south side of the lower Beth-horon. And the boundary was drawn *thence*, and 14 wound about the corner of the sea southward, from the hill that *lieth* before Beth-horon southward; and the extremities thereof were at Kirjath-baal (which *is* Kirjath-jearim), a city of the children of Judah: this *was* the west quarter. And 15 the south quarter *was* from the end of Kirjath-jearim; and the boundary went out on the west, and went out to the well of waters of Nephtoah. And the boundary came down to the 16 end of the mountain that *lieth* before the valley of the son of Hinnom, *and* which *is* in the valley of the giants on the north, and descended to the valley of Hinnom, to the side of the Jebusites on the south, and descended to En-rogel, and 17 was drawn from the north, and went forth to En-shemesh, and went forth toward Geliloth, which *is* over against the ascent of Adummim, and descended to the stone of Bohan the son of Reuben, and passed along toward the side over 18 against Arabah northward, and went down unto Arabah.

19 And the boundary passed along to the side of Beth-hoglah northward; and the extremities of the boundary were at the north tongue *of land* of the salt sea, at the south end of the
20 Jordan: this *was* the southern boundary. And the Jordan was the boundary of it on the east side. This *was* the inheritance of the children of Benjamin,. by its boundaries
21 round about, according to their families. Now the cities of the tribe of the children of Benjamin, according to their families, were Jericho, and Beth-hoglah, and the valley of
23 Keziz, and Beth-arabah, and Zemaraim, and Beth-el, and
24 Avim, and Parah, and Ophrah, and Chephar-haammonai, and
25 Ophni, and Gaba; twelve cities with their villages. Gibeon,
26 and Ramah, and Beeroth, and Mizpeh, and Chephirah, and
28 Mozah, and Rekem, and Irpeel, and Taralah, and Zelah, Eleph, and the Jebusites (which *is* Jerusalem), Gibeath, *and* Kirjath; fourteen cities with their villages. This *is* the inheritance of the children of Benjamin, according to their families.

1 CHAP. XIX.—And the second lot came forth to Simeon, for the tribe of the children of Simeon according to their families; and their inheritance was within the inheritance of
2 the children of Judah. And they had in their inheritance,
3 Beer-sheba, and Moladah, and Hazar-shual, and Balah, and
5 Azem, and Eltolad, and Bethul, and Hormah, and Ziklag, and
6 Beth-marcaboth, and Hazar-susah, and Beth-lebaoth, and
7 Sharuhen; thirteen cities and their villages. Ain, Remmon,
8 and Ether, and Ashan; four cities and their villages, and all the villages that *were* round about these cities, to Baalath-beer, Ramath of the south. This *is* the inheritance of the tribe of the children of Simeon according to their families.
9 Out of the portion of the children of Judah *was* the inheritance of the children of Simeon: for the part of the children of Judah was too much for them; therefore the children of Simeon had their inheritance within the inheritance of them.
10 And the third lot came up for the children of Zebulun, according to their families: and the boundary of their in-
11 heritance was unto Sarid: and their boundary went up toward the sea, and Maralah, and reached to Dabbasheth, and
12 reached to the torrent that *is* before Jokneam; and turned from Sarid eastward, toward the sun-rising, unto the boundary of Chisloth-tabor, and then goeth out to Daberath, and
13 goeth up to Japhia, and from thence passeth on along on the

east to Gittah-hepher, to Ittah-kazin, and goeth out to Rim- mon, which extendeth to Neah: and the boundary com- 14 passeth it on the north side to Hannathon; and its extremities are in the valley of Jiphthah-el: and Kattath, and Nahallal, 15 and Shimron, and Idalah, and Beth-lehem: twelve cities with their villages. This *is* the inheritance of the children 16 of Zebulun according to their families, these cities with their villages.

And the fourth lot came forth to Issachar, for the children 17 of Issachar according to their families. And their boundary 18 was toward Jezreel, and Chesulloth, and Shunem, and Ha- 19 phraim, and Shihon, and Anaharath, and Rabbith, and Kishion, 20 and Abez, and Remeth, and En-gannim, and En-haddah, 21 and Beth-pazzez. And the boundary reacheth to Tabor, 22 and Shahazimah, and Beth-shemesh; and the extremities of their boundary were at Jordan: sixteen cities with their villages. This *is* the inheritance of the tribe of the children 23 of Issachar, according to their families, the cities and their villages.

And the fifth lot came forth for the tribe of the children of 24 Asher according to their families. And their boundary was 25 Helkath, and Hali, and Beten, and Achshaph, and Alam- 26 melech, and Amad, and Misheal, and reacheth to Carmel westward, and to Shihor-libnath, and turneth toward the sun- 27 rising to Beth-dagon, and reacheth to Zebulun, and to the valley of Jiphthah-el, toward the north side of Beth-emek, and Neiel, and goeth out to Cabul on the left hand, and 28 Hebron, and Rehob, and Hammon, and Kanah, *even* unto great Sidon; and *then* the boundary turneth to Ramah, and to 29 the strong city Tyre; and the boundary turneth to Hosah; and its extremities are at the sea, from the coast to Achzib: Ummah also, and Aphek, and Rehob: twenty and two cities 30 with their villages. This *is* the inheritance of the tribe of 31 the children of Asher according to their families, these cities with their villages.

The sixth lot came forth to the children of Naphtali, *even* 32 for the children of Naphtali according to their families. And their boundary was from Heleph, from Allon to Zaanan- 33 nim, and Adami, Nekeb, and Jabneel, unto Lakum; and its extremities were at Jordan; and *then* the boundary turneth 34 westward to Aznoth-tabor, and goeth out from thence to Hukkok, and reacheth to Zebulun on the south side, and reacheth to Asher on the west side, and to Judah upon the

35 Jordan toward the sun-rising. And the fenced cities *are*
36 Ziddim, Zer, and Hammath, Rakkath, and Chinneroth, and
37 Adamah, and Ramah, and Hazor, and Kedesh, and Edrei,
38 and En-hazor, and Iron, and Migdal-el, Horem, and Beth-anath, and Beth-shemesh; nineteen cities with their villages.
39 This *is* the inheritance of the tribe of the children of Naphtali according to their families, the cities and their villages.
40 *And* the seventh lot came forth for the tribe of the
41 children of Dan according to their families. And the boundary of their inheritance was Zorah, and Eshtaol,
42 and Ir-shemesh, and Shaalabbin, and Ajalon, and Jethlah,
44 and Elon, and Thimnathah, and Ekron, and Eltekeh,
45 and Gibbethon, and Baalath, and Jehud, and Bene-berak,
46 and Gath-rimmon, and Me-jarkon, and Rakkon, with the
47 boundary before Japho. And the boundary of the children of Dan went out beyond them; for the children of Dan went up to fight against Leshem, and took it, and smote it with the edge of the sword, and possessed it, and dwelt therein, and called Leshem, Dan, after the name of Dan their
48 father. This *is* the inheritance of the tribe of the children of Dan according to their families, these cities with their villages.
49 When they had made an end of dividing the land for inheritance, according to their boundaries, the children of Israel gave an inheritance to Joshua the son of Nun among
50 them: according to the word of Jehovah, they gave him the city which he asked, *even* Timnath-serah in mount Ephraim; and he built the city, and dwelt therein.
51 These *are* the inheritances which Eleazar the priest, and Joshua the son of Nun, and the heads of the fathers of the tribes of the children of Israel, divided for an inheritance by lot in Shiloh before Jehovah, at the door of the tent of meeting. So they made an end of dividing the land.

1 CHAP. XX.—Jehovah spake also to Joshua, saying,
2 "Speak to the children of Israel, saying, 'Appoint for yourselves cities of refuge, concerning which I spake to you by
3 the hand of Moses; that the slayer that killeth *any* person unawares *and* unwittingly may flee thither; and they shall
4 be your refuge from the avenger of blood. And when he that fleeth unto one of those cities shall stand at the entering of the gate of the city, and shall declare his cause in the ears of the elders of that city, they shall take

him into the city, unto them, and give him a place, that he may dwell among them. And if the avenger of blood 5 pursue after him, then they shall not deliver the slayer up into his hand; because he smote his neighbour unwittingly, and hated him not beforetime. And he shall dwell in that 6 city, until he stand before the congregation for judgment, *and* until the death of the high priest that shall be in those days: then shall the slayer return, and come to his own city, and to his own house, to the city whence he fled.'" And they appointed Kadesh in Galilee in mount Naphtali, 7 and Shechem in mount Ephraim, and Kirjath-arba (which *is* Hebron), in the mountainous country of Judah. And be- 8 yond Jordan by Jericho eastward, they assigned Bezer in the desert upon the plain out of the tribe of Reuben, and Ramoth in Gilead out of the tribe of Gad, and Golan in Bashan out of the tribe of Manasseh. These were the cities appointed 9 for all the children of Israel, and for the stranger that sojourneth among them, that whosoever killeth *any* person unawares might flee thither, and not die by the hand of the avenger of blood, until he stood before the congregation.

CHAP. XXI.—Then came near the heads of the fathers 1 of the Levites unto Eleazar the priest, and unto Joshua the son of Nun, and unto the heads of the fathers of the tribes of the children of Israel; and they spake unto them at 2 Shiloh in the land of Canaan, saying, "Jehovah commanded by the hand of Moses to give us cities to dwell in, with the suburbs thereof for our cattle." And the children of Israel 3 gave unto the Levites out of their inheritance, at the commandment of Jehovah, these cities and their suburbs. And the lot came forth for the families of the Kohathites : 4 and the children of Aaron the priest, *which were* of the Levites, had by lot, out of the tribe of Judah, and out of the tribe of Simeon, and out of the tribe of Benjamin, thirteen cities. And the rest of the children of Kohath *had* by 5 lot, out of the families of the tribe of Ephraim, and out of the tribe of Dan, and out of the half of the tribe of Manasseh, ten cities. And the children of Gershon *had* by lot, out of the 6 families of the tribe of Issachar, and out of the tribe of Asher, and out of the tribe of Naphtali, and out of the half of the tribe of Manasseh in Bashan, thirteen cities. The 7 children of Merari, by their families, *had*, out of the tribe of Reuben, and out of the tribe of Gad, and out of the tribe

JOSHUA XXI.

8 of Zebulun, twelve cities. And the children of Israel gave by lot unto the Levites these cities with their suburbs, as
9 Jehovah commanded by the hand of Moses. And they gave out of the tribe of the children of Judah, and out of the tribe of the children of Simeon, these cities which are *here*
10 mentioned by name, which the children of Aaron, *being* of the families of the Kohathites, *who were* of the children
11 of Levi, had: for theirs was the first lot. And they gave them the city of Arba, the father of Anak (which *city is* Hebron), in the mountainous country of Judah, with the
12 suburbs thereof round about it. But the fields of the city, and the villages thereof, gave they to Caleb the son of
13 Jephunneh for his possession. Thus they gave to the children of Aaron the priest, Hebron with her suburbs, *to be* a city of refuge for the slayer; and Libnah with her suburbs,
14 and Jattir with her suburbs, and Eshtemoa with her suburbs,
15 and Holon with her suburbs, and Debir with her suburbs,
16 and Ain with her suburbs, and Juttah with her suburbs, *and* Beth-shemesh with her suburbs; nine cities out of those
17 two tribes. And out of the tribe of Benjamin, Gibeon with
18 her suburbs, Geba with her suburbs, Anathoth with her
19 suburbs, and Almon with her suburbs; four cities. All the cities of the children of Aaron, the priests, *were* thirteen
20 cities with their suburbs. And the families of the children of Kohath, the Levites which remained of the children of Kohath, even they had the cities of their lot out of the tribe
21 of Ephraim. For they gave them Shechem with her suburbs in mount Ephraim, *to be* a city of refuge for the slayer; and
22 Gezer with her suburbs, and Kibzaim with her suburbs, and
23 Bethhoron with her suburbs; four cities. And out of the tribe of Dan, Eltekeh with her suburbs, Gibbethon with her
24 suburbs, Aijalon with her suburbs, Gath-rimmon with her
25 suburbs; four cities. And out of the half of the tribe of Manasseh, Taanach with her suburbs, and Gath-rimmon with her
26 suburbs; two cities. All the cities *were* ten, with their suburbs, for the families of the children of Kohath that remained.
27 And unto the children of Gershon, of the families of the Levites, out of the *other* half of the tribe of Manasseh, *they gave* Golan in Bashan with her suburbs *to be* a city of refuge for the slayer; and Beesh-terah with her suburbs; two cities.
28 And out of the tribe of Issachar, Kishon with her suburbs,
29 Dabareh with her suburbs, Jarmuth with her suburbs, En-
30 gannim with her suburbs; four cities. And out of the

tribe of Asher, Mishal with her suburbs, Abdon with her suburbs, Helkath with her suburbs, and Rehob with her ³¹ suburbs; four cities. And out of the tribe of Naphtali, ³² Kedesh in Galilee with her suburbs, *to be* a city of refuge for the slayer; and Hammoth-dor with her suburbs, and Kartan with her suburbs; three cities. All the cities of the ³³ Gershonites, according to their families, *were* thirteen cities with their suburbs.

And unto the families of the children of Merari, the rest ³⁴ of the Levites, out of the tribe of Zebulun, Jokneam with her suburbs, and Kartah with her suburbs, Dimnah with her ³⁵ suburbs, Nahalal with her suburbs; four cities. And out of ³⁶ the tribe of Reuben, Bezer with her suburbs, and Jahazah with her suburbs, Kedemoth with her suburbs and Mephaath ³⁷ with her suburbs; four cities. And out of the tribe of Gad, ³⁸ Ramoth in Gilead with her suburbs, *to be* a city of refuge for the slayer; and Mahanaim with her suburbs, Heshbon ³⁹ with her suburbs, Jazer with her suburbs; four cities in all. So all the cities for the children of Merari, by their families, ⁴⁰ which were remaining of the families of the Levites, were, *by* their lot, twelve cities.

All the cities of the Levites within the possession of the ⁴¹ children of Israel *were* forty and eight cities with their suburbs. These cities were every one with their suburbs ⁴² round about them: thus *were* all these cities.

And Jehovah gave to Israel all the land which he sware to ⁴³ give to their fathers; and they possessed it, and dwelt therein. And Jehovah gave them rest round about, accord- ⁴⁴ ing to all that he sware to their fathers; and there stood not a man of all their enemies before them; Jehovah delivered all their enemies into their hand. There failed not ought of ⁴⁵ any good thing which Jehovah had spoken to the house of Israel; all came to pass.

CHAP. XXII.—Then Joshua called the Reubenites, and ¹ the Gadites, and the half of the tribe of Manasseh, and ² said to them, " Ye have observed all that Moses the servant of Jehovah commanded you, and have obeyed my voice in all that I commanded you: ye have not left your brethren ³ these many days unto this day, but have kept the charge of the commandment of Jehovah your God.

And now Jehovah your God hath given rest to your ⁴ brethren, as he promised them: therefore now return, and go

to your tents, to the land of your possession, which Moses the servant of Jehovah gave you on the other side of the
5 Jordan. But take diligent heed to do the commandment and the law, which Moses the servant of Jehovah charged you, to love Jehovah your God, and to walk in all his ways, and to keep his commandments, and to cleave unto him, and to serve him with all your heart and with all your soul."
6 So Joshua blessed them, and sent them away: and they
7 went to their tents. (Now, to the *one* half of the tribe of Manasseh, Moses had given *possession* in Bashan; but to the *other* half thereof Joshua gave *possession* among their brethren on this side of the Jordan westward.) And when Joshua sent them away also to their tents, then he blessed
8 them; and he spake to them, saying, "Return with much riches to your tents, and with very much cattle, with silver, and with gold, and with brass, and with iron, and with very much raiment: divide the spoil of your enemies with your brethren."
9 Then the children of Reuben, and the children of Gad, and the half of the tribe of Manasseh, returned, and departed from the children of Israel out of Shiloh, which is in the land of Canaan, to go to the country of Gilead, to the land of their possession, of which they were possessed, according to the word of Jehovah by the hand of Moses.
10 And when they came to the regions of the Jordan, that are in the land of Canaan, the children of Reuben, and the children of Gad, and the half of the tribe of Manasseh, built there an altar by the Jordan, a great altar to behold.
11 And the children of Israel heard say, "Lo, the children of Reuben, and the children of Gad, and the half of the tribe of Manasseh, have built an altar over against the land of Canaan, in the borders of the Jordan, at the passage of the
12 children of Israel." And when the children of Israel heard *of it*, the whole assembly of the children of Israel gathered themselves together at Shiloh, to go up to war
13 against them. And the children of Israel sent to the children of Reuben, and to the children of Gad, and to the half of the tribe of Manasseh, into the land of Gilead, Phinehas,
14 the son of Eleazar the priest; and with him ten princes, a prince of each chief house throughout all the tribes of Israel; and each one *was* a head of the house of their fathers among the thousands of Israel.
15 And they came to the children of Reuben, and to the

children of Gad, and to the half of the tribe of Manasseh,
unto the land of Gilead; and they spake with them, saying,
"Thus saith the whole congregation of Jehovah, 'What ¹⁶
transgression *is* this that ye have committed against the God
of Israel, by turning away this day from following Jehovah,
by building for yourselves an altar, so as to rebel this day
against Jehovah? *Is* the iniquity of Peor too little for us, ¹⁷
from which we are not cleansed until this day, although there
was a plague in the congregation of Jehovah, but that ye must ¹⁸
turn away this day from following Jehovah? and it will be,
seeing ye rebel to-day against Jehovah, that to-morrow he
will be wroth with the whole congregation of Israel. But, ¹⁹
if the land of your possession be unclean, *then* pass over to
the land of the possession of Jehovah, wherein the tabernacle
of Jehovah dwelleth, and take possession among us; but
rebel not against Jehovah, nor rebel against us, in building
for yourselves an altar, besides the altar of Jehovah our God.
Did not Achan the son of Zerah commit a transgression in ²⁰
respect of the devoted thing, so that wrath fell on all the
assembly of Israel, and that man perished not alone in his
iniquity?'" Then the children of Reuben, and the children ²¹
of Gad, and the half of the tribe of Manasseh, answered and
said to the heads of the thousands of Israel, "Jehovah, God ²²
of gods, Jehovah, God of gods, he himself knoweth, and Israel
he shall know, (save us not this day!) if *it be* in rebellion, or
if in transgression against Jehovah, that we have built us an ²³
altar to turn from following Jehovah, or if to offer thereon
burnt-offering or meal-offering, or if to offer peace-offerings
thereon: let Jehovah himself make inquisition; and if we have ²⁴
not *rather* done it for fear of *this* thing, saying, 'In time to
come your children might say to our children, What have ye
to do with Jehovah God of Israel? For Jehovah hath made ²⁵
the Jordan a boundary between us and you; ye children of
Reuben, and children of Gad, ye have no part in Jehovah:
so shall your children make our children cease from fearing
Jehovah. Therefore we said, Let us now prepare to build us ²⁶
an altar, not for burnt-offering, nor for sacrifice; but *that* it ²⁷
may be a witness between us and you, and our generations
after us, that we might do the service of Jehovah before him
with our burnt-offerings, and with our sacrifices, and with
our peace-offerings; that your children may not say to our
children in time to come, 'Ye have no part in Jehovah.'
Therefore said we, that it shall be, when they should *so* say ²⁸

to us, or to our generations in time to come, that we may say *again*, 'Behold the pattern of the altar of Jehovah, which our fathers made, not for burnt-offerings, nor for sacrifices; but it
29 *is* a witness between us and you.' Far be it from us that we should rebel against Jehovah, and turn this day from following Jehovah, to build an altar for burnt-offerings, for meal-offerings, or for sacrifices, besides the altar of Jehovah our God
30 that *is* before his tabernacle." And when Phinehas the priest, and the princes of the congregation, and heads of the thousands of Israel who *were* with him, heard the words that the children of Reuben, and the children of Gad, and the chil-
31 dren of Manasseh, spake, it pleased them. And Phinehas the son of Eleazar the priest said to the children of Reuben, and to the children of Gad, and to the children of Manasseh, "This day we perceive that Jehovah is among us, because ye have not committed this transgression against Jehovah: now ye have delivered the children of Israel out of the hand
32 of Jehovah." And Phinehas the son of Eleazar the priest, and the princes, returned from the children of Reuben, and from the children of Gad, out of the land of Gilead, to the land of Canaan, to the children of Israel, and brought them
33 word again. And the thing pleased the children of Israel; and the children of Israel blessed God, and did *no longer* think of going up against them in battle, to destroy the land
34 wherein the children of Reuben and Gad dwelt. And the children of Reuben, and the children of Gad, called the altar *Ed* [TESTIMONY]: "Because it is a testimony between us that Jehovah is God."

1 CHAP. XXIII.—And it came to pass a long time after that Jehovah had given rest to the Israelites from all their enemies round about, that Joshua grew old *and* far advanced
2 in age. And Joshua called for all the Israelites, for their elders, and for their chiefs, and for their judges, and for their
3 officers, and said to them, "I am become old *and* far advanced in age: and ye have seen all that Jehovah your God hath done unto all these nations because of you: for
4 Jehovah your God is he that hath fought for you. Lo, I have divided to you by lot these nations that remain, to be an inheritance for your tribes, from the Jordan, even to the great sea westward, and from all the nations that I have cut off.
5 And Jehovah your God, will himself expel them from before you, and drive them from out of your sight; and ye

shall possess their land, as Jehovah your God hath promised you. Be ye therefore very courageous, to keep and to do 6 all that is written in the book of the law of Moses, that ye turn not aside from it to the right hand or to the left; that 7 ye come not among these nations, these that remain among you; neither make mention of the name of their gods, nor cause to swear *by them,* nor serve them, nor bow yourselves unto them; but cleave to Jehovah your God, as ye have done 8 unto this day. For Jehovah hath driven out from before 9 you great nations and strong: but as for you, no man hath been able to stand before you to this day. One man of you 10 shall chase a thousand: for Jehovah your God, himself fighteth for you, as he hath promised you. Take good 11 heed therefore to yourselves, that ye love Jehovah your God. Else if ye shall in any wise go back, and cleave unto the 12 remnant of these nations, *even* these that remain among you, and shall make marriages with them, and go in unto them, and they to you; know assuredly that Jehovah your God 13 will no more drive out any of these nations from before you; but they shall be snares and traps to you, and scourges in your sides, and thorns in your eyes, until ye perish from off this good land, which Jehovah your God hath given you. And, lo, this day I am going the way of all the earth; 14 and ye know in all your hearts, and in all your souls, that not one thing hath failed of all the good things which Jehovah your God spake concerning you; all are come to pass unto you; not one thing hath failed thereof. There- 15 fore, as all good things are come upon you, which Jehovah your God promised you; so shall Jehovah bring upon you all evil things, until he have destroyed you from off this good land which Jehovah your God hath given you. When ye have transgressed the covenant of Jehovah your 16 God, which he commanded you, and have gone and served other gods, and bowed yourselves to them; then shall the anger of Jehovah be kindled against you, and ye shall perish quickly from off the good land which he hath given to you."

CHAP. XXIV.—And Joshua gathered all the tribes of 1 Israel to Shechem, and called for the elders of Israel, and for their chiefs, and for their judges, and for their officers; and they presented themselves before God. And Joshua 2 said to all the people, "Thus saith Jehovah God of Israel,

JOSHUA XXIV.

'Your fathers dwelt from of old on the other side of the river, *even* Terah the father of Abraham, and the father of Nachor; and they served other gods. But I took your father Abraham from the other side of the river, and led him through all the land of Canaan, and multiplied his seed, and gave him Isaac. And I gave to Isaac, Jacob and Esau; and I gave to Esau mount Seir, that he might possess it; but Jacob and his sons went down into Egypt.

I sent Moses also and Aaron, and I plagued Egypt, according to that which I did in the midst of it: and afterward I brought you out. And I brought your fathers out of Egypt, and ye came unto the sea; and the Egyptians pursued after your fathers with chariots and horsemen unto the Red Sea. And when they cried to Jehovah, he put darkness between you and the Egyptians, and brought the sea upon them, and covered them; and your eyes have seen what I did in Egypt. And ye dwelt in the desert a long season; and I brought you into the land of the Amorites, which dwelt on the other side of the Jordan; and they fought with you; and I gave them into your hand, that ye might possess their land; and I destroyed them from before you. Then Balak the son of Zippor, king of Moab, arose and warred against Israel, and sent and called Balaam the son of Beor to curse you: but I would not hearken unto Balaam; therefore he blessed you still: so I delivered you out of his hand.

And ye went over the Jordan, and came to Jericho, and the men of Jericho fought against you, the Amorites, and the Perizzites, and the Canaanites, and the Hittites, and the Girgashites, the Hivites, and the Jebusites; and I delivered them into your hand. And I sent the hornet before you, which drove them out from before you, *even* the two kings of the Amorites; *but* not with thy sword, nor with thy bow. And I have given you a land for which ye did not labour, and cities which ye built not, and ye dwell in them; of the vineyards and oliveyards which ye planted not, do ye eat.' Now therefore fear Jehovah, and serve him in sincerity and in truth: and put away the gods which your fathers served on the other side of the river, and in Egypt; and serve ye Jehovah. And if it seem evil to you to serve Jehovah, choose you this day whom you will serve; whether the gods which your fathers served, who *were* on the other side of the river, or the gods of the Amorites, in whose land ye dwell: but as for me and my house, we will serve Jehovah."

And the people answered and said, "Far be it from us that we should forsake Jehovah, to serve other gods; for Jehovah our God, he it is who brought us up, and our fathers, out of the land of Egypt, from the house of bondage, and who did those great signs in our sight, and preserved us in all the way wherein we went, and among all the people through whom we passed: and Jehovah drove out from before us all the peoples, even the Amorites who dwelt in the land: Jehovah we will serve; for he is our God."

And Joshua said to the people, "Ye cannot serve Jehovah, for he is a holy God; he is a jealous God; he will not forgive your transgressions nor your sins. When ye forsake Jehovah, and serve strange gods, then he will turn and do you hurt, and consume you, after that he hath done you good." And the people said to Joshua, "Nay, Jehovah we will serve." Then Joshua said to the people, "Ye are witnesses against yourselves that ye have chosen you Jehovah, to serve him." And they said, "*We are* witnesses." "Now therefore put away," *said he*, "the strange gods which are among you, and incline your heart to Jehovah God of Israel." And the people said to Joshua, "Jehovah our God will we serve, and his voice will we obey."

So Joshua made a covenant with the people that day, and appointed to them a statute and an ordinance in Shechem. And Joshua wrote these words in the book of the law of God. He then took a great stone, and set it up there under a terebinth tree, that was by the sanctuary of Jehovah. And Joshua said to all the people, "Lo, this stone shall be a testimony against us; for it hath heard all the words of Jehovah which he spake unto us: it shall be therefore a testimony against you, lest ye deny your God." So Joshua let the people depart, every man unto his inheritance.

And it came to pass after these things, that Joshua the son of Nun, the servant of Jehovah, died, *being* a hundred and ten years old. And they buried him in the territory of his inheritance in Timnath-serah, which is in mount Ephraim, on the north side of the hill of Gaash.

And Israel served Jehovah all the days of Joshua, and all the days of the elders that outlived Joshua, and who had known all the works of Jehovah, that he had done for Israel.

32 And the bones of Joseph, which the children of Israel had brought up out of Egypt, they buried in Shechem, in a parcel of ground which Jacob bought of the sons of Hamor, the father of Shechem, for a hundred pieces of silver; and it
33 became the inheritance of the children of Joseph. And Eleazar, the son of Aaron, died; and they buried him in the hill of Phinehas his son, which had been given to him in mount Ephraim.

THE BOOK OF JUDGES.

CHAP. I.—Now it came to pass after the death of 1 Joshua, that the children of Israel enquired of Jehovah, saying, "Who shall go up for us against the Canaanites first, to fight against them?" And Jehovah said, "Judah shall 2 go up: lo! I have delivered the land into his hand." Then 3 Judah said to Simeon his brother, "Come up with me into my lot, that we may fight against the Canaanites; and I likewise will go with thee into thy lot." So Simeon went with him. And Judah went up; and Jehovah delivered the 4 Canaanites and the Perizzites into their hand: and they slew of them in Bezek ten thousand men. And they found 5 Adoni-bezek in Bezek; and they fought against him, and they slew the Canaanites and the Perizzites. But Adoni- 6 bezek fled: and they pursued him, and caught him, and cut off his thumbs and his great toes. And Adoni-bezek said, 7 "Three-score and ten kings, having their thumbs and their great toes cut off, gathered *their meat* under my table: as I have done, so God hath requited me." And they brought him to Jerusalem, and there he died.

And the children of Judah fought against Jerusalem, and 8 took it, and smote it with the edge of the sword, and set the city on fire. And afterwards the children of Judah went 9 down to fight against the Canaanites, that dwelt in the mountainous country, and in the south, and in the lowland. And Judah went against the Canaanites that dwelt in 10 Hebron (now the name of Hebron before was Kirjath-arba), and they slew Sheshai, and Ahiman, and Talmai. And 11 thence he went against the inhabitants of Debir (now the name of Debir before *was* Kirjath-sepher): and Caleb said, 12 "He that smiteth Kirjath-sepher, and taketh it, to him will I give Achsah my daughter for a wife." And Othniel the son 13 of Kenaz, Caleb's younger brother, took it: and he gave

JUDGES I.

14 him Achsah his daughter for a wife. And when she came *to him*, she persuaded him to ask of her father a field: and she alighted from her ass; and Caleb said unto her,
15 "What wouldest thou?" And she said to him, "Give me a blessing: for thou hast given me a south land, give me also springs of water." And Caleb gave her the upper springs and the lower springs.
16 Now the children of the Kenite, the father-in-law of Moses, went up out of the city of palm-trees with the children of Judah into the wilderness of Judah, which is on the south of Arad: and they went and dwelt among the people.
17 And Judah went with Simeon his brother, and they slew the Canaanites that inhabited Zephath, and they devoted it *to destruction:* (And the name of the city was called Hormah
18 [THE DEVOTED CITY].) Also Judah took Gaza with its boundary, and Askelon with its boundary, and Ekron with its
19 boundary. And Jehovah was with Judah, and he drove out *the inhabitants of* the mountainous country, but could not drive out the inhabitants of the lowland, because they had
20 chariots of iron. And they gave Hebron to Caleb, as Moses
21 said: and he expelled thence the three sons of Anak. And the children of Benjamin did not drive out the Jebusites that inhabited Jerusalem; but the Jebusites dwell with the children
22 of Benjamin in Jerusalem unto this day. And the *house* of Joseph, they also went up against Beth-el: and Jehovah was
23 with them. And the *house* of Joseph sent to explore Beth-
24 el: (now the name of the city before was Luz.) And the spies saw a man coming out of the city; and they said to him, "Show us, we pray thee, the entrance into the city, and we
25 will deal kindly with thee." And he showed them the entrance into the city, and they smote the city with the edge of the sword; but they let go the man and all his family.
26 And the man went into the land of the Hittites, and built a city, and called the name thereof Luz: that is its name unto
27 this day. And Manasseh did not drive out *the inhabitants of* Beth-sheam and its towns, nor of Taanach and its towns, nor the inhabitants of Dor and its towns, nor the inhabitants of Ibleam and its towns, nor the inhabitants of Megiddo and its towns: for the Canaanite was content to dwell in
28 that land. And when the Israelites were strong, they put the Canaanites under tribute, and did not utterly drive them
29 out. And Ephraim did not drive out the Canaanites that dwelt in Gezer; but the Canaanites dwelt in Gezer among

them. Zebulun did not drive out the inhabitants of 30
Kitron, nor the inhabitants of Nahalol; but the Canaanites
dwelt among them, and became tributaries. Asher did 31
not drive out the inhabitants of Accho, nor the inhabitants
of Zidon, nor of Ahlab, nor of Achzib, nor of Helbah, nor
of Aphik, nor of Rehob; but the Asherites dwelt among 32
the Canaanites, the inhabitants of the land; for they did not
drive them out. Naphtali did not drive out the inhabit- 33
ants of Beth-shemesh, nor the inhabitants of Beth-anath;
but he dwelt among the Canaanites, the inhabitants of the
land: nevertheless the inhabitants of Beth-shemesh and
of Beth-anath became tributaries unto them. And the 34
Amorites forced the children of Dan into the mountainous
country: for they would not suffer them to cóme down to the
valley; but the Amorites were content to dwell in mount 35
Heres in Aijalon, and in Shaalbim; yet the hand of the
house of Joseph prevailed, so that they became tributaries.
And the boundary of the Amorites was from the going up to 36
Akrabbim, from Selah, and upward.

CHAP. II.—And a messenger of Jehovah came up from 1
Gilgal to Bochim, and said, "I brought you up out of Egypt,
and have brought you into the land which I sware to your
fathers; and I said, 'I will never break my covenant with
you.' But ye shall make no covenant with the inhabitants 2
of this land; ye shall throw down their altars: yet ye have
not obeyed my voice: why have ye done this? Wherefore 3
I also say, 'I will not drive them out from before you; but
they shall be *as thorns* in your sides, and their gods shall be
a snare unto you.'" And when the messenger of Jehovah 4
spake these words to all the children of Israel, the people
lifted up their voice, and wept. And they called the name 5
of that place Bochim [WEEPING] : and they sacrificed there
to Jehovah.

Now when Joshua had let the people go, the children of 6
Israel went every man to his inheritance to possess the land.
And the people served Jehovah all the days of Joshua, and 7
all the days of the elders that outlived Joshua, who had seen
all the great works of Jehovah, that he did for Israel. And 8
Joshua the son of Nun, the servant of Jehovah, died, *being* a
hundred and ten years old. And they buried him in the 9
boundary of his inheritance in Timnath-serah in the mount of
Ephraim, on the north side of the hill Gaash. And also all 10

that generation were gathered unto their fathers: and there arose another generation after them, which knew not Jeho-
11 vah, nor yet the works which he had done for Israel. And the children of Israel did evil in the sight of Jehovah, and
12 served Baalim; and forsook Jehovah God of their fathers, who brought them out of the land of Egypt, and followed other gods, of the gods of the peoples that were round about them, and bowed themselves down unto them, and provoked
13 Jehovah to anger. And they forsook Jehovah, and served
14 Baal and Ashtaroth. And the anger of Jehovah was kindled against the Israelites, and he delivered them into the hands of spoilers who spoiled them, and he sold them into the hands of their enemies round about, so that they could not any
15 longer stand before their enemies. Whithersoever they went out, the hand of Jehovah was against them for evil, as Jehovah had said, and as Jehovah had sworn to them: and
16 they were greatly distressed. Nevertheless Jehovah raised up Judges, who delivered them out of the hand of those
17 that spoiled them. And yet they would not hearken to their Judges, but they went astray after other gods, and bowed themselves down unto them: they turned quickly out of the way in which their fathers had walked, obeying the com-
18 mandments of Jehovah; *but* they did not so. And when Jehovah raised them up Judges, then Jehovah was with the Judge, and delivered them out of the hand of their enemies all the days of the Judge: for it repented Jehovah because of their groanings, by reason of those that oppressed them
19 and vexed them. And when the Judge was dead, they returned and became more corrupt than their fathers, in following other gods to serve them, and to bow down to them: they ceased not from their own doings, nor from their per-
20 verse way. So the anger of Jehovah was kindled against the Israelites; and he said, "Because this people hath transgressed my covenant which I commanded their fathers, and
21 have not hearkened to my voice, I also will not henceforth drive out from before them any one of the nations which
22 Joshua left when he died; that through them I may prove the Israelites, whether they will keep the way of Jehovah, to
23 walk therein, as their fathers kept it, or not." Therefore Jehovah left those nations, without driving them out hastily; neither delivered he them into the hand of Joshua.

1 CHAP. III.—Now these are the nations which Jehovah

left, by which to prove *the Israelites;* (as many *of them* as had not known all the wars of Canaan; only that the generations of the children of Israel might be taught to know war, at the least such as before knew nothing thereof;) *namely,* five lords of the Philistines, and all the Canaanites, and the Zidonians, and the Hivites that dwelt in mount Lebanon, from mount Baal-hermon unto the entering in of Hamath. And by these the Israelites were to be proved, that it might be known whether they would hearken to the commandments of Jehovah, which he commanded their fathers by the hand of Moses. So the children of Israel dwelt among the Canaanites, Hittites, and Amorites, and Perizzites, and Hivites, and Jebusites: and they took their daughters to be their wives, and gave their daughters to their sons, and served their gods. Thus the children of Israel did evil in the sight of Jehovah, and forgot Jehovah their God, and served Baalim and the *idols of the* groves. Therefore the anger of Jehovah was kindled against the Israelites, and he sold them into the hand of Chushan-rishathaim king of Mesopotamia; and the children of Israel served Chushan-rishathaim eight years. Then the children of Israel cried to Jehovah, and Jehovah raised up a deliverer to the children of Israel, who delivered them, Othniel the son of Kenaz, Caleb's younger brother. And the spirit of Jehovah came upon him, and he judged Israel, and went out to war: and Jehovah delivered Chushan-rishathaim king of Mesopotamia into his hand; and his hand prevailed against Chushan-rishathaim. And the land had rest forty years: and Othniel the son of Kenaz died.

And the children of Israel did evil again in the sight of Jehovah: and Jehovah strengthened Eglon the king of Moab against the Israelites, because they had done evil in the sight of Jehovah. And he gathered unto him the children of Ammon and Amalek, and went and smote Israel, and they took possession of the City of Palm-trees. So the children of Israel served Eglon the king of Moab eighteen years. But the children of Israel cried to Jehovah, and Jehovah raised up for them a deliverer, Ehud the son of Gera, a Benjaminite, a man left-handed: and by him the children of Israel sent a present to Eglon the king of Moab. Now Ehud had made him a dagger, which had two edges, of the length of a cubit: and he girded it under his raiment upon his right thigh. And he brought the present to Eglon king of Moab: (now

18 Eglon was a very fat man.) And when he had made an end of offering the present, he sent away the people that bare 19 the present. But he himself turned again from the quarries that were near Gilgal, and said, "I have a secret errand to thee, O king:" who said, "Keep silence." And all that 20 stood by him went out from him. Then Ehud came to him; and he was sitting in a summer chamber, which he had for himself, alone; and Ehud said, "I have a message from God 21 to thee," and he arose out of *his* seat. And Ehud put forth his left hand, and took the dagger from his right thigh, and 22 thrust it into his belly. And the haft also went in after the blade; and the fat closed upon the blade, so that he could not draw the dagger out of his belly; and the dirt came out. 23 Then Ehud went forth through the porch, and shut the 24 doors of the chamber upon him, and fastened them. When he was gone out, his servants came; and when they saw that, lo, the doors of the chamber were fastened, they said, 25 "Surely he covereth his feet in his summer chamber." And they waited till they were ashamed; and lo, he opened not the doors of the chamber: therefore they took a key and opened them: and lo, their lord was fallen down dead 26 on the ground. But Ehud had escaped while they were waiting, and passed beyond the quarries, and escaped unto 27 Seirath. And when he was come, he blew a trumpet in the mountain of Ephraim, and the children of Israel went down 28 with him from the mountain, and he before them. And he said to them, "Follow me; for Jehovah hath delivered your enemies the Moabites into your hand." And they went down after him, and took possession of the fords of the Jordan toward Moab, and suffered not a man to pass over. 29 And they slew of the Moabites at that time about ten thousand men, all strong, and all men of valour; and not 30 one escaped. So Moab was humbled that day under the hand of Israel. And the land had rest fourscore years. 31 And after him was Shamgar, the son of Anath, who slew of the Philistines six hundred men with an ox-goad: and he also delivered Israel.

1 CHAP. IV.—And the children of Israel again did evil in 2 the sight of Jehovah, when Ehud was dead. And Jehovah sold them into the hand of Jabin king of Canaan, who reigned in Hazor; the captain of whose host was Sisera, who dwelt 3 in Harosheth of the Nations. And the children of Israel

cried to Jehovah: for he had nine hundred chariots of iron: and he grievously oppressed the children of Israel during twenty years. And Deborah a prophetess, the wife of Lapi- 4 doth, judged Israel at that time. And she sat under the 5 palm-tree of Deborah, between Ramah and Beth-el in the mountain of Ephraim; and the children of Israel came up to her for judgment. And she sent and called Barak, the 6 son of Abinoam, out of Kedesh-Naphtali, and said to him, "Hath not Jehovah God of Israel commanded, *saying*, ' Go, and draw toward mount Tabor, and take with thee ten thousand men of the children of Naphtali and of the children of Zebulun; and I will draw unto thee, to the 7 torrent Kishon, Sisera, the captain of Jabin's army, with his chariots and his multitude; and I will deliver him into thy hand?'" And Barak said to her, "If thou wilt go 8 with me, then I will go; but if thou wilt not go with me, I will not go." And she said, "I will surely go with thee: 9 yet the honour shall not be thine for the way that thou goest; for Jehovah will sell Sisera into the hand of a woman." And Deborah arose, and went with Barak to Kedesh.

And Barak called Zebulun and Naphtali to Kedesh; and he 10 went up with ten thousand men following him: and Deborah went up with him. (Now Heber the Kenite, *who* was of the 11 children of Hobab, the father-in-law of Moses, had separated himself from the Kenites, and pitched his tent at the terebinth tree of Zaanaim, which is by Kedesh.) And it 12 was told to Sisera that Barak, the son of Abinoam, was gone up to mount Tabor. Then Sisera gathered together all his 13 chariots, nine hundred chariots of iron, and all the people that were with him, from Harosheth of the Nations unto the torrent Kishon. And Deborah said to Barak, "Arise; for 14 this is the day, in which Jehovah hath delivered Sisera into thy hand: is not Jehovah gone out before thee?" So Barak went down from mount Tabor, and ten thousand men after him. And Jehovah confounded Sisera, and all his 15 chariots, and all his host with the edge of the sword, before Barak; so that Sisera alighted from his chariot, and fled on foot. But Barak pursued after the chariots, and after the 16 host, unto Harosheth of the Nations: and all the host of Sisera fell by the edge of the sword; not even one was left. But Sisera fled on foot to the tent of Jael the wife of 17 Heber the Kenite: for there was peace between Jabin the king of Hazor and the house of Heber the Kenite. And 18

Jael went out to meet Sisera, and said to him, "Turn in, my lord, turn in to me; fear not:" and when he had turned
19 in to her into the tent, she covered him with a mantle. And he said to her, "Give me, I pray thee, a little water to drink; for I am thirsty:" and she opened the bottle of milk, and
20 gave him drink, and covered him. Again he said to her, "Stand in the door of the tent; and if any one should come and inquire of thee, and say, 'Is there any man here?' thou
21 shalt say, No one." Then Jael, the wife of Heber, took the tent-pin, and took the hammer in her hand, and went softly unto him, and smote the pin into his temples, and fastened it into the ground; (for he was fast asleep, and weary:) so
22 he died. And, lo, as Barak pursued Sisera, Jael came out to meet him, and said to him, "Come, and I will shew thee the man whom thou art seeking." And when he came in to her *tent,* lo, Sisera lay dead, and the pin was in his tem-
23 ples. So God subdued on that day Jabin the king of Ca-
24 naan before the children of Israel. And the hand of the children of Israel prospered, and continued to prevail against Jabin the king of Canaan, until they had destroyed Jabin king of Canaan.

1 CHAP. V.—Then sang Deborah and Barak, the son of Abinoam, on that day, saying,

2 "For the chieftainship of the chiefs in Israel,
For the willing self-offering of the people,
Praise ye Jehovah!
3 Hear, ye kings; listen, ye princes:
I, *even* I, will sing to Jehovah;
I will sing with an instrument to Jehovah God of Israel.

4 O Jehovah, when thou wentest forth from Seir,
When thou marchedst forth from the field of Edom,
The earth trembled,
The heavens also dropped,
The clouds also dropped water.
5 The mountains melted at the presence of Jehovah,
This Sinai at the presence of Jehovah, God of Israel.

6 In the days of Shamgar son of Anath,
In the days of Jael, deserted were the highways,
And travellers went through by-paths.

Rulers had ceased in Israel, they had ceased, 7
Till I Deborah arose,
Till I arose, a mother in Israel.
They had chosen for themselves new gods; 8
Then was there war at the gates.
Was a shield or a spear to be seen,
Among forty thousand *men* in Israel?
My heart is toward the leaders of Israel, 9
Who offered themselves willingly among the people.
Praise ye Jehovah!
Ye who ride on dappled she-asses, 10
Ye who sit on carpets,
And ye who walk on the road, sing!
Without the noise of archers at the watering places. 11
There shall they acknowledge the righteous acts of Jehovah,
The righteous acts of his rulers in Israel.
Then went down to the gates the people of Jehovah.

Awake, awake, Deborah; 12
Awake, awake, utter a song!
Arise, Barak,
And lead captive thy prisoners, son of Abinoam!

Then came down a remnant against the powerful; 13
The people of Jehovah came down to me against the mighty;
From Ephraim whose root is in Amalek; 14
After thee, Benjamin, among thy people.
From Machir came down leaders,
And from Zebulun they who hold the staff of the commander.
The princes also of Issachar were with Deborah; 15
And as Issachar, so Barak:
He rushed into the valley on foot.
At the brooks of Reuben great were the deliberations: 16
Why didst thou abide within the sheepfolds,
To listen to the bleatings of the flocks?
At the brooks of Reuben great were the deliberations.
Gilead abode beyond the Jordan: 17
And Dan, why did he remain among the ships?
Asher sat still on the sea-shore,
And abode among his harbours.

18   Zebulun was the people that jeoparded its life unto the death;
    And Naphtali in the high places of the field.

19   Kings came, they fought;
    Then fought the kings of Canaan,
    At Taanach by the waters of Megiddo.
    A fragment of silver they took not away.
20   From the heavens fought the stars,
    From their courses they fought against Sisera.
21   The torrent Kishon carried them away;
    That torrent of ancient times, the torrent Kishon.

    My soul, go on thy way with strength.

22   Then stamped the hoofs of the horses
    In the wheelings, the wheelings of their mighty ones.
23   'Curse ye Meroz,' saith the messenger of Jehovah,
    'Bitterly curse ye its inhabitants;
    Because they came not to the aid of Jehovah,
    To the aid of Jehovah among the mighty.'
24   Blessed above *all* women be Jael,
    The wife of Heber the Kenite;
    Above *all* women dwelling in tents be she blessed.
    Water he asked for, milk she gave;
25   In a noble bowl she brought forth curdled milk.
    She put forth her hand to the tent-pin,
26   And her right hand to the workman's hammer,
    And she smote Sisera with the hammer; she shattered his head,
    And she struck and pierced his temples.
27   Between her feet he bowed, he fell, he lay down;
    Between her feet he bowed, he fell;
    Where he bowed he fell, struck dead.

28   Through a window looked forth the mother of Sisera,
    And exclaimed through a lattice,
    'Why delayeth his chariot to come?
    Why tarry the wheels of his chariots?'
29   The wisest of her ladies answered her,
    Yea, she returned answer to herself:
30   'Have they not prevailed? *Are they not* dividing the spoil;

D D

A damsel, two damsels for every mighty man?
A spoil of various colours for Sisera,
A spoil of various colours of embroidery,
Of various colours, of double embroidery,
For the neck of him who taketh the spoil.'

So perish all thy enemies, O Jehovah! 31
But may they who love him be as the going forth of the sun in his might!" And the land had rest forty years.

CHAP. VI.—And the children of Israel did evil in the sight 1 of Jehovah; and Jehovah delivered them into the hand of the Midianites seven years. And the hand of the Midianites pre- 2 vailed against Israel: *and* because of the Midianites the children of Israel made for themselves the dens which are in the mountains, and caves, and strong holds. And *so* it was when 3 the Israelites had sown, the Midianites came up, with the Amalekites, and the children of the east, even these came up against them; and they encamped against them, and de- 4 stroyed the produce of the land, till thou come unto Gaza; and left no sustenance for the Israelites, neither sheep, nor oxen, nor asses. For they came up with their cattle, and 5 their tents, and they came as locusts for multitude: both they and their camels were without number; and they entered into the land to lay it waste. And the Israelites 6 were greatly impoverished by the Midianites; and the children of Israel cried to Jehovah. And when the children of 7 Israel cried to Jehovah because of the Midianites, Jehovah 8 sent a prophet to the children of Israel, who said to them, "Thus saith Jehovah God of Israel, 'I brought you up from Egypt, and brought you forth out of the house of bondage; and I delivered you out of the hand of the Egyptians, and 9 out of the hand of all that oppressed you, and drove them out from before you, and gave you their land: and I said to you, 10 I am Jehovah your God: fear not the gods of the Amorites, in whose land ye dwell: but ye have not obeyed my voice.'"

And there came an angel of Jehovah, and sat under the 11 terebinth tree which was in Ophrah, that belonged to Joash the Abi-ezrite: now Gideon his son was threshing wheat in the wine-press, to hide it from the Midianites. And the 12 angel of Jehovah appeared to him, and said to him, "Jehovah is with thee, thou mighty man of valour." And Gideon 13 said to him, "Oh, my Lord, if Jehovah be with us, why then

hath all this befallen us? and where are all his wonders
which our fathers told us of, saying, 'Did not Jehovah
bring us up from Egypt?' but now Jehovah hath forsaken
us, and delivered us into the hands of the Midianites."
14 And Jehovah looked upon him, and said, "Go in this thy
might, and thou shalt save Israel from the hand of the Mi-
15 dianites: have not I sent thee?" And he said unto him,
"Oh, my Lord, wherewith shall I save Israel? Lo, my
family is the poorest in Manasseh, and I am the least in my
16 father's house." And Jehovah said to him, "Surely I will
be with thee, and thou shalt smite the Midianites as one
17 man." And he said to him, "If now I have found favour
in thy sight, then show me a sign that thou talkest with me.
18 Depart not hence, I pray thee, until I come to thee, and
bring forth my present, and set it before thee." And he
19 said, "I will tarry until thou come again." And Gideon
went in, and made ready a kid, and unleavened cakes of an
ephah of flour: the flesh he put in a basket, and he put the
broth in a pot, and brought it out to him under the terebinth
20 tree, and presented it. And the angel of God said to him,
"Take the flesh and the unleavened cakes, and lay them
upon this rock, and pour out the broth." And he did so.
21 Then the angel of Jehovah put forth the end of the staff
that was in his hand, and touched the flesh and the unleavened cakes; and fire rose up out of the rock, and consumed
the flesh and the unleavened cakes. Then the angel of
22 Jehovah departed out of his sight. And when Gideon perceived that he was an angel of Jehovah, Gideon said, "Alas,
O Lord Jehovah! because I have seen an angel of Jehovah
23 face to face." And Jehovah said to him, "Peace be to thee;
24 fear not: thou shalt not die." Then Gideon built an altar
there to Jehovah, and called it Jehovah-shalom [JEHOVAH IS
PEACE]: unto this day it is yet in Ophrah of the Abi-ezrites.
25 And the same night Jehovah said to him, "Take thy father's
young bullock, and a second bullock seven years old, and
throw down the altar of Baal that thy father hath, and cut
26 down the grove that is by it; and build an altar to Jehovah
thy God upon the top of this rock, in the ordered manner,
and take the second bullock, and offer a burnt sacrifice with
27 the wood of the grove which thou shalt cut down." Then
Gideon took ten men of his servants, and did as Jehovah had
said to him: but because he feared his father's household, and
the men of the city, he could not do it by day, so he did it

by night. And when the men of the city arose early in the morning, lo, the altar of Baal was cast down, and the grove was cut down that was by it, and the second bullock was offered upon the altar that was built. And they said one to another, "Who hath done this thing?" And when they inquired and asked, they said, "Gideon the son of Joash hath done this thing." Then the men of the city said to Joash, "Bring out thy son, that he may die; because he hath cast down the altar of Baal, and because he hath cut down the grove that was by it." And Joash said to all that stood before him, "Will ye contend for Baal? will ye save him? he that will contend for him, let him be put to death whilst it is yet morning: if he be a god, let him contend for himself, because he hath cast down his altar." Therefore on that day he was called Jerubbaal [LET BAAL CONTEND], when it was said, "Let Baal contend against him, because he hath thrown down his altar."

Then all the Midianites, and the Amalekites, and the children of the east, were gathered together, and went over, and encamped in the valley of Jezreel. But the Spirit of Jehovah came upon Gideon, and he blew a trumpet; and the Abi-ezrites mustered after him. And he sent messengers throughout all Manasseh, who also mustered after him; and he sent messengers to Asher, and to Zebulun, and to Naphtali; and they came up to meet them. Now Gideon had said to God, "If thou wilt save Israel by my hand, as thou hast said, lo, I will put a fleece of wool on the threshing-floor; if the dew be on the fleece only, and it be dry upon all the ground *beside*, then shall I know that thou wilt save Israel by my hand, as thou hast said." And it was so: for he rose up early on the morrow, and pressed the fleece together, and wrung the dew out of the fleece, a bowl-full of water. And Gideon said to God, "Let not thy anger be kindled against me, and I will speak but this once. Let me try, I pray thee, but this once with the fleece; let it now be dry only upon the fleece, and upon all the ground let there be dew." And God did so that night: for it was dry upon the fleece only, and there was dew on all the ground.

CHAP. VII.—Then Jerubbaal (who is Gideon), and all the people that were with him, rose up early, and encamped beside the well of Harod: and the host of the Midianites

were on the north side of them, by the hill of Moreh, in the
2 valley. And Jehovah said to Gideon, "The people that are with thee are too many for me to give the Midianites into their hands, lest the Israelites vaunt themselves against me,
3 saying, 'My own hand hath saved me.' Now, therefore, proclaim in the ears of the people, saying, 'Whosoever is fearful and trembling, let him return, and depart early from mount Gilead.'" And there returned of the people twenty and
4 two thousand, and there remained ten thousand. And Jehovah said to Gideon, "The people are yet *too* many; bring them down to the water, and I will prove them for thee there: and it shall be, that of whom I shall say to thee, 'This shall go with thee,' he shall go with thee; and of whomsoever I say to thee, 'This shall not go with thee,' he
5 shall not go." So he brought down the people to the water: and Jehovah said to Gideon, "Every one that lappeth of the water with his tongue, as a dog lappeth, him shalt thou set by himself; and every one that boweth down upon his knees
6 to drink." And the number of them that lapped, with their hand to their mouth, were three hundred men: but all the rest of the people bowed down upon their knees to drink
7 water. And Jehovah said to Gideon, "By the three hundred men that lapped will I save you, and deliver the Midianites into thy hand; and let all the *other* people go each man to his own place."
8 So the people took victuals in their hand, and their trumpets; and he sent all *the rest of* the Israelites each man to his tent, and retained those three hundred men. And the host
9 of Midian was below him in the valley. And the same night, Jehovah said to him, "Arise, go down into the camp; for I
10 have delivered it into thy hand. But if thou fear to go down, go thou with Phurah thy servant down to the camp,
11 and thou shalt hear what they say; and afterward shall thy hands be strengthened to go down to the camp." So he went down with Phurah his servant to the outermost of the
12 armed men that were in the camp. And the Midianites, and the Amalekites, and all the children of the east, lay along in the valley like locusts for multitude; and their camels were without number, as the sand by the sea-side for multi-
13 tude. And when Gideon was come, lo, a man was telling a dream to his companion, and he said, "Lo, I dreamed a dream, and, lo, a cake of barley-bread rolled through the camp of the Midianites, and came to the tent, and struck it

so that it fell, and overturned it, so that the tent lay along." And his companion answered and said, "This is nothing 14 else but the sword of Gideon the son of Joash, a man of Israel: into his hand hath God delivered the Midianites, and all the camp." And when Gideon heard the telling of 15 the dream, and the interpretation thereof, he bowed himself down, and returned into the camp of the Israelites, and said, "Arise, for Jehovah hath delivered into your hand the camp of the Midianites." And he divided the three hundred 16 men into three companies, and he put a trumpet into every man's hand, with empty pitchers, and torches within the pitchers; and he said to them, "Look on me, and do like- 17 wise: and, lo, when I come to the outside of the camp, as I do, so do ye. When I blow with a trumpet, I and all that 18 are with me, then blow ye the trumpets also on every side of all the camp, and say, 'For Jehovah, and for Gideon.'"

So Gideon, and the hundred men that were with him, 19 came to the outside of the camp, in the beginning of the middle watch; (for they had but newly set the watch:) and they blew the trumpets, and brake the pitchers that were in their hands. And the three companies blew the trumpets, 20 and brake the pitchers, and held the torches in their left hands, and the trumpets in their right hands to blow with; and they cried, "The sword of Jehovah and of Gideon." And they stood every man in his place round about the 21 camp: and all the host ran, and cried, and fled.

And the three hundred blew the trumpets, and Jehovah 22 set every man's sword against his fellow, even throughout the whole camp: and the host fled to Beth-shaittah in Zererath, *and* to the border of Abel-meholah, at Tabbath. Then the men of Israel gathered themselves 23 together out of Naphtali, and out of Asher, and out of all Manasseh, and pursued the Midianites. And Gideon sent 24 messengers throughout all Mount Ephraim, saying, "Come down against the Midianites, and take possession before them of the waters unto Beth-barah and the Jordan." Then all the men of Ephraim gathered themselves together, and took possession of the waters unto Beth-barah and the Jordan. And they took two princes of the Midianites, 25 Oreb and Zeeb; and they slew Oreb upon the rock Oreb, and Zeeb they slew at the wine-press of Zeeb, and pursued the Midianites, and brought the heads of Oreb and Zeeb to Gideon beyond the Jordan.

JUDGES VIII.

1 CHAP. VIII.—And the men of Ephraim said to him, "What is this which thou hast done to us, that thou calledst us not when thou wentest to fight with the Midianites?" And
2 they rebuked him sharply. And he said to them, "What have I done now in comparison of you? Is not the gleaning of the grapes of Ephraim better than the vintage of
3 Abi-ezer? God hath delivered into your hands the princes of Midian, Oreb and Zeeb: and what have I been able to do in comparison of you?" Then their anger was abated toward him, when he had said that.
4 And Gideon came to the Jordan, *and* passed over, he, and the three hundred men that were with him, faint, yet
5 pursuing. And he said to the men of Succoth, "Give, I pray you, loaves of bread to the people that follow me; for they are faint, and I am pursuing after Zebah and
6 Zalmunna, kings of Midian." But the princes of Succoth said, "Are the hands of Zebah and Zalmunna now in thy
7 hand, that we should give bread to thy army?" And Gideon said, "Therefore, when Jehovah shall have delivered Zebah and Zalmunna into my hand, then I will tear your flesh with the thorns of the desert and with briers."
8 And he went up thence to Penuel, and spake to them in the same manner: and the men of Penuel answered him as
9 the men of Succoth had answered. And he spake also to the men of Penuel, saying, "When I come again in peace, I will break down this tower."
10 Now Zebah and Zalmunna were in Karkor, and their hosts with them, about fifteen thousand men, all that were left of the entire hosts of the children of the east: for there had fallen one hundred and twenty thousand men that drew
11 the sword. And Gideon went up by the way of them that dwelt in tents, on the east of Nobah and Jogbehah, and smote the host; for the host thought themselves secure.
12 And Zebah and Zalmunna fled, and he pursued them, and took the two kings of Midian, Zebah and Zalmunna,
13 and discomfited all the host. And Gideon, the son of Joash,
14 returned from battle, from the ascent of Heres, and he caught a young man of the men of Succoth, and inquired of him: and he wrote down for him the princes of Succoth,
15 and its elders, threescore and seventeen men. And he came to the men of Succoth, and said, "Lo, Zebah and Zalmunna, concerning whom ye did upbraid me, saying, 'Are the hands of Zebah and Zalmunna now in thy hand,

that we should give bread to thy men who are weary?'"
And he took the elders of the city, and thorns of the desert 16
and briers, and with them he chastised the men of Succoth.
And he beat down the tower of Penuel, and slew the men 17
of the city. Then said he to Zebah and Zalmunna, "What 18
sort of men were they whom ye slew at Tabor?" And
they answered, "As thou art, so were they; each of them
resembled the children of a king." And he said, "They 19
were my brethren, the sons of my mother: *as* Jehovah
liveth, if ye had saved them alive, I would not slay you."
And he said to Jether his first-born son, "Rise up, slay 20
them:" but the youth drew not his sword; for he was
afraid, because he was yet a youth. Then Zebah and Zal- 21
munna said, "Rise thou, and fall upon us: for as the man
is, so is his strength." And Gideon arose, and slew Zebah
and Zalmunna, and took away the ornaments that were on
their camels' necks.

Then the men of Israel said to Gideon, "Rule thou over us, 22
both thou and thy son, and thy son's son also; since thou
hast delivered us from the hand of the Midianites." But 23
Gideon said to them, "I will not rule over you, neither shall
my son rule over you: Jehovah shall rule over you." And 24
Gideon said to them, "I would desire a request of you, that
ye would give me every man the ear-rings of his booty:"
(for they had golden ear-rings, because they were Ishmaelites.)
And they answered, "We will willingly give them." And 25
they spread a garment, and cast therein every man the
ear-rings of his booty. And the weight of the golden ear- 26
rings that he requested was a thousand and seven hundred
shekels of gold; beside ornaments, and collars, and purple
raiment that was on the kings of Midian, and beside the
chains that were about their camels' necks. And Gideon 27
made an ephod thereof, and put it in his city, in Ophrah;
and all Israel went astray thither after it: and it was a snare
to Gideon, and to his house. Thus were the Midianites sub- 28
dued before the children of Israel, so that they lifted up
their heads no more. And the land had rest forty years in
the days of Gideon.

And Jerubbaal, the son of Joash, went and dwelt in his 29
own house. And Gideon had seventy sons who came from 30
his loins: for he had many wives. And his concubine also, 31
who was in Shechem, bore to him a son, whose name he
called Abimelech. And Gideon, the son of Joash, died in 32

a good old age, and was buried in the sepulchre of Joash his father, in Ophrah of the Abi-ezrites.

33 And it came to pass, as soon as Gideon was dead, that the children of Israel turned again, and went astray after Baalim,
34 and made Baal-berith their god. And the children of Israel remembered not Jehovah their God, who had delivered them
35 out of the hands of all their enemies on every side: neither shewed they kindness to the house of Jerubbaal, namely, Gideon, according to all the goodness which he had shewed to Israel.

1 CHAP. IX.—And Abimelech, the son of Jerubbaal, went to Shechem to his mother's brethren, and spoke with them, and with all the family of the house of his mother's father,
2 saying, "Speak, I pray you, in the ears of all the men of Shechem, 'Which is better for you, that all the sons of Jerubbaal, seventy persons, reign over you, or that one reign over you?' remember also that I am your bone and
3 your flesh." And his mother's brethren spake of him in the ears of all the men of Shechem all these words: and their hearts inclined to follow Abimelech; for they said,
4 "He *is* our brother." And they gave him seventy *pieces* of silver out of the house of Baal-berith; with which Abime-
5 lech hired vain and light persons, who followed him. And he went to his father's house at Ophrah, and slew his brethren, the son of Jerubbaal, *being* seventy persons, upon one stone: but Jotham, the youngest son of Jerubbaal, remained; for he had hidden himself.
6 And all the men of Shechem gathered together, and all the house of Millo, and went and made Abimelech king, by the terebinth tree by the pillar that was near Shechem.
7 And when they told it to Jotham, he went and stood on the top of mount Gerizim, and lifted up his voice, and cried, and said to them, "Hearken to me, ye men of Shechem, that
8 God may hearken to you. The trees went forth to anoint a king over them: and they said to the olive-tree, 'Reign
9 thou over us.' But the olive-tree said to them, 'Shall I forego my richness, wherewith by me they honour God
10 and man, and go to bear sway over the trees?' Then the trees said to the fig-tree, 'Come thou *and* reign over us.'
11 But the fig-tree said to them, 'Shall I forego my sweetness, and my good fruit, and go to bear sway over the trees?'
12 Then said the trees to the vine, 'Come thou, *and* reign

over us.' And the vine said to them, 'Shall I forego my 13 wine, which cheereth God and man, and go to bear sway over the trees?' Then said all the trees to the bramble, 14 'Come thou, *and* reign over us.' And the bramble said to 15 the trees, 'If in truth ye anoint me king over you, come *and* put your trust in my shade; but if not, fire shall come out of the bramble, and devour the cedars of Lebanon.' Now therefore, if ye have done truly and sincerely in that 16 ye have made Abimelech king, and if ye have dealt well toward Jerubbaal and his house, and have done to him according to the deserving of his hands; (for my father fought 17 for you, and adventured his life without reserve, and delivered you out of the hand of the Midianites; and ye are risen up 18 against my father's house this day, and have slain his sons, seventy persons, upon one stone, and have made Abimelech, the son of his maid-servant, king over the men of Shechem, because he *is* your brother;) if then ye have dealt truly and 19 sincerely with Jerubbaal and with his house this day, *then* rejoice ye in Abimelech, and let him also rejoice in you; but if not, fire shall come out from Abimelech, and devour 20 the men of Shechem, and the house of Millo; and fire shall come out from the men of Shechem, and from the house of Millo, and devour Abimelech." Then Jotham fled speedily, 21 and went to Beer, and dwelt there, for fear of Abimelech his brother.

When Abimelech had reigned three years over Israel, 22 then God sent an evil spirit between Abimelech and the men 23 of Shechem; and the men of Shechem dealt treacherously with Abimelech; that the violence *done* to the seventy sons 24 of Jerubbaal might come, and their blood be laid upon Abimelech their brother, who slew them; and upon the men of Shechem, who had aided him in the killing of his brethren. So the men of Shechem set liers in wait for him 25 on the top of the mountains, and they robbed all that came along that way by them; and it was told Abimelech. And 26 Gaal, the son of Ebed, came with his brethren, and went over to Shechem: and the men of Shechem put their confidence in him. And they went out into the fields, and 27 gathered their vineyards, and trod out *the grapes*, and made merry, and went into the house of their god, and ate and drank, and cursed Abimelech. And Gaal, the son of Ebed, 28 said, "Who is Abimelech, and who is Shechem, that we should serve him? Is not he the son of Jerubbaal? and

Zebul his officer? Serve ye the men of Hamor, the father
29 of Shechem; for why should we serve him? And oh that
this people were under my hand! then would I remove
Abimelech." And he said to Abimelech, "Increase thy
30 army, and come out." And when Zebul, the ruler of the
city, heard the words of Gaal, the son of Ebed, his anger
31 was kindled. And he sent messengers to Abimelech,
secretly, saying, "Lo, Gaal the son of Ebed, and his
brethren, are come to Shechem; and, lo, they are fortifying
32 the city against thee. Now, therefore, rise up by night,
thou and the people that is with thee, and lie in wait in the
33 field: and in the morning, as soon as the sun is up, thou
shalt rise early and attack the city: and, lo, *when* he
and the people that is with him come out against thee, then
34 mayest thou do to them as thou shalt find occasion." And
Abimelech rose up, and all the people that were with him,
by night, and they laid wait against Shechem in four com-
35 panies. And Gaal, the son of Ebed, went out and stood in
the entering of the gate of the city; and Abimelech rose
up, and the people that were with him, from lying in wait.
36 And when Gaal saw the people, he said to Zebul, "Lo,
people are coming down from the top of the mountains."
And Zebul said to him, "Thou seest the shadow of the
37 mountains as *if they were* men." But Gaal spake again, and
said, "Lo, people are coming down from the summit of the
land, and another company is coming by the terebinth tree
38 of Meonenim." Then said Zebul to him, "Where is now
thy mouth, with the speech which thou saidst, 'Who is Abimelech, that we should serve him?'. Is not this the people that
thou hast despised? go out, I pray *thee* now, and fight with
39 them." And Gaal went out before the men of Shechem,
40 and fought with Abimelech. And Abimelech pursued him,
and he fled before him; and many fell slain, unto the entering
41 of the gate. And Abimelech remained at Arumah: and
Zebul thrust out Gaal and his brethren, that they should
42 not dwell in Shechem. But on the morrow the people went
43 out into the field; and it was told to Abimelech. And he
took the people, and divided them into three companies, and
laid wait in the field, and looked, and, lo, the people were
come forth out of the city; and he rose up against them, and
44 smote them. And Abimelech, and the company that was
with him, rushed forward, and stood in the entering of the
gate of the city: and the two *other* companies ran upon all

who were in the fields and slew them. And Abimelech 45 fought against the city all that day: and he took the city, and slew the people that were therein, and beat down the city, and sowed it with salt.

And when all the men of the tower of Shechem heard 46 that, they entered into a hold of the house of the god Berith. And it was told to Abimelech that all the men of the tower 47 of Shechem were gathered together. And Abimelech went 48 up to mount Zalmon, he and all the people that were with him; and Abimelech took an axe in his hand, and cut down a bough from the trees, and took it, and laid *it* on his shoulder, and said to the people that were with him, "What ye have seen me do, make haste, do as I *have done*." And all the people likewise cut down every man his bough, 49 and followed Abimelech, and put *them* to the hold, and set the hold on fire upon them; so that all the men of the tower of Shechem died also, about a thousand men and women.

Then went Abimelech to Thebez, and encamped against 50 Thebez, and took it. But there was a strong tower within 51 the city, and thither fled all the men and women, and all those of the city, and shut it upon themselves, and went up to the top of the tower. And Abimelech came to the tower 52 and fought against it, and went near to the door of the tower to burn it with fire. And a certain woman cast a 53 piece of a millstone upon Abimelech's head, and shattered his scull. Then he called hastily to the young man his 54 armour-bearer, and said to him, "Draw thy sword, and slay me, that men say not of me, 'A woman slew him.'" And his young man thrust him through, and he died. And when 55 the men of Israel saw that Abimelech was dead, they departed every man to his place. Thus God requited the 56 wickedness of Abimelech, which he did to his father, in slaying his seventy brethren; and all the wickedness of 57 the men of Shechem did God requite upon their heads: and upon them came the curse of Jotham the son of Jerubbaal.

CHAP. X.—And after Abimelech there arose, to defend 1 Israel, Tola the son of Puah, the son of Dodo, a man of Issachar; and he dwelt in Shamir in mount Ephraim. And he judged Israel twenty-three years, and died, and was 2 buried in Shamir.

3 And after him arose Jair a Gileadite, and judged Israel
4 twenty-two years. And he had thirty sons that rode on thirty young asses, and they had thirty cities, which are called Havoth-jair [THE VILLAGES OF JAIR] unto this day,
5 which *are* in the land of Gilead. And Jair died, and was buried in Camon.
6 And the children of Israel did evil again in the sight of Jehovah, and served Baalim, and Ashtaroth, and the gods of Syria, and the gods of Zidon, and the gods of Moab, and the gods of the children of Ammon, and the gods of the
7 Philistines, and forsook Jehovah, and served not him. And the anger of Jehovah was kindled against Israel, and he sold them into the hands of the Philistines, and into the hands of
8 the children of Ammon. And that year they vexed and oppressed the children of Israel; eighteen years *they vexed* all the children of Israel that were beyond the Jordan, in the land
9 of the Amorites, which is in Gilead; moreover, the children of Ammon passed over the Jordan to fight also against Judah, and against Benjamin, and against the house of Ephraim;
10 so that Israel was greatly distressed. And the children of Israel cried to Jehovah, saying, "We have sinned against thee, because we have forsaken our God, and also served
11 Baalim." And Jehovah said to the children of Israel, "Did not I *deliver you* from the Egyptians, and from the Amorites, from the children of Ammon, and from the Philistines?
12 The Zidonians also, and the Amalekites, and the Maonites, oppressed you; and ye cried to me, and I delivered you out
13 of their hand. Yet ye have forsaken me, and served other
14 gods: wherefore I will deliver you no more. Go and cry to the gods whom ye have chosen; let them deliver you in
15 the time of your distress." And the children of Israel said to Jehovah, "We have sinned; do thou unto us whatsoever seemeth good unto thee; deliver us only, we pray thee, this
16 day." And they put away the strange gods from among them, and served Jehovah; and his soul was grieved for the misery of Israel.
17 Then the children of Ammon were gathered together, and encamped in Gilead; and the children of Israel assembled
18 themselves together, and encamped in Mizpeh. And the people and princes of Gilead said one to another, "Who is the man that will begin to fight against the children of Ammon? he shall be chief over all the inhabitants of Gilead."

CHAP. XI.—Now Jephthah the Gileadite was a mighty 1 man of valour, and he *was* the son of a harlot: and Gilead begat Jephthah. And Gilead's wife bare him sons; and 2 when his wife's sons were grown up, they thrust out Jephthah, and said to him, "Thou shalt not inherit in our father's house; for thou art the son of a strange woman." So 3 Jephthah fled from his brethren, and dwelt in the land of Tob; and there were gathered idle men to Jephthah, and went out with him. And in process of time, the children of 4 Ammon made war against the Israelites. And when the 5 children of Ammon made war against the Israelites, the elders of Gilead went to fetch Jephthah out of the land of Tob; and they said to Jephthah, " Come, and be our captain, 6 that we may fight with the children of Ammon." And 7 Jephthah said to the elders of Gilead, "Did ye not hate me, and expel me out of my father's house? and why are ye come to me now when ye are in distress?" And the elders 8 of Gilead said to Jephthah, " Therefore we turn to thee now, that thou mayest go with us, and fight against the children of Ammon, and be our chief over all the inhabitants of Gilead." And Jephthah said to the elders of Gilead, " If 9 ye bring me home again to fight against the children of Ammon, and Jehovah deliver them before me, shall I be your chief?" And the elders of Gilead said to Jephthah, "Je- 10 hovah be witness between us, if we do not so according to thy words." Then Jephthah went with the elders of Gilead, 11 and the people made him chief and captain over them: and Jephthah uttered all his words before Jehovah in Mizpeh.

And Jephthah sent messengers to the king of the children 12 of Ammon, saying, "What hast thou to do with me, that thou art come against me to fight in my land?" And the king 13 of the children of Ammon answered the messengers of Jephthah, "Because the Israelites took away my lands when they came up out of Egypt, from the Arnon even unto the Jabbok, and unto the Jordan: now, therefore, restore those *lands* again peaceably." And Jephthah sent messengers again 14 to the king of the children of Ammon, and said to him, 15 " Thus saith Jephthah, the Israelites took not away the land of Moab, nor the land of the children of Ammon: but 16 when the Israelites came up from Egypt, and walked through the desert unto the Red Sea, and came to Kadesh; then 17 the Israelites sent messengers to the king of Edom, saying, ' Let us, we pray thee, pass through thy land:' but the

king of Edom would not hearken *to them.* And they sent
also to the king of Moab; but he would not *hearken to them:*
18 so the Israelites abode in Kadesh. Then they went along
through the desert, and compassed the land of Edom and
the land of Moab, and came by the east side of the land of
Moab, and encamped on the other side of the Arnon, but
came not within the boundary of Moab: for the Arnon *was*
19 the boundary of Moab. And the Israelites sent messengers
to Sihon king of the Amorites, the king of Heshbon; and
the Israelites said to him, 'Let us pass, we pray thee,
20 through thy land unto our own place.' But Sihon would
not trust the Israelites to pass through his coast; but Sihon
gathered all his people together, and encamped in Jahaz, and
21 fought against the Israelites. And Jehovah, God of Israel,
delivered Sihon and all his people into the hand of the
Israelites, and they smote them: so the Israelites took possession of all the land of the Amorites, the inhabitants of
22 that country. And they took possession of all the boundaries
of the Amorites, from the Arnon even unto the Jabbok, and
23 from the desert even unto the Jordan. So now Jehovah
God of Israel hath dispossessed the Amorites from before
his people the Israelites, and shouldest thou take possession
24 of it? Wilt not thou possess that which Chemosh thy god
hath given thee to possess? So whomsoever Jehovah our
God shall drive out from before us, them will we possess.
25 And now, art thou anything better than Balak the son of
Zippor, king of Moab? did he ever strive against the
26 Israelites, or did he ever fight against them, while the
Israelites dwelt in Heshbon and its towns, and in Aroer and
its towns, and in all the cities that are along the banks of
the Arnon, three hundred years? why therefore did ye not
27 recover them within that time? Wherefore I have not
sinned against thee, but thou doest me wrong to war against
me: Jehovah the Judge be judge this day between the chil-
28 dren of Israel and the children of Ammon." However the
king of the children of Ammon hearkened not to the words
of Jephthah which he sent to him.
29 Then the spirit of Jehovah came upon Jephthah; and he
passed over Gilead and Manasseh, and he passed over Mizpeh
of Gilead, and from Mizpeh of Gilead he passed over *unto*
30 the children of Ammon. And Jephthah vowed a vow to
Jehovah, and said, "If thou shalt without fail deliver the
31 children of Ammon into my hands, then whatsoever cometh

forth of the doors of my house to meet me, when I return in peace from the children of Ammon, shall surely be Jehovah's, and I will offer it up for a burnt-offering." So 32 Jephthah passed over to the children of Ammon, to fight against them; and Jehovah delivered them into his hands. And he smote them from Aroer, even till thou come to 33 Minnith, to the entrance of twenty cities, and unto the plain of the vineyards, with a very great slaughter. Thus the children of Ammon were humbled before the children of Israel.

And Jephthah came to Mizpeh to his house, and, lo, his 34 daughter came out to meet him with timbrels and with dances; and she was his only child: beside her he had neither son nor daughter. And when he saw her, he rent 35 his clothes, and said, "Alas, my daughter! thou hast brought me very low, and thou art one of them that trouble me: for I have opened my mouth to Jehovah, and I cannot go back." And she said to him, "My father, hast thou 36 opened thy mouth to Jehovah? Do to me according to that which hath proceeded out of thy mouth; since Jehovah hath taken vengeance for thee of thy enemies, the children of Ammon." And she said to her father, "Let this thing 37 be done for me: let me alone two months, that I may go up and down upon the mountains, and bewail my virginity, I and my companions." And he said, "Go." And he sent her away for two months; and she went with her 38 companions, and bewailed her virginity upon the mountains. And at the end of two months, she returned to her father, 39 who did with her *according* to his vow which he had vowed; and she knew no man. And it was a custom in Israel, for 40 the daughters of Israel to go yearly to lament the daughter of Jephthah the Gileadite four days in a year.

CHAP. XII.—And the men of Ephraim gathered them- 1 selves together, and passed over *the Jordan* northward, and said to Jephthah, "Wherefore passedst thou over to fight against the children of Ammon, and didst not call us to go with thee? we will burn thy house over thee with fire." And Jephthah said to them, "I and my people were at great 2 strife with the children of Ammon; and when I called you, ye delivered me not out of their hands. And when I saw 3 that ye delivered me not, I put my life in my hands, and passed over against the children of Ammon, and Jehovah

delivered them into my hand. Wherefore then are ye come
4 up to me this day to fight against me?" Then Jephthah
gathered together all the men of Gilead, and fought with
the Ephraimites: and the men of Gilead smote the
Ephraimites, because they said, "Ye Gileadites *are* fugitives
of Ephraim among the Ephraimites, *and* among the Manas-
5 sites." And the Gileadites took possession of the fords of the
Jordan before the Ephraimites; and when any one of those
Ephraimites who had escaped, said, "Let me go over," the
men of Gilead said to him, "Art thou an Ephraimite?"
6 If he said, "No;" then said they to him, "Say now Shib-
boleth;" and he said "Sibboleth:" for he could not rightly
pronounce it. Then they took him, and slew him at the fords
of Jordan; and there fell at that time of the Ephraimites
forty-two thousand.
7 And Jephthah judged Israel six years: then Jephthah the
Gileadite died, and was buried in *one of* the cities of Gilead.
9 And after him Ibzan of Bethlehem judged Israel. And he
had thirty sons, and thirty daughters, *whom* he sent abroad;
and he brought thirty daughters from abroad for his sons;
10 and he judged Israel seven years. Then Ibzan died and
was buried at Beth-lehem.
11 And after him Elon a Zebulonite judged Israel; and he
12 judged Israel ten years. And Elon the Zebulonite died, and
was buried in Aijalon, in the country of Zebulun.
13 And after him Abdon, the son of Hillel a Pirathonite,
14 judged Israel. And he had forty sons, and thirty grandsons,
who rode on seventy young asses; and he judged Israel eight
15 years. And Abdon, the son of Hillel the Pirathonite, died,
and was buried in Pirathon, in the land of Ephraim, in the
mount of the Amalekites.

1 CHAP. XIII.—And the children of Israel did evil again
in the sight of Jehovah; and Jehovah delivered them into
2 the hand of the Philistines, forty years. Now there was a
certain man of Zorah, of the family of the Danites, whose
name *was* Manoah; and his wife was barren, and bare not.
3 And the angel of Jehovah appeared to the woman and said
to her, "Lo, now, thou art barren, and bearest not;
4 but thou shalt conceive, and bear a son. Now therefore beware, I pray thee, and drink not wine nor strong drink, and
5 eat not any *thing* unclean: for, lo, thou shalt conceive,
and bear a son; and no razor shall come on his head; for

E E

the child shall be a Nazarite to God from the womb; and he shall begin to deliver Israel out of the hand of the Philistines." Then the woman came, and told her husband, say-⁶ ing, "A man of God came to me, and his countenance was like the countenance of an angel of God, very terrible; but I asked him not whence he was, neither told he me his name. But he said to me, 'Lo, thou shalt conceive, and bear a son; ⁷ and now drink no wine nor strong drink, neither eat any *thing* unclean: for the child shall be a Nazarite to God from the womb to the day of his death.'" Then Manoah en-⁸ treated Jehovah, and said, "O my Lord, let the man of God whom thou didst send come again to us, and teach us what we shall do to the child that shall be born." And God ⁹ hearkened to the voice of Manoah; and the angel of God came again to the woman as she was sitting in the field; but Manoah her husband was not with her. And the woman ¹⁰ ran in haste, and told her husband, and said to him, "Lo, the man hath appeared to me, who came to me the *other* day." So Manoah arose, and went after his wife, and came to the man, ¹¹ and said to him, "*Art* thou the man that spakest to the woman?" And he said, "I am." And Manoah said, "Now ¹² when thy words shall have come to pass, what shall be the training of the child, and what shall he do?" And the ¹³ angel of Jehovah said to Manoah, "Of all that I said to the woman let her beware. She may not eat of any *thing* ¹⁴ that cometh of the vine, neither may she drink wine or strong drink, nor eat any *thing* unclean: all that I commanded her she must observe." And Manoah said to the ¹⁵ angel of Jehovah, "I pray thee, let us detain thee until we shall have made ready a kid for thee." And the angel ¹⁶ of Jehovah said to Manoah, "Though thou detain me, I will not eat of thy bread; but if thou wilt offer a burnt-offering, thou must offer it to Jehovah." Now Manoah knew not that it was an angel of Jehovah. And Ma-¹⁷ noah said to the angel of Jehovah, "What is thy name, that, when thy sayings come to pass, we may do thee honour?" And the angel of Jehovah said to him, "Why ¹⁸ askest thou thus after my name, seeing it is secret?" So ¹⁹ Manoah took a kid, with a meal-offering, and offered it upon a rock to Jehovah: and a wondrous thing was done, while Manoah and his wife were looking on. For when the flame ²⁰ went up towards heaven from off the altar, the angel of Jehovah ascended in the flame of the altar; and Manoah and

his wife were looking on, and they fell on their faces to
21 the ground. When the angel of Jehovah no more appeared
to Manoah and to his wife, then Manoah knew that he was
22 an angel of Jehovah. And Manoah said to his wife, "We
23 shall surely die, because we have seen God." But his wife
said to him, "If Jehovah had desired to kill us, he would
not have received a burnt-offering and a meal-offering at our
hands; neither would he have showed us all these things,
nor would he, in that case, have told us *such things* as these."
24 And the woman bare a son, and called his name Samson;
25 and the child grew, and Jehovah blessed him. And the Spirit
of Jehovah began to move him at times in the camp of Dan,
between Zorah and Eshtaol.

1 CHAP. XIV.—And Samson went down to Timnath, and
saw a woman in Timnath of the daughters of the Philistines.
2. And he came up and told his father and his mother, and said,
"I have seen a woman in Timnath of the daughters of the
3 Philistines; now, therefore, get her for me to wife." Then
his father and his mother said unto him, "Is there no woman among the daughters of thy brethren, or among all my
people, that thou wouldst go to take a wife of the uncircumcised Philistines?" And Samson said to his father, "Get
4 her for me; for she pleaseth me well." But his father and
his mother knew not that it was of Jehovah that he sought
an occasion against the Philistines; for at that time the Philis-
5 tines had dominion over the Israelites. Then went Samson
down, and his father and his mother, to Timnath, and came
to the vineyards of Timnath; and, lo, a young lion roared
6 against him. And the Spirit of Jehovah came mightily
upon him, and he rent him, as he would have rent a kid,
though he had nothing in his hand; but he told not his
7 father or his mother what he had done. And he went down,
and talked with the woman; and she pleased Samson well.
8 And after a time he returned to take her, and he turned aside
to see the remains of the lion; and, lo, there was a swarm of
9 bees and honey in the remains of the lion. And he took of
it in his hands, and went on eating, and came to his father
and mother, and he gave them, and they did eat; but he
told them not that he had taken the honey out of the re-
10 mains of the lion. So his father went down to the woman;
and Samson made there a feast; for so used the young men
11 to do. And when they saw him they brought thirty com-

panions to be with him. And Samson said to them, "I 12 will now put forth a riddle to you: if you can certainly expound it to me within the seven days of the feast, and find it out, then I will give you thirty vests of fine linen, and thirty changes of garments: but if ye cannot expound it 13 to me, then ye shall give me thirty vests of fine linen, and thirty changes of garments." And they said to him, "Put forth thy riddle, that we may hear it." And he said to them, 14 "Out of the eater came forth meat, and out of the strong came forth sweetness." And they could not in three days expound the riddle. And on the seventh day, they said to 15 Samson's wife, "Entice thy husband, that he may expound unto us the riddle, lest we burn thee and thy father's house with fire: have ye invited us to make us poor? Is it not so?" And Samson's wife wept before him, and said, 16 "Thou dost but hate me, and lovest me not: thou hast put forth a riddle to the children of my people, and hast not told it to me." And he said to her, "Lo, I have not told *it* to my father nor to my mother, and shall I tell *it* to thee?" And she wept before him the seven days that the feast 17 lasted; and on the seventh day he told her, because she pressed him earnestly; and she told the riddle to the children of her people. And the men of the city said to him 18 on the seventh day, before the sun went down, "What is sweeter than honey? and what is stronger than a lion?" And he said to them, "If ye had not plowed with my heifer, ye had not found out my riddle." And the Spirit of 19 Jehovah came upon him, and he went down to Ashkelon, and slew thirty men of them, and took their spoil, and gave changes of garments to those who had expounded the riddle: and his anger was kindled, and he went up to his father's house. But Samson's wife was *given* to his companion, 20 whom he had made his friend.

CHAP. XV.—And some time after, in the days of wheat 1 harvest, Samson visited his wife, with a kid; and he said, "Let me go in to my wife into the chamber:" but her father would not suffer him to go in. And her father said, 2 "I verily thought that thou hadst utterly hated her; therefore I gave her to thy companion. Is not her younger sister fairer than she? take her, I pray thee, instead of her." And Samson said concerning them, "Now shall I be more 3 blameless than the Philistines, though I do them a mischief."

JUDGES XV.

4 So Samson went and caught three hundred jackalls, and took fire-brands, and turned *them* tail to tail, and put a fire-brand
5 in the midst between two tails. And when he had set the brands on fire, he let them go into the standing corn of the Philistines, and burnt up both the shocks and also
6 the standing corn, with the vineyards and olives. Then the Philistines said, "Who hath done this?" And they answered, "Samson, the son-in-law of the Timnite, because he had taken his wife, and given her to his companion." And the Philistines came up, and burnt her and her father with
7 fire. And Samson said to them, "Since ye have done this,
8 I will be avenged of you; and after that I will cease." And he smote them hip and thigh with a great slaughter.

Then he went down and dwelt in a cavern of the rock Etam.
9 And the Philistines went up, and encamped in Judah, and
10 spread themselves in Lehi. And the men of Judah said, "Why are ye come up against us?" And they answered, "To bind Samson are we come up, to do to him as he hath
11 done to us." Then three thousand men of Judah went to the cavern of the rock Etam, and said to Samson, "Knowest thou not that the Philistines are rulers over us? what is this that thou hast done to us?" And he said to them, "As
12 they did to me, so have I done to them." And they said to him, "We are come down to bind thee, that we may deliver thee into the hands of the Philistines." And Samson said to them, "Swear to me, that ye will not fall upon me your-
13 selves." And they spake to him, saying, "No; but we will bind thee fast, and deliver thee into their hand; but assuredly we will not kill thee." And they bound him with
14 two new cords, and brought him up from the rock. When he came to Lehi, the Philistines shouted on meeting him; and the Spirit of Jehovah came mightily upon him; and the cords that were upon his arms became as flax that was burnt
15 with fire, and his bands loosed from off his hands. And he found a fresh jaw-bone of an ass, and he put forth his
16 hand and took it, and with it he slew a thousand men. Then Samson said,

"With the jaw-bone of an ass, heaps upon heaps,

With the jaw-bone of an ass have I slain a thousand men."
17 And when he had made an end of speaking, he cast away the jaw-bone out of his hand, and called that place Ra-
18 math-lehi [THE HILL OF THE JAW-BONE]. And he was very thirsty, and called on Jehovah, and said, "Thou hast

given this great deliverance into the hand of thy servant: and now shall I die for thirst, and fall into the hand of the uncircumcised?" But God clave the hollow place in Lehi, 19 and there came out of it water; and when he had drunk, his spirit came again, and he revived: wherefore he called its name En-hakkore [THE FOUNTAIN OF THE INVOKER], which is in Lehi unto this day. And he judged Israel, in the 20 days of the Philistines, twenty years.

CHAP. XVI.—Then went Samson to Gaza, and saw 1 there a harlot, and went in to her. *And it was told* the Ga- 2 zites, saying, "Samson is come hither." And they compassed *him* in, and laid wait for him all night in the gate of the city; and kept themselves quiet all the night, saying, "In the morning, when it is day, we will kill him." And 3 Samson lay till midnight; but at midnight he arose, and laid hold of the doors of the gate of the city, and the two posts, and pulled them up with the bar, and put them upon his shoulders, and carried them up to the top of a hill that is opposite to Hebron.

And it came to pass after this, that he loved a woman in 4 the valley of Sorek, whose name was Delilah. And the 5 lords of the Philistines came up to her, and said to her, "Entice him, and see wherein his great strength lieth, and by what means we may prevail against him, that we may bind him so as to weaken him; and we will give thee, every one of us, eleven hundred *pieces* of silver." And Delilah said 6 to Samson, "Tell me, I pray thee, in what thy great strength lieth, and with what thou mightest be bound so as to weaken thee." And Samson said to her, "If they bind me with 7 seven green willow-twigs that were never dried, then shall I be weak, and be as a *common* man." Then the lords of the 8 Philistines brought up to her seven green willow-twigs which had not been dried, and she bound him with them. (Now 9 *there were* men lying in wait, abiding with her in the chamber.) And she said to him, "The Philistines are upon thee, Samson." And he brake the willow-twigs, as a thread of tow is broken when it toucheth the fire: so his strength was not known. Then Delilah said to Samson, "Lo, thou 10 hast mocked me, and told me lies: now tell me, I pray thee, with what thou mightest be bound." And he said to 11 her, "If they bind me fast with new ropes that have never been used, then shall I be weak, and be as a *common* man."

JUDGES XVI.

12 Delilah therefore took new ropes, and bound him with them, and said to him, " The Philistines are upon thee, Samson." (Now there were men lying in wait abiding in the chamber.)
13 And he brake them from off his arms like a thread. And Delilah said to Samson, " Hitherto thou hast mocked me, and told me lies: tell me with what thou mightest be bound." And he said to her, " If thou weave the seven locks of my
14 head with the web." And she fastened them with the pin, and said to him, " The Philistines are upon thee, Samson." And he awaked out of his sleep, and went away with the pin
15 of the beam, and with the web. And she said to him, " How canst thou say, I love thee, when thy heart is not with me? thou hast mocked me these three times, and hast
16 not told me in what thy great strength *lieth*." And when she pressed him daily with her words, and urged him, *so* that
17 his soul was vexed unto death, he told her all his mind, and said to her, "There hath not come a razor upon my head; for I *have been* a Nazarite to God from my mother's womb: if I be shaven, then my strength will go from me, and I
18 shall become weak, and be like all *other* men." And when Delilah saw that he had told her all his mind, she sent and called for the lords of the Philistines, saying, " Come up once more; for he hath told me all his mind." Then the lords of the Philistines came up to her, and brought money
19 in their hand. And she made him sleep upon her knees; and she called for a man, and caused him to shave off the seven locks of his head; and she began to weaken him, and his
20 strength went from him. And she said, " The Philistines are upon thee, Samson." And he awoke out of his sleep, and said, " I will go forth as at former times, and shake myself." For he knew not that Jehovah had departed from
21 him. But the Philistines took him, and put out his eyes, and brought him down to Gaza, and bound him with fetters of brass; and he did grind in the prison-house.
22 And the hair of his head began to grow again after he
23 was shaven. Then the lords of the Philistines gathered them together to offer a great sacrifice to Dagon their god, and to rejoice; for they said, " Our god hath delivered Sam-
24 son our enemy into our hand." And when the people saw him, they praised their god; for they said, " Our god hath delivered into our hands our enemy, and the destroyer of
25 our country, who slew many of us." And when their hearts were merry, they said, " Call for Samson, that he may make

us sport." And they called for Samson out of the prison-house; and he made them sport; and they set him between the pillars. And Samson said to the young man who held 26 him by the hand, "Suffer me to feel the pillars on which the house standeth, that I may lean upon them." Now the house was full of men and women; and all the 27 lords of the Philistines were there: and there were upon the roof about three thousand men and women, who were looking on while Samson made sport. And Samson called to 28 Jehovah, and said, "O Lord Jehovah, remember me, I pray thee, and strengthen me, I pray thee, only this once, O God, that I may be at once avenged of the Philistines for my two eyes." Then Samson took hold of the two middle pillars on 29 which the house stood, and on which it was borne up, of the one with his right hand, and of the other with his left. And Samson said, "Let me die with the Philistines." And 30 he bowed himself with *all his* might; and the house fell upon the lords, and upon all the people that were therein: so the dead whom he slew at his death were more than those whom he had slain in his life. Then his brethren, and 31 all the house of his father, came down, and took him, and brought *him* up, and buried him between Zorah and Eshtaol, in the burying-place of Manoah his father. Now he had judged Israel twenty years.

CHAP. XVII.—And there was a man of mount Ephraim, 1 whose name was Micah. And he said to his mother, "The 2 eleven hundred *shekels* of silver that were taken from thee, about which thou didst utter imprecations, and spakest also in my hearing, lo, the silver is with me; I took it." And his mother said, "Blessed be thou of Jehovah, my son." And when he had restored the eleven hundred *shekels* of 3 silver to his mother, his mother said, "I had wholly dedicated the silver to Jehovah, from my hand, for my son, to make a graven image and a molten image; now, therefore, I will return it to thee." But he gave back the money to his 4 mother; and his mother took two hundred *shekels* of silver, and gave them to the founder, who made thereof a graven image and a molten image; and they were in the house of Micah. And the man Micah had a house of God, and he 5 made an ephod, and teraphim, and consecrated one of his sons to be his priest. In those days there was no king in 6 Israel; every man did what was right in his own eyes. Now 7

there was a young man out of Beth-lehem-judah, of the family of Judah, who was a Levite, who had sojourned there.
8 And the man departed from the city, from Beth-lehem-judah, to sojourn where he could find *a place;* and as he journeyed
9 he came to mount Ephraim, to the house of Micah. And Micah said to him, "Whence comest thou?" And he said to him, "I am a Levite of Beth-lehem-judah, and I am
10 going to sojourn where I may find a place." And Micah said to him, "Dwell with me, and be to me a father and a priest, and I will give thee ten *shekels* of silver by the year, and a suit of apparel, and thy victuals." So the Levite went in.
11 And the Levite was content to dwell with the man; and the
12 young man was to him as one of his sons. And Micah consecrated the Levite; and the young man became his
13 priest, and was in the house of Micah. Then said Micah, "Now I know that Jehovah will do me good, since I have a Levite for a priest."

1 CHAP. XVIII.—In those days there was no king in Israel; and in those days the tribe of the Danites sought for themselves an inheritance to dwell in; for unto that day an inheritance had not fallen to them among the tribes of Israel.
2 So the children of Dan sent of their family five men from their territory, men of valour, from Zorah, and from Eshtaol, to spy out the land, and to search it; and they said to them, "Go, search the land; and they came to mount Ephraim, by
3 the house of Micah, and they lodged there. When they were near the house of Micah, they knew the voice of the young man the Levite; and they turned in thither, and said to him, "Who brought thee hither? and what art thou doing
4 in this *place?* and what hast thou here?" And he said to them, "Thus and thus Micah dealeth with me, and he hath
5 hired me, and I am his priest." And they said to him, "Ask counsel, we pray thee, of God, that we may know
6 whether our way which we go shall be prosperous." And the priest said to them, "Go in peace: before Jehovah is your way in which ye are going."

7 Then the five men departed, and came to Laish, and saw the people that were therein, that they dwelt securely after the manner of the Zidonians, quiet and secure; and *there was* no one that possessed control in the land, that might put *them* to shame in *any* thing: and they were far from the Zidonians, and had no dispute with *any* man.

And they came to their brethren to Zorah and Eshtaol; 8
and their brethren said to them, "What have ye *to say?*"
And they said, "Arise, and let us go up against them; for 9
we have seen the land, and, behold, it is very good: and *are*
ye still? Be not slothful to go, to enter to possess the
land. When ye go, ye will come to a people secure, and to 10
a large land; for God hath given it into your hands; a place
where there is no want of any thing that is in the earth."
And there went thence of the family of the Danites, out of 11
Zorah and out of Eshtaol, six hundred men furnished with
weapons of war. And they went up, and encamped in Kir- 12
jath-jearim, in Judah; wherefore they called that place Ma-
haneh-Dan [THE CAMP OF DAN], to this day: lo, it is
behind Kirjath-jearim. And they passed thence to mount 13
Ephraim, and came to the house of Micah. Then the five 14
men that went to spy out the country of Laish began to
speak, and said to their brethren, "Do ye know that there
is in these houses an ephod, and teraphim, and a graven
image, and a molten image? Now, therefore, consider what
ye have to do." And they turned thither, and came to the 15
house of the young man the Levite, to the house of Micah,
and saluted him. And the six hundred men furnished with 16
their weapons of war, who *were* of the children of Dan,
stood by the entrance of the gate. And the five men that 17
went to spy out the land went up, *and* came in thither, *and*
took the graven image, and the ephod, and the teraphim, and
the molten image; and the priest stood at the entrance of the
gate, with the six hundred men *that were* appointed with
weapons of war. And these went into Micah's house, and 18
fetched the graven image, the ephod, and teraphim, and the
molten image. Then said the priest unto them, "What are
ye doing?" And they said to him, "Be silent; lay thy 19
hand upon thy mouth, and go with us, and be to us a father
and a priest: is it better for thee to be a priest to the house
of one man, or to be a priest to a tribe and a family in
Israel?" And the priest's heart was glad; and he took the 20
ephod, and the teraphim, and the graven image, and went in
the midst of the people. So they turned and departed, and 21
put the little ones, and the cattle, and the carriage, before
them. They had gone a good way from the house of Micah, 22
when the men that were in the houses near to Micah's house
were called together, and overtook the children of Dan.
And they cried to the children of Dan; and they turned 23

their faces, and said to Micah, "What *aileth* thee, that ye
24 have been called together?" And he said, " Ye have taken
away my gods which I made, and the priest, and ye are gone
away; and what have I more? and what is this that ye say
25 to me, 'What *aileth* thee?'" And the children of Dan
said to him, " Let not thy voice be heard among us, lest
men bitter in spirit run upon thee, and thy life be taken
26 away, with the lives of thy household." So the children
of Dan went their way; and when Micah saw that they
were too strong for him, he turned, and went back to his
27 house. And they took what Micah had made, and the priest
whom he had, and came to Laish, to a people quiet and secure: and they smote them with the edge of the sword, and
28 burnt the city with fire. And there was no deliverer, because
it was far from Zidon, and they had no dispute with any
man; and it was in the valley that is by Beth-rehob. And
29 they built a city, and dwelt therein. And they called the
name of the city Dan, after the name of Dan their father,
who was born to Israel: but the name of the city was Laish
30 at the first. And the children of Dan set up the graven
image; and Jonathan the son of Gershom, the son of Moses,
he and his sons were priests to the tribe of Dan until the
31 day of the captivity of the land. And they set them up
Micah's graven image, which he made, all the time that the
house of God was in Shiloh.

1 CHAP. XIX.—And in those days, when there was no
king in Israel, there was a certain Levite sojourning on the
side of mount Ephraim, who took to himself a concubine
2 out of Beth-lehem-judah. And his concubine played the
harlot against him, and went away from him to her father's
house to Beth-lehem-judah, and was there four whole
3 months. And her husband arose, and went after her, to
speak kindly to her, *and* to bring her again, having his servant with him, and a couple of asses; and she brought him
into her father's house; and when the father of the damsel
4 saw him, he rejoiced to meet him. And his father-in-law,
the damsel's father, retained him; and he abode with him
three days: so they did eat and drink, and lodged there.
5 And on the fourth day, when they arose early in the morning,
he rose up to depart; and the damsel's father said to his son-
in-law, "Comfort thy heart with a morsel of bread, and
6 afterward go your way." And they sat down, and ate and

drank both of them together: for the damsel's father had said to the man, "Be content, I pray thee, and tarry all night, and let thy heart be merry." And when the man 7 rose up to depart, his father-in-law urged him; therefore he lodged there again. And he arose early in the morning on 8 the fifth day to depart; and the damsel's father said, "Comfort thy heart, I pray thee." And they tarried until after noon, and they ate both of them. And when the man rose 9 up to depart, he and his concubine and his servant, his father-in-law, the damsel's father, said to him, "Lo now, the day draweth toward evening; I pray you tarry all night: behold, the day groweth to an end; lodge here, that thy heart may be merry; and to-morrow be early on your way, that thou mayest go home." But the man would not tarry 10 that night, but rose up and departed, and came over against Jebus (which is Jerusalem): and there were with him two asses saddled; his concubine also was with him. *And* when 11 they were by Jebus, the day was far spent; and the servant said to his master, "Come, I pray thee, and let us turn into this city of the Jebusites, and lodge in it." And his master said to him, "We will not turn aside hither into the city of 12 an alien, that is not of the children of Israel; we will pass over to Gibeah." And he said to his servant, "Come, and 13 let us draw near to one of these places to lodge all night, in Gibeah, or in Ramah." And they passed on and went their 14 way; and the sun went down upon them *when they were* by Gibeah, which belongeth to Benjamin. And they turned 15 aside thither, to go in *and* to lodge in Gibeah; and when he went in, he sat down in a street of the city; for no man took them into his house to lodge. And, lo, there came an old 16 man from his work out of the field at even, who was also of mount Ephraim; and he sojourned in Gibeah: but the men of the place were Benjaminites. And when he raised his 17 eyes, he saw a way-faring man in the street of the city: and the old man said, "Whither goest thou? and whence comest thou?" And he said to him, "We are passing from Beth- 18 lehem-judah toward the side of mount Ephraim; thence *am* I: and I went to Beth-lehem-judah, but I *am now* going to the house of Jehovah; and there is no man that receiveth me to his house. Yet there is both straw and provender for our 9 asses; and there is bread and wine also for me, and for thy handmaid, and for the young man who is with thy servant: there is no want of any thing." And the old man said, 20

"Peace be with thee: howsoever, let all thy wants be upon me; only lodge not in the street." So he brought him into his house, and gave provender to the asses; and they washed their feet, and ate and drank. They were making their hearts merry, when lo, men of the city, sons of Belial, surrounded the house, beat at the door, and spake to the master of the house, the old man, saying, "Bring forth the man that came into thy house, that we may know him." And the man, the master of the house, went out to them, and said to them, "Nay, my brethren, I pray you, do not so wickedly; seeing that this man is côme into my house, do not this folly. Lo, *here is* my daughter, a maiden, and his concubine; them I will bring out now, and humble ye them, and do with them what seemeth good to you; but to this man do not so vile a thing." But the men would not hearken to him: so the man took his concubine, and brought her forth to them; and they knew her, and abused her all the night until the morning: and when the day began to dawn, they let her go. Then came the woman, at the dawn of day, and fell down at the door of the man's house where her husband was, till it was light. And her husband rose up in the morning, and opened the doors of the house, and went out to go his way; and, lo, the woman his concubine was fallen down at the door of the house, and her hands were upon the threshold. And he said to her, "Rise, and let us be going:" but she answered not. Then the man took and put her upon an ass, and the man rose up, and went to his own place. And when he was come into his house, he took a knife, and laid hold on his concubine, and divided her, together with her bones, into twelve pieces, and sent her into all the borders of Israel. And all who saw it said, "No such deed hath been done or seen from the day that the children of Israel came up out of the land of Egypt unto this day: consider of it, take advice, and speak *your minds.*"

CHAP. XX.—Then all the children of Israel went out, and the congregation was gathered together as one man, from Dan even to Beer-sheba, with the land of Gilead, unto Jehovah in Mizpeh. And the chief of all the people, of all the tribes of Israel, presented themselves in the assembly of the people of God, four hundred thousand footmen that drew the sword. And the children of Benjamin heard that the children of Israel were gone up to Mizpeh. Then said the children of Israel, "Tell us, how was this wickedness?" And the Levite, the husband of the woman who was slain, answered and said, "I came into Gibeah that belongeth to Benjamin, I and my concubine, to lodge: And the men of Gibeah rose against me, and surrounded the house upon me by night, *and* thought to kill *me*; *and* my concubine have they forced, that she is dead. And I took my concubine, and cut her in pieces, and sent her throughout all the country of the inheritance of Israel: for they have committed lewdness and folly in Israel. Behold, ye are all children of Israel; give here your advice and counsel." And all the people arose as one man, saying, "We will not any *of us* go to his tent, neither will we any *of us* turn into his house; but now, this *shall be* the thing which we will do to Gibeah, we will go up by lot against it; and we will take ten men of a hundred throughout all the tribes of Israel, and a hundred of a thousand, and a thousand of ten thousand, to fetch victual for the people, that they may do, when they come to Gibeah of Benjamin, according to all the folly that they have wrought in Israel." So all the men of Israel were gathered against the city, knit together as one man. And all the tribes of Israel sent men through all the tribe of Benjamin, saying, "What wickedness *is* this that is done among you? Now therefore deliver up the men, sons of Belial, who are in Gibeah, that we may put them to death, and put away evil from Israel." But the children of Benjamin would not hearken to the voice of their brethren the children of Israel; but the children of Benjamin gathered themselves together out of the cities unto Gibeah, to go out to battle against the children of Israel. And the children of Benjamin were numbered at that time, out of the cities, twenty-six thousand men that drew the sword, beside the inhabitants of Gibeah, who were numbered seven hundred chosen men. Among all this people there were seven hundred chosen men left-handed; every one could sling stones at a hair, and not miss. And the men of Israel, beside Benjamin, were numbered four hundred thousand men that drew the sword: all these *were* men of war.

And the children of Israel arose, and went up to the house of God, and asked counsel of God, and said, "Which of us shall go up first to the battle against the children of Benjamin?" And Jehovah said, "Judah *shall go up* first." And the children of Israel rose up in the morning, and encamped against

20 Gibeah. And the men of Israel went out to battle against Benjamin; and the men of Israel put themselves in array to
21 fight against them at Gibeah. And the children of Benjamin came forth out of Gibeah, and destroyed down to the ground of the Israelites that day, twenty-two thousand
22 men. And the people, the men of Israel, encouraged themselves, and set their battle again in array, in the place where
23 they put themselves in array the first day. (And the children of Israel had gone up, and wept before Jehovah until the evening, and had asked counsel of Jehovah, saying, "Shall I go up again to battle against the children of Benjamin my brother?" And Jehovah said, "Go up against him.")
24 And the children of Israel came near against the children
25 of Benjamin the second day. And Benjamin went forth against them out of Gibeah the second day, and destroyed down to the ground, of the children of Israel again, eighteen
26 thousand men; all these drew the sword. Then all the children of Israel, and all the people, went up, and came unto the house of God, and wept, and sat there before Jehovah, and fasted that day until the evening, and offered
27 burnt-offerings and peace-offerings before Jehovah. And the children of Israel inquired of Jehovah (for the ark of
28 the covenant of God *was* there in those days; and Phinehas, the son of Eleazar, the son of Aaron, stood before it in those days), saying, "Shall I yet again go out to battle against the children of Benjamin my brother, or shall I cease?" And Jehovah said, "Go up; for to-morrow I will deliver
29 them into thy hand." And the Israelites set liers in wait
30 round about Gibeah. And the children of Israel went up against the children of Benjamin on the third day, and put
31 themselves in array against Gibeah, as at other times. And the children of Benjamin went out against the people, *and* were drawn away from the city; and they began to smite of the people *and* kill, as at other times, in the highways (of which one goeth up to the house of God, and the other to
32 Gibeah in the field), about thirty men of Israel. And the children of Benjamin said, "They are smitten down before us, as at the first." But the children of Israel said, "Let us flee, and draw them from the city, into the highways."
33 And all the men of Israel rose up out of their place, and put themselves in array at Baal-tamar; and the liers in wait of Israel came forth out of their place, *even* out of the open
34 fields of Gibeah. And there came against Gibeah ten thou-

sand chosen men out of all Israel, and the battle was sore;
but they knew not that evil *was* near them. And Jehovah 35
smote Benjamin before Israel; and the children of Israel
destroyed of the Benjaminites that day twenty-five thousand
one hundred men: all these drew the sword. So the chil- 36
dren of Benjamin saw that they were smitten; for the men
of Israel gave way before the Benjaminites, because they
trusted to the liers in wait whom they had set beside Gibeah.
And the liers in wait hasted, and rushed upon Gibeah; and 37
the liers in wait spread themselves along, and smote all the
city with the edge of the sword. Now there was an ap- 38
pointed signal between the men of Israel and the liers in
wait, that they should make a great flame with smoke rise
up out of the city. So when the men of Israel retreated in 39
the battle, the Benjaminites began to smite *and* kill of the
men of Israel about thirty persons; for they said, "Surely
they are smitten down before us, as *in* the first battle." But 40
when the flame began to arise up out of the city with a pillar
of smoke, the Benjaminites looked behind them, and, behold,
the flame of the city ascended up to the heavens. And 41
when the men of Israel turned again, the men of Benjamin
were amazed: for they saw that evil was come upon them.
Therefore they turned before the men of Israel unto the way 42
of the desert; but the battle overtook them; and those who
came out of the cities they destroyed in the midst of it.
They inclosed the Benjaminites round about; they chased 43
them from their resting-place; they trode them down till
over against Gibeah toward the sun-rising. And there fell 44
of Benjamin eighteen thousand men: all these *were* men of
valour. And they turned and fled toward the desert unto 45
the rock of Rimmon; and they gleaned of them in the
highways five thousand men; and pursued hard after them
unto Gidom, and slew two thousand men of them. So that 46
all who fell that day of Benjamin were twenty-five thousand
men that drew the sword: all these *were* men of valour.
But six hundred men turned, and fled to the desert unto 47
the rock Rimmon, and abode in the rock Rimmon four
months. And the men of Israel turned again upon the 48
children of Benjamin, and smote them with the edge of the
sword, men and beast of *every* city, and all that was found:
also they set on fire all the cities to which they came.

CHAP. XXI.—Now the men of Israel had sworn in 1

Mizpeh, saying, There shall not any of us give his daughter
2 unto a Benjaminite to wife. And the people came to the
house of God, and abode there till evening before God, and
3 lifted up their voices, and wept greatly; and said, "O
Jehovah, God of Israel, why is this come to pass in Israel,
that there should be to-day one tribe wanting in Israel?"
4 And on the morrow, the people rose early, and built there an
5 altar, and offered burnt-offerings and peace-offerings. And
the children of Israel said, "Who *is there* among all the
tribes of Israel that came not up with the assembly unto
Jehovah?" for they had made a great oath concerning him
that came not up to Jehovah to Mizpeh, saying, "He shall
6 surely be put to death." And the children of Israel repented them concerning Benjamin their brother, and said,
7 "There is one tribe cut off from Israel this day. How shall
we do for wives for those that remain, seeing we have sworn
by Jehovah, that we will not give them of our daughters for
8 wives?" And they said, "What one *is there* of the tribes
of Israel that came not up to Mizpeh to Jehovah?" And
lo, there came none to the camp from Jabesh-gilead to the
9 assembly. For the people were numbered, and, lo, *there were*
10 none of the inhabitants of Jabesh-gilead there. And the
congregation sent thither twelve thousand of the most
valiant men, and commanded them, saying, "Go and smite
the inhabitants of Jabesh-gilead with the edge of the sword,
11 with the women and the children. And this *is* the thing
that ye shall do, ye shall utterly destroy every male, and
12 every woman that hath lain by man." And they found
among the inhabitants of Jabesh-gilead four hundred young
virgins, who had known no man by lying with any male;
and they brought them to the camp to Shiloh, which is in
13 the land of Canaan. Then the whole congregation sent *some*
to speak to the children of Benjamin who were in the rock
14 of Rimmon, and to call peaceably unto them. And the
Benjaminites returned at that time; and they gave them
wives which they had saved alive of the women of Jabesh-
15 gilead: and yet so they sufficed them not. And the people
repented them concerning the Benjaminites because Jehovah
16 had made a breach in the tribes of Israel. Then the
elders of the congregation said, "How shall we do for wives
for those that remain, seeing the women are destroyed out of
Benjamin?" And they said, "*There must be* an inheritance
17 for those who have escaped of the Benjaminites, that a tribe

be not destroyed out of Israel. But we may not give them 18 wives of our daughters; for the children of Israel have sworn, saying, 'Cursed be he that giveth a wife to a Benjaminite.'" Then they said, "Lo, there is a yearly feast of 19 Jehovah in Shiloh, which *is* on the north side of Beth-el, on the east side of the highway that goeth up from Beth-el to Shechem, and on the south of Lebonah." Therefore they 20 advised the children of Benjamin, saying, " Go and lie in wait in the vineyards; and see, and, lo, if the daughters of 21 Shiloh come out to dance in dances, then come ye out of the vineyards, and catch you every man his wife of the daughters of Shiloh, and go to the land of Benjamin. And when 22 their fathers or their brethren come unto us to complain, we will say to them, 'Be favourable to them for our sakes; because we reserved not to each man his wife in the war; for ye did not give *wives* to them; in which case ye would have been guilty.'" And the children of Benjamin did so, and took 23 for themselves wives according to their number, of those that danced, whom they caught; and they went and returned to their inheritance, and repaired the cities, and dwelt in them. And the children of Israel departed thence at that time, 24 every man to his tribe, and to his family; and they went out thence every man to his inheritance.

In those days there was no king in Israel: every man 25 did what was right in his own eyes.

THE BOOK OF RUTH.

1 CHAP. I.—Now in the days when the Judges ruled, there was a famine in the land. And a certain man of Beth-lehem of Judah went to sojourn in the country of 2 Moab, he, and his wife, and his two sons. And the name of the man was Elimelech, and the name of his wife Naomi, and the name of his two sons Mahlon and Chilion, Ephrathites of Beth-lehem of Judah. And they went into the 3 country of Moab, and continued there. And Elimelech, Naomi's husband, died; and she was left with her two sons. 4 And they took for themselves wives of the women of Moab; the name of the one was Orphah, and the name of the other Ruth. And when they had dwelled there about ten 5 years, Mahlon and Chilion died also, even both of them; and the woman was bereaved of her two sons and her husband. 6 Then she arose, with her daughters-in-law, that she might return from the country of Moab; for she had heard in the country of Moab that Jehovah had visited his people by 7 giving them bread. So she went from the place where she was, and her two daughters-in-law with her; and they went 8 on the way to return into the land of Judah. And Naomi said to her two daughters-in-law, "Go, return each of you to her mother's house: may Jehovah deal kindly with you, 9 as ye have dealt with the dead, and with me. Jehovah grant that ye may find rest, each of you in the house of her husband." Then she kissed them; and they lifted up their 10 voice, and wept. And they said to her, "Surely we will re-11 turn with thee unto thy people." And Naomi said, "Return, my daughters, why will ye go with me? Are there yet any sons in my womb, who might be your husbands? 12 Return, my daughters, go your way; for I am too old to have a husband. If I should say, I have hope; should I have a husband even this night, and should I also bear sons; 3 would ye wait for them until they were grown? would ye

stay for them from having husbands? Nay, my daughters;
for it grieveth me much, for your sakes, that the hand of
Jehovah is gone out against me." And they lifted up their 14
voice, and wept again. And Orphah kissed her mother-in-
law; but Ruth clave to her. And she said, "Behold, thy 15
sister-in-law has returned to her people, and to her gods;
return thou after thy sister-in-law." And Ruth said, 16
"Entreat me not to leave thee, by returning from following thee; for whither thou goest, I will go, and where
thou lodgest, I will lodge; thy people *shall be* my people,
and thy God my God. Where thou diest will I die, 17
and there will I be buried. May Jehovah do so to me,
and more also, *if aught* but death part thee and me!"
When she saw that she was firmly resolved to go with her, 18
she ceased to speak to her. So they two went until they 19
came to Beth-lehem. And when they were come to Beth-
lehem, all the city was moved about them, and said, "Is
this Naomi?" And she said to them, "Call me not Naomi 20
[PLEASANTNESS], call me Mara [BITTERNESS]; for the
Almighty hath dealt very bitterly with me. I went out full, 21
and Jehovah hath brought me home again empty. Why
then call ye me Naomi, since Jehovah hath testified against
me, and the Almighty hath afflicted me?"

Thus Naomi returned, and Ruth the Moabitess, her 22
daughter-in-law, returned with her out of the country of
Moab; and they came to Beth-lehem in the beginning of
the barley-harvest.

CHAP. II.—Now Naomi had a kinsman of her hus- 1
band's, a man of great wealth, of the family of Elimelech;
and his name was Boaz. And Ruth the Moabitess said to 2
Naomi, "Let me now go to the field, and glean ears of corn
after him in whose sight I shall find favour." And she
said to her, "Go, my daughter." And she went, and came, 3
and gleaned in the field after the reapers; and it chanced
that she lighted on a part of the field which belonged to
Boaz, who was of the family of Elimelech. And, behold, 4
Boaz came from Beth-lehem, and said to the reapers, "May
Jehovah be with you!" And they answered him, "May
Jehovah bless thee!" Then said Boaz to his servant who 5
was set over the reapers, "Whose damsel is that?" And 6
the servant who was set over the reapers answered and said,
"It is the Moabitish damsel that returned with Naomi out

7 of the country of Moab: and she said, 'I pray thee, let me glean and gather among the sheaves after the reapers:' so she came, and hath continued even from the morning 8 until now, she hath tarried but little in the house." Then said Boaz to Ruth, "Hearest thou not, my daughter? Go not to glean in another field, neither go hence, but abide 9 here near my maidens. Keep thine eyes on the field that they are reaping, and go thou after them. Have I not charged the young men that they shall not touch thee? and when thou art thirsty, go to the vessels, and drink of 10 what the young men have drawn." Then she fell on her face, and bowed herself to the ground, and said to him, "Why have I found favour in thine eyes, that thou should-11 est take knowledge of me, and I an alien?" And Boaz answered and said to her, "All that thou hast done to thy mother-in-law since the death of thy husband, hath been fully told to me: and *how* thou hast left thy father and thy mother, and the land of thy nativity, and art come unto a 12 people which thou knewest not before. May Jehovah recompense thy deeds, and may a full reward be given to thee by Jehovah God of Israel, under whose wings thou art come 13 to trust." Then she said, "Let me find favour in thy sight, my lord, for thou hast comforted me, and hast spoken friendly to thy handmaid, though I be not like one of thy 14 handmaids." And Boaz said to her, "At meal-time come thou hither, and eat of the bread, and dip thy morsel in the vinegar." So she sat down beside the reapers: and he reached her parched *corn*, and she did eat, and was satisfied and left. 15 And when she was risen up to glean, Boaz commanded his young men, saying, "Let her glean even among the sheaves, 16 and reproach her not; and let fall also *some* of the handfuls on purpose for her, and leave them, that she may glean them; 17 and rebuke her not." So she gleaned in the field until evening, and she beat out what she had gleaned; and it was about an 18 ephah of barley. And she took it up, and went into the city; and her mother-in-law saw what she had gleaned; and she brought forth, and gave to her that which she had reserved 19 after she was satisfied. And her mother-in-law said to her, "Where hast thou gleaned to-day? and where wroughtest thou? Blessed be he that did take knowledge of thee!" And she shewed her mother-in-law with whom she had wrought, and said, "The man's name with whom I wrought to-day is 20 Boaz." And Naomi said to her daughter-in-law, "Blessed

of Jehovah may he be who hath not left off his kindness to the living and to the dead." And Naomi said to her, "The man is near of kin to us, one of our next kinsmen." And 21 Ruth the Moabitess said, "He said to me also, 'Thou must keep near my servants until they have ended all my harvest.'" And Naomi said to Ruth her daughter-in-law, "*It* 22 *is* good, my daughter, that thou go out with his maidens, that they come not upon thee in any other field." So she 23 kept near the maidens of Boaz to glean, to the end of barley-harvest, and of wheat-harvest; but she dwelt with her mother-in-law.

CHAP. III.—Then Naomi her mother-in-law said to her, 1 "My daughter, shall I not seek rest for thee, that it may be well with thee? And now is not Boaz of our kindred, with 2 whose maidens thou wast? Lo, he winnoweth barley in the threshing-floor, to-night. Wash thyself, therefore, and 3 anoint thee, and put thy raiment upon thee, and go down to the threshing-floor: make not thyself known to the man, until he shall have done eating and drinking. And when 4 he lieth down, thou shalt mark the place where he shall lie, and thou shalt go in, and uncover his feet, and lie down; and he will tell thee what thou shalt do." And she said to 5 her, "All that thou sayest to me I will do."

And she went down unto the threshing-floor, and did ac- 6 cording to all that her mother-in-law bade her. And when 7 Boaz had eaten and drunk, and his heart was joyful, he went to lie down at the end of the heap of corn; and she came softly, and uncovered his feet, and lay down. And at midnight the 8 man was afraid, and turned himself; and, lo, a woman was lying at his feet. And he said, "Who art thou?" And 9 she answered, "I am Ruth thy handmaid; spread therefore thy skirt over thy handmaid; for thou art a near kinsman." And he said, "Blessed be thou of Jehovah, my daughter; 10 thou hast shewed more kindness in the latter end than in the beginning, inasmuch as thou followedst not young men, whether poor or rich. And now, my daughter, fear not; I 11 will do for thee all that thou requirest; for all the city of my people knoweth that thou art a virtuous woman. And 12 now, although it is true that I am a near kinsman, yet there is a kinsman nearer than I. Remain this night, and in the 13 morning, if he will perform to thee the part of a kinsman, well; let him do the kismann's part; bpt if he will not do

the part of a kinsman to thee, then will I do the part of a kinsman to thee, as Jehovah liveth: lie down until the
14 morning." And she lay at his feet until the morning; and she rose up before a man could know his neighbour. And he said, "Let it not be known that a woman came into the
15 threshing-floor." Also he said, "Bring the veil that is upon thee, and hold it." And when she held it, he measured six *measures* of barley, and he placed it upon her; and she
16 went into the city. And when she came to her mother-in-law, she said, "Who art thou, my daughter?" And she
17 told her all that the man had done to her. And she said, "These six *measures* of barley gave he to me; for he said to me, 'Go not empty-handed to thy mother-in-law.'"
18 Then said she, "Sit still, my daughter, until thou know how the matter will turn out; for the man will not rest until he have finished the matter this day."

1 CHAP. IV.—Then went Boaz up to the city gate, and sat down there: and, lo, the kinsman, of whom Boaz had spoken, came by; to whom he said, "Ho, such-a-one! turn aside, sit down here." And he turned aside, and sat down.
2 And he took ten men of the elders of the city, and said,
3 "Sit ye down here." And they sat down. And he said to the kinsman, "Naomi, who hath returned from the country of Moab, sold a piece of land, which belonged to our brother
4 Elimelech: and I thought fit to make this known to thee, saying, 'Buy it before the inhabitants, and before the elders of my people.' If thou wilt redeem *it*, redeem *it*; but if thou wilt not redeem *it*, *then* tell me, that I may know: for there is none to redeem *it* besides thee; and I am after
5 thee." And he said, "I will redeem *it*." Then said Boaz, "When thou buyest the field from the hand of Naomi, thou must buy also Ruth the Moabitess, the wife of the dead, to
6 raise up the name of the dead upon his inheritance." Then the kinsman said, "I cannot redeem it for myself, lest I injure my own inheritance: redeem thou my right to thy-
7 self; for I cannot redeem *it*." (Now this was *the custom* in former time in Israel, in redeeming and in exchanging, to confirm all things: a man pulled off his shoe, and gave it to
8 his neighbour; and this was a testimony in Israel.) Therefore the kinsman said to Boaz, "Buy it for thyself," and he
9 pulled off his shoe. And Boaz said to the elders, and to all the people, "Ye are witnesses this day that I have bought all

that was Elimelech's, and all that was Chilion's and Mahlon's, from the hand of Naomi. Ruth also the Moabitess, 10 the wife of Mahlon, have I bought to be my wife, to raise up the name of the dead upon his inheritance, that the name of the dead be not cut off from among his brethren, and from the gate of his place: ye are witnesses this day." And all the people that were in the gate, and the elders, said, 11 "*We are* witnesses. May Jehovah make the woman who cometh into thy house like Rachel and like Leah, which two did build the house of Israel; and mayest thou get wealth in Ephratah, and be famous in Beth-lehem; and may thy house 12 be like the house of Pharez (whom Tamar bare to Judah), of the seed which Jehovah shall give thee of this young woman." So Boaz took Ruth, and she was his wife; and 13 when he went in unto her, Jehovah gave her conception, and she bare a son. And the women said to Naomi, "Blessed 14 be Jehovah who hath not left thee this day without a kinsman, and his name shall be famous in Israel. And he shall 15 be to thee a restorer of *thy* life, and a nourisher of thy old age: for thy daughter-in-law who loveth thee, who is better to thee than seven sons, hath borne him *a child*." And 16 Naomi took the child, and laid it in her bosom, and became nurse to it. And the women her neighbours gave it a name, 17 saying, "There is a son born to Naomi;" and they called his name Obed: he was the father of Jesse, the father of David.

Now these are the descendants of Pharez: Pharez begat 18 Hezron, and Hezron begat Ram, and Ram begat Amminadab, 19 and Amminadab begat Nahshon, and Nahshon begat Salmon, 20 and Salmon begat Boaz, and Boaz begat Obed, and Obed 22 begat Jesse, and Jesse begat David.

END OF FIRST VOLUME.

www.ingramcontent.com/pod-product-compliance
Lightning Source LLC
Chambersburg PA
CBHW020526300426
44111CB00008B/558